PERSPECTIVES IN PHILOSOPHY

A Book of Readings   Third Edition

TEEN DAYS

N. BECK *Clark University*

HOLT, RINEHART AND WINSTON
New York   Chicago   San Francisco   Atlanta
Dallas   Montreal   Toronto   London   Sydney

Library of Congress Cataloging in Publication Data

Beck, Robert Nelson, 1924-   ed.
    Perspectives in philosophy.

    Includes bibliographies.
    1. Philosophy—Introductions. I. Title.
BD31.B38   1975   108   74-20804
ISBN 0-03-089645-2

PREFACE

A textbook of selections is one of the tools of learning. It will be utilized in a variety of ways by students and instructors, who give the materials form and seek to comprehend the living thought rather than repeat the dead word. But this does not mean that the materials themselves should be relatively formless.

As an alternative to the introductory textbook of selections that is based on a "problems" approach to philosophy, this volume is organized in terms of positions or schools of philosophy. The concept of a philosophical position is admittedly a difficult one and clearly seems to be "open textured." Generally, I think, a position should be defined in terms of a "continuity of intention," to use Professor Urban's phrase, rather than through identity of conclusions. Vague, then, as the idea of a school is bound to be, it nevertheless can like all classificatory devices be a useful pedagogical instrument. If internal differences and variety are not suppressed, and if thinking of "isms" is seen as a means to understanding rather than its end, an introduction to philosophy through the study of major alternative positions will have its unique values.

All determination is negation, and all selection reflects something of the arbitrary. Teachers will note that not all important philosophic schools have been—or could be—included, and that some major thinkers are not represented. There is also some validity to the viewpoint that the greatest philosophers transcend schools—though in fact such transcendence usually leads to the founding of another school. Generally, the aim of selection in this textbook has been to provide as firm a basis for further study as possible and, for those for whom a "problems" course is the only elective in philosophy, to offer a valid terminal experience.

It is to help secure these educational goals that the selections in this anthology have been set out by positions. Thus it is possible for the readings themselves to show the basic themes of a philosophy, and in an order that can serve effective learning because it aids fuller description of issues by providing their context and wider exploration of connections by juxtaposing selections on various topics within a structure of relationships. Such structuring, needless to say, is not intended to be an overstructuring, nor to encourage students to think in terms of slogans and isms. Quite the opposite is the case: problems, issues, and alternatives are and should remain the center of attention. Yet when a setting of approach, terms, and conclusions is helpful, it should be utilized. Nor need any perspective be considered rigid: there are differences among its representatives (consider existentialism), and frequently the study of specific issues leads to clarification of the general concepts in a position. By becoming aware of these and similar matters, the student gains greater opportunity to develop insight and philosophical maturity.

Introductory material is provided to guide students in their reading and understanding of the selections. Brief bibliographical notes follow each section to aid in further reading, should students desire to pursue beyond the introductory level the ideas presented in the selections. A selected glossary of some of the important terms used by authors is included at the end of the book.

February 1975   R. N. B.

CONTENTS

THEMATIC CONTENTS

PHILOSOPHY OF MAN

SCIENCE

RELIGION

CRITIQUES

SUMMARIES

Chapter One

The Encounter with Philosophy

Descartes · Kant · Quine

Philosophy, like religion, seems to defy precise definition. The complexity and diversity of the subject is an initial difficulty; another difficulty is that individual philosophers view the task of philosophy differently, and usually make their definitions part of their general philosophic positions. Nor is etymology fully helpful: "philosophy" is derived from the Greek *philein*, to love, and *sophia*, wisdom; but the meaning of wisdom is somewhat obscure, and the definition reflects Greek rather than other views of philosophy. Perhaps one should ask "what is philosophy?" after, rather than before, exposure to the field.

Still, there is some common ground between philosophy in a technical sense and our ordinary experience. For when we use the word philosophical apart from books and classes, we generally are trying to point to some idea as essentially "important." (Occasionally, someone might mean a vague, abstract, or even irrelevant idea. We shall not refer to this meaning, though it is understandable. Sometimes philosophical writing does impress one in just this way!) To be sure, what is important to one person may be completely unimportant to another. Variation in importance may also be found in social movements and historical periods. The Middle Ages took it to be extremely important to understand rightly such ideas as faith, revelation, and salvation; the contemporary civil rights movement has highlighted such notions as oppression, power, violence, and justice. This is not to say that concern about some ideas—for example, human happiness, or truth—is not relatively permanent and pervasive in human experience.

Philosophical talk and thinking, then, deal with what is important as this question arises or is forced upon us by the conditions of life. The interconnection of life experiences and the sensed importance of ideas, programs, and alternatives also gives us the basic meaning of another commonly used word, relevance. One needs to be a bit careful, though, in judgments about what is or is not relevant. It

1

may be, if we seek to justify our views, that seemingly very general and abstract ideas like being, meaning, truth, good, and justice are critically relevant to very specific issues like abortion, civil rights, and self-identity, if only we work and reflect enough to find that relevance.

We have noted that the question of importance has differed from age to age, and has arisen in different social and cultural contexts. This generalization has application today. The context in which we are most likely to begin philosophizing is our rapidly changing, industrialized, and populous society. Literature describing contemporary society, with its special problems and dilemmas, is vast, and you have undoubtedly been introduced to it in some of your previous studies. Many of the conclusions of these social studies are factual or scientific; others, however, have undoubtedly been identified as involving a sense of importance, and thus as suggesting philosophy or philosophical thinking.

Why Philosophy?

If philosophical thinking is sometimes suggested by other studies, the answer to this question might simply be, because some problems and statements are philosophical and because our human experience raises them. But this is not wholly helpful until we define philosophical. Earlier we used the vague word importance, but it will not do without qualification. After all, other disciplines like physics, mathematics, and history also deal with what is important to them and to aspects of human experience. What makes an issue or activity philosophical is that it is related to clarification and justification (a reason why), that it is generic or general in not being limited to one recognized discipline, and, some philosophers would say, that it is ultimate in the sense that no more basic principles or grounds for its justification can be given. Reflect for a moment on some important issue, say civil rights or abortion, on which you have read. Writers on these issues attempt to give you truths, to be meaningful, to base their statements on evidence, to propose something good or of value. Each of these concepts, truth, meaning, evidence, value, is generally recognized as philosophical. The activity of analyzing, clarifying, and sometimes synthesizing them, is what philosophy is about.

The Field of Philosophy

Philosophy, then, deals with generic problems of human experience, and philosophers maintain that their work with these problems has a direct and relevant bearing on specific issues of human concern. A general characterization of philosophical activity, even if tentative and introductory, may be further helpful in delineating our field of study and distinguishing it from other types of inquiry. Looking back over the history of philosophy, we discover that philosophers have attempted to investigate four distinguishable though interrelated lines of thought.

They have sought to work out some inclusive conception of the universe in all its aspects, including man's place in it. Here philosophers have been synthetic. Making use of the beliefs of common sense and the results of science, and adding to them the insights of our moral, esthetic, and religious experiences, they have undertaken to "see life steadily and see it whole." The inquiry has also been speculative, advancing hypotheses that seem to transcend the deliverances of ordinary experience. To put it briefly, philosophy in this activity is the attempt to give a comprehensive theory of reality as a whole.

Phenomenology is the technical name for a second philosophical activity. Here the interest of the philosopher has been not so much speculative as descriptive, and descriptive in a complete and, at least initially, uninterpretive sense. Many facets of our experience are not immediately obvious, and some are neither clear to common sense nor studied by the natural sciences. Still others may be so muddied by inherited beliefs and interpretations that the philosopher feels obliged to return to the data, to the facts themselves. Facts must be revealed, the implicit made explicit, and the misinterpreted or uninterpreted brought forward for examination.

Besides these two activities, there has been a third that, unlike the others, is closer to the etymology of philosophy. Philosophers have sometimes tried to provide not only a vision of the world in which we live, but standards and guides for individual and social action as well. The principles of right and wrong, the ideals of associative life, the meaning of the good life—such normative concerns have been central to the philosopher's search for wisdom.

In pursuit of the real and the ideal, synoptically and descriptively, philosophers have usually engaged in a fourth activity that we shall call analysis. Perhaps less exciting, yet essential to the philosophic spirit, analysis has included a critical assessment of the assumptions or presuppositions and of the methods upon which common sense, the sciences, and even philosophy rely. Analytic inquiries have also been directed toward key terms like "real," "true," "good," "matter," "mind," "space," and "time," which play a central role in all systematic thinking. Here the philosopher—whatever his ultimate goal may be—is simply searching for fundamental clarity and understanding.

These four activities—the speculative, the descriptive, the normative, and the analytic—describe the philosopher's work. But how shall we view the interrelationships of these activities? Some philosophers would answer that they are all parts of an inclusive philosophic activity, and any philosophy that aims to be truly adequate must include all of them, as did those of the great classical philosophers like Plato, Aristotle, Spinoza, and Hegel. Another group of philosophers would regard these activities not as parts but as different kinds of philosophy, the implication being that the student must choose one kind from among them. This is the view held by many philosophers today. Some follow the lead of men like Moritz Schlick, arguing that philosophy can be neither speculative, descriptive, nor normative, and that it should therefore limit itself to the activity of analysis. Ludwig Wittgenstein, whose views we will study later, saw philosophy as a kind of analysis of language, and he believed that a therapeutic clarification of our concepts would result from it. Others, such as the followers of John Dewey, contend that philosophy's chief business is normative, that it should be primarily "a search for the ends and values that give direction to our collective human activities." Only a relatively few contemporary thinkers, such as those influenced by Alfred North Whitehead, urge that philosophy should return to its original speculative interests as well.

While there are differences among philosophers regarding philosophy itself, there is nevertheless relative agreement on the divisions or areas of philosophical concern. Here again we shall give only introductory statements about these divisions, and allow the selections to develop them. First is the discipline named *metaphysics*. Metaphysics can be defined as the general theory of reality. Among the questions it has traditionally asked are, What is the nature of reality? Is reality one or many? and, Is reality purposive or mechanical? It is usually subdivided into the following fields: *ontology*, or theory of being; *cosmology*, or theory of the cosmos; *rational psychology*, or theory of mind and mind's place in nature; *rational theology*, or theory of divinity; and *axiology*, or theory of values and of the place of values in reality. Generally, the methods in metaphysical investigation have been speculative rather than experimental; frequently, metaphysics and speculation have been taken as synonymous.

The second major subdivision of philosophy is *epistemology*, or theory of knowledge. It questions, What is the nature of knowledge? What is the source of knowledge? and, What is the criterion of knowledge? A third subdivision is usually called the *normative sciences*, chiefly because it deals with problems of value in relation to rules or standards. The major normative sciences are *logic*, the study of arguments; *ethics*, the study of the individual good; *social philosophy*, the study of the social good; *esthetics*, the normative science of art and the beautiful; and *philosophy of religion*, the philosophic examination of religious beliefs and practices. Last is a group of studies to which no special name has been traditionally given, but which we shall call the "philosophies of." They are alike in that each of them begins with some limited area of experience and then seeks to relate that area to a general philosophic position. The philosophy of science is one study from this group that is included in this volume.

The Study of Philosophical Positions

We shall turn shortly from introductory talk about philosophy to talk in philosophy. In so doing, we shall meet problems which are among the most important a human being can face, and with which many of the best minds of Western culture have wrestled. But before we do this, one or two additional introductory remarks need to be made.

One of the characteristics of philosophy is that it generally proceeds with its work by reference to traditions which are cultivated over long periods of time. Even the most individualistic and creative philosopher thinks in this way. Because of this fact, this text, unlike most others, is organized in terms of positions or schools of philosophy. Some explanation of the rationale for this organization may help your reading and understanding. Although the concept of a philosophical school or position is somewhat loose and open-textured, an anthology constructed to take major alternatives into account has several advantages for your understanding of philosophical issues. In this anthology, you can explore the context within which key terms in arguments are defined or clarified, follow the development of approaches and conclusions in their interrelatedness, and, most important of all, develop greater sophistication in handling and reflecting upon the problems of philosophy.

In addition to the observation about philosophers working by reference to traditions, a second observation can be made that philosophical positions become identified with certain basic presuppositions or "theses." A philosophical stand is identified as, say, realist or materialist, through its relationship to them. At the beginning of each perspective below, these theses are spelled out. The selections which follow amplify, develop, and apply the theses in a variety of philosophical fields of study. But these theses not only serve to classify positions, they also indicate what a philosophical position takes to be most basic and important in the effort toward philosophical understanding. Realists, for example, argue that an understanding of being and its principles has this central role for philosophy, while linguistic philosophers take attention to and understanding of language as fundamental. The constitutive beliefs of a philosophy may not agree with your own judgments about importance. But even in disagreement, perhaps through it, we expand our intellectual horizons.

A third observation about philosophy is that it quickly moves from specific issues to general, abstract conceptions. Like other human beings, philosophers are concerned, for example, about race relations, penal reform, and honest government. Their work and interest, however, soon focus not so much on these issues as on the general ideas they involve. In these cases they represent the ideal of justice, the concept of punishment, the nature of authority and power. Indeed, one of the marks of philosophic talent, even greatness, is the ability to discover and clarify fundamental ideas in such a way that in turn they clarify the particular details of our lives. Our study of philosophy will explore these general ideas as various philosophical traditions and positions have enunciated them, and we will trace some of their implications for other selected problems. Of course we cannot cover all the issues that may concern you, and you should always feel free to ask your instructor about the bearing of philosophical ideas on matters that interest you.

In order to attain such educational goals as philosophical understanding and insight, the selections in this anthology have been set out by positions. Thus it is possible for the readings themselves to show the basic themes of a philosophy. The order is meant to serve effective learning because it aids fuller description of issues by providing their context and a wider exploration of connections by juxtaposing selections on various topics within a structure of relationships. But such structuring, it must be emphasized, is not intended to be an overstructuring, nor to encourage you to think in terms of slogans and isms. Indeed the opposite is the case: problems, issues, alternatives are and must remain the center of attention. It is critically more important for you to follow and assess the argument than to classify it as materialist or existentialist. Still, when a setting of approach, terms, and conclusions is helpful, it should be utilized. Nor need any perspective be considered rigid; there are differences among its representatives (consider existentialism), and frequently the study of specific issues leads to clarification of the general concepts in a position. By becoming aware of these and similar matters, the student gains greater opportunity to develop insight and philosophical maturity—which are substantial goals for an introductory course in philosophy.

Three Philosophical Problems

Although we have just mentioned the study of philosophical positions, we are beginning our work with selections on three basic philosophical problems, the nature of man, the good, and the real. These topics are central for many philosophers, and they are also frequently considered to have a bearing on the understanding of issues of contemporary social interest. You may want to consider how a problem such as social justice might be related to the nature of man and the concept of good.

Apart from such connections, these issues are important in themselves, and we shall be returning to them many times throughout our study. Now, however, our reading is directed to them as examples of philosophical reasoning. You will want to follow each author in identifying the problem with which he is dealing, the argument he constructs toward its resolution, and you will want to begin asking whether the writer is developing a position which you might find acceptable.

1 The Nature of Man

René Descartes (1596-1650)

One of the recurring problems amid the many tensions of the contemporary world is the nature of man—the kind of being he is, the critical problems of identity and meaning he faces, the relations to others and the world which affect his being. In this first introductory selection, we turn to the writings of a widely known philosopher for an exploration of this problem.

Born in 1596, Descartes lived at the beginning of what historians term the modern world, with its science, technology, and mass society. His times were similar to ours in many ways, for they were marked by rapid social and intellectual change. Skeptical views about knowledge and values were common, and older traditional ideas were being discarded. Descartes and many others believed that new and more adequate philosophical understanding was needed both to refute skepticism and to provide an interpretation of the new modes of experience. Though his philosophy was and continues to be debated, Descartes is often referred to as the father of modern philosophy.

As an example of philosophical reasoning, this selection should be studied with regard to its reasoning as well as its content. Descartes is constructing an argument by searching for premises, and inferring conclusions. He is "doing philosophy," though his work is subject to evaluation. The argument he constructs begins with the problem of knowledge. Descartes is asking if and where real knowledge, certain and indubitable, is to be found. After a systematic survey of possibilities ("methodological doubt"), he is led to the conclusion that only his self-consciousness or mind is known with certainty, as in his famous phrase, "I think, therefore I am."

Next Descartes asks, What is this "I"? He finds that it is the conscious processes of thinking, willing, doubting, feeling, and so on. But are we not beings with bodies as well as minds? Indeed we are, Descartes answers, but we are or have bodies in a different way from our being minds. Descartes therefore concludes that our human being is a composition of two realities or substances, one mental, the other physical and material.

This conclusion is not without its difficulties. Even Descartes' contemporaries asked him how these two realities, mind and matter, relate to each other. But the argument Descartes developed has nevertheless remained profoundly influential, and the clear and readable form in which it is expressed (a virtue not common to all philosophers) makes it an interesting introduction to philosophical work.

Several years have now elapsed since I first became aware that I had accepted, even from my youth, many false opinions for true, and that consequently what I afterward based on such principles was highly doubtful; and from that time I was convinced of the necessity of undertaking once in my life to rid myself of all the opinions I had adopted, and of commencing anew the work of building from the foundation, if I desired to establish a firm and abiding superstructure in the sciences. But as this enterprise appeared to me to be one of great magnitude, I waited until I had attained an age so mature as to leave me no hope that at any stage of life more advanced I should be better able to execute my design. On this account, I have delayed so long that I should henceforth consider I was doing wrong were I still to consume in deliberation any of the time that now re-

mains for action. To-day, then, since I have opportunely freed my mind from all cares [and am happily disturbed by no passions],[1] and since I am in the secure possession of leisure in a peaceable retirement, I will at length apply myself earnestly and freely to the general overthrow of all my former opinions. . . .

I . . . will proceed by casting aside all that admits of the slightest doubt, not less than if I had discovered it to be absolutely false; and I will continue always in this track until I shall find something that is certain, or at least, if

The selection is from the First, Second, and Sixth of Descartes's *Meditations on The First Philosophy* (tr. John Veitch) (Washington: M. Walter Dunne, 1901).

[1 Brackets in the text have been used by the translator to indicate phrases in the French edition of the *Meditations* not found in the Latin version. *Ed.*]

I can do nothing more, until I shall know with certainty that there is nothing certain. Archimedes, that he might transport the entire globe from the place it occupied to another, demanded only a point that was firm and immovable; so, also, I shall be entitled to entertain the highest expectations, if I am fortunate enough to discover only one thing that is certain and indubitable.

I suppose, accordingly, that all the things which I see are false (fictitious); I believe that none of those objects which my fallacious memory represents ever existed; I suppose that I possess no senses; I believe that body, figure, extension, motion, and place are merely fictions of my mind. What is there, then, that can be esteemed true? Perhaps this only, that there is absolutely nothing certain.

But how do I know that there is not something different altogether from the objects I have now enumerated, of which it is impossible to entertain the slightest doubt? Is there not a God, or some being, by whatever name I may designate him, who causes these thoughts to arise in my mind? But why suppose such a being, for it may be I myself am capable of producing them? Am I, then, at least not something? But I before denied that I possessed senses or a body; I hesitate, however, for what follows from that? Am I so dependent on the body and the senses that without these I cannot exist? But I had the persuasion that there was absolutely nothing in the world, that there was no sky and no earth, neither minds nor bodies; was I not, therefore, at the same time, persuaded that I did not exist? Far from it; I assuredly existed, since I was persuaded. But there is I know not what

being, who is possessed at once of the highest power and the deepest cunning, who is constantly employing all his ingenuity in deceiving me. Doubtless, then, I exist, since I am deceived; and, let him deceive me as he may, he can never bring it about that I am nothing, so long as I shall be conscious that I am something. So that it must, in fine, be maintained, all things being maturely and carefully considered, that this proposition (*pronunciatum*) I am, I exist, is necessarily true each time it is expressed by me, or conceived in my mind.

But I do not yet know with sufficient clearness what I am, though assured that I am; and hence, in the next place, I must take care, lest perchance I inconsiderately substitute some other object in room of what is properly myself, and thus wander from truth, even in that knowledge (cognition) which I hold to be of all others the most certain and evident. For this reason, I will now consider anew what I formerly believed myself to be, before I entered on the present train of thought; and of my previous opinion I will retrench all that can in the least be invalidated by the grounds of doubt I have adduced, in order that there may at length remain nothing but what is certain and indubitable. What then did I formerly think I was? Undoubtedly I judged that I was a man. But what is a man? Shall I say a rational animal? Assuredly not; for it would be necessary forthwith to inquire into what is meant by animal, and what by rational, and thus, from a single question, I should insensibly glide into others, and these more difficult than the first; nor do I now possess enough of leisure to warrant me in wasting my time amid subtleties of this sort. I prefer here to attend to the thoughts that sprung up of themselves in my mind, and were inspired by my own nature alone, when I applied myself to the consideration of what I was. In the first place, then, I thought that I possessed a countenance, hands, arms, and all the fabric of members that appears in a corpse, and which I called by the name of body. It further occurred to me that I was nourished, that I walked, perceived, and thought, and all those actions I referred to the soul; but what the soul itself was I either did not stay to consider, or, if I did, I imagined that it was something extremely rare and subtile, like wind, or flame, or ether, spread through my grosser parts. As regarded the body, I did not even doubt of its nature, but thought I distinctly knew it, and if I had wished to describe it according to the notions I then entertained, I should have explained myself in this manner: By body I understand all that can be terminated by a certain figure; that can be comprised in a certain place, and so fill a certain space as therefrom to exclude every other body; that can be perceived either by touch, sight, hearing, taste, or smell; that can be moved in different ways, not indeed of itself, but by something foreign to it by which it is touched [and from which it receives the impression]; for the power of self-motion, as likewise that of perceiving and thinking, I held as by no means pertaining to the nature of body; on the contrary, I was somewhat astonished to find such faculties existing in some bodies.

But [as to myself, what can I now say that I am], since I suppose there exists an extremely powerful, and, if I may so speak, malignant being, whose whole endeavors are directed toward deceiving me? Can I affirm that I possess any one of all those attributes of which I have lately spoken as belonging to the nature of body? After attentively considering them in my own mind, I find none of them that can properly be said to belong to myself. To recount them were idle and tedious. Let us pass, then, to the attributes of the soul. The first mentioned were the powers of nutrition and walking; but, if it be true that I have no body, it is true likewise that I am capable neither of walking nor of being nourished. Perception is another attribute of the soul; but perception too is impossible without the body; besides, I have frequently, during sleep, believed that I perceived objects which I afterward observed I did not in reality perceive. Thinking is another attribute of the soul; and here I discover what properly belongs to myself. This alone is inseparable from me. I am—I exist: this is certain; but how often? As often as I think; for perhaps it would even happen, if I should wholly cease to think, that I should at the same time altogether cease to be. I now admit nothing that is not necessarily true. I am therefore, precisely speaking, only a thinking thing, that is, a mind (*mens sive animus*), understanding, or reason, terms whose signification was before unknown to me. I am, however, a real thing, and really existent; but what thing? The answer was, a thinking thing. The question now arises, am I aught besides? I will stimulate my imagination with a view to discover whether I am not still something more than a thinking being. Now it is plain I am not the assemblage of members called the human body; I am not a thin and penetrating air diffused through all these members, or wind, or flame, or vapor, or breath, or any of all the things I can imagine; for I supposed that all these were not, and, without changing the supposition, I find that I still feel assured of my existence.

But it is true, perhaps, that those very things which I suppose to be nonexistent, because they are unknown to me, are not in truth different from myself whom I know. This is a point I cannot determine, and do not now enter into any dispute regarding it. I can only judge of things that are known to me: I am conscious that I exist, and I who know that I exist inquire into what I am. It is, however, perfectly certain that the knowledge of my existence, thus precisely taken, is not dependent on things, the existence of which is as yet unknown to me: and consequently it is not dependent on any of the things I can feign in imagination. Moreover, the phrase itself, I frame an image (*effingo*), reminds me of my error; for I should in truth frame one if I were to imagine myself to be anything, since to imagine is nothing more than to contemplate the figure or image of a corporeal thing; but I already know that I exist, and that it is possible at the same time that all those images, and in general all that relates to the nature of body, are merely dreams [or chimeras]. From this I discover that it is not more reasonable to say, I will excite my imagination that I may know more distinctly what I am, than to express myself as follows: I am now awake, and perceive something real; but because my perception is not sufficiently clear, I will of express pur-

pose go to sleep that my dreams may represent to me the object of my perception with more truth and clearness. And, therefore, I know that nothing of all that I can embrace in imagination belongs to the knowledge which I have of myself, and that there is need to recall with the utmost care the mind from this mode of thinking, that it may be able to know its own nature with perfect distinctness.

But what, then, am I? A thinking thing, it has been said. But what is a thinking thing? It is a thing that doubts, understands, [conceives], affirms, denies, wills, refuses; that imagines also, and perceives. Assuredly it is not little, if all these properties belong to my nature. But why should they not belong to it? Am I not that very being who now doubts of almost everything; who, for all that, understands and conceives certain things; who affirms one alone as true, and denies the others; who desires to know more of them, and does not wish to be deceived; who imagines many things, sometimes even despite his will; and is likewise percipient of many, as if through the medium of the senses. Is there nothing of all this as true as that I am, even although I should be always dreaming, and although he who gave me being employed all his ingenuity to deceive me? Is there also any one of these attributes that can be properly distinguished from my thought, or that can be said to be separate from myself? For it is of itself so evident that it is I who doubt, I who understand, and I who desire, that it is here unnecessary to add anything by way of rendering it more clear. And I am as certainly the same being who imagines; for although it may be (as I before supposed) that nothing I imagine is true, still the power of imagination does not cease really to exist in me and to form part of my thought. In fine, I am the same being who perceives, that is, who apprehends certain objects as by the organs of sense, since, in truth, I see light, hear a noise, and feel heat. But it will be said that these presentations are false, and that I am dreaming. Let it be so. At all events it is certain that I seem to see light, hear a noise, and feel heat; this cannot be false, and this is what in me is properly called perceiving (*sentire*), which is nothing else than thinking. From this I begin to know what I am with somewhat greater clearness and distinctness than heretofore. . . .

To commence this examination accordingly, I here remark, in the first place, that there is a vast difference between mind and body, in respect that body, from its nature, is always divisible, and that mind is entirely indivisible. For in truth, when I consider the mind, that is, when I consider myself in so far only as I am a thinking thing, I can distinguish in myself no parts, but I very clearly discern that I am somewhat absolutely one and entire; and although the whole mind seems to be united to the whole body, yet, when a foot, an arm, or any other part is cut off, I am conscious that nothing has been taken from my mind; nor can the faculties of willing, perceiving, conceiving, etc., properly be called its parts, for it is the same mind that is exercised [all entire] in willing, in perceiving, and in conceiving, etc. But quite the opposite holds in, corporeal or extended things; for I cannot imagine any one of them [how small soever it may be], which I

cannot easily sunder in thought, and which, therefore, I do not know to be divisible. This would be sufficient to teach me that the mind or soul of man is entirely different from the body, if I had not already been apprised of it on other grounds.

I remark, in the next place, that the mind does not immediately receive the impression from all the parts of the body, but only from the brain, or perhaps even from one small part of it, viz, that in which the common sense (*sensus communis*) is said to be, which as often as it is affected in the same way gives rise to the same perception in the mind, although meanwhile the other parts of the body may be diversely disposed, as is proved by innumerable experiments, which it is unnecessary here to enumerate.

I remark, besides, that the nature of body is such that none of its parts can be moved by another part a little removed from the other, which cannot likewise be moved in the same way by any one of the parts that lie between those two, although the most remote part does not act at all. As, for example, in the cord A, B, C, D, [which is in tension], if its last part D, be pulled, the first part A, will not be moved in a different way than it would be were one of the intermediate parts B or C to be pulled, and the last part D meanwhile to remain fixed. And in the same way, when I feel pain in the foot, the science of physics teaches me that this sensation is experienced by means of the nerves dispersed over the foot, which, extending like cords from it to the brain, when they are contracted in the foot, contract at the same time the inmost parts of the brain in which they have their origin, and excite in these parts a certain motion appointed by nature to cause in the mind a sensation of pain, as if existing in the foot; but as these nerves must pass through the tibia, the leg, the loins, the back, and neck, in order to reach the brain, it may happen that although their extremities in the foot are not affected, but only certain of their parts that pass through the loins or neck, the same movements, nevertheless, are excited in the brain by this motion as would have been caused there by a hurt received in the foot, and hence the mind will necessarily feel pain in the foot, just as if it had been hurt; and the same is true of all the other perceptions of our senses.

I remark, finally, that as each of the movements that are made in the part of the brain by which the mind is immediately affected, impresses it with but a single sensation, the most likely supposition in the circumstances is, that this movement causes the mind to experience, among all the sensations which it is capable of impressing upon it, that one which is the best fitted, and generally the most useful for the preservation of the human body when it is in full health. But experience shows us that all the perceptions which nature has given us are of such a kind as I have mentioned; and accordingly, there is nothing found in them that does not manifest the power and goodness of God. Thus, for example, when the nerves of the foot are violently or more than usually shaken, the motion passing through the medulla of the spine to the innermost parts of the brain affords a sign to the mind on which it experiences a sensation, viz., of pain, as if it were in the foot, by which the mind is ad-

monished and excited to do its utmost to remove the cause of it as dangerous and hurtful to the foot. It is true that God could have so constituted the nature of man as that the same motion in the brain would have informed the mind of something altogether different: the motion might, for example, have been the occasion on which the mind became conscious of itself, in so far as it is in the brain, or in so far as it is in some place intermediate between the foot and the brain, or, finally, the occasion on which it perceived some other object quite different, whatever that might be; but nothing of all this would have so well contributed to the preservation of the body as that which the mind actually feels. In the same way, when we stand in need of drink, there arises from this want a certain parchedness in the throat that moves its nerves, and by means of them the internal parts of the brain; and this movement affects the mind with the sensation of thirst, because there is nothing on that occasion which is more useful for us than to be made aware that we have need of drink for the preservation of our health; and so in other instances.

Whence it is quite manifest that, notwithstanding the sovereign goodness of God, the nature of man, in so far as it is composed of mind and body, cannot but be sometimes fallacious. For, if there is any cause which excites, not in the foot, but in some one of the parts of the nerves that stretch from the foot to the brain, or even in the brain itself, the same movement that is ordinarily created when the foot is ill affected, pain will be felt, as it were, in the foot, and the sense will thus be naturally deceived; for as the same movement in the brain can but impress the mind with the same sensation, and as this sensation is much more frequently excited by a cause which hurts the foot than by one acting in a different quarter, it is reasonable that it should lead the mind to feel pain in the foot rather than in any other part of the body. And if it sometimes happens that the parchedness of the throat does not arise, as is usual, from drink being necessary for the health of the body, but from quite the opposite cause, as is the case with the dropsical, yet it is much better that it should be deceitful in that instance, than if, on the contrary, it were continually fallacious when the body is well-disposed; and the same holds true in other cases.

2 The Problem of Good
Immanuel Kant (1726-1806)

A great many, perhaps most, of the personal and social issues which concern us include questions of what is good in contrast to what is evil. We say that social justice is good, that racism is evil, and we debate and wonder whether abortion is good or evil. The general concept presupposed in all these matters is that of the good, and we turn next to one philosophical study of that concept in the writings of Immanuel Kant.

Kant is one of the most influential philosophers in the entire history of thought. In addition to his studies in ethics, he wrote on almost every area of philosophy. The themes which pervade his ethical writings are found in the selection below. Kant was convinced, first, that the only value which is completely good, good without qualification, is the good will, which he defines as a will which is obedient to duty. The second theme is expressed in the phrase, "respect for personality." Kant believed that respect for persons is the highest duty for the good will. He also believed that these two theses are interconnected, and he attempts in these pages to show this connection as well. Finally, Kant illustrates his conclusions through four examples which, though debatable, may be helpful in understanding his views.

Nothing can possibly be conceived in the world, or even out of it, which can be called good, without qualification, except a Good Will. Intelligence, wit, judgment, and the other *talents* of the mind, however they may be named, or courage, resolution, perseverance, as qualities of temperament, are undoubtedly good and desirable in many re-

The selection is from Immanuel Kant, *Fundamental Principles of the Metaphysics of Morals* (tr. T. K. Abbott) (London: Longmans, Green, [1873] 1909).

spects; but these gifts of nature may also become extremely bad and mischievous if the will which is to make use of them, and which, therefore, constitutes what is called *character*, is not good. It is the same with the *gifts of fortune*. Power, riches, honor, even health, and the general well-being and contentment with one's condition which is called *happiness*, inspire pride, and often presumption, if there is not a good will to correct the influence of these on the mind, and with this also to rectify the whole principle of acting, and adapt it to its end. The sight of a being who is not adorned with a single feature of a pure and good will, enjoying unbroken prosperity, can never give pleasure to an impartial rational spectator. Thus a good will appears to constitute the indispensable condition even of being worthy of happiness.

There are even some qualities which are of service to this good will itself, and may facilitate its action, yet which have no intrinsic unconditional value, but always presuppose a good will, and this qualifies the esteem that we justly have for them, and does not permit us to regard them as absolutely good. Moderation in the affections and passions, self-control, and calm deliberation are not only good in many respects, but even seem to constitute part of the intrinsic worth of the person; but they are far from deserving to be called good without qualification, although they have been so unconditionally praised by the ancients. For without the principles of a good will, they may become extremely bad; and the coolness of a villain not only makes him far more dangerous, but also directly makes him more abominable in our eyes than he would have been without it.

A good will is good not because of what it performs or effects, not by its aptness for the attainment of some proposed end, but simply by virtue of the volition, that is, it is good in itself, and considered by itself is to be esteemed much higher than all that can be brought about by it in favor of any inclination, nay, even of the sum-total of all inclinations. Even if it should happen that, owing to special disfavor of fortune, or the niggardly provision of a step-motherly nature, this will should wholly lack power to accomplish its purpose, if with its greatest efforts it should yet achieve nothing, and there should remain only the good will (not, to be sure, a mere wish, but the summoning of all means in our power), then, like a jewel, it would still shine by its own light, as a thing which has its whole value in itself. Its usefulness or fruitlessness can neither add to nor take away anything from this value. It would be, as it were, only the setting to enable us to handle it the more conveniently in common commerce, or to attract to it the attention of those who are not yet connoisseurs, but not to recommend it to true connoisseurs, or to determine its value.

We have then to develop the notion of a will which deserves to be highly esteemed for itself, and is good without a view to anything further, a notion which exists already in the sound natural understanding, requiring rather to be cleared up than to be taught, and which in estimating the value of our actions always takes the first place, and constitutes the condition of all the rest. In order to do this, we will take the notion of duty, which includes that of a good will, although implying certain subjective restrictions and hindrances. These, however, far from concealing it, or rendering it unrecognizable, rather bring it out by contrast, and make it shine forth so much the brighter. . . .

If we attend to the experience of men's conduct, we meet frequent and, as we ourselves allow, just complaints that one cannot find a single certain example of the disposition to act from pure duty. Although many things are done in *conformity* with what *duty* prescribes, it is nevertheless always doubtful whether they are done strictly *from duty*, so as to have a moral worth. Hence there have at all times been philosophers who have altogether denied that this disposition actually exists at all in human actions, and have ascribed everything to a more or less refined self-love. Not that they have on that account questioned the soundness of the conception of morality; on the contrary, they spoke with sincere regret of the frailty and corruption of human nature, which though noble enough to take as its rule an idea so worthy of respect, is yet too weak to follow it, and employs reason, which ought to give it the law only for the purpose of providing for the interest of the inclinations, whether singly or at the best in the greatest possible harmony with one another.

But in order that in this study we may not merely advance by the natural steps from the common moral judgment (in this case very worthy of respect) to the philosophical, as has been already done, but also from a popular philosophy, which goes no further than it can reach by groping with the help of examples, to metaphysic (which does not allow itself to be checked by anything empirical, and as it must measure the whole extent of this kind of rational knowledge, goes as far as ideal conceptions, where even examples fail us), we must follow and clearly describe the practical faculty of reason, from the general rules of its determination to the point where the notion of duty springs from it.

Everything in nature works according to laws. Rational beings alone have the faculty of acting according *to the conception* of laws, that is according to principles, *i.e.* have a *will*. Since the deduction of actions from principles requires *reason*, the will is nothing but practical reason. If reason infallibly determines the will, then the actions of such a being which are recognized as objectively necessary are subjectively necessary also, *i.e.* the will is a faculty to choose *that only* which reason independent of inclination recognizes as practically necessary, *i.e.* as good. But if reason of itself does not sufficiently determine the will, if the latter is subject also to subjective conditions (particular impulses) which do not always coincide with the objective conditions; in a word, if the will does not *in itself* completely accord with reason (which is actually the case with men), then the actions which objectively are recognized as necessary are subjectively contingent, and the determination of such a will according to objective laws is *obligation*, that is to say, the relation of the objective laws to a will that is not thoroughly good is conceived as the determination of the will of a rational being by principles of reason, but which the will from its nature does not of necessity follow.

The conception of an objective principle, in so far as it is obligatory for a will, is called a command (of reason), and the formula of the command is called an Imperative.

All imperatives are expressed by the word *ought* [or *shall*], and thereby indicate the relation of an objective law of reason to a will, which from its subjective constitution is not necessarily determined by it (an obligation). They say that something would be good to do or to forbear, but they say it to a will which does not always do a thing because it is conceived to be good to do it. That is practically *good*, however, which determines the will by means of the conceptions of reason, and consequently not from subjective causes, but objectively, that is on principles which are valid for every rational being as such. It is distinguished from the *pleasant*, as that which influences the will only by means of sensation from merely subjective causes, valid only for the sense of this or that one, and not as a principle of reason, which holds for every one.

A perfectly good will would therefore be equally subject to objective laws (viz. laws of good), but could not be conceived as *obliged* thereby to act lawfully, because of itself from its subjective constitution it can only be determined by the conception of good. Therefore no imperatives hold for the Divine will, or in general for a *holy* will; *ought* is here out of place, because the volition is already of itself necessarily in unison with the law. Therefore imperatives are only formulæ to express the relation of objective laws of all volition to the subjective imperfection of the will of this or that rational being, *e.g.* the human will.

Now all *imperatives* command either *hypothetically* or *categorically*. The former represent the practical necessity of a possible action as means to something else that is willed (or at least which one might possibly will). The categorical imperative would be that which represented an action as necessary of itself without reference to another end, *i.e.*, as objectively necessary.

Since every practical law represents a possible action as good, and on this account, for a subject who is practically determinable by reason, necessary, all imperatives are formulæ determining an action which is necessary according to the principle of a will good in some respects. If now the action is good only as a means *to something else*, then the imperative is *hypothetical*; if it is conceived as good *in itself* and consequently as being necessarily the principle of a will which of itself conforms to reason, then it is *categorical*.

Accordingly the hypothetical imperative only says that the action is good for some purpose, *possible* or *actual*. In the first case it is a Problematical, in the second an Assertorial practical principle. The categorical imperative which declares an action to be objectively necessary in itself without reference to any purpose, *i.e.* without any other end, is valid as an Apodictic (practical) principle.

Whatever is possible only by the power of some rational being may also be conceived as a possible purpose of some will; and therefore the principles of action as regards the means necessary to attain some possible purpose are in fact infinitely numerous. All sciences have a practical part, consisting of problems expressing that some end is possible for us, and of imperatives directing how it may be attained. These may, therefore, be called in general imperatives of Skill. Here there is no question whether the end is rational and good, but only what one must do in order to attain it. The precepts for the physician to make his patient thoroughly healthy, and for a poisoner to ensure certain death, are of equal value in this respect, that each serves to effect its purpose perfectly. Since in early youth it cannot be known what ends are likely to occur to us in the course of life, parents seek to have their children taught a *great many things*, and provide for their *skill* in the use of means for all sorts of arbitrary ends, of none of which can they determine whether it may not perhaps hereafter be an object to their pupil, but which it is at all events *possible* that he might aim at; and this anxiety is so great that they commonly neglect to form and correct their judgment on the value of the things which may be chosen as ends.

There is *one* end, however, which may be assumed to be actually such to all rational beings (so far as imperatives apply to them, viz. as dependent beings), and, therefore, one purpose which they not merely *may* have, but which we may with certainty assume that they all actually *have* by a natural necessity, and this is *happiness*. The hypothetical imperative which expresses the practical necessity of an action as means to the advancement of happiness is Assertorial. We are not to present it as necessary for an uncertain and merely possible purpose, but for a purpose which we may presuppose with certainty and *à priori* in every man, because it belongs to his being. Now skill in the choice of means to his own greatest well-being may be called *prudence*, in the narrowest sense. And thus the imperative which refers to the choice of means to one's own happiness, *i.e.* the precept of prudence, is still always *hypothetical*; the action is not commanded absolutely,

but only as means to another purpose.

Finally, there is an imperative which commands a certain conduct immediately, without having as its condition any other purpose to be attained by it. This imperative is Categorical. It concerns not the matter of the action, or its intended result, but its form and the principle of which it is itself a result; and what is essentially good in it consists in the mental disposition, let the consequence be what it may. This imperative may be called that of Morality.

When I conceive a hypothetical imperative, in general I do not know beforehand what it will contain until I am given the condition. But when I conceive a categorical imperative, I know at once what it contains. For as the imperative contains besides the law only the necessity that the maxims shall conform to this law, while the law contains no conditions restricting it, there remains nothing but the general statement that the maxim of the action should conform to a universal law, and it is this conformity alone that the imperative properly represents as necessary.

There is therefore but one categorical imperative, namely, this: *Act only on that maxim whereby thou canst at the same time will that it should become a universal law.*

Now if all imperatives of duty can be deduced from this one imperative as from their principle, then, although it should remain undecided whether what is called duty is not merely a vain notion, yet at least we shall be able to show what we understand by it and what this notion means.

Since the universality of the law according to which effects are produced constitutes what is properly called *na-*

ture in the most general sense (as to form), that is the existence of things so far as it is determined by general laws, the imperative of duty may be expressed thus: *Act as if the maxim of thy action were to become by thy will a universal law of nature.*

We will now enumerate a few duties, adopting the usual division of them into duties to ourselves and to others, and into perfect and imperfect duties.

1. A man reduced to despair by a series of misfortunes feels wearied of life, but is still so far in possession of his reason that he can ask himself whether it would not be contrary to his duty to himself to take his own life. Now he inquires whether the maxim of his action could become a universal law of nature. His maxim is: From self-love I adopt it as a principle to shorten my life when its longer duration is likely to bring more evil than satisfaction. It is asked then simply whether this principle founded on self-love can become a universal law of nature. Now we see at once that a system of nature of which it should be a law to destroy life by means of the very feeling whose special nature it is to impel to the improvement of life would contradict itself, and therefore could not exist as a system of nature; hence that maxim cannot possibly exist as a universal law of nature, and consequently would be wholly inconsistent with the supreme principle of all duty.

2. Another finds himself forced by necessity to borrow money. He knows that he will not be able to repay it, but sees also that nothing will be lent to him, unless he promises stoutly to repay it in a definite time. He desires to make this promise, but he has still so much conscience as to ask himself: Is it not unlawful and inconsistent with duty to get out of a difficulty in this way? Suppose, however, that he resolves to do so, then the maxim of his action would be expressed thus: When I think myself in want of money, I will borrow money and promise to repay it, although I know that I never can do so. Now this principle of self-love or of one's own advantage may perhaps be consistent with my whole future welfare; but the question now is, Is it right? I change then the suggestion of self-love into a universal law, and state the question thus: How would it be if my maxim were a universal law? Then I see at once that it could never hold as a universal law of nature, but would necessarily contradict itself. For supposing it to be a universal law that everyone when he thinks himself in a difficulty should be able to promise whatever he pleases, with the purpose of not keeping his promise, the promise itself would become impossible, as well as the end that one might have in view in it, since no one would consider that anything was promised to him, but would ridicule all such statements as vain pretences.

3. A third finds in himself a talent which with the help of some culture might make him a useful man in many respects. But he finds himself in comfortable circumstances, and prefers to indulge in pleasure rather than to take pains in enlarging and improving his happy natural capacities. He asks, however, whether his maxim of neglect of his natural gifts, besides agreeing with his inclination to indulgence, agrees also with what is called duty. He sees then that a system of nature could indeed subsist with such a universal law although men (like the South Sea island-

ers) should let their talents rest, and resolve to devote their lives merely to idleness, amusement, and propagation of their species—in a word, to enjoyment; but he cannot possibly *will* that this should be a universal law of nature, or be implanted in us as such by a natural instinct. For, as a rational being, he necessarily wills that his faculties be developed, since they serve him, and have been given him, for all sorts of possible purposes.

4. A fourth, who is in prosperity, while he sees that others have to contend with great wretchedness and that he could help them, thinks: What concern is it of mine? Let everyone be as happy as Heaven pleases, or as he can make himself; I will take nothing from him nor even envy him, only I do not wish to contribute anything to his welfare or to his assistance in distress! Now no doubt if such a mode of thinking were a universal law, the human race might very well subsist, and doubtless even better than in a state in which everyone talks of sympathy and goodwill, or even takes care occasionally to put it into practice, but, on the other side, also cheats when he can, betrays the rights of men, or otherwise violates them. But although it is possible that a universal law of nature might exist in accordance with that maxim, it is impossible to *will* that such a principle should have the universal validity of a law of nature. For a will which resolved this would contradict itself, inasmuch as many cases might occur in which one would have need of the love and sympathy of others, and in which, by such a law of nature, sprung from his own will, he would deprive himself of all hope of the aid he desires.

These are a few of the many actual duties, or at least what we regard as such, which obviously fall into two classes on the one principle that we have laid down. We must be *able to will* that a maxim of our action should be a universal law. This is the canon of the moral appreciation of the action generally. Some actions are of such a character that their maxim cannot without contradiction be even *conceived* as a universal law of nature, far from it being possible that we should *will* that it *should* be so. In others this intrinsic impossibility is not found, but still it is impossible to *will* that their maxim should be raised to the universality of a law of nature, since such a will would contradict itself. It is easily seen that the former violate strict or rigorous (inflexible) duty; the latter only laxer (meritorious) duty. Thus it has been completely shown by these examples how all duties depend as regards the nature of the obligation (not the object of the action) on the same principle.

If now we attend to ourselves on occasion of any transgression of duty, we shall find that we in fact do not will that our maxim should be a universal law, for that is impossible for us; on the contrary, we will that the opposite should remain a universal law, only we assume the liberty of making an *exception* in our own favor or (just for this time only) in favor of our inclination. Consequently if we considered all cases from one and the same point of view, namely, that of reason, we should find a contradiction in our own will, namely, that a certain principle should be objectively necessary as a universal law, and yet subjectively should not be universal, but admit of exceptions. As, however, we at one moment regard our action from the point of view of a will wholly conformed to reason, and then again look at the same action from the point of view of a will affected by inclination, there is not really any contradiction, but an antagonism of inclination to the precept of reason, whereby the universality of the principle is changed into a mere generality, so that the practical principle of reason shall meet the maxim half way. Now, although this cannot be justified in our own impartial judgment, yet it proves that we do really recognize the validity of the categorical imperative and (with all respect for it) only allow ourselves a few exceptions, which we think unimportant and forced from us.

We have thus established at least this much, that if duty is a conception which is to have any import and real legislative authority for our actions, it can only be expressed in categorical, and not at all in hypothetical imperatives. We have also, which is of great importance, exhibited clearly and definitely for every practical application the content of the categorical imperative, which must contain the principle of all duty if there is such a thing at all. We have not yet, however, advanced so far as to prove *à priori* that there actually is such an imperative, that there is a practical law which commands absolutely of itself, and without any other impulse, and that the following of this law is duty.

The question then is this: Is it a necessary law *for all rational beings* that they should always judge of their actions by maxims of which they can themselves will that they should serve as universal laws? If it is so, then it must be connected (altogether *à priori*) with the very conception of the will of a rational being generally. But in order to discover this connection we must, however reluctantly, take a step into metaphysic, although into a domain of it which is distinct from speculative philosophy, namely, the metaphysic of morals.

The will is conceived as a faculty of determining oneself to action *in accordance with the conception of certain laws.* And such a faculty can be found only in rational beings. Now that which serves the will as the objective ground of its self-determination is the *end*, and if this is assigned by reason alone, it must hold for all rational beings. On the other hand, that which merely contains the ground of possibility of the action of which the effect is the end, this is called the *means.* The subjective ground of the desire is the *spring*, the objective ground of the volition is the *motive*; hence the distinction between subjective ends which rest on springs, and objective ends which depend on motives valid for every rational being. Practical principles are *formal* when they abstract from all subjective ends; they are *material* when they assume these, and therefore particular springs of action. The ends which a rational being proposes to himself at pleasure as *effects* of his actions (material ends) are all only relative, for it is only their relation to the particular desires of the subject that gives them their worth, which therefore cannot furnish principles universal and necessary for all rational beings and for every volition, that is to say practical laws. Hence all these relative ends can give rise only to hypothetical imperatives.

Supposing, however, that there were something *whose existence* has *in itself* an absolute worth, something which, being *an end in itself*, could be a source of definite laws, then in this and this alone would lie the source of a possible categorical imperative, *i.e.* a practical law.

Now I say: man and generally any rational being *exists* as an end in himself, *not merely as a means* to be arbitrarily used by this or that will, but in all his actions, whether they concern himself or other rational beings, must be always regarded at the same time as an end. All objects of the inclinations have only a conditional worth; for if the inclinations and the wants founded on them did not exist, then their object would be without value. But the inclinations themselves being sources of want are so far from having an absolute worth for which they should be desired, that, on the contrary, it must be the universal wish of every rational being to be wholly free from them. Thus the worth of any object which is *to be acquired* by our action is always conditional. Beings whose existence depends not on our will but on nature's, have nevertheless, if they are rational beings, only a relative value as means, and are therefore called *things*; rational beings, on the contrary, are called *persons*, because their very nature points them out as ends in themselves, that is as something which must not be used merely as means, and so far therefore restricts freedom of action (and is an object of respect). These, therefore, are not merely subjective ends whose existence has a worth *for us* as an effect of our action, but *objective ends*, that is things whose existence is an end in itself: an end moreover for which no other can be substituted, which they should subserve *merely* as means, for otherwise nothing whatever would pos-

sess *absolute worth*; but if all worth were conditioned and therefore contingent, then there would be no supreme practical principle of reason whatever.

If then there is a supreme practical principle or, in respect of the human will, a categorical imperative, it must be one which, being drawn from the conception of that which is necessarily an end for everyone because it is *an end in itself*, constitutes an *objective* principle of will, and can therefore serve as a universal practical law. The foundation of this principle is: *rational nature exists as an end in itself*. Man necessarily conceives his own existence as being so: so far then this is a *subjective* principle of human actions. But every other rational being regards its existence similarly, just on the same rational principle that holds for me: so that it is at the same time an objective principle, from which as a supreme practical law all laws of the will must be capable of being deduced. Accordingly the practical imperative will be as follows: *So act as to treat humanity, whether in thine own person or in that of any other, in every case as an end withal, never as means only.* We will now inquire whether this can be practically carried out.

To abide by the previous examples: *Firstly*, under the head of necessary duty to oneself: He who contemplates suicide should ask himself whether his action can be consistent with the idea of humanity *as an end in itself*. If he destroys himself in order to escape from painful circumstances, he uses a person merely as *a means* to maintain a tolerable condition up to the end of life. But a man is not a thing, that is to say, something which can be used merely as means, but must in all his actions be always considered as an end in himself. I cannot, therefore, dispose in any way of a man in my own person so as to mutilate him, to damage or kill him. (It belongs to ethics proper to define this principle more precisely, so as to avoid all misunderstanding, *e.g.* as to the amputation of the limbs in order to preserve myself; as to exposing my life to danger with a view to preserve it, etc. This question is therefore omitted here.)

Secondly, as regards necessary duties, or those of strict obligation, towards others; he who is thinking of making a lying promise to others will see at once that he would be using another man *merely as a means* without the latter containing at the same time the end in himself. For he whom I propose by such a promise to use for my own purposes cannot possibly assent to my mode of acting towards him, and therefore cannot himself contain the end of this action. This violation of the principle of humanity in other men is more obvious if we take in examples of attacks on the freedom and property of others. For then it is clear that he who transgresses the rights of men intends to use the person of others merely as means, without considering that as rational beings they ought always to be esteemed also as ends, that is, as beings who must be capable of containing in themselves the end of the very same action.

Thirdly, as regards contingent (meritorious) duties to oneself; it is not enough that the action does not violate humanity in our own person as an end in itself, it must also *harmonize with* it. Now there are in humanity capacities of greater perfection which belong to the end that nature has in view in regard to humanity in ourselves as the subject: to neglect these might perhaps be consistent with the *maintenance* of humanity as an end in itself, but not with the *advancement* of this end.

Fourthly, as regards meritorious duties towards others: the natural end which all men have is their own happiness. Now humanity might indeed subsist, although no one should contribute anything to the happiness of others, provided he did not intentionally withdraw anything from it; but after all, this would only harmonize negatively, not positively, with *humanity as an end in itself*, if everyone does not also endeavor, as far as in him lies, to forward the ends of others. For the ends of any subject which is an end in himself, ought as far as possible to be *my* ends also, if that conception is to have its *full* effect with me.

3 On What There Is

Willard V. O. Quine (1908-   )

All of us at some time or other have said that some things are, other things are not. The general question behind these statements is, What do we mean by "are" or "exists" and "are not?" It is just this question which occupies the author of the following selection. Quine is a distinguished American philosopher who has written widely on this and related questions, as well as an original logician. The latter accounts in part for the seemingly mysterious way Quine states his conclusion, that to be is to be the value of a variable. But he explains the meaning of this expression, and shows how it clarifies the nature of the "ontology" one happens to accept.

*A curious thing about the ontological problem is its simplicity. It can be put in three Anglo-Saxon monosyllables: "What is there?" It can be answered, moreover, in a word—"Everything"—and everyone will accept this answer as true. However, this is merely to say that there is what there is. There remains room for disagreement over cases: and so the issue has stayed alive down the centuries.

Suppose now that two philosophers, McX and I, differ over ontology. Suppose McX maintains there is something which I maintain there is not. McX can, quite consistently with his own point of view, describe our difference of opinion by saying that I refuse to recognize certain entities. I should protest of course that he is wrong in his formulation of our disagreement, for I maintain that there are no entities, of the kind which he alleges, for me to recognize: but my finding him wrong in his formulation of our disagreement is unimportant, for I am committed to considering him wrong in his ontology anyway.

When *I* try to formulate our differ-

ence of opinion, on the other hand, I seem to be in a predicament. I cannot admit that there are some things which McX countenances and I do not, for in admitting that there are such things I should be contradicting my own rejection of them.

It would appear, if this reasoning were sound, that in any ontological dispute the proponent of the negative side suffers the disadvantage of not being able to admit that his opponent disagrees with him.

This is the old Platonic riddle of nonbeing. Non-being must in some sense be, otherwise what is it that there is not? This tangled doctrine might be nicknamed *Plato's beard*: historically it has proved tough, frequently dulling the edge of Occam's razor.[1]

It is some such line of thought that leads philosophers like McX to impute being where they might otherwise be quite content to recognize that there is nothing. Thus, take Pegasus. If Pegasus *were* not, McX argues, we should not be talking about anything when we use the word; therefore it would be nonsense to say even that Pegasus is not. Thinking to show thus that the denial of Pegasus cannot be coherently maintained, he concludes that Pegasus is.

McX cannot, indeed, quite persuade himself that any region of space-time,

The selection is from Willard Van Orman Quine, "On What There Is," *The Review of Metaphysics*, 1(1948), pp. 21-36, with omissions. Used by permission of the Editor and author.

* This is a revised version of a paper which was presented before the Graduate Philosophy Club of Yale University on May 7, 1948. The latter paper, in turn, was a revised version of one which was presented before the Graduate Philosophical Seminary of Princeton University on March 15.

[1 The name frequently given to a logical principle stated by the English Franciscan theologian, William of Occam or Ockham (1280-1349). The principle is that entities should not be multiplied beyond necessity. *Ed.*]

near or remote, contains a flying horse of flesh and blood. Pressed for further details on Pegasus, then, he says that Pegasus is an idea in men's minds. Here, however, a confusion begins to be apparent. We may for the sake of argument concede that there is an entity, and even a unique entity (though this is rather implausible), which is the mental Pegasus-idea; but this mental entity is not what people are talking about when they deny Pegasus.

McX never confuses the Parthenon with the Parthenon-idea. The Parthenon is physical; the Parthenon-idea is mental (according any way to McX's version of ideas, and I have no better to offer). The Parthenon is visible; the Parthenon-idea is invisible. We cannot easily imagine two things more unlike, and less liable to confusion, than the Parthenon and the Parthenon-idea. But when we shift from the Parthenon to Pegasus, the confusion sets in—for no other reason than that McX would sooner be deceived by the crudest and most flagrant counterfeit than grant the non-being of Pegasus.

The notion that Pegasus must be, because it would otherwise be nonsense to say even that Pegasus is not, has been seen to lead McX into an elementary confusion. Subtler minds, taking the same precept as their starting point, come out with theories of Pegasus which are less patently misguided than McX's, and correspondingly more difficult to eradicate. One of these subtler minds is named, let us say, Wyman. Pegasus, Wyman maintains, has his being as an unactualized possible. When we say of Pegasus that there is no such thing, we are saying, more precisely, that Pegasus does not have the special

attribute of actuality. Saying that Pegasus is not actual is on a par, logically, with saying that the Parthenon is not red; in either case we are saying something about an entity whose being is unquestioned.

Wyman, by the way, is one of those philosophers who have united in ruining the good old word 'exist'. Despite his espousal of unactualized possibles, he limits the word 'existence' to actuality—thus preserving an illusion of ontological agreement between himself and us who repudiate the rest of his bloated universe. We have all been prone to say, in our common-sense usage of 'exist', that Pegasus does not exist, meaning simply that there is no such entity at all. If Pegasus existed he would indeed be in space and time, but only because the word 'Pegasus' has spatio-temporal connotations, and not because 'exists' has spatio-temporal connotations. If spatio-temporal reference is lacking when we affirm the existence of the cube root of 27, this is simply because a cube root is not a spatio-temporal kind of thing, and not because we are being ambiguous in our use of 'exist'. However, Wyman, in an ill-conceived effort to appear agreeable, genially grants us the non-existence of Pegasus and then, contrary to what *we* meant by non-existence of Pegasus, insists that Pegasus *is*. Existence is one thing, he says, and subsistence is another. The only way I know of coping with this obfuscation of issues is to *give* Wyman the word 'exist'. I'll try not to use it again; I still have 'is'. So much for lexicography; let's get back to Wyman's ontology.

Wyman's overpopulated universe is in many ways unlovely. It offends the aesthetic sense of us who have a taste for desert landscapes, but this is not the worst of it. Wyman's slum of possibles is a breeding ground for disorderly elements. Take, for instance, the possible fat man in that doorway; and, again, the possible bald man in that doorway. Are they the same possible man, or two possible men? How do we decide? How many possible men are there in that doorway? Are there more possible thin ones than fat ones? How many of them are alike? Or would their being alike make them one? Are no *two* possible things alike? Is this the same as saying that it is impossible for two things to be alike? Or, finally, is the concept of identity simply inapplicable to unactualized possibles? But what sense can be found in talking of entities which cannot meaningfully be said to be identical with themselves and distinct from one another? These elements are well nigh incorrigible. By a Fregean therapy of individual concepts, some effort might be made at rehabilitation; but I feel we'd do better simply to clear Wyman's slum and be done with it.

Possibility, along with the other modalities of necessity and impossibility and contingency, raises problems upon which I do not mean to imply that we should turn our backs. But we can at least limit modalities to whole statements. We may impose the adverb 'possibly' upon a statement as a whole, and we may well worry about the semantical analysis of such usage: but little real advance in such analysis is to be hoped for in expanding our universe to include so-called *possible entities*. I suspect that the main motive for this expansion is simply the old notion that Pegasus, e.g., must be because it would otherwise be nonsense to say even that he is not.

Still, all the rank luxuriance of Wyman's universe of possibles would seem to come to naught when we make a slight change in the example and speak not of Pegasus but of the round square cupola on Berkeley College. If, unless Pegasus were, it would be nonsense to say that he is not, then by the same token, unless the round square cupola on Berkeley College were, it would be nonsense to say that it is not. But, unlike Pegasus, the round square cupola on Berkeley College cannot be admitted even as an unactualized *possible*. Can we drive Wyman now to admitting also a realm of unactualizable impossibles? If so, a good many embarrassing questions could be asked about them. We might hope even to trap Wyman in contradictions, by getting him to admit that certain of these entities are at once round and square. But the wily Wyman chooses the other horn of the dilemma and concedes that it is nonsense to say that the round square cupola on Berkeley College is not. He says that the phrase 'round square cupola' is meaningless.

Wyman was not the first to embrace this alternative. The doctrine of the meaninglessness of contradictions runs away back. The tradition survives, moreover, in writers such as Wittgenstein[2] who seem to share none of Wyman's motivations. Still I wonder whether the first temptation to such a doctrine may not have been substantially the motivation which we have observed in Wyman. Certainly the doctine has no intrinsic appeal; and it has led its devotees to such quixotic ex-

---

[2 Ludwig Wittgenstein, whose thought is discussed in Chapter Six. *Ed.*]

tremes as that of challenging the method of proof by *reductio ad absurdum*[3]—a challenge in which I seem to detect a quite striking *reductio ad absurdum eius ipsius.*

Moreover, the doctrine of meaninglessness of contradictions has the severe methodological drawback that it makes it impossible, in principle, ever to devise an effective test of what is meaningful and what is not. It would be forever impossible for us to devise systematic ways of deciding whether a string of signs made sense—even to us individually, let alone other people—or not. For, it follows from a discovery in mathematical logic, due to Church,[4] that there can be no generally applicable test of contradictoriness.

I have spoken disparagingly of Plato's beard, and hinted that it is tangled. I have dwelt at length on the inconveniences of putting up with it. It is time to think about taking steps.

Russell,[5] in his theory of so-called singular descriptions, showed clearly how we might meaningfully use seeming names without supposing that the entities allegedly named be. The names to which Russell's theory directly applies are complex descriptive names such as 'the author of *Waverly*', 'the present King of France', 'the round square cupola on Berkeley College'. Russell analyzes such phrases systematically as frag-

ments of the whole sentences in which they occur. The sentence 'The author of *Waverly* was a poet', e.g., is explained as a whole as meaning 'Someone (better: something) wrote *Waverly* and was a poet, and nothing else wrote *Waverly*'. (The point of this added clause is to affirm the uniqueness which is implicit in the word 'the', in '*the* author of *Waverly*'.) The sentence 'The round square cupola on Berkeley College is pink' is explained as 'Something is round and square and is a cupola on Berkeley College and is pink, and nothing else is round and square and a cupola on Berkeley College'.

The virtue of this analysis is that the seeming name, a descriptive phrase, is paraphrased *in context* as a so-called incomplete symbol. No unified expression is offered as an analysis of the descriptive phrase, but the statement as a whole which was the context of that phrase still gets its full quota of meaning —whether true or false.

The unanalyzed statement 'The author of *Waverly* was a poet' contains a part, 'the author of *Waverly*', which is wrongly supposed by McX and Wyman to demand objective reference in order to be meaningful at all. But in Russell's translation, 'Something wrote *Waverly* and was a poet and nothing else wrote *Waverly*', the burden of objective reference which had been put upon the descriptive phrase is now taken over by words of the kind that logicians call bound variables, variables of quantification: namely, words like 'something', 'nothing', 'everything'. These words, far from purporting to be names specifically of the author of *Waverly*, do not purport to be names at all; they refer to entities generally, with a kind of studied

---

[3 "Reduction to absurdity": a method of proof of a proposition by proof or disproof of its contradictory. *Ed.*]

[4 Alonzo Church, distinguished American logician. *Ed.*]

[5 Bertrand Russell, noted British philosopher and logician. *Ed.*]

ambiguity peculiar to themselves. These quantificational words or bound variables are of course a basic part of language, and their meaningfulness, at least in context, is not to be challenged. But their meaningfulness in no way presupposes there being either the author of *Waverly* or the round square cupola on Berkeley College or any other specifically preassigned objects.

Where descriptions are concerned, there is no longer any difficulty in affirming or denying being. 'There *is* the author of *Waverly*' is explained by Russell as meaning 'Someone (or, more strictly, something) wrote *Waverly* and nothing else wrote *Waverly*'. 'The author of *Waverly* is not' is explained, correspondingly, as the alternation 'Either each thing failed to write *Waverly* or two or more things wrote *Waverly*.' This alternation is false, but meaningful; and it contains no expression purporting to designate the author of *Waverly*. The statement 'The round square cupola on Berkeley College is not' is analyzed in similar fashion. So the old notion that statements of non-being defeat themselves goes by the board. When a statement of being or non-being is analyzed by Russell's theory of descriptions, it ceases to contain any expression which even purports to name the alleged entity whose being is in question, so that the meaningfulness of the statement no longer can be thought to presuppose that there be such an entity.

Now what of 'Pegasus'? This being a word rather than a descriptive phrase, Russell's argument does not immediately apply to it. However, it can easily be made to apply. We have only to rephrase 'Pegasus' as a description, in any way that seems adequately to single out our idea: say 'the winged horse that was captured by Bellerophon'. Substituting such a phrase for 'Pegasus', we can then proceed to analyze the statement 'Pegasus is', or 'Pegasus is not', precisely on the analogy of Russell's analysis of 'The author of *Waverly* is' and 'The author of *Waverly* is not'. . . .

We can very easily involve ourselves in ontological commitments, by saying, e.g., that *there is something* (bound variable) which red houses and sunsets have in common; or that *there is something* which is a prime number between 1000 and 1010. But this is, essentially, the *only* way we can involve ourselves in ontological commitments: by our use of bound variables. The use of alleged names is no criterion, for we can repudiate their namehood at the drop of a hat unless the assumption of a corresponding entity can be spotted in the things we affirm in terms of bound variables. Names are in fact altogether immaterial to the ontological issue, for I have shown, in connection with 'Pegasus' and 'pegasize', that names can be converted to descriptions, and Russell has shown that descriptions can be eliminated. Whatever we say with help of names can be said in a language which shuns names altogether. To be is, purely and simply, to be the value of a variable. In terms of the categories of traditional grammar, this amounts roughly to saying that to be is to be in the range of reference of a pronoun. Pronouns are the basic media of reference; nouns might better have been named pro-pronouns. The variables of quantification, 'something', 'nothing', 'everything', range over our whole ontology, whatever it may be; and we are convicted of a particular ontological presupposition if, and only if, the alleged presupposition has to be reckoned among the entities over which our variables range in order to render one of our affirmations true.

We may say, e.g., that some dogs are white, and not thereby commit ourselves to recognizing either doghood or whiteness as entities. 'Some dogs are white' says that some things that are dogs are white; and, in order that this statement be true, the things over which the bound variable 'something' ranges must include some white dogs, but need not include doghood or whiteness. On the other hand, when we say that some zoölogical species are cross-fertile, we are committing ourselves to recognizing as entities the several species themselves, abstract though they be. We remain so committed at least until we devise some way of so paraphrasing the statement as to show that the seeming reference to species on the part of our bound variable was an avoidable manner of speaking.

If I have been seeming to minimize the degree to which in our philosophical and unphilosophical discourse we involve ourselves in ontological commitments, let me then emphasize that classical mathematics, as the example of primes between 1000 and 1010 clearly illustrates, is up to its neck in commitments to an ontology of abstract entities. Thus it is that the great mediaeval controversy over universals[6] has flared up anew in the modern philosophy of mathematics. The issue is clearer now than of old, because we now have a more explicit standard whereby to decide what ontology a given theory or form of discourse is committed to: a theory is committed to those and only those entities to which the bound variables of the theory must be capable of referring in order that the affirmations made in the theory be true.

Because this standard of ontological presupposition did not emerge clearly in the philosophical tradition, the modern philosophical mathematicians have not on the whole recognized that they were debating the same old problem of universals in a newly clarified form. But the fundamental cleavages among modern points of view on foundations of mathematics do come down pretty explicitly to disagreements as to the range of entities to which the bound variables should be permitted to refer....

I have argued that the sort of ontology we adopt can be consequential—notably in connection with mathematics, although this is only an example. Now how are we to adjudicate among rival ontologies? Certainly the answer is not provided by the semantical formula "To be is to be the value of a variable"; this formula serves rather, conversely, in testing the conformity of a given remark or doctrine to a prior ontological standard. We look to bound variables in connection with ontology not in order to know what there is, but in order to know what a given remark or doctrine, ours or someone else's, *says* there is; and this much is quite properly a problem involving language. But what there is is another question....

Our acceptance of an ontology is, I think, similar in principle to our accep-

---

[6 A controversy over the status of universal concepts ("man," "red," etc.). Three alternative theories were developed: *nominalism*, that universals are only ideas; *realism*, that universals have real, objective existence independent of ideas; and *conceptualism*, that universals are both in ideas and in things. *Ed.*]

tance of a scientific theory, say a system of physics: we adopt, at least insofar as we are reasonable, the simplest conceptual scheme into which the disordered fragments of raw experience can be fitted and arranged. Our ontology is determined once we have fixed upon the over-all conceptual scheme which is to accommodate science in the broadest sense; and the considerations which determine a reasonable construction of any part of that conceptual scheme, e.g. the biological or the physical part, are not different in kind from the considerations which determine a reasonable construction of the whole. To whatever extent the adoption of any system of scientific theory may be said to be a matter of language, the same—but no more—may be said of the adoption of an ontology.

BIBLIOGRAPHICAL NOTE

The philosophy section of any college library will offer the student a great variety of materials on philosophic issues. Some familiarity with that section will aid one's study and an appreciation of philosophy immensely. Bibliographical notes in this text are designed only to help initiate such familiarity; their suggestions should be pursued as far as one's interests and available resources permit.

Almost any introductory textbook in philosophy will have materials on the nature and meaning of philosophy. Texts differ greatly in their approaches, emphases, and even in their definitions and understanding of the philosophic enterprise, but sampling them is rewarding. Two brief and easily available books on the nature of philosophy are Elmer Sprague, *What Is Philosophy?* (New York, 1961), and Henry Johnstone, *What Is Philosophy?* (New York, 1965). Other anthologies which might be consulted include W. T. Blackstone, *Meaning and Existence* (New York, 1971); Edwards and Pap, *A Modern Introduction to Philosophy* (New York, 3rd ed., 1973); Mandelbaum *et al.*, *Philosophic Problems* (New York, 1967); and J. Margolis, *An Introduction to Philosophy* (New York, 1968). A good text maintaining a high level of philosophical work is Errol Harris, *Fundamentals of Philosophy* (New York, 1969). Also of value on the meaning of philosophy (as well as on a great number of other topics) are such standard reference works as the *Encyclopaedia Britannica*; J. M. Baldwin (ed.), *Dictionary of Philosophy and Psychology*, 3 vols. (New York, 1901, 1902); J. Hastings (ed.), *Encyclopedia of Religion and Ethics*, 12 vols. (New York, 1908); D. D. Runes (ed.), *Dictionary of Philosophy* (New York, 1942); and P. Edwards (ed.), *The Encyclopedia of Philosophy*, 8 vols. (New York, 1967).

Classical Realism

Plato · Aristotle · Copleston · Wild
Cicero · Gilson · D'Arcy · Maritain
St. Anselm · St. Thomas Aquinas · Williams

One of the oldest and most continuously active movements in philosophy is classical realism. It is termed "classical" both to indicate its origins in Greek thought and to distinguish it from other realistic movements such as Scottish realism and the American new realism. It is called "realism" because its basic doctrine holds that there is a world of real existence, independent of man, which can be known by the human intellect. Such a proposition may seem to be only "common sense," and the realist would urge that his position is one which acknowledges and remains true to the beliefs of the common man. But realism is not simply common sense; for in its efforts to articulate the deliverances of ordinary experience, it becomes a technically developed philosophy.

The fundamental theses of this philosophy may be divided into three groups.[1] First, realists believe that metaphysics is a valid and important discipline—indeed, that it is the central philosophical activity. They define metaphysics as the science of being, and a concern for being and its principles will be found throughout realist writings. Furthermore, realists believe that experience shows that both material and immaterial beings exist; no reduction of one mode of being to another is possible. In their epistemology realists urge that these beings can be known by the human mind as they are in themselves. Thus truth can be grasped by man, and it is universal, absolute, and eternal. Truth is achieved through a cognitive union of the intellect and its objects. In the areas of individual and social action, realists find that knowledge—especially that which treats human nature—provides mankind with reliable and unchanging norms of good and evil.

---

[1] These theses are part of the platform of a contemporary professional organization, the Association for Realistic Philosophy. See John Wild (ed.), *The Return to Reason* (Chicago: Henry Regnery Co., 1953), pp. 357–363.

In developing these theses, realists have adopted a common and basic technical vocabulary whose key terms include "substance," "form," "matter," "essence," and "existence." Such terms were utilized by the Greek philosophers Plato and Aristotle, and we find in their writings an effort to define and explain them. Realists through the centuries have been guided by the thought of these Greek thinkers; even today they believe that important truths are contained in the Greek philosophic tradition, and that that tradition merits careful and continuous study. Hence it is necessary for our study of realism to begin with selections from Plato and Aristotle.

INTRODUCTION

The general problem of Plato's dialogue *The Republic,* from which the first selection is taken, is that of justice. In attempting to determine its meaning, Plato is led to assert that justice, which must be based on knowledge, will be achieved only when rulers become philosophers. This however raises the question of the meaning of "philosopher," which leads Plato to a statement of the "Theory of Forms," his most distinctive philosophic tenet.

Socrates, spokesman in the dialogue, defines the philosopher as a lover of wisdom. But what is a lover of wisdom? He is one who has, or loves, knowledge, one who has a passion for truth. But what, again, is the meaning of this reply? Seeking to explain his answer, Socrates points out that there is a difference between one who dreams and one who does not, in that the dreamer mistakes an appearance for a reality. The philosopher as a pursuer of truth has an object before him which his thought is seeking. And that natural object of his thought is the real.

Again we must ask, however, what this real is. It must be something, Socrates asserts, which *is.* But a thing which *is* cannot be something which comes into being, changes, and then passes away and is no more. What *is* is permanent and unchanging. Nothing with these characteristics is found in the world of nature, the world observed by the senses; and this leads Plato to assert that reality belongs not to the sense world which is always in a state of flux, but rather to a world of forms, to a world of intelligible objects known by the "mind's eye," and perfect, immutable, and eternal. Consider a brief illustration of what Plato is saying: a bridge is constructed of materials like steel and concrete; but it is not only material, for it embodies certain laws or principles involving stresses and strains, gravitation, and so on. The bridge itself, belonging to the sense world, may endure for a long time, but it is not eternal. The mathematical and physical laws, however, known and utilized by the engineer, do not perish when the bridge does; they are eternal and hence, for Plato, they are the real, not the mortar and steel.

Thus in his Theory of Forms, Plato holds a dualistic metaphysics of the real and sense worlds. In maintaining this view, he raises such problems as those of truth, knowledge, form, and reality which have continued to be important to philosophers. Plato's solutions have remained suggestive too, and their influence has been felt not only by realists, but by philosophers of other persuasions as well. Some, in fact, would classify Plato as an idealist rather than a realist. However this point is settled, the following pages discuss a concept, namely form, that is central to realism.

1 The Theory of Forms
Plato (428-348)

[SOCRATES.] Now, if we are to have a chance of escaping from the assailants you speak of, I think it essential to give them our definition of "philosophers," and shew whom we mean, when we venture to assert that such persons ought to govern; in order that, their character having been made thoroughly apparent, we may be able to defend ourselves by demonstrating that it is the natural province of these men to embrace philosophy, and take the lead in a state, and the province of all others to let philosophy alone, and follow the lead of the former.

[GLAUCON.] Yes, it is a fit time, he said, to give this definition.

Come then, follow my steps, and let us try if we can in some way or other satisfactorily expound our notion.

Lead on.

Will it be necessary to remind you, or do you remember without it, that when we state that a man loves some object, we are bound to shew, if the statement be correct, that he does not love one part of that object to the exclusion of another, but that he takes delight in the whole?

I require to be reminded, it seems: for I do not quite understand you.

Such a confession, Glaucon, would have been more appropriate in another person. A man of your amorous nature ought not to forget that a boy-loving, susceptible person is in some way or other attracted and excited by the charms of all who are in their bloom, and thinks they all deserve his attentions and addresses. Is not this the manner in which you behave to your favorites? You will praise a boy with a turned-up nose as having a winning look; the hooked nose of another you consider king-like; while a third, whose nose is between the two extremes, has a beautifully proportioned face: the dark, you say, have a manly look, the fair are children of the gods: and who do you suppose coined the phrase "olive-pale" but a lover who could palliate and easily put up with paleness, when he found it on the cheek of youth? In one word, you invent all kinds of excuses, and employ every variety of expression, sooner than reject any that are in the flower and prime of life.

If you wish, replied Glaucon, to found on my case an assertion that the amatively disposed thus act, I will allow you to do so for the argument's sake.

To take another illustration; do you now observe that those who are fond of

The selection is from Book V of *The Republic of Plato* (trs. John Llewelyn Davies and David James Vaughan) (London: Macmillan and Company, Ltd., 1895), pp. 187–196.

wine behave in a precisely similar manner, finding some excuse or other to admire every sort of wine?

Yes, certainly.

And you doubtless have seen how persons who love honor will command a company, if they cannot lead an army, and in default of being honored by great and important personages, are glad to receive the respect of the little and the insignificant; so covetous are they of honor in any shape.

Precisely so.

Then answer me yes or no to this: when we describe a man as having a longing for something, are we to assert that he longs after the whole class that the term includes, or only after one part, to the exclusion of another?

He longs after the whole.

Then shall we not maintain that the philosopher, or the lover of wisdom, is one who longs for wisdom, not partially, but wholly?

True.

So that if a person makes difficulties about his studies, especially while he is young and unable to discriminate between what is profitable and what is not, we shall pronounce him to be no lover of learning or of wisdom; just as when a man is nice about his eating, we deny that he is hungry or desirous of food, and instead of describing him as fond of eating, we call him a bad feeder.

Yes, and we shall be right in doing so.

On the other hand, when a man is ready and willing to taste every kind of knowledge, and addresses himself joyfully to his studies with an appetite which never can be satiated, we shall justly call such a person a philosopher, shall we not?

To which Glaucon replied, You will find your description includes a great number and a strange company. All the lovers of sights, I conclude, are philosophers, because they take pleasure in acquiring knowledge; and those who delight in hearing, are a very singular set to reckon among philosophers,— those, I mean, who will never, if they can help it, be present at a philosophical discussion, or any similar entertainment, but are unfailing attendants at every Dionysian festival, whether held in town or country, and run about as if they had let out their ears on hire to listen to all the choruses of the season. Are we then to give the title of philosophers to all these people, as well as to others who have a taste for any similar studies, and to the professors of small arts?

Certainly not, I replied: we must call them counterfeit philosophers.

And whom, he asked, do you call genuine philosophers?

Those who love to see truth, I answered.

In that, he said, you cannot be wrong: but will you explain what you mean?

That would be not at all easy, with a different questioner: but you, I imagine, will make me the admission I require.

What is it?

That since beauty is the opposite of deformity, they are two things.

Of course they are.

Then since they are two, each of them taken separately is one thing.

That also is true.

The same thing may be said likewise of justice and injustice, good and evil, and all general conceptions. Each of them in itself is one thing, but by the intermixture with actions and bodies and with one another, through which they are everywhere made visible, each appears to be many things.

You are right.

By the help of this principle, then, I draw a distinction between those whom you described just now as lovers of sights, lovers of arts, and practical persons, on the one hand, and on the other, those about whom we are now inquiring, to whom alone we can rightly give the name of philosophers.

Explain what you mean.

Why, I suppose that those who love seeing and hearing admire beautiful sounds, and colors, and forms, and all artistic products into which these enter; but the nature of beauty in itself their understanding is unable to behold and embrace.

Yes, it certainly is as you say.

But those who are capable of reaching to the independent contemplation of abstract beauty will be rare exceptions, will they not?

They will indeed.

Therefore if a man recognizes the existence of beautiful things, but disbelieves in abstract beauty, and has not the power to follow should another lead the way to the knowledge of it, is his life, think you, a dreaming or a waking one? Just consider. Is it not dreaming when a person, whether asleep or awake, mistakes the likeness of anything for the real thing of which it is a likeness?

I confess I should say that a person in that predicament was dreaming.

Take again the opposite case, of one who acknowledges an abstract beauty, and has the power to discern both this essence and the objects into which it enters, and who never mistakes such objects for the essence, nor the essence for the objects; does such a person, think you, live a dreaming or a waking life?

A waking life, undoubtedly.

If so, shall we not be right in calling the mental process of the latter knowledge, because he really knows; and that of the former, opinion, because he merely opines?

Yes, perfectly right.

Well then, should this person, whom we describe as opining, but not knowing, grow wroth with us, and contend that what we say is not true, shall we be able to appease his indignation and gently convince him, disguising from him the fact that he is in an unsound state?

That were certainly desirable.

Come then, consider what we are to say to him. Would you like us to make certain inquiries of him, premising that if he really does know anything, we shall not in the least grudge him his knowledge?—on the contrary, we shall be truly glad to find that it is so. But answer us this question, we shall say: When a man knows, does he know something or nothing? Be so good, Glaucon, as to make answer in his behalf.

My answer will be, that he knows something.

Something that exists, or does not exist?

Something that exists: for how could a thing that does not exist be known?

Are we then quite sure of this fact, in whatever variety of ways we might examine it, that what completely exists may be completely known, whereas that which has no existence at all must be wholly unknown?

We are perfectly sure of it.

Good: now, if there be anything so constituted, as at the same time to be and not to be, must it not lie somewhere between the purely existent and the absolutely non-existent?

It must.

Well then, as knowledge is correlative to the existent, and the negation of knowledge necessarily to the non-existent, must we not try to find something intermediate between science and ignorance, if there is anything of the kind, to correspond to this that is intermediate between the existent and the non-existent?

Yes, by all means.

Do we speak of opinion as a something?

Undoubtedly we do.

Do we consider it a faculty distinct from science or identical with it?

Distinct from it.

Therefore opinion is appointed to one province and science to another, each acting according to its own peculiar power.

Just so.

Is it not the nature of science, as correlative to the existent, to know how the existent exists? But first there is a distinction which I think it necessary to establish.

What is that?

We shall hold that faculties, as a certain general class, are the things whereby we, and every other thing, are able to do whatever we can do: for example, I call sight and hearing faculties, if you happen to understand the special conception which I wish to describe.

I do understand it.

Then let me tell you what view I take of them. In a faculty I do not see either color, or form, or any of those qualities that I observe in many other things, by regarding which I can in many cases distinguish to myself between one thing and another. No, in a faculty I look only to its province and its function, and thus I am led to call it in each case by this name, pronouncing those faculties to be identical whose provinces and functions are identical, and those diverse whose provinces and functions are diverse. But pray, how do you proceed?

Just in the same way.

Now then, return with me, my excellent friend. Under what general term do you class science? Do you make it a faculty?

Yes I do; it is of all the faculties the most powerful.

Well, is opinion a faculty; or are we to refer it to some other denomination?

Not to any other: for that whereby we are able to opine, can only be opinion.

Well, but a little while ago you admitted that science and opinion are not identical.

Why how could a sensible man identify the fallible with the infallible?

Very good: so we are clearly agreed that opinion is a thing distinct from science?

It is.

If so, each of them has by its nature a different province, and a different efficacy.

The inference is inevitable.

Science, I believe, has for its province to know the nature of the existent.

Yes.

And the province of opinion is, we say, to opine.

Yes.

Does opinion take cognizance of precisely that material which science knows? In other words, is the object-matter of opinion identical with that of science? or is that impossible?

It is impossible, after the admissions we have made; that is, if it be granted that different faculties have different provinces, and that both opinion and science are faculties, and that the two are distinct,—all which we affirm. These premises make it impossible to identify the object-matter of science and that of opinion.

Then, if the existent is the object-matter of knowledge, that of opinion must be something other than the existent?

It must.

Well then, does opinion exercise itself upon the non-existent, or is it impossible to apprehend even in opinion that which does not exist? Consider—does not the person opining carry his thought towards something? Or is it possible to have an opinion, but an opinion about nothing?

It is impossible.

Then the person who opines has an opinion about some one thing?

Yes.

Well, but the non-existent could not be called some one thing; it might, on the contrary, with the greatest truth be styled nothing.

Just so.

But to the non-existent we were constrained to assign ignorance, and to the existent, knowledge.

And rightly.

Then neither the existent nor the non-existent is the object of opinion?

No.

Therefore opinion cannot be either ignorance or knowledge.

Apparently not.

Then does it lie beyond either of these, so as to surpass either knowledge in certainty or ignorance in uncertainty?

It does neither.

Then tell me, do you look upon opinion as something more dusky than knowledge, more luminous than ignorance?

Yes, it is strongly so distinguished from either.

And does it lie within these extremes?

Yes.

Then opinion must be something between the two.

Precisely so.

Now a little while back, did we not say, that if anything could be found so constituted as at the same time to be and not to be, it must lie between the purely existent and the absolutely not existent, and must be the object neither of science nor yet of ignorance, but of a third faculty, which should be similarly discovered in the interval between science and ignorance?

We did.

But now we have discovered between these two a faculty which we call opinion.

We have.

It will remain then for us, apparently, to find what that is which partakes both of being and of not being, and which cannot be rightly said to be either of these absolutely; in order that, should it discover itself to us, we may justly proclaim it to be the object of opinion; thus assigning extremes to extremes, and means to means. Am I not right?

You are.

These positions then being laid down, I shall proceed to interrogate that worthy man who denies the existence of anything absolutely beautiful, or any form of abstract beauty, which for ever continues the same and unchangeable, though he acknowledges a variety of beautiful objects,—that lover of sights, who cannot endure to be told that beauty is one, and justice one, and so on of the rest: —My good sir, I shall say, of all these beautiful things, is there one which may not appear ugly? Of all these just things, is there one which may not appear unjust? Or of these holy things, one which may not appear unholy?

No, answered Glaucon: they must inevitably appear in a certain sense both fair and foul, both just and unjust, both holy and unholy.

Again, may not the many double things be considered halves just as well as doubles?

Just as well.

In the same way, have the things which we describe as great, small, light, heavy, any better claim to these titles, than to their opposites?

No, they will always be equally entitled to either.

Would it be more correct, then, to predicate of those many objects, that each of them is, or is not, that which it is said to be?

You remind me of the conundrums with a contradiction in them, that are proposed at table, and of the children's riddle[1] about the eunuch who threw at the bat, hinting darkly with what he hit it, and on what it sat: for the things in question have the same ambiguous character, and one cannot positively conceive of them as either being or not being, as both being and not being, or as neither.

Can you tell then, said I, what to do with them, or where they may be better put than in the interspace between being and not being? For I presume they will not appear either darker than the non-existent, and so more non-existent, or more luminous than the existent, and therefore more existent.

You are perfectly right.

Hence we have discovered, apparently, that the mass of notions, current among the mass of men, about beauty, justice, and the rest, roam about between the confines of pure existence and pure non-existence.

We have.

And we before admitted, that if anything of this kind should be brought to light, it ought to be described as the object of opinion, and not of knowledge, —these intermediate rovers being caught by the intermediate faculty.

We did make this admission.

Therefore, when people have an eye for a multitude of beautiful objects, but can neither see beauty in itself, nor follow those who would lead them to it, —when they behold a number of just things, but not justice in itself, and so in every instance, we shall say they have in every case an opinion, but no real knowledge of the things about which they opine.

It is a necessary inference.

---

[1] The riddle is thus given by the Scholiast: "A tale is told, that a man and not a man, seeing and not seeing a bird and not a bird, seated on wood and not on wood, hit it and did not hit it with a stone and not a stone." It is partly explained in the text, and we leave the further solution of it to the reader. [Translators' note.]

But what, on the other hand, must **we say** of those who contemplate things **as they** are in themselves, and as they **exist** ever permanent and immutable? **Shall** we not speak of them as knowing, not opining?

That also is a necessary inference.

Then shall we not assert that such persons admire and love the objects of knowledge,—the others, the objects of opinion? For we have not forgotten, have we, that we spoke of these latter as loving and looking upon beautiful sounds and colors and the like, while they will not hear of the existence of an abstract beauty?

We have not forgotten it.

Shall we commit any fault then, if we call these people philodoxical rather than philosophical, that is to say, lovers of opinion rather than lovers of wisdom? And will they be very much offended with us for telling them so?

No, not if they will take my advice: for it is wrong to be offended with the truth.

Those therefore that set their affections on that which in each case really exists, we must call not philodoxical, but philosophical?

Yes, by all means.

2 The Theory of Substance
Aristotle (384-322)

Known simply as The Philosopher in the Middle Ages, Aristotle developed one of the truly major philosophies of our civilization. He began his career as a student in Plato's Academy, remaining there for nearly twenty years and undoubtedly accepting the main tenets of Platonism. Toward the end of that period, however, Aristotle began to differ from his master, and upon Plato's death he left the Academy to develop his own position.

There were differences in temperament between the two philosophers which were at least partly responsible for their differences in thought. Plato was more mystical—his philosophy has appealed to mystics through the centuries—whereas Aristotle, perhaps influenced by his birth into a medical family, was more empirical, more scientific, more concerned with the experienced world.

This concern led Aristotle finally to reject the Platonic dualism and to assert that reality is the concrete, individual thing: this man, this stone, this animal. He uses the word "ousia," or substance, to refer to the truly real. But because individuals alone are real, the principles explaining and accounting for them must therefore be intrinsic ones. Aristotle's metaphysical analysis uncovers four factors "that make a thing what it is"—namely, a material, formal, efficient, and final cause. Further, since change is a universal characteristic of things, Aristotle turns to its analysis and finds its explanation in the concepts of potency and actuality.

[i. *The science of being.*] There is a science which investigates being as being and the attributes which belong to this in virtue of its own nature. Now this is not the same as any of the so-called special sciences; for none of these others treats universally of being as being. They cut off a part of being and investigate the attribute of this part; this is what the mathematical sciences for instance do. Now since we are seeking the first principles and the highest causes, clearly there must be some thing to which these belong in virtue of its own nature. If then those who sought the elements of existing things were seeking these same principles, it is necessary that the elements must be elements of being not by accident but just because it *is* being. Therefore it is of being as being that we also must grasp the first causes.

[ii. *The meanings of being.*] There are many senses in which a thing may be said to "be," but all that "is" is related to one central point, one definite kind of thing, and is not said to "be" by a mere ambiguity. Everything which is healthy is related to health, one thing in the sense that it preserves health, another in the sense that it produces it, another in the sense that it is a symptom of health, another because it is capable of it. And that which is medical is relative to the medical art, one thing being called medical because it possesses it, another because it is naturally adapted to it, another because it is a function of the medical art. And we shall find other words used similarly to these. So, too, there are many senses in which a thing is said to be, but all refer to one starting-point; some things are said to be because they are substances, others be-

The selection is from Aristotle's *Metaphysica* (tr. W. D. Ross), 2nd ed., Vol. VIII of *The Works of Aristotle* (ed. W. D. Ross) (Oxford: The Clarendon Press, 1928). Used by permission of the Clarendon Press, Oxford.

cause they are affections of substance, others because they are a process towards substance, or destructions or privations or qualities of substance, or productive or generative of substance, or of things which are relative to substance, or negations of one of these things or of substance itself. It is for this reason that we say even of non-being that it *is* non-being. As, then, there is one science which deals with all healthy things, the same applies in the other cases also. For not only in the case of things which have one common notion does the investigation belong to one science, but also in the case of things which are related to one common nature; for even these in a sense have one common notion. It is clear then that it is the work of one science also to study the things that are, *qua* being. —But everywhere science deals chiefly with that which is primary, and on which the other things depend, and in virtue of which they get their names. If, then, this is substance, it will be of substances that the philosopher must grasp the principles and the causes.

[iii. *The meanings of substance.*] We call "substance" (1) the simple bodies, i.e. earth and fire and water and everything of the sort, and in general bodies and the things composed of them, both animals and divine beings, and the parts of these. All these are called substance because they are not predicated of a subject but everything else is predicated of them. (2) That which, being present in such things as are not predicated of a subject, is the cause of their being, as the soul is of the being of an animal. (3) The parts which are present in such things, limiting them and marking them as individuals, and by whose destruction the whole is destroyed, as the body is by the destruction of the plane, as some[1] say, and the plane by the destruction of the line; and in general number is thought by some[1] to be of this nature; for if it is destroyed, they say, nothing exists, and it limits all things. (4) The essence, the formula of which is a definition, is also called the substance of each thing.

It follows, then, that "substance" has two senses, (*A*) the ultimate substratum, which is no longer predicated of anything else, and (*B*) that which, being a "this," is also separable and of this nature is the shape or form of each thing.

[iv. *The four causes of being.*] "Cause" means (1) that from which, as immanent material, a thing comes into being, e.g. the bronze is the cause of the statue and the silver of the saucer, and so are the classes which include these. (2) The form or pattern, i.e. the definition of the essence, and the classes which include this (e.g. the ratio 2:1 and number in general are causes of the octave), and the parts included in the definition. (3) That from which the change or the resting from change first begins; e.g. the adviser is a cause of the action, and the father a cause of the child, and in general the maker a cause of the thing made and the change-producing of the changing. (4) The end, i.e. that for the sake of which a thing is; e.g. health is the cause of walking. For "Why does one walk?" we say; "that one may be healthy"; and in speaking thus we think we have given the cause. The same is true of all the means that intervene before the end,

when something else has put the process in motion, as e.g. thinning or purging or drugs or instruments intervene before. health is reached; for all these are for the sake of the end, though they differ from one another in that some are instruments and others are actions.

These, then, are practically all the senses in which causes are spoken of, and as they are spoken of in several senses it follows both that there are several causes of the same thing, and in no accidental sense (e.g. both the art of sculpture and the bronze are causes of the statue not in respect of anything else but *qua* statue; not, however, in the same way, but the one as matter and the other as source of the movement), and that things can be causes of one another (e.g. exercise of good condition, and the latter of exercise; not, however, in the same way, but the one as end and the other as source of movement). Again, the same thing is the cause of contraries; for that which when present causes a particular thing, we sometimes charge, when absent, with the contrary, e.g. we impute the shipwreck to the absence of the steersman, whose presence was the cause of safety; and both—the presence and the privation—are causes as sources of movement.

[v. *The types of change.*] Of things which change, some change in an accidental sense, like that in which "the musical" may be said to walk, and others are said, without qualification, to change, because something in them changes, i.e. the things that change in parts; the body becomes healthy, because the eye does. But there is something which is by its own nature moved directly, and this is the essentially mov-

----

[1] The Pythagoreans and Plato.

able. The same distinction is found in the case of the mover; for it causes movement either in an accidental sense or in respect of a part of itself or essentially. There is something that directly causes movement; and there is something that is moved, also the time in which it is moved, and that from which and that into which it is moved. But the forms and the affections and the place, which are the terminals of the movement of moving things, are unmovable, e.g. knowledge or heat; it is not heat that is a movement, but heating. Change which is not accidental is found not in all things, but between contraries, and their intermediates, and between contradictories. We may convince ourselves of this by induction.

That which changes changes either from positive into positive, or from negative into negative, or from positive into negative, or from negative into positive. (By positive I mean that which is expressed by an affirmative term.) Therefore there must be three changes; for that from negative into negative is not change, because (since the terms are neither contraries nor contradictories) there is no opposition. The change from the negative into the positive which is its contradictory is generation—absolute change absolute generation, and partial change partial generation; and the change from positive to negative is destruction—absolute change absolute destruction, and partial change partial destruction. If, then, "that which is not" has several senses, and movement can attach neither to that which implies putting together or separating,[2]

nor to that which implies potency and is opposed to that which is in the full sense[3] (true, the not-white or not-good *can* be moved *incidentally*, for the not-white might be a man; but that which is not a particular thing at all can in no wise be moved), that which is not cannot be moved (and if this is so, generation cannot be movement; for that which is not *is* generated; for even if we admit to the full that its generation is accidental, yet it is true to say that "not-being" is predicable of that which is generated absolutely).[4] Similarly *rest* cannot belong to that which is not. These consequences, then, turn out to be awkward, and also this, that everything that is moved is in a place, but that which is not is not in a place; for then it would be somewhere. Nor is destruction movement; for the contrary of movement is movement or rest, but the contrary of destruction is generation. Since every movement is a change, and the kinds of change are the three named above, and of these those in the way of generation and destruction are not movements, and these are the changes from a thing to its contradictory, it follows that only the change from positive into positive is movement. And the positives are either contrary or intermediate (for even privation must be regarded as contrary), and are expressed by an affirmative term, e.g. "naked" or "toothless" or "black."

---

[2] i.e. to "that which is not" in the sense of "the judgment which is false."

[3] i.e. a thing cannot be moved when it does not exist actually, but exists potentially.

[4] i.e. even if the not-being (privation) which is the starting-point of generation can exist only as an accident of prime matter, still not-being *is* the starting-point of absolute generation (i.e. generation of a substance, not of a quality).

[vi. *The nature of actuality.*] Since we have treated of the kind of potency which is related to movement, let us discuss actuality—what, and what kind of thing, actuality is. For in the course of our analysis it will also become clear, with regard to the potential, that we not only ascribe potency to that whose nature it is to move something else, or to be moved by something else, either without qualification or in some particular way, but also use the word in another sense, which is the reason of the inquiry in the course of which we have discussed these previous senses also. Actuality, then, is the existence of a thing not in the way which we express by "potentially"; we say that potentially, for instance, a statue of Hermes is in the block of wood and the half-line is in the whole, because it might be separated out, and we call even the man who is not studying a man of science, if he is capable of studying; the thing that stands in contrast to each of these exists actually. Our meaning can be seen in the particular cases by induction, and we must not seek a definition of everything but be content to grasp the analogy, that it is as that which is building is to that which is capable of building, and the waking to the sleeping, and that which is seeing to that which has its eyes shut but has sight, and that which has been shaped out of the matter to the matter, and that which has been wrought up to the unwrought. Let actuality be defined by one member of this antithesis, and the potential by the other. But all things are not said in the *same sense* to exist actually, but only by analogy—as A is in B or to B, C is in D or to D; for some are as movement

to potency, and the others as substance to some sort of matter.

[vii. *The priority of the actual.*] From our discussion of the various senses of "prior," it is clear that actuality is prior to potency. And I mean by potency not only that definite kind which is said to be a principle of change in another thing or in the thing itself regarded as other, but in general every principle of movement or of rest. For nature also is in the same genus as potency; for it is a principle of movement—not, however, in something else but in the thing itself *qua* itself. To all such potency, then, actuality is prior both in formula and in substantiality; and in time it is prior in one sense, and in another not.

(1) Clearly it is prior in formula; for that which is in the primary sense potential is potential because it is possible for it to become active; e.g. I mean by "capable of building" that which can build, and by "capable of seeing" that which can see, and by "visible" that which can be seen. And the same account applies to all other cases, so that the formula and the knowledge of the one must precede the knowledge of the other.

(2) In time it is prior in this sense: the actual which is identical in species though not in number with a potentially existing thing is prior to it. I mean that to this particular man who now exists actually and to the corn and to the seeing subject the matter and the seed and that which is capable of seeing, which are potentially a man and corn and seeing, but not yet actually so, are prior in time; but prior in time to these are other actually existing things, from which they were produced. For from the po-

tentially existing the actually existing is always produced by an actually existing thing, e.g. man from man, musician by musician; there is always a first mover, and the mover already exists actually. We have said in our account of substance that everything that is produced is something produced from something and by something, and that the same in species as it.

This is why it is thought impossible to be a builder if one has built nothing or a harper if one has never played the harp; for he who learns to play the harp learns to play it by playing it, and all other learners do similarly. And thence arose the sophistical quibble, that one who does not possess a science will be doing that which is the object of the science; for he who is learning it does not possess it. But since, of that which is coming to be, some part must have come to be, and, of that which, in general, is changing, some part must have changed (this is shown in the treatise on movement), he who is learning must, it would seem, possess some part of the science. But *here* too, then, it is clear that actuality is in this sense also, viz. in order of generation and of time, prior to potency.

But (3) it is also prior in substantiality; firstly, because the things that are posterior in becoming are prior in form and in substantiality (e.g. man is prior to boy and human being to seed; for the one already has its form, and the other has not), and because everything that comes to be moves towards a principle, i.e. an end (for that for the sake of which a thing is, is its principle, and the becoming is for the sake of the end), and the actuality is the end, and it is for

the sake of this that the potency is acquired. For animals do not see in order that they may have sight, but they have sight that they may see. And similarly men have the art of building that they may build, and theoretical science that they may theorize; but they do not theorize that they may have theoretical science, except those who are learning by practice; and these do not theorize except in a limited sense, or because they have no need to theorize. Further, matter exists in a potential state, just because it may come to its form; and when it exists *actually*, then it is in its form. And the same holds good in all cases, even those in which the end is a movement. And so, as teachers think they have achieved their end when they have exhibited the pupil at work, nature does likewise. For if this is not the case, we shall have Pauson's Hermes over again, since it will be hard to say about the knowledge, as about the figure in the picture, whether it is within or without.[5] For the action is the end, and the actuality is the action. And so even the *word* "actuality" is derived from "action," and points to the complete reality.

And while in some cases the exercise is the ultimate thing (e.g. in sight the ultimate thing is seeing, and no other product besides this results from sight), but from some things a product follows (e.g. from the art of building there results a house as well as the act of building), yet none the less the act is in the former case the end and in the latter more of an end than the potency is. For

---

[5] The reference is apparently to a tricky painting in which the figure was painted so as to stand out in high relief.

the act of building is realized in the thing that is being built, and comes to be, and is, at the same time as the house.

Where, then, the result is something apart from the exercise, the actuality is in the thing that is being made, e.g. the act of building is in the thing that is being built and that of weaving in the thing that is being woven, and similarly in all other cases, and in general the movement is in the thing that is being moved; but where there is no product apart from the actuality, the actuality is present in the agents, e.g. the act of seeing is in the seeing subject and that of theorizing in the theorizing subject and the life is in the soul (and therefore well-being also; for it is a certain kind of life).

Obviously, therefore, the substance or form is actuality. According to this argument, then, it is obvious that actuality is prior in substantial being to potency; and as we have said, one actuality always precedes another in time right back to the actuality of the eternal prime mover.

EPISTEMOLOGY

Realists hold generally that reality is knowable, that the human mind can therefore attain truth, and that it can do so with certainty. When we know an object, we both know that we know it, and we know it as knowable. To explain these assertions, F. C. Copleston develops in the following selection the classical Thomistic epistemology, which in turn is based largely on the thought of Aristotle.

Knowledge begins in sense and proceeds from the perception through the image to the idea or concept. Corresponding to and responsible for this process are various powers of the soul: the sense organ, the common sense, the imagination, and the active and passive intellects. We may illustrate the process as it occurs within the soul: an object is perceived by the sense of sight, and therewith the sensible form of the object is received. This form is presented by the common sense to the imagination, where an image is developed which bears the intelligible form. Next the active intellect picks out this form or universal concept from the image and impresses it on the passive intellect where it is known as a universal.

In this process there is synthesis, abstraction, and continuity. There is continuity in that the concept or intelligible form is implicit in the sense-perception and is in the end known explicitly in the intellect. There is an act of abstraction, for the intellect knows the object according to the latter's own form or essence. And there is synthesis, for the act of knowing is one in which the powers of the soul work together to achieve the universal concept.

The concept of truth is developed within this context. Predicated primarily of judgments, and therefore primarily in the mind, truth is defined as the conformity between mind and thing. But can the intellect grasp truth? Realists answer yes, holding with Aquinas that in knowing truth the mind, by reflecting on its own act, is aware that it can attain truth. And how is this to be proven? Summarizing, Copleston writes that "we do not need any further guarantee of our ability to attain truth than our awareness or recognition of the fact that we do in fact attain it."

3 Knowing and Reality

F. C. Copleston (1907-   )

The first stage in the acquisition of knowledge is sense-perception. Our organs of sense are affected by external objects, and we receive sense-impressions. The eye, for example, sees colors or color-patches; but it would not do so unless it were affected by its object acting on it through a medium. It receives an impression, therefore, and undergoes a physical alteration. The process of sensation cannot, however, be reduced to a mere physical change. "If physiological change sufficed for sensation, all natural bodies would have sensations when they underwent change" (*S.T.*, Ia, 78, 3). Sensation is a psychophysical process in which a sensible "form" is received.

If we consider the level of the individual external senses in itself, it is true to say that there are only discrete sense-impressions. The sense of sight, says Aquinas, is able to distinguish one color from another (the impression of green is different from the impression of blue); but the sense of sight is quite

unable to compare and distinguish colors from sounds, since it does not hear. It is obvious, however, that even animals synthesize their sense-impressions. The dog perceives a man and achieves a synthesis of the different sense-impressions of sight, hearing, smell and touch. It is therefore clear that even at the level of purely sensitive life there takes place a synthesis of the data of the different external senses. Aquinas therefore postulates interior "senses" by means of which this synthesis is achieved. The word "sense" may seem peculiar, because we are accustomed to use the word only in reference to what Aquinas calls the five external senses; but by using the word he intends to indicate that the power or faculty of which he speaks belongs to the level of sensitive life and is found in animals as well as in human beings.

The function of distinguishing and collating the data of the various external senses is performed by the general sense (*sensus communis*). We must also postulate an imaginative power which conserves the forms received by the senses. Again, the animal is able to apprehend, for example, that something is useful to it. A dog apprehends that a particular man is friendly or unfriendly. We shall

The selection is from F. C. Copleston, *Aquinas* (Harmondsworth: Penguin Books, Ltd., 1955), pp. 173-178 and 46-51. Copyright © F. C. Copleston, 1955. Used by permission of the publisher.

thus have to postulate a power or disposition to apprehend these facts (the *vis aestimativa*) and a power of conserving such apprehensions (the *vis memorativa*). In postulating all these powers or faculties Aquinas relied very largely on Aristotle, and we may well ask in what precise sense, if any, we are justified in speaking of different "faculties" or "interior senses." But the point to which I wish to draw attention is Aquinas' insistence on the work of synthesis that goes on in cognition. The synthesis of which I have been speaking takes place at the level of sensitive life, and it must not be taken to mean a conscious, deliberate synthesis; but that a synthesis does take place is a fact which scarcely admits of doubt.

Although, however, the synthesis which takes place on the sensitive level is in some sense common to animals and to men, this does not mean that sensitive cognition is identical in both. I have already quoted a passage from the *De potentia* (3, 11 *ad* 1), where Aquinas says that sensitive life, though generically the same in animals as in men, is not specifically the same, since it is "much higher" in the latter, "as is clear in the case of touch and in the case of the interior senses." Thus according to Aquinas what corresponds in human beings to the *vis aestimativa* in animals deserves a special name, since more than instinct is involved: and he calls it the *vis cogitativa*. He was aware that in human perception sense and reason are both involved. But it does not follow that an attempt to abstract or isolate what belongs to the level of sense-life from what belongs to the level of reason is misguided or useless.

· For Aquinas an explanation is needed of the transition from sensitive to rational or intellectual cognition. The senses apprehend particular objects, and images, even if confused, are particular. The mind, however, has universal concepts; it apprehends in abstraction the forms of things. We therefore have on the one hand sensitive apprehension of the particular and on the other intellectual cognition of the universal. This does not mean that universals as such have any extramental existence. There are, for example, only particular human beings; there is no such thing as an existent universal man, nor can there be. But individual human beings possess, Aquinas was convinced, specifically similar essences, and this similarity of essence is the objective foundation of the universal concept of man, which enables us to predicate the same term of individual human beings, saying, for example, that John is a man and that Peter is also a man. But even when we suppose this view of universals, namely that universals as such exist in the mind and not extra-mentally, the problem still remains, how is the universal concept formed? What is the process by which the universal concept is formed? It cannot be explained as a purely passive process, passive, that is to say, on the mind's part. For the mind, being immaterial, cannot be directly affected by a material thing or by the image. It is necessary to postulate an activity on the mind's part, in order to explain how the universal concept is formed from the material provided by sense-experience. In other words, on the rational level there takes place a further stage of the process of synthesis involved in human cognition, and an analysis of this further stage is required.

Aquinas employs the Aristotelian distinction between the active and passive intellects, two distinct functions of the mind. According to him the active intellect "illumines" the image of the object apprehended by the senses; that is to say, it actively reveals the formal and potentially universal element which is implicitly contained in the image. It then abstracts this potentially universal element and produces in the passive intellect what Aquinas calls the *species impressa*. The passive intellect reacts to this determination by the active intellect, and the result is the *species expressa*, the universal concept in the full sense. This language is certainly unfamiliar and therefore difficult to follow; but what Aquinas has in mind is more or less this. The human intellect has no store of innate ideas: it is in potentiality to possessing ideas or concepts. Considered in this light, the intellect is passive. And its concepts must be derived in some way from the data provided by the senses, exterior and interior. But the senses provide particular impressions of particular objects, together with the images to which these impressions give rise, whereas concepts are universal in character. We must suppose, then, that the intellect as active picks out, as it were, the potentially universal element in the image, the synthesized reproduction in the imagination of the data of the different senses. Thus the intellect as active abstracts the universal essence of man from a particular image, leaving out the particularizing notes which confine the image to being the image of this or that particular man, and impresses it on the

intellect as passive. And so the universal concept is born.

In the process of synthesis and abstraction there is therefore continuity, from the primary sense-impressions up to the universal concept. The mediating point between the data of sense and the universal concept is for Aquinas the image. And it is important to realize that when he talks about images in this connection he is not speaking of arbitrarily constructed images like the image of a unicorn. In our sense-experience of, say, Peter, the eye sees color-patches, the ear hears sounds, and so on. These sense-impressions are, however, synthesized in the form of the "image." And it is from this synthesis that the universal, "man," is, according to Aquinas, abstracted. That which is primarily known by the mind is, however, the universal, that is the form, as apprehended in Peter. Peter is known as a man. It is only secondarily that the mind apprehends the universal precisely as universal. That is to say, it is only secondarily that it apprehends the universal as predictable not only of Peter but also of James and John and every other individual human being. To speak of "abstraction" is not, therefore, for Aquinas to cut off the life of the intellect from that of the senses and to say that the mind knows only its own ideas. The universal concept is primarily the modification of the intellect by which a thing (Peter for example) is known according to its form or essence.

As we have seen earlier, Aquinas held that the mind is dependent on the image, not only in the formation of its ideas but also in their employment, in the sense that there is no thinking without the use of images or symbols. Since the mind is active and possesses the power of active reflection, it is not confined to the knowledge of material things; but at the same time it can know immaterial things only in so far as material things are related to them and reveal them. Moreover, in thinking about immaterial things we cannot dispense with the use of images or symbols. We can recognize the inadequacy of the images based on sense-experience, but we cannot get rid of them. We cannot conceive immaterial things, even when their existence is known by revelation, except on an analogy with visible things, though we can attempt to purify our ideas of them. "Images necessarily accompany our knowledge in this present life, however spiritual the knowledge may be: for even God is known by us through the images of His effects (in creatures)" (*De malo*, 16, 8, *ad* 3). Again, "the image is a principle of our knowledge. It is that from which our intellectual activity begins, not simply as a transitory stimulus, but as a permanent foundation of intellectual activity . . . And so when the imagination is impeded, so also is our theological knowledge" (*In librum Boethii de Trinitate*, 6, 2, *ad* 5).

A point to be noticed is that truth and falsity are predicated primarily neither of sense-impressions nor of concepts but of judgments. We can hardly speak of error in the case of a particular sense apprehending its own proper object, unless perhaps the organ is impaired; but inasmuch as Aquinas is prepared to speak of the senses "judging," he is also prepared to speak of truth and falsity at the sense-level. We might say, for example, that an animal misjudged the distance, distance being

only indirectly apprehended by the senses. But though a "judgment" of sense may be true or false, according as it corresponds or not with reality, its truth or falsity is not reflectively apprehended at the sense-level. "Truth is primarily in the mind . . . It is defined as conformity between the mind and the thing. Hence to know this conformity is to know truth. Sense, however, does not know truth as such. For although sight has the likeness of a visible thing it does not know the correspondence between the thing seen and its perception of it. The mind, however, can know its own conformity with an intelligible thing, not simply by apprehending its essence, but it makes a judgment about the thing . . . It is then that it first knows and enunciates truth . . . And so, strictly speaking, it is in the mind's judgments that truth is found and not in sensation, nor in the intellectual apprehension of an essence" (*S.T.*, Ia, 16, 2). I may have a true perception of Peter as white; but it is not of this perception as such that truth is primarily predicated. It is the judgment that Peter is white which is strictly speaking "true." Aquinas does, indeed, speak of things as "true," as, being, for example, conformed to the mind of the Creator. But in the *De veritate* and elsewhere he carefully distinguishes the various senses in which he uses the word "true" and states that truth is primarily found in the mind's act of judging. . . .

According to Aquinas it is in the act of knowing truth that the mind is aware of its ability to attain truth. Truth is predicated primarily of propositions; or, as he puts it, truth is found primarily in the judgment. Now, there are indubitable propositions, the truth of which cannot really be doubted, though they can, of course, be verbally denied. "The whole is greater than any of its parts" would be a case in point. And in recognizing the truth of such indubitable propositions the mind recognizes both the fact that it knows their truth and that it is its own nature to be conformed to reality and so to know. In a rather cryptic passage Aquinas states that truth is a resultant of the activity of the mind, when the mind's judgment is about the thing as it is. Truth is known by the mind according as the mind reflects on its act, not only as knowing its act but also as knowing the relation of conformity between the act and the thing (*proportionem eius ad rem*). This indeed cannot be known unless the nature of the act itself is known; and this in turn cannot be known unless the nature of the active principle, that is, of the mind itself, is known, to whose nature it pertains to be conformed to reality (to things, *rebus*). Therefore "the mind knows truth according as it reflects on itself" (*De veritate*, 1, 9). Thus the mind knows its own power of attaining truth by reflecting on itself in the act of knowing truth. Aquinas' point of view was that sometimes at least we know something with certainty, that we know that we know it and that in knowing it we know that the object is knowable. It may be objected that this point of view is uncritical and naïve on the ground that it amounts to accepting the ordinary man's spontaneous conviction that he can attain truth and often does so. But the point is that for Aquinas the ordinary man's conviction on this matter is not simply "naïve." It is in the act of knowing that the mind's ability to

know is recognized; and it is recognized by the ordinary man. The philosopher can reflect on this recognition and make explicit what for the ordinary man is implicit. And this procedure can be called "second reflection." The passage quoted above is an instance of second reflection. But the "reflection" about which the passage speaks is not itself philosophic reflection: it is what we may call "first reflection," the awareness of knowing truth which at least sometimes accompanies the ordinary man's mental activity. In other words, the philosopher can reflect on the ordinary man's awareness of attaining truth, but he has not at his disposal some extraordinary and special means of proving that we can know truth or that "knowledge" is knowledge. If a philosopher were to comment that in this case we can never prove that we can attain truth and that if we cannot prove it we can never know it, Aquinas might reply that the sort of proof which the philosopher is looking for is inherently useless and indeed impossible, but that it does not follow that we cannot both attain truth and also know that we can attain it. We do not need any further guarantee of our ability to attain truth than our awareness or recognition of the fact that we do in fact attain it. . . .

It would, however, be a mistake to interpret Aquinas' appeal to the ordinary man's awareness of attaining truth as equivalent to saying that whenever anyone thinks that he knows the truth he does in fact know it. In the case of some propositions there can be no error, but this does not mean that we cannot enunciate false propositions while believing them to be true. If I say "That object in the distance is a tree," my statement may turn out to be false, even though I now believe it to be true. But though error is possible, Aquinas did not regard this possibility as any valid reason for unlimited skepticism. In cases where there is a possibility of error or where there is reason to suspect error Aquinas speaks of a "resolution to first principles." But we must not interpret "first principles" as meaning exclusively the first principles of logic and mathematics. True, if we have reason to suspect that there is an error in our mathematical reasoning, we have to go back and retrace our steps. But under "first principles" in the present connection Aquinas includes actual sense-perception. "Because the first principle of our knowledge is sense, it is necessary to reduce in some way to sense all things about which we judge" (*De veritate,* 1, 2, 3, *ad* 2). If my statement that the object in the field is a tree is open to doubt, the way to resolve the doubt or to correct the error is to look more closely. It may be said that this does not touch the problem whether all sense-perception may not be illusory. But I do not think that Aquinas would have had much patience with a problem of this kind. The term "illusion" has meaning for us only in contrast with what is not illusion and is known not to be illusion, and the word "false" has meaning for us only in contrast with the word "true." And we know the meaning of the word "true" because we enunciate and know that we enunciate true propositions. Again, the word "knowledge" is meaningful for us because we actually know. And to ask whether the knowledge we have is "really" knowledge is to pursue a profitless inquiry. Of course, if when we ask

whether what we think to be knowledge is "really" knowledge, we mean to ask whether knowing that there is a cat under the table is "mathematical knowledge," the answer is that it is not. And if we insist that only the conclusions of mathematical demonstrations can properly be said to be "known," it follows that knowledge of non-mathematical truths is not knowledge. But all we are doing is to propose a peculiar use of the words "know" and "knowledge" which is different from the normal use and which has little, if anything, to recommend it. In other words, I suggest that Aquinas would have considerable sympathy with those modern philosophers who examine with the aid of linguistic analysis[1] what precisely is being asked when it is asked whether all that we take to be knowledge may not be something other than knowledge, whether all sense-perception may not be illusory, whether all experience may not be a dream, and so on.

For Aquinas, therefore, it is in actually knowing something that we know and that the object is knowable. And he was convinced that further reflection shows that the object is knowable or intelligible because and in so far as it has being. The truth that being is intelligible is revealed in the concrete act of knowing anything, though its expression in the form of an abstract proposition is the work of reflection. And this is for Aquinas the reason why the mind goes forward confidently to investigate reality, whether in the sciences or in philosophy. And if his philosophical interpretation of the

---

[1On linguistic philosophy, see Chapter Six. *Ed.*]

world forms in some sense a system, the reason why it does so is not for him that reality is forced into a preconceived and presupposed mould but that the world is in itself an intelligible system and that this intelligible system discloses itself to the reflective mind. It is rather that the system is imposed on the mind by reality than that the mind reads a system into phenomena.

METAPHYSICS

The metaphysical analyses of Plato and, especially, Aristotle are utilized by Professor Wild to explain the being of the objects of nature and human experience. His statement is developed through attention to the fact of change, and he incorporates the substance-accident and form-matter distinctions first fully discussed by Aristotle. In the first part of the selection is a review of these concepts. Change, Professor Wild observes, always involves three factors: matter, form, and privative form. The first of these accounts for the continuity present in change, the latter two for the change itself. The further distinction between substance and accident is required to analyze changes where a basic structure abides but change happens to it ("accidental change"), and change where the structure itself of something changes ("substantial change").

Yet another distinction is necessary, however—namely, that of essence and existence. These terms received their fullest treatment within the realistic tradition by St. Thomas Aquinas. The immediate data of experience, realists hold, involve more than form and matter, for as beings they all exist in opposition to nonbeing. Hence the need for essence-existence: essence, or what a thing is, separates kinds of entities, whereas the act of existence separates entities from nonbeing. The exploration of these principles is, therefore, Professor Wild's second concern.

4 Being, Essence, and Existence
John Wild (1902–1973)

The object of general metaphysics is being as such. The facts we there observe apply to any being whatsoever, whether finite or infinite, changing or immutable, multiple or one. Now we must turn to an existential analysis of the entities which are presented to us in our imme-

diate experience. How do these entities exist? Are they changing or immutable? Do they exist in themselves or in something else distinct from them? Are they one or many? Is their existence atomic and self-enclosed or incomplete and tendential? Is their existence necessary or contingent? These basic questions cannot be answered by any of the sciences restricted to non-pervasive data. They are philosophical questions which can be scientifically answered only by

The selection is from John Wild, "Phenomenology and Metaphysics," in *The Return to Reason*, edited by John Wild, copyright 1953 by Henry Regnery Company. Used by permission of the publisher.

a careful description and analysis of the philosophical data which constitutively pervade the whole field of experience. Let us now turn to these peculiar, existential data and attempt such an analysis.

How do the entities of our experience exist? They are evidently finite, mutable, and multiple. We shall start with the data of mutability, then turn to those of multiplicity, and conclude with a brief discussion of the more basic datum of finitude which underlies both.

A. The datum of change. Unlike existence, the datum of change is not all-pervasive. There is nothing about existence as such which requires that any existent entity must be mutable. Nevertheless, change does pervade the data of human experience. The extended objects of nature are constantly undergoing those modes of physical change which are peculiar to them. I feel many kinds of psychophysical change proceeding within myself, and through the agencies of human communication I am aware of those manifold modes of social and cultural change which make up the complex web of human history. From this it is clear that change is too pervasive a datum to fall within the restricted province of any one of the special sciences. Each science studies only a special kind of change from its own special point of view.

Modern philosophy has not been clearly aware of its own peculiar data but has been deeply impressed by the positivistic view that every datum belongs to the special province of some restricted science. Hence when one raises the fundamental question: *What is change?* even in philosophical literature, he looks in vain for an intelligible answer. Many philosophers, like Dewey, insist upon the universal occurrence of what they call process and flux. But they seem almost wholly unaware of the need for a philosophical analysis and explanation of this peculiar and complex, philosophic datum. Instead of analysis, they give us merely synonyms. . . .

In the realistic analysis of change, first suggested by Aristotle, three sources of change are always recognized: two opposed structural principles (such as green and red) to account for the discontinuity, and one potential or dispositional principle (matter) to account for the continuity. When this third, dispositional principle is not clearly recognized, change is reduced to the pure discontinuity of succession, first one specific determination and then another opposed determination, annihilation and creation *ex nihilo*. On this view, the end of a process would have nothing in common with the beginning, and anything could come out of anything. But there is a vast array of empirical evidence against this conclusion. You cannot make a silk purse out of a sow's ear nor a poplar tree from an apple seed. Change is continuous as well as discontinuous.

What, then, are the major kinds of change? If we stick close to the data, we shall be forced to recognize two types in particular which are so important that we shall single them out for a brief analysis.

B. Accidental change and the distinction of substance and accident. At the present time, there are several deepseated misconceptions of substance and accident. Since this topic is treated more thoroughly elsewhere, we shall confine ourselves here to a brief consideration of these major misunderstandings, which are three in number.

The first is a widespread impression that the distinction of substance from accident is derived primarily from epistemological considerations and must be defended, if it is to be defended at all, on the basis of epistemological evidence. On this view, the accidental properties of a thing are supposed to be directly sensed. The realist is held to believe that back of these accidents, underlying them, is a noumenal x, or substance, in which they inhere like separate pins in an underlying pincushion. This conception is far removed from any realistic conception of substance and accident.

In the first place, this distinction is concerned not with epistemological facts but with dynamic facts. It is required to explain not the structure of knowledge but the structure of change. As we have just noted, there is a factor of continuity in all types of change. But in certain types, this continuous factor is constituted by a complex, formal pattern (or essence) which persists throughout the process. At the level of inorganic nature, where our entitative knowledge is less exact, we cannot clearly grasp the formal unity of what is changing. But in the case of individual plants and animals, we can grasp something of this substantial structure. As the roots are extended, the stalk grows, and the buds ripen and fall, the plant endures as a single, corporeal, living entity.

Somewhere between the simplest physical transformations and the processes of life, certain forms of unified structure have gained sufficient domination over limited bits of matter to enable them to persist through the various accidental transformations to which they are subject. Thus I am directly aware of various evolutions and transformations, resulting in the gain or loss of accidental properties, as long as my life endures. But I am also aware of the fact that I myself persist through these changes as a corporeal, living, human substance. This is an example of accidental change in which the continuity is provided by a unified, formal structure, partially expressed in the specific definition of the entity.

In the second place, substance and accident cannot be accurately understood as separate entities, merely juxtaposed with, or inhering in, one another as pins in a pincushion. This atomistic conception utterly fails to do justice to the situation. Substance is not a *thing,* and accident another *thing,* which happen to be joined. Neither is a thing. Each of them is a correlative principle which exists only by virtue of its fusion with the other. The only thing is the concrete entity constituted by this fusion.

Each principle contributes something to the whole entity. Thus its identity and individuation are derived from the substantial component, its changing qualities from the accidental component. But it is precisely the *whole, composite entity* which is individuated and qualified, not merely a part. It is entirely wrong to think of the substance as a fixed atom, remaining lifeless and inert as the accidental changes sweep by it. This is a complete perversion of the facts. It is the whole entity which changes, and every constitutive phase of the entity is involved in this change, the substance as providing it with continuity and individuality, the accidents as providing it with novelty and discontinuity.

Finally, in the third place, it is clear from their correlative structure that neither substance nor accident can be known without the other. It is as impossible to know accidents without substance as to know a father without any children. This is a pure figment of atomistic thought. But what of human sensation? Surely it is aware of the pure color green, the middle-C sound, which are accidents, but not of that mysterious something I know not what, which John Locke[1] confused with substance.

This last phrase is correct. Sensation knows nothing of *substance*. But neither does it know anything of *accident*. The color green is the object of a universal concept. It is never sensed. What is sensed is a complex flux of quantitative and qualitative characters confused together in an unanalyzed blur. Substance and accident are implicit in this blur. But they can be clearly apprehended and distinguished only through a rational analysis of this sensory confusion. Substance is the formal unity which persists throughout the concrete change. The accidents come and go.

C. Substantial change and the distinction of matter and form. The accidental changes we have so far been considering affect the whole, concrete,

changing entity. They do not affect the formal essence which maintains the substantial unity of the entity throughout these accidental transformations. There is another more radical type of change, however, which results in the generation or destruction of the entity and which, therefore, does penetrate to the very essence. The death of my cat is not an accidental change, for he does not survive the process. My cat has ceased to be. Nevertheless, the data show that this process is not wholly discontinuous. The carcass remains, and while it consists of new substances not in existence before, there is something in them which was once in the cat.

This matter, or capacity to be possessed by different substantial forms, underlies any process of substantial change and supplies it with a minimum continuity. Thus in order to account for the continuity which characterizes even the most radical changes of nature, including the evolution of new species from earlier forms, we must recognize a further composition in the very essence of any natural entity which has come into existence by a process of evolution. On the one hand, its essence must consist of a certain formal structure marking off this entity from other species, which disappears when the entity is destroyed. But there must be another essential part which existed before and which will outlast the entity. This must be a capacity or potency, able to exist under divergent forms and able to unite both essence and accidents together into a single, material unity.

Here again it is most important to notice how this hylomorphic composition in the essence of any evolutionary entity must be distorted by any atomis-

---

[1 The reference is to the philosopher, John Locke (1632–1704), the first great British empiricist. *Ed.*]

tic mode of analysis. Matter is not one thing, and form another. The essence is no mere addition of quantitative atoms. Matter and form are correlative principles, each of which exists only by virtue of the other. It is true that this matter may exist under some other form than that which now possesses it. But it cannot exist as an atom by itself alone. Similarly, the form can be found apart from *this* matter, but never apart from matter. Each is a vectorial principle, intrinsically correlative to something distinct from itself, and each contributes something to the whole concrete entity which is thus constituted. The matter sustains the entity and gives it an individual position in nature, while the form specifically characterizes the entity as a whole.

Thus in order to account for the pervasive datum of change, we are forced to recognize a fourfold composition in the structure of the simplest conceivable dynamic entity. First (unless it was created *ex nihilo*), this entity must include a matter from which it continuously evolved. It must also include an essential form, marking it off from other *kinds* of entity, which must be in possession of the matter as long as the entity endures, from the moment of its generation to that of its extinction. The matter, when given existence in union with such a form, is a complete substance, which is then capable of undergoing accidental transformations by which further existent properties are gained or lost without the destruction of the entity. These principles are not entities, but vectorial factors by which a concrete natural entity exists. Matter cannot exist without form, nor form without matter. Substance exists only with accidents, and accidents only in substance.

We must now turn to an even more basic composition which is required by another immediate datum of experience —multiplicity.

D. The problem of the one and the many: essence and existence. An *order* is a unity in multiplicity. The data of change present us with a certain type of order, a temporal multiplicity of determinations united by matter, or by substantial form in the case of accidental change. In order to account for these immediate data, we are forced to recognize in any concrete changing entity the distinct, component principles of matter and form, substance and accident. But at any given moment we are also presented with an even more basic *static* order, as we may call it—a multiplicity of diverse entities, all of which share in existence. On the one hand, each entity is distinct from, and opposed to, the rest. So they are a multiplicity. But on the other hand, they all share in that existence which opposes them all to nothing. In this respect they are one. How can they be both many and one?

Consider my own being. I am directly aware of myself as radically distinct from all the other entities surrounding me. They are not what I am, and I am not what they are. This is an immediate datum of experience, thrust upon me with inexorable constraint. I cannot question it without also questioning, if I am consistent, all other data as well, and thus abandoning the whole attempt to know. But there is another datum also thrust upon me with equal constraint. This is the datum of existence which pervades both self and not-self. The others exist as much as I. Existence is shared in common. But how is this possible? How can the same entity be both diverse and similar to the very same entities? Unless we are to fall into a radical monism which denies the datum of multiplicity, or into a radical, atomistic pluralism which denies the datum of shared existence, we must find an answer to this problem of the one and the many.

There is only one way of solving this problem. That is by inferring another and even more basic composition in the complex structure of a finite entity. This means that an absolutely *simple* Democritean atom, or Humean impression,[2] is impossible. Such a simple, atomic entity cannot exist among others even for an instant. A simple, finite entity cannot be both similar to, and distinct from, the very same entities. But the actual entities now existing at this instant are both similar to, and distinct from, the rest. Hence they are not simple. Each must include something within it, essense, by which it is wholly divorced from other entities, and something else, existence, by which it is opposed to nothing and in this respect similar to the rest.

Each of these principles is correlative. Neither can be adequately conceived apart from the other. Existence is always the existence *of* something (an essence), and essence is always the distinct character *of* something existent. When we conceive of an essence not

[2 The references are to Democritus' atomic theory (see materialism/naturalism below) and to David Hume's theory of knowledge (see below under positivism). *Ed.*]

actualized, which we call a possibility, we conceive of it as something that *might be* actualized, and therefore in relation to existence. Furthermore, in any actual thing these two principles are fused together in such a way that each determines the entity as a whole. In my concrete totality I am marked off from other entities, and every phase of my being is pervaded by my existence.

The essence as such is atomistic and self-enclosed. In the second place, it is nontendential and inactive. One essence as such does not tend to other essences, nor can it diffuse anything to another. Each is simply *what it is*. Finally, the determinate parts of a concrete essence are more readily grasped by the human mind. Hence, as has been recently noted, there has been a strong tendency in the history of Western thought to emphasize essence at the expense of existence, which is less easily abstracted and fixed by the human mind in clear and distinct definitions by universal concepts. As a result of this tendency, Western thought has been peculiarly prone to philosophies of radical pluralism and logical atomism, which view the world as a set of distinct entities entirely divorced from one another and which have great difficulty in focusing the active, causal phases of being which spring from existence rather than from essence.

This essentialist tendency leads to significant distortions and over-simplifications of philosophical doctrine, for existence is more ultimate and more perfect than essence. Essence without existence, though it may be brought before the mind very easily as a logical abstraction, in reality is nothing at all. It is only by virtue of existence that essence emerges from its causes and ceases to be nothing. Though less easily grasped than essence, existence is actually possessed in common by all the data of experience, indeed by anything whatsoever, whether in human experience or not. Furthermore, it is active and diffusive, never atomistic, self-enclosed, and insular, like the essential aspect of finite being. These active, tendential, and causal phases of concrete entities are due to existence rather than to essence. They are expressed in our language by verbs rather than by nouns. It is to these existential aspects of finite being that we must now turn.

E. Tendency and causation. Activity is a special kind of change, namely, that which originates within a finite entity. The organization and partial completion of such activity within the entity is *tendency*.

The existence of such tendencies within all the entities we experience is confirmed by a vast wealth of direct evidence. First of all, we constantly feel within ourselves such tendencies as hunger, thirst, curiosity, and so forth. Through communication with others, we discover such tendencies in them. In the case of subhuman entities, with which communication is impossible, we find that similar entities act and behave in similar ways. Unless we assume constant, self-originating tendencies, determined by similar, formal structures, we cannot explain the myriad facts revealed by what is called induction.

That these tendencies originate within the entity is confirmed by evidence which shows that a given entity will go on behaving in a constant manner even though the surrounding conditions may vary over a wide range. Otherwise, the prediction of what a given entity will do in a hitherto unobserved situation would be impossible. As long as its structure endures, fire tends to burn, ice to cool, and so on. Every natural entity constantly tends to act in ways which are determined by its essential structure. What is the explanation of this constant, tendential factor?

It cannot be explained by reference to essence alone, for as we have seen, essence, like a Humean impression, is always insular, self-enclosed, and exclusive. Tendency is an urge that reaches out beyond essence to more being not yet possessed. Hence it is due to existence rather than to essence, for it is by existence that the finite entity is allied to others beyond itself. As soon as existence is fused with a determinate, restricted essence, it bubbles over as an active tendency toward further existence. But the specific form of this tendency is determined by the essence. Each tends beyond its essence because of its existence.

But the character of this tendency is due to its essence. Each divergent kind of thing has correspondingly divergent tendencies. Inorganic things have simpler tendencies, corresponding to their simpler nature. Plants have their constant, vegetative tendencies, and individual human beings all possess tendencies to live in human ways determined by their human nature. This basic urge is the root of what is called human obligation, and the realization of these essential tendencies is the standard of human goodness. Any entity is in a sound or healthy state only in so far as it realizes its essential tendencies. Good is no mere property or essence, but an *existential category*—the active realization of a given nature.[3]

Tendency is, therefore, a necessary result of essence and existence together. It must be recognized as a distinct factor in the complex structure of any finite entity. There are two distinct types of tendency, the immanent and the transitive. Immanent tendencies not only originate but are also completed within the active agent. Thus the tendency to knowledge in man is completed within the knowing agent without

---

[3] Hence for a realist there is no radical separation of fact from value. What is *universally* and essentially good for man is determined by his tendential nature, certainly a fact. He is in a good condition when this nature is realized, in a bad condition when this is thwarted.

any change being produced in the environment. Such purely immanent tendencies are, however, very rare. Most tendencies are transitive in character. Such tendencies originate within a given entity, but then pass out of it to effect changes in surrounding entities by which alone the original tendency is realized.

This transitive realization of tendency, which is diffused to other entities, is commonly referred to as *causal efficacy,* or more properly as *efficient causation.* Many of these causal influences are directly observed. Others are inferred. They are expressed in the natural laws or principles of science, which show the dependence of one kind of entity on another. No finite entity can exist by itself; but it is dependent upon other entities in myriad ways.

This raises an important question concerning the whole collection of finite entities which constitutes the world of nature. Can it exist alone? Or is it dependent on something extrinsic?

ETHICS

Realistic ethics is marked by three basic principles. The first is called the law of nature or the natural law. The natural law, realists hold, prescribes the good for man and, as we shall see later, for society. It is not based simply on subjective interests or desires, but rather on the very nature of man and the universe he inhabits. Therefore realists argue that the natural law is not arbitrarily constructed by any human groups, but rather it is discovered by human reason as embedded in the nature of man and things. This makes the natural law objective or independent of particular circumstance and interest, and universal in the sense that it applies to all men everywhere.

The second principle of realist ethics is happiness or well-being. This principle refers to the perfection of our human nature which is the goal of all moral effort. But such perfection is achieved only by the development of proper habits. Good habits are called virtues; bad habits, vices. Virtue is thus the third principle of realist ethics. It is the primary internal cause of happiness, and human activity in accordance with virtue is the very definition of happiness itself.

The following selection is from Aristotle's major ethical work, the *Nicomachean Ethics.* It includes a discussion of happiness, a description of the virtues related to and derived from Aristotle's view of man, and a statement of man's highest good as the exercise of his highest capacity, contemplative reason. These Aristotelian concepts have remained the basis of realistic ethics to the present day.

5 Happiness and Virtue
Aristotle (384-322)

Book I. The Good or the End

1. Every art and every kind of inquiry, and likewise every act and purpose, seems to aim at some good: and so it has been well said that the good is that at which everything aims.

But a difference is observable among these aims or ends. What is aimed at is sometimes the exercise of a faculty, sometimes a certain result beyond that exercise. And where there is an end beyond the act, there the result is better than the exercise of the faculty.

Now since there are many kinds of actions and many arts and sciences, it follows that there are many ends also; *e.g.* health is the end of medicine, ships of ship-building, victory of the art of war, and wealth of economy.

But when several of these are subordinated to some one art or science, —as the making of bridles and other trappings to the art of horsemanship, and this in turn, along with all else that the soldier does, to the art of war, and so on, then the end of the master-art is always more desired than the ends of the subordinate arts, since these are pursued for its sake. And this is equally true whether the end in view be the mere exercise of a faculty or something beyond that, as in the above instances.

2. If then in what we do there be some end which we wish for on its own account, choosing all the others as means to this, but not every end without exception as a means to something else (for so we should go on *ad infinitum,* and desire would be left void and objectless), this evidently will be the good or the best of all things. And surely from a practical point of view it much concerns us to know this good; for then, like archers shooting at a definite mark, we shall be more likely to attain what we want.

If this be so, we must try to indicate roughly what it is, and first of all to which of the arts or sciences it belongs.

It would seem to belong to the supreme art or science, that one which most of all deserves the name of master-art or master-science.

Now Politics[1] seems to answer to this description. For it prescribes which of the sciences a state needs, and which each man shall study, and up to what point; and to it we see subordinated even the highest arts, such as economy, rhetoric, and the art of war.

Since then it makes use of the other

The selection is from the translation by F. H. Peters, *The Nicomachean Ethics of Aristotle* (7th ed.) (London: Kegan Paul, Trench, Trübner and Co., Ltd., 1898), Books I, II, and VI, with omissions.

[1 Aristotle uses the term "politics" for the general study of human life, of which ethics or the study of the individual good is a part. *Ed.*]

practical sciences, and since it further ordains what men are to do and from what to refrain, its end must include the ends of the others, and must be the proper good of man.

For though this good is the same for the individual and the state, yet the good of the state seems a grander and more perfect thing both to attain and to secure; and glad as one would be to do this service for a single individual, to do it for a people and for a number of states is nobler and more divine.

This then is the aim of the present inquiry, which is a sort of political inquiry. . . .

4. Since—to resume—all knowledge and all purpose aims at some good, what is this which we say is the aim of Politics; or, in other words, what is the highest of all realizable goods?

As to its name, I suppose nearly all men are agreed; for the masses and the men of culture alike declare that it is happiness, and hold that to "live well" or to "do well" is the same as to be "happy."

But they differ as to what this happiness is, and the masses do not give the same account of it as the philosophers.

The former take it to be something palpable and plain, as pleasure or wealth or fame; one man holds it to be this, and another that, and often the same man is of different minds at different times, after sickness it is health, and in poverty it is wealth; while when they are impressed with the consciousness of their ignorance, they admire most those who say grand things that are above their comprehension.

Some philosophers, on the other hand, have thought that, beside these several good things, there is an "absolute" good which is the cause of their goodness.

As it would hardly be worth while to review all the opinions that have been held, we will confine ourselves to those which are most popular, or which seem to have some foundation in reason. . . .

5. . . . It seems that men not unreasonably take their notions of the good or happiness from the lives actually led, and that the masses who are the least refined suppose it to be pleasure, which is the reason why they aim at nothing higher than the life of enjoyment.

For the most conspicuous kinds of life are three: this life of enjoyment, the life of the statesman, and, thirdly, the contemplative life.

The mass of men show themselves utterly slavish in their preference for the life of brute beasts, but their views receive consideration because many of those in high places have the tastes of Sardanapalus.

Men of refinement with a practical turn prefer honor; for I suppose we may say that honor is the aim of the statesman's life.

But this seems too superficial to be the good we are seeking: for it appears to depend upon those who give rather than upon those who receive it; while we have a presentiment that the good is something that is peculiarly a man's own and can scarce be taken away from him.

Moreover, these men seem to pursue honor in order that they may be assured of their own excellence, at least, they wish to be honored by men of sense, and by those who know them, and on the ground of their virtue or excellence.

It is plain, then, that in their view, at any rate, virtue or excellence is better than honor; and perhaps we should take this to be the end of the statesman's life, rather than honor.

But virtue or excellence also appears too incomplete to be what we want; for it seems that a man might have virtue and yet be asleep or be inactive all his life, and, moreover, might meet with the greatest disasters and misfortunes; and no one would maintain that such a man is happy, except for argument's sake. But we will not dwell on these matters now, for they are sufficiently discussed in the popular treatises.

The third kind of life is the life of contemplation: we will treat of it further on.

As for the money-making life, it is something quite contrary to nature; and wealth evidently is not the good of which we are in search, for it is merely useful as a means to something else. So we might rather take pleasure and virtue or excellence to be ends than wealth; for they are chosen on their own account. But it seems that not even they are the end, though much breath has been wasted in attempts to show that they are. . . .

7. Leaving these matters, then, let us return once more to the question, what this good can be of which we are in search.

It seems to be different in different kinds of action and in different arts, one thing in medicine and another in war, and so on. What then is the good in each of these cases? Surely that for the sake of which all else is done. And that in medicine is health, in war is victory, in building is a house, a different thing in each different case, but always, in whatever we do and in whatever we choose, the end. For it is always for the sake of the end that all else is done.

If then there be one end of all that man does, this end will be the realizable good, or these ends, if there be more than one.

By this generalization our argument is brought to the same point as before. This point we must try to explain more clearly.

We see that there are many ends. But some of these are chosen only as means, as wealth, flutes, and the whole class of instruments. And so it is plain that not all ends are final.

But the best of all things must, we conceive, be something final.

If then there be only one final end, this will be what we are seeking, or if there be more than one, then the most final of them.

Now that which is pursued as an end in itself is more final than that which is pursued as means to something else, and that which is never chosen as means than that which is chosen both as an end in itself and as means, and that is strictly final which is always chosen as an end in itself and never as means.

Happiness seems more than anything else to answer to this description: for we always choose it for itself, and never for the sake of something else; while honor and pleasure and reason, and all virtue or excellence, we choose partly indeed for themselves (for, apart from any result, we should choose each of them), but partly also for the sake of happiness, supposing that they will help to make us happy. But no one chooses happiness for the sake of these things, or as a means to anything else at all. . . .

But perhaps the reader thinks that though no one will dispute the statement that happiness is the best thing in the world, yet a still more precise definition of it is needed.

This will best be gained, I think, by asking, What is the function of man? For as the goodness and the excellence of a piper or a sculptor, or the practicer of any art, and generally of those who have any function or business to do, lies in that function, so man's good would seem to lie in his function, if he has one.

But can we suppose that, while a carpenter or a cobbler has a function and a business of his own, man has no business and no function assigned him by nature? Nay, surely as his several members, eye and hand and foot, plainly have each his own function, so we must suppose that man also has some function over and above all these.

What then is it?

Life evidently he has in common even with the plants, but we want that which is peculiar to him. We must exclude, therefore, the life of mere nutrition and growth.

Next to this comes the life of sense; but this too he plainly shares with horses and cattle and all kinds of animals.

There remains then the life whereby he acts—the life of his rational nature, with its two sides or divisions, one rational as obeying reason, the other rational as having and exercising reason.

But as this expression is ambiguous, we must be understood to mean thereby the life that consists in the exercise of the faculties; for this seems to be more properly entitled to the name.

The function of man, then, is exercise of his vital faculties [or soul] on one side in obedience to reason, and on the other side with reason.

But what is called the function of a man of any profession and the function of a man who is good in that profession are generically the same, e.g., of a harper and of a good harper; and this holds in all cases without exception, only that in the case of the latter his superior excellence at his work is added; for we say a harper's function is to harp, and a good harper's to harp well.

(Man's function then being, as we say, a kind of life—that is to say, exercise of his faculties and action of various kinds with reason—the good man's function is to do this well and beautifully [or nobly]. But the function of anything is done well when it is done in accordance with the proper excellence of that thing.)

If this be so the result is that the good of man is exercise of his faculties in accordance with excellence or virtue, or, if there be more than one, in accordance with the best and most complete virtue.

But there must also be a full term of years for this exercise; for one swallow or one fine day does not make a spring, nor does one day or any small space of time make a blessed or happy man. . . .

13. Since happiness is an exercise of the vital faculties in accordance with perfect virtue or excellence, we will now inquire about virtue or excellence; for this will probably help us in our inquiry about happiness. . . .

The virtue or excellence that we are to consider is, of course, the excellence of man; for it is the good of man and the happiness of man that we started to seek. And by the excellence of man I mean excellence not of body, but of soul; for happiness we take to be an activity of the soul.

If this be so, then it is evident that the statesman must have some knowledge of the soul, just as the man who is to heal the eye or the whole body must have some knowledge of them, and that the more in proportion as the science of the state is higher and better than medicine. But all educated physicians take much pains to know about the body.

As statesmen [or students of Politics], then, we must inquire into the nature of the soul, but in so doing we must keep our special purpose in view and go only so far as that requires; for to go into minuter detail would be too laborious for the present undertaking.

Now, there are certain doctrines about the soul which are stated elsewhere with sufficient precision, and these we will adopt.

Two parts of the soul are distinguished, an irrational and a rational part.

Whether these are separated as are the parts of the body or any divisible thing, or whether they are only distinguishable in thought but in fact inseparable, like concave and convex in the circumference of a circle, makes no difference for our present purpose.

Of the irrational part, again, one division seems to be common to all things that live, and to be possessed by plants —I mean that which causes nutrition and growth; for we must assume that all things that take nourishment have a faculty of this kind, even when they are embryos, and have the same faculty when they are full grown; at least, this is more reasonable than to suppose that they then have a different one.

The excellence of this faculty, then, is plainly one that man shares with other beings, and not specifically human. . . .

But there seems to be another vital principle that is irrational, and yet in some way partakes of reason. In the case of the continent and of the incontinent man alike we praise the reason or the rational part, for it exhorts them rightly and urges them to do what is best; but there is plainly present in them another principle besides the rational one, which fights and struggles against the reason. For just as a paralyzed limb, when you will to move it to the right, moves on the contrary to the left, so is it with the soul; the incontinent man's impulses run counter to his reason. Only whereas we see the refractory member in the case of the body, we do not see it in the case of the soul. But we must nevertheless, I think, hold that in the soul too there is something beside the reason, which opposes and runs counter to it (though in what sense it is distinct from the reason does not matter here).

It seems, however, to partake of reason also, as we said: at least, in the continent man it submits to the reason; while in the temperate and courageous man we may say it is still more obedient; for in him it is altogether in harmony with the reason.

The irrational part, then, it appears, is twofold. There is the vegetative faculty, which has no share of reason; and the faculty of appetite or of desire in general, which in a manner partakes of reason or is rational as listening to reason and submitting to its sway, rational in the sense in which we speak of rational obedience to father or friends, not in the sense in which we speak of rational apprehension of mathematical truths. But all advice and all rebuke and exhortation testify that the irrational part is in some way amenable to reason.

If then we like to say that this part, too, has a share of reason, the rational part also will have two divisions: one rational in the strict sense as possessing reason in itself, the other rational as listening to reason as a man listens to his father.

Now, on this division of the faculties is based the division of excellence; for we speak of intellectual excellences and of moral excellences; wisdom and understanding and prudence we call intellectual, liberality and temperance we call moral virtues or excellences. When we are speaking of a man's moral character we do not say that he is wise or intelligent, but that he is gentle or temperate. But we praise the wise man, too, for his habit of mind or trained faculty; and a habit or trained faculty that is praiseworthy is what we call an excellence or virtue.

Book II. Moral Virtue

1. Excellence, then, being of these two kinds, intellectual and moral, intellectual excellence owes its birth and growth mainly to instruction, and so requires time and experience, while moral excellence is the result of habit or custom (ἔθος), and has accordingly in our language received a name formed by a slight change from ἔθος.

From this it is plain that none of the moral excellences or virtues is implanted in us by nature; for that which is by nature cannot be altered by training. For instance, a stone naturally tends to fall downwards, and you could not train it to rise upwards, though you tried to do so by throwing it up ten thousand times, nor could you train fire to move downwards, nor accustom anything which naturally behaves in one way to behave in any other way.

The virtues, then, come neither by nature nor against nature, but nature gives the capacity for acquiring them, and this is developed by training. . . .

We may safely assert that the virtue or excellence of a thing causes that thing both to be itself in good condition and to perform its function well. The excellence of the eye, for instance, makes both the eye and its work good; for it is by the excellence of the eye that we see well. So the proper excellence of the horse makes a horse what he should be, and makes him good at running, and carrying his rider, and standing a charge.

If, then, this holds good in all cases, the proper excellence or virtue of man will be the habit or trained faculty that makes a man good and makes him perform his function well.

How this is to be done we have already said, but we may exhibit the same conclusion in another way, by inquiring what the nature of this virtue is.

Now, if we have any quantity, whether continuous or discrete, it is possible to take either a larger [or too large], or a smaller [or too small], or an equal [or fair] amount, and that either absolutely or relatively to our own needs.

By an equal or fair amount I understand a mean amount, or one that lies between excess and deficiency.

By the absolute mean, or mean relatively to the thing itself, I understand that which is equidistant from both extremes, and this is one and the same for all.

By the mean relatively to us I understand that which is neither too much nor too little for us; and this is not one and the same for all.

For instance, if ten be larger [or too large] and two be smaller [or too small], if we take six we take the mean relatively to the thing itself [or the arithmetical mean]; for it exceeds one extreme by the same amount by which it is exceeded by the other extreme; and this is the mean in arithmetical proportion.

But the mean relatively to us cannot be found in this way. If ten pounds of food is too much for a given man to eat, and two pounds too little, it does not follow that the trainer will order him six pounds: for that also may perhaps be too much for the man in question, or too little; too little for Milo, too much for the beginner. The same holds true in running and wrestling.

And so we may say generally that a master in any art avoids what is too much and what is too little, and seeks for the mean and chooses it—not the absolute but the relative mean.

If, then, every art or science perfects its work in this way, looking to the mean and bringing its work up to this standard (so that people are wont to say of a good work that nothing could be taken from it or added to it, implying that excellence is destroyed by excess or deficiency, but secured by observing the mean; and good artists, as we say, do in fact keep their eyes fixed on this in all that they do), and if virtue, like nature, is more exact and better than any art, it follows that virtue also must aim at the mean—virtue of course

meaning moral virtue or excellence; for it has to do with passions and actions, and it is these that admit of excess and deficiency and the mean. For instance, it is possible to feel fear, confidence, desire, anger, pity, and generally to be affected pleasantly and painfully, either too much or too little, in either case wrongly; but to be thus affected at the right times, and on the right occasions, and towards the right persons, and with the right object, and in the right fashion, is the mean course and the best course, and these are characteristics of virtue. And in the same way our outward acts also admit of excess and deficiency, and the mean or due amount.

Virtue, then, has to deal with feelings or passions and with outward acts, in which excess is wrong and deficiency also is blamed, but the mean amount is praised and is right—both of which are characteristics of virtue.

Virtue, then, is a kind of moderation (μεστότης τις), inasmuch as it aims at the mean or moderate amount (τὸ μέσον).

Again, there are many ways of going wrong (for evil is infinite in nature, to use a Pythagorean[2] figure, while good is finite), but only one way of going right; so that the one is easy and the other hard—easy to miss the mark and hard to hit. On this account also, then, excess and deficiency are characteristic of vice, hitting the mean is characteristic of virtue:

Goodness is simple, ill takes any shape.

Virtue, then, is a habit or trained

[2 Aristotle refers here to a doctrine of Pythagoras (c. 522–497), a pre-Socratic philosopher, mathematician, and religious leader. *Ed.*]

faculty of choice, the characteristic of which lies in moderation or observance of the mean relatively to the persons concerned, as determined by reason, *i.e.* by the reason by which the prudent man would determine it. And it is a moderation, firstly, inasmuch as it comes in the middle or mean between two vices, one on the side of excess, the other on the side of defect; and, secondly, inasmuch as, while these vices fall short of or exceed the due measure in feeling and in action, it finds and chooses the mean, middling, or moderate amount.

Regarded in its essence, therefore, or according to the definition of its nature, virtue is a moderation or middle state, but viewed in its relation to what is best and right it is the extreme of perfection.

But it is not all actions nor all passions that admit of moderation; there are some whose very names imply badness, as malevolence, shamelessness, envy, and, among acts, adultery, theft, murder. These and all other like things are blamed as being bad in themselves, and not merely in their excess or deficiency. It is impossible therefore to go right in them; they are always wrong: rightness and wrongness in such things (*e.g.* in adultery) does not depend upon whether it is the right person and occasion and manner, but the mere doing of any one of them is wrong.

It would be equally absurd to look for moderation or excess or deficiency in unjust, cowardly, or profligate conduct; for then there would be moderation in excess or deficiency, and excess in excess, and deficiency in deficiency.

The fact is that just as there can be no excess or deficiency in temperance or courage, because the mean or mod-

erate amount is, in a sense, an extreme, so in these kinds of conduct also there can be no moderation or excess or deficiency, but the acts are wrong however they be done. For, to put it generally, there cannot be moderation in excess or deficiency, nor excess or deficiency in moderation. . . .

Book VI. The Intellectual Virtues

1. . . . The virtues or excellences of the mind or soul, it will be remembered, we divided into two classes, and called the one moral and the other intellectual. The moral excellences or virtues we have already discussed in detail; let us now examine the other class, the intellectual excellences, after some preliminary remarks about the soul.

We said before that the soul consists of two parts, the rational and the irrational part. We will now make a similar division of the former, and will assume that there are two rational faculties: (1) that by which we know those things that depend on invariable principles, (2) that by which we know those things that are variable. For to generically different objects must correspond generically different faculties, if, as we hold, it is in virtue of some kind of likeness or kinship with their objects that our faculties are able to know them.

Let us call the former the scientific or demonstrative, the latter the calculative or deliberative faculty. For to deliberate is the same as to calculate, and no one deliberates about things that are invariable. One division then of the rational faculty may be fairly called the calculative faculty. . . .

6. Science is a mode of judging that deals with universal and necessary truths; but truths that can be demon-

strated depend upon principles, and (since science proceeds by demonstrative reasoning) every science has its principles. The principles, then, on which the truths of science depend cannot fall within the province of science, nor yet of art or prudence; for a scientific truth is one that can be demonstrated, but art and prudence have to do with that which is variable.

Nor can they fall within the province of wisdom; for it is characteristic of the wise man to have a demonstrative knowledge of certain things.

But the habits of mind or formed faculties by which we apprehend truth without any mixture of error, whether in the domain of things invariable or in the domain of things variable, are science, prudence, wisdom, and reason. If then no one of the first three (prudence, science, wisdom) can be the faculty which apprehends these principles, the only possible conclusion is that they are apprehended by reason.

7. The term sophia (wisdom) is sometimes applied in the domain of the arts to those who are consummate masters of their art; *e.g.* it is applied to Phidias as a master of sculpture, and to Polyclitus for his skill in portrait-statues; and in this application it means nothing else than excellence of art or perfect development of the artistic faculty.

But there are also men who are considered wise, not in part nor in any particular thing (as Homer says in the Margites—

Him the gods gave no skill with
  spade or plough,
Nor made him wise in aught),

but generally wise. In this general sense, then, wisdom plainly will be the most perfect of the sciences.

The wise man, then, must not only know what follows from the principles of knowledge, but also know the truth about those principles. Wisdom, therefore, will be the union of [intuitive] reason with [demonstrative] scientific knowledge, or scientific knowledge of the noblest objects with its crowning perfection, so to speak, added to it. For it would be absurd to suppose that the political faculty or prudence is the highest of our faculties, unless indeed man is the best of all things in the universe.

SOCIAL PHILOSOPHY

Just as there are universal and objective principles of the individual good, so there are for the realist such principles of the common or social good. The traditional name for that principle of right order in society is justice. Philosophic problems connected with this ideal include questions of definition, of implication, of relationships to other social ideals such as freedom and equality, and of the status and authority of the ideal. Realists begin this discussion with Aristotle's definition of justice as fairness (which was later restated by the Roman jurist Justinian as giving every man his due). Realists also assert, with Aristotle and Cicero, that the roots of Justice are in Nature or the structure of things and of man. They are opposed to any view that right and justice are founded simply on men's opinions or on convention. And, because there is but a single definition of man, so can there be but a single definition of justice for all men. Virtue, as Aristotle taught, is nature perfected. Justice is similarly an ideal for the perfection of man's associative nature. The principles of justice become embodied in law, which is the measure and "right reason" of human acts. The good state, finally, is that state whose actual positive law reflects and embodies the Law of Reason which is Justice.

6 Nature and Justice
Cicero (106-43)

MARCUS. I shall seek the root of Justice in Nature, under whose guidance our whole discussion must be conducted.

ATTICUS. Quite right. Surely with her as our guide, it will be impossible for us to go astray.

MARCUS. Do you grant us, then, Pomponius (for I am aware of what Quintus thinks), that it is by the might of the immortal gods, or by their nature, reason, power, mind, will, or any other term which may make my meaning clearer, that all Nature is governed? For if you do not admit it, we must begin our argument with this problem before taking up anything else.

ATTICUS. Surely I will grant it, if you insist upon it. . . .

MARCUS. I will not make the argument long. Your admission leads us to this: that animal which we call man, endowed with foresight and quick intelligence, complex, keen, possessing memory, full of reason and prudence, has been given a certain distinguished status by the supreme God who created him; for he is the only one among so many different kinds and varieties of living beings who has a share in reason and thought, while all the rest are deprived of it. But what is more divine, I will not say in man only, but in all heaven and earth, than reason? And reason, when it is full grown and perfected, is rightly called wisdom. Therefore, since there is nothing better than reason, and since it exists both in man and God, the first common possession of man and God is reason. But those who have reason in common must also have right reason in common. And since right reason is Law, we must believe that men have Law also in common with the gods. Further, those who share Law must also share Justice; and those who share these are to be regarded as members of the same commonwealth. If indeed they obey the same authorities and powers, this is true in a far greater degree; but as a matter of fact they do obey this celestial system, the divine mind, and the God of transcendent power. Hence we must now conceive of this whole universe as one commonwealth of which both gods and men are members.

And just as in States distinctions in legal status are made on account of the

The selection is reprinted by permission of the publishers from the Loeb Classical Library edition, translated by Clinton Walker Keyes, Cicero, *De Re Publica, De Legibus* (Cambridge, Mass.: Harvard University Press, 1928), pp. 319–367 and 379–387, with omissions.

blood relationships of families, so in the universe the same thing holds true, but on a scale much vaster and more splendid, so that men are grouped with Gods on the basis of blood relationship and descent. For when the nature of man is examined, the theory is usually advanced (and in all probability it is correct) that through constant changes and revolutions in the heavens, a time came which was suitable for sowing the seed of the human race. And when this seed was scattered and sown over the earth, it was granted the divine gift of the soul. For while the other elements of which man consists were derived from what is mortal, and are therefore fragile and perishable, the soul was generated in us by God. Hence we are justified in saying that there is a blood relationship between ourselves and the celestial beings; or we may call it a common ancestry or origin. Therefore among all the varieties of living beings, there is no creature except man which has any knowledge of God, and among men themselves there is no race either so highly civilized or so savage as not to know that it must believe in a god, even if it does not know in what sort of god it ought to believe. Thus it is clear that man recognizes God because, in a way, he remembers and recognizes the source from which he sprang.

Moreover, virtue exists in man and God alike, but in no other creature besides; virtue, however, is nothing else than Nature perfected and developed to its highest point; therefore there is a likeness between man and God. As this is true, what relationship could be closer or clearer than this one? For this reason, Nature has lavishly yielded such a wealth of things adapted to man's con-

venience and use that what she produces seems intended as a gift to us, and not brought forth by chance; and this is true, not only of what the fertile earth bountifully bestows in the form of grain and fruit, but also of the animals; for it is clear that some of them have been created to be man's slaves, some to supply him with their products, and others to serve as his food. Moreover innumerable arts have been discovered through the teachings of Nature; for it is by a skilful imitation of her that reason has acquired the necessities of life. Nature has likewise not only equipped man himself with nimbleness of thought, but has also given him the senses, to be, as it were, his attendants and messengers; she has laid bare the obscure and none too [obvious][1] meanings of a great many things, to serve as the foundations of knowledge, as we may call them; and she has granted us a bodily form which is convenient and well suited to the human mind. For while she has bent the other creatures down toward their food, she has made man alone erect, and has challenged him to look up toward heaven, as being, so to speak, akin to him, and his first home. . . .

The points which are now being briefly touched upon are certainly important; but out of all the material of the philosophers' discussions, surely there comes nothing more valuable than the full realization that we are born for Justice, and that right is based, not upon men's opinions, but upon Nature. This fact will immediately be plain if you once get a clear conception of man's

---

[1] Brackets indicate gaps in Cicero's text. The words within brackets have been supplied by editors of Cicero.

fellowship and union with his fellow-men. For no single thing is so like an-other, so exactly its counterpart, as all of us are to one another. Nay, if bad habits and false beliefs did not twist the weaker minds and turn them in whatever direction they are inclined, no one would be so like his own self as all men would be like all others. And so, however we may define man, a single definition will apply to all. This is a sufficient proof that there is no dif-ference in kind between man and man; for if there were, one definition could not be applicable to all men; and indeed reason, which alone raises us above the level of the beasts and enables us to draw inferences, to prove and disprove, to discuss and solve problems, and to come to conclusions, is certainly com-mon to us all, and, though varying in what it learns, at least in the capacity to learn it is invariable. For the same things are invariably perceived by the senses, and those things which stimu-late the senses stimulate them in the same way in all men; and those rudi-mentary beginnings of intelligence to which I have referred, which are im-printed on our minds, are imprinted on all minds alike; and speech, in the mind's interpreter, though differing in the choice of words, agrees in the senti-ments expressed. In fact, there is no human being of any race who, if he finds a guide, cannot attain to virtue.

The similarity of the human race is clearly marked in its evil tendencies as well as in its goodness. For pleasure also attracts all men; and even though it is an enticement to vice, yet it has some likeness to what is naturally good. For it delights us by its lightness and agreeableness; and for this reason, by

an error of thought, it is embraced as something wholesome. It is through a similar misconception that we shun death as though it were a dissolution of nature, and cling to life because it keeps us in the sphere in which we were born; and that we look upon pain as one of the greatest of evils, not only because of its cruelty, but also because it seems to lead to the destruction of nature. In the same way, on account of the simi-larity between moral worth and renown, those who are publicly honored are con-sidered happy, while those who do not attain fame are thought miserable. Troubles, joys, desires, and fears haunt the minds of all men without distinc-tion, and even if different men have different beliefs, that does not prove, for example, that it is not the same quality of superstition that besets those races which worship dogs and cats as gods, as that which torments other races. But what nation does not love courtesy, kindliness, gratitude, and re-membrance of favors bestowed? What people does not hate and despise the haughty, the wicked, the cruel, and the ungrateful? Inasmuch as these consider-ations prove to us that the whole human race is bound together in unity, it fol-lows, finally, that knowledge of the principles of right living is what makes men better. . . .

The next point, then, is that we are so constituted by Nature as to share the sense of Justice with one another and to pass it on to all men. And in this whole discussion I want it understood that what I shall call Nature is [that which is implanted in us by Nature]; that, however, the corruption caused by bad habits is so great that the sparks of fire, so to speak, which Nature has kindled in us are extinguished by this corruption, and the vices which are their opposites spring up and are established. But if the judgments of men were in agreement with Nature, so that, as the poet says, they considered "nothing alien to them which concerns mankind," then Justice would be equally observed by all. For those creatures who have received the gift of reason from Nature have also received right reason, and therefore they have also received the gift of Law, which is right reason applied to command and prohibition. And if they have received Law, they have received Justice also. Now all men have received reason; therefore all men have received Justice. Consequently Socrates was right when he cursed, as he often did, the man who first separated utility from Justice; for this separation, he complained, is the source of all mischief. . . .

Now all this is really a preface to what remains to be said in our discussion, and its purpose is to make it more easily understood that Justice is inherent in Nature. . . .

QUINTUS. You certainly need to say very little more on that head, for from what you have already said, Atticus is convinced, and certainly I am, that Nature is the source of Justice.

ATTICUS. How can I help being convinced, when it has just been proved to us, first, that we have been provided and equiped with what we may call the gifts of the gods; next, that there is only one principle by which men may live with one another, and that this is the same for all, and possessed equally by all; and, finally, that all men are bound together by a certain natural feeling of kindliness and good-will, and also by a partnership in Justice? Now that we have admitted the truth of these conclusions, and rightly, I think, how can we separate Law and Justice from Nature? . . .

MARCUS. But the most foolish notion of all is the belief that everything is just which is found in the customs or laws of nations. Would that be true, even if these laws had been enacted by tyrants? If the well-known Thirty had desired to enact a set of laws at Athens, or if the Athenians without exception were delighted by the tyrants' laws, that would not entitle such laws to be regarded as just, would it? No more, in my opinion, should that law be considered just which a Roman interrex proposed, to the effect that a dictator might put to death with impunity any citizen he wished, even without a trial. For Justice is one; it binds all human society, and is based on one Law, which is right reason applied to command and prohibition. Whoever knows not this Law, whether it has been recorded in writing anywhere or not, is without Justice.

But if Justice is conformity to written laws and national customs, and if, as the same persons claim, everything is to be tested by the standard of utility, then anyone who thinks it will be profitable to him will, if he is able, disregard and violate the laws. It follows that Justice does not exist at all, if it does not exist in Nature, and if that form of it which is based on utility can be overthrown by that very utility itself. And if Nature is not to be considered the foundation of Justice, that will mean the destruction [of the virtues on which human society depends]. For where then will there be a place for generosity, or love of country, or loyalty, or the inclination to be of service to others or to show gratitude for favors received? For these virtues originate in our natural inclination to love our fellow-men, and this is the foundation of Justice. Otherwise not merely consideration for men but also rites and pious observances in honor of the gods are done away with; for I think that these ought to be maintained, not through fear, but on account of the close relationship which exists between man and God. But if the principles of Justice were founded on the decrees of peoples, the edicts of princes, or the decisions of judges, then Justice would sanction robbery and adultery and forgery of wills, in case these acts were approved by the votes or decrees of the populace. But if so great a power belongs to the decisions and decrees of fools that the laws of Nature can be changed by their votes, then why do they not ordain that what is bad and baneful shall be considered good and salutary? Or, if a law can make Justice out of Injustice, can it not also make good out of bad? But in fact we can perceive the difference between good laws and bad by referring them to no other standard than Nature; indeed, it is not merely Justice and Injustice which are distinguished by Nature, but also and without exception things which are honorable and dishonorable. For since an intelligence common to us all makes things known to us and formulates them in our minds, honorable actions are ascribed by us to virtue, and dishonorable actions to vice; and only a madman would conclude that these judgments are matters of opinion, and not fixed by Nature. For even what we, by a misuse of the term, call the virtue of a tree or of a horse, is not a matter

of opinion, but is based on Nature. And if that is true, honorable and dishonorable actions must also be distinguished by Nature. For if virtue in general is to be tested by opinion, then its several parts must also be so tested; who, therefore, would judge a man of prudence and, if I may say so, hard common sense, not by his own character but by some external circumstance? For virtue is reason completely developed; and this certainly is natural; therefore everything honorable is likewise natural. For just as truth and falsehood, the logical and illogical, are judged by themselves and not by anything else, so the steadfast and continuous use of reason in the conduct of life, which is virtue, and also inconstancy, which is vice, [are judged] by their own nature.

[Or, when a farmer judges the quality of a tree by nature,] shall we not use the same standard in regard to the characters of young men? Then shall we judge character by Nature, and judge virtue and vice, which result from character, by some other standard? But if we adopt the same standard· for them, must we not refer the honorable and the base to Nature also? Whatever good thing is praiseworthy must have within itself something which deserves praise, for goodness itself is good by reason not of opinion but of Nature. For, if this were not true, men would also be happy by reason of opinion; and what statement could be more absurd than that? Wherefore since both good and evil are judged by Nature and are natural principles, surely honorable and base actions must also be distinguished in a similar way and referred to the standard of Nature. But we are confused by the variety of men's beliefs and by their disagreements, and because this same variation is not found in the senses, we think that Nature has made these accurate, and say that those things about which different people have different opinions and the same people not always identical opinions are unreal. However, this is far from being the case. For our senses are not perverted by parent, nurse, teacher, poet, or the stage, nor led astray by popular feeling; but against our minds all sorts of plots are constantly being laid, either by those whom I have just mentioned, who, taking possession of them while still tender and unformed, color and bend them as they wish, or else by that enemy which lurks deep within us, entwined in our every sense—that counterfeit of good, which is, however, the mother of all evils—pleasure. Corrupted by her allurements, we fail to discern clearly what things are by Nature good, because the same seductiveness and itching does not attend them.

To close now our discussion of this whole subject, the conclusion, which stands clearly before our eyes from what has already been said, is this: Justice and all things honorable are to be sought for their own sake. And indeed all good men love fairness in itself and Justice in itself, and it is unnatural for a good man to make such a mistake as to love what does not deserve love for itself alone. . . .

. . . It is certainly true that, since Law ought to be a reformer of vice and an incentive to virtue, the guiding principles of life may be derived from it. It is therefore true that wisdom is the mother of all good things; and from the Greek expression meaning "the love of

wisdom" philosophy has taken its name. And philosophy is the richest, the most bounteous, and the most exalted gift of the immortal gods to humanity. For she alone has taught us, in addition to all other wisdom, that most difficult of all things—to know ourselves. This precept is so important and significant that the credit for it is given, not to any human being, but to the god of Delphi. For he who knows himself will realize, in the first place, that he has a divine element within him, and will think of his own inner nature as a kind of consecrated image of God; and so he will always act and think in a way worthy of so great a gift of the gods, and, when he has examined and thoroughly tested himself, he will understand how nobly equipped by Nature he entered life, and what manifold means he possesses for the attainment and acquisition of wisdom. For from the very first he began to form in his mind and spirit shadowy concepts, as it were, of all sorts, and when these have been illuminated under the guidance of wisdom, he perceives that he will be a good man, and, for that very reason, happy. For when the mind, having attained to a knowledge and perception of the virtues, has abandoned its subservience to the body and its indulgence of it, has put down pleasure as if it were a taint of dishonor, has escaped from all fear of death or pain, has entered into a partnership of love with its own, recognizing as its own all who are joined to it by Nature; when it has taken up the worship of the gods and pure religion, has sharpened the vision both of the eye and of the mind so that they can choose the good and reject the opposite—a virtue which is called prudence because it foresees—

then what greater degree of happiness can be described or imagined? And further, when it has examined the heavens, the earth, the seas, the nature of the universe, and understands whence all these things came and whither they must return, when and how they are destined to perish, what part of them is mortal and transient and what is divine and eternal; and when it almost lays hold of the ruler and governor of the universe, and when it realizes that it is not shut in by [narrow] walls as a resident of some fixed spot, but is a citizen of the whole universe, as it were of a single city—then in the midst of this universal grandeur, and with such a view and comprehension of nature, ye immortal gods, how well it will know itself, according to the precept of the Pythian Apollo! . . .

II

MARCUS. Once more, then, . . . let us look at the character and nature of Law, for fear that, though it must be the standard to which we refer everything, we may now and then be led astray by an incorrect use of terms, and forget the rational principles on which our laws must be based. . . .

I find that it has been the opinion of the wisest men that Law is not a product of human thought, nor is it any enactment of peoples, but something eternal which rules the whole universe by its wisdom in command and prohibition. Thus they have been accustomed to say that Law is the primal and ultimate mind of God, whose reason directs all things either by compulsion or restraint. Wherefore that Law which the gods have given to the human race has been justly praised; for it is the reason and mind of a wise lawgiver applied to command and prohibition.

QUINTUS. You have touched upon this subject several times before. But please make the character of this heavenly Law clear to us, so that the waves of habit may not carry us away and sweep us into the common mode of speech on such subjects.

MARCUS. Ever since we were children, Quintus, we have learned to call, "If one summon another to court," and other rules of the same kind, laws. But we must come to the true understanding of the matter, which is as follows: this and other commands and prohibitions of nations have the power to summon to righteousness and away from wrongdoing; but this power is not merely older than the existence of nations and States, it is coeval with that God who guards and rules heaven and earth. For the divine mind cannot exist without reason, and divine reason cannot but have this power to establish right and wrong. . . . For reason did exist, derived from the Nature of the universe, urging men to right conduct and diverting them from wrongdoing, and this reason did not first become Law when it was written down, but when it first came into existence; and it came into existence simultaneously with the divine mind. Wherefore the true and primal Law, applied to command and prohibition, is the right reason of supreme Jupiter.

QUINTUS. I agree with you, brother, that what is right and true is also eternal, and does not begin or end with written statutes.

MARCUS. Therefore, just as that divine mind is the supreme Law, so, when [reason] is perfected in man [that also is Law; and this perfected reason exists] in the mind of the wise man; but those rules which, in varying forms and for the need of the moment, have been formulated for the guidance of nations, bear the title of laws rather by favor than because they are really such. For every law which really deserves that name is truly praiseworthy, as they prove by approximately the following arguments. It is agreed, of course, that laws were invented for the safety of citizens, the preservation of States, and the tranquillity and happiness of human life, and that those who first put statutes of this kind in force convinced their people that it was their intention to write down and put into effect such rules as, once accepted and adopted, would make possible for them an honorable and happy life; and when such rules were drawn up and put in force, it is clear that men called them "laws." From this point of view it can be readily understood that those who formulated wicked and unjust statutes for nations, thereby breaking their promises and agreements, put into effect anything but "laws." It may thus be clear that in the very definition of the term "law" there inheres the idea and principle of choosing what is just and true. I ask you then, Quintus, according to the custom of the philosophers: if there is a certain thing, the lack of which in a State compels us to consider it no State at all, must we consider this thing a good?

QUINTUS. One of the greatest goods, certainly.

MARCUS. And if a State lacks Law, must it for that reason be considered no State at all?

QUINTUS. It cannot be denied.

MARCUS. Then Law must necessarily be considered one of the greatest goods.

QUINTUS. I agree with you entirely.

MARCUS. What of the many deadly, the many pestilential statutes which nations put in force? These no more deserve to be called laws than the rules a band of robbers might pass in their assembly. For if ignorant and unskilful men have prescribed deadly poisons instead of healing drugs, these cannot possibly be called physicians' prescriptions; neither in a nation can a statute of any sort be called a law, even though the nation, in spite of its being a ruinous regulation, has accepted it. Therefore Law is the distinction between things just and unjust, made in agreement with that primal and most ancient of all things, Nature; and in conformity to Nature's standard are framed those human laws which inflict punishment upon the wicked but defend and protect the good.

ESTHETICS

Aristotle distinguished three types of science: the theoretical, which deals with knowledge referring to things known; the practical, which deals with knowledge in reference to human action; and the productive, which deals with knowledge of art. The following selection by a well-known contemporary Thomist is concerned with the ontology of painting, and more especially with the problem of artistic creation.

As the art object is an existent, Professor Gilson applies Aristotelian and Thomistic metaphysical concepts to the understanding of that being. The artist, he notes, produces a being: his act is creative, although not in the absolute sense in which God is creative. Yet apart from the creative activity of the artist, the world would lose those existents which he produces and would therefore be a poorer place. This is why the death of a great· artist is such a loss to the world, for actual existence is always at stake in the artist's work.

7 Art and Reality
Étienne Gilson (1884-1974)

The notion of form is familiar to painters, but it presupposes other notions whose presence in their mind is certain, even though it is not always perceived with complete clarity. The obscurity of these notions is due to their high degree of abstraction, itself inseparable from the mystery of being. Yet the most elementary esthetic experience attests the reality of their objects.

Let us consider music. Its very existence presupposes that of silence. We recognize as nonmusically gifted the well-known class of persons whom music inspires at once with an irresistible urge to talk. The reason for this is that talking is making noise and that to make noise is to make music impossible. Hence, on a larger scale, the many precautions taken by the conductors of orchestras to ensure complete silence at the beginning of any concert or any operatic performance. The existence of musical sounds presupposes the absolute nothingness of all other sounds. In this sense, music can be said to be created *ex nihilo musicae*, just about as the

world is said to have been created by God from a nothingness of world, or as being was first created from a nothingness of being. There is nothing paradoxical in such statements. On the contrary, they could rather be reproached with stating what is too obvious to stand in need of restatement—namely, that the nonmusic that is silence is a prerequisite for the creation of music.

Let us now consider the poet. Confronted as he is with his sheet of white paper, he sees it as the place of infinite poetic possibilities, any one of which can materialize precisely because none of them is already there. The same remark applies to the canvas, wood panel, or wall selected by the painter as the support of his future painting. Whatever its nature, the first care of the painter will be to prime it—that is, to lay on it a coating or preparation that will ensure its perfect uniformity and neutrality with respect to any possible pattern of lines and colors it may have later on to receive. This initial nothingness of figures corresponds to the nothingness of sounds that is the silence created by conductors at the beginning of a musical performance. Like music, painting can be said to be, in a certain sense, created from nothing.[1]

The selection is from *Painting and Reality*, by Étienne Gilson, Bollingen Series xxxv, no. 4 in The A. W. Mellon Lectures in the Fine Arts (copyright © 1957 by the Trustees of the National Gallery of Art, Washington, D.C.), reprinted by permission of Princeton University Press: pp. 113–21.

[1] It is remarkable that modern artists have sometimes spontaneously resorted to the language of Holy Scripture in expressing their

After priming his canvas, the first thing usually done by a painter is to sketch an outline of his future work. This, of course, is an extremely complex operation in which intelligence, imagination, and draftsmanship are equally involved, but we can arbitrarily simplify it to facilitate analysis. More precisely, we can consider in it the sole initial motion of the hand whereby a painter (or a child) delineates the first outline on a sheet of white paper. Even reduced to these simple terms, the question evokes at once such a variety of answers that it remains necessary to make a further choice or, at least, to adopt a certain order.

Expressed in the simplest possible terms, the result of this initial operation is to make "some thing" appear where, heretofore, there was "no thing." This is what is meant by the term "creation" when it is applied to works of art. In this, art is unique, and the fact is especially evident in the case of the plastic arts such as design, drawing, engraving, or painting.

In a loose sense, all the productions of the human mind can be called its creations. Science is something added to nature by the minds of scientists, but it is not another thing added by scientists to the world of already existing things. Science is not an artifact. It is not even a mental image of reality that we could conceive as duplicating and enriching it in the mind of the scientist. As a construction of the mind, science remains contained within the very reality it strives to describe. And what is true of science is also true of philosophy, particularly of metaphysics. The aim and scope of philosophy is to know the ultimate nature of reality. At a different level, and by methods different from those of science, metaphysics, too, is essentially speculative; its ultimate aim and purpose is not to produce a new being, or thing, but rather, to know given reality exactly as it is. To the extent that it is art, painting is an activity specifically different from both scientific and metaphysical cognition.[2]

This does not mean that there is no art in science and that a philosopher cannot be, at the same time, an artist.[3] The unity of the human mind is such that, just as there is intellectual knowledge in all that man does, or makes, there seldom is complete absence of art in what man knows. Elegance is a quality highly prized in mathematical demonstrations. The same elegance is perceptible in the dialogues of Plato, so

own experience on this point. For instance, speaking of his glass pictures, which he began by drawing with a needle on a blackened piece of glass, Paul Klee found it natural to say: "I begin logically with chaos, that is only natural" (Grohmann, *Paul Klee*, p. 115). Speaking of Piet Mondrian: "To create emptiness is the principal act. And this is true creation, because this emptiness is positive; it contains the germ of the absolutely new." (Michel Seuphor, *L'Art abstrait*, p. 120.)

[2] See E. Gilson, "Art et métaphysique," *Revue de métaphysique et de morale*, XXIII, No. 1 bis (Jan. 1916), 244–46.

[3] Thomas Aquinas has noted that "even in speculative matters there is something by way of work"; we *make* speeches, reasonings, demonstrations, expositions, etc. The arts related to the operations of the mind, and in which the body does not share, are called, for this very reason, *liberal* arts: *Summa theologiae*, Ia, IIae, 57, 3, reply to obj. 3. On the many different answers given to the question "What is art?" see the excellent ch. III, "The Meanings of Art," in Thomas Munro, *The Arts and Their Interrelations*, pp. 49–109.

much so that some of them—for instance, his *Symposium*—constitute in themselves exceptionally perfect specimens of literary art. But this is not our question. Even if it is truly esthetic in nature, mathematical elegance is entirely at the service of cognition: it aims to achieve an expression of truth highly satisfactory to the mind. As to such works of art as Plato's *Symposium,* what of philosophy they contain could be stated in a much simpler, shorter, and less artistic way without losing any of its truth value, although it would lose all its beauty and much of its persuasive force. But this reduction of art to any kind of cognitive process is particularly impossible in the case of painting. The work of the painter is there, materially present in space, for everyone to see. While a scientist is explaining his science, he himself and his science occupy the same place in the lecture room; when a painter presents his works to the public, he himself and his paintings do not occupy the same space in the exhibition room. This is what we mean in saying that the art of painting is not a particular species included in the genus "cognition."

This point is of decisive importance, and the answers to so many other problems depend upon it that we should not let important difficulties pass unnoticed. One of the best known follows from the popular definition of art commonly attributed to the novelist Émile Zola: art is a fragment of nature seen through a temperament. If this were true, nothing would be more common than artistic creativity, for, indeed, each and every man has a temperament through which he cannot help seeing nature, but very few men are endowed by nature with the gifts that it takes to create works of art worthy of the name. This elementary confusion lies at the origin of many pseudo-artistic vocations. The most exquisite sensitiveness to natural beauty requires neither science, nor philosophy, nor even any kind of intellectual culture in general; between the charm of nature and ourselves, there is nothing, but between our sensibility and any painting that we may attempt to do, there is art. In the case of painting, art is not nature seen through a temperament; rather, it is the ability to create a new being that nobody would ever see, either in nature or otherwise, unless the art of the painter caused it to exist.

A similar formula, attributed to Francis Bacon, defines art as "man added to nature" (*homo additus naturae*), and it raises similar difficulties. Like so many other brilliant definitions, this one does not bear the acid test of critical examination. Since man is part and parcel of nature, he cannot be added to it. Rather than as man added to nature, art should be conceived as man adding to nature, or, better still, as nature enriching itself by all the additions that it receives at the hands of man. As has been said, the painter is neither a philosopher nor a scientist in whose mind nature mirrors itself; but he is not, at the same time, one of those engineers whose cleverness harnesses the forces of nature and puts them at our disposal; he is one of the creative forces of nature, in this sense at least, that he gives existence to certain beings that, in nature, nothing else than himself could possibly have produced. And not only nothing else, but no one else. It is not evident that, at the present stage of scientific progress, the premature death of a great scientist renders impossible the scientific discoveries that a longer life would have enabled him to make. On the contrary, the death of an artist certainly brings to a close the production of the kind of painting that bears the imprint of his hand. Many men can now know the paintings and enjoy them, but no other man than himself could cause them to exist. The lineage of these beings, which resemble one another as the children of the same father, is not extinct, and neither the admiration nor the zeal and cleverness of his most faithful pupils will ever increase it by a single unit. The creative artist is for us the only empirically observable example of a force analogous to the still more mysterious one in virtue of which the works of nature come into being. No painting, drawing, or etching done by anyone else will ever replace those which a still longer life would have enabled Matisse himself to create. The death of a great painter is an irretrievable loss of substance for the world.[4]

In the light of what precedes, it may well be asked if paintings should simply be classified among the artifacts. And, indeed, they are artifacts, at least in the sense that they are products of human workmanship; but even granting that all paintings are artifacts, it cannot be granted that all artifacts are works of art. Considered as a genus, artifacts include, besides works of art properly so called, the densely populated class of the many and manifold tools, instruments, and machines due to the inventiveness and skill of *homo faber*. Now, whatever their differences, all these tools, instruments, and machines have this in common, that their final cause lies outside themselves. Not one of them is made for its own sake. One does not look at a timepiece (taken precisely qua timepiece) except to know what time it is. An ornamented shotgun may well be considered a work of art, but then it is no longer seen as a shotgun, whose intrinsic qualities, taken precisely qua shotgun, are foreign to the notions of ornamentation and decoration. Not so in the case of paintings. We call "tool" anything that serves as a means to an end, but, precisely, a painting cannot be used as a means to any end extrinsic to itself. A painting is not there to permit any kind of operation to be performed such as carrying goods or persons, talking from a distance, or shooting game. There is nothing that one can do *with* a painting. True enough, there is something that one can do *about* it, but, precisely, there is only one such thing, and it is to look at it. If he considers a painting as a means to any other end than its contemplation, a man does not see it as a work of art. He may look at it as an art dealer looks at the particular brand of merchandise he tries to sell, or as an investor looks at a more or less promising kind of stock. He may even consider it something to be talked about, if he is a lecturer; or something to be written about, if he is an art historian

---

[4] See the epigraph (borrowed from Gabriele d'Annunzio's *Il Fuoco*) to our essay of 1915 on "Art et métaphysique": "Ah, Stelio, t'aspettavo! Riccardo Wagner è morto. Il mondo parve diminuito di valore." ("Ah, Stelio, I was waiting for you. Richard Wagner is dead. The world seemed to have lost some of its value.") This page was written on the very day the Toronto radio announced the death of Henri Matisse (November 5, 1954).

or an art critic.[5] In every one of these cases, the end of the work of art lies outside it, as in money, in a lecture to give, in an article or in a book to write; consequently, in every one of these cases, the work of art will be used as a means to another end; it will cease to act as a work of art.

We can now return to our question and give it an answer. The question was: in what sense is it true to say that the term "creation" fittingly designates the initial operation of artists, and quite especially of painters? The answer is: because the immediate and direct effect of such an operation is to cause something to be or, in simpler terms, because the effect of such an operation is the actual existence of a new "being." Here again a comparison with theology can help, not at all because we should attempt in any way to deduce esthetics from theology, but rather, on the contrary, because in certain matters theology has based its inferences upon the experience of artists as well as upon the nature of art. Such is particularly the case with the notion of creation. In his *Timaeus,* under the form of a mythical narrative, Plato has presented the world as the work of a divine artist whom he called the Demiurge. We shall have later on to ask ourselves what light this

dialogue throws on the nature of artistic production; for our present problem, it will prove more important to consider the notion of creation such as, on the strength of Biblical data, the Christian theologians have understood it.

If we leave aside the history of this religious notion and consider it merely as it became at the very time it reached its point of perfection, this notion points out the act by which a certain being causes other beings to be. Strictly speaking, only one being can thus be the cause of existence for other beings— namely, God, who, because he himself is the pure act of being, is eminently able to impart actual existence. Obviously, no artist can create his works, as God does, from an absolute nothingness of existence. Some material must be at his disposal before he begins his work; even the forms he creates are the forms of something, and he has seen them in nature, or in the art of his predecessors, before he himself began to create.[6] Moreover, the kind of existence an artist imparts to his works always presupposes his own existence, which, unlike that of God, is a received one. Inciden-

---

[5] Critics themselves do not like discussing the question of their own attitude toward works of art. It seems hardly possible to consider their position as identical with that of common art lovers. Critics are at their best when they deal with works of art with which they used to be familiar before they began to speak, or to write, as critics. At any rate, to look at a painting *in view of* writing about it must somewhat interfere with the esthetic apprehension of the work in question.

[6] This point is forcefully developed by Delacroix in his *Journal,* p. 386 (March 1, 1859), particularly: "But not only did these great men create nothing in the proper sense of the word, which means making *something* out of *nothing,* but in order to form their talent, or prevent it from getting rusty, they had to imitate their predecessors and, consciously or unconsciously, to imitate them almost unceasingly." Delacroix himself always had Rubens in mind; Manet could not forget Velázquez during his "Spanish period," and Picasso, perhaps the most inexhaustible source of new forms in our own times, cannot help remembering somebody or something else's style the very moment he is inventing a style of his own.

tally, this is the reason why esthetics need not carry its investigations beyond the philosophical level of ontology to the properly theological level of the divine act of existing. The actual existence of the matter to be informed by the art of the painter, as well as that of the painter himself, are two necessary prerequisites for the very possibility of art. The problems that belong to esthetics presuppose the fact that there are works of art, and although esthetics can investigate the mode of being proper to this specific class of artifacts, its inquiry stops at the level of substantial being specified and determined by its form. Actual existence is presupposed as already given, for all its ingredients, from the very beginning of the operation.

This does not mean that actual existence is not at stake in the making of a painting. The actual existence of the painting to be done is the final result that the artist intends to achieve. Since God alone is the pure act of being, no secondary cause, be it even the art of a creative artist, can conjure up a new being from total nonbeing. But the artist himself, his art, the matter and the forms he puts to use, all are enjoying an actual existence they have received from the Prime Cause. Artists can impart or communicate to their works the actual existence that is their own. Some pen drawings by Corot are enough to give existence to charming landscapes that seem to be made from nothing, and almost with nothing. An etching done from a pen drawing by Pieter Brueghel succeeds in educing the most complex landscape from the blank surface of a plate. The mere interplay of the lines, ordered as they are by a supremely

lucid imagination, even permits him to pretend that the very Journey to Emmaus is included in this creation of his hand. In this sense, the production of plastic works of art truly extends to their very existence. Himself an existent, the painter is an efficient cause of actual existence for other existents.[7]

These notions will have to be reconsidered at a different level in discussing the proper kind of causality a painter exercises with respect to his works. For the present, let it suffice to observe that thus to relate art to metaphysics, and even to theology, is by no means to attempt a deduction of art from these lofty sciences. On the contrary, when theologians started from the visible world in order to conceive, as best they could, the invisible nature of God, they first borrowed from art the pattern of the most perfect kind of causality given in human experience, and then transcended it in order to make it attributable to God. In their effort to do so, the theologians have unveiled to us the very Idea of what an absolute artistic creation would be: an act in which, be-

---

[7] "To act is nothing else than to communicate that by which the acting being is in act" (Thomas Aquinas, *De potentia,* qu. 2, art. 1, answer). Thomas presently adds to this: "to the extent that it is possible." Now, God, who is the Prime Cause, is the pure act of Being. Consequently, "all the created causes communicate in one single effect, which is actual existence [*esse*], although each one of them has its own effects, by which they differ from one another. For instance, heat makes something to be hot, and an architect causes a house to be [*aedificator facit domum esse*]. Created causes thus agree in this, that they cause being [*conveniunt ergo in hoc quod causant esse*], but they differ in this, that while fire causes fires, an architect causes a house" (qu. 7, art. 2 answer).

cause the intellect, the power, the will, and the art of the artist are identically one with his own act of being, the total cause of the total effect is included. Artistic creation is not such an act, but it remains for us the least imperfect image there is of what the theologians call creation. And no wonder, since it is found at the origin of the notion that the theologians have formed of it. Supposing, therefore, that painters can communicate existence to their own works, we must now ascertain the sense in which it is true to say that, because they also produce forms, painters truly produce beings.

PHILOSOPHY OF MAN

Under the heading "philosophy of man," philosophers consider a number of questions that can be asked about man: his nature and status in the universe, his distinctive characteristics, his relationships to other beings, and his own constitution. This last question is often referred to as the "mind-body" problem, and in many ways it is the focal point of concern in philosophy of man. This and the other selections under this heading concentrate on that problem—though they do not, of course, exclude reference to other questions.

Stressing realistic concepts, M. C. D'Arcy understands man in terms of form and matter. To be sure, in man is found soul on the rational level, which opens up to man the possibilities of knowledge, goodness, and truth. It is because of these possibilities that man is more than a material being. But man is not two beings—mind and body—either: he is rather one being constituted by the substantial union of form and matter. Like all forms, the soul is the determining principle of the body, yet it has operations independent of the body as well. Thus anti-Cartesian in spirit and analysis, the realistic view of man is monistic without being reductionistic in the sense of denying mind any substance or operations of its own.

8 Form, Matter, and Man

M. C. D'Arcy (1888-   )

Man is differentiated from animals by the gift of reason. He is a rational animal, and if we consult one side of

The selection is from M. C. D'Arcy, *Thomas Aquinas* (London: Ernest Benn, Ltd., 1930). Used by permission of the Oxford University Press.

him he seems to be nothing more than a superior animal. St. Thomas probably tends to exaggerate the influence of heredity, of temperament and bodily dispositions on human character and conduct, and he is enabled to do this without fear because of his theory of the relation of the soul to the body. The two are conjoined so as to make one being, the human being, as form with matter. This mode of relationship, which stands in strong opposition to that of the soul inhabiting a body already formed and taking charge of it, determines the whole treatment of human nature. It aroused strong opposition at the time, and without a doubt a consistent application of the theory leads to some surprising results.

Despite the criticism sometimes made, it is certain that St. Thomas in calling the soul the form of the body, does not intend to belittle it. Up to now we have been moving within the realm of matter; even the sensitive soul with all its powers was bounded by space and time and material organs. But now, with the coming of the rational soul, a completely new world is opened; mind has no physical organ, however much it may be conditioned by the brain and senses; it is infinite in its capacity and so extends beyond the visible and temporal world; its act is so immanent that it can reflect upon itself, be aware of its own nature through its activities, and know also the intelligible nature of the entire universe. Its good, therefore, is not judged by personal pleasure or utility but by absolute goodness and truth. As St. Thomas says: "But in those things which have knowledge, each one is determined to its own natural being by its natural form, in such a manner that it is nevertheless receptive of the species of other things; for example, sense receives the species of all things sensible, and the intellect of all things intelligible, so that the soul of man is, in a way, all things by sense and intellect; and thereby, those things that have knowledge, in a way, approach to a likeness to God, in whom

all things pre-exist, as Dionysius says."[1] Again, to bring out the change that has taken place, he is fond of comparing the reason of man with *materia prima*. Just as in the region of the physical world prime matter is nothing more than a reaching out to form, a capacity to be filled, so in the spiritual world the mind of man begins in darkness as a power receptive of the universe of truth. A physical substance is perfected and at the same time limited by its form; it is itself and nothing else; it suffers therefore from individualism and its good is selfish. But a being with a mind can enter the whole world and make it its life; it is *quodammodo omnia*. It can know other things as they are in themselves, not as they appear to it or merely is so far as they minister to its private well-being. It does not indeed absorb the actual existent things which live their life independently; it knows them after the fashion of a mind, not possessed of intuition, to wit, through ideas or "intentional" forms; that is to say it possesses them immanently, both as a perfection of itself and as they are in themselves.

Because man is endowed with this new power St. Thomas calls him a denizen of two worlds, a horizon or meeting-place. He is not, like the angels, pure spirit; he is not, like the animals, purely material. He is both in one with all the advantages and disadvantages of such a lot. Whereas some of his contemporaries were inclined to regard the body as a necessary evil, and to advocate the Platonic flight from it as an ideal, St. Thomas shows himself a true humanist in his defence of it. As one of the most discerning of modern

---

[1] *S. Theol.*, Ia., q. 80, a. 1.

writers on Thomism has remarked, it cannot be said of him as it was said of Plotinus, that he hated to be a man.[2] He is neither a misanthropist nor a Stoic, and if his adversaries charged him with underestimating the soul, he could retort that they failed to appreciate the whole of human nature. The Augustinians elevated the soul into a complete and independent substance, itself composed of matter and form, and on this account they were—so St. Thomas thought—prevented from doing justice to the substantial union of the body with the soul. It is not our body which feels, nor our mind which thinks, but we, as single human beings, who feel and think. The theory of substantial union by matter and form was then of great moment to him, and explains why he is unwontedly vigorous in his defence of it against the Augustinians, and particularly the Averrhoists, led by Siger de Brabant.[3] The

latter committed the additional grave crime of quoting Aristotle as a witness on their side. What precisely the Averrhoists held, and which of the two interpretations of the famous text of Aristotle in the *De Anima,* theirs or that of St. Thomas, be right, it is not easy to say. St. Thomas accuses them of a doctrine which is incompatible with Christianity, a single separate intellect, which is that of the species, humanity, thinking in a succession of individuals. He rejects this both as an incorrect interpretation of Aristotle and as an absurd theory. "It is impossible," he says, "for many distinct individuals to have one form, as it is impossible for them to have one existence, for the form is the principle of existence." Again, if there were one intellect for all men then "the distinction between Socrates and Plato would be no other than that of one man with a tunic and another with a cloak, which is absurd"; and lastly, "the diversity of phantasms which are in this one and that one would not cause a diversity of intellectual operations in this man and that man."

The substantial union of matter and form is then, in his eyes, the only possible explanation, and it is interesting to see that he argues to this view in logical continuation from what he has said of physical and living substances. The soul is, by definition, the substantial form of a physical living organism. "It is clear that the first thing by which the body lives is the soul. And as life appears through various operations in different degrees of living things, that whereby

---

[2] P. Rousselot, *L'Espirit de St. Thomas. Etudes,* Vol. 128, 1911, pp. 627–34. P. Rousselot gives as an illustration of the humanism of St. Thomas his remark that "man is bound by a kind of natural debt to live with others merrily, *ut aliis delectabiliter convivat,*" and refers also to his view that even in the state of innocence there would have been generation. "I answer that in the state of innocence there would have been generation in order to multiply the human race; otherwise the sin of man would have been very necessary, seeing that so much good has followed." And on the manner of generation he writes: "Not because there would have been less sensible pleasure as some say; for the purer the nature, the greater would have been the sensible pleasure." [Plotinus (205–270) produced a significant philosophic and religious system which included Platonic and mystical elements. *Ed.*]

[3 Followers of Averroes (1126–1198), an important commentator on Aristotle's works, whose interpretation of the Aristotelian view

of man as sharing in one intellect common to all men denied the doctrine of personal immortality. *Ed.*]

we primarily perform each of all these vital actions is the soul. For the soul is the primary principle of our nourishment, feeling, and local movement; and likewise the primary principle whereby we understand. Therefore this principle by which we primarily understand, whether it be called the intellect or the intellectual soul, is the form of the body."[4] From this it is clear that St. Thomas does not start with the notion of the human soul as a kind of mysterious entity which has got to be fitted somehow into a body. He begins by regarding it as the form of the body, the determining and active principle of the body. Are we, then, to think of it as nothing more than a principle of organisation and unity? No, he answers, because on inspection we find that this does not altogether meet the case. There is no reason why a soul should be not only the determining principle of a body but also have an operation independent of that body. "Aristotle does not say that the soul is the act of a body only, but the act of a physical organic body which has life potentially; and that this potentiality does not reject the soul." Form can reach such a degree of immanence that it is self-conscious, and with this self-consciousness the soul can become and be itself by becoming all things immaterially; and we may add that the fact that "man can know all things and apprehend the immaterial and universal" is for St. Thomas a decisive proof in itself that the intellect is not a bodily activity.

There is nothing, therefore, against the possibility of a form having a side to it which is immaterial, and in the human soul facts show that this is the case. The intellectual operation proves, he says, that the soul must be both incorporeal and subsistent. By our intellect we can know all corporeal things; now, if knowledge were in any way corporeal this would not happen, because the particular kind of body it would have to be would prevent it from knowing all else indifferently, as a sick man's tongue being vitiated by a feverish and bitter humour is insensible to anything sweet, and everything seems bitter to it. Again, if the intellect had a particular bodily organ, then it could not know all objects as they are in themselves, but only relatively to the particular and determinate nature of that organ. Now the intellect testifies to us in its very act that it knows reality not pragmatically but truly, that is, as it is in itself. Furthermore, it knows objects precisely by abstracting from them all that renders them material, removing them out of space and time, and considering them according to their form, absolutely and universally. Lastly, the immanent activity of the subject revealing itself in self-consciousness, in the power to reflect upon itself and realise itself in the identity of a lived and living idea or form, cannot without contradiction be attributed to any purely material or corporeal form.

If, therefore, there is an activity without a bodily organ and independent of the body, it must have as its subject what is also independent or subsistent. "Only a self-subsisting thing can have an operation of its own; for nothing can operate but what is actual." Looking at human life St. Thomas, like Crusoe, has found the footprint of mind, and the paradox of mind is that the universality

---

[4] *S. Theol.*, Ia., q. 26, a. 4.

of its outlook corresponds with a greater inner concentration or selfhood.[5] In the lowest orders of reality unity is only just discernible, and the function of form as determinant is almost wholly external; two pins are very much alike; the form is easily destroyed and is multiple and monotonous. In living things the form grows in power, the unity is richer, less passive and less isolated. The sensitive being has more autonomy than the vegetative, but the form is still occupied and absorbed in its own private affairs. In the rational soul freedom and universality for the first time emerge, and a new order begins, the monad life. The whole world can be reflected and enjoyed in consciousness, and in that consciousness the form is face to face not only with the universe but with itself. In man this blaze of consciousness is subdued and darkened by the co-partnership of the body. St. Thomas calls him a creature of two worlds; the connatural object of his mind is the sensible thing, or rather material form, known by the aid of the senses; he is still passive to experience; he has to grow to self-knowledge and perfection, and learn laboriously the natures of external things, remedying the lack of intuition by discursive reasoning, deductive and inductive, and filling out the intelligible world of essences he dimly apprehends with the help of quantitative methods suited to his senses. He is hung, therefore, in St. Thomas' vision, halfway between the world of body and the world of spirit, and if on one side he is kin to the animals and the earth, he is also neighbour to the angels, those pure forms, lighted from within and each comprising a complete and specific world of beauty and image of the divine.

Such then is his analysis of the rational soul and of human nature. To sum up, man is one being, composed of matter and form; there can be only one form in a substance, as it is the form which determines the substance to be what it is. The soul in man is the form of the body, determining it to be a human body; but the soul has an activity which intrinsically is immaterial—and this is proved by the fact that it has no material organ and that its object is the universal and absolute—therefore the soul itself, the subject of this activity, must be immaterial and subsistent. Subsistence means that it has a life of its own, and as this life is not that of a complete being but of a form looking by nature to this or that body, it is to be described as an incomplete substance. Not every particular substance is a hypostasis or person, but that alone which has the complete nature of its species. "Hence, a hand or a foot is not called a hypostasis or person; nor likewise is the soul alone so called, since it is a part of the human species."[6]

---

[5] *Contra Gent.*, II, 68.

[6] *S. Theol.*, Ia., q. 75, a. 4.

PHILOSOPHY OF SCIENCE

As a philosophy basing itself on a metaphysics of being, realism faces the problem of relating itself to the natural sciences. Both metaphysics and science claim to give us knowledge of the physical order, both claim to be supreme in the sense of not being dependent on other disciplines for their own conclusions. How then are science and metaphysics related? Is there inevitable conflict between them, or can distinctions between them be made so that any apparent conflict is removed?

Professor Maritain, another Thomist, addresses himself to this problem, seeking to clarify the relations among science (or, as he calls it, empiriological physics), philosophy of nature, and metaphysics. The study of nature, he argues, belongs to the first order of abstraction or intellectual consideration. Philosophy of nature or ontological physics deals with mutable being as such and its principles, while empiriological physics deals with a description of phenomena within the order of physical nature. To the second order of abstraction belongs mathematics, the science of quantity. Metaphysics, the science of being as such, is a third abstraction.

Given this analysis, Maritain believes that no conflict can exist among these disciplines. They are ordered hierarchically, with metaphysics at the top; but each has its own problems, its own methods, and, within the proper limits of each, its own validity.

9   Science and Nature
Jacques Maritain (1882-1973)

The conflict between philosophy and science leads to a central problem; that of the philosophy of nature. Ought there to be a philosophy of nature which is distinct at one and the same time from metaphysics and the special sciences? What are its characteristics, its nature and definition, its spirit? As these questions are of rather a technical order, the aridity of the exposition which they demand will be excused. They are not

The selection is reprinted with the permission of Charles Scribner's Sons and of Geoffrey Bles, Ltd., from Jacques Maritain, *Science and Wisdom*, pp. 34–36, 39, 50–55, and 60–64.

easy because they reach us charged with historical implications and associations. Is not the philosophy of nature what Aristotle called physics? Did not the idea of physics cover, for antiquity, the whole province of the natural sciences? Is not the ruin of the Aristotelian explanations of natural phenomena also the ruin of the whole of Aristotelian physics—and hence of the philosophy of nature? And hence, ought not the place of physics in Aristotle's sense to be occupied still for us today by physics, but by physics as understood in the sense of Einstein, Planck and Louis de Broglie: or more generally by the body of the sciences of the phenomena of nature, called simply Science by the modern world. Such are the connections and liaisons which are involved in the theoretical questions of which I propose to treat.

These questions are fundamental and not easy. We need not hesitate to say that they are of first rate importance for human wisdom. We ought not to neglect the problem of the philosophy of nature. Of all speculative wisdom it is the humblest, the nearest the world of sense, the least perfect. It is not even a form of wisdom in the pure and simple sense of the word, it is wisdom only in the order of mobile and corruptible things. But this is precisely the order most proportioned to our rational nature. This wisdom, which is not even purely and simply wisdom, is the first which is offered in the progressive ascending movement of our thought. And that is why it has such importance for us— precisely because it is at the lowest rung of the ladder of φιλία τῆς σοφίας [the love of wisdom].

In what ways can the real enter within us? There are but two, one natural, the other supernatural: the senses, and the divine Spirit. When we are concerned with the light which descends from heaven it is not metaphysics which is primary, but the highest and purely spiritual wisdom, by which we are enabled to open our soul and being and to receive something which enters into us according to the gift of grace. And if it is a question of the light which springs from earth, it is likewise not metaphysics which is primary, but an inferior wisdom bound up with sense perception and strictly dependent on experience: because it is through the senses that we are open to things, and

something enters us, according to our natural mode of knowing.

Metaphysics lies halfway between. It is not directly open, as the platonists taught, to an intuition of divine things. The intuition with which it deals lies at the summit of the process of visualization or abstraction which begins with the sensible order. It is in itself and formally independent of the philosophy of nature, being superior to it and ruling it. But materially, and *quoad nos*, it presupposes it: not of course in its perfect statement, but at least in its first positions. . . .

Thus it would be quite vain to try to evade the problem of the philosophy of nature. This problem must be regarded squarely and we must try to treat it for its own sake, in point of doctrine. Here the metaphysician of knowledge faces two questions. Should there be a philosophy of nature distinct from the sciences of natural phenomena? (This is the question *an sit*.) And in what exactly does it consist? (This is the question *quid sit*.) A whole volume would be needed to treat them fully. I shall only indicate in the shortest possible way the conclusions I believe we ought to reach.

To reply to the first question we must distinguish—at the first degree of intellectual abstraction, in the order of knowledge of sensible reality—two ways of constructing concepts and of analyzing the real: the analysis we have already called ontological, and the analysis which we have called empiriological, of sensible reality. In the first case we are dealing with an ascending analysis towards intelligible being, in which the sensible plays an indispensable part, but in attendance on intelligible being. In the second case we are dealing with a descending synthesis towards the sensible, towards the observable as such. Not of course that the mind then ceases to have to do with being, which is impossible, but being passes into the service of the sensible, the observable and above all of the measurable, becomes an unknown element assuring the constancy of certain sensible determinations and of certain standards, or assuring the value of certain *entia rationis* with a foundation *in re*.

In one case one seeks a definition by ontological characteristics, by the constituent elements of an intelligible nature or essence—so obscurely that only at times does one grasp this essence. In the other case, one tries to define by possibilities of observation and measurement, by the performance of physical operations: here the permanent possibility of sensible verification and measurement plays for the scientist a part similar to that played by the essence for the philosopher.

This distinction once understood, it is easy to understand that knowledge of the empiriological kind, that is to say, the sciences of natural phenomena, needs to be completed by knowledge of the ontological kind, that is to say, by a philosophy of nature. For these sciences imply, as Meyerson[1] has shown so well, an ontological aspiration and an ontological reference—which they do not satisfy. They aim at being (as real) and they mistrust it (as intelligible) and fall back on sensible phenomena; in such a way that, to constitute themselves in accord with their pure epistemological type, they are in a certain sense obliged to go counter to the inclination of the intellect.

The sciences of phenomena thus bear witness to the fact that nature is knowable and that they only know it in an essentially unsatisfying way. In this measure, therefore, they require to be completed by another knowledge of the same sensible universe, which will be an ontological knowledge—in truth, a philosophy of nature. Not only do we say that the sciences deepen and quicken the desire of the intelligence to pass to deeper and higher truths, just as the philosophy of nature itself quickens the desire of the intelligence to pass to metaphysics, but we say also that inasmuch as they are knowledge ordered to a certain term, the experimental sciences require to be completed, not of course so far as concerns their own proper rule of explanation, or the formal object which *specifies* them, but in regard to the term in which they issue, which is the sensible and the real. In so far as it is mutable and corruptible, the latter is known in an essentially unsatisfying way with the help of the vocabulary which is proper to empiriological knowledge. Thus, this knowledge must be completed by another which exists at the first degree of intellectual abstraction and will grasp the intelligibility of the real which is thus proposed to it.

Moreover, the inverse is equally true. The philosophy of nature must be completed by the experimental sciences. It does not provide for us by itself alone a complete knowledge of the real in which it issues, that is to say, of sensible nature. Because by its very structure, this knowledge of the ontological kind—and on this point ancient philosophers were not

---

[1] Cf. Emile Meyerson's work on the philosophy of science, *Identity and Reality*, tr. Kate Loewenberg (New York, 1962). *Ed.*]

clear—must withdraw any claim to explain the detail of phenomena or to exploit the phenomenal wealth of nature. From this point of view one may say that the great modern scientific movement since Galileo has delivered philosophy and ontological knowledge from a whole body of duties which it took upon itself and which in reality did not belong to it. . . .

Let us now turn to the second question. In accord with definitions more rigorous than those we have been using up till now, and in the light of Thomist epistemological principles, let us ask ourselves in what the philosophy of nature consists.

The Thomists reply, with Cajetan:[2] it is a form of knowledge whose proper object is that which moves, mutable being as such. Thus its proper object is being, being which is analogous and which imbues all generic and specific diversifications—that is why it is a philosophy—but not being as such, or being in its own intelligible mystery, which is the object of the metaphysician. The object of the philosophy of nature is being taken in the conditions which affect it in the necessitous and divided universe which is the material universe, being in the mystery of its becoming and mutability, of movement in space whereby bodies are in interaction, of substantial generation and corruption—the chief mark of their ontological structure; of the movement of vegetative growth in which is manifested the ascent of matter to the order of living things. But we have need of further precisions.

We have already noticed that antiquity did not distinguish, or distinguished very inadequately, the philosophy of nature from the sciences of nature. Warned by the progress of these sciences we must put the accent on this distinction, without however forcing it. What ought we to say on this subject? It seems to me that two points of doctrine need to be stressed. In the first place the philosophy of nature belongs to the same degree of abstractive visualization or intellectual vision as the sciences of nature: and that is why, as I have already mentioned, it is fundamentally different from metaphysics. In the second place, however, it differs from the natural sciences in an essential and specific way. . . .

And so I come to the second of the two points mentioned above. How is the philosophy of nature distinguished from the natural sciences? The considerations we have already discussed show clearly that the philosophy of nature is distinguished from the natural sciences in an essential and specific way.

What is the ultimate principle of the specification of the sciences? Thomist logicians tell us that it is the typical mode according to which the definitions are formed: *modus definiendi*.

If this be so, it is clear that in the generic sphere of intelligibility in the first order of abstraction, the notions and definitions which emerge on the one hand from empiriological analysis, where everything is primarily resolved in the observable, and on the other hand from ontological analysis where everything is primarily resolved in intelligible being, answer to specifically distinct modes of knowledge. The conceptual vocabulary of the philosophy of nature and that of the natural sciences are different in type.

[2 The reference is to Cardinal Cajetan (1468–1534), author of many important commentaries on St. Thomas Aquinas. *Ed.*]

Even if they happen to be translated externally by the same words the mental *verbum* signified by one and the same word is formed in each case in a way typically different. The philosophy of nature differs specifically from the natural sciences. Now let us try to reach a more precise definition, on the lines of Thomist epistemology. I will spare the reader the apparatus of technical distinctions which are required before beginning, and will only say that as I understand it the philosophy of nature ought to be defined as follows: 1. The appeal of intelligibility *(ratio formalis quae)* to which it answers, is mutability: it deals with mutable being as mutable, *ens sub ratione mobilitatis.* 2. Its objective light is an ontological mode of analysis and conceptualization, a way of abstracting and defining which, while it has an intrinsic reference to sense perception, aims at the intelligible essence. And it is for this reason that it differs specifically from the natural sciences.

Thus the object of natural philosophy does not lie in the detailed phenomena of sensible things but in intelligible being itself *as mutable,* that is to say, as capable of generation and corruption: or again its object lies in the differences of being which it can decipher (while aiming at intelligible nature but without sacrificing sense data) in the world of ontological mutability.

At this point it is appropriate to describe the spirit and method of natural philosophy. I will touch on one aspect of this question. It goes without saying that natural philosophy ought to make use of facts which are themselves philosophical, that is to say, established and evaluated in the proper light of philosophy. Because a fact can only yield what

it contains; and philosophical conclusions can only be drawn from philosophical premises and from facts which have themselves a philosophical value. Ordinary observation, criticized philosophically, can furnish many facts of this kind.

But what ought to be the relationship between the philosophy of nature and scientific facts? Two errors need to be carefully avoided.

The first error consists in expecting philosophical criteria from rough scientific facts. By rough scientific facts I mean scientific facts which have not been philosophically *treated.* As long as they are illuminated only by the light which originally made them discernible in the real and useful to the scientist these facts only interest the scientist, and not the philosopher. The scientist is right if he forbids the philosopher to touch them, and claims them for himself alone. It is an illusion to think that a philosophical discussion can be invalidated by an appeal to scientific facts which have not been examined in the light of philosophy. . . .

The second error would be to reject scientific facts, to try to construct a natural philosophy independent of them, and to maintain a natural philosophy isolated from the sciences. This tendency, it is worth noticing, is inevitable if the philosophy of nature is confounded with metaphysics. In such a case one tries to give to the philosophy of nature the freedom with regard to detailed scientific fact which is proper to metaphysics.[3] In reality, one is not likely

[3] This does not mean that metaphysics can ignore science. But though it needs to keep in contact with the sciences (through the medium of natural philosophy) this

to reach a metaphysic of *sensibilia,* but will run the risk of having a metaphysic of ignorance.

The truth is that the philosopher must make use of scientific facts on condition that they are examined and interpreted philosophically: thanks to which philosophical facts already established may be confirmed, and other philosophical facts may be discovered. By bringing scientific facts into contact with philosophical knowledge already acquired elsewhere and with philosophical first principles, and bringing an objective philosophical light to bear on them, an intelligible content can be deduced from them which can be handled by philosophy.

But here a question may well be asked. If it is true that the philosophy of nature requires to be completed by the sciences and needs for its confirmation or advancement to derive philosophical facts from the material of scientific fact,

---

contact is not for the sake of the argumentation that is proper to the metaphysician, but rather for his general information; for his knowledge of the world and his scientific imagery which, where dispositive or material causality is concerned, are vital for his thought.

must it not also accept as a consequence a certain law of aging and renewal? Of course this does not mean substantial change. There is a substantial continuity between the philosophy of nature as it appeared to Aristotle and as it appears to us. But in its passage it has undergone many changes; it has grown old and has been renewed. So that even as a form of knowledge it is much more dependent on time than is metaphysics.

Here we have an indication of the difference in their formal objects and formal values. A metaphysical treatise, if it be pure (though in fact it always contains allusions to the state of the sciences when it was written, to human opinions and so forth), can cross the centuries. But how long can a treatise on experimental physics or biology last? Twenty years, ten years, two years, the life-span of a horse, of a dog, of the grub of a cockchafer. And a treatise on the philosophy of nature can at the maximum endure a lifetime, and even then it must be periodically revised, supposing it appears in successive editions. This is because it needs to have intimate contact with the phenomenal sciences, and these sciences renew themselves much more rapidly than philosophy.

PHILOSOPHY OF RELIGION

The problem of God as the highest Being is central in realist writings, and a number of the preceding selections have raised this question. Plato discussed the problem in his dialogues, Aristotle provided the metaphysical concepts for the realist's treatment of it and suggested proofs of God's existence, and St. Anselm and St. Thomas Aquinas presented compact but forceful arguments for God's existence. The following selections from them contain material of extreme importance in realistic thinking.

The arguments rest upon the realistic analysis of being with its concepts of cause, essence and existence, and actuality and potentiality. St. Anselm's argument, named the ontological argument, attempts to make an inference from the idea of a Perfect Being to the existence of that Being. It presupposes the concept of degrees of being, and finds its inspiration in Platonic sources. (Plato in fact hinted at such an argument.) St. Thomas, however, rejected Anselm's argument; proceeding rather from Aristotelian premises, he argues that proofs must begin with characteristics of the world actually met in human experience and made explicit by metaphysical analysis. The important five arguments for God which he offers begin from such characteristics: motion, causality, contingency, the gradation of things, and order. These, however, are incomplete and unintelligible in themselves and require the intellect to proceed to a conclusion wherein the existence of God is asserted. The five arguments he expounds are rightfully called the classical proofs of God's existence.

10 The Ontological Argument
St. Anselm (1033-1109)

Chapter II
Truly there is a God, although the fool hath said in his heart, There is no God.

And so, Lord, do thou, who dost give understanding to faith, give me, so far as thou knowest it to be profitable, to understand that thou art as we believe; and that thou art that which we believe. And, indeed, we believe that thou art a being than which nothing greater can be conceived. Or is there no such nature, since the fool hath said in his heart, there is no God? (Psalms xiv. 1). But, at any rate, this very fool, when he hears of this being of which I speak—a being than which nothing greater can be conceived—understands what he hears, and what he understands is in his understanding; although he does not understand it to exist.

For, it is one thing for an object to be in the understanding, and another to

The selection is from St. Anselm, *Proslogium* (tr. Sidney Norton Deane) (Chicago: The Open Court Publishing Co., 1903), pp. 7–9.

understand that the object exists. When a painter first conceives of what he will afterwards perform, he has it in his understanding, but he does not yet understand it to be, because he has not yet performed it. But after he has made the painting, he both has it in his understanding, and he understands that it exists, because he has made it.

Hence, even the fool is convinced that something exists in the understanding, at least, than which nothing greater can be conceived. For, when he hears of this, he understands it. And whatever is understood, exists in the understanding. And assuredly that, than which nothing greater can be conceived, cannot exist in the understanding alone. For, suppose it exists in the understanding alone: then it can be conceived to exist in reality; which is greater.

Therefore, if that, than which nothing greater can be conceived, exists in the understanding alone, the very being, than which nothing greater can be conceived, is one, than which a greater can be conceived. But obviously this is impossible. Hence, there is no doubt that there exists a being, than which nothing greater can be conceived, and it exists both in the understanding and in reality.

Chapter III

God cannot be conceived not to exist. —God is that, than which nothing greater can be conceived.—That which can be conceived not to exist is not God.

And it assuredly exists so truly, that it cannot be conceived not to exist. For, it is possible to conceive of a being which cannot be conceived not to exist; and this is greater than one which can be conceived not to exist. Hence, if that, than which nothing greater can be conceived, can be conceived not to exist, it is not that, than which nothing greater can be conceived. But this is an irreconcilable contradiction. There is, then,

so truly a being than which nothing greater can be conceived to exist, that it cannot even be conceived not to exist; and this being thou art, O Lord, our God.

So truly, therefore, dost thou exist, O Lord, my God, that thou canst not be conceived not to exist; and rightly. For, if a mind could conceive of a being better than thee, the creature would rise above the Creator; and this is most absurd. And, indeed, whatever else there is, except thee alone, can be conceived not to exist. To thee alone, therefore, it belongs to exist more truly than all other beings, and hence in a higher degree than all others. For, whatever else exists does not exist so truly, and hence in a less degree it belongs to it to exist. Why, then, has the fool said in his heart, there is no God (Psalms xiv. 1), since it is so evident, to a rational mind, that thou dost exist in the highest degree of all? Why, except that he is dull and a fool?

11 Five Ways to God

St. Thomas Aquinas (1225-1274)

FIRST ARTICLE

Whether the Existence of God is Self-Evident?

We proceed thus to the First Article:—
Objection 1. It seems that the Existence of God is self-evident. Those things are said to be self-evident to us the knowledge of which is naturally im-

planted in us, as we can see in regard to first principles. But the Damascene[1] says that, *the knowledge of God is naturally implanted in all.* Therefore the Existence of God is self-evident.

Objection 2. Further, those things are said to be self-evident which are known as soon as the terms are known, which the Philosopher says is true of the first

The selection is from Question II of Part I of St. Thomas Aquinas, *Summa Theologica* (New York: Benziger Brothers, Inc., 1911), pp. 19–27. Used by permission of the publisher.

[1 The reference is to John of Damascus (d. before 754), whose writings include a complete system of theology founded on the teachings of the church fathers and councils. His work was known by St. Thomas. *Ed.*]

principles of demonstration. Thus, when the nature of a whole and of a part is known, it is at once recognized that every whole is greater than its part. But as soon as the signification of the word "God" is understood, it is at once seen that God exists. For by this word is signified that thing than which nothing greater can exist. But that which exists actually and mentally is greater than that which exists only mentally. Therefore, because as soon as the word "God" is understood it exists mentally, it also follows that it exists actually. Therefore the proposition that God exists is self-evident.

Objection 3. Further, the existence of Truth is self-evident; for whoever denies the existence of Truth concedes that Truth does not exist. Now, if Truth does not exist, then the proposition "Truth does not exist" is true. But if there is anything true, there must be Truth. God is Truth itself: *I am the way, the truth, and the life* (John xiv. 6). Therefore the proposition that God exists is self-evident.

On the contrary, No one can mentally admit the opposite of what is self-evident; as is clear from the Philosopher, concerning the first principles of demonstration. The opposite of the proposition "God is" can be mentally admitted: *The fool hath said in his heart, There is no God* (Ps. lii. I). Therefore, that God exists is not self-evident.

I answer that, A thing can be self-evident in either of two ways; on the one hand, self-evident in itself, though not to us; on the other, self-evident in itself, and to us. A proposition is self-evident because the predicate is included in the notion of the subject, as "Man is an animal," for animal is contained in the formal idea of man. If, therefore, the essence of the predicate and subject be known to all, the proposition will be self-evident to all; as is clear with regard to the first principles of demonstration, the terms of which are common things that no one is ignorant of, such as being and non-being, whole and part, and such like. If there are some to whom the essence of the predicate and subject are unknown, the proposition will be self-evident in itself, but not to those who do not know the meaning of the predicate and subject of the proposition. Therefore, it happens, as Boethius[2] says, that there are some mental concepts self-evident only to the learned, as that incorporeal substances are not in space. Therefore I say that this proposition, "God exists," of itself is self-evident, for the predicate is the same as the subject; because God is His Own Existence. Forasmuch as we do not know the Essence of God, the proposition is not self-evident to us; but need to be proved by such things as are more evident to us, though less evident in their nature—namely, by effects.

Reply Objection 1. To know that God exists in a general and indefinite way is implanted in us by nature, inasmuch as God is man's beatitude. For man naturally desires happiness, and what is naturally desired by a man must be naturally known to him. This, however, is not to know absolutely that God exists; as to know that someone is approaching is not the same as to know that Peter is approaching, even though it is Peter who is approaching; for many

---

[2 The reference is to Boethius (470–525), an important and influential commentator on Aristotle and Cicero. *Ed.*]

there are who imagine that man's perfect good (which is happiness) consists in riches, and others in pleasures, and others in something else.

Reply Objection 2. Perhaps not everyone who hears of this word "God" may understand it to signify something than which nothing better can be imagined, seeing that some have believed God to be a body. Yet, granted that everyone understands by this word "God" is signified something than which nothing greater can be imagined, nevertheless, it does not therefore follow that he understands that what the word signifies exists actually, but only that it exists mentally. Nor can it be argued logically that it actually exists, unless it be admitted that there exists something than which nothing greater can be imagined; and this precisely is not admitted by those who hold that God does not exist.

Reply Objection 3. The existence of truth in a general way is self-evident, but the existence of a Primal Truth is not self-evident to us.

SECOND ARTICLE

Whether It Can Be Demonstrated that God Exists?

We proceed thus to the Second Article:—

Objection 1. It seems that the existence of God cannot be demonstrated; for it is an article of Faith that God exists. But what is of Faith cannot be demonstrated, because a demonstration produces knowledge; whereas Faith is of the unseen (Heb. xi. i). Therefore it cannot be demonstrated that God exists.

Objection 2. Further, the essence is the middle term of demonstration. But we cannot know in what God's essence

consists, but solely in what it does not consist; as the Damascene says. Therefore we cannot demonstrate that God exists.

Objection 3. Further, if the existence of God were demonstrated, this could only be from His effects. But the effects are not proportionate to Him, since He is infinite and His effects are finite; and between the finite and infinite there is no proportion. Therefore, since a cause cannot be demonstrated by an effect not proportionate to it, it seems that the existence of God cannot be demonstrated.

On the contrary, The Apostle says: *The invisible things of God are clearly seen, being understood by the things that are made* (Rom. i. 20). But this would not be unless the existence of God could be demonstrated through the things that are made; for the first thing we must know of anything is, whether it exists.

I answer that, Demonstration can be made in two ways: One is through the cause, and is called *a priori,* and this is to argue from what is prior absolutely. The other is through the effect, and is called a demonstration *a posteriori;* this is to argue from what is prior relatively only to us. When an effect is better known to us than its cause, from the effect we proceed to the knowledge of the cause. From every effect the existence of a proportionate cause can be demonstrated, so long as its effects are better known to us. Since every effect depends upon its cause, if the effect exists, the cause must have preexisted. Hence the existence of God, in so far as it is not self-evident to us, can be demonstrated from those of His effects which are known to us.

Reply Objection 1. The existence of God and other like truths about God, which can be known by natural reason, are not articles of Faith, but are preambles to the articles; for Faith presupposes natural knowledge, even as grace presupposes nature, and perfection supposes something that can be perfected. Nevertheless, there is nothing to prevent a man, who cannot grasp its proof, accepting, as a matter of Faith, something in itself capable of being known and demonstrated.

Reply Objection 2. When the existence of a cause is demonstrated from an effect, this effect takes the place of the definition of the cause in proof of the cause's existence. This is especially the case in regard to God, because, in order to prove the existence of anything, it is necessary to accept as a middle term the meaning of the word, and not its essence, for the question of its essence follows on the question of its existence. The names given to God are derived from His effects; consequently, in demonstrating the existence of God from His effects, we may take for the middle term the meaning of the word "God."

Reply Objection 3. From effects not proportionate to the cause no perfect knowledge of that cause can be obtained. Yet from every effect the existence of the cause can be demonstrated, and so we can demonstrate the existence of God from His effects; though from them we cannot perfectly know God as He is in His own Essence.

THIRD ARTICLE

Whether God Exists?

We proceed thus to the Third Article:—

Objection 1. It seems that God does not exist; because if one of two contraries be infinite, the other would be altogether destroyed. But the word "God" means that He is infinite goodness. If, therefore, God existed, there would be no evil discoverable; but there is evil in the world. Therefore God does not exist.

Objection 2. Further, it is superfluous to suppose that, what can be accounted for by a few principles has been produced by many. But it seems that everything that appears in the world can be accounted for by other principles, supposing God did not exist. For all natural things can be reduced to one principle, which is nature; and all things that happen intentionally can be reduced to one principle, which is human reason, or will. Therefore there is no need to suppose God's existence.

On the contrary, It is said in the person of God: *I am Who am* (Exod. iii. 14).

I answer that, The existence of God can be proved in five ways.

The first and more manifest way is the argument from motion. It is certain and evident to our senses that some things are in motion. Whatever is in motion is moved by another, for nothing can be in motion except it have a potentiality for that towards which it is being moved; whereas a thing moves inasmuch as it is in act. By "motion" we mean nothing else than the reduction of something from a state of potentiality into a state of actuality. Nothing, however, can be reduced from a state of potentiality into a state of actuality, unless by something already in a state of actuality. Thus that which is actually hot as fire, makes wood, which is potentially hot, to be actually hot, and thereby moves and changes it. It is not possible that the same thing should be at once in a state of actuality and potentiality from the same point of view, but only from different points of view. What is actually hot cannot simultaneously be only potentially hot; still, it is simultaneously potentially cold. It is therefore impossible that from the same point of view and in the same way anything should be both moved and mover, or that it should move itself. Therefore, whatever is in motion must be put in motion by another. If that by which it is put in motion be itself put in motion, then this also needs be put in motion by another, and that by another again. This cannot go on to infinity, because then there would be no first mover, and, consequently, no other mover—seeing that subsequent movers only move inasmuch as they are put in motion by the first mover; as the staff only moves because it is put in motion by the hand. Therefore it is necessary to arrive at a First Mover, put in motion by no other; and this everyone understands to be God.

The second way is from the formality of efficient causation. In the world of sense we find there is an order of efficient causation. There is no case known (neither is it, indeed, possible) in which a thing is found to be the efficient cause of itself; for so it would be prior to itself which is impossible. In efficient causes it is not possible to go on to infinity, because in all efficient causes following in order, the first is the cause of the intermediate cause, and the intermediate is the cause of the ultimate cause, whether the intermediate cause be several, or one only. To take away the cause is to take away the effect. Therefore, if there be no first cause among efficient causes, there will be no ultimate cause, nor any intermediate. If in efficient causes it is possible to go on

to infinity, there will be no first efficient cause, neither will there be an ultimate effect, nor any intermediate efficient causes; all of which is plainly false. Therefore it is necessary to put forward a First Efficient Cause, to which everyone gives the name of God.

The third way is taken from possibility and necessity, and runs thus. We find in nature things that could either exist or not exist, since they are found to be generated, and then to corrupt; and, consequently, they can exist, and then not exist. It is impossible for these always to exist, for that which can one day cease to exist must at sometime have not existed. Therefore, if everything could cease to exist, then at one time there could have been nothing in existence. If this were true, even now there would be nothing in existence, because that which does not exist only begins to exist by something already existing. Therefore, if at one time nothing was in existence, it would have been impossible for anything to have begun to exist; and thus even now nothing would be in existence—which is absurd. Therefore, not all beings are merely possible, but there must exist something the existence of which is necessary. Every necessary thing either has its necessity caused by another, or not. It is impossible to go on to infinity in necessary things which have their necessity caused by another, as has been already proved in regard to efficient causes. Therefore we cannot but postulate the existence of some being having itself its own necessity, and not receiving it from another, but rather causing in others their necessity. This all men speak of as God.

The fourth way is taken from the gradation to be found in things. Among beings there are some more and some less good, true, noble, and the like. But "more" and "less" are predicated of different things, according as they resemble in their different ways something which is in the degree of "most," as a thing is said to be hotter according as it more nearly resembles that which is hottest; so that there is something which is truest, something best, something noblest, and, consequently, something which is uttermost being; for the truer things are, the more truly they exist. What is most complete in any genus is the cause of all in that genus; as fire, which is the most complete form of heat, is the cause whereby all things are made hot. Therefore there must also be something which is to all beings the cause of their being, goodness, and every other perfection; and this we call God.

The fifth way is taken from the governance of the world; for we see that things which lack intelligence, such as natural bodies, act for some purpose, which fact is evident from their acting always, or nearly always, in the same way, so as to obtain the best result. Hence it is plain that not fortuitously, but designedly, do they achieve their purpose. Whatever lacks intelligence cannot fulfil some purpose, unless it be directed by some being endowed with intelligence and knowledge; as the arrow is shot to its mark by the archer. Therefore some intelligent being exists by whom all natural things are ordained towards a definite purpose; and this being we call God.

Reply Objection 1. As Augustine says: *Since God is wholly good, He would not allow any evil to exist in His works, unless His omnipotence and goodness were such as to bring good even out of evil.* This is part of the infinite goodness of God, that He should allow evil to exist, and out of it produce good.

Reply Objection 2. Since nature works out its determinate end under the direction of a higher agent, whatever is done by nature must needs be traced back to God, as to its first cause. So also whatever is done designedly must also be traced back to some higher cause other than human reason or will, for these can suffer change and are defective; whereas things capable of motion and of defect must be traced back to an immovable and self-necessary first principle.

CRITIQUE

Central to our study of classical realism has been the problem and analysis of being, and uppermost in that analysis have been the principles of form and matter. Not all philosophers, however, have been satisfied with the realistic account of form, and in the following selection Donald C. Williams, an outstanding professor of philosophy at Harvard, discusses some of the problems in that account.

Williams' own position is a kind of materialism (which we shall study in the next section) he sometimes calls actualism.[1] From this position, he finds that the

---

[1] That is, reality is composed of material structures wholly actual and thus excluding potentialities and possibilities.

notion of structure is the one acceptable element in the realist's analysis of form, though structure is not unambiguously related to form in Aristotelian metaphysics. The rest of the analysis—form and matter, hierarchy, pure form—Williams finds highly problematic.

12 The Problem of Form
Donald C. Williams (1899-   )

Some such contrast as that of form and matter would be common intellectual property, no doubt, even if Aristotle and Kant had not made such relentless metaphysics of it. As things are, the Aristotelian notion in particular has probably affected more human beings than any other philosophic concept. Few doctrines are easier to explain in a textbook paragraph; almost none is harder to understand in detail and principle. This does not disturb the traditionalist for whom its antiquity and versatility *in usum ecclesiae* [in ecclesiastical use] put it above serious criticism, nor the modernist for whom its association with exploded science has made it beneath contempt. It is a trial, however, to two ingenuous sorts of citizen, the classical scholar who wishes to decipher what Aristotle was driving at, and the student of ontology who is looking for principles to explain things by. I have no pretensions to classical scholarship, so it was a certain involvement of the latter sort which set me plodding in some of the Peripatetic tracks. I am accordingly grateful for opportunity to put the issue before better informed persons, hoping that if I can interest them with an outsider's canvass of some things which Aristotle may have meant, they will help toward some verdict on the truth of the business.[1]

The trouble seems to have lain at the roots of the doctrine, growing out of Greek common sense and older philosophies where it was vague and legendary except for the materialistic version which Aristotle could not abide. This native obscurity the Aristotelian school cultivated like a fine flower by means of the famous method of analogy of proportionality. Form, we are told, is to matter as the shape of the statue is to its bronze, as the educated man to the uneducated, as health is to gall and phlegm, and as specific difference is to genus, and so on for a repertory of illustrations repeated with dreamy obstinacy for centuries. This leaves us, of course, at the mercy of the Philosopher's thumping errors of fact; but more seriously it is delusive in principle, because any pair of

The selection is from Donald C. Williams, "Form and Matter," *The Philosophical Review*, 67(1958), pp. 291-302, with omissions. Used by permission of the Editor and author.

[1] This was written for a meeting of the Society for Ancient Greek Philosophy at Harvard University on December 27, 1957. Though not unaffected by certain clues and countersuggestions kindly offered there, I think they do not yet demand any substantial revision of this inventory.

things "are to" one another, that is, are related, in a virtual infinity of ways, and in any finite set of such pairs countless of these relations will resemble and countless will differ. An arithmetical proportion is perfectly intelligible, though unexciting, because the abstractions are already familiar and we understand just what relations are being compared. The philosophical method of analogy, however, starts at the other end, expecting to identify the intended relation or its grounds from only the statement or hunch that it is one among those shared in a set of pairs; and it lacks just what makes the predigested arithmetical proportion reliable. In abeyance of the abstraction which the method is used to avoid, only with good luck could Aristotle have identified the same respect of resemblance among all his pairs of pairs to begin with, and only with more luck could we identify the same respect after him.

One reason why the mystery has nevertheless seldom silenced us in the classroom is, of course, the conventional pretense that anyone who took the trouble to look the subject up would find it all worked out somewhere. But there is a better reason in our easy access to at least one version of the distinction which is not analogical but abstract and clear: form is structure, and matter is what has or enters into the structure; and the structure of anything is a relation or a set of relations or a sum of relations among its parts. Each part or term is designatable as "matter" for the form, "content" for the structure; but "the" matter or content for it is strictly the polyad of terms, or set of parts, subject to the relation, and less strictly is their sum, the concrete thing minus the stipulated relations. The same complex of relations thus relates the parts, is the form for which they are matter, and is the form *of* the total thing, parts and relations together.

The principle of structure, I think, is indeed the one substantive element in the Aristotelian notion, and is what gives professional dignity and endurance to it. The standard pedagogic epitome of hylomorphism is that "the matter is the stuff a thing is made of, the form is the way it is put together." And prominent in the secular scholar's offhand description of Aristotelian form is "intelligible structure."[2] Greek culture seems to have been fascinated with order and rhythm of arrangement and resemblance —aesthetically, mathematically, and then metaphysically. The "forms" advocated by the Pythagoreans and Democritus were configurations with countable junctures, and Plato after them continually thought of his Forms as like a carpenter's plan which the world's lumber is arranged to match. Of Aristotle's words for form, the majority—εἶδος, ἰδέα, γένος (194b 26), παράδειγμα, λόγος (996b 7), φύσις (193b 17), and even μορφή—might by then have meant

---

[2] Thus Professor Morrow in the Runes *Dictionary of Philosophy* (New York, 1942), art. "Form"; W. D. Ross, *Aristotle* (London, 1930), p. 74; etc. Ostensible quotations from Aristotle hereinafter are mostly from the Ross translations. My documentation is a little sporadic because most of the allusions are commonplaces, to ideas much repeated in Aristotle's works, or familiar resultants of many dispersed remarks. The references are meant mainly to identify the phases of Aristotle's argument which are intended, mainly in the *Physics* (184-267) and *Metaphysics* (980-1093), rather than to be proofs of my interpretation.

almost anything, but most of them were redolent of the structuralistic tradition, I should suppose, and his σχῆμα must have reminded his colleagues of his own "figures" of the syllogism and of Democritus' use of the word for essential principles which had to be structures of the plainest spatiotemporal sort, while the occasional τάξις is confirmatory evidence. His first official example of a formal cause is the ratio 2:1 (194b 27), and a little later we hear that "all excellences depend upon particular relations" (246b 4). His favorite illustrations are "arrangements" or "structures" in the literal sense that they have been arranged or constructed, either by themselves, as living things are, or by art, like the statue, the rudder, the house. The shape of the statue, I need hardly point out, consists of the distances and directions among its parts; and though Aristotle's science of mixed and blended qualities is more elusive, if we once can credit such metaphysical pharmacy we must grant that the results would be "structures" in the broad and proper sense. The great avatar, Kant, finally, who plumed himself that he was using the Aristotelian distinction, made no bones about it that "form" is relational structure.

Many of the very discrepancies and vacillations in the Aristotelian corpus only confirm the structuralistic interpretation, for they are just what structuralism would make natural. Thus Aristotle writes of "the" form of a thing, as if it had just the one form, whereas anything demonstrably has a virtual infinity of structures—every set of a thing's parts providing as many structures as there are relations among them, and there being a stupendous if not infinite num-ber of sets of parts. But this is the sort of wholesome lapse made by people who unquestionably are thinking about structure and would explain that by "the structure" they mean some special or salient structure, much as Aristotle concedes that in strictness a thing has many forms if we count nonessential ones. Our interpretation explains, again, Aristotle's mild wonder that the form not merely in some degree depends causally on the matter but sometimes *includes* the matter (1033a 4)—a saw by definition must consist of iron (200b 6), though a man, I gather, need not consist of meat (1036b 5). For it is customary, and doubtless indispensable, to count qualities of terms as constitutive of structures and even of relations, as the specific colors of parts of a flag, no less than their locations and contrasts, are essential to its pattern. Then again we explain Aristotle's quandary about whether the form of a thing is, as he often says, a part or constituent of it (1033b 19, e.g.), or, as he says at least once, not a part but a "principle" of unity (1041b 30). For what we confront here is the primordial and subtle difficulty for any analytic philosophy, which Russell was to wrestle with again in his *Principles of Mathematics*,[3] that while the relations among the parts of a thing are in a sense constituents too, and though we can list the relations with the terms, the form with the matter, we thus leave out, that is, fail to convey, what can only be expressed not by a list but by a proposition: how the relations are operative, that they relate these terms in this order, that the form is of

3 Bertrand Russell, *Principles of Mathematics* (New York, 1943), p. 141.

this matter. Aristotle's apparent belief (983b, etc.), approved by Ross as well as by more religious champions,[4] that for this reason form is an "immaterial" principle in a sense hostile to philosophic materialism is a mistake, since the problem of relationality is as integral to physical structures as to spiritual ones, but it too is the kind of error to be expected if "form" means relational structure.

There is a profounder deterrent to the structuralistic interpretation of form in that the Aristotelian, who belittles relations as "least of all a kind of entity" (1088a 22), and at a showdown denies that substances can so much as contain actual parts to be related (1002a 20, 1040b 5), cannot with good grace admit relational pattern into the very core and essence of things. But this barrier to our hypothesis must go down anyhow, not just because the Aristotelian canon of relations demonstrably requires general revision, but because the Aristotelian relaxes it here himself. The irony is that though Aristotle and his Scholastics seldom or never say that a form is a structure consisting of relations among a thing's parts, they say not only that the form and matter are parts but that they are related parts. Aristotle does this tacitly when he introduces form and matter by analogy, for he defines analogy as a resemblance of rela-

tions. He does it expressly when he calls form and matter "relative" because of how they causally depend on each other (194b 9). Neo-Thomists labor it most when they insist that form and matter can be understood only by their "transcendental relation" and "the hylomorphic structure" this composes.[5] If the μορφή now is a structure too, the hylomorphic structure is the relation between relations and their terms, and it deserves the title "transcendental" if only because *its* terms belong to different categories or types.

That a form consists of relations, and that it is related to its matter, are two senses in which the form-matter distinction may be said to be "relative," but most famous is a third way, that what is form relatively to one batch of being may be matter relatively to another, and this on the whole our structuralism also accommodates, finding in it again only about the degree and kind of error one would expect—to quote Aristotle's way of condescending to his predecessors (993a 16, etc.)—in the lisping infancy of philosophy. For Aristotle is right enough that structurally a man is to his organs as each organ is to its tissues, and as these are to the cosmic elements, namely, in that he consists of them in a certain combination. We need only guard against saying that *this* relation is that of form to matter; it is only that of whole to part, a structural relation at one level being not a term for but a constituent of a term for a structural relation at the next "higher" level. Only when the inclusive relations relate the included relations themselves is it

---

[4] Ross, *Aristotle*, p. 172; introduction to his edition of the *Metaphysics* (Oxford, 1953), I, p. cxiii; Jacques Maritain, *Introduction to Philosophy* (New York, 1930), p. 167. Aristotle in the passages I cite is complaining that the pre-Socratics were obsessed with "the material cause"; but in fact, of course, they wanted to explain everything by differences of *structure*.

[5] See Louis de Raeymaeker, *Philosophie de l'être* (Louvain, 1947), pp. 191, etc.

strictly true that the form at one level is matter for the next level, and this is a refinement which Aristotle, who found it hard enough to instruct the Athenians about plain everyday relations of things, can be excused from elucidating.

Very quickly now, however, the hierarchical theme which haunts all Aristotelianism joins with others of its dominant motives to carry us to where the structural interpretation fits so badly that either the philosophy is sadly in error about the nature of structure or it does not intend to equate form with structure after all. In the latter event it is a nice and hard duty to guess what it does intend. The departures are in two main directions, one which makes form in a clear-cut technical way a more general concept than structure, another which makes it, in a more obscure, elevating, and influential way, a more special concept.

The technical departure is most manifest, perhaps, at the supposed top and bottom of the form-matter hierarchy. A modern analyst, if he did not think the pattern of part and whole ran to infinity up and down, would hold that the top of the hierarchy is the structure of the world whole, into which everything enters as matter and which enters as matter into nothing, and that the bottom is supplied by terms into which no structure enters but which together enter into all structures. Being devoid of relational character, the latter must have or be simple qualia. Our analyst might sympathize with Aristotle's quest for primitive stuffs and qualities to provide content for things, and certainly would join him in reprehending Plato's disembodied Forms, which threaten the absurdity, not just of qualities without instances,

but of relations without terms, a wilder notion than lefts without rights. But what Aristotle in fact does, of course, is so gratuitously different from this that centuries of custom have not lessened the shock of it on critical minds. In defiance of his own tireless complaints against Plato, he affirms a top form which, so far from having everything for its matter, has no matter, but is pure form, and at the bottom end, where we might now expect, to match his form without matter, a matter without form, that is, consisting of terms which *have* no relations, we find instead neither this which his new thesis requires, nor the terms merely containing no relations which strict structuralism requires, but a stuff devoid both of structures and of qualities. This alone is prime matter, everything else, including the structureless qualia, being "form." I don't lodge the usual objection, which I think is false, that such a substratum is inconceivable, nor even object, what I think is true, that it provides a clumsy and incredible theory of predication. The fault is that the scheme has confounded together two quite distinct principles, the more special notion of relational composition, and the more general notion of predication or attribution. Though we grant that a man's body "is to" his organs as an organ is to its tissues and as the tissues are to constituent simple qualia, now when we have got down to the qualia we are at the end of that hierarchy or proportionality; by hypothesis there cannot be anything to which the qualia have the "ratio" the tissue has to them. That Aristotle has skipped to a fundamentally different principle is witnessed by how many modern analysts would think it imperative that relations should have terms but preposterous that qualities must inhere in a substratum. If Aristotle wants to say the latter too, as is his right, he must suppose that qualitative predication is itself an elementary structure, to yield still a different hierarchy, where the last structure is the union of quale and substratum, which are thus irreducibly and coequally prime matters.

Losing his way in the twilight of the analogical hierarchy was perhaps a main occasion for Aristotle's extending the title of "form" from structures to all characters or predicates, but it surely was not the only one. For though he often plays fast and loose with whether form or matter is preeminently a "this" (1042a 29, 1049a 26, 1070a 11), when he seriously distinguishes "this" from "such," the matter is the "this" (190b 25, 999a 33), the particular subject, and the form is the "such" (1033b 22, 1038b 35), the characterizing attribute, just any such entity as "determines" a subject, in whatever category —structure, quale, or even the subject's relation to something outside itself (1042b 23, 1043a 7). To be a form is to be abstract and universal: to be abstract in that it cannot exist separately, "in itself," but only "in another"; and to be a universal either actually and directly; identically present in each of many instances, as the school books generally say Aristotle held, and as I think was his conspicuous intention, or indirectly, by the operationalist idea fathered on him by the Thomists, that the form is anyhow the element in the thing which is fit to become a universal when the mind "abstracts" it. These specifications confirm that a quale is as truly a form as a structure is, since warmth, for example, is as incapable of existing without a subject, and as capable of existing in many subjects, as humanity or triangularity.

Aristotle's use of "form" in senses more hospitable than the notion of structure would permit does not, however, hinder him from a use which confines it to senses more special and honorific than structure requires and indeed than it can well support. In the new senses to be a "form" is a prerogative capable of degrees, some forms are more formish than others, and *the* form, the essential form, of a thing is its most formish form. And whereas the extension of the idea of form from structure to all characters seems only an incident in Aristotle's exposition, its specialization to apply properly only to superlative and prerogative forms is altogether central and entrancing. It is, however, correspondingly obscure, and I propose to follow now only the one clue, given by Aristotle's pretty plain relegation of qualia to the foot of the analogical ladder, that what is "form" in the special sense must be at least a structure, and to ask then whether the prerogatives assigned to it can be defined by traits of structure or even consistently grafted on them. In this connection we might have hoped to get light on prerogative "form" from the cognate notion of prerogative "essence" (οὐσία; τὸ τά ἦν εἶναι) which Aristotle often equates with it (1032b 1, 1044a 36, etc.), but I am convinced that a course proceeding in the opposite direction has anyhow the advantage of *obscurius per obscurum*.

There is nothing in the fundamental conception of structure to dictate what might count as more structure. Typically, I suppose, we would mean by "more structure" a structure which pleases or entertains us. We call a thing "deformed" or "amorphous" if we don't like or don't notice the shape, and "shapely" if we do, much as we describe a person or a thing as "quality" if it is of good quality and "classy" if of a desirable class. But even if we conjecture that professorial lickerishness first decided Aristotle on his verdict, quite ungrounded otherwise, that the form of wine is superior to the form of vinegar (1044b 33), still he must have been trying to apply a general principle of a more serious kind. The most obvious of objective associations of "higher form" would be with two abstractly logical sorts of "superiority," each a sort of inclusiveness, which loomed large to him already. One is taxonomic, by which the "higher" form, whether quale or structure, would be the more general one, of the greatest extension. The old philosophies, never very sound on extension and intension, were often victimized by this, but it can't be the main Aristotelian reliance, for it makes the most abstract and indeterminate character the "highest," and Aristotle is very repetitive that the genus is not more form than but is matter for the species (1024b 7, 1038a 6, etc.). The other logical criterion of inclusiveness is the strictly hylomorphic one, constituted not by how many instances a universal has, but by the scope of a particular relationship—the criterion by which in a hierarchy of nested matters and forms, the forms of wholes are "higher" than the forms of their parts. This has at least perspicuity and decorum, explaining why qualia gravitate to the bottom, and making the big-

gest things the loftiest ones. But "higher" here too is only a logical trope which, no matter what Aristotle may sometimes have thought, entails none of the Aristotelian prerogatives. The organization of a human cell may in some significant way be "higher" than that of a molecule in it, and the organization of a man "higher" than of the cell, but the state's form, in spite of Aristotle's occasional anticipation of the Hegelian view, is not superior to that of the individual, and the human race is pandemonium. That nothing important could have followed from rank in the hierarchy is evident when we remember that there can be a square figure whose elements are circles, or a circle composed of squares, or a circle of circles, or a square of squares. (The degrees of form, therefore, since they coincide with nothing else we have found so far, call for still another explication of the maxim that the idea of form is "relative," that is, that it is comparative.) . . .

I still think that the only tolerably strict sense of "more structure" is complexity, conceived as some function of number, variety, and degree of constituent relations. But I shall take advantage of the historical and sentimental justification for using "higher form" or "amount (or degree) of structure in the special (or honorific) sense" to stand for organization, tentatively understood, or half-understood, as complexity-cum-simplicity, even though we have no notion about such essential factors in it as how much complexity in one dimension is equipollent with how much simplicity in another.

SUMMARY

Classical realism, we have seen, may be called a philosophy of being, in that it places the concept of being and its metaphysical analysis at the center of philosophical concern. Other philosophies, of course, wish to claim this title also; but not all of them, the realist believes, can rightfully do so. This concluding selection presents a realist's conviction that metaphysics is a valid human enterprise, that the first concept of being is its fundamental problem, and that the Aristotelian-Thomistic tradition, among all philosophies, is closest to a true analysis of that concept.

Writing as a philosopher in the contemporary world, Professor Gilson is aware of a variety of criticisms that have been leveled against the speculative metaphysics which lies at the heart of realism. He especially singles out the antimetaphysical position of the German philosopher Immanuel Kant who had argued that metaphysics, in attempting to determine the principles of being that underlie experience, necessarily surpasses the bounds of the valid employment of human reason. Kant's philosophy concludes with the assertion that speculative metaphysics is impossible, and hence it is one of many philosophies which issue in skepticism about metaphysical knowledge. Some of these positions we shall examine later.

Professor Gilson is convinced that these skeptical philosophies either overlook or misuse the first concept of being. There is a fundamental intuition of being that lies at the basis of metaphysical thinking, but the meaning and implications of being have frequently been distorted by philosophers. True and fruitful metaphysical thinking, he concludes, is possible only if the first principle of being is firmly grasped and retained by the metaphysician; and this general conclusion is the basic reply which the realist would give to William's critique.

13 Being and Realism
Étienne Gilson (1884-1974)

By his very nature, man is a metaphysical animal. . . . Since man is essentially rational, the constant recurrence of metaphysics in the history of human knowledge must have its explanation in the very structure of reason itself. In other words, the reason why man is a metaphysical animal must lie somewhere in the nature of rationality. Many centuries before Kant, philosophers had stressed the fact that there is more in rational knowledge than we find in sensible experience. The typical attributes of scientific knowledge, that is universality and necessity, are not to be found in sensible reality, and one of the most generally received explanations is that they come to us from our very

---

The selection is reprinted with the permission of Charles Scribner's Sons and of Sheed and Ward, Ltd., from Étienne Gilson, *The Unity of Philosophical Experience* copyright 1937 Charles Scribner's Sons, Sheed and Ward, Ltd., pp. 307–316, with omissions.

power of knowing. As Leibniz[1] says, there is nothing in the intellect that has not first been in sense, except the intellect itself. As Kant was the first both to distrust metaphysics and to hold it to the unavoidable, so was he also the first to give a name to human reason's remarkable power to overstep all sensible experience. He called it the *transcendent* use of reason and denounced it as the permanent source of our metaphysical illusions. Let us retain the term suggested by Kant; it will then follow that whether such knowledge be illusory or not, there is, in human reason, a natural aptness, and consequently a natural urge, to transcend the limits of experience and to form transcendental notions by which the unity of knowledge may be completed. These are metaphysical notions, and the highest of them all is that of the cause of all causes, or first cause, whose discovery has been for centuries the ambition of the metaphysicians. . . . *Metaphysics is the knowledge gathered by a naturally transcendent reason in its search for the first principles, or first causes, of what is given in sensible experience.*

This is, in fact, what metaphysics is, but what about its validity? The Kantian conclusion that metaphysical knowledge is illusory by its own nature was not a spontaneous offspring of human reason. If metaphysical speculation is a shooting at the moon, philosophers have always begun by shooting at it; only after missing it have they said that there was no moon, and that it was a waste of time to shoot at it. Skepticism is defeat-

[1 G. W. Leibniz (1646–1716), influential German philosopher whose thought has been referred to as the dawning consciousness of the modern world (Dewey). *Ed.*]

ism in philosophy, and all defeatisms are born of previous defeats. When one has repeatedly failed in a certain undertaking, one naturally concludes that it was an impossible undertaking. I say naturally, but not logically, for a repeated failure in dealing with a given problem may point to a repeated error in discussing the problem rather than to its intrinsic insolubility.

The question then arises: should the repeated failures of metaphysics be ascribed to metaphysics itself, or to metaphysicians? It is a legitimate question, and one that can be answered in the light of philosophical experience. For indeed that experience itself exhibits a remarkable unity. If our previous analyses are correct, they all point to the same conclusion, that metaphysical adventures are doomed to fail when their authors substitute the fundamental concepts of any particular science for those of metaphysics. Theology, logic, physics, biology, psychology, sociology, economics, are fully competent to solve their own problems by their own methods; on the other hand, however, and this must be our . . . conclusion: *as metaphysics aims at transcending all particular knowledge, no particular science is competent either to solve metaphysical problems, or to judge their metaphysical solutions.*

Of course, Kant would object that, so far, his own condemnation of metaphysics still holds good, for he never said that metaphysical problems could be solved in that way; he merely said that they could not be solved at all. True, but it is also true that his condemnation of metaphysics was not the consequence of any personal attempt to reach the foundations of metaphysical knowledge. Kant busied himself with questions about metaphysics, but he had no metaphysical interests of his own. Even during the first part of his career there was always some book between this professor and reality. To him, nature was in the books of Newton, and metaphysics in the books of Wolff.[2] Anybody could read it there; Kant himself had read it, and it boiled down to this, that there are three metaphysical principles or transcendental ideas of pure reason: an immortal soul to unify psychology; freedom to unify the laws of cosmology; and God to unify natural theology. Such, to Kant, was metaphysics; a second-hand knowledge, for which he was no more personally responsible than for the physics of Newton. Before allowing Kant to frighten us away from metaphysics, we should remember that what he knew about it was mere hearsay.

In fact, what Kant considered as the three principles of metaphysics were not principles, but conclusions. The real principles of metaphysics are the first notions through which all the subsequent metaphysical knowledge has to be gathered. What these first notions are cannot be known unless we begin by bringing forth some metaphysical knowledge; then we can see how it is made and, lastly, we can form an estimate of its value. Now our analysis of the concrete working of various metaphysical minds clearly suggests that the principles of metaphysics are very different from the three transcendental ideas of Kant. The average metaphysician usually overlooks them because, though he aims at the discovery of the ultimate ground of reality as a whole, he attempts to explain the whole by one of its parts. Then he fails and he ascribes his failure to metaphysics, little aware of the fact that now is the proper time for him to metaphysicize, for the most superficial reflection on his failure would take him to the very root of metaphysics.

When Thales[3] said, six centuries before Christ, that everything is water, though he certainly did not prove his thesis, he at least made it clear that reason is naturally able to conceive all that is as being basically one and the same thing, and that such a unification of reality cannot be achieved by reducing the whole to one of its parts. Instead of drawing that conclusion, the successors of Thales inferred from his failure that he had singled out the wrong part. Thus Anaximenes said that it was not water, but air. It still did not work. Then Heraclitus said it was fire, and as there were always objections, the Hegel of the time appeared, who said that the common stuff of all things was the *indeterminate,* that is, the initial fusion of all the contraries from which all the rest had been evolved. Anaximander thus completed the first philosophical cycle recorded by the history of Western culture. The description of the later cycles could not take us further, for it is already clear, from a mere inspection of the first, that the human mind must be possessed of an aptitude to conceive all things as the same, but always fails in its endeavor to conceive all things as

[2 The reference is to Christian Wolff (1697–1754), professor of mathematics at Halle and an outstanding philosopher of the German Enlightenment. *Ed.*]

[3 M. Gilson refers in this paragraph to some of the major pre-Socratic philosophers and their basic doctrines: Thales (6th cen., B.C.), Anaximenes (6th cen., B.C.), Heraclitus (a.536-470), and Anaximander (6th cen., B.C.) *Ed.*]

being the same as one of them. In short, *the failures of the metaphysicians flew from their unguarded use of a principle of unity present in the human mind.*

This new conclusion brings us face to face with the last and truly crucial problem: what is it which the mind is bound to conceive both as belonging to all things and as not belonging to any two things in the same way? Such is the riddle which every man is asked to read on the threshold of metaphysics. It is an easy one, as, after all, was that of the Sphinx; yet many a good man has failed to say the word, and the path to the metaphysical Sphinx is strewn with the corpses of philosophers. The word is —Being. Our mind is so made that it cannot formulate a single proposition without relating it to some being. Absolute nothingness is strictly unthinkable, for we cannot even deny an existence unless we first posit it in the mind as something to be denied. "If any man," says J[onathan] Edwards, "thinks that he can conceive well enough how there should be nothing, I will engage, that what he means by nothing, is as much something, as anything that he ever thought of in his life." This, I think, is true. But if it is true that human thought is always about being; that each and every aspect of reality, or even of unreality, is necessarily conceived as being, or defined in reference to being, it follows that the understanding of being is the first to be attained, the last into which all knowledge is ultimately resolved and the only one to be included in all our apprehensions. What is first, last and always in human knowledge is its first principle, and its constant point of reference. Now if metaphysics is knowledge dealing with the first principles and the first causes themselves, we

can safely conclude that *since being is the first principle of all human knowledge, it is a fortiori the first principle of metaphysics.*

The classical objection to this statement is that, from such a vague idea as that of being, no distinct knowledge can be deduced. This is true, but it is not an objection. To describe being as the "principle of knowledge," does not mean that all subsequent knowledge can be analytically deduced from it, but rather that being is the first knowledge through which all subsequent knowledge can be progressively acquired. As soon as it comes into touch with sensible experience the human intellect elicits the immediate intuition of being: X is, or exists; but from the intuition *that* something is, the knowledge of *what* it is, beyond the fact that it is something, cannot possibly be deduced, nor is it the task of the intellect to deduce it. The intellect does not deduce, it intuits, it sees, and, in the light of intellectual intuition, the discursive power of reason slowly builds up from experience a determinate knowledge of concrete reality. Thus, in the light of immediate evidence, the intellect sees that something is, or exists; that what exists is that which it is; that which is, or exists, cannot be and not be at one and the same time; that a thing either is, or it is not, and no third supposition is conceivable; last, but not least, that being only comes from being, which is the very root of the notion of causality. Reason has not to prove any one of these principles, otherwise they would not be principles, but conclusions; but it is by them that reason proves all the rest. Patiently weaving the threads of concrete knowledge, reason adds to the intellectual evidence of being and of its properties the science of *what* it is. The first principle brings with it, therefore, both the certitude that metaphysics is the science of being as being, and the abstract laws according to which that science has to be constructed. Yet the principle of a certain knowledge is not that knowledge; and the first principle of human knowledge does not bring us a ready-made science of metaphysics, but its principle and its object.

The twofold character of the intellectual intuition of being, to be given in any sensible experience, and yet to transcend all particular experience, is both the origin of metaphysics and the permanent occasion of its failures. If being is included in all my representations, no analysis of reality will ever be complete unless it culminates in a science of being, that is in metaphysics. On the other hand, the same transcendency which makes the first principle applicable to all experience entails at least the possibility of overstepping the limits by which concrete and particular existences are distinguished. This indeed is more than an abstract possibility, it is a temptation, precisely because it is true that the notion of Being applies to all real or possible experience. Yet, if it is also true that everything is what it is, and nothing else, existence belongs to each and every thing in a truly unique manner, as its own existence, which can be shared in by nothing else. Such is the first principle, both universally applicable, and never applicable twice in the same way. When philosophers fail to perceive either its presence or its true nature, their initial error will pervade the whole science of being, and bring about the ruin of philosophy.

When, owing to some fundamental scientific discovery, a metaphysically minded man first grasps the true nature of a whole order of reality, what he is thus grasping for the first time is but a particular determination of being at large. Yet the intuition of being is always there, and if our philosopher fails to discern its meaning, he will fall a victim to its contagious influence. That which is but a particular determination of being, or *a* being, will be invested with the universality of being itself. In other words, a particular essence will be credited with the universality of being, and allowed to exclude all the other aspects of reality. This is precisely what happened to Abailard, to Ockham, to Descartes, to Kant and to Comte. They were truly laboring under a transcendental delusion; Kant himself knew it, but he was wrong in thinking that such an illusion was unavoidable, for it can be avoided; and he was still more wrong in viewing that illusion as the source of metaphysics, for it is not its source but the cause of its destruction; and not only of the destruction of metaphysics, but, for the same reason and at the same time, of the ruin of the very science which has thus been unduly generalized. If every order of reality is defined by its own essence, and every individual is possessed of its own existence, to encompass the universality of being within the essence of this or that being is to destroy the very object of metaphysics; but to ascribe to the essence of this or that being the universality of being itself, is to stretch a particular science beyond its natural limits and to make it a caricature of metaphysics. In short, and this will be our last conclusion: *all the failures of metaphysics should be traced to the fact, that the first principle of human knowledge has been either overlooked or misused by the metaphysicians.*

BIBLIOGRAPHICAL NOTE

Systematic introductions to classical realistic philosophy may be found in such volumes as Jacques Maritain, *An Introduction to Philosophy* (London, 1930); John Wild, *Introduction to Realistic Philosophy* (New York, 1948); H. D. Gardeil, *Introduction to the Philosophy of St. Thomas Aquinas* (tr. J. A. Otto), 4 vols. (St. Louis, 1956 and later); and R. J. Kreyche, *First Philosophy* (New York, 1959). A Thomist introduction to philosophy which relies less heavily on Aristotelian concepts is James E. Royce, *Man and Meaning* (New York: McGraw-Hill, Inc., 1969). Very readable is Henry B. Veatch's *Aristotle: A Contemporary Appreciation* (Bloomington: Indiana University Press, 1974); more advanced is Felix Grayeff, *Aristotle and his School* (New York: Barnes & Noble, 1974). For further intensive study, the student must turn to the basic texts of the great figures in classical realism, Plato, Aristotle, and St. Thomas Aquinas. Their works are available in many editions and compilations. Of value in studying them are such commentaries as A. E. Taylor, *Plato, the Man and His Work*, 4th ed. (New York, 1956); G. M. A. Grube, *Plato's Thought* (Boston, 1958); W. D. Ross, *Aristotle*, 5th ed. (London, 1949); F. C. Copleston, *Aquinas* (Penguin Books, 1955); Jacques Maritain, *Saint Thomas Aquinas* (London, 1933); and Étienne Gilson, *The Christian Philosophy of St. Thomas Aquinas* (New York, 1956). A naturalistic commentary on Aristotle is found in J. H. Randall, *Aristotle* (New York, 1960); and recent interpretations of Plato have been given by Gilbert Ryle and J. N. Findlay. Many works exist on the history of realism, especially of the medieval period; see, for example, Maurice de Wulf, *History of Medieval Philosophy* (New York, 1909), the interpretive and excellent study by Gilson, *The Spirit of Medieval Philosophy* (New York, 1940), and J. R. Weinberg, *A Short History of Medieval Philosophy* (Princeton, 1964). Contemporary work by thinkers of realistic persuasion is found in such volumes as John Wild (ed.), *The Return to Reason* (Chicago, 1953), the Proceedings of the American Catholic Philosophical Association, and the many publications of Maritain and Gilson, who have written on all the major areas of philosophical concern. An interesting, though advanced, development in realism is found in Louis de Raeymaeker, *The Philosophy of Being* (tr. E. H. Ziegelmeyer) (St. Louis, 1961). Contemporary studies by realists may also be found in such journals as *The International Philosophical Quarterly, The Modern Schoolman*, and *The Thomist*.

Chapter Three

Materialism/ Naturalism

Lucretius · Bacon · Peirce · Alexander
Perry · Marx · Dewey · Smart
Cohen · Santayana · Brightman · Nagel

The position developed in the selections in this third Part is known sometimes as materialism, sometimes as naturalism. However named, two propositions define the basic orientation of this philosophy: (1) nature is all there is; there is no supernatural being, realm, or entity, and (2) scientific method is the most reliable means of inquiry for men to use in exploring nature. The first statement indicates that materialism is antithetical to all forms of supernaturalism and that it seeks to understand the various dimensions of experience in the context of nature alone. The second points to a relation between materialism and science that is of both historical and contemporary importance.

Among the varieties of materialism, it is possible to distinguish two major emphases. The first, and older, view is materialism, which holds that the real is matter or energy, motion, time, and space, and that all phenomena can be reduced to these terms. The word "naturalism" is frequently used to denote a second emphasis, which otherwise has no special name. Naturalism cannot always be sharply separated from materialism, although it is generally viewed as a distinct philosophy. For the naturalist, materialism presents too narrow a view of nature, for he finds nature much more complex and varied than an account in terms of matter and motion would seem to show. His aim is rather to describe accurately and fully the variety of levels within nature and to resist the tendency to make severe reductions of these levels to more primitive ones.

The ties between philosophy and science are very important in the rise of contemporary materialism even though a link with science has been present from the beginnings of materialism. Arising primarily in the seventeenth century, modern science involved a new methodology for man to follow and offered as well a new promise to man for the control of experience. The method itself has been of as much, and perhaps more, importance than the actual results of science. Yet among the results, too, are special achievements upon which materialism has based itself. One of these, the theory of evolution, is of special significance for naturalism, for it provided a theory in terms of which the naturalist could develop a fully naturalistic, yet nonreductive account of the higher and more human levels of experience.

No compact definition of materialism is wholly adequate; for just as nature is changing and evolving, so materialism too is not a fixed, closed system of propositions. Guided by science, it offers only a tentative and cautious statement about the general traits of existence. In proposing its metaphysical visions, materialism belongs to that group of philosophic schools which finds ultimate generalization an important activity of man. It would separate itself, however, from philosophies that divorce themselves from science to offer what, from its point of view, are unguarded or dogmatic statements about things. It would also be suspicious of distinctions between "appearance and reality." The goal of materialistic thinking is rather only that vision of man and nature which responsible inquiry will justify.

INTRODUCTION

Materialism in the ancient world found expression in the thought of four major thinkers: Leucippus (a. 450), Democritus (460–360), Epicurus (341–270), and Lucretius. With these men materialism took an atomistic direction, and the proposition that atoms and the void are real is perhaps the basic assertion of the entire school.

The most complete extant statement of ancient materialism is found in the poem by Lucretius, *On the Nature of Things*. Writing under the direct inspiration of Epicurus, Lucretius presents an interesting motivation for turning to philosophy. Mankind's greatest fear, he writes, is the fear of death and of possible punishment in the hereafter. It is therefore necessary to develop a metaphysics in which the mortality of man is so guaranteed that he can pursue without distraction the Epicurean moral ideal of a life free from disturbance in the mind and of pain in the body. These needs are met in the hypothesis of materialistic atomism.

The essential assertions of Lucretius can be briefly summarized. Only atoms and the void are real. They are also both eternal and infinite. Mind, composed of atoms in motion, is corporeal and perishable. Death, being the end of sensation as well as the dissolution of the atomic structure known as man, is consequently of no concern to man. The following selection elaborates upon these theses and includes a number of interesting arguments in their support.

1 Classical Materialism

Lucretius (98-54)

I shall proceed to discourse to thee[1] of the whole system of heaven and the gods, and unfold to thee the first principles of all things, from which nature produces, develops, and sustains all, and into which she again resolves them at their dissolution: these, in explaining our subject, we are accustomed to call matter, and the generative bodies of things, and to designate as the seeds of *all* things, and to term them primary bodies, because from them *as* primary all things are derived.

[For the whole nature of the gods must necessarily, of itself, enjoy immortality in absolute repose, separated, and far removed, from our affairs; for, exempt from all pain, exempt from perils, all-sufficient in its own resources, *and* needing nothing from us, it is neither propitiated by services *from the good,* nor affected with anger *against the bad.*][2]

When the life of men lay foully groveling before *our* eyes, crushed beneath the weight of a Religion, who displayed her head from the regions of the sky, lowering over mortals with terrible aspect, a man of Greece[3] was the first that

dared to raise mortal eyes against *her,* and first to make a stand against *her.* Him neither tales of gods, nor thunderbolts, nor heaven itself with its threatening roar, repressed, but roused the more the active energy of his soul, *so* that he should desire to be the first to break the close bars of nature's portals. Accordingly the vivid force of his intellect prevailed, and proceeded far beyond the flaming battlements of the world, and in mind and thought traversed the whole immensity of space; hence triumphant, he declares to us what can arise *into being,* and what can not; in fine, in what way the powers of all things are limited, only a deeply-fixed boundary assigned to each. By which means Religion, brought down under *our* feet, is bruised in turn; and *his* victory sets us on a level with heaven. . . .

Wilt thou too, overcome by the frightful tales of bards, ever seek to turn away from me? *Surely not;* for doubtless I, even now, could invent for thee many dreams, which might disturb the tenor of thy life, and confound all thy enjoyments with terror. And with reason too *under the present system of belief;* for did men *but* know that there was a fixed limit to their woes, they would be able, in some measure, to defy the religious fictions and menaces of the poets; *but* now, since we must fear eternal punishment at death, there is no mode, no means, of resisting *them.* For men know not what the nature of the soul is; whether it is engendered *with us,* or whether, on the contrary, it is infused into us at our birth, whether it perishes

---

The selection is from Books I and III of Lucretius' *On the Nature of Things* (tr. John Selby Watson) (London: Henry G. Bohn, 1851).

[1 The poem is addressed to a member of the family of Memmius, possibly the member to whom Cicero wrote letters. *Ed.*]

[2 Brackets have been used by the translator to indicate possibly misplaced lines. *Ed.*]

[3 The reference is to Epicurus, who is greatly praised throughout the poem. *Ed.*]

with us, dissolved by death, or whether it haunts the gloomy shades and vast pools of Orcus, or whether, by divine influence, it infuses itself into other animals, as our Ennius[4] sung, who first brought from pleasant Helicon a crown of never-fading leaf, which should be distinguished in fame throughout the Italian tribes of men. . . .

This terror and darkness of the mind, therefore, it is not the rays of the sun, or the bright shafts of day, that must dispel, but reason and the contemplation of nature; of which our first principle shall hence take its commencement, THAT NOTHING IS EVER DIVINELY GENERATED FROM NOTHING. For thus *it is that* fear restrains all men, because they observe many things effected on the earth and in heaven, of which effects they can by no means see the causes, and *therefore* think that they are wrought by a divine power. For which reasons, when we shall have *clearly* seen that NOTHING AN BE PRODUCED FROM NOTHING, we shall then have a more accurate perception of that of which we are in search, and *shall understand* whence each individual thing is generated, and how all things are done without the agency of the gods.

For if *things* came forth from nothing, every kind *of thing* might be produced from all things; nothing would require seed. In the first place, men might spring from the sea; the scaly tribe, and birds, *might spring* from the earth; herds, and other cattle, might burst from the sky; the cultivated fields, as well as the deserts, might contain every kind of wild animal, without any settled *law of* pro-

[4 A Pythagorean who thought that the soul of Homer had passed into himself. *Ed.*]

duction: nor would the same fruits be constant to the *same* trees, but would be changed; *and* all *trees* might bear all *kinds of fruit.* Since, when there should not be generative elements for each *production,* how could a certain parent-producer remain invariable for *all individual* things? But now, because all things are severally produced from certain seeds, *each* is produced, and comes forth into the regions of light, from that spot in which the matter, and first elements of each, subsist. And for this cause all things cannot be produced from all, inasmuch as there are distinct *and peculiar* faculties in certain substances. . . .

Add, too, that nature resolves each thing into its own *constituent* elements, and DOES NOT REDUCE ANY THING TO NOTHING.

For if any thing were perishable in all its parts, every thing might *then* dissolve, being snatched suddenly from before our eyes; for there would be no need of force to produce a separation of its parts, and break *their* connection. Whereas now, since all things individually consist of eternal seed, nature does not suffer the destruction of any thing to be seen, until such power assail them as to sever them with a blow, or penetrate inwardly through the vacant spaces, and dissolve *the parts.*

Besides, if time utterly destroys whatever things it removes through length of age, consuming all their *constituent* matter, whence does Venus restore to the light of life the race of animals according to their kinds? Whence does the variegated earth nourish and develop them, when restored, affording them sustenance according to their kinds? Whence do pure fountains, and eternal rivers *flowing* from afar, supply the sea?

Whence does the ether feed the stars? For infinite time already past, and *length of* days, ought to have consumed all things which are of mortal consistence: but if *those elements,* of which this sum of things consists and is renewed, have existed through that *long* space, and that past duration of time, they are assuredly endowed with an immortal nature. Things therefore cannot return to nothing.

Further, the same force and cause might destroy all things indiscriminately, unless an eternal matter held them more or less bound by mutual connection. For a *mere* touch, indeed, would be a sufficient cause of destruction, supposing that there were no *parts* of eternal consistence, *but all perishable,* the union of which any force might dissolve. But now, because various connections of elements unite together, and matter is eternal, things continue of unimpaired consistence, until some force of sufficient strength be found to assail them, proportioned to the texture of each. No thing, therefore, relapses into nonexistence, but all things at dissolution return to the first principles of matter. . . .

Attend, now, *further:* since I have shown that things cannot be produced from nothing, and also that, when produced, *they cannot* return to nothing, yet, lest haply thou shouldst begin to distrust my words, because the primary particles of things cannot be discerned by the eye, hear, in addition, what substances thou thyself must necessarily confess to exist, although impossible to be seen.

In the first place, the force of the wind, when excited, lashes the sea, agitates the tall ships, and scatters the clouds; at times, sweeping over *the earth* with an impetuous hurricane, it strews the plains with huge trees, and harasses the mountain-tops with forest-rending blasts; so *violently* does the deep chafe with fierce roar and rage with menacing murmur. The winds, then, are invisible bodies, which sweep the sea, the land, the clouds of heaven, and, agitating *them,* carry *them* along with a sudden tornado. Not otherwise do they rush forth, and spread destruction, than *as* when a body of liquid water is borne along in an overwhelming stream, which a vast torrent from the lofty mountains swells with large rain-floods, dashing together fragments of woods and entire groves; nor can the strong bridges sustain the sudden force of the sweeping water, with such overwhelming violence does the river, turbid with copious rain, rush against the *opposing* mounds; it scatters ruin with a mighty uproar, and rolls huge rocks under its waters; it rushes on *triumphant* wheresoever any thing opposes its waves. Thus, therefore, must the blasts of the wind also be borne along; which (when, like a mighty flood, they have bent their force in any direction) drive all things before them, and overthrow them with repeated assaults, and sometimes catch them up in a writhing vortex and rapidly bear them off in a whirling hurricane. Wherefore, I repeat, the winds are substances, *though* invisible, since in their effects, and modes of *operation,* they are found to rival mighty rivers, which are of manifest bodily substance.

Moreover we perceive various odors of objects, and yet never see them approaching our nostrils. Nor do we behold violent heat, or distinguish cold with our eyes; nor are we in the habit of viewing sounds; all which things, however, must of necessity consist of a corporeal nature, since they have the power of striking the senses: FOR NOTHING, EXCEPT BODILY SUBSTANCE, CAN TOUCH OR BE TOUCHED.

Further, garments, when suspended upon a shore on which waves are broken, grow moist; the same, when spread out in the sun, become dry; yet neither has it been observed how the moisture of the water settled in them, nor, on the other hand, how it escaped under the influence of the heat. The moisture, therefore, is dispersed into minute particles, which our eyes can by no means perceive.

Besides, in the course of many revolutions of the sun, a ring upon the finger is made somewhat thinner by wearing *it;* the fall of the drop from the eaves hollows a stone; the crooked share of the plough, *though* made of iron, imperceptibly decreases in the fields; even the stone pavements of the streets we see worn by the feet of the multitude; and the brazen statues, *which stand* near the gates, show their right hands made smaller by the touch of people frequently saluting them, and passing by. These objects, therefore, after they have been worn, we observe to become diminished; but what particles take their departure on each particular occasion, jealous nature has withheld from us the faculty of seeing.

Lastly, whatever *substances* time and nature add little by little to objects, obliging them to increase gradually, *those substances* no acuteness of vision, *however earnestly* exerted, can perceive; nor, moreover, whatever *substances* waste away through age and decay; nor can you discern what the rocks, which overhang the sea, *and are* eaten by the corroding salt *of the ocean,* lose every time

that they are washed by the waves. Nature, therefore, carries on her operations by imperceptible particles.

Nor, however, are all things held enclosed by corporeal substance; for there is a VOID in things; *a truth* which it will be useful for you, in reference to many points, to know; and which will prevent you from wandering in doubt, and from perpetually inquiring about the ENTIRE OF THINGS, and from being distrustful of my words. Wherefore, *I say,* there is space INTANGIBLE, EMPTY, and VACANT. If this were not the case, things could by no means be moved; for that which is the quality of body, *namely,* to obstruct and to oppose, would be present *at all times, and would be exerted* against all *bodies;* nothing, therefore, would be able to move forward, since nothing would begin to give way. But now, throughout the sea and land and heights of heaven, we see many things moved before our eyes in various ways *and* by various means, which, if there were no void, would not so much want *their* active motion, *as being* deprived *of it,* as they would, *properly speaking,* never by any means have been produced at all; since matter, crowded together on all sides, would have remained at rest, *and have been unable to act. . . .*

As it is, therefore, all nature of itself has consisted, *and consists,* of two parts; for there are bodily substances, and vacant *space,* in which these *substances* are situate, and in which they are moved in different directions. For the common perception *of all men* shows that there is corporeal consistence; of *the existence of* which, unless the belief shall be first firmly established, there will be no *principle* by reference to which we may succeed, by any means whatever, in settling the mind with argument concerning matters not obvious to sense.

To proceed then, if there were no place, and *no* space which we call vacant, bodies could not be situated any where, nor could at all move any whither in different directions; a fact which we have shown to you a little before.

Besides, there is nothing which you can say is separate from all bodily substance, and distinct from empty space; which would, indeed, be as it were a third kind of nature. For whatsoever shall exist, must *in* itself be something, either of large bulk, or ever so diminutive, provided it be at all; when, if it shall be *sensible to* the touch, however light and delicate, it will increase the number of bodies, and be ranked in the multitude of them; but if it shall be intangible, inasmuch as it cannot hinder in any part any object proceeding to pass through it, it *then,* you may be sure, will be the empty space which we call a vacuum.

Moreover, whatsoever shall exist of itself, will either *do* something, or will be obliged TO SUFFER other things acting upon it, or will *simply be,* so that other things may exist and be done in it. But nothing can DO or SUFFER without *being possessed of* bodily substance, nor, moreover, afford place *for acting and suffering,* unless *it be* empty and vacant space. No third nature, therefore, *distinct* in itself, besides vacant space and material substance, can possibly be left *undiscovered* in the sum of things; no *third kind of being,* which can at any time fall under *the notice of* our senses, or which any one can find out by the exercise of his reason. . . .

In the first place, since a two-fold nature of two things, *a two-fold nature, or rather two natures* extremely dissimilar,

has been found to exist, *namely,* matter, and space in which every thing is done, it must necessarily be that each exists by itself for itself, *independently of the other,* and pure *from admixture;* for wheresoever there is empty space, which we call a vacuum, there is no matter, *and,* likewise, wheresoever matter maintains itself, there by no means exists empty space. Original substances are therefore solid and without vacuity.

Furthermore, since in things which are produced, *or compounded of matter,* there is *found* empty space, solid matter must exist around it; nor can any thing be proved by just argument to conceal vacuity, and to contain *it* within its body, unless you admit that that which contains *it* is a solid. But that *solid* can be nothing but a combination of matter, *such* as may have the power of keeping a vacuity enclosed. *That* matter, therefore, which consists of solid body, may be eternal, while other *substances, which are only compounds of this matter,* may be dissolved.

In addition, too, if there were no space to be vacant and unoccupied, all *space* would be solid. On the other hand, unless there were certain bodies to fill up completely the *places* which they occupy, all space, which *any where* exists, would be an empty void. Body, therefore, is evidently distinct from empty space, *though each has its place* alternately; since *all space* neither exists entirely full, nor, again, *entirely* empty. There exist, therefore, certain bodies which can *completely fill the places which they occupy,* and distinguish empty space from full.

These bodies, *which thus completely fill space,* can neither be broken in pieces *by* being struck with blows externally, nor, again, can be decomposed *by* being penetrated internally; nor can they be made to yield *if* attempted by any other method; a *principle* which we have demonstrated to you a little above; for neither does it seem possible for any thing to be dashed in pieces without a vacuum, nor to be broken, nor to be divided into two by cutting; nor to admit moisture, nor, moreover, subtle cold, nor penetrating fire, by which *operations and means* all things *compounded* are dissolved. And the more any thing contains empty space within it, the more it yields when thoroughly tried by these means. If, therefore, the primary atoms are solid and without void, they must of necessity be eternal.

Again, unless there had been eternal matter, all things, before this time, would have been utterly reduced to nothing; and whatsoever *objects* we behold would have been reproduced from nothing. But since I have shown above, that nothing can be produced from nothing, and that that which has been produced *cannot* be resolved into nothing, the primary elements must be of an imperishable substance, into which *primary elements* every body may be dissolved, so that matter may be supplied for the reproduction of things. The primordial elements, therefore, are of pure solidity; nor could they otherwise, preserved, *as they have been,* for ages, repair things, *as they have done,* through *that* infinite space of time *which has elapsed since the commencement of this material system.* . . .

But since I have taught that atoms of matter, entirely solid, pass to-and-fro perpetually, unwasted through *all* time; come now, *and* let us unravel whether there be any limit to their aggregate, or

not; also, let us look into that which has been found *to be* vacancy, or the room and space in which things severally are done, *and learn* whether the whole is entirely limited, or extends unbounded and unfathomably profound.

All that exists, therefore, *I affirm,* is bounded in no direction; for, *if it were bounded,* it must have some extremity; but it appears that there cannot be an extremity of any thing, unless there be something beyond, which may limit it; so that there may appear *to be some line* farther than which this faculty of our sense (*i. e. our vision*) cannot extend. Now, since it must be confessed that there is nothing beyond the WHOLE, *the whole* has no extremity; nor does it matter at what part of it you stand, *with a view to being distant from its boundary;* inasmuch as, whatever place any one occupies, he leaves the WHOLE just as much boundless in every direction. . . .

Besides, Nature herself prevents the WHOLE OF THINGS from being able to provide bounds for itself, inasmuch as she compels body to be bounded by *that which is* vacuum, and that which is vacuum to be bounded by body; that so, by *this* alternate *bounding of one by the other,* she may render ALL infinite. Else, moreover, if one or other of these did not bound the other by its simple nature, so that *one of them, the vacuum for instance,* should extend unlimited, neither the sea, nor the land, nor the bright temples of heaven, nor the race of mortals, nor the sacred persons of the gods, could subsist for the small space of an hour. For the body of matter, driven abroad from its union, would be borne dispersed through the mighty void, or rather, in such a case, never having been united, would *never* have produced any thing, since, when *originally* scattered, it could not have been brought together.

For certainly neither the primary elements of things disposed themselves severally in their own order, by *their own counsel or* sagacious understanding; nor, assuredly, did they agree among themselves what motions each should produce; but because, being many, and changed in many ways, they are for an infinite *space of time* agitated, being acted upon by forces, throughout the WHOLE, *they thus,* by experiencing movements and combinations of every kind, at length settle into such positions, by which means (*i.e. positions*) this SUM *of things,* being produced, exists. And *this sum of things,* when it was once thrown into suitable motions, being also maintained *in that state* through many long years, causes that the rivers recruit the greedy sea with large floods of water, and that the earth, cherished by the heat of the sun, renews *its* productions; also that the race of living creatures flourishes undecayed, and that the gliding fires of heaven live. Which *effects atoms* could by no means produce, unless an abundant supply of matter could arise from the infinite *of space,* whence every thing *that is produced* is accustomed to repair in time the parts lost. . . .

These things if you shall understand, led on by *my* humble effort (for one *proposition* will appear plain from another), dark night will not prevent your progress, *or hinder you* from seeing clearly into the last *depths* of nature; so *effectually* will truths kindle light for truths.

And since I have shown of what kind the primordial atoms of all things are, and how, differing in *their* various forms,

and actuated by motion from all eternity, they fly *through the void of space* of their own accord; and *since I have also demonstrated* by what means all individual things may be produced from them; the nature of the MIND and of the SOUL now seems, next to these subjects, *proper* to be illustrated in my verses. . . .

I now affirm that the mind and soul are held united with one another, and form of themselves one nature *or substance;* but that *that which* is as it were the head, and *which* rules in the whole body, is the reason, *the thinking or intellectual part* which we call mind and understanding; and this remains seated in the middle portion of· the breast. For here dread and terror throb; around these parts joys soothe; here therefore is the understanding and mind. The other part of the soul, *or vital power,* distributed through the whole body, obeys, and is moved according to the will and impulse of the mind. And *this rational or intellectual part* thinks of itself alone, and rejoices for itself, *at times* when nothing *of the kind* moves either *the rest of* the soul or the body. And as when the head or the eye, when pain affects it, is troubled in us, *and as part of us, but* we are not afflicted throughout the whole body, so the mind is sometimes grieved itself *alone,* and is *sometimes* excited with joy, when the other part of the soul, *diffused* through the limbs and joints, is stimulated by no new sensation. But when the mind is more *than ordinarily* shaken by violent terror, we see the whole soul, throughout the *several* members, sympathize with it, and perspirations and paleness, in consequence, arise over the whole body, and the tongue rendered powerless and the voice die away; *while we find* the eyes darkened, the ears ringing, *and* the limbs sinking underneath.

Furthermore, we often see men faint *altogether* from terror of mind; *so* that any one may easily understand from this, that with the mind is united the soul, which, when it has been acted upon by the power of the mind, then influences and affects the body.

This same *course of* reasoning teaches us that the nature *or substance* of the mind and soul is corporeal; for when *this nature or substance* is seen to impel the limbs, to rouse the body from sleep, and to change the countenance, and to guide and turn about the whole man;— of which *effects* we see that none can be produced without touch, and that touch, moreover, *can*not *take place* without body;—must we not admit that the mind and soul are of a corporeal nature?

Besides, you see that the mind suffers with the body, and sympathizes for us with the body. *Thus,* if the violent force of a dart, driven into *the body,* the bones and nerves being divided, does not hurt the life *itself,* yet there follows a languor, and a kind of agreeable inclination-to-sink to the ground, and *when we are* on the ground, a perturbation *and giddiness* which is produced in the mind, and sometimes, as it were, an irresolute desire to rise. It therefore necessarily follows that the nature of the mind is corporeal, since it is made to suffer by corporeal weapons and violence. . . .

And now attend. That thou mayest understand that living creatures have minds, and subtle souls, BORN and PERISHABLE, I will proceed to arrange verses worthy of thy life *and virtues, verses* collected during a long time, and prepared with sweet labor. *And* thou, *my friend,* take care to include both of them under one name, *whichsoever of the two I may use;* and, for example, when I proceed to speak of the soul, teaching that it is mortal, suppose that I also speak of the mind; inasmuch as they are one by mutual *combination,* and their substance is united.

In the first place, since I have shown that the *soul, being* subtle, consists of minute particles, and is composed of much smaller atoms than the clear fluid of water, or mist, or smoke; (for it far surpasses *those bodies* in susceptibility-of-motion, and is more readily impelled when acted upon from a slight cause; inasmuch as *both the mind and soul* are moved by the *mere* images of smoke and mist; as when, lulled in sleep, we see high altars exhale with vapor, and carry up smoke; since doubtless these phantasms are produced in us;) now, therefore, *I say,* since, when vessels are broken to pieces, you see water flow about, and *any other* liquid run away; and since, *also,* mist and smoke disperse into the air; *you must* conclude that the soul is likewise scattered abroad, and is dissipated much sooner *than mist and smoke,* and more easily resolved into *its* original elements, when it *has* once *been* withdrawn from the body of a man, *and* has taken its departure. . . .

Death, therefore, is nothing, nor at all concerns us, since the nature *or substance* of the soul is *to be* accounted mortal. And as, in past time, we felt no anxiety, when the Carthaginians gathered on all sides to fight *with our forefathers, and* when all things under the lofty air of heaven, shaken with the dismaying tumult of war, trembled with dread; and *men* were uncertain to the sway of which *power* every thing human, by land and by sea, was to fall; so, when we shall cease to be, when there shall be a separation of the body and soul of which we are conjointly composed, it is certain that to us, who shall not then exist, nothing will by any possibility happen, or excite our feeling, not even if the earth shall be mingled with the sea, and the sea with the heaven.

2 The Method of Science
Sir Francis Bacon (1561-1626)

The close affinity between naturalism and science has already been noted, and in fact there are signs of this relation in Lucretius. But the rise of modern science in the seventeenth century makes this affinity clearer and more important.

Sir Francis Bacon is often referred to as the prophet of modern science. No scientist himself, he nevertheless expressed with vigor and clarity the basic impulse of the new methodology. For Bacon, knowledge, when properly conceived, is power. But in the past, knowledge has been improperly conceived. Human reason, left to itself and unchecked, is prone to a variety of errors. What is needed is a method that will provide such checks; and these Bacon finds in scientific induction and experiment.

1. Man, as the minister and interpreter of nature, does and understands as much as his observations on the order of nature, either with regard to things or the mind, permit him, and neither knows nor is capable of more.

2. The unassisted hand and the understanding left to itself possess but little power. Effects are produced by the means of instruments and helps, which the understanding requires no less than the hand; and as instruments either promote or regulate the motion of the hand, so those that are applied to the mind prompt or protect the understanding.

The selection is from Book I of Bacon's *Novum Organon* (New York: The Colonial Press, 1900).

3. Knowledge and human power are synonymous, since the ignorance of the cause frustrates the effect; for nature is only subdued by submission, and that which in contemplative philosophy corresponds with the cause in practical science becomes the rule.

19. There are and can exist but two ways of investigating and discovering truth. The one hurries on rapidly from the senses and particulars to the most general axioms, and from them, as principles and their supposed indisputable truth, derives and discovers the intermediate axioms. This is the way now in use. The other constructs its axioms from the senses and particulars, by ascending continually and gradually, till it finally arrives at the most general

axioms, which is the true but unattempted way.

26. We are wont, for the sake of distinction, to call that human reasoning which we apply to nature the anticipation of nature (as being rash and premature), and that which is properly deduced from things the interpretation of nature.

36. We have but one simple method of delivering our sentiments, namely, we must bring men to particulars and their regular series and order, and they must for a while renounce their notions, and begin to form an acquaintance with things.

37. Our method and that of the skeptics agree in some respects at first setting out, but differ most widely, and are completely opposed to each other in their conclusion; for they roundly assert that nothing can be known; we, that but a small part of nature can be known, by the present method; their next step, however, is to destroy the authority of the senses and understanding, whilst we invent and supply them with assistance.

38. The idols and false notions which have already preoccupied the human understanding, and are deeply rooted in it, not only so beset men's minds that they become difficult of access, but even when access is obtained will again meet and trouble us in the instauration of the sciences, unless mankind when forewarned guard themselves with all possible care against them.

39. Four species of idols beset the human mind, to which (for distinction's sake) we have assigned names, calling the first Idols of the Tribe, the second Idols of the Den, the third Idols of the Market, the fourth Idols of the Theatre.

40. The formation of notions and axioms on the foundation of true induction is the only fitting remedy by which we can ward off and expel these idols. It is, however, of great service to point them out; for the doctrine of idols bears the same relation to the interpretation of nature as that of the confutation of sophisms does to common logic.

41. The idols of the tribe are inherent in human nature and the very tribe or race of man; for man's sense is falsely asserted to be the standard of things; on the contrary, all the perceptions both of the senses and the mind bear reference to man and not to the universe, and the human mind resembles those uneven mirrors which impart their own properties to different objects, from which rays are emitted and distort and disfigure them.

42. The idols of the den are those of each individual; for everybody (in addition to the errors common to the race of man) has his own individual den or cavern, which intercepts and corrupts the light of nature, either from his own peculiar and singular disposition, or from his education and intercourse with others, or from his reading, and the authority acquired by those whom he reverences and admires, or from the different impressions produced on the mind, as it happens to be preoccupied and predisposed, or equable and tranquil, and the like; so that the spirit of man (according to its several dispositions) is variable, confused, and, as it were, actuated by chance; and Heraclitus said well that men search for knowledge in lesser worlds, and not in the greater or common world.

43. There are also idols formed by the reciprocal intercourse and society of

man with man, which we call idols of the market, from the commerce and association of men with each other; for men converse by means of language, but words are formed at the will of the generality, and there arises from a bad and unapt formation of words a wonderful obstruction to the mind. Nor can the definitions and explanations with which learned men are wont to guard and protect themselves in some instances afford a complete remedy—words still manifestly force the understanding, throw everything into confusion, and lead mankind into vain and innumerable controversies and fallacies.

44. Lastly, There are idols which have crept into men's minds from the various dogmas of peculiar systems of philosophy, and also from the perverted rules of demonstration, and these we denominate idols of the theatre: for we regard all the systems of philosophy hitherto received or imagined, as so many plays brought out and performed, creating fictitious and theatrical worlds. Nor do we speak only of the present systems, or of the philosophy and sects of the ancients, since numerous other plays of a similar nature can be still composed and made to agree with each other, the causes of the most opposite errors being generally the same. Nor, again, do we allude merely to general systems, but also to many elements and axioms of sciences which have become inveterate by tradition, implicit credence, and neglect. We must, however, discuss each species of idols more fully and distinctly in order to guard the human understanding against them.

45. The human understanding, from its peculiar nature, easily supposes a greater degree of order and equality in things than it really finds; and although many things in nature be sui generis and most irregular, will yet invent parallels and conjugates and relatives, where no such thing is. Hence the fiction, that all celestial bodies move in perfect circles, thus rejecting entirely spiral and serpentine lines (except as explanatory terms). Hence also the element of fire is introduced with its peculiar orbit, to keep square with those other three which are objects of our senses. The relative rarity of the elements (as they are called) is arbitrarily made to vary in tenfold progression, with many other dreams of the like nature. Nor is this folly confined to theories, but it is to be met with even in simple notions.

46. The human understanding, when any proposition has been once laid down (either from general admission and belief, or from the pleasure it affords), forces everything else to add fresh support and confirmation; and although most cogent and abundant instances may exist to the contrary, yet either does not observe or despises them, or gets rid of and rejects them by some distinction, with violent and injurious prejudice, rather than sacrifice the authority of its first conclusions. It was well answered by him[1] who has shown in a temple the votive tablets suspended by such as had escaped to peril of shipwreck, and was pressed as to whether he would then recognize the power of the gods, by an inquiry. But where are the portraits of those who have perished in

[1 The reference is to Diagoras of Melos, surnamed the Atheist, who flourished in the Fifth Century B.C. Although religious in his youth, he is said to have become an atheist because a great wrong done to him was left unpunished by the gods. *Ed.*]

spite of their vows? All superstition is much the same, whether it be that of astrology, dreams, omens, retributive judgment, or the like, in all of which the deluded believers observe events which are fulfilled, but neglect and pass over their failure, though it be much more common. But this evil insinuates itself still more craftily in philosophy and the sciences, in which a settled maxim vitiates and governs every other circumstance, though the latter be much more worthy of confidence. Besides, even in the absence of that eagerness and want of thought (which we have mentioned), it is the peculiar and perpetual error of the human understanding to be more moved and excited by affirmatives than negatives, whereas it ought duly and regularly to be impartial; nay, in establishing any true axiom the negative instance is the most powerful.

48. The human understanding is active and cannot halt or rest, but even, though without effect, still presses forward. Thus we cannot conceive of any end or external boundary of the world, and it seems necessarily to occur to us that there must be something beyond. Nor can we imagine how eternity has flowed on down to the present day, since the usually received distinction of an infinity, a parte ante and a parte post cannot hold good; for it would thence follow that one infinity is greater than another, and also that infinity is wasting away and tending to an end. There is the same difficulty in considering the infinite divisibility of lines arising from the weakness of our minds, which weakness interferes to still greater disadvantage with the discovery of causes; for although the greatest generalities in nature must be positive, just as they are

found, and in fact not causable, yet the human understanding, incapable of resting, seeks for something more intelligible. Thus, however, whilst aiming at further progress, it falls back to what is actually less advanced, namely, final causes; for they are clearly more allied to man's own nature, than the system of the universe, and from this source they have wonderfully corrupted philosophy. But he would be an unskilful and shallow philosopher who should seek for causes in the greatest generalities, and not be anxious to discover them in subordinate objects.

49. The human understanding resembles not a dry light, but admits a tincture of the will and passions, which generate their own system accordingly; for man always believes more readily that which he prefers. He, therefore, rejects difficulties for want of patience in investigation; sobriety, because it limits his hope; the depths of nature, from superstition; the light of experiment, from arrogance and pride, lest his mind should appear to be occupied with common and varying objects; paradoxes, from a fear of the opinion of the vulgar; in short, his feelings imbue and corrupt his understanding in innumerable and sometimes imperceptible ways.

50. But by far the greatest impediment and aberration of the human understanding proceeds from the dullness, incompetency, and errors of the senses; since whatever strikes the senses preponderates over everything, however superior, which does not immediately strike them. Hence contemplation mostly ceases with sight, and a very scanty, or perhaps no regard is paid to invisible objects. The entire operation, therefore, of spirits enclosed in tangible bodies is

concealed, and escapes us. All that more delicate change of formation in the parts of coarser substances (vulgarly called alteration, but in fact a change of position in the smallest particles) is equally unknown; and yet, unless the two matters we have mentioned be explored and brought to light, no great effect can be produced in nature. Again, the very nature of common air, and all bodies of less density (of which there are many) is almost unknown; for the senses are weak and erring, nor can instruments be of great use in extending their sphere or acuteness—all the better interpretations of nature are worked out by instances, and fit and apt experiments, where the senses only judge of the experiment, the experiment of nature and the thing itself.

51. The human understanding is, by its own nature, prone to abstraction, and supposes that which is fluctuating to be fixed. But it is better to dissect than abstract nature; such was the method employed by the school of Democritus, which made greater progress in penetrating nature than the rest. It is best to consider matter, its conformation, and the changes of that conformation, its own action, and the law of this action or motion; for forms are a mere fiction of the human mind, unless you will call the laws of action by that name.

52. Such are the idols of the tribe, which arise either from the uniformity of the constitution of man's spirit, or its prejudices, or its limited faculties or restless agitation, or from the interference of the passions, or the incompetency of the senses, or the mode of their impressions.

53. The idols of the den derive their origin from the peculiar nature of each individual's mind and body, and also from education, habit, and accident; and although they be various and manifold, yet we will treat of some that require the greatest caution, and exert the greatest power in polluting the understanding.

55. The greatest and, perhaps, radical distinction between different men's dispositions for philosophy and the sciences is this, that some are more vigorous and active in observing the differences of things, others in observing their resemblances; for a steady and acute disposition can fix its thoughts, and dwell upon and adhere to a point, through all the refinements of differences, but those that are sublime and discursive recognize and compare even the most delicate and general resemblances; each of them readily falls into excess, by catching either at nice distinctions or shadows of resemblance.

56. Some dispositions evince an unbounded admiration of antiquity, others eagerly embrace novelty, and but few can preserve the just medium, so as neither to tear up what the ancients have correctly laid down, nor to despise the just innovations of the moderns. But this is very prejudicial to the sciences and philosophy, and instead of a correct judgment we have but the factions of the ancients and moderns. Truth is not to be sought in the good fortune of any particular conjecture of time, which is uncertain, but in the light of nature and experience, which is eternal. Such factions, therefore, are to be abjured, and the understanding must not allow them to hurry it on to assent.

58. Let such, therefore, be our precautions in contemplation, that we may ward off and expel the idols of the den, which mostly owe their birth either to some predominant pursuit, or, secondly,

to an excess in synthesis and analysis, or, thirdly, to a party zeal in favor of certain ages, or, fourthly, to the extent of narrowness of the subject. In general, he who contemplates nature should suspect whatever particularly takes and fixes his understanding, and should use so much the more caution to preserve it equable and unprejudiced.

59. The idols of the market are the most troublesome of all, those namely which have entwined themselves round the understanding from the associations of words and names. For men imagine that their reason governs words, whilst, in fact, words react upon the understanding; and this has rendered philosophy and the sciences sophistical and inactive. Words are generally formed in a popular sense, and define things by those broad lines which are most obvious to the vulgar mind; but when a more acute understanding, or more diligent observation is anxious to vary those lines, and to adapt them more accurately to nature, words oppose it. Hence the great and solemn disputes of learned men often terminate in controversies about words and names, in regard to which would be better (imitating the caution of mathematicians) to proceed more advisedly in the first instance, and to bring such disputes to a regular issue by definitions. Such definitions, however, cannot remedy the evil in natural and material objects, because they consist themselves of words, and these words produce others; so that we must necessarily have recourse to particular instances, and their regular series and arrangement, as we shall mention when we come to the mode and scheme of determining notions and axioms.

62. The idols of the theatre, or of theories, are numerous, and may, and perhaps will, be still more so. For unless men's minds had been now occupied for many ages in religious and theological considerations, and civil governments (especially monarchies), had been averse to novelties of that nature even in theory (so that men must apply to them with some risk and injury to their own fortunes, and not only without reward, but subject to contumely and envy), there is no doubt that many other sects of philosophers and theorists would have been introduced, like those which formerly flourished in such diversified abundance amongst the Greeks. For as many imaginary theories of the heavens can be deduced from the phenomena of the sky, so it is even more easy to found many dogmas upon the phenomena of philosophy—and the plot of this our theatre resembles those of the poetical, where the plots which are invented for the stage are more consistent, elegant, and pleasurable than those taken from real history.

In general, men take for the groundwork of their philosophy either too much from a few topics, or too little from many; in either case their philosophy is founded on too narrow a basis of experiment and natural history, and decided on too scanty grounds. For the theoretic philosopher seizes various common circumstances by experiment, without reducing them to certainty or examining and frequently considering them, and relies for the rest upon meditation and the activity of his wit.

There are other philosophers who have diligently and accurately attended to a few experiments, and have thence presumed to deduce and invent systems of philosophy, forming everything to conformity with them.

A third set, from their faith and religious veneration, introduce theology and traditions; the absurdity of some among them having proceeded so far as to seek and derive the sciences from spirits and genii. There are, therefore, three sources of error and three species of false philosophy; the sophistic, empiric, and superstitious.

95. Those who have treated of the sciences have been either empirics or dogmatical. The former like ants only heap up and use their store, the latter like spiders spin out their own webs. The bee, a mean between both, extracts matter from the flowers of the garden and the field, but works and fashions it by its own efforts. The true labor of philosophy resembles hers, for it neither relies entirely nor principally on the powers of the mind, nor yet lays up in the memory the matter afforded by the experiments of natural history and mechanics in its raw state, but changes and works it in the understanding. We have good reason, therefore, to derive hope from a closer and purer alliance of these faculties (the experimental and rational) than has yet been attempted.

99. Again, even in the abundance of mechanical experiments, there is a very great scarcity of those which best inform and assist the understanding. For the mechanic, little solicitous about the investigation of truth, neither directs his attention, nor applies his hand to anything that is not of service to his business. But our hope of further progress in the sciences will then only be well founded, when numerous experiments shall be received and collected into natural history, which, though of no use in themselves, assist materially in the dis-

covery of causes and axioms; which experiments we have termed enlightening, to distinguish them from those which are profitable. They possess this wonderful property and nature, that they never deceive or fail you; for being used only to discover the natural cause of some object, whatever be the result, they equally satisfy your aim by deciding the question.

104. Nor can we suffer the understanding to jump and fly from particulars to remote and most general axioms (such as are termed the principles of arts and things), and thus prove and make out their intermediate axioms according to the supposed unshaken truth of the former. This, however, has always been done to the present time from the natural bent of the understanding, educated too, and accustomed to this very method, by the syllogistic mode of demonstration. But we can then only augur well for the sciences, when the ascent shall proceed by a true scale, and successive steps, without interruption or breach, from particulars to the lesser axioms, thence to the intermediate (rising one above the other), and lastly, to the most general. For the lowest axioms differ but little from bare experiments; the highest and most general (as they are esteemed at present), are notional, abstract, and of no real weight. The intermediate are true, solid, full of life, and upon them depend the business and fortune of mankind; beyond these are the really general, but not abstract, axioms, which are truly limited by the intermediate.

We must not then add wings, but rather lead and ballast to the understanding, to prevent its jumping or flying, which has not yet been done; but whenever this takes place, we may entertain greater hopes of the sciences.

105. In forming axioms, we must invent a different form of induction from that hitherto in use; not only for the proof and discovery of principles (as they are called), but also of minor, intermediate, and, in short, every kind of axioms. The induction which proceeds by simple enumeration is puerile, leads to uncertain conclusions, and is exposed to danger from one contradictory instance, deciding generally from too small a number of facts, and those only the most obvious. But a really useful induction for the discovery and demonstration of the arts and sciences, should separate nature by proper rejections and exclusions, and then conclude for the affirmative, after collecting a sufficient number of negatives. Now this has not been done, nor even attempted, except perhaps by Plato, who certainly uses this form of induction in some measure, to sift definitions and ideas. But much of what has never yet entered the thoughts of man must necessarily be employed, in order to exhibit a good and legitimate mode of induction or demonstration, so as even to render it essential for us to bestow more pains upon it than have hitherto been bestowed on syllogisms. The assistance of induction is to serve us not only in the discovery of axioms, but also in defining our notions. Much indeed is to be hoped from such an induction as has been described.

EPISTEMOLOGY

Materialism not only is interested in historical interpretations of science such as that of Bacon, but it continues both to be concerned with the philosophy of science and to base itself upon scientific method. It is not surprising, therefore, that in his epistemology the materialist proposes that science is man's only sure path to knowledge. A more recent statement of this position is given in the following selection by the American thinker Charles Sanders Peirce. His interpretation of science is pragmatic, in that he believes that thinking always begins in doubt or felt tensions and aims at consequences that will remove such doubt. Pragmatism means for him that the conceived consequences involved in an idea constitute the meaning of the idea.

Peirce characterizes doubt as a state of irritation that we seek to overcome; and he calls the process of removing doubt and establishing belief "inquiry." Three methods, followed by the great majority of mankind, produce sure belief but not necessarily true belief. He calls them the method of tenacity, of authority, and the a priori method. Only a fourth, the scientific method, presents any distinction of a right and a wrong way, according to Peirce, and thus allows for true as well as sure belief. Science accomplishes this because, unlike the other methods, it involves a new conception—namely, that of Reality.

In another place, Peirce shows how this new concept of Reality is related to truth. The great hope of all thinking, he says, is that what are initially divergent views held by different investigators will in the process of inquiry tend toward one and the same conclusion. Then "the opinion which is fated to be ultimately agreed to by all who investigate, is what we mean by truth, and the object represented in this opinion is the real."

Although his influence on materialism has been great, Peirce was not himself a materialist. In fact, he admired in some ways absolute idealism, believing that although the logic of idealists is bad, their conclusions are essentially right. Yet it is Peirce's work in logic and the philosophy of science rather than in metaphysics that has had the predominant influence.

3 Inquiry and Belief
C. S. Peirce (1839-1914)

Few persons care to study logic, because everybody conceives himself to be proficient enough in the art of reasoning already. But I observe that this satisfaction is limited to one's own ratiocination, and does not extend to that of other men.

We come to the full possession of our power of drawing inferences the last of all our faculties, for it is not so much a natural gift as a long and difficult art. The history of its practice would make a grand subject for a book. The medieval schoolmen, following the Romans, made logic the earliest of a boy's studies after grammar, as being very easy. So it was, as they understood it. Its fundamental principle, according to them, was, that all knowledge rests on either authority or reason; but that whatever is deduced by reason depends ultimately on a premise derived from authority. Accordingly, as soon as a boy was perfect in the syllogistic procedure, his intellectual kit of tools was held to be complete.

To Roger Bacon, that remarkable mind who in the middle of the thirteenth century was almost a scientific man, the schoolmen's conception of reasoning appeared only an obstacle to truth. He saw that experience alone teaches anything —a proposition which to us seems easy to understand, because a distinct conception of experience has been handed down to us from former generations; which to him also seemed perfectly clear, because its difficulties had not yet unfolded themselves. Of all kinds of experience, the best, he thought, was interior illumination, which teaches many things about Nature which the external senses could never discover, such as the transubstantiation of bread.

Four centuries later, the more celebrated Bacon, in the first book of his "Novum Organum," gave his clear account of experience as something which must be opened to verification and re-examination. But, superior as Lord Bacon's conception is to earlier notions, a modern reader who is not in awe of his grandiloquence is chiefly struck by the inadequacy of his view of scientific pro-

The selection is from Pierce's article, "The Fixation of Belief," *The Popular Science Monthly*, 12 (1877–1878), pp. 1–15, with omissions.

cedure. That we have only to make some crude experiments, to draw up briefs of the results in certain blank forms, to go through these by rule, checking off everything disproved and setting down the alternatives, and that thus in a few years physical science would be finished up—what an idea! "He wrote on science like a Lord Chancellor," indeed.

The early scientists, Copernicus, Tycho Brahe, Kepler, Galileo and Gilbert, had methods more like those of their modern brethren. Kepler undertook to draw a curve through the places of Mars; and his greatest service to science was in impressing on men's minds that this was the thing to be done if they wished to improve astronomy; that they were not to content themselves with inquiring whether one system of epicycles was better than another but that they were to sit down by the figures and find out what the curve, in truth, was. He accomplished this by his incomparable energy and courage, blundering along in the most inconceivable way (to us), from one irrational hypothesis to another, until, after trying twenty-one of these, he fell, by the mere exhaustion of his invention, upon the orbit which a mind well furnished with the weapons of modern logic would have tried almost at the outset.

In the same way, every work of science great enough to be remembered for a few generations affords some exemplification of the defective state of the art of reasoning of the time when it was written; and each chief step in science has been a lesson in logic. It was so when Lavoisier and his contemporaries took up the study of Chemistry. The old chemist's maxim had been, "Lege, lege,

lege, labora, ora, et relege." Lavoisier's method was not to read and pray, not to dream that some long and complicated chemical process would have a certain effect, to put it into practice with dull patience, after its inevitable failure, to dream that with some modification it would have another result, and to end by publishing the last dream as a fact: his way was to carry his mind into his laboratory, and to make of his alembics and cucurbits instruments of thought, giving a new conception of reasoning as something which was to be done with one's eyes open, by manipulating real things instead of word and fancies. . . .

The object of reasoning is to find out, from the consideration of what we already know, something else which we do not know. Consequently, reasoning is good if it be such as to give a true conclusion from true premises, and not otherwise. Thus, the question of validity is purely one of fact and not of thinking. A being the premises and B being the conclusion, the question is, whether these facts are really so related that if A is B is. If so, the inference is valid; if not, not. It is not in the least the question whether, when the premises are accepted by the mind, we feel an impulse to accept the conclusion also. It is true that we do generally reason correctly by nature. But that is an accident; the true conclusion would remain true if we had no impulse to accept it; and the false one would remain false, though we could not resist the tendency to believe in it. . . .

That which determines us, from given premises, to draw one inference rather than another, is some habit of mind, whether it be constitutional or acquired. The habit is good or otherwise, according as it produces true conclusions from true premises or not; and an inference is regarded as valid or not, without reference to the truth or falsity of its conclusion specially, but according as the habit which determines it is such as to produce true conclusions in general or not. The particular habit of mind which governs this or that inference may be formulated in a proposition whose truth depends on the validity of the inferences which the habit determines; and such a formula is called a *guiding principle* of inference. Suppose, for example, that we observe that a rotating disk of copper quickly comes to rest when placed between the poles of a magnet, and we infer that this will happen with every disk of copper. The guiding principle is, that what is true of one piece of copper is true of another. Such a guiding principle with regard to copper would be much safer than with regard to many other substances— brass, for example. . . .

We generally know when we wish to ask a question and when we wish to pronounce a judgment, for there is a dissimilarity between the sensation of doubting and that of believing.

But this is not all which distinguishes doubt from belief. There is a practical difference. Our beliefs guide our desires and shape our actions. The Assassins, or followers of the Old Man of the Mountain, used to rush into death at his least command, because they believed that obedience to him would insure everlasting felicity. Had they doubted this, they would not have acted as they did. So it is with every belief, according to its degree. The feeling of believing is a more or less sure indication of there being established in our nature some habit which

will determine our actions. Doubt never has such an effect.

Nor must we overlook a third point of difference. Doubt is an uneasy and dissatisfied state from which we struggle to free ourselves and pass into the state of belief; while the latter is a calm and satisfactory state which we do not wish to avoid, or to change to a belief in anything else. On the contrary, we cling tenaciously, not merely to believing, but to believing just what we do believe.

Thus, both doubt and belief have positive effects upon us, though very different ones. Belief does not make us act at once, but puts us into such a condition that we shall behave in a certain way, when the occasion arises. Doubt has not the least effect of this sort, but stimulates us to action until it is destroyed. This reminds us of the irritation of a nerve and the reflex action produced thereby; while for the analogue of belief, in the nervous system, we must look to what are called nervous associations—for example, to that habit of the nerves in consequence of which the smell of a peach will make the mouth water.

The irritation of doubt causes a struggle to attain a state of belief. I shall term this struggle *inquiry,* though it must be admitted that this is sometimes not a very apt designation.

The irritation of doubt is the only immediate motive for the struggle to attain belief. It is certainly best for us that our beliefs should be such as may truly guide our actions so as to satisfy our desires; and this reflection will make us reject any belief which does not seem to have been so formed as to insure this result. But it will only do so by creating a doubt in the place of that belief. With the doubt, therefore, the struggle begins, and with the cessation of doubt it ends. Hence, the sole object of inquiry is the settlement of opinion. We may fancy that this is not enough for us, and that we seek not merely an opinion, but a true opinion. But put this fancy to the test, and it proves groundless; for as soon as a firm belief is reached we are entirely satisfied, whether the belief be false or true. And it is clear that nothing out of the sphere of our knowledge can be our object, for nothing which does not affect the mind can be a motive for a mental effort. The most that can be maintained is, that we seek for a belief that we shall *think* to be true. But we think each one of our beliefs to be true, and, indeed, it is mere tautology to say so. . . .

If the settlement of opinion is the sole object of inquiry, and if belief is of the nature of a habit, why should we not attain the desired end, by taking any answer to a question, which we may fancy, and constantly reiterating it to ourselves, dwelling on all which may conduce to that belief, and learning to turn with contempt and hatred from anything which might disturb it? The simple and direct method is really pursued by many men. I remember once being entreated not to read a certain newspaper lest it might change my opinion upon free-trade. "Lest I might be entrapped by its fallacies and misstatements," was the form of expression. "You are not," my friend said, "a special student of political economy. You might, therefore, easily be deceived by fallacious arguments upon the subject. You might, then, if you read this paper, be led to believe in protection. But you admit that free-trade is the true doctrine; and you do not wish to believe what is not true." I have often

known this system to be deliberately adopted. Still oftener, the instinctive dislike of an undecided state of mind, exaggerated into a vague dread of doubt, makes men cling spasmodically to the views they already take. The man feels that, if he only holds to his belief without wavering, it will be entirely satisfactory. Nor can it be denied that a steady and immovable faith yields great peace of mind. It may, indeed, give rise to inconveniences, as if a man should resolutely continue to believe that fire would not burn him, or that he would be eternally damned if he received his *ingesta* otherwise than through a stomach-pump. But then the man who adopts this method will not allow that its inconveniences are greater than its advantages. He will say, "I hold steadfastly to the truth and the truth is always wholesome." . . .

But this method of fixing belief, which may be called the method of tenacity, will be unable to hold its ground in practice. The social impulse is against it. The man who adopts it will find that other men think differently from him, and it will be apt to occur to him in some saner moment that their opinions are quite as good as his own, and this will shake his confidence in his belief. This conception, that another man's thought or sentiment may be equivalent to one's own, is a distinctly new step, and a highly important one. It arises from an impulse too strong in man to be suppressed, without danger of destroying the human species. Unless we make ourselves hermits, we shall necessarily influence each other's opinions; so that the problem becomes how to fix belief, not in the individual merely, but in the community.

Let the will of the state act, then, instead of that of the individual. Let an institution be created which shall have for its object to keep correct doctrines before the attention of the people, to reiterate them perpetually, and to teach them to the young; having at the same time power to prevent contrary doctrines from being taught, advocated, or expressed. Let all possible causes of a change of mind be removed from men's apprehensions. Let them be kept ignorant, lest they should learn of some reason to think otherwise than they do. Let their passions be enlisted, so that they may regard private and unusual opinions with hatred and horror. Then, let all men who reject the established belief be terrified into silence. Let the people turn out and tar-and-feather such men, or let inquisitions be made into the manner of thinking of suspected persons, and, when they are found guilty of forbidden beliefs, let them be subjected to some signal punishment. When complete agreement could not otherwise be reached, a general massacre of all who have not thought in a certain way has proved a very effective means of settling opinion in a country. If the power to do this be wanting, let a list of opinions be drawn up, to which no man of the least independence of thought can assent, and let the faithful be required to accept all these propositions, in order to segregate them as radically as possible from the influence of the rest of the world.

This method has, from the earliest times, been one of the chief means of upholding correct theological and political doctrines, and of preserving their universal or catholic character. In Rome, especially, it has been practised from the days of Numa Pompilius to those of Pius Nonus. This is the most perfect example in history; but wherever there is a priesthood—and no religion has been without one—this method has been more or less made use of. Wherever there is an aristocracy, or a guild, or any association of a class of men whose interests depend, or are supposed to depend, on certain propositions, there will be inevitably found some traces of this natural product of social feeling. Cruelties always accompany this system; and when it is consistently carried out, they become atrocities of the most horrible kind in the eyes of any rational man. Nor should this occasion surprise, for the officer of a society does not feel justified in surrendering the interests of that society for the sake of mercy, as he might his own private interests. It is natural, therefore, that sympathy and fellowship should thus produce a most ruthless power.

In judging this method of fixing belief, which may be called the method of authority, we must, in the first place, allow its immeasurable mental and moral superiority to the method of tenacity. Its success is proportionately greater; and, in fact, it has over and over again worked the most majestic results. The mere structures of stone which it has caused to be put together—in Siam, for example, in Egypt, and in Europe—have many of them a sublimity hardly more than rivalled by the greatest works of Nature. And, except the geological epochs, there are no periods of time so vast as those which are measured by some of these organized faiths. If we scrutinize the matter closely, we shall find that there has not been one of their creeds which has remained always the same; yet the change is so slow as to be imperceptible during one person's life, so that individual belief remains sensibly fixed. For the mass of mankind, then, there is perhaps no better method than this. If it is their highest impulse to be intellectual slaves, then slaves they ought to remain.

But no institution can undertake to regulate opinions upon every subject. Only the most important ones can be attended to, and on the rest men's minds must be left to the action of natural causes. This imperfection will be no source of weakness so long as men are in such a state of culture that one opinion does not influence another—that is, so long as they cannot put two and two together. But in the most priest-ridden states some individuals will be found who are raised above that condition. These men possess a wider sort of social feeling; they see that men in other countries and in other ages have held to very different doctrines from those which they themselves have been brought up to believe; and they cannot help seeing that it is the mere accident of their having been taught as they have, and of their having been surrounded with the manners and associations they have, that has caused them to believe as they do and not far differently. Nor can their candor resist the reflection that there is no reason to rate their own views at a higher value than those of other nations and other centuries; thus giving rise to doubts in their minds.

They will further perceive that such doubts as these must exist in their minds with reference to every belief which seems to be determined by the caprice either of themselves or of those who originated the popular opinions. The willful adherence to a belief, and the arbitrary forcing of it upon others, must, therefore, both be given up. A different new method of settling opinions must be adopted, that shall not only produce an impulse to believe, but shall also decide what proposition it is which is to be believed. Let the action of natural preferences be unimpeded, then, and under their influence let men, conversing together and regarding matters in different lights, gradually develop beliefs in harmony with natural causes. This method resembles that by which conceptions of art have been brought to maturity. The most perfect example of it is to be found in the history of metaphysical philosophy. Systems of this sort have not usually rested upon any observed facts, at least not in any great degree. They have been chiefly adopted because their fundamental propositions seemed "agreeable to reason." This is an apt expression; it does not mean that which agrees with experience, but that which we find ourselves inclined to believe. Plato, for example, finds it agreeable to reason that the distances of the celestial spheres from one another should be proportional to the different lengths of strings which produce harmonious chords. Many philosophers have been led to their main conclusions by considerations like this; but this is the lowest and least developed form which the method takes, for it is clear that another man might find Kepler's theory, that the celestial spheres are proportional to the inscribed and circumscribed spheres of the different regular solids, more agreeable to *his* reason. But the shock of opinions will soon lead men to rest on preferences of a far more universal nature. Take, for example, the doctrine that man only acts selfishly—that is, from the consideration that acting in one way will afford him more pleasure than acting in another. This rests on no fact in the world, but it has had a wide acceptance as being the only reasonable theory.

This method is far more intellectual and respectable from the point of view of reason than either of the others which we have noticed. But its failure has been the most manifest. It makes of inquiry something similar to the development of taste; but taste, unfortunately, is always more or less a matter of fashion, and accordingly metaphysicians have never come to any fixed agreement, but the pendulum has swung backward and forward between a more material and a more spiritual philosophy, from the earliest times to the latest. And so from this, which has been called the *a priori* method, we are driven, in Lord Bacon's phrase, to a true induction. We have examined into this *a priori* method as something which promised to deliver our opinions from their accidental and capricious element. But development, while it is a process which eliminates the effect of some casual circumstances, only magnifies that of others. This method, therefore, does not differ in a very essential way from that of authority. The government may not have lifted its finger to influence my convictions; I may have been left outwardly quite free to choose, we will say, between monogamy and polygamy, and, appealing to my conscience only, I may have concluded that the latter practice is in itself licentious. But when I come to see that the chief obstacle to the spread of Christianity among a people of as high culture as the Hindoos has been a conviction of the immorality of our way of treating women, I cannot help seeing that, though governments do not interfere, sentiments in their development will be very greatly determined by accidental causes. Now,

there are some people, among whom I must suppose that my reader is to be found, who, when they see that any belief of theirs is determined by any circumstance extraneous to the facts, will from that moment not merely admit in words that that belief is doubtful, but will experience a real doubt of it, so that it ceases in some degree to be a belief.

To satisfy our doubts, therefore, it is necessary that a method should be found by which our beliefs may be caused by nothing human, but by some external permanency—by something upon which our thinking has no effect. Some mystics imagine that they have such a method in a private inspiration from on high. But that is only a form of the method of tenacity, in which the conception of truth as something public is not yet developed. Our external permanency would not be external, in our sense, if it was restricted in its influence to one individual. It must be something which affects, or might affect, every man. And, though these affections are necessarily as various as are individual conditions, yet the method must be such that the ultimate conclusion of every man shall be the same. Such is the method of science. Its fundamental hypothesis, restated in more familiar language, is this: There are Real things, whose characters are entirely independent of our opinions about them; those realities affect our senses according to regular laws, and, though our sensations are as different as are our relations to the objects, yet, by taking advantage of the laws of perception, we can ascertain by reasoning how things really are; and any man, if he have sufficient experience and he reason enough about it, will be led to the one True conclusion. The new conception here involved is that of Reality. It may be asked how I know that there are any realities. If this hypothesis is the sole support of my method of inquiry, my method of inquiry must not be used to support my hypothesis. The reply is this: 1. If investigation cannot be regarded as proving that there are Real things, it at least does not lead to a contrary conclusion; but the method and the conception on which it is based remain ever in harmony. No doubts of the method, therefore, necessarily arise from its practice, as is the case with all the others. 2. The feeling which gives rise to any method of fixing belief is a dissatisfaction at two repugnant propositions. But here already is a vague concession that there is some *one* thing to which a proposition should conform. Nobody, therefore, can really doubt that there are realities, for, if he did, doubt would not be a source of dissatisfaction. The hypothesis, therefore, is one which every mind admits. So that the social impulse does not cause men to doubt it. 3. Everybody uses the scientific method about a great many things, and only ceases to use it when he does not know how to apply it. 4. Experience of the method has not led us to doubt it, but, on the contrary, scientific investigation has had the most wonderful triumphs in the way of settling opinion. These afford the explanation of my not doubting the method or the hypothesis which it supposes; and not having any doubt, nor believing that anybody else whom I could influence has, it would be the merest babble for me to say more about it. If there be anybody with a living doubt upon the subject, let him consider it. . . .

This is the only one of the four methods which presents any distinction of a right and a wrong way. If I adopt the method of tenacity and shut myself out from all influences, whatever I think necessary to doing this is necessary according to that method. So with the method of authority: the state may try to put down heresy by means which, from a scientific point of view, seem very ill-calculated to accomplish its purposes; but the only test *on that method* is what the state thinks, so that it cannot pursue the method wrongly. So with the *a priori* method. The very essence of it is to think as one is inclined to think. All metaphysicians will be sure to do that, however they may be inclined to judge each other to be perversely wrong. The Hegelian system recognizes every natural tendency of thought as logical, although it be certain to be abolished by counter-tendencies. Hegel thinks there is a regular system in the succession of these tendencies, in consequence of which, after drifting one way and the other for a long time, opinion will at last go right. And it is true that metaphysicians get the right ideas at last; Hegel's system of Nature represents tolerably the science of that day; and one may be sure that whatever scientific investigation has put out of doubt will presently receive *a priori* demonstration on the part of the metaphysicians. But with the scientific method the case is different. I may start with known and observed facts to proceed to the unknown; and yet the rules which I follow in doing so may not be such as investigation would approve. The test of whether I am truly following the method is not an immediate appeal to my feelings and purposes, but, on the contrary, itself involves the application of the method. Hence it is that bad reasoning as well as good reasoning is possible; and this fact is the foundation of the practical side of logic.

METAPHYSICS

Materialists differ in their metaphysical writings and outlooks, depending on whether they tend to speculativeness or caution in their generalizations about nature. The following selection from the work of the British philosopher Samuel Alexander belongs to the more speculative group, and is naturalistic in emphasis.

Alexander views nature as a cosmic process within which are critical points where new qualities emerge and where, therefore, new levels of nature develop. To sketch this view quickly: the original matrix of nature is the space-time continuum. From space-time have emerged the levels of primary qualities, secondary qualities, life, and mind. The next level of nature, not yet emerged, and whose characteristic qualities cannot therefore be described, is called deity. Alexander insists that these various levels are true emergents and he holds that there are thus limits to attempts to explain them. In the selection he illustrates his point by reference to the emergence of life from physico-chemical properties. Life, he writes, is resolvable without remainder into these properties, but life is not *merely* such. There is a new property, that of life itself, which has emerged from them. The scientist, then, must be careful not to fall into a "metaphysical mania" by asking unanswerable questions; rather, he must accept the mystery of facts in an attitude not unhappily called "natural piety."

4 Emergence and the Levels of Nature

Samuel Alexander (1859-1938)

I do not mean by natural piety exactly what Wordsworth[1] meant by it—the reverent joy in nature, by which he wished that his days might be bound to each other—though there is enough connection with his interpretation to justify me

---

The selection is from Alexander's article, "Natural Piety," *The Hibbert Journal,* 20 (1921–1922), pp. 609–621, with omissions. Used by permission of the Editor.

[1 In the fragment beginning "My heart leaps up" and ending
    The Child is Father of the man:
And I could wish my days to be
    Bound each to each by natural piety.

He also used the phrase in *The Excursion,* Bk. III, line 266:
    Such acquiescence neither doth imply
    In me, a meekly-blending spirit soothed
By natural piety; nor a lofty mind
By philosophic discipline prepared
For calm subjection to acknowledged
    law. *Ed.*]

in using his phrase. The natural piety I am going to speak of is that of the scientific investigator, by which he accepts with loyalty the mysteries which he cannot explain in nature and has no right to try to explain. I may describe it as the habit of knowing when to stop in asking questions of nature. The limits to the right of asking questions are drawn differently for different purposes. They are not the same in science as in ordinary intercourse between men in conversation. I may recall an incident in the life of Dr. Johnson.[2] I was once present, says Boswell, when a gentleman (perhaps it was Boswell himself) asked so many (questions), as "What did you do, sir?" "What did you say, sir?" that at last he grew enraged, and said, "I will not be put to the *question*. Don't you consider, sir, that these are not the manners of a gentleman? I will not be baited with *what* and *why*. What is this? What is that? Why is a cow's tail long? Why is a fox's tail bushy?" Boswell adds that the gentleman, who was a good deal out of countenance, said, "Why, sir, you are so good, that I venture to trouble you." JOHNSON. "Sir, my being so *good* is no reason why you should be so *ill*." The questions which Johnson regarded as typically offensive in conversation about the cow's and the fox's tail might quite legitimately be asked in science, and I fancy, answered by a naturalist without any particular difficulty. There is a mental disease known as the questioning or metaphysical mania, which cannot accept anything, even the most trivial, without demanding explanation. Why do I stand here where I stand? Why is a

glass a glass, a chair a chair? How is it that men are only of the size they are? Why not as big as houses? etc. (I quote from William James.[3]) Now the very life of knowledge depends on asking questions. Is it not called inquiry? And its limits are not drawn by considerations of politeness or by shrinking from insanity. But it does recognize that, however far it may push its explanations, the world presents characters which must be accepted reverently as beyond explanation, though they do not pass understanding. And I call this habit of acceptance of nature by the name of natural piety, because simple-minded religion is accustomed to speak of events for which it can find no reason as the will of God. . . .

[The features which can be] traced in human affairs; new creations which lend an unexplained and strange flavor to existing institutions and remodel them; external habits and ways of life retained but their inward meaning transformed; immense complexities of elements, hitherto chaotic, now gathering themselves together and as it were flowering into some undreamed simplicity; these features are found in the nature of which man is but the latest stage. Nature is "stratified," and if we apply to it our customary conceptions of growth and development, we can regard it as a geological formation with a history. But the comparison is still inadequate; for new geological strata are but fresh deposits laid down upon the subjacent ones, not drawing from them their new life. Nature is rather a history of organic growth of species, in which the new type

---

[2] Dr. Samuel Johnson (1709-1784), British man of letters. James Boswell (1740-1795) was Johnson's biographer. *Ed.*]

[3] William James (1842-1910), American psychologist and philosopher, and one of the founders of pragmatism. *Ed.*]

of organism is the outgrowth of the older type, and continues the earlier life into a form at once more complex and more highly simplified. As there is in the animal world or the plant world a hierarchy of forms, so in nature there is a hierarchy of qualities which are characteristics of various levels of development. There are, if I may borrow a metaphor used by Mr. Sellars of Michigan in his recent book,[4] "critical points" in the unfolding of Nature when she gathers up her old resources for a new experiment and breeds a new quality of existence. The earliest of these qualities of being which is familiar to us is that of physical matter, whatever we are to suppose it is that materiality consists in. Other well-marked levels are those of chemical structure and behavior, and life, which is the quality of things which behave physiologically.

I am not concerned to offer a complete enumeration of these levels of existence with their distinguishing qualities. The three qualities mentioned are but a selection. Every attempt at completeness raises questions of difficulty. Certain, however, it is now that mere physical materiality is a highly developed stage, late in the history of the world: that there are forms of submaterial being, and the line between the submaterial and the material is not for me to draw. Neither is it for me to say whether electrons are the lowest existences in the scale. Again, beyond life, some have maintained that mind is itself a new quality which arises out of life, while others treat consciousness merely as a function of all life, and for

them consciousness and life are one, and accordingly all the knowing on which we pride ourselves so much is in the end only a special form of vital behavior. There is another debatable question. To me, colors and sounds and tastes and all the sensible characters of material things appear to be resident in things themselves; and colored existence to be a critical point in nature. When a physical body is such that the light which it sends out to our eyes has a determinate wave-length, that body is red. To others, and they are the majority, the color depends upon the possession by the percipient of eyes. These questions I need not raise in this place because they take us away from the central theme into historic problems which have occupied physics and philosophy from the days of Galileo and before. There is still another matter I leave open. Life is without doubt such a critical point in nature. Are the various gradations of life, first of all the difference of plants and animals as a whole, and next the marked differences of kinds among animals and plants themselves, to be regarded likewise? The differences which part a humble amoeba or hydra from the monkey, or even from the lizard or crab, are vast. Are they critical differences? All I need answer is that if they are not, at least the outgrowth of the higher from the lower forms of life helps us mightily to understand the outgrowth at the critical point of the higher level of quality from the lower. Further, if it is right to treat colors as real qualities, not dependent for existence on the physiological organs; which are but instruments in that case for apprehending, not for creating them; if this is so, the different kinds of colors—red, green, and the rest—are comparable to the species of animals or

---

[4 The reference is to the American philosopher Roy Wood Sellars and his book, *Evolutionary Naturalism* (Chicago, 1922). *Ed.*]

plants, and if they do not mark a change of level they mark differences upon that level. All these matters of debate I leave aside, in order to insist on the vital feature of nature that she does exhibit critical changes of quality, which mark new syntheses, that we can but note. We may and must observe with care out of what previous conditions these new creations arise. We cannot tell why they should assume these qualities. We can but accept them as we find them, and this acceptance is natural piety.

These bodies with new qualities, these "creative syntheses," which arise at critical points from a lower level of existence, are therefore no mere mechanical resultants of their lower conditions. If they were they would have merely the quality of their antecedents or components, as the component pulls upon a body along the sides of a parallelogram are equivalent to a resultant pull along the diagonal. Even the chemical combination of sodium and sulphuric acid, though it leads to something new and its process is not purely mechanical, does but issue in a new chemical body, just as the pairing of two living beings may lead to a new variety, but still a variety of living being. They are, therefore, after the usage of the late George Henry Lewes, described as emergents by Mr. Lloyd Morgan, with whom I have for many years shared this conception of things, which he has expounded with a simplicity and lucidity beyond my powers in a chapter of his book, *Instinct and Experience,* and with particular force in the address with which he inaugurated the independent section of Psychology at the recent meeting of the British Association at Edinburgh (1921).

Without attempting to take in the whole field of nature, I will confine myself here to life, considered as an emergent from the realm of physico-chemical bodies. A living body is, according to this conception, a physico-chemical body of a certain degree and kind of complexity, whose actions may severally be viewed as physical or chemical, but taken in their integration, or entirety (to borrow a word of Lord Haldane's), have the quality of life. Life is therefore resoluble without remainder into physico-chemical processes; but it cannot be treated as *merely* physico-chemical. Certain of its functions may be referred to physical or chemical laws, but it is not these separable processes which constitute life. Life exists only when we have that particular collocation of such physico-chemical actions which we know as living. It is the special co-ordination which conditions the appearance or creation of the new quality of life. We might therefore be disposed to describe the living body indifferently as being a physico-chemical body which is *also* vital, or as being vital and *also* physico-chemical. In reality only the second designation is satisfactory. The first would imply that a certain grouping of such processes remain no more than physical and chemical, that life is not something new but a name for this integration, whereas it is a new quality conditioned by and equivalent to the particular complexity of integration. Given life, we can hope to resolve it into its physico-chemical equivalent. We can even hope to reproduce partially or wholly by artificial means the existence of life. It is well known, for instance, that certain foams or emulsions of oil have exhibited streaming movements like those of living protoplasm. But life has been already attained, and it is our clue to the invention of the necessary machinery. Given mere physical and chemical processes, we can only generate life when we have hit upon the requisite form of integration. Thus life is *also* physico-chemical, because in its separable activities it is comparable with other physico-chemical processes. But it is not *merely* physico-chemical, because merely physico-chemical processes are not alive, and they do not give us life until the requisite complexity of integrations is attained. . . .

The emergence of life with this new collocation of conditions implies that life is continuous with chemical, physical, and mechanical action. To be more explicit, the living body is also physical and chemical. It surrenders no claim to be considered a part of the physical world. But the new quality of life which it possesses is neither chemical nor mechanical, but something new. Thus the parts of the living body have color but life is not colored, and they are material but life itself is not material, but only the body which is alive is material. The lower conditions out of whose collocations life emerges supply a body as it were to a new soul. The specific characters which they possess are not continued into the new soul. The continuity which exists between life and the material does not mean that the material is carried over into life. There would not in that case be continuity between the living body as a new emergent and its predecessors; the living body would be nothing more than an elaborate material mechanism, which would illustrate material action, but could not claim a position of privilege. The characters which *are* continued from the lower level into

life are not the specific qualities of the lower level; they are rather those characters which all existence shares in common, such as existence in time and space, intensity, capacity of affecting other existences, all which belong to life as much as to matter. . . .

We are to combine in our thoughts this fundamental unity with the recognition of emergent qualities which can only be accepted but cannot be accounted for. One difficulty in the way of effecting this combination in our thought is the idea that if the world is a determinate growth, each new creation determined by its predecessors on a lower level, the history of the world must be capable of prediction, according to the famous assertion of Laplace.[5] But this conclusion does not follow. Laplace's calculator might foresee that at a certain point a certain complexity might arise, whose actions were capable of measurement and would be those of living things. He could never affirm that this form of action would have the quality of life, unless he lived to see. He might predict ethereal waves but could not predict them to be light; still less that a material body would be material or when touched by light would be red, or even merely look red to a living body with eyes. All known forms of action could be predicted in their measurable characters, but never in their emergent ones. Not even God, if we suppose a God presiding over the birth of the world, in

[5 Pierre Simon Laplace (1749-1827), French mathematician and astronomer who produced a systematized theory of celestial mechanics that would in principle allow mathematical prediction of any event. Once, when asked whether a God was required to complete his explanatory theory, he replied, "I have no need of that hypothesis." *Ed.*]

accordance with the conception of the crudest theism, could predict what these emergent qualities would be; he could only accept them like ourselves when the world he made had originated them.

I have chosen as illustrating the attitude of natural piety our acceptance of the emergence of these qualities. They remain for ever a mysterious fact. But they are after all only a part of the mystery which encompasses us and which we have no right to ask to penetrate. They are themselves related to simpler conditions, which it is the object of science to discover. Some persons have even supposed, following the precedent of the early Greek philosophers, and in particular of the chief Pythagorean speaker in Plato's great dialogue, the *Timaeus,* that all these features in the world are but specifications of some ultimate stuff of which the world is made. If this were true, it might be repugnant to the feelings of some, but natural piety would accept it, as it accepts the law of gravitation, or the law of the progression in the forms of life according to evolution, whatever the law of evolution may turn out to be; or as it would accept, if we are compelled to think so, that the four-dimensional space-time in which we live is bent in the neighborhood of matter. All science attempts to connect the variegated phenomena of the world by expressing them in terms of measurable motions. It seems to take the color and richness from the world of secondary sensible qualities and expresses them in terms of primary qualities which in the end are terms of space and time. It does not, nor does it pretend to remove, the mystery of these qualities, and in all its explanations it does but bring us in face of other mysteries which we must needs accept.

We are thus forever in presence of miracles; and as old Nathan said, the greatest of all miracles is that the genuine miracles should be so familiar. And here I interpolate a remark, not altogether irrelevant to my subject, upon the uses of great men. The emergence of qualities is the familiar miracle, but great men, and in particular great men of science, are for ever enlarging our mysteries, simplifying them and extending their scope, as when they record the law of attraction, or the idea which lies at the basis of the notion of relativity. And thus with their fresher insight they keep for us our sense of piety to nature alive. Compared with other men they are like the springs of a river. . . .

The mystery of facts, whether these facts are the individual facts of experience or the larger universal facts which are scientific laws, or such facts, more comprehensive still, as may be discovered by a prudent and scientific philosophy, is the last word of knowledge. The reverent temper which accepts them is the mood of natural piety.

ETHICS

Man's moral life, the materialist holds, is as natural as life itself; it must therefore be understood as natural to him. Ralph Barton Perry attempts to make this formulation in the following selection. When life emerges in nature, it introduces a bias that in turn produces value in an otherwise valueless cosmos. That bias is interest, which produces struggle—the organism seeks to preserve itself and to have its demands satisfied—and the distinction of good and bad. Goodness then is simply the fulfillment of interest, or the satisfaction of desire. Morality, in turn, produces a community of interests or a civilization, for it involves choices so as to mass interests in the struggle of life against a reluctant nature.

5 Ethical Naturalism
Ralph Barton Perry (1876-1957)

The moral affair of men, a prolonged and complicated historical enterprise, is thrown into historical relief upon the background of a mechanical cosmos. Nature, as interpreted by the inorganic sciences, presents a spectacle of impassivity. It moves, transforms, and radiates, on every scale and in all its gigantic range of temporal and spatial distance, utterly without loss or gain of value. One cannot rightly attribute to such a world even the property of neglect or brutality. Its indifference is absolute.

Such a world is devoid of value because of the elimination of the bias of life. Where no interest is at stake, changes can make no practical difference; where no claims are made, there can be neither fortune nor calamity, neither comedy nor tragedy. There is no object of applause or resentment, if there be nothing in whose behalf such judgments may be urged.

But with the introduction of life, even the least particle of it, the rudest bit of protoplasm that ever made the venture,

nature becomes a new system with a new center. The organism inherits the earth; the mechanisms of nature become its environment, its resources in the struggle to keep for a time body and soul together. The mark of life is partiality for itself. If anything is to become an object of solicitude, it must first announce itself through acting in its own behalf. With life thus instituted there begins the long struggle of interest against inertia and indifference, that war of which civilization itself is only the latest and most triumphant phase.

Nature being thus enlivened, the simpler terms of value now find a meaning. A living thing must suffer calamities or achieve successes; and since its fortunes are *good* or *bad* in the most elementary sense that can be attached to these conceptions, it is worth our while to consider the matter with some care. An *interest,* or unit of life, is essentially an organization which consistently acts for its own preservation. It deals with its environment in such wise as to keep itself intact and bring itself to maturity; appropriating what it needs, and avoiding or destroying what threatens it with injury. The interest so functions as to supply itself with the means whereby it may continue to exist and function. This is the principle of action which may be generalized from its behavior, and through which it may be distinguished within the context of nature. Now the term *interest* being construed in this sense, we may describe goodness as *fulfilment of interest*. The description will perhaps refer more clearly to human life, if for the term *interest* we substitute the term *desire*. Goodness would then consist in the *satisfaction of desire*. In other words, things are good because desired, not desired because good. To say that one desires things because one needs them, or likes them, or admires them, is redundant; in the end one simply desires certain things, that is, one possesses an interest or desire which they fulfil. There are as many varieties of goodness as there are varieties of interest; and to the variety of interest there is no end.

Strictly speaking, goodness belongs to an interest's actual state of fulfilment. This will consist in an activity, exercised by the interest, but employing the environment. With a slight shift of emphasis, goodness in this absolute sense will attach either to interest in so far as nourished by objects, as in the case of hunger appeased, or to objects in so far as assimilated to interest, as in the case of food consumed. It follows that goodness in a relative sense, in the sense of "good for," will attach to whatever *conduces* to good in the absolute sense; that is, actions and objects, such as agriculture and bread, that lead directly or indirectly to the fulfilment of interest. But "good" and "good for," like their opposite "bad" and "bad for," are never sharply distinguishable, because the imagination anticipates the fortunes of interests, and transforms even remote contingencies into actual victory or defeat.

Through their organization into life, the mechanisms of nature thus take on the generic quality of good and evil. They either serve interests or oppose them; and must be employed and assimilated, or avoided and rejected accordingly. Events which once indifferently happened are now objects of hope and fear, or integral parts of success and failure.

But that organization of life which denotes the presence of morality has not yet been defined. The isolated interest extricates itself from mechanism; and, struggling to maintain itself, does, it is true, divide the world into good and bad, according to its uses. But the moral drama opens only when interest meets interest; when the path of one unit of life is crossed by that of another. Every interest is compelled to recognize other interests, on the one hand as parts of its environment, and on the other hand as partners in the general enterprise of life. Thus there is evolved the *moral* idea, or principle of action, according to which *interest allies itself with interest in order to be free-handed and powerful* against the common hereditary enemy, the heavy inertia and the incessant wear of the cosmos. Through morality a plurality of interests becomes an *economy*, or *community of interests*.

I have thus far described the situation as though it were essentially a social one. But while, historically speaking, it is doubtless always social in one of its aspects, the essence of the matter is as truly represented within the group of interests sustained by a single organism, when these, for example, are united in an individual life-purpose. Morality is that procedure in which several interests, whether they involve one or more physical organisms, are so adjusted as to function as one interest, more massive in its support, and more coherent and united in the common task of fulfilment. Interests morally combined are not destroyed or superseded, as are mechanical forces, by their resultant. The power of the higher interest is due to a summing of incentives emanating from the contributing interests; it can perpetuate itself only through keeping these interests alive. The most spectacular instance of this is government, which functions as one, and yet derives its power from an enormous variety of different interests, which it must foster and conserve as the sources of its own life. In all cases the strength of morality must lie in its liberality and breadth.

Morality is simply the forced choice between suicide and abundant life. When interests war against one another they render the project of life, at best a hard adventure, futile and abortive. I hold it to be of prime importance for the understanding of this matter to observe that from the poorest and crudest beginnings, morality is *the massing of interests against a reluctant cosmos*. Life has been attended with discord and mutual destruction, but this is its failure. The first grumbling truce between savage enemies, the first collective enterprise, the first peaceful community, the first restraint on gluttony for the sake of health, the first suppression of ferocity for the sake of a harder blow struck in cold blood, these were the first victories of morality. They were moral victories in that they organized life into more comprehensive unities, making it a more formidable thing, and securing a more abundant satisfaction. The fact that life thus combined and weighted, was hurled

against life, was the lingering weakness, the deficiency which attends upon all partial attainment. The moral triumph lay in the positive access of strength.

Let us now correct our elementary conceptions of value so that they may apply to moral value. The fulfilment of a simple isolated interest is good, but only *the fulfilment of an organization of interests* is morally good. Such goodness appears in the realization of an individual's systematic purpose or in the well-being of a community. That it virtually implies one ultimate good, the fulfilment of the system of all interests, must necessarily follow; although we cannot at present deal adequately with that conclusion.

The quality of moral goodness, like the quality of goodness in the fundamental sense, lies not in the nature of any class of objects, but in any object or activity whatsoever, in so far as this provides a fulfilment of interest or desire. In the case of moral goodness this fulfilment must embrace a group of interests in which each is limited by the others. Its value lies not only in fulfilment, but also in adjustment and harmony. And this value is independent of the special subject-matter of the interests. Moralists have generally agreed that it is impossible to conceive moral goodness exclusively in terms of any special interest, even such as honor, power, or wealth. There is no interest so rare or so humble that its fulfilment is not morally good, provided that fulfilment forms part of the systematic fulfilment of a group of interests. . . .

There is an old and unprofitable quarrel between those who identify, and those who contrast, morality with *nature*. To adjudicate this quarrel, it is necessary to define a point at which nature somehow exceeds herself. Strictly speaking, it is as arbitrary to say that morality, which arose and is immersed in nature, is not natural, as to say that magnetism and electricity are not natural. If nature be defined in terms of the categories of any stage of complexity, all beyond will wear the aspect of a miracle. It would be proper to dismiss the question as only a trivial matter of terminology, did not the discussion of it provide an occasion for alluding to certain confused notions that have obtained wide currency. . . .

If one insists still upon drawing a line between cosmical and moral forces, let it be drawn at the point where there first arises that unstable complex called life. Life does in a sense oppose itself to the balance of nature. To hold itself together, it must play at parry and thrust with the very forces which gave it birth. Once having happened, it so acts as to persist. But it should be remarked that this opposition between the careless and rough course of the cosmos, the insidious forces of dissolution, on the one hand, and the self-preserving care of the organism on the other, is present absolutely from the outset of life.

Vegetable and animal organisms do, it is true, adapt themselves to the environment; but their adaptation is essentially a method of using and modifying the environment in their own favor, precisely as is the case with human action. Therefore Huxley's sharp distinction between natural plant life and man's artificial garden is misleading.

"The tendency of the cosmic process," he says, "is to bring about the adjustment of the forms of plant life to the current conditions; the tendency of the horticultural process is the adjustment of the conditions to the needs of the forms of plant life which the gardener desires to raise."[1] But this is to ignore the basal fact, which is that plant life in any form is a defiance of current conditions. Art has already begun when natural processes assume a form that feeds itself, reproduces itself, and grows. The first organisms have only a local footing; they are rooted in the soil, and can turn to their advantage only the conditions characteristic of a time and place. Eventually there evolves a more resourceful unit of life, like the gardener with his cultivated plants, who is capable of inhabiting nature at large. But the method is still the same, that of playing off nature against nature; only it is now done on a larger scale, and in a more aggressive and confident spirit. The need of concession to the demands of locality is reduced, through a concession once and for all to the wider processes of nature. But in relation to its environment, life is never wholly constructive, as it is never wholly passive. Whether it appears in the form of vegetation or civilization, it always involves both an adaptation of nature to itself and of itself to nature.

Morality, then, is natural if life is natural; for it is defined by the same essential principles. It is related to life as a later to an earlier phase of one development. The organization of life answers the self-preservative impulse with which life begins; that the deliberate fulfilment of a human purpose is only life grown strong enough through organization to conduct a larger and more adventurous enterprise.

[1 Perry refers to the work of the renowned English scientist Thomas Henry Huxley (1825–1895) who devoted himself to a defense of evolutionism. *Ed.*]

SOCIAL PHILOSOPHY

Up to this point in our study, we have distinguished two forms of materialism. In the writings of Karl Marx, we meet a third kind, variously called historical, dialectical, or economic materialism. The basic thesis of Marx's position is that the primary forces in human life are economic, chiefly the relations arising out of economic production (which constitute the "material" basis of life). All other social phenomena—law, government, justice, property, even our social consciousness—are determined and moulded by economic relations. Marx did not stop with economic analysis. He projected a future in which man, if he were to reshape economic phenomena, could achieve a society which would be adequate to his nature. This goal is to be realized, partly by recognizing the class structure of society and the inevitable conflict of classes, and thereafter by working toward the abolition of classes and their economic base, namely the private ownership of the means of production.

Marx remained primarily a social philosopher, and did not produce a systematic materialist metaphysics, although his doctoral dissertation was on ancient materialism. As later Marxist philosophers have done metaphysics, however, they have generally been inclined to materialism. Not all materialists and naturalists, it should be added, accept Marxist social philosophy.

6 The Material Basis of Life
Karl Marx (1818-1883)

The first work undertaken for the solution of the question that troubled me, was a critical revision of Hegel's "Philosophy of Law"; the introduction to that work appeared in the "Deutsch-Französische Jahrbücher," published in Paris in 1844. I was led by my studies to the conclusion that legal relations as well as forms of state could neither be understood by themselves, nor explained by the so-called general progress of the human mind, but that they are rooted in the material conditions of life, which are summed up by Hegel after the fashion of the English and French of the eighteenth century under the name "civic society"; the anatomy of that civic society is to be sought in political economy. The study of the latter which I had taken up in Paris, I continued at Brussels whither I emigrated on account of an order of expulsion issued by Mr. Guizot. The general conclusion at which I arrived and which, once reached, continued to serve as the leading thread in my studies, may be briefly summed up as follows: In the social production which men carry on they enter into

The selection is from Karl Marx, *A Contribution to the Critique of Political Economy*, tr. N. I. Stone (Chicago: Charles H. Kerr and Co., 1904), and *Manifesto of the Communist Party* by Marx and Engels (Chicago: Charles H. Kerr and Co., 1888).

definite relations that are indispensable and independent of their will; these relations of production correspond to a definite stage of development of their material powers of production. The sum total of these relations of production constitutes the economic structure of society —the real foundation, on which rise legal and political superstructures and to which correspond definite forms of social consciousness. The mode of production in material life determines the general character of the social, political and spiritual processes of life. It is not the consciousness of men that determines their existence, but, on the contrary, their social existence determines their consciousness. At a certain stage of their development, the material forces of production in society come in conflict with the existing relations of production, or—what is but a legal expression for the same thing—with the property relations within which they had been at work before. From forms of development of the forces of production these relations turn into their fetters. Then comes the period of social revolution. With the change of the economic foundation the entire immense superstructure is more or less rapidly transformed. In considering such transformations the distinction should always be made between the material transformation of the economic conditions of production which can be determined with the precision of natural science, and the legal, political, religious, aesthetic or philosophic—in short ideological forms in which men become conscious of this conflict and fight it out. Just as our opinion of an individual is not based on what he thinks of himself, so can we not judge of such a period of transformation by its own consciousness; on the contrary, this consciousness must rather be explained from the contradictions of material life, from the existing conflict between the social forces of production and the relations of production. No social order ever disappears before all the productive forces, for which there is room in it, have been developed; and new higher relations of production never appear before the material conditions of their existence have matured in the womb of the old society. Therefore, mankind always takes up only such problems as it can solve; since, looking at the matter more closely, we will always find that the problem itself arises only when the material conditions necessary for its solution already exist or are at least in the process of formation. In broad outlines we can designate the Asiatic, the ancient, the feudal, and the modern bourgeois methods of production as so many epochs in the progress of the economic formation of society. The bourgeois relations of production are the last antagonistic form of the social process of production—antagonistic not in the sense of individual antagonism, but of one arising from conditions surrounding the life of individuals in society; at the same time the productive forces developing in the womb of bourgeois society create the material conditions for the solution of that antagonism. This social formation constitutes, therefore, the closing chapter of the prehistoric stage of human society.

The history of all hitherto existing society is the history of class struggles.

Freeman and slave, patrician and plebeian, lord and serf, guild-master and journeyman, in a word, oppressor and oppressed, stood in constant opposition to one another, carried on an uninterrupted, now hidden, now open fight, a fight that each time ended, either in a revolutionary re-constitution of society at large, or in the common ruin of the contending classes.

In the earlier epochs of history, we find almost everywhere a complicated arrangement of society into various orders, a manifold gradation of social rank. In ancient Rome we have patricians, knights, plebians, slaves; in the Middle Ages, feudal lords, vassals, guildmasters, journeymen, apprentices, serfs; in almost all of these classes, again, subordinate gradations.

The modern bourgeois society that has sprouted from the ruins of feudal society has not done away with class antagonisms. It has but established new classes, new conditions of oppression, new forms of struggle in place of the old ones.

Our epoch, the epoch of the bourgeoisie, possesses, however, this distinctive feature: it has simplified the class antagonisms. Society as a whole is more and more splitting up into two great hostile camps, into two great classes directly facing each other: Bourgeoisie and Proletariat. . . .

Each step in the development of the bourgeoisie was accompanied by a corresponding political advance of that class. An oppressed class under the sway of the feudal nobility, an armed and self-governing association in the mediaeval commune, here independent urban republic (as in Italy and Germany), there taxable "third estate" of the monarchy (as in France), afterwards, in the period of manufacture proper, serving either the semi-feudal or the absolute monarchy as a counterpoise against the nobility, and, in fact, cornerstone of the great monarchies in general, the bourgeoisie has at last, since the establishment of Modern Industry and of the world-market, conquered for itself, in the modern representative State, exclusive political sway. The executive of the modern State is but a committee for managing the common affairs of the whole bourgeoisie.

The bourgeoisie, historically, has played a most revolutionary part.

The bourgeoisie, wherever it has got the upper hand, has put an end to all feudal, patriarchal, idyllic relations. It has pitilessly torn asunder the motley feudal ties that bound man to his "natural superiors," and has left remaining no other nexus between man and man than naked self-interest, than callous "cash payment." It has drowned the most heavenly ecstasies of religious fervour, of chivalrous enthusiasm, of philistine sentimentalism, in the icy water of egotistical calculation. It has resolved personal worth into exchange value and in place of the numberless indefeasible chartered freedoms, has set up that single, unconscionable freedom—Free Trade. In one word, for exploitation, veiled by religious and political illusions, it has substituted naked, shameless, direct, brutal exploitation.

The bourgeoisie has stripped of its halo every occupation hitherto honoured and looked up to with reverent awe. It has converted the physician, the lawyer, the priest, the poet, the man of science, into its paid wage-labourers.

The bourgeoisie has torn away from the family its sentimental veil, and has reduced the family relation to a mere money relation.

The bourgeoisie has disclosed how it came to pass that the brutal display of vigour in the Middle Ages, which Reactionists so much admire, found its fitting complement in the most slothful indolence. It has been the first to show what man's activity can bring about. It has accomplished wonders far surpassing Egyptian pyramids, Roman aqueducts, and Gothic cathedrals; it has conducted expeditions that put in the shade all former Exoduses of nations and crusades.

The bourgeoisie cannot exist without constantly revolutionising the instruments of production, and thereby the relations of production, and with them the whole relations of society. Conservation of the old modes of production in unaltered form, was on the contrary, the first condition of existence for all earlier industrial classes. Constant revolutionising of production, uninterrupted disturbance of all social conditions, everlasting uncertainty and agitation distinguish the bourgeois epoch from all earlier ones. All fixed, fastfrozen relations, with their train of ancient and venerable prejudices and opinions, are swept away, all new-formed ones become antiquated before they can ossify. All that is solid melts into air, all that is holy is profaned, and man is at last compelled to face with sober senses, his real conditions of life, and his relations with his kind.

The need of a constantly expanding market for its products chases the bourgeoisie over the whole surface of the globe. It must nestle everywhere, settle everywhere, establish connexions everywhere. . . .

The bourgeoisie, during its rule of scarce one hundred years, has created more massive and more colossal productive forces than have all preceding generations together. Subjection of Nature's forces to man, machinery, application of chemistry to industry and agriculture, steam-navigation, railways, electric telegraphs, clearing of whole continents for cultivation, canalisation of rivers, whole populations conjured out of the ground—what earlier century had even a presentiment that such productive forces slumbered in the lap of social labour?

We see then: the means of production and of exchange, on whose foundation the bourgeoisie built itself up, were generated in feudal society. At a certain stage in the development of these means of production and of exchange, the conditions under which feudal society produced and exchanged, the feudal organisation of agriculture and manufacturing industry, in one word, the feudal relations of property became no longer compatible with the already developed productive forces; they became so many fetters. They had to be burst asunder; they were burst asunder.

Into their place stepped free competition, accompanied by a social and political constitution adapted to it, and by the economical and political sway of the bourgeois class.

A similar movement is going on before our own eyes. Modern bourgeois society with its relations of production, of exchange and of property, a society that has conjured up such gigantic means of production and of exchange, is like the sorcerer, who is no longer able to control the powers of the nether world whom he has called up by his spells. For many a decade past the history of industry and commerce is but the history of the revolt of modern productive forces against modern conditions of production, against the property relations that are the conditions for the existence of the bourgeoisie and of its rule. It is enough to mention the commercial crises that by their periodical return put on its trial, each time more threateningly, the existence of the entire bourgeois society. In these crises a great part not only of the existing products, but also of the previously created productive forces, are periodically destroyed. In these crises there breaks out an epidemic that, in all earlier epochs, would have seemed an absurdity—the epidemic of over-production. Society suddenly finds itself put back into a state of momentary barbarism; it appears as if a famine, a universal war of devastation had cut off the supply of every means of subsistence; industry and commerce seem to be destroyed; and why? Because there is too much civilisation, too much means of subsistence, too much industry, too much commerce. The productive forces at the disposal of society no longer tend to further the development of the conditions of bourgeois property; on the contrary, they have become too powerful for these conditions, by which they are fettered, and so soon as they overcome these fetters, they bring disorder into the whole of bourgeois society, endanger the existence of bourgeois property. The conditions of bourgeois society are too narrow to comprise the wealth created by them. And how does the bourgeoisie get over these crises? On the one hand by enforced destruction of a mass of productive forces; on the other, by the conquest of new markets, and by the more thorough exploitation of the old

ones. That is to say, by paving the way for more extensive and more destructive crises, and by diminishing the means whereby crises are prevented.

The weapons with which the bourgeoisie felled feudalism to the ground are now turned against the bourgeoisie itself.

But not only has the bourgeoisie forged the weapons that bring death to itself; it has also called into existence the men who are to wield those weapons—the modern working class—the proletarians.

In proportion as the bourgeoisie, *i.e.*, capital, is developed, in the same proportion is the proletariat, the modern working class, developed—a class of labourers, who live only so long as they find work, and who find work only so long as their labour increases capital. These labourers, who must sell themselves piecemeal, are a commodity, like every other article of commerce, and are consequently exposed to all the vicissitudes of competition, to all the fluctuations of the market.

Owing to the extensive use of machinery and to division of labour, the work of the proletarians has lost all individual character, and, consequently, all charm for the workman. He becomes an appendage of the machine, and it is only the most simple, most monotonous, and most easily acquired knack, that is required of him. Hence, the cost of production of a workman is restricted, almost entirely, to the means of subsistence that he requires for his maintenance, and for the propagation of his race. But the price of a commodity, and therefore also of labour, is equal to its cost of production. In proportion, therefore, as the repulsiveness of the work increases, the wage decreases. Nay more, in proportion as the use of machinery and division of labour increases, in the same proportion the burden of toil also increases, whether by prolongation of the working hours, by increase of the work exacted in a given time or by increased speed of the machinery, etc.

Modern industry has converted the little workshop of the patriarchal master into the great factory of the industrial capitalist. Masses of labourers, crowded into the factory, are organised like soldiers. As privates of the industrial army they are placed under the command of a perfect hierarchy of officers and sergeants. Not only are they slaves of the bourgeois class, and of the bourgeois State; they are daily and hourly enslaved by the machine, by the overlooker, and, above all, by the individual bourgeois manufacturer himself. The more openly this despotism proclaims gain to be its end and aim, the more petty, the more hateful and the more embittering it is. . . .

The proletariat goes through various stages of development. With its birth begins its struggle with the bourgeoisie. At first the contest is carried on by individual labourers, then by the workpeople of a factory, then by the operatives of one trade, in one locality, against the individual bourgeois who directly exploits them. They direct their attacks not against the bourgeois conditions of production, but against the instruments of production themselves; they destroy imported wares that compete with their labour, they smash to pieces machinery, they set factories ablaze, they seek to restore by force the vanished status of the workman of the Middle Ages.

At this stage the labourers still form an incoherent mass scattered over the whole country, and broken up by their mutual competition. If anywhere they unite to form more compact bodies, this is not yet the consequence of their own active union, but of the union of the bourgeoisie, which class, in order to attain its own political ends, is compelled to set the whole proletariat in motion, and is moreover yet, for a time, able to do so. At this stage, therefore, the proletarians do not fight their enemies, but the enemies of their enemies, the remnants of absolute monarchy, the landowners, the non-industrial bourgeois, the petty bourgeoisie. Thus the whole historical movement is concentrated in the hands of the bourgeoisie; every victory so obtained is a victory for the bourgeoisie.

But with the development of industry the proletariat not only increases in number; it becomes concentrated in greater masses, its strength grows, and it feels that strength more. The various interests and conditions of life within the ranks of the proletariat are more and more equalised, in proportion as machinery obliterates all distinctions of labour, and nearly everywhere reduces wages to the same low level. The growing competition among the bourgeois, and the resulting commercial crises, make the wages of the workers ever more fluctuating. The unceasing improvement of machinery, ever more rapidly developing, makes their livelihood more and more precarious; the collisions between individual workmen and individual bourgeois take more and more the character of collisions between two classes. Thereupon the workers begin to form combinations (Trades' Unions) against the bourgeois; they club together in order to keep up the rate of wages; they found permanent associations in order to make provision beforehand for these occasional revolts. Here and there the contest breaks out into riots.

Now and then the workers are victorious, but only for a time. The real fruit of their battles lies, not in the immediate result, but in the ever-expanding union of the workers. This union is helped on by the improved means of communication that are created by modern industry and that place the workers of different localities in contact with one another. It was just this contact that was needed to centralise the numerous local struggles, all of the same character, into one national struggle between classes. But every class struggle is a political struggle. And that union, to attain which the burghers of the Middle Ages, with their miserable highways, required centuries, the modern proletarians, thanks to railways, achieve in a few years.

This organisation of the proletarians into a class, and consequently into a political party, is continually being upset again by the competition between the workers themselves. But it ever rises up again, stronger, firmer, mightier. It compels legislative recognition of particular interests of the workers, by taking advantage of the divisions among the bourgeoisie itself. Thus the ten-hours' bill in England was carried.

Altogether collisions between the classes of the old society further, in many ways, the course of development of the proletariat. The bourgeoisie finds itself involved in a constant battle. At first with the aristocracy; later on, with those portions of the bourgeoisie itself, whose interests have become antagonistic to the progress of industry; at all times, with the bourgeoisie of foreign countries. In all these battles it sees itself compelled to appeal to the proletariat, to ask for its help, and thus, to drag it into the political arena. The bourgeoisie itself, therefore, supplies the proletariat with its own elements of political and general education, in other words, it furnishes the proletariat with weapons for fighting the bourgeoisie.

Further, as we have already seen, entire sections of the ruling classes are, by the advance of industry, precipitated into the proletariat, or are at least threatened in their conditions of existence. These also supply the proletariat with fresh elements of enlightenment and progress.

Finally, in times when the class struggle nears the decisive hour, the process of dissolution going on within the ruling class, in fact within the whole range of old society, assumes such a violent, glaring character, that a small section of the ruling class cuts itself adrift, and joins the revolutionary class, the class that holds the future in its hands. Just as, therefore, at an earlier period, a section of the nobility went over to the bourgeoisie, so now a portion of the bourgeoisie goes over to the proletariat, and in particular, a portion of the bourgeois ideologists, who have raised themselves to the level of comprehending theoretically the historical movement as a whole.

Of all the classes that stand face to face with the bourgeoisie today, the proletariat alone is a really revolutionary class. The other classes decay and finally disappear in the face of Modern Industry; the proletariat is its special and essential product.

The lower middle class, the small manufacturer, the shopkeeper, the artisan, the peasant, all these fight against the bourgeoisie, to save from extinction their existence as fractions of the middle class. They are therefore not revolutionary, but conservative. Nay more, they are reactionary, for they try to roll back the wheel of history. If by chance they are revolutionary, they are so only in view of their impending transfer into the proletariat, they thus defend not their present, but their future interests, they desert their own standpoint to place themselves at that of the proletariat.

The "dangerous class," the social scum, that passively rotting mass thrown off by the lowest layers of old society, may, here and there, be swept into the movement by a proletarian revolution, its conditions of life, however, prepare it far more for the part of a bribed tool of reactionary intrigue.

In the conditions of the proletariat, those of old society at large are already virtually swamped. The proletarian is without property; his relation to his wife and children has no longer anything in common with the bourgeois family-relations; modern industrial labour, modern subjection to capital, the same in England as in France, in America as in Germany, has stripped him of every trace of national character. Law, morality, religion, are to him so many bourgeois prejudices, behind which lurk in ambush just as many bourgeois interests.

All the preceding classes that got the upper hand, sought to fortify their already acquired status by subjecting society at large to their conditions of appropriation. The proletarians cannot become masters of the productive forces of society, except by abolishing their own previous mode of appropriation, and thereby also every other previous mode of appropriation. They have nothing of their own to secure and to fortify; their mission is to destroy all previous securities for, and insurances of, individual property.

All previous historical movements were movements of minorities, or in the interest of minorities. The proletarian movement is the self-conscious, independent movement of the immense majority, in the interests of the immense majority. The proletariat, the lowest stratum of our present society, cannot stir, cannot raise itself up, without the whole superincumbent strata of official society being sprung into the air.

Though not in substance, yet in form, the struggle of the proletariat with the bourgeoisie is at first a national struggle. The proletariat of each country must, of course, first of all settle matters with its own bourgeoisie.

In depicting the most general phases of the development of the proletariat, we traced the more or less veiled civil war, raging within existing society, up to the point where that war breaks out into open revolution, and where the violent overthrow of the bourgeoisie lays the foundation for the sway of the proletariat.

Hitherto, every form of society has been based, as we have already seen, on the antagonism of oppressing and oppressed classes. But in order to oppress a class, certain conditions must be assured to it under which it can, at least, continue its slavish existence. The serf, in the period of serfdom, raised himself to membership in the commune, just as the petty bourgeois, under the yoke of feudal absolutism, managed to develop into a bourgeois. The modern labourer, on the contrary, instead of rising with the progress of industry, sinks deeper and deeper below the conditions of existence of his own class. He becomes a pauper, and pauperism develops more rapidly than population and wealth. And here it becomes evident, that the bourgeoisie is unfit any longer to be the ruling class in society, and to impose its conditions of existence upon society as an over-riding law. It is unfit to rule because it is incompetent to assure an existence to its slave within his slavery, because it cannot help letting him sink into such a state, that it has to feed him, instead of being fed by him. Society can no longer live under this bourgeoisie, in other words, its existence is no longer compatible with society.

The essential condition for the existence, and for the sway of the bourgeois class, is the formation and augmentation of capital; the condition for capital is wage-labour. Wage-labour rests exclusively on competition between the labourers. The advance of industry, whose involuntary promoter is the bourgeoisie, replaces the isolation of the labourers, due to competition, by their revolutionary combination, due to association. The development of Modern Industry, therefore, cuts from under its feet the very foundation on which the bourgeoisie produces and appropriates products. What the bourgeoisie, therefore, produces, above all, is its own grave-diggers. Its fall and the victory of the proletariat are equally inevitable.

ESTHETICS

Life is more than science, even though science for the materialist is the most reliable way to knowledge. Among the other dimensions of experience is the esthetic. As with morality, materialists treat art and the esthetic within nature and experience rather than going beyond them.

The writings of John Dewey provide such a materialist or naturalist interpretation. Dewey defines experience as the interaction of organism and environment, a doing and an undergoing. But experience must be distinguished from *an* experience, for things are not always composed to produce the latter. An experience is had only when the materials experienced lead to completion and fulfillment.

A work of art produces such an experience, for its different parts fuse in a unity without losing their own characters, and the unity involves a single pervasive quality. The esthetic experience is thus a total, integrated experience, intrinsically worthwhile, of an emotionally satisfying quality. Dewey points out, however, that art is not alone in producing this quality; thinking, for example, is like art in this respect, differing from art only in its materials.

7 Art as Experience
John Dewey (1859-1952)

Experience is the result, the sign, and the reward of that interaction of organism and environment which, when it is carried to the full, is a transformation of interaction into participation and communication. Since sense-organs with their connected motor apparatus are the means of this participation, any and every derogation of them, whether practical or theoretical, is at once effect and cause of a narrowed and dulled life-experience. Oppositions of mind and body, soul and matter, spirit and flesh all have their origin, fundamentally, in fear of what life may bring forth. They are marks of contraction and withdrawal. Full recognition, therefore, of the continuity of the organs, needs and basic impulses of the human creature with his animal forbears, implies no necessary reduction of man to the level of the brutes. On the contrary, it makes possible the drawing of a groundplan of human experience upon which is erected the superstructure of man's marvelous and distinguishing experience. What is distinctive in man makes it possible for him to sink below the level of the beasts. It also makes it possible for him to carry to new and unprecedented heights that unity of sense and impulse, of brain and

eye and ear, that is exemplified in animal life, saturating it with the conscious meanings derived from communication and deliberate expression. . . .

Experience occurs continuously, because the interaction of live creature and environing conditions is involved in the very process of living. Under conditions of resistance and conflict, aspects and elements of the self and the world that are implicated in this interaction qualify experience with emotions and ideas so that conscious intent emerges. Oftentimes, however, the experience had is inchoate. Things are experienced but not in such a way that they are composed into *an* experience. There are distraction and dispersion; what we observe and what we think, what we desire and what we get, are at odds with each other. We put our hands to the plow and turn back; we start and then we stop, not because the experience has reached the end for the sake of which it was initiated but because of extraneous interruptions or of inner lethargy.

In contrast with such experience, we have *an* experience when the material experienced runs its course to fulfillment. Then and then only is it integrated within and demarcated in the general stream of experience from other experiences. A piece of work is finished in a way that is satisfactory; a problem receives its solution; a game is played through; a situation, whether that of eating a meal, playing a game of chess, carrying on a conversation, writing a

The selection is from pp. 22–44, with omissions, of *Art as Experience* by John Dewey. Copyright 1934 by John Dewey. Published by Minton, Balch & Co. and George Allen & Unwin, Ltd. Used by permission of G. P. Putnam's Sons and of George Allen & Unwin, Ltd.

book, or taking part in a political campaign, is so rounded out that its close is a consummation and not a cessation. Such an experience is a whole and carries with it its own individualizing quality and self-sufficiency. It is *an* experience.

Philosophers, even empirical philosophers, have spoken for the most part of experience at large. Idiomatic speech, however, refers to experiences each of which is singular, having its own beginning and end. For life is no uniform uninterrupted march or flow. It is a thing of histories, each with its own plot, its own inception and movement toward its close, each having its own particular rhythmic movement; each with its own unrepeated quality pervading it throughout. A flight of stairs, mechanical as it is, proceeds by individualized steps, not by undifferentiated progression, and an inclined plane is at least marked off from other things by abrupt discreteness.

Experience in this vital sense is defined by those situations and episodes that we spontaneously refer to as being "real experiences"; those things of which we say in recalling them, "that *was* an experience." It may have been something of tremendous importance—a quarrel with one who was once an intimate, a catastrophe finally averted by a hair's breadth. Or it may have been something that in comparison was slight —and which perhaps because of its very slightness illustrates all the better what is to be an experience. There is that meal in a Paris restaurant of which one says "that *was* an experience." It stands out as an enduring memorial of what food may be. Then there is that storm one went through in crossing the Atlantic—the storm that seemed in its

fury, as it was experienced, to sum up in itself all that a storm can be, complete in itself, standing out because marked out from what went before and what came after.

In such experiences, every successive part flows freely, without seam and without unfilled blanks, into what ensues. At the same time there is no sacrifice of the self-identity of the parts. A river, as distinct from a pond, flows. But its flow gives a definiteness and interest to its successive portions greater than exist in the homogeneous portions of a pond. In an experience, flow is from something to something. As one part leads into another and as one part carries on what went before, each gains distinctness in itself. The enduring whole is diversified by successive phases that are emphases of its varied colors.

Because of continuous merging, there are no holes, mechanical junctions, and dead centers when we have *an* experience. There are pauses, places of rest, but they punctuate and define the quality of movement. They sum up what has been undergone and prevent its dissipation and idle evaporation. Continued acceleration is breathless and prevents parts from gaining distinction. In a work of art, different acts, episodes, occurrences melt and fuse into unity, and yet do not disappear and lose their own character as they do so—just as in a genial conversation there is a continuous interchange and blending, and yet each speaker not only retains his own character but manifests it more clearly than is his wont.

An experience has a unity that gives it its name, that meal, that storm, that rupture of friendship. The existence of this unity is constituted by a single *quality* that pervades the entire experience in spite of the variation of its constituent parts. This unity is neither emotional, practical, nor intellectual, for these terms name distinctions that reflection can make within it. In discourse *about* an experience, we must make use of these adjectives of interpretation. In going over an experience in mind *after* its occurrence, we may find that one property rather than another was sufficiently dominant so that it characterizes the experience as a whole. There are absorbing inquiries and speculations which a scientific man and philosopher will recall as "experiences" in the emphatic sense. In final import they are intellectual. But in their actual occurrence they were emotional as well; they were purposive and volitional. Yet the experience was not a sum of these different characters; they were lost in it as distinctive traits. No thinker can ply his occupation save as he is lured and rewarded by total integral experiences that are intrinsically worth while. Without them he would never know what it is really to think and would be completely at a loss in distinguishing real thought from the spurious article. Thinking goes on in trains of ideas, but the ideas form a train only because they are much more than what an analytic psychology calls ideas. They are phases, emotionally and practically distinguished, of a developing underlying quality; they are its moving variations, not separate and independent like Locke's and Hume's so-called ideas and impressions, but are subtle shadings of a pervading and developing hue. . . .

Hence *an* experience of thinking has its own esthetic quality. It differs from those experiences that are acknowledged to be esthetic, but only in its materials. The material of the fine arts consists of qualities; that of experience having intellectual conclusion are signs or symbols having no intrinsic quality of their own, but standing for things that may in another experience be qualitatively experienced. The difference is enormous. It is one reason why the strictly intellectual art will never be popular as music is popular. Nevertheless, the experience itself has a satisfying emotional quality because it possesses internal integration and fulfillment reached through ordered and organized movement. This artistic structure may be immediately felt. In so far, it is esthetic. What is even more important is that not only is this quality a significant motive in undertaking intellectual inquiry and in keeping it honest, but that no intellectual activity is an integral event (is *an* experience) unless it is rounded out with this quality. Without it, thinking is inconclusive. In short, esthetic cannot be sharply marked off from intellectual experience since the latter must bear an esthetic stamp to be itself complete.

The same statement holds good of a course of action that is dominantly practical, that is, one that consists of overt doings. It is possible to be efficient in action and yet not have a conscious experience. The activity is too automatic to permit of a sense of what it is about and where it is going. It comes to an end but not to a close or consummation in consciousness. Obstacles are overcome by shrewd skill, but they do not feed experience. There are also those who are wavering in action, uncertain, and inconclusive like the shades in classic literature. Between the poles of aimlessness and mechanical efficiency, there lie those courses of action in which through successive deeds there runs a sense of growing meaning conserved and accumulating toward an end that is felt as accomplishment of a process. . . . There is interest in completing an experience. The experience may be one that is harmful to the world and its consummation undesirable. But it has esthetic quality.

The Greek identification of good conduct with conduct having proportion, grace, and harmony, the *kalon-agathon,* is a more obvious example of distinctive esthetic quality in moral action. One great defect in what passes as morality is its anesthetic quality. Instead of exemplifying wholehearted action, it takes the form of grudging piecemeal concessions to the demands of duty. But illustrations may only obscure the fact that any practical activity will, provided that it is integrated and moves by its own urge to fulfillment, have esthetic quality.

. . . In much of our experience we are not concerned with the connection of one incident with what went before and what comes after. There is no interest that controls attentive rejection or selection of what shall be organized into the developing experience. Things happen, but they are neither definitely included nor decisively excluded; we drift. We yield according to external pressure, or evade and compromise. There are beginnings and cessations, but no genuine initiations and concludings. One thing replaces another, but does not absorb it and carry it on. There is experience, but so slack and discursive that it is not *an* experience. Needless to say, such experiences are anesthetic.

Thus the non-esthetic lies within two limits. At one pole is the loose succession that does not begin at any particular place and that ends—in the sense of ceasing—at no particular place. At the other pole is arrest, constriction, proceeding from parts having only a mechanical connection with one another. There exists so much of one and the other of these two kinds of experience that unconsciously they come to be taken as norms of all experience. Then, when the esthetic appears, it so sharply contrasts with the picture that has been formed of experience, that it is impossible to combine its special qualities with the features of the picture and. the esthetic is given an outside place and status. The account that has been given of experience dominantly intellectual and practical is intended to show that there is no such contrast involved in having an experience; that, on the contrary, no experience of whatever sort is a unity unless it has esthetic quality.

The enemies of the esthetic are neither the practical nor the intellectual. They are the humdrum; slackness of loose ends; submission to convention in practice and intellectual procedure. Rigid abstinence, coerced submission, tightness on one side and dissipation, incoherence and aimless indulgence on the other, are deviations in opposite directions from the unity of an experience. Some such considerations perhaps induced Aristotle to invoke the "mean proportional" as the proper designation of what is distinctive of both virtue and the esthetic. He was formally correct. "Mean" and "proportion" are, however, not self-explanatory, nor to be taken over in a prior mathematical sense, but are properties belonging to an experience that has a developing movement toward its own consummation. . . .

I have spoken of the esthetic quality that rounds out an experience into completeness and unity as emotional. The reference may cause difficulty. We are given to thinking of emotions as things as simple and compact as are the words by which we name them. Joy, sorrow, hope, fear, anger, curiosity, are treated as if each in itself were a sort of entity that enters full-made upon the scene, an entity that may last a long time or a short time, but whose duration, whose growth and career, is irrelevant to its nature. In fact emotions are qualities, when they are significant, of a complex experience that moves and changes. I say, when they are *significant,* for otherwise they are but the outbreaks and eruptions of a disturbed infant. All emotions are qualifications of a drama and they change as the drama develops. Persons are sometimes said to fall in love at first sight. But what they fall into is not a thing of that instant. What would love be were it compressed into a moment in which there is no room for cherishing and for solicitude? The intimate nature of emotion is manifested in the experience of one watching a play on the stage or reading a novel. It attends the development of a plot; and a plot requires a stage, a space, wherein to develop and time in which to unfold. Experience is emotional but there are no separate things called emotions in it.

By the same token, emotions are attached to events and objects in their movement. They are not, save in pathological instances, private. And even an "objectless" emotion demands something beyond itself to which to attach itself, and thus it soon generates a delusion in lack of something real. Emo-

tion belongs of a certainty to the self. But it belongs to the self that is concerned in the movement of events toward an issue that is desired or disliked. We jump instantaneously when we are scared, as we blush on the instant when we are ashamed. But fright and shamed modesty are not in this case emotional states. Of themselves they are but automatic reflexes. In order to become emotional they must become parts of an inclusive and enduring situation that involves concern for objects and their issues. The jump of fright becomes emotional fear when there is found or thought to exist a threatening object that must be dealt with or escaped from. The blush becomes the emotion of shame when a person connects, in thought, an action he has performed with an unfavorable reaction to himself of some other person. . . .

There are, therefore, common patterns in various experiences, no matter how unlike they are to one another in the details of their subject matter. There are conditions to be met without which an experience cannot come to be. The outline of the common pattern is set by the fact that every experience is the result of interaction between a live creature and some aspect of the world in which he lives. A man does something; he lifts, let us say, a stone. In consequence he undergoes, suffers, something: the weight, strain, texture of the surface of the thing lifted. The properties thus undergone determine further doing. The stone is too heavy or too angular, not solid enough; or else the properties undergone show it is fit for the use for which it is intended. The process continues until a mutual adaptation of the self and the object emerges and that particular experience comes to a close. What is true of this simple instance is true, as to form, of every experience. The creature operating may be a thinker in his study and the environment with which he interacts may consist of ideas instead of a stone. But interaction of the two constitutes the total experience that is had, and the close which completes it is the institution of a felt harmony.

An experience has pattern and structure, because it is not just doing and undergoing in alternation, but consists of them in relationship. To put one's hand in the fire that consumes it is not necessarily to have an experience. The action and its consequence must be joined in perception. This relationship is what gives meaning; to grasp it is the objective of all intelligence. The scope and content of the relations measure the significant content of an experience.

PHILOSOPHY OF MAN

Materialism from its beginnings in ancient Greece to the present day has sought to explain and understand phenomena in the objective, material terms of contemporary science. Lucretius thought of man (and mind) as composed, like everything else, of atoms; an eighteenth century materialist spoke of "man the machine;" and twentieth century materialists view man as a physiologically-defined organism.

If man is so defined, what is to be said about mind, consciousness, or mental acts? Along with Professor Smart, many contemporary materialists answer simply that conscious processes are brain processes. Thus they posit an identity of mind and brain which maintains the consistency of their materialism. Smart takes this identity to be a factual one, and hence his writing in this selection is directed primarily against objections to that identity.

8 Materialism and Consciousness

J. J. C. Smart (1920-   )

. . . I wish to argue for the view that conscious experiences are simply *brain processes*. This is a view which almost every elementary student of philosophy is taught to refute. I shall try to show that the standard refutations of the view are fallacious.

The selection is from J. J. C. Smart, *Philosophy and Scientific Realism*, London and New York, 1963. Used by permission of Routledge and Kegan Paul, Ltd., and Humanities Press, Inc.

Many of our ordinary psychological concepts seem to refer to inner processes. Of course this is not so with all of them. Some of them seem to be able to be elucidated in a behaviouristic way: to say that someone is vain is to say that he tends to show off, or look at himself often in the mirror, or something of that sort. To say that he is interested in mathematics is to say that he has a tendency to read mathematical books, to work out problems, to talk in terms of mathematical analogies, and so on. Similarly with the emotions: 'anger,' 'fear,' 'joy,' and the like can plausibly be said to refer to characteristic behaviour patterns. Again various adverbial phrases can be elucidated in a behaviouristic way. As Ryle has pointed out, the phrase 'thinking what he is doing' in 'he is driving the car thinking what he is doing' refers to certain tendencies to behave in various ways: for example, to apply the brakes when one sees a child about to run on to the road. To drive a car thinking what you are doing is not like walking and whistling. You can walk without whistling and you can whistle without walking, but you cannot do the 'thinking what you are doing' part of 'driving the car thinking what you are doing' without the driving of the car. (Similarly, you can walk gracefully, but you cannot do the being graceful part of the performance without doing the walking part of it.) This helps to elucidate the well-known difficulty of thinking without words. Certain kinds of thinking are pieces of intelligent talking to oneself. Consider the way in which I 'thinkingly' wrote the last sentence. I can no more do the 'thinking' part without the talking (or writing) part than a man can do the being graceful part apart from the walking (or some equivalent activity).

If all our psychological concepts were capable of a behaviouristic or quasi-behaviouristic analysis this would be congenial for physicalism. . . . Unfortunately, however, there are a good many psychological concepts for which a behaviouristic account seems impossible.

Suppose that I report that I am having an orange-yellow roundish after-image. Or suppose again that I report that I

have a pain. It seems clear that the content of my report cannot be exclusively a set of purely behavioural facts. There seems to be some element of 'pure inner experience' which is being reported, and to which only I have direct access. You can observe my behaviour, but only I can be aware of my own after-image or my own pain. I suspect that the notion of a 'pain' is partly akin to that of an emotion: that is, the notion of pain seems essentially to involve the notion of distress, and distress is perhaps capable of an elucidation in terms of a characteristic behaviour pattern. But this is not all that a pain is: there is an immediately felt sensation which we do not have in other cases of distress. (Consider by contrast the distress of a mother because her son goes out gambling. The son gives his mother much pain, but he does not necessarily give her *a* pain.) In the case of the after-image there is not this 'emotional' component of distress, and it seems easier to consider such 'neat' inner experiences. I shall therefore concentrate on the case where I report the experience of having an after-image. . . .

The first argument against the identification of experiences and brain processes can be put as follows: Aristotle, or for that matter an illiterate peasant, can report his images and aches and pains, and yet nevertheless may not know that the brain has anything to do with thinking. (Aristotle thought that the brain was an organ for cooling the blood.) Therefore what Aristotle or the peasant reports cannot *be* a brain process, though it can, of course, be something which is (unknown to Aristotle or the peasant) causally connected with a brain process.

The reply to this argument is simply this: when I say that experiences are brain processes I am asserting this *as a matter of fact*. I am not asserting that 'brain process' is part of what we *mean* by 'experience.' A couple of analogies will show what is wrong with the argument. Suppose that a man is acquainted with Sir Walter Scott and knows him as 'the author of *Waverley*.' He may never have heard of Ivanhoe. Yet the author of *Waverley* can be (and was) the very same person as the author of *Ivanhoe*. Again, consider lightning. According to modern science, lightning is a movement of electric charges from one ionised layer of cloud to another such layer or to the earth. This is what lightning really is. This fact was not known to Aristotle. And yet Aristotle presumably knew the meaning of the Greek word for 'lightning' perfectly well.

I wish to make it clear that I have used these examples mainly to make a *negative* point: I do not wish to claim that the relation between the expression 'I am having an after image' and 'there is such-and-such a brain process going on in me' is in *all* respects like that between 'there is the author of *Waverley*' and 'there is the author of *Ivanhoe*,' or like that between 'that is lightning' and 'that is a motion of electric charges.' The point I wish to make at present is simply that these analogies show the weakness of the . . . argument against identifying experiences and brain processes. I am, however, suggesting also that it may be the true nature of our inner experiences, as revealed by science, to be brain processes, just as to be a motion of electric charges is the true nature of lightning, what lightning really is. Neither the case of lightning nor the case of inner experiences is like that of explaining a footprint by reference to a burglar. It is not the true nature of a footprint to be a burglar.

In short, there can be contingent statements of the form 'A is identical with B,' and a person may know that something is an A without knowing it is a B. An illiterate peasant might well be able to talk about his sensations without knowing about his brain processes, just as he can talk about lightning, though he knows nothing about lightning... . .

A related objection which is sometimes put up against the brain process thesis runs as follows. It will be pointed out that the hypothesis that sensations are connected with brain processes shares the tentative character of all scientific hypotheses. It is possible, though in the highest degree unlikely, that our present physiological theories will one day be given up, and it will seem as absurd to connect sensations with the brain as it now does to connect them with the heart. It follows that when we report a sensation we are not reporting a brain process.

This argument falls to the ground once it is realised that assertions of identity can be factual and contingent. The argument certainly does prove that when I say 'I have a yellowish-orange after-image' I cannot *mean* that I have such-and-such a brain process. (Any more than that if a man says 'there goes the author of *Waverley*' he *means* 'there goes the author of *Ivanhoe*.' The two sentences are not inter-translatable.) But the argument does not prove that what we report (*e.g.* the having of an after-image) is not *in fact* a brain process. It could equally be said that it is conceivable (though in the highest degree unlikely) that the electrical theory of lightning should be given up. This shows indeed that 'that is lightning' does not *mean* the same as 'that is a motion of electric charges.' But for all that, lightning is *in fact* a motion of electric charges. . . . Now it may be said that if we identify an experience and a brain process and if this identification is, as I hold it is, a *contingent* or *factual* one, then the experience must be identified as having some property not logically deducible from the properties whereby we identify the brain process. To return to our analogy of the contingent identification of the author of *Waverley* with the author of *Ivanhoe*. If the property of being the author of *Waverley* is the analogue of the neurophysiological properties of a brain process, what is the analogue of the property of being author of *Ivanhoe?* There is an inclination to say: 'an irreducible, emergent, introspectible property.'

How do I get round this objection? I do so as follows. The man who reports a yellowish-orange after-image does so in effect as follows: '*What is going on in me is like what is going on in me when* my eyes are open, the lighting is normal, etc., etc., and there really is a yellowish-orange patch on the wall.' In this sentence the word 'like' is meant to be used in such a way that something can be like itself: an identical twin is not only like his brother but is like himself too. With this sense of 'like' the above formula will do for a report that one is having a veridical sense datum too. Notice that the italicised words '*what is going on in me is like what is going on in me when* . . .' are topic-neutral. A dualist will think that what is going on in him when he reports an experience is in fact a non-physical process (though his report does not say that it is), an ancient Greek may think that it is a process in his heart, and I think that it is a process in my brain. The report itself is neutral to all these possibilities. This extreme 'openness' and 'topic neutrality' of reports of experiences perhaps explains why the 'raw feels' or immediate qualia of internal experiences have seemed so elusive. 'What is going on in me is like what is going on in me when . . .' is a colourless phrase, just as the word 'somebody' is colourless. If I say 'somebody is coming through the garden' I may do so because I see my wife coming through the garden. Because of the colourless feel of the word 'somebody' a very naïve hearer (like the king in *Alice in Wonderland*, who got thoroughly confused over the logical grammar of 'nobody') might suspect that 'somebody is coming through the garden' is about some very elusive and ghostly entity, instead of, in fact, that very colourful and flesh and blood person, my wife.

For this account to be successful, it is necessary that we should be able to report two processes as like one another without being able to say in what respect they are alike. An experience of having an after-image may be classified as like the experience I have when I see an orange, and this likeness, on my view, must consist in a similarity of neuro-physiological patterns. But of course we are not immediately aware of the pattern; at most we are able to report the similarity. Now it is tempting, when we think in a metaphysical and *a priori* way, to suppose that reports of similarities can be made only on a basis of the conscious apprehension of the features in respect of which these similarities subsist. But when we think objectively about the human being as a functioning mechanism this metaphysical supposition may come to seem unwarranted. It is surely more easy to construct a mechanism which will record (on a punched tape, for example) bare similarities in a class of stimuli than it is to construct a machine which will provide a report of the features in which these similarities consist. It therefore seems to me quite possible that we should be able to make reports to the effect that 'what is going on in me is like what goes on in me when . . .' without having any idea whatever of what in particular is going on in me (*e.g.* whether a brain process, a heart process, or a spiritual process).

I must make it clear that I am not producing the phrase 'What is going on in me is like what goes on in me when . . .' as a *translation* of a sensation report. It is rather meant to give in an informal way what a sensation report purports to be about. For example, it has been objected that it is no good translating 'I have a pain' as 'what is going on in me is like what goes on when a pin is stuck into me,' since, to put it crudely, pains have nothing in particular to do with pins, and certainly someone might learn the word 'pain' without ever having learned the word 'pin.' When, however, I say that 'I have a pain' is to the effect of 'what is going on in me is like what goes on in me when a pin is stuck into me,' my intention is *simply* to indicate the way in which learning to make sensation reports is learning to report likenesses and unlikenesses of various internal processes. There is indeed no need to learn the word 'pain' by having a pin stuck into one. A child may,

for example, be introduced to the word 'pain' when he accidentally grazes his knee. But sensation talk must be learned with reference to some environmental stimulus situation or another. Certainly it need not be any *particular* one, such as the sticking in of pins.

The above considerations also show how we can reply to another objection which is commonly brought against the brain-process theory. The experience, it will be said, is not in physical space, whereas the brain process is. Hence the experience is not a brain process. This objection seems to beg the question. If my view is correct the experience *is* in physical space: in my brain. The truth behind the objection is that the experience is not reported as something spatial. It is reported only (in effect) in terms of 'what is going on in me is like what goes on in me when. . . .' This report is so 'open' and general that it is indeed neutral between my view that what goes on in me goes on in physical space and the psychophysical dualist's view that what goes on in me goes on in a nonspatial entity. This is without prejudice to the statement that what goes on in me is something which in fact *is* in physical space. On my view sensations do in fact have all sorts of neurophysiological properties. For they are neurophysiological processes. . . .

We must now pass on to consider another objection. This is that our experiences are private, immediately known only to ourselves, whereas brain processes are public, observable (in principle) by any number of external observers. If someone sincerely says that he is having a certain experience, then no one can contradict him. But if the physiologist reports something in the brain, then it is always *in principle* possible to say: 'Perhaps you are mistaken; you may be having an illusion or hallucination or something of the sort.' It will be remembered that I suggested that in reporting sensations we are in fact reporting likenesses and unlikenesses of brain processes. Now it may be objected (as has been done by K.E.M. Baier): 'Suppose that you had some electro-encephalograph fixed to your brain, and you observed that, according to the electro-encephalograph, you did *not* have the sort of brain process that normally goes on when you have a yellow sense datum. Nevertheless, if you had a yellow sense datum you would not give up the proposition that you had such a sense datum, no matter *what* the

encephalograph said.' This part of the objection can be easily answered. I simply reply that the brain-process theory was put forward as a factual identification, not as a logically necessary one. I can therefore agree that it is logically possible that the electro-encephalograph experiment should turn out as envisaged in the objection, but I can still believe *that this will never in fact happen.* If it did happen I should doubtless give up the brain-process theory. . . .

[However], it is incumbent on anyone who wishes to dispute the brain-process theory to produce experiences which are known to possess irreducibly 'psychic' properties, not merely 'topic neutral' ones. So far I do not think that anyone has done so.

PHILOSOPHY OF SCIENCE

Throughout their writings materialists have stressed the role and importance of scientific thought for their philosophy. Now, with Morris R. Cohen and Ernest Nagel, we must inquire into the fundamental features of that thought for a fuller understanding of science and its method. The selection explains a number of key terms in scientific method such as fact, observation, hypothesis, deduction, evidence, and verification. The ideals of science are seen to be system, self-correction, utility, and truth. Finally, the authors note both the limits and the value of science: limits, for human beings are not omniscient; yet value, for in requiring detachment and disinterestedness science may be seen as "the finest flower and test of a liberal civilization."

9 The Value of Science
M. R. Cohen (1880-1947) and Ernest Nagel (1901-   )

[Earlier in the book,] we asserted that the method of science is free from the limitations and willfulness of the alternative methods for settling doubt which we there rejected. Scientific method, we declared, is the most assured technique

The selection is from pp. 391–396 and 399–403 of *An Introduction to Logic and Scientific Method* by Morris R. Cohen and Ernest Nagel; copyright, 1934, by Harcourt, Brace & World, Inc., and Routledge & Kegan Paul, Ltd. Used by permission of the publishers.

man has yet devised for controlling the flux of things and establishing stable beliefs. What are the fundamental features of this method? We have already examined in some detail different constituent parts of it. Let us in this final chapter bring together the more important threads of our discussions.

Facts and Scientific Method. The method of science does not seek to impose the desires and hopes of men upon the flux of things in a capricious manner. It may indeed be employed to satisfy the desires of men. But its successful use depends upon seeking, in a deliberate manner, and irrespective of what men's desires are, to recognize, as well as to take advantage of, the structure which the flux possesses.

1. Consequently, scientific method aims to discover what the facts truly are, and the use of the method must be guided by the discovered facts. But, as we have repeatedly pointed out, what the facts are cannot be discovered without reflection. Knowledge of the facts cannot be equated to the brute immediacy of our sensations. When our skin comes into contact with objects having high temperatures or with liquid air, the immediate experiences may be similar. We cannot, however, conclude without error that the temperatures of the substances touched are the same. Sensory experience sets the *problem* for knowledge, and just because such experience is immediate and final it must become informed by reflective analysis before knowledge can be said to take place.

2. Every inquiry arises from some felt problem, so that no inquiry can even get under way unless some selection or sifting of the subject matter has taken place. Such selection requires, we have been urging all along, some hypothesis, preconception, prejudice, which guides the research as well as delimits the subject matter of inquiry. Every inquiry is specific in the sense that it has a definite problem to solve, and such solution terminates the inquiry. It is idle to collect "facts" unless there is a problem upon which they are supposed to bear.

3. The ability to formulate problems whose solution may also help solve other problems is a rare gift, requiring extraordinary genius. The problems which meet us in daily life can be solved, if they can be solved at all, by the application of scientific method. But such problems do not, as a rule, raise far-reaching issues. The most striking applications of scientific method are to be found in the various natural and social sciences.

4. The "facts" for which every inquiry reaches out are propositions for whose truth there is considerable evidence. Consequently what the "facts" are must be determined by inquiry, and cannot be determined antecedently to inquiry. Moreover, what we believe to be the facts clearly depends upon the stage of our inquiry. There is therefore no sharp line dividing facts from guesses or hypotheses. During any inquiry the status of a proposition may change from that of hypothesis to that of fact, or from that of fact to that of hypothesis. Every so-called fact, therefore, *may* be challenged for the evidence upon which it is asserted to be a fact, even though no such challenge is actually made.

Hypotheses and Scientific Method. The method of science would be impossible if the hypotheses which are suggested as solutions could not be elaborated to reveal what they imply. The full meaning of a hypothesis is to be discovered in its implications.

1. Hypotheses are suggested to an inquirer by something in the subject matter under investigation, and by his previous knowledge of other subject matters. No rules can be offered for obtaining fruitful hypotheses, any more than rules can be given for discovering significant problems.

2. Hypotheses are required at every stage of an inquiry. It must not be forgotten that what are called general principles or laws (which may have been confirmed in a previous inquiry) can be applied to a present, still unterminated inquiry only with some risk. For they may not in fact be applicable. The general laws of any science function as hypotheses, which guide the inquiry in all its phases.

3. Hypotheses can be regarded as suggestions of possible connections between actual facts or imagined ones. The question of the truth of hypotheses need not, therefore, always be raised. The necessary feature of a hypothesis, from this point of view, is that it should be statable in a determinate form, so that its implications can be discovered by logical means.

4. The number of hypotheses which may occur to an inquirer is without limit, and is a function of the character of his imagination. There is a need, therefore, for a technique to choose between the alternative suggestions, and to make sure that the alternatives are in fact, and not only in appearance, *differ-ent* theories. Perhaps the most important and best explored part of such a technique is the technique of formal inference. For this reason, the structure of formal logic has been examined at some length. The object of that examination has been to give the reader an adequate sense of what formal validity means, as well as to provide him with a snyoptic view of the power and range of formal logic.

5. It is convenient to have on hand—in storage, so to speak—different hypotheses whose consequences have been carefully explored. It is the task of mathematics to provide and explore alternative hypotheses. Mathematics receives hints concerning what hypotheses to study from the natural sciences; and the natural sciences are indebted to mathematics for suggestions concerning the type of order which their subject matter embodies.

6. The deductive elaboration of hypotheses is not the sole task of scientific method. Since there is a plurality of possible hypotheses, it is the task of inquiry to determine which of the possible explanations or solutions of the problem is in best agreement with the facts. Formal considerations are therefore never sufficient to establish the material truth of any theory.

7. No hypothesis which states a general proposition can be demonstrated as absolutely true. We have seen that all inquiry which deals with matters of fact employs probable inference. The task of such investigations is to select that hypothesis which is the most probable on the factual evidence; and it is the task of further inquiry to find other factual evidence which will increase or decrease

the probability of such a theory.

Evidence and Scientific Method. Scientific method pursues the road of systematic doubt. It does not doubt *all* things, for this is clearly impossible. But it does question whatever lacks adequate evidence in its support.

1. Science is not satisfied with psychological certitude, for the mere intensity with which a belief is held is no guarantee of its truth. Science demands and looks for logically adequate grounds for the propositions it advances.

2. No single proposition dealing with matters of fact is beyond every significant doubt. No proposition is so well supported by evidence that other evidence may not increase or decrease its probability. However, while no single proposition is indubitable, the body of knowledge which supports it, and of which it is itself a part, is better grounded than any alternative body of knowledge.

3. Science is thus always ready to abandon a theory when the facts so demand. But the facts must really demand it. It is not unusual for a theory to be modified so that it may be retained in substance even though "facts" contradicted an earlier formulation of it. Scientific procedure is therefore a mixture of a willingness to change, and an obstinacy in holding on to, theories apparently incompatible with facts.

4. The verification of theories is only approximate. Verification simply shows that, within the margin of experimental error, the experiment is *compatible* with the verified hypothesis.

System in the Ideal of Science. The ideal of science is to achieve a systematic

interconnection of facts. Isolated propositions do not constitute a science. Such propositions serve merely as an opportunity to find the logical connection between them and other propositions.

1. "Common sense" is content with a miscellaneous collection of information. As a consequence, the propositions it asserts are frequently vague, the range of their application is unknown, and their mutual compatibility is generally very questionable. The advantages of discovering a system among facts is therefore obvious. A condition for achieving a system is the introduction of accuracy in the assertions made. The limit within which propositions are true is then clearly defined. Moreover, inconsistencies between propositions asserted become eliminated gradually because propositions which are part of a system must support and correct one another. The extent and accuracy of our information is thus increased. In fact, scientific method differs from other methods in the accuracy and number of facts it studies.

2. When, as frequently happens, a science abandons one theory for another, it is a mistake to suppose that science has become "bankrupt" and that it is incapable of discovering the structure of the subject matter it studies. Such changes indicate rather that the science is progressively realizing its ideal. For such changes arise from correcting previous observations or reasoning, and such correction means that we are in possession of more reliable facts.

3. The ideal of system requires that the propositions asserted to be true should be connected without the introduction of further propositions for which

the evidence is small or nonexistent. In a system the number of unconnected propositions and the number of propositions for which there is no evidence are at a minimum. Consequently, in a system the requirements of simplicity, as expressed in the principle of Occam's razor,[1] are satisfied in a high degree. For that principle declares that entities should not be multiplied beyond necessity. This may be interpreted as a demand that whatever is capable of proof should be proved. But the ideal of system requires just that.

4. The evidence for propositions which are elements in a system accumulates more rapidly than that for isolated propositions. The evidence for a proposition may come from its own verifying instances, or from the verifying instances of *other* propositions which are connected with the first in a system. It is this systematic character of scientific theories which gives such high probabilities to the various individual propositions of a science.

The Self-Corrective Nature of Scientific Method.   Science does not desire to obtain conviction for its propositions in *any* manner and at *any* price. Propositions must be supported by logically acceptable evidence, which must be weighed carefully and tested by the well-known canons of necessary and probable inference. It follows that the *method* of science is more stable, and more important to men of science, than any particular result achieved by its means.

[1 The reference is to a logical principle stated by the English Franciscan theologian, William of Occam or Ockham (1280–1349). The principle itself is given in the text. *Ed.*]

1. In virtue of its method, the enterprise of science is a self-corrective process. It appeals to no special revelation or authority whose deliverances are indubitable and final. It claims no infallibility, but relies upon the methods of developing and testing hypotheses for assured conclusions. The canons of inquiry are themselves discovered in the process of reflection, and may themselves become modified in the course of study. The method makes possible the noting and correction of errors by continued application of itself.

2. General propositions can be established only by the method of repeated sampling. Consequently, the propositions which a science puts forward for study are either confirmed in all possible experiments or modified in accordance with the evidence. It is this self-corrective nature of the method which allows us to challenge any proposition, but which also assures us that the theories which science accepts are more probable than any alternative theories. By not claiming more certainty than the evidence warrants, scientific method succeeds in obtaining more logical certainty than any other method yet devised.

3. In the process of gathering and weighing evidence, there is a continuous appeal from facts to theories or principles, and from principles to facts. For there is nothing intrinsically indubitable, there are no absolutely first principles, in the sense of principles which are self-evident or which must be known prior to everything else.

4. The method of science is thus essentially circular. We obtain evidence for principles by appealing to empirical material, to what is alleged to be "fact";

and we select, analyze, and interpret empirical material on the basis of principles. In virtue of such give and take between facts and principles, everything that is dubitable falls under careful scrutiny at one time or another. . . .

The Limits and the Value of Scientific Method. The desire for knowledge for its own sake is more widespread than is generally recognized by anti-intellectualists. It has its roots in the animal curiosity which shows itself in the cosmological questions of children and in the gossip of adults. No ulterior utilitarian motive makes people want to know about the private lives of their neighbors, the great, or the notorious. There is also a certain zest which makes people engage in various intellectual games or exercises in which one is required to find out something. But while the desire to know is wide, it is seldom strong enough to overcome the more powerful organic desires, and few indeed have both the inclination and the ability to face the arduous difficulties of scientific method in more than one special field. The desire to know is not often strong enough to sustain critical inquiry. Men generally are interested in the results, in the story or romance of science, not in the technical methods whereby these results are obtained and their truth continually is tested and qualified. Our first impulse is to accept the plausible as true and to reject the uncongenial as false. We have not the time, inclination, or energy to investigate everything. Indeed, the call to do so is often felt as irksome and joy-killing. And when we are asked to treat our cherished beliefs as mere hypotheses, we rebel as violently as when those dear to us are insulted. This provides the ground for various movements that are hostile to rational scientific procedure (though their promoters do not often admit that it is science to which they are hostile).

Mystics, intuitionists, authoritarians, voluntarists, and fictionalists are all trying to undermine respect for the rational methods of science. These attacks have always met with wide acclaim and are bound to continue to do so, for they strike a responsive note in human nature. Unfortunately they do not offer any reliable alternative method for obtaining verifiable knowledge. The great French writer Pascal opposed to logic the spirit of subtlety or finesse (*esprit géometrique* and *esprit de finesse*) and urged that the heart has its reasons as well as the mind, reasons that cannot be accurately formulated but which subtle spirits apprehend none the less.

Men as diverse as James Russell Lowell and George Santayana are agreed that:

> The soul is oracular still,

and

> It is wisdom to trust the heart . . .
> To trust the soul's invincible surmise.

Now it is true that in the absence of omniscience we must trust our soul's surmise; and great men are those whose surmises or intuitions are deep or penetrating. It is only by acting on our surmise that we can procure the evidence in its favor. But only havoc can result from confusing a surmise with a proposition for which there is already evidence. Are all the reasons of the heart sound? Do all oracles tell the truth? The sad history of human experience is distinctly discouraging to any such claim. Mystic intuition may give men absolute subjective certainty, but can give no proof that contrary intuitions are erroneous. It is obvious that when authorities conflict we must weigh the evidence in their favor logically if we are to make a rational choice. Certainly, when a truth is questioned it is no answer to say, "I am convinced," or, "I prefer to rely on this rather than on another authority." The view that physical science is no guide to proof, but is a mere fiction, fails to explain why it has enabled us to anticipate phenomena of nature and to control them. These attacks on scientific method receive a certain color of plausibility because of some indefensible claims made by uncritical enthusiasts. But it is of the essence of scientific method to limit its own pretension. Recognizing that we do not know everything, it does not claim the ability to solve all of our practical problems. It is an error to suppose, as is often done, that science denies the truth of all unverified propositions. For that which is unverified today may be verified tomorrow. We may get at truth by guessing or in other ways. Scientific method, however, is concerned with verification. Admittedly the wisdom of those engaged in this process has not been popularly ranked as high as that of the sage, the prophet, or the poet. Admittedly, also, we know of no way of supplying creative intelligence to those who lack it. Scientists, like all other human beings, may get into ruts and apply their techniques regardless of varying circumstances. There will always be formal procedures which are fruitless. Definitions and formal distinctions may be a sharpening of tools without

the wit to use them properly, and statistical information may conform to the highest technical standards and yet be irrelevant and inconclusive. Nevertheless, scientific method is the only way to increase the general body of tested and verified truth and to eliminate arbitrary opinion. It is well to clarify our ideas by asking for the precise meaning of our words, and to try to check our favorite ideas by applying them to accurately formulated propositions. . . .

In general the chief social condition of scientific method is a widespread desire for truth that is strong enough to withstand the powerful forces which make us cling tenaciously to old views or else embrace every novelty because it is a change. Those who are engaged in scientific work need not only leisure for reflection and material for their experiments, but also a community that respects the pursuit of truth and allows freedom for the expression of intellectual doubt as to its most sacred or established institutions. Fear of offending established dogmas has been an obstacle to the growth of astronomy and geology and other physical sciences; and the fear of offending patriotic or respected sentiment is perhaps one of the strongest hindrances to scholarly history and social science. On the other hand, when a community indiscriminately acclaims every new doctrine the love of truth becomes subordinated to the desire for novel formulations.

On the whole it may be said that the safety of science depends on there being men who care more for the justice of their methods than for any results obtained by their use. For this reason it is unfortunate when scientific research in the social field is largely in the hands of those not in a favorable position to oppose established or popular opinion.

We may put it the other way by saying that the physical sciences can be more liberal because we are sure that foolish opinions will be readily eliminated by the shock of facts. In the social field, however, no one can tell what harm may come of foolish ideas before the foolishness is finally, if ever, demonstrated. None of the precautions of scientific method can prevent human life from being an adventure, and no scientific investigator knows whether he will reach his goal. But scientific method does enable large numbers to walk with surer step. By analyzing the possibilities of any step or plan, it becomes possible to anticipate the future and adjust ourselves to it in advance. Scientific method thus minimizes the shock of novelty and the uncertainty of life. It enables us to frame policies of action and of moral judgment fit for a wider outlook than those of immediate physical stimulus or organic response.

Scientific method is the only effective way of strengthening the love of truth. It develops the intellectual courage to face difficulties and to overcome illusions that are pleasant temporarily but destructive ultimately. It settles differences without any external force by appealing to our common rational nature. The way of science, even if it is up a steep mountain, is open to all. Hence, while sectarian and partisan faiths are based on personal choice or temperament and divide men, scientific procedure unites men in something nobly devoid of all pettiness. Because it requires detachment, disinterestedness, it is the finest flower and test of a liberal civilization.

PHILOSOPHY OF RELIGION

Religion, like art and morality, is understood by the naturalist or materialist within the contexts of experience and nature. He makes no reference to the supernatural in his treatments of these subjects, for his basic metaphysical orientation disallows such reference. Though it may seem strange to treat religion without the supernatural, there are nevertheless many sensitive and discerning studies of religion by naturalists. Among them is that by George Santayana.

The selection is taken from Santayana's five-volume work, *The Life of Reason.* Reason for him is the seat of all ultimate values. Historical religions, Santayana observes, have also pursued ultimate value, although unlike reason, they have been unsuccessful in that pursuit. The cause of this failure lies in the fact that religion pursues truth through the imagination. Hence, it is allied to poetry; and, as with poetry, we must therefore judge religions as better or worse depending on the moral plane to which they lift their adherents, but never as true or false.

10 Reason and Religion

George Santayana (1863-1952)

Experience has repeatedly confirmed that well-known maxim of Bacon's, that "a little philosophy inclineth man's mind to atheism, but depth in philosophy bringeth men's minds about to religion." In every age the most comprehensive thinkers have found in the religion of their time and country something they could accept, interpreting and illustrating that religion so as to give it depth and universal application. Even the heretics and atheists, if they have had profundity, turn out after a while to be forerunners of some new orthodoxy. What they rebel against is a religion alien to their nature; they are atheists only by accident, and relatively to a convention which inwardly offends them, but they yearn mightily in their own souls after the religious acceptance of a world interpreted in their own fashion. So it appears in the end that their atheism and loud protestation were in fact the hastier part of their thought, since what emboldened them to deny the poor world's faith was that they were too impatient to understand it. Indeed, the enlightenment common to young wits and worm-eaten old satirists, who plume themselves on detecting the scientific ineptitude of religion—something which the blindest half see—is not nearly enlightened enough: it points to notorious facts incompatible with religious tenets literally taken, but it leaves unexplored the habits of thought from which those tenets sprang, their original meaning, and their true function. Such studies would bring the skeptic face to face with the mystery and pathos of mortal existence. They would make him understand why religion is so profoundly moving and in a sense so profoundly just.. There must needs be something humane and necessary in an influence that has become the most general sanction of virtue, the chief occasion for art and philosophy, and the source, perhaps, of the best human happiness. If nothing, as Hooker said, is "so malapert as a splenetic religion," a sour irreligion is almost as perverse.

At the same time, when Bacon penned the sage epigram we have quoted he forgot to add that the God to whom depth in philosophy brings back men's minds is far from being the same from whom a little philosophy estranges them. It would be pitiful indeed if mature reflection bred no better conceptions than those which have drifted down the muddy stream of time, where tradition and passion have jumbled everything together. Traditional conceptions, when they are felicitous, may be adopted by the poet, but they must be purified by the moralist and disintegrated by the philosopher. Each religion, so dear to those whose life it sanctifies, and fulfilling so necessary a function in the society that has adopted

The selection is reprinted with the permission of Charles Scribner's Sons from *The Life of Reason: Reason in Religion* by George Santayana, copyright 1905 Charles Scribner's Sons; renewal copyright 1933 George Santayana; and with the permission of Constable and Company, Ltd., pp. 3–14.

it, necessarily contradicts every other religion, and probably contradicts itself. What religion a man shall have is a historical accident, quite as much as what language he shall speak. In the rare circumstances where a choice is possible, he may, with some difficulty, make an exchange; but even then he is only adopting a new convention which may be more agreeable to his personal temper but which is essentially as arbitrary as the old.

The attempt to speak without speaking any particular language is not more hopeless than the attempt to have a religion that shall be no religion in particular. A courier's or a dargoman's speech may indeed be often unusual and drawn from disparate sources, not without some mixture of personal originality; but that private jargon will have a meaning only because of its analogy to one or more conventional languages and its obvious derivation from them. So travellers from one religion to another, people who have lost their spiritual nationality, may often retain a neutral and confused residuum of belief, which they may egregiously regard as the essence of all religion, so little may they remember the graciousness and naturalness of that ancestral accent which a perfect religion should have. Yet a moment's probing of the conceptions surviving in such minds will show them to be nothing but vestiges of old beliefs, creases which thought, even if emptied of all dogmatic tenets, has not been able to smooth away at its first unfolding. Later generations, if they have any religion at all, will be found either to revert to ancient authority, or to attach themselves spontaneously to something wholly novel

and immensely positive, to some faith promulgated by a fresh genius and passionately embraced by a converted people. Thus every living and healthy religion has a marked idiosyncrasy. Its power consists in its special and surprising message and in the bias which that revelation gives to life. The vistas it opens and the mysteries it propounds are another world to live in; and another world to live in—whether we expect ever to pass wholly into it or no— is what we mean by having a religion.

What relation, then, does this great business of the soul, which we call religion, bear to the Life of Reason? That the relation between the two is close seems clear from several circumstances. The Life of Reason is the seat of all ultimate values. Now the history of mankind will show us that whenever spirits at once lofty and intense have seemed to attain the highest joys, they have envisaged and attained them in religion. Religion would therefore seem to be a vehicle or a factor in rational life, since the ends of rational life are attained by it. Moreover, the Life of Reason is an ideal to which everything in the world should be subordinated; it establishes lines of moral cleavage everywhere and makes right eternally different from wrong. Religion does the same thing. It makes absolute moral decisions. It sanctions, unifies, and transforms ethics. Religion thus exercises a function of the Life of Reason. And a further function which is common to both is that of emancipating man from his personal limitations. In different ways religions promise to transfer the soul to better conditions. A supernaturally favored kingdom is to be established for posterity upon earth, or for all the faithful in heaven, or the soul is to be freed by repeated purgations from all taint and sorrow, or it is to be lost in the absolute, or it is to become an influence and an object of adoration in the places it once haunted or wherever the activities it once loved may be carried on by future generations of its kindred. Now reason in its ways lays before us all these possibilities: it points to common objects, political and intellectual, in which an individual may lose what is mortal and accidental in himself and immortalize what is rational and human; it teaches us how sweet and fortunate death may be to those whose spirit can still live in their country and in their ideas; it reveals the radiating effects of action and the eternal objects of thought.

Yet the difference in tone and language must strike us, so soon as it is philosophy that speaks. That change should remind us that even if the function of religion and that of reason coincide, this function is performed in the two cases by very different organs. Religions are many, reason one. Religion consists of conscious ideas, hopes, enthusiasms, and objects of worship; it operates by grace and flourishes by prayer. Reason, on the other hand, is a mere principle or potential order, on which, indeed, we may come to reflect, but which exists in us ideally only, without variation or stress of any kind. We conform or do not conform to it; it does not urge or chide us, nor call for any emotions on our part other than those naturally aroused by the various objects which it unfolds in their true nature and proportion. Religion brings some order into life by weighing it with new materials. Reason adds to the nat-

ural materials only the perfect order which it introduces into them. Rationality is nothing but a form, an ideal constitution which experience may more or less embody. Religion is a part of experience itself, a mass of sentiments and ideas. The one is an inviolate principle, the other a changing and struggling force. And yet this struggling and changing force of religion seems to direct man toward something eternal. It seems to make for an ultimate harmony within the soul and for an ultimate harmony between the soul and all the soul depends upon. So that religion, in its intent, is a more conscious and direct pursuit of the Life of Reason than is society, science, or art. For these approach and fill out the ideal life tentatively and piecemeal, hardly regarding the goal or caring for the ultimate justification of their instinctive aims. Religion also has an instinctive and blind side, and bubbles up in all manner of chance practices and intuitions; soon, however, it feels its way toward the heart of things, and, from whatever quarter it may come, veers in the direction of the ultimate.

Nevertheless, we must confess that this religious pursuit of the Life of Reason has been singularly abortive. Those within the pale of each religion may prevail upon themselves to express satisfaction with its results, thanks to a fond partiality in reading the past and generous draughts of hope for the future; but any one regarding the various religions at once and comparing their achievements with what reason requires, must feel how terrible is the disappointment which they have one and all prepared for mankind. Their chief anxiety has been to offer imaginary remedies for mortal ills, some of which are incurable essentially, while others might have been really cured by well-directed effort. The Greek oracles, for instance, pretended to heal our natural ignorance, which has its appropriate though difficult cure, while the Christian vision of heaven pretended to be an antidote to our natural death, the inevitable correlate of birth and of a changing and conditioned existence. By methods of this sort little can be done for the real betterment of life. To confuse intelligence and dislocate sentiment by gratuitous fictions is a short-sighted way of pursuing happiness. Nature is soon avenged. An unhealthy exaltation and a one-sided morality have to be followed by regrettable reactions. When these come, the real rewards of life may seem vain to a relaxed vitality, and the very name of virtue may irritate young spirits untrained in any natural excellence. Thus religion too often debauches the morality it comes to sanction, and impedes the science it ought to fulfil.

What is the secret of this ineptitude? Why does religion, so near to rationality in its purpose, fall so far short of it in its texture and in its results? The answer is easy: Religion pursues rationality through the imagination. When it explains events or assigns causes, it is an imaginative substitute for science. When it gives precepts, insinuates ideals, or remolds aspiration, it is an imaginative substitute for wisdom—I mean for the deliberate and impartial pursuit of all good. The conditions and the aims of life are both represented in religion poetically, but this poetry tends to arrogate to itself literal truth and moral authority, neither of which it possesses. Hence the depth and importance of religion become intelligible no less than its contradictions and practical disasters. Its object is the same as that of reason, but its method is to proceed by intuition and by unchecked poetical conceits. These are repeated and vulgarized in proportion to their original fineness and significance, till they pass for reports of objective truth and come to constitute a world of faith, superposed upon the world of experience and regarded as materially enveloping it, if not in space at least in time and in existence. The only truth of religion comes from its interpretation of life, from its symbolic rendering of that moral experience which it springs out of and which it seeks to elucidate. Its falsehood comes from the insidious misunderstanding which clings to it, to the effect that these poetic conceptions are not merely representations of experience as it is or should be, but are rather information about experience or reality elsewhere—an experience and reality which, strangely enough, supply just the defects betrayed by reality and experience here.

Thus religion has the same original relation to life that poetry has; only poetry, which never pretends to literal validity, adds a pure value to existence, the value of a liberal imaginative exercise. The poetic value of religion would initially be greater than that of poetry itself, because religion deals with higher and more practical themes, with sides of life which are in greater need of some imaginative touch and ideal interpretation than are those pleasant or pompous things which ordinary poetry dwells upon. But this initial advantage is neutralized in part by the abuse to which religion is subject, whenever its symbolic rightness is taken for scientific truth.

Like poetry, it improves the world only by imagining it improved, but not content with making this addition to the mind's furniture—an addition which might be useful and ennobling—it thinks to confer a more radical benefit by persuading mankind that, in spite of appearances, the world is really such as that rather arbitrary idealization has painted it. This spurious satisfaction is naturally the prelude to many a disappointment, and the soul has infinite trouble to emerge again from the artificial problems and sentiments into which it is thus plunged. The value of religion becomes equivocal. Religion remains an imaginative achievement, a symbolic representation of moral reality which may have a most important function in vitalizing the mind and in transmitting, by way of parables, the lessons of experience. But it becomes at the same time a continuous incidental deception; and this deception, in proportion as it is strenuously denied to be such, can work indefinite harm in the world and in the conscience.

On the whole, however, religion should not be conceived as having taken the place of anything better, but rather as having come to relieve situations which, but for its presence, would have been infinitely worse. In the thick of active life, or in the monotony of practical slavery, there is more need to stimulate fancy than to control it. Natural instinct is not much disturbed in the human brain by what may happen in that thin superstratum of ideas which commonly overlays it. We must not blame religion for preventing the development of a moral and natural science which at any rate would seldom have appeared; we must rather thank

it for the sensibility, the reverence, the speculative insight which it has introduced into the world.

We may therefore proceed to analyze the significance and the function which religion has had at its different stages, and, without disguising or in the least condoning its confusion with literal truth, we may allow ourselves to enter as sympathetically as possible into its various conceptions and emotions. They have made up the inner life of many sages, and of all those who without great genius or learning have lived steadfastly in the spirit. The feeling of reverence should itself be treated with reverence, although not at a sacrifice of truth, with which alone, in the end, reverence is compatible. Nor have we any reason to be intolerant of the partialities and contradictions which religions display. Were we dealing with a science, such contradictions would have to be instantly solved and removed; but when we are concerned with the poetic interpretation of experience, contradiction means only variety, and variety means spontaneity, wealth of resource, and a nearer approach to total adequacy.

If we hope to gain any understanding of these matters we must begin by taking them out of that heated and fanatical atmosphere in which the Hebrew tradition has enveloped them. The Jews had no philosophy, and when their national traditions came to be theoretically explicated and justified, they were made to issue in a puerile scholasticism and a rabid intolerance. The question of monotheism, for instance, was a terrible question to the Jews. Idolatry did not consist in worshipping a god who, not being ideal, might be unworthy of worship, but rather in recognizing other gods than the one worshipped in Jerusalem. To the Greeks, on the contrary, whose philosophy was enlightened and ingenuous, monotheism and polytheism seemed perfectly innocent and compatible. To say God or the gods was only to use different expressions for the same influence, now viewed in its abstract unity and correlation with all existence, now viewed in its various manifestations in moral life, in nature, or in history. So that what in Plato, Aristotle, and the Stoics meets us at every step—the combination of monotheism with polytheism—is no contradiction, but merely an intelligent variation of phrase to indicate various aspects or functions in physical and moral things. When religion appears to us in this light its contradictions and controversies lose all their bitterness. Each doctrine will simply represent the moral plane on which they live who have devised or adopted it. Religions will thus be better or worse, never true or false. We shall be able to lend ourselves to each in turn, and seek to draw from it the secret of its inspiration.

CRITIQUE

In spite of their support in much of our contemporary scientific and technological world, the basic theses of materialism on the primacy of matter and the methodological supremacy of science have their sharp critics. One of them, Edgar S. Brightman, takes issue with both theses, finding the first reductive and the second dogmatic. Brightman is aware of the varieties of materialism, and even surveys some of them. While he particularly focuses his observations on naturalism, his critique really extends to materialism as a whole.

Brightman's own philosophic position is a form of idealism known as personalism. Rather than asserting the primacy of matter, personalism holds that conscious personality provides the best clues we have about the nature of reality. We turn to the study of idealism in the next section.

11 The Limits of Naturalism
Edgar S. Brightman (1884-1953)

In one positive respect, modern naturalism is a marked advance over ancient materialism or even over nineteenth century mechanism and atomism. From

---

The selection is from Edgar S. Brightman, *Nature and Values* (New York: Abingdon-Cokesbury Press, 1945), pp. 97-109. Copyright renewal 1973 by Irma Fall Brightman. Used by permission of Abingdon Press.

Democritus to "nineteenth century physics," the atom was the fundamental unit of materialism. The atoms were solid, impenetrable, and eternal; they were in constant motion, although there was no clear reason why they should move. But from the middle of the nineteenth century on—under the combined influence of Darwin, of Marx, and of the new physics—materialists began to see that the old solid atoms were superfluous; they began to talk of a world of energy, of fields of force, or of events. Materialism became "Diamat" (dialectical materialism) or naturalism, with the stress on evolution and activity. Atoms ceased to be solid; they became fields of force. Modern naturalists, like R. W. Sellars, think of existence as activity.[1] W. R. Dennes speaks of the shift in recent naturalism "from such categories as matter and motion to the categories 'event,' 'quality,' and 'relation.' "[2] Such writers as Samuel Alexander and John Dewey, as well as R. W. Sellars, have developed an "evolutionary naturalism" which lays stress on what has become well known as "emergent" evolution. Naturalists are, of late, also emphasizing continuity among the activities or processes of nature;[3] and they are no longer regarding that continuity as merely mechanical.[4]

In so far as naturalists regard nature as a world of living activity, evolution, and continuous process, they are moving away from traditional naturalism to points of view which have been characteristic of idealists, and especially of personalists. Berkeley, Leibniz, Hegel, Lotze, and Bowne have consistently defined being as activity. The conception of development became dominant in modern philosophy through Hegel. The law of continuity (the *lex continui*) was a contribution of the panpsychistic personalist, Leibniz. Some of the modern thinkers for whom the idea of emergent or creative evolution has come to be of central importance started out with more or less naturalistic bias, but have moved far in the direction of idealism or personalistic theism. This is true of Bergson,[5] of Lloyd Morgan,[6] and of Whitehead.[7]

It appears, consequently, that the first two traits of naturalism which we have examined are strongly emphasized by naturalists and are sometimes claimed by them as their sole property, but that they are in no sense purely naturalistic. In truth, the revolt against dogma and the belief in nature as a realm of continuous, living, evolving activity are characteristic of idealism and are accepted by most philosophical theists. No one need regret that there are increasing signs of what Bosanquet once called "the meeting of extremes in contemporary philosophy." On the other hand, it would be a great mistake to suppose that the extremes have met, that naturalism has become idealism, and that there is no longer any issue at

---

[1] See the expressions "what, in existence, is a local activity" and "the activations of agents" in Sellars, "Dewey on Materialism," *Philosophy and Phenomenological Research,* III (1943), 383.

[2] See Dennes in Krikorian, *Naturalism and the Human Spirit* (New York: Columbia University Press, 1944), p. 271.

[3] See the discussions of continuity by Thelma Z. Lavine (citing and supporting Dewey) and Herbert W. Schneider, in *ibid.,* pp. 183-84, 124-25.

[4] Life as "purposive behavior" is not to be "turned into mechanism," nor mechanism into life. Such is the substance of Y. H. Krikorian's view, *ibid.,* p. 245.

[5] *The Two Sources of Morality and Religion* (New York: Henry Holt & Co., 1935).
[6] *Emergent Evolution* (New York: Henry Holt & Co., 1923).
[7] *Process and Reality* (New York: The Macmillan Co., 1929).

stake between them. Naturalism is one world and idealism is another; but recent developments have made it increasingly difficult to define the limits of each. Naturalism is no longer what its defenders or its critics in the nineteenth century took it to be. It is today in a state of ferment and transition. If it is "one world," it may well be called a world of confused issues. Let us try to find some order in the chaos.

Naturalism, we have just said, is a world of confused issues. The root of the confusion, as has been pointed out already, lies in the failure of naturalists to arrive at a clear definition of what they mean by nature. When they identify nature with the physical world disclosed by the senses, nature is easily contrasted with supernature, the physical with the spiritual. Obviously we do not perceive duty or love of God by our senses. When naturalists hold that nature defined as the object of sense perception is all that there is, their denial of the supernatural has a meaning: namely, that all experiences which are not sensory are illusory or purely subjective. But if naturalists define nature as all that there is, without giving any other definition of nature than mere inclusiveness or allness, then it is meaningless for such naturalists to attack supernaturalism. If nature is all, then, conceivably, God and prayer and miracles are realities or processes within nature, and they could not intelligibly be called supernatural. Until naturalists become more exact in definition this area of confusion will remain unclarified, and no one will know clearly what they assert when they assert nature or what they deny when they deny the supernatural.

There is a second area of confusion when naturalists talk about scientific method. When a man of science, undefiled by naturalistic philosophy (or any other!), speaks of scientific method, he usually means first of all the method of his own science, whether it be physics or chemistry or biology or geology or astronomy. Some sciences, such as logic and mathematics, are chiefly concerned with the principles of necessary deduction; their methods are independent of any particular sensory experiences, and rest solely on the experiences of reasoning. Hence they are called formal. Usually when we speak of scientific method we mean the method common to the natural sciences. Their scientific method includes observation (of sense data or objects), accurate description, hypothesis, prediction, and experiment.[8] The description, the hypothesis, and the experiment are more scientific the more accurate they are; and in most sciences mathematics is the best possible measure of accuracy. Yet scientific method varies with the subject matter. In astronomy, experiment is impossible; the heavenly bodies are observed but not tampered with. Nevertheless astronomy is perhaps the most remarkable of all sciences in its predictions. Geology, likewise, must forego experiment, but it also foregoes prediction, except in a very rough sense; its use of mathematics is not comparable with that in physics or astrophysics.

Scientific method, therefore, cannot rightly be conceived in any narrow sense.

---

[8] For an important treatment of the topic by a logical positivist, see Hans Reichenbach, *Experience and Prediction* (Chicago: University of Chicago Press, 1938). [On positivism, see Section V below. *Ed.*]

For many years I have been convinced that one of the chief obstacles both to understanding among scientists and also to understanding between scientists and the general public is the tendency of some scientists to judge other fields in terms of the methods used in their own field. Some sociologists interpret mathematics and morals solely from the sociological point of view; some psychologists interpret philosophy and religion solely from the psychological point of view. This tendency results in nothing but confusion and misunderstanding. The sociologist who thinks of morals only as mores or the psychologist who supposes that all religion is only rationalization will never understand either morals or religion. His method prevents him from trying to understand them. Any provincial restriction, which requires the exclusive use of one scientific method and one only for all types of subject matter, is worthy of being called methodological dogmatism.[9] A physical dogmatist would insist that numbers and thoughts must be treated as matter in motion; and he would rightly be laughed out of court as being incompetent in the fields of mathematics and psychology.

It is of the utmost importance, therefore, to distinguish what is common to all scientific method from what is peculiar to the methods of one field. As we have seen, naturalists rightly reject the method of anathema and of authoritative pronouncements in favor of an appeal to experience, if not always to experiment; for no experimental operations can be performed on the sun or the geological past. If naturalists mean by their appeal to scientific method no more than that all beliefs must be tested by a clear and exact appeal to experience, I quite agree with them. Their method is the method of Jesus, who said, "By their fruits ye shall know them," and their appeal is the appeal of the man born blind: "Whereas I was blind, now I see."[10]

The great trouble with naturalists, however, is that as soon as they begin to talk about scientific method they begin to manifest symptoms of methodological dogmatism. Y. H. Krikorian, the editor of naturalism's most comprehensive manifesto, illustrates this in his chapter on "A Naturalistic View of Mind."[11] He defines naturalism as holding a "basic belief" in "the universal application of the experimental method," which he calls objective. Since he goes on to criticize Hocking and Maritain, who recognize something "supersensible," it is clear that Krikorian means by "objective" the same as "sensible" or "sensory." But if experimental method be of "universal application," why not apply it to supersensible experience? Krikorian has committed the fallacy of methodological dogmatism, because he has called his method "universal" and then restricted it to the field of his special interest.

Method means, literally, a "road

[9] See E. S. Brightman, "What Constitutes a Scientific Interpretation of Religion?" in *Journal of Philosophy*, **XXIII** (1926), 250-58, where the subject is discussed more fully.

[10] See John 9:25. Because of my appeal to experience, I have been called a naturalist by one theological reviewer, and another has expressed doubt whether I was a naturalist or a liberal. The present book should clear the fog.

[11] *Op. cit.*, pp. 242-69, especially the first pages of the chapter.

after," that is, a pursuit of something. Scientific method is a pursuit of facts, laws, and truths in special fields. Philosophical method is a pursuit of facts, laws, and truths pertaining to experience as a whole. If naturalists make a philosophy out of a method which excludes all facts except those accessible to our senses, they contradict the very nature of philosophy and mutilate experience by refusing to admit experiences which are not of the kind which they prefer. Each science must, of course, exclude facts irrelevant to it; physics must exclude all moral, religious, and metaphysical judgments from its experiments and laws. But to declare that facts which are irrelevant to the particular purposes of physics, or of any other special science, are therefore not facts is to deny the very evidence of experience. It is both unusual and encouraging to note that Ray Lepley in a recent book has declared that verification should not be restricted to "empirical [sensory] operations of testing," but should include methods of "critical reflective thinking . . . and the like."[12]

Naturalists, we see, are confused about whether scientific method restricts us to the physical and sensory or allows a more adequate view of experience. They are also confused about the results of scientific method. Their confusion at this point is not purely arbitrary but rests on a dilemma which experience forces on everyone. On the one hand we have to act: existential theologians and pragmatists would agree with personalists at this point. Life demands decisions. On the other hand, life does not

furnish sufficient light for perfect decisions. Only in purely formal sciences, like logic and mathematics, is there logical necessity; but all judgments about persons or societies or things or values are to some extent tentative. The evidence is never all in. Neither science nor philosophy, much less common sense, can give us absolute knowledge.

Here is the dilemma. We must decide; yet we never can decide with perfect knowledge. If we decide to wait for perfect knowledge, even that decision is imperfectly grounded. If we decide to act without perfect knowledge, we may be wrong. This dilemma is inherent in the human situation and there is no escape. We cannot avoid the necessity of decision; and we cannot avoid the possibility of being wrong. If someone tells us that he has perfect knowledge, we, just as we are, have to decide whether to believe him; and a Protestant conscience always has to decide whether or not to accept Catholic theory.

There is, therefore, a sense in which all decisions made by man must be tentative, subject to further light. Science and religion agree in principle on this point. The scientist holds all his hypotheses lightly, being perfectly willing to abandon any hypothesis which is refuted by new experimental evidence. The religious believer knows that his beliefs are something seen "through a glass, darkly," and are "but broken lights of Thee." All human decisions and creeds are subject to divine correction. God knows it better.

Naturalists, however, take this truth of the tentativeness of all human knowledge and press it to extremes, or, rather, they treat it arbitrarily. In so far as they see—like Dewey in *The Quest for Cer-*

---

[12] See his *The Verifiability of Value*, pp. 20-21.

tainty or Bosley in *The Quest for Religious Certainty*—that we cannot attain absolute finality, they are on solid ground. But when they infer that, because the scientific method requires open-mindedness, it therefore prohibits any commitments, they become confused.

This confusion is especially manifest in the fields of ethics, religion, and metaphysics. If the tentativeness of scientific methods means that commitment is forbidden, then no consistent naturalist could be depended on to keep a contract, to be loyal to his country, or even to believe sincerely in the operational method. Ethical decisions are necessary, even in the absence of perfect knowledge. So, too, it is necessary to decide what attitude one is to assume toward religion, and in principle a naturalist who commits himself to irreligion is in at least as precarious a position as one who commits himself to religion; and, practically speaking, everyone must commit himself to one or the other of these views. The typical naturalistic tentativeness manifests itself especially in regard to metaphysics. Naturalistic refusal to pass any metaphysical judgments is called positivism.

At this point there is a basic confusion about the meaning of tentativeness. If tentativeness means a complete suspension of judgment and a refusal to try any experiment, it means total cessation of thought and of progress; and this is exactly what consistent positivism means regarding knowledge of God and even of human personality, to say nothing of nature itself. But if tentativeness means search for the truth, commitment to truth now apprehended, and willingness to learn new truth as well as to

criticize old beliefs, then it is at least as sound to have faith in God in this spirit as it is to develop a science or to be committed to naturalistic method.

By way of summary, it may be said that we find among naturalists a twofold confusion about scientific method: an uncertainty about the restriction of that method to sensory data and an uncertainty about the practical effects of the open-mindedness inherent in scientific method. When scientific method is allowed to face all the facts including values and ideals, and when open-mindedness is seen to include and require decisions and commitments, naturalism is greatly weakened. It ceases to be an effective foe of theistic belief.

A third area of confusion in naturalistic thought centers about the conception of reason. Naturalists talk much about intelligence, meaning by intelligence the application of scientific method. At the same time, many naturalists are very dubious of system and of any attempt at inclusiveness in thought.[13]

The best way to clarify the situation here is to propose an inclusive definition of reason, as distinguished from the special applications of reason to one field or another. We suggest that reason

---

[13] There are, of course, exceptions to this. Naturalists like R. W. Sellars or D. C. Williams aim sincerely to be systematic and inclusive. Ernest Nagel, following Duhein, holds that "only systems of beliefs can be put to a definitive test," and he calls this "a commonplace" (see Krikorian, *op. cit.*, p. 240). Abraham Edel hopes for "the most systematic account of the field" (*ibid.*, p. 69). But Sidney Hook would rule out system and inclusiveness by assigning values to "the viscera" (*ibid.*, p. 41; but cf. p. 57). See Brightman, *A Philosophy of Religion* (New York: Prentice-Hall, Inc., 1940), pp. 232-33, n. 34.

is an ideal of completely coherent thinking and living, never fully realized, never merely static, yet always imperative in its claims. It is the supreme court of the mind. It consists of the following norms:

Be consistent (eliminate all contradictions).

Be systematic (discover all relevant relations).

Be inclusive (weigh all available experiences).

Be analytic (consider all the elements of which every complex consists).

Be synoptic (relate all the elements of any whole to its properties as a whole).

Be active (use experimental method).

Be open to alternatives (consider many possible hypotheses).

Be critical (test and verify or falsify hypotheses).

Be decisive (be committed to the best available hypothesis).

This analysis of reason speaks for itself. The inevitable conclusion is that if one appeals to reason he appeals to systematic thought; if he does not appeal to reason he cannot be reasoned with. Naturalists need to give much more consideration to the structure and function of reason.

A fourth confusion in naturalistic thought is its inability to choose between positivism and metaphysics. A consistent positivist is a kind of idealist: all knowledge is based on verifiable sensory experience. This is Berkeleianism[14] minus God. But on the other hand, constant traffic with sensations leads naturalists toward materialism or at least

toward "physical realism," and so to an anti-idealistic metaphysics. The naturalist is in unstable equilibrium between subjective idealism and objective materialism. Whichever decision the naturalist makes leads him to conflict with many of his own principles and with fellow naturalists.

A fifth confusion, closely related to the fourth, is concerned with consciousness. Among many naturalists, extreme behaviorism is popular, with its denial of consciousness, although many others are willing to grant to consciousness a place in nature. Yet there is a peculiar aversion to facing the facts of consciousness. Mr. Dewey, for example, in the Krikorian volume has spoken about "alleged facts of and about mind, consciousness, self, and so forth."[15] He objects not only to "subject" and "person," but even to "sensations" and "sense-data." Krikorian declares that "mind must be analyzed as behavior" and as "anticipatory response," yet he freely admits "consciousness";[16] with one breath he concedes that there are "immediate feelings," and with another he identifies the unity which is "the whole mind" with "the biological organism."[17] Is an immediate feeling a biological fact? Further confusion in this connection lies in the use of the word "experience," which Dewey, in *Experience and Nature*, used so broadly as to include under it many processes of nature which do not fall in any sense within human consciousness. Clarity can be achieved only if our conscious-

[14 For Bishop Berkeley's views, see the next section. *Ed.*]

15 *Op. cit.*, p. 4.

16 *Ibid.*, p. 252.

17 *Ibid.*, p. 269, cf. p. 266.

ness is recognized to be exactly what we experience in our awareness, and is not confused or identified with its causes or objects or setting, either in the bodily organism or in the wider system of nature.

The sixth confusion in the world of naturalism is *one* in which all the other confusions culminate—confusion about God.

Naturalists reject belief in God as "unverifiable," yet they stretch their concept of verification to include knowledge of the past and of the interior of the moon. As applied to God, verification is taken rigorously; as applied to the past and the moon, it is taken loosely. They reject belief in God as supernatural; yet many of them admit the validity of values and ideals which are at least supersensible, and they are not prepared to define "supernatural" clearly. They object to the commitment required by faith in God, but do not hesitate to commit themselves to human love, democracy, and operational method. They avow experimental method, yet refuse to extend it to spiritual realms, and decline to experiment with God. It is

almost true that the Orient has experimented only with God, and the Occident only with nature. Nothing but confusion can arise from this one-sidedness! Naturalists reject God because he is connected with ecclesiastical tradition. They do not appear to see that it is just as irrational to reject a belief merely because it is traditional as it is to accept it for the same reason. Nor do they seem to realize adequately either the value of social institutions or the need of reforming them if they are in error. Naturalists argue that belief in God is unimportant even if true, because they hold that the belief makes no practical difference. They thus ignore the practical differences made by love to an eternal Friend, by the peace and power that arises in mystical union (call it yoga or *unio mystica* or what you will), by prayer, by heightened confidence in the triumph of ideals, by religious fellowship in social institutions.

In so far as naturalism is a caution against superstition and wishful thinking it is a wholesome force. In so far as it is a skeptical rejection of God, it is based on confusion.

SUMMARY

Materialism or naturalism, we have seen, is a speculative vision of man and the cosmos grounded, the naturalist believes, on methods of responsible inquiry. Professor Ernest Nagel provides an important summary statement of this vision in the following selection. He finds two theses central to naturalism: the primacy of organized matter, and the plurality of things and events. Man's career and destiny must, therefore, be seen as taking place within nature. Professor Nagel also examines two objections to naturalism: first, that in relying on the methods of science, naturalism has "stacked the cards" in its favor; second, in committing itself to science, naturalism rests on a faith similar to religious faith. He finds these objections unwarranted; and he concludes his reconsideration of naturalism by stating that among the possible philosophies open to men's belief, naturalism is best supported by the evidence.

12 Naturalism Reconsidered

Ernest Nagel (1901-   )

The past quarter century has been for philosophy in many parts of the world a period of acute self-questioning, engendered in no small measure by developments in scientific and logical thought, and in part no doubt by fundamental changes in the social order. In any event, there has come about a general loss of confidence in the competence of philosophy to provide by way of a distinctive intellectual method a basic ground-plan of the cosmos, or for that matter to contribute to knowledge of any primary subject matter except by becoming a specialized positive science and subjecting itself to the discipline of empirical inquiry. Although the abysses of human ignorance are undeniably profound, it has also become apparent that ignorance, like actual knowledge, is of many special and heterogeneous things; and we have come to think, like the fox and unlike the hedgehog of whom Mr. Isaiah Berlin has recently reminded us,[1] that there are a great many things which are already known or remain to be discovered, but that there is no one "big thing" which, if known, would make everything else coherent and unlock the mystery of creation. In consequence, many of us have ceased to emulate the great system-builders in the history of philosophy. In partial imitation of the strategy of modern science, and in the hope of achieving responsibly held conclusions about matters concerning which we could acquire genuine competence, we have tended to become specialists in our professional activities. We have come to direct our best energies to the resolution of limited problems and puzzles that emerge in the analysis of scientific and ordinary discourse, in the evaluation of claims to knowledge, in the interpretation of validation of ethical and esthetic judgments, and in the assessment of types of human experience. I hope I shall not be regarded as offensive in stating my impression that the majority of the best minds among us have turned away from the conception of the philosopher as the spectator of all time and existence, and have concentrated on restricted but manageable questions, with almost deliberate unconcern for the bearing of their often minute investigations upon an inclusive view of nature and man. . . .

On the other hand, philosophers like other men conduct their lives within the framework of certain comprehensive if

---

[1 This reference is to the use by Sir Isaiah Berlin in his book, *The Hedgehog and the Fox* (London, 1953), of a line from the Greek poet Archilochus: "The fox knows many things, but the hedgehog knows one big thing." *Ed.*]

The selection is from Ernest Nagel,"Naturalism Reconsidered," *Proceedings of the American Philosophical Association,* 28 (1954–1955), pp. 5–17, with omissions. Reprinted in Nagel, *Logic Without Metaphysics,* Copyright 1956 by The Free Press, a corporation. Used by permission of the American Philosophical Association, The Free Press, and the author.

not always explicit assumptions about the world they inhabit. These assumptions color evaluations of major ideals and proposed policies. I also suspect that the directions taken by analyses of specific intellectual problems are frequently if subtly controlled by the expressed or tacit beliefs philosophers hold concerning the over-all nature of things, by their views on human destiny, and by their conceptions of the scope of human reason. But conversely, resolutions of special problems made plausible by recent philosophical analysis, as well as by the findings of various positive sciences, seem to me to support certain broad generalizations about the cosmos and to disconfirm others. It is clearly desirable that such basic intellectual commitments, which are at once the matrix and the outcome of inquiries into specific problems, be made as explicit as possible. A philosopher who is a reflective man by profession, certainly owes it to himself to articulate, if only occasionally, what sort of world he thinks he inhabits, and to make clear to himself where approximately lies the center of his convictions.

The discharge of the important obligation which is mine this evening, seems to me an appropriate occasion for stating as simply and as succinctly as I can the substance of those intellectual commitments I like to call "naturalism." The label itself is of no importance, but I use it partly because of its historical associations, and partly because it is a reminder that the doctrines for which it is a name are neither new nor untried. With Santayana, I prefer not to accept in philosophic debate what I do not believe when I am not arguing; and naturalism as I con-

strue it merely formulates what centuries of human experience have repeatedly confirmed. At any rate, naturalism seems to me a sound generalized account of the world encountered in practice and in critical reflection, and a just perspective upon the human scene. I wish to state briefly and hence with little supporting argument what I take to be its major tenets, and to defend it against some recent criticisms.

Claims to knowledge cannot ultimately be divorced from an evaluation of the intellectual methods used to support those claims. It is nevertheless unfortunate that in recent years naturalists in philosophy have so frequently permitted their allegiance to a dependable method of inquiry to obscure their substantive views on things in general. For it is the inclusive intellectual image of nature and man which naturalism supplies that sets it off from other comprehensive philosophies. In my conception of it, at any rate, naturalism embraces a generalized account of the cosmic scheme and of man's place in it, as well as a logic of inquiry.

I hasten to add, however, that naturalism does not offer a theory of nature in the sense that Newtonian mechanics, for example, provides a theory of motion. Naturalism does not, like the latter, specify a set of substantive principles with the help of which the detailed course of concrete happenings can be explained or understood. Moreover, the principles affirmed by naturalism are not proposed as competitors or underpinnings for any of the special theories which the positive sciences assert. Nor, finally, does naturalism offer its general view of nature and man as the product of some special philosophical mode of knowing. The account of things proposed by naturalism is a distillation from knowledge acquired in the usual way in daily encounters with the world or in specialized scientific inquiry. Naturalism articulates features of the world which, because they have become so obvious, are rarely mentioned in discussions of special subject matter, but which distinguish our actual world from other conceivable worlds. The major affirmations of naturalism are accordingly meager in content; but the principles affirmed are nevertheless effective guides in responsible criticism and evaluation.

Two theses seem to me central to naturalism as I conceive it. The first is the existential and causal primacy of organized matter in the executive order of nature. This is the assumption that the occurrence of events, qualities and processes, and the characteristic behaviors of various individuals, are contingent on the organization of spatio-temporally located bodies, whose internal structures and external relations determine and limit the appearance and disappearance of everything that happens. That this is so, is one of the best-tested conclusions of experience. We are frequently ignorant of the special conditions under which things come into being or pass away; but we have also found repeatedly that when we look closely, we eventually ascertain at least the approximate and gross conditions under which events occur, and we discover that those conditions invariably consist of some more or less complex organization of material substances. Naturalism does not maintain that only what is material exists, since many things noted in experience, for example, modes of action, relations of meaning, dreams, joys, plans, aspirations, are not as such material bodies or organizations of material bodies. What naturalism does assert as a truth about nature is that though *forms* of behavior or *functions* of material systems are indefeasibly parts of nature, forms and functions are not themselves agents in their own realization or in the realization of anything else. In the conception of nature's processes which naturalism affirms, there is no place for the operation of disembodied forces, no place for an immaterial spirit directing the course of events, no place for the survival of personality after the corruption of the body which exhibits it.

The second major contention of naturalism is that the manifest plurality and variety of things, of their qualities and their functions, are an irreducible feature of the cosmos, not a deceptive appearance cloaking some more homogeneous "ultimate reality" or transempirical substance, and that the sequential orders in which events occur or the manifold relations of dependence in which things exist are *contingent* connections, not the embodiments of a fixed and unified pattern of logically necessary links. The existential primacy of organized matter does not make illusory either the relatively permanent or the comparatively transient characters and forms which special configurations of bodies may possess. In particular, although the continued existence of the human scene is precarious and is dependent on a balance of forces that doubtless will not endure indefinitely, and even though its distinctive traits are not pervasive throughout space, it is nonetheless as much a part of the "ultimate" furniture of the world, and is as genuine a sample of what "really" exists, as are atoms and stars. There undoubtedly occur integrated systems of bodies, such as biological organisms, which have the capacity because of their material organization to maintain themselves and the direction of their characteristic activities. But there is no positive evidence, and much negative evidence, for the supposition that all existential structures are teleological systems in this sense, or for the view that whatever occurs is a phase in a unitary, teleologically organized, and all-inclusive process or system. . . . In brief, if naturalism is true, irreducible variety and logical contingency are fundamental traits of the world we actually inhabit. The orders and connections of things are all accessible to rational inquiry; but these orders and connections are not all derivable by deductive methods from any set of premises that deductive reason can certify.

It is in this framework of general ideas that naturalism envisages the career and destiny of man. Naturalism views the emergence and the continuance of human society as dependent of physical and physiological conditions that have not always obtained, and that will not permanently endure. But it does not in consequence regard man and his works as intrusions into nature, any more than it construes as intrusions the presence of heavenly bodies or of terrestrial protozoa. The stars are no more foreign to the cosmos than are men, even if the conditions for the existence of both stars and men are realized only occasionally or only in a few regions. Indeed, the conception of human life as a war with nature, as a struggle with an implacable foe that has doomed man to extinction, is but an inverted theology, with a malicious Devil in the seat of Omnipotence. It is a conception that is immodest as well as anthropomorphic in the importance it imputes to man in the scheme of things.

On the other hand, the affirmation that nature is man's "home" as much as it is the "home" of anything else, and the denial that cosmic forces are *intent* on destroying the human scene, do not warrant the interpretation that every sector of nature is explicable in terms of traits known to characterize only human individuals and human actions. Man undoubtedly possesses characteristics which are shared by everything that exists; but he also manifests traits and capacities that appear to be distinctive of him. Is anything gained but confusion when all forms of dependence between things, whether animate or inanimate, and all types of behaviors they display, are subsumed under distinctions that have an identifiable content only in reference to the human psyche? Measured by the illumination they bring, there is nothing to differentiate the thesis that human traits are nothing but the properties of bodies which can be formulated exclusively in the language of current physical theory, from the view that every change and every mode of operation, in whatever sector of the cosmos it may be encountered, is simply an illustration of some category pertinent to the description of human behavior. . . .

Human nature and history, in short, are *human* nature and history, not the history and nature of anything else, however much knowledge of other things contributes to a just appraisal of what man is. In particular, the adequacy of proposed ideals for human life must be judged, not in terms of their causes and origins, but in reference to how the pursuit and possible realization of ideals contribute to the organization and release of *human* energies. Men are animated by many springs of action, no one of which is intrinsically good or evil; and a moral ideal is the imagined satisfaction of some complex of impulses, desires, and needs. When ideals are handled responsibly, they therefore function as hypotheses for achieving a balanced exercise of human powers. Moral ideals are not self-certifying, any more than are the theories of the physical sciences; and evidence drawn from experienced satisfactions is required to validate them, however difficult may be the process of sifting and weighing the available data. Moral problems arise from a conflict of specific impulses and interests. They cannot, however, be effectively resolved by invoking standards derived from the study of nonhuman nature, or of what is allegedly beyond nature. If moral problems can be resolved at all, they can be resolved only in the light of specific human capacities, historical circumstance and acquired skills, and the opportunities (revealed by an imagination disciplined by knowledge) for altering the physical and social environment and for redirecting habitual behaviors. Moreover, since human virtues are in part the products of the society in which human powers are matured, a naturalistic moral theory is at the same time a critique of civilization, that is, a critique of the institutions that channel human energies, so as to exhibit the possibilities and limitations of various forms and arrangements of society for bringing enduring satisfactions to individual human careers.

These are the central tenets of what I take to be philosophical naturalism. They are tenets which are supported by compelling empirical evidence, rather than dicta based on dogmatic preference. In my view of it, naturalism does not dismiss every other different conception of the scheme of things as logically impossible; and it does not rule out all alternatives to itself on a priori grounds. It is possible, I think, to conceive without logical inconsistency a world in which disembodied forces are dynamic agents, or in which whatever happens is a manifestation of an unfolding logical pattern. In such possible worlds it would be an error to be a naturalist. But philosophy is not identical with pure mathematics, and its ultimate concern is with the actual world, even though philosophy must take cognizance of the fact that the actual world contains creatures who can envisage possible worlds and who employ different logical procedures for deciding which hypothetical world is the actual one. It is partly for this reason that contemporary naturalists devote so much attention to methods of evaluating evidence. When naturalists give their allegiance to the method of intelligence commonly designated as the method of modern empirical science, they do so because that method appears to be the most assured way of achieving reliable knowledge.

As judged by that method, the evidence in my opinion is at present conclusive for the truth of naturalism, and it is tempting to suppose that no one familiar with the evidence can fail to acknowledge that philosophy. Indeed, some commentators there are who assert that all philosophies are at bottom only expressions in different idioms of the same conceptions about the nature of things, so that the strife of philosophic systems is mainly a conflict over essentially linguistic matters. Yet many thinkers for whom I have a profound respect explicitly reject naturalism, and their espousal of contrary views seems to me incompatible with the irenic claim that we really are in agreement on fundamentals.

Although I do not have the time this evening to consider systematically the criticisms currently made of naturalism, I do wish to examine briefly two repeatedly voiced objections which, if valid, would in my opinion seriously jeopardize the integrity and adequacy of naturalism as a philosophy. Stated summarily, the first objection is that in relying exclusively on the logico-empirical method of modern science for establishing cognitive claims, naturalists are in effect stacking the cards in their own favor, since thereby all alternative philosophies are antecedently disqualified. It is maintained, for example, that naturalism rejects any hypothesis about transempirical causes or time-transcending spiritual substances as factors in the order of things, not because such hypotheses are actually shown to be false, but simply because the logic of proof adopted dismisses as irrelevant any evidence which might establish them.

This criticism does not seem to me to have merit: the logico-empirical method of evaluating cognitive claims to which naturalists subscribe does not eliminate by fiat any hypothesis about existence for which evidence can be procured, that is, evidence that in the last resort can be obtained through sensory or introspective observation. Thus, anyone who asserts a hypothesis postulating a transempirical ground for all existence, presumably seeks to understand in terms of that ground the actual occurrences in nature, and to account thereby for what

actually happens as distinct from what is merely imagined to happen. There must therefore be some connection between the postulated character of the hypothetical transempirical ground, and the empirically observable traits in the world around us; for otherwise the hypothesis is otiose, and not relevant to the spatio-temporal processes of nature. This does not mean, as some critics of naturalism suppose the latter to maintain, that the hypothetical transempirical ground must be characterized exclusively in terms of the observable properties of the world, any more than that the sub-microscopic particles and processes which current physical theory postulates must be logical constructions out of the observable traits of macroscopic objects. But it does mean that unless the hypothesis implies, even if only by a circuitous route, some statements about empirical data, it is not adequate to the task for which it is proposed. If naturalists reject hypotheses about transempirical substances, they do not do so arbitrarily. They reject such hypotheses either because their relevance to the going concerns of nature is not established, or because, though their relevance is not in question, the actual evidence does not support them.

Nor does naturalism dismiss as unimportant and without consideration experiences such as of the holy, of divine illumination, or of mystical ecstasy, experiences which are of the greatest moment in the lives of many men, and which are often taken to signify the presence and operation of some purely spiritual reality. Such experiences have dimensions of meaning for those who have undergone them, that are admittedly not on par with the import of more common experiences like those of physical hunger, general well-being, or feelings of remorse and guilt. Yet such experiences are nonetheless events among other events; and though they may be evidence for something, their sheer occurrence does not certify *what* they are evidence for, any more than the sheer occurrence of dreams, hopes, and delusions authenticates the actual existence of their ostensible objects. In particular, whether the experience labelled as an experience of divine illumination is evidence for the existence of a divinity, is a question to be settled by inquiry, not by dogmatic affirmations or denials. . . .

There is, however, a further objection to naturalism, to the effect that in committing itself to the logic of scientific proof, it is quite analogous to religious belief in resting on unsupported and indemonstrable faith. For that logic allegedly involves assumptions like the uniformity of nature or similar principles which transcend experience, cannot be justified empirically, and yet provide the premises that constitute the ultimate warrant for the conclusions of empirical inquiry. But if naturalism is thus based on unprovable articles of faith, on what cogent grounds can it reject a different conception of the true order of governance of events which rests on a different faith?

I cannot here deal adequately with the complex issues raised by this objection. Its point is not satisfactorily turned by claiming, as some have done, that instead of being articles of faith, the alleged indemonstrable postulates of scientific method are simply rules of the scientific game which *define* what in that game is to be understood by the words "knowledge" and "evidence." As I see it, however, the objection has force only for those whose ideal of reason is demonstration, and who therefore refuse to dignify anything as genuine knowledge unless it is demonstrable from self-luminous and self-evident premises. But if, as I also think, that ideal is not universally appropriate, and if, furthermore, a *wholesale* justification for knowledge and its methods is an unreasonable demand and a misplaced effort, the objection appears as quite pointless. . . .

It is almost painful to have to make a point of the elementary fact that whatever may happen to be the range of special interests and sensibilities of individual naturalists, there is no incompatibility, whether logical or psychological, between maintaining that warranted knowledge is secured only through the use of a definite logical method, and recognizing that the world can be experienced in many other ways than by knowing it. It is a matter of record that outstanding exponents of naturalism, in our own time as well as in the past, have exhibited an unequaled and tender sensitivity to the esthetic and moral dimensions of human experience; and they have been not only movingly eloquent celebrants of the role of moral idealism and of intellectual and esthetic contemplation in human life, but also vigorous defenders of the distinctive character of these values against facile attempts to reduce them to something else.

It seems to me singularly inept, moreover, to indict naturalism as a philosophy without a sense for the tragic aspects of life. For unlike many worldviews, naturalism offers no cosmic consolation for the unmerited defeats and undeserved sufferings which all men experience in one form or another. It has never sought to conceal its view of human destiny as an episode between two oblivions. To be sure, naturalism is not a philosophy of despair. For one facet in its radical pluralism is the truth that a human good is nonetheless a good, despite its transitory existence. There doubtless are foolish optimists among those professing naturalism, though naturalism has no monopoly in this respect, and it is from other quarters that one usually receives glad tidings of a universal nostrum. But in any event, neither the pluralism so central to naturalism, nor its cultivation of scientific reason, is compatible with any dogmatic assumption to the effect that men can be liberated from *all* the sorrows and evils to which they are now heirs, through the eventual advances of science and the institution of appropriate physical and social innovations. Indeed, why suppose that a philosophy which is wedded to the use of the sober logic of scientific intelligence, should thereby be committed

to the dogma that there are no irremediable evils? On the contrary, human reason is potent only against evils that are *remediable*. At the same time, since it is impossible to decide responsibly, *antecedent* to inquiry, *which* of the many human ills can be mitigated if not eradicated by extending the operations of scientific reason into human affairs, naturalism is not a philosophy of *general* renunciation, even though it recognizes that it is the better part of wisdom to be equably resigned to what, in the light of available evidence, cannot be avoided. Human reason is not an omnipotent instrument for the achievement of human goods; but it is the only instrument we do possess, and it is not a contemptible one. Although naturalism is acutely sensitive to the actual limitations of rational effort, those limitations do not warrant a romantic philosophy of general despair, and they do not blind naturalism to the possibilities implicit in the exercise of disciplined reason for realizing human excellence.

BIBLIOGRAPHICAL NOTE

A broad historical survey of materialism is given in F. H. Lange's *History of Material-ism* (New York, 1926), although naturalists frequently give their own interpretive views of that history; see, for example, Santayana's essay on Lucretius in *Three Philo-sophical Poets* (Cambridge, 1910). A great number of volumes trace the rise of modern science, including its philosophical assumptions, from the seventeenth century to the present. Among the most valuable of these works are Herbert Butterfield's *The Origins of Modern Science* (New York, 1951), A. R. Hall, *The Scientific Revolution* (Boston, 1954), and J. J. Kockelmans, *Philosophy of Science: The Historical Background* (New York, 1968). The varieties of naturalism, including those of a pragmatic temper, are represented in such works as Samuel Alexander, *Space, Time and Deity*, 2 vols. (Lon-don, 1920); John Dewey's many books, including especially *Experience and Nature* (Chicago, 1925); J. B. Pratt, *Naturalism* (New Haven, 1939); the writings of San-tayana; F. J. E. Woodbridge, *Nature and Mind* (New York, 1937); J. H. Randall, Jr., *Nature and Historical Experience* (New York, 1958); Patrick Romanell, *Toward a Critical Naturalism* (New York, 1958); and S. P. Lamprecht, *The Metaphysics of Naturalism* (New York, 1967). Two of these thinkers, Dewey and Santayana, are included in the series of volumes, The Library of Living Philosophers, edited by P. A. Schilpp. Two older anthologies may also be of interest to the student: R. W. Sellars, V. J. McGill, and M. Farber (eds.), *Philosophy for the Future* (New York, 1949), and Y. H. Krikorian (eds.), *Naturalism and the Human Spirit* (New York, 1944). More recent writers on materialism or scientific realism, as the position is also some-times called, include Wilfred Sellars and J. J. C. Smart. Appropriate articles in *The Encyclopedia of Philosophy* are also helpful.

Chapter Four

Idealism

Berkeley · Hegel · Blanshard · Royce
Bradley · Barker · Croce · Lewis
Harris · Sorley · Moore · Hartshorne

One of the major philosophic alternatives to realism and materialism is idealism. Although there are anticipations of idealism in ancient thought, the flowering of idealism has occurred in the last three centuries. Like realism, idealism is an explicitly metaphysical philosophy, in that it believes that speculative knowledge of reality is both possible and important. Unlike realism, however, which focuses its attention on principles of being like substance and essence, as well as the objective norms grounded in being, idealism bases itself on the centrality of mind and its activity in knowledge, being, and value. Against materialists, idealists argue that scientific method is too narrow a base for a philosophic position: value experience, for example, must also be considered.

These basic concerns suggest an introductory characterization of idealism. As a metaphysics, idealism holds that the real is mind or the mindlike; as an epistemology, it holds that knowledge is a result of mind's creative activity; and in axiology and related disciplines, it holds the mind-dependence of values. In sum, to use a quotation from W. M. Urban, the term "idealism" applies to "any theory which maintains that the universe is throughout the work or embodiment of mind."

Although idealists generally accept this description of their position, they do differ in their respective emphases. These differences provide a convenient basis for distinguishing four varieties of idealism. There are, first, mentalists or subjective idealists who, following Bishop Berkeley, deny the reality of material substance, asserting rather that physical objects—"all the choir of heaven and furniture of the earth"—are of such being as mind itself. A second group of idealists are the absolutists, who urge that certain logical concepts like system or universal best characterize reality. A third school seeks to uncover the presuppositions or "transcendental conditions" of experience; in finding them in mind and its activities, they belong to the idealist perspective. Finally, there are philosophers who argue that values are in some sense objective and part of the nature of reality; yet, because value implies mind, they draw the idealist conclusion that reality is in its essence spiritual.

These idealist assertions are expanded and developed in the selections that follow. We shall also trace the implications of the idealist argument in a number of areas of philosophy, just as we have done in the case of realism and naturalism. Throughout this chapter, however—and here idealism again differs from realism —we shall be dealing with a position that is not so clearly or directly related to "common sense" as realism claims to be. Indeed, the brief characterization of idealism given in this introduction may seem to be presenting a paradoxical philosophy, to say the least. Yet there is a "driving force" in idealism such that many of the best minds of history have been attracted to it as the most adequate expression of the nature of reality. Professor Hartshorne has provided an interpretive summary of this force, and it appears as the summary selection. As we examine the idealists' solution of some of the same problems that realists and materialists face, and continue to compare and relate the alternatives, we enter into the dialogue between positions and arguments which philosophy most essentially is.

INTRODUCTION

Historically, a major source of idealistic thought is the writings of Bishop George Berkeley, Anglican divine and philosopher; for although much of his argumentation is directed toward the intellectual positions of his day, he nevertheless formulated a basic philosophic vision from which idealists take inspiration even if they revise that formulation severely. Berkeley was motivated to engage in philosophical work by what he considered to be the rising materialism, with its threats to religion, that stemmed from the scientific advances of his day and the philosophical elaborations thereof.

Materialism, the philosophy which as we have seen holds that only material substance, or matter, is real, seemed to Berkeley to follow from certain philosophical assumptions such as the distinction between primary and secondary qualities. Primary qualities are those qualities of an object such as size and mass that can be measured mathematically; secondary qualities are the *qualia* such as a color or sound that are experienced by a perceiver. Furthermore, it was believed that the former are qualities of the object itself, whereas the latter depend on the perceiver and are relative to him. Matter and primary qualities thus seem to be "objective," whereas mind and secondary qualities seem to be "subjective." The tendency to believe that matter alone is real, and that mind has only a derivative being, follows closely on these distinctions.

Is this tendency, as well as its presuppositions, justified? Berkeley believes not. If we examine experience carefully, we find that an object, say a desk, is only a bundle of qualities: shape, color, weight, and so on. Now what of the supposed independence of primary qualities? Are they not just as much ideas as colors? And are they not, therefore, just as dependent on the perceiver as secondary qualities? To both questions Berkeley answers yes. The desk is a bundle of qualities or ideas, ideas depend for their existence on the perceiver, therefore the desk's existence depends on its being perceived. In his famous formula, *esse* is *percipi*, Berkeley concludes that only perceivers or spirits—one Infinite, many finite—are real. Nature, the realm of objects, exists as God's perceptions; all being, in fact, is ideal.

To such an argument there will be, of course, objections, and Berkeley considers some of these himself. They will bear careful attention for an understanding of the argument itself.

1 The Rejection of Matter
George Berkeley (1685-1753)

1. It is evident to any one who takes a survey of the *objects of human knowledge,* that they are either *ideas* actually imprinted on the senses; or else such as are perceived by attending to the passions and operations of the mind; or lastly, *ideas* formed by help of memory and imagination—either compounding, dividing, or barely representing those originally perceived in the aforesaid ways. By sight I have the ideas of light and colors, with their several degrees and variations. By touch I perceive hard and soft, heat and cold, motion and resistance; and of all these more and less either as to quantity or

The selection follows the text of the second edition of the "Principles of Human Knowledge," in A. C. Fraser (ed.), *The Works of George Berkeley,* 4 vols. (Oxford: Clarendon Press, 1901), Vol. I, pp. 257–279, with omissions.

degree. Smelling furnishes me with odors; the palate with tastes; and hearing conveys sounds to the mind in all their variety of tone and composition.

And as several of these are observed to accompany each other, they come to be marked by one name, and so to be reputed as one *thing.* Thus, for example, a certain color, taste, smell, figure and consistence having been observed to go together, are accounted one distinct thing, signified by the name apple; other collections of ideas constitute a stone, a tree, a book, and the like sensible things; which as they are pleasing or disagreeable excite the passions of love, hatred, joy, grief, and so forth.

2. But, besides all that endless variety of ideas or objects of knowledge, there is likewise Something which knows or perceives them; and exercises divers operations, as willing, imagining, re-

membering, about them. This perceiving, active being is what I call *mind, spirit, soul,* or *myself.* By which words I do not denote any one of my ideas, but a thing entirely distinct from them, wherein they exist, or, which is the same thing, whereby they are perceived; for the existence of an idea consists in being perceived.

3. That neither our thoughts, nor passions, nor ideas formed by the imagination, exist without the mind is what everybody will allow. And to me it seems no less evident that the various sensations or ideas imprinted on the Sense, however blended or combined together (that is, whatever objects they compose), cannot exist otherwise than in a mind perceiving them. I think an intuitive knowledge may be obtained of this, by any one that shall attend to what is meant by the term *exist* when applied to sensible things. The table I write on I say exists; that is, I see and feel it: and if I were out of my study I should say it existed; meaning thereby that if I was in my study I might perceive it, or that some other spirit actually does perceive it. There was an odor, that is, it was smelt; there was a sound, that is, it was heard; a color or figure, and it was perceived by sight or touch. This is all that I can understand by these and the like expressions. For as to what is said of the *absolute* existence of unthinking things, without any relation to their being perceived, that is to me perfectly unintelligible. Their *esse* is *percipi;* nor is it possible they should have any existence out of the minds or thinking things which perceive them.

4. It is indeed an opinion strangely prevailing amongst men, that houses, mountains, rivers, and in a word all sensible objects, have an existence, natural or real, distinct from their being perceived by the understanding. But, with how great an assurance and acquiescence soever this Principle may be entertained in the world, yet whoever shall find in his heart to call it in question may, if I mistake not, perceive it to involve a manifest contradiction. For, what are the forementioned objects but the things we perceive by sense? and what do we perceive besides our own ideas or sensations? and is it not plainly repugnant that any one of these, or any combination of them, should exist unperceived?

5. If we thoroughly examine this tenet it will, perhaps, be found at bottom to depend on the doctrine of *abstract ideas.* For can there be a nicer strain of abstraction than to distinguish the existence of sensible objects from their being perceived, so as to conceive them existing unperceived? Light and colors, heat and cold, extension and figures—in a word the things we see and feel—what are they but so many sensations, notions, ideas, or impressions on the sense? and is it possible to separate, even in thought, any of these from perception? For my part, I might as easily divide a thing from itself. I may, indeed, divide in my thoughts, or conceive apart from each other, those things which perhaps I never perceived by sense so divided. Thus, I imagine the trunk of a human body without the limbs, or conceive the smell of a rose without thinking on the rose itself. So far, I will not deny, I can abstract; if that may properly be called *abstraction* which extends only to the conceiving separately such objects as it is possible may really exist or be actually perceived

asunder. But my conceiving or imagining power does not extend beyond the possibility of real existence or perception. Hence, as it is impossible for me to see or feel anything without an actual sensation of that thing, so is it impossible for me to conceive in my thoughts any sensible thing or object distinct from the sensation or perception of it.

6. Some truths there are so near and obvious to the mind that a man need only open his eyes to see them. Such I take this important one to be, viz. that all the choir of heaven and furniture of the earth, in a word all those bodies which compose the mighty frame of the world, have not any subsistence without a mind; that their *being* is to be perceived or known; that consequently so long as they are not actually perceived by me, or do not exist in my mind, or that of any other created spirit, they must either have no existence at all, or else subsist in the mind of some Eternal Spirit: it being perfectly unintelligible, and involving all the absurdity of abstraction, to attribute to any single part of them an existence independent of a spirit. To be convinced of which, the reader need only reflect, and try to separate in his own thoughts the *being* of a sensible thing from its *being perceived.*

7. From what has been said it is evident there is not any other Substance than *Spirit,* or that which perceives. But, for the fuller proof of this point, let it be considered the sensible qualities are color, figure, motion, smell, taste, and such like, that is, the ideas perceived by sense. Now, for an idea to exist in an unperceiving thing is a manifest contradiction; for to have an idea is all one as to perceive: that therefore wherein color, figure, and the like qualities exist must perceive them. Hence it is clear there can be no unthinking substance or *substratum* of those ideas.

8. But, say you, though the ideas themselves do not exist without the mind, yet there may be things like them, whereof they are copies or resemblances; which things exist without the mind, in an unthinking substance. I answer, an idea can be like nothing but an idea; a color or figure can be like nothing but another color or figure. If we look but never so little into our thoughts, we shall find it impossible for us to conceive a likeness except only between our ideas. Again, I ask whether those supposed *originals,* or external things, of which our ideas are the pictures or representations, be themselves perceivable or no? If they are, then *they* are ideas, and we have gained our point: but if you say they are not, I appeal to any one whether it be sense to assert a color is like something which is invisible; hard or soft, like something which is intangible; and so of the rest.

9. Some there are who make a distinction betwixt *primary* and *secondary* qualities. By the former they mean extension, figure, motion, rest, solidity or impenetrability, and number; by the latter they denote all other sensible qualities, as colors, sounds, tastes, and so forth. The ideas we have of these last they acknowledge not to be the resemblances of anything existing without the mind, or unperceived; but they will have our ideas of the *primary qualities* to be patterns or images of things which exist without the mind, in an unthinking substance which they call Matter. By Matter, therefore, we are to understand an

inert, senseless substance, in which extension, figure, and motion do actually subsist. But it is evident, from what we have already shewn, that extension, figure, and motion are only ideas existing in the mind, and that an idea can be like nothing but another idea; and that consequently neither they nor their archetypes can exist in an unperceiving substance. Hence, it is plain that the very notion of what is called *Matter* or *corporeal substance,* involves a contradiction in it. . . .

18. But, though it were possible that solid, figured, moveable substances may exist without the mind, corresponding to the ideas we have of bodies, yet how is it possible for us to know this? Either we must know it by Sense or by Reason. As for our senses, by them we have the knowledge only of our sensations, ideas, or those things that are immediately perceived by sense, call them what you will: but they do not inform us that things exist without the mind, or unperceived, like to those which are perceived. This the materialists themselves acknowledge. It remains therefore that if we have any knowledge at all of external things, it must be by reason inferring their existence from what is immediately perceived by sense. But what reason can induce us to believe the existence of bodies without the mind, from what we perceive, since the very patrons of Matter themselves do not pretend there is any necessary connection betwixt them and our ideas? I say it is granted on all hands (and what happens in dreams, frenzies, and the like, puts it beyond dispute) that it is possible we might be affected with all the ideas we have now, though no bodies existed without resembling them.

Hence it is evident the supposition of external bodies is not necessary for the producing our ideas; since it is granted they are produced sometimes, and might possibly be produced always, in the same order we see them in at present, without their concurrence.

19. But, though we might possibly have all our sensations without them, yet perhaps it may be thought easier to conceive and explain the manner of their production, by supposing external bodies in their likeness rather than otherwise; and so it might be at least probable there are such things as bodies that excite their ideas in our minds. But neither can this be said. For, though we give the materialists their external bodies, they by their own confession are never the nearer knowing how our ideas are produced; since they own themselves unable to comprehend in what manner body can act upon spirit, or how it is possible it should imprint any idea in the mind. Hence it is evident the production of ideas or sensations in our minds, can be no reason why we should suppose Matter or corporeal substances; since that is acknowledged to remain equally inexplicable with or without this supposition. If therefore it were possible for bodies to exist without the mind, yet to hold they do so must needs be a very precarious opinion; since it is to suppose, without any reason at all, that God has created innumerable beings that are entirely useless, and serve to no manner of purpose.

20. In short, if there were external bodies, it is impossible we should ever come to know it; and if there were not, we might have the very same reasons to think there were that we have now. Suppose—what no one can deny possi-

ble—an intelligence, without the help of external bodies, to be affected with the same train of sensations or ideas that you are, imprinted in the same order and with like vividness in his mind. I ask whether that intelligence hath not all the reason to believe the existence of Corporeal Substances, represented by his ideas, and exciting them in his mind, that you can possibly have for believing the same thing? Of this there can be no question. Which one consideration were enough to make any reasonable person suspect the strength of whatever arguments he may think himself to have, for the existence of bodies without the mind. . . .

23. But, say you, surely there is nothing easier than for me to imagine trees, for instance, in a park, or books existing in a closet, and nobody by to perceive them. I answer, you may so, there is no difficulty in it. But what is all this, I beseech you, more than framing in your mind certain ideas which you call *books* and *trees,* and at the same time omitting to frame the idea of any one that may perceive them? But do not you yourself perceive or think of them all the while? This therefore is nothing to the purpose: it only shews you have the power of imagining, or forming ideas in your mind; but it does not shew that you can conceive it possible the objects of your thought may exist without the mind. To make out this, it is necessary that you conceive them existing unconceived or unthought of; which is a manifest repugnancy. When we do our utmost to conceive the existence of external bodies, we are all the while only contemplating our own ideas. But the mind, taking no notice of itself, is deluded to think it can and does

conceive bodies existing unthought of, or without the mind, though at the same time they are apprehended by, or exist in, itself. A little attention will discover to any one the truth and evidence of what is here said, and make it unnecessary to insist on any other proofs against the existence of *material substance.* . . .

34. Before we proceed any farther it is necessary we spend some time in answering Objections which may probably be made against the Principles we have hitherto laid down. In doing of which, if I seem too prolix to those of quick apprehensions, I desire I may be excused, since all men do not equally apprehend things of this nature; and I am willing to be understood by every one.

First, then, it will be objected that by the foregoing principles all that is real and substantial in nature is banished out of the world, and instead thereof a chimerical scheme of *ideas* takes place. All things that exist exist only in the mind; that is, they are purely notional. What therefore becomes of the sun, moon, and stars? What must we think of houses, rivers, mountains, trees, stones; nay, even of our own bodies? Are all these but so many chimeras and illusions on the fancy?— To all which, and whatever else of the same sort may be objected, I answer, that by the Principles premised we are not deprived of any one thing in nature. Whatever we see, feel, hear, or any wise conceive or understand, remains as secure as ever, and is as real as ever. There is a *rerum natura,* and the distinction between realities and chimeras retains its full force. . . .

35. I do not argue against the existence of any one thing that we can ap-

prehend, either by sense or reflection. That the things I see with my eyes and touch with my hands do exist, really exist, I make not the least question. The only thing whose existence we deny is that which *philosophers* call Matter or corporeal substance. And in doing of this there is no damage done to the rest of mankind, who, I dare say, will never miss it. The Atheist indeed will want the color of an empty name to support his impiety; and the Philosophers may possibly find they have lost a great handle for trifling and disputation.

36. If any man thinks this detracts from the existence or reality of things, he is very far from understanding what hath been premised in the plainest terms I could think of. Take here an abstract of what has been said:—There are spiritual substances, minds, or human souls, which will or excite ideas in themselves at pleasure; but these are faint, weak, and unsteady in respect of others they perceive by sense: which, being impressed upon them according to certain rules or laws of nature, speak themselves the effects of a Mind more powerful and wise than human spirits. These latter are said to have *more reality* in them than the former;—by which is meant that they are more affecting, orderly, and distinct, and that they are not fictions of the mind perceiving them. And in this sense the sun that I see by day is the real sun, and that which I imagine by night is the idea of the former. In the sense here given of *reality,* it is evident that every vegetable, star, mineral, and in general each part of the mundane system, is as much a *real being* by our principles as by any other. Whether others mean anything by the term *reality* different from what I do, I entreat them to look into their own thoughts and see.

37. It will be urged that thus much at least is true, to wit, that we take away all *corporeal substances.* To this my answer is, that if the word *substance* be taken in the vulgar sense, for a *combination* of sensible qualities, such as extension, solidity, weight, and the like —this we cannot be accused of taking away: but if it be taken in a philosophic sense, for the support of accidents or qualities without the mind—then indeed I acknowledge that we take it away, if one may be said to take away that which never had any existence, not even in the imagination.

38. But after all, say you, it sounds very harsh to say we eat and drink ideas, and are clothed with ideas. I acknowledge it does so—the word *idea* not being used in common discourse to signify the several combinations of sensible qualities which are called *things;* and it is certain that any expression which varies from the familiar use of language will seem harsh and ridiculous. But this doth not concern the truth of the proposition, which in other words is no more than to say, we are fed and clothed with those things which we perceive immediately by our senses. The hardness or softness, the color, taste, warmth, figure, and suchlike qualities, which combined together constitute the several sorts of victuals and apparel, have been shewn to exist only in the mind that perceives them: and this is all that is meant by calling them *ideas;* which word, if it was as ordinarily used as *thing,* would sound no harsher nor more ridiculous than it. I am not for disputing about the propriety, but the

truth of the expression. If therefore you agree with me that we eat and drink and are clad with the immediate objects of sense, which cannot exist unperceived or without the mind, I shall readily grant it is more proper or conformable to custom that they should be called *things* rather than *ideas.*

39. If it be demanded why I make use of the word *idea,* and do not rather in compliance with custom call them *things;* I answer, I do it for two reasons: —First, because the term *thing,* in contradistinction to *idea,* is generally supposed to denote somewhat existing without the mind: Secondly, because *thing* hath a more comprehensive signification than *idea,* including spirits, or thinking things, as well as ideas. Since therefore the objects of sense exist only in the mind, and are withal thoughtless and inactive, I chose to mark them by the word *idea;* which implies those properties.

40. But, say what we can, some one perhaps may be apt to reply, he will still believe his senses, and never suffer any arguments, how plausible soever, to prevail over the certainty of them. Be it so; assert the evidence of sense as high as you please, we are willing to do the same. That what I see, hear, and feel doth exist, that is to say, is perceived by me, I no more doubt than I do of my own being. But I do not see how the testimony of sense can be alleged as a proof for the existence of anything which is *not* perceived by sense. We are not for having any man turn skeptic and disbelieve his senses; on the contrary, we give them all the stress and assurance imaginable; nor are there any principles more opposite to Skepticism than those we have laid down, as shall be hereafter clearly shewn.

41. *Secondly,* it will be objected that there is a great difference betwixt real fire for instance, and the idea of fire, betwixt dreaming or imagining oneself burnt, and actually being so. . . . This and the like may be urged in opposition to our tenets.—To all which the answer is evident from what hath been already said; and I shall only add in this place, that if real fire be very different from the idea of fire, so also is the real pain that it occasions very different from the idea of the same pain, and yet nobody will pretend that real pain either is, or can possibly be, in an unperceiving thing, or without the mind, any more than its idea.

2 Philosophy and Spirit
G. W. F. Hegel (1770-1831)

The second major historical source of idealism is the philosophy of Hegel, a many-sided, encyclopedic, and at times difficult position. Hegel's emphasis, though idealistic, is rather different from Berkeley's, and hence the term "absolute idealism" is used of it as against Berkeley's subjective idealism or mentalism.

Philosophy, as Hegel understood it, is the attempt to think concretely; that is, to think of experience in all its manifold relations. ("Abstract" thinking is that wherein we drop consideration of some relations in order to concentrate on others.) It is simply an effort to view experience as a whole; and until we have a conception of the whole, our thinking remains partial and inadequate. "The true is the whole" is one of Hegel's basic assertions.

Philosophy leads us, Hegel believes, to grasp things as Subject, not just as substance. That is, reality in Hegel's view is not static identity, but the self-development of an essential nature. Such development is made possible by mediation and relationship, and is characterized by Hegel as "dialectical." This means that development is a unifying of opposites—a mediation—and is also an unfolding of stages. The stages of the dialectic include the thesis, or abstract starting point; the antithesis, or opposite; and the synthesis, which unifies thesis and antithesis. Hegel carries the dialectic into all areas of experience, and it ultimately involves all things in an inclusive, concrete whole which is the Absolute. The Absolute is the name of all entities worked out into interrelated actuality. It is also Spirit or the realm of concrete unity existing in-and-for itself and incorporating and mediating all oppositions.

The tracing of the systematic development of the Absolute becomes the basic task of philosophy. Hegel asserts that philosophy must take the form of science (in its etymological sense of systematic knowledge, not of course as modern experimental science), and be set out as a system. The laws of thought and being, in fact, are ultimately one, so that concrete thought grasps concrete reality.

In the case of a philosophical work it seems not only superfluous, but, in view of the nature of philosophy, even inappropriate and misleading to begin, as writers usually do in a preface, by explaining the end the author had in mind, the circumstances which gave rise to the work, and the relation in which the writer takes it to stand to other treatises on the same subject, written by his predecessors or his contemporaries. For whatever it might be suitable to state about philosophy in a preface—say, an historical sketch of the main drift and point of view, the general content and results, a string of desultory assertions and assurances about the truth—this cannot be accepted as the form and manner in which to expound philosophical truth.

Moreover, because philosophy had its being essentially in the element of that universality which encloses the particular within it, the end or final result seems, in the case of philosophy more than in that of other sciences, to have absolutely expressed the complete fact itself in its very nature; contrasted with that the mere process of bringing it to light would seem, properly speaking, to have no essential significance. On the other hand, in the general idea of e.g. anatomy—the knowledge of the parts of the body regarded as lifeless— we are quite sure we do not possess the objective concrete fact, the actual content of the science, but must, over and

The selection is from G. W. F. Hegel, *Phenomenology of Mind*, 2nd ed. Tr. T. R. Baillie. Humanities Press, New York, and George Allen & Unwin Ltd., London, 1931. Used by permission of the publishers.

above, be concerned with particulars. Further, in the case of such a collection of items of knowledge, which has no real right to the name of science, any talk about purpose and such-like generalities is not commonly very different from the descriptive and superficial way in which the contents of the science— these nerves and muscles, etc.—are themselves spoken of. In philosophy, on the other hand, it would at once be felt incongruous were such a method made use of and yet shown by philosophy itself to be incapable of grasping the truth.

In the same way too, by determining the relation which a philosophical work professes to have to other treatises on the same subject, an extraneous interest is introduced, and obscurity is thrown over the point at issue in the knowledge of the truth. The more the ordinary mind takes the opposition between true and false to be fixed, the more is it accustomed to expect either agreement or contradiction with a given philosophical system, and only to see reason for the one or the other in any explanatory statement concerning such a system. It does not conceive the diversity of philosophical systems as the progressive evolution of truth; rather, it sees only contradiction in that variety. The bud disappears when the blossom breaks through, and we might say that the former is refuted by the latter; in the same way when the fruit comes, the blossom may be explained to be a false form of the plant's existence, for the fruit appears as its true nature in place of the blossom. These stages are not merely differentiated; they supplant one another as being incompatible with one

another. But the ceaseless activity of their own inherent nature makes them at the same time moments of an organic unity, where they not merely do not contradict one another, but where one is as necessary as the other; and this equal necessity of all moments constitutes alone and thereby the life of the whole. But contradiction as between philosophical systems is not wont to be conceived in this way; on the other hand, the mind perceiving the contradiction does not commonly know how to relieve it or keep it free from its onesidedness, and to recognize in what seems conflicting and inherently antagonistic the presence of mutually necessary moments.

The demand for such explanations, as also the attempts to satisfy this demand, very easily pass for the essential business philosophy has to undertake. Where could the inmost truth of a philosophical work be found better expressed than in its purposes and results? and in what way could these be more definitely known than through their distinction from what is produced during the same period by others working in the same field? If, however, such procedure is to pass for more than the beginning of knowledge, if it is to pass for actually knowing, then we must, in point of fact, look on it as a device for avoiding the real business at issue, an attempt to combine the appearance of being in earnest and taking trouble about the subject with an actual neglect of the subject altogether. For the real subject-matter is not exhausted in its purpose, but in working the matter out; nor is the mere result attained the concrete whole itself, but the result along with the process of arriving at it. The purpose by itself is a lifeless universal, just as the general drift is a mere activity in a certain direction, which is still without its concrete realization; and the naked result is the corpse of the system which has left its guiding tendency behind it. Similarly, the distinctive difference of anything is rather the boundary, the limit, of the subject; it is found at that point where the subject-matter stops, or it is what this subject-matter is *not*. To trouble oneself in this fashion with the purpose and results, and again with the differences, the positions taken up and judgments passed by one thinker and another, is therefore an easier task than perhaps it seems. For instead of laying hold of the matter in hand, a procedure of that kind is all the while away from the subject altogether. Instead of dwelling within it and becoming absorbed by it, knowledge of that sort is always grasping at something else; such knowledge, instead of keeping to the subject-matter and giving itself up to it, never gets away from itself. The easiest thing of all is to pass judgment on what has a solid substantial content; it is more difficult to grasp it, and most of all difficult to do both together and produce the systematic exposition of it.

The beginning of culture and of the struggle to pass out of the unbroken immediacy of naïve psychical life has always to be made by acquiring knowledge of universal principles and points of view, by striving, in the first instance, to work up simply to the *thought* of the subject-matter in general, not forgetting at the same time to give reasons for supporting it or refuting it, to apprehend the concrete riches and fullness contained in its various determinate qualities, and to know how to furnish a coherent, orderly account of it and a responsible judgment upon it. This beginning of mental cultivation will, however, very soon make way for the earnestness of actual life in all its fullness, which leads to a living experience of the subject-matter itself; and when, in addition, conceptual thought strenuously penetrates to the very depths of its meaning, such knowledge and style of judgment will keep their due place in everyday thought and conversation.

The systematic development of truth in scientific form can alone be the true shape in which truth exists. To help to bring philosophy nearer to the form of science—that goal where it can lay aside the name of *love* of knowledge and be actual *knowledge*—that is what I have set before me. The inner necessity that knowledge should be science lies in its very nature; and the adequate and sufficient explanation for this lies simply and solely in the systematic exposition of philosophy itself. The external necessity, however, so far as this is apprehended in a universal way, and apart from the accident of the personal element and the particular occasioning influences affecting the individual, is the same as the internal: it lies in the form and shape in which the process of time presents the existence of its moments. To show that the time process does raise philosophy to the level of scientific system would, therefore, be the only true justification of the attempts which aim at proving that philosophy must assume this character; because the temporal process would thus bring out and lay bare the necessity of it, nay, more, would at the same time be carrying out that very aim itself. . . .

In my view—a view which the developed exposition of the system itself can alone justify—everything depends on grasping and expressing the ultimate truth not as Substance but as Subject as well. At the same time we must note that concrete substantiality implicates and involves the universal or the immediacy of knowledge itself, as well as that immediacy which is being, or immediacy *qua* object *for* knowledge. If the generation which heard God spoken of as the One Substance[1] was shocked and revolted by such a characterization of his nature, the reason lay partly in the instinctive feeling that in such a conception self-consciousness was simply submerged, and not preserved. But partly, again, the opposite position, which maintains thinking to be merely subjective thinking, abstract universality as such, is exactly the same bare uniformity, is undifferentiated, unmoved substantiality.[2] And even if, in the third place, thought combines with itself the being of substance, and conceives immediacy or intuition (*Anschauung*) as thinking, it is still a question whether this intellectual intuition does not fall back into that inert, abstract simplicity, and exhibit and expound reality itself in an unreal manner.[3]

The living substance, further, is that being which is truly subject, or, what is the same thing, is truly realized and actual (*wirklich*) solely in the process of positing itself, or in mediating with its own self its transitions from one state or position to the opposite. As subject

it is pure and simple negativity, and just on that account a process of splitting up what is simple and undifferentiated, a process of duplicating and setting factors in opposition, which [process] in turn is the negation of this indifferent diversity and of the opposition of factors it entails. True reality is merely this process of reinstating self-identity, of reflecting into its own self in and from its other, and is not an original and primal unity as such, not an immediate unity as such. It is the process of its own becoming, the circle which presupposes its end as its purpose, and has its end for its beginning; it becomes concrete and actual only by being carried out, and by the end it involves. . . .

The truth is the whole. The whole, however, is merely the essential nature reaching its completeness through the process of its own development. Of the Absolute it must be said that it is essentially a result, that only at the end is it what it is in very truth; and just in that consists its nature, which is to be actual, subject, or self-becoming, self-development. Should it appear contradictory to say that the Absolute has to be conceived essentially as a result, a little consideration will set this appearance of contradiction in its true light. The beginning, the principle, or the Absolute, as at first or immediately expressed, is merely the universal. If we say "all animals," that does not pass for zoology; for the same reason we see at once that the words absolute, divine, eternal, and so on do not express what is implied in them; and only mere words like these, in point of fact, express intuition as the immediate. Whatever is more than a word like that, even the mere transition to a proposi-

---

[1] Spinoza.

[2] Kant and Fichte.

[3] Schelling.

tion, is a form of mediation, contains a process towards another state from which we must return once more. It is this process of mediation, however, that is rejected with horror, as if absolute knowledge were being surrendered when more is made of mediation than merely the assertion that it is nothing absolute, and does not exist in the Absolute.

This horrified rejection of mediation, however, arises as a fact from want of acquaintance with its nature, and with the nature of absolute knowledge itself. For mediating is nothing but self-identity working itself out through an active self-directed process; or, in other words, it is reflection into self, the aspect in which the ego is for itself, objective to itself. It is pure negativity, or, reduced to its utmost abstraction, the process of bare and simple becoming. The ego, or becoming in general, this process of mediating, is, because of its being simple, just immediacy coming to be, and is immediacy itself. We misconceive therefore the nature of reason if we exclude reflection or mediation from ultimate truth, and do not take it to be a positive moment of the Absolute. It is reflection which constitutes truth the final result, and yet at the same time does away with the contrast between result and the process of arriving at it. For this process is likewise simple, and therefore not distinct from the form of truth, which consists in appearing as simple in the result; it is indeed just this restoration and return to simplicity. While the embryo is certainly, in itself, implicitly a human being, it is not so explicitly, it is not by itself a human being (*für sich*); man is explicitly man only in the form of developed and cul-

tivated reason, which has made itself to be what it is implicitly. Its actual reality is first found here. But this result arrived at is itself simple immediacy; for it is self-conscious freedom, which is at one with itself, and has not set aside the opposition it involves and left it there, but has made its account with it and become reconciled to it.

What has been said may also be expressed by saying that reason is purposive activity. The exaltation of so-called nature at the expense of thought misconceived, and more especially the rejection of external purposiveness, have brought the idea of purpose in general into disrepute. All the same, in the sense in which Aristotle, too, characterizes nature as purposive activity, purpose is the immediate, the undisturbed, the unmoved which is self-moving; as such it is subject. Its power of moving, taken abstractly, is its existence for itself, or pure negativity. The result is the same as the beginning solely because the beginning is purpose. Stated otherwise, what is actual and concrete is the same as its inner principle or notion simply because the immediate *qua* purpose contains within it the self or pure actuality. The realized purpose, or concrete actuality, is movement and development unfolded. But this very unrest is the self; and it is one and the same with that immediacy and simplicity characteristic of the beginning just for the reason that it is the result, and has returned upon itself—while this latter again is just the self, and the self is self-referring and self-relating identity and simplicity. . . .

Among the many consequences that follow from what has been said, it is of importance to emphasize this, that knowledge is only real and can only be set forth fully in the form of science, in the form of system; and further, that a so-called fundamental proposition or first principle of philosophy, even if it is true, is yet none the less false just because and in so far as it is merely a fundamental proposition, merely a first principle. It is for that reason easily refuted. The refutation consists in bringing out its defective character; and it *is* defective because it is merely the universal, merely a principle, the beginning. If the refutation is complete and thorough, it is derived and developed from the nature of the principle itself, and not accomplished by bringing in from elsewhere other counter assurances and chance fancies. It would be strictly the development of the principle, and thus the completion of its deficiency, were it not that it misunderstands its own purport by taking account solely of the negative aspect of what it seeks to do, and is not conscious of the positive character of its process and result. The really positive working out of the beginning is at the same time just as much the very reverse, it is a negative attitude towards the principle we start from, negative, that is to say, of its one-sided form, which consists in being primarily immediate, a mere purpose. It may therefore be regarded as a refutation of what constitutes the basis of the system; but more correctly it should be looked at as a demonstration that the *basis* or principle of the system is in point of fact merely its *beginning*.

That the truth is only realized in the form of system, that substance is essentially subject, is expressed in the idea which represents the Absolute as Spirit (*Geist*)—the grandest conception of all, and one which is due to modern times and its religion. Spirit is alone Reality. It is the inner being of the world, that which essentially is, and is *per se;* it assumes objective, determinate form, and enters into relations with itself—it is externality (otherness), and exists for self; yet, in this determination, and in its otherness, it is still one with itself—it is self-contained and self-complete, in itself and for itself at once. This self-containedness, however, is first something known by us, it is implicit in its nature (*an sich*); it is Substance spiritual. It has to become self-contained *for itself,* on its own account; it must be knowledge of spirit, and must be consciousness of itself as spirit. This means, it must be presented to itself as an object, but at the same time straightway annul and transcend this objective form; it must be its own object in which it finds itself reflected. So far as its spiritual content is produced by its own activity, it is only *we* [the thinkers] who know spirit to be for itself, to be objective to itself; but in so far as spirit knows itself to be for itself, then this self-production, the pure notion, is the sphere and element in which its objectification takes effect, and where it gets its existential form. In this way it is in its existence aware of itself as an object in which its own self is reflected. Mind, which, when thus developed, knows itself to be mind, is science. Science is its realization, and the kingdom it sets up for itself in its own native element.

EPISTEMOLOGY

Two questions in epistemology can be distinguished: that of the criterion of truth, and of the nature of truth. By many idealists they are both answered in the theory of coherence. As a criterion of truth, coherence means that a proposition is to be considered true in terms of its consistent and systematic relationship to other propositions. As a theory of the nature of truth, coherence means that truth itself is a coherent system of propositions—a system such that, as Professor Blanshard writes, no proposition is arbitrary and every proposition is entailed by the others.

In support of his conviction that coherence does define the nature of truth, Professor Blanshard distinguishes the immanent end of thought, systematic vision, from the transcendent end which is fulfillment in an object. But, he argues, these ends must be one: the pursuit of thought's own ideal must at the same time be an apprehension of the real. This involves, then, a metaphysical theory that the immanent end of thought is a clue to the nature of things; in other words, that reality is an ordered, systematic, and intelligible structure, and that truth too is such a structure.

3 Truth as Coherence

Brand Blanshard (1892-   )

1. It has been contended in the last chapter that coherence is in the end our sole criterion of truth. We have now to face the question whether it also gives us the nature of truth. We should be clear at the beginning that these are different questions, and that one may reject coherence as the definition of truth while accepting it as the test. It is conceivable that one thing should be an accurate index of another and still be extremely different from it. There have been philosophers who held that pleasure was an accurate gauge of the

amount of good in experience, but that to confuse good with pleasure was a gross blunder. There have been a great many philosophers who held that for every change in consciousness there was a change in the nervous system and that the two corresponded so closely that if we knew the laws connecting them we could infallibly predict one from the other; yet it takes all the hardihood of a behaviorist to say that the two are the same. Similarly it has been held that though coherence supplies an infallible measure of truth, it would be a very grave mistake to identify it with truth.

2. The view that truth *is* coherence rests on a theory of the relation of thought to reality; and since this is the central problem of the theory of knowl-

The selection is from Brand Blanshard, *The Nature of Thought*, 2 vols. (London: George Allen & Unwin Ltd.; New York: The Macmillan Company, 1939), Vol. II, pp. 260–269. Used by permission of the publishers.

edge, to begin one's discussion by assuming the answer to it or by trying to make one out of whole cloth would be somewhat ridiculous. But as this was our main problem in the long discussions of Book II, we may be pardoned here for brevity. First we shall state in *résumé* the relation of thought to reality that we were there driven to accept, and sketch the theory of truth implicit in it. We shall then take up one by one the objections to this theory and ask if they can pass muster.

To think is to seek understanding. And to seek understanding is an activity of mind that is marked off from all other activities by a highly distinctive aim. This aim, as we saw in our chapter on the general nature of understanding, is to achieve systematic vision, so to apprehend what is now unknown to us as to relate it, and relate it necessarily, to what we know already. We think to solve problems; and our method of solving problems is to build a bridge of intelligible relation from the continent of our knowledge to the island we wish to include in it. Sometimes this bridge is causal, as when we try to explain a disease; sometimes teleological, as when we try to fathom the move of an opponent over the chess board; sometimes geometrical, as in Euclid. But it is always systematic; thought in its very nature is the attempt to bring something unknown or imperfectly known into a sub-system of knowledge, and thus also into that larger system that forms the world of accepted beliefs. That is what explanation is. *Why* is it that thought desires this ordered vision? Why should such a vision give satisfaction when it comes? To these questions there is no answer, and if there were, it would be

an answer only because it had succeeded in supplying the characteristic satisfaction to this unique desire.

But may it not be that what satisfies thought fails to conform to the real world? Where is the guarantee that when I have brought my ideas into the form my ideal requires, they should be *true?* Here we come round again to the tortured problem of Book II. In our long struggle with the relation of thought to reality we saw that if thought and things are conceived as related only externally, then knowledge is luck; there is no necessity whatever that what satisfies intelligence should coincide with what really is. It may do so, or it may not; on the principle that there are many misses to one bull's-eye, it more probably does not. But if we get rid of the misleading analogies through which this relation has been conceived, of copy and original, stimulus and organism, lantern and screen, and go to thought itself with the question what reference to an object means, we get a different and more hopeful answer. To think of a thing is to get that thing itself in some degree within the mind. To think of a color or an emotion is to have that within us which if it *were developed and completed*, would identify itself with the object. In short, if we accept its own report, thought is related to reality as the partial to the perfect fulfilment of a purpose. The more adequate its grasp the more nearly does it approximate, the more fully does it realize in itself, the nature and relations of its objects.

3. Thought thus appears to have two ends, one immanent, one transcendent. On the one hand it seeks fulfilment in a special kind of satisfaction, the satis-

faction of systematic vision. On the other hand it seeks fulfilment in its object. Now it was the chief contention of our second book that these ends are one. Indeed unless they are accepted as one, we could see no alternative to skepticism. If the pursuit of thought's own ideal were merely an elaborate self-indulgence that brought us no nearer to reality, or if the apprehension of reality did not lie in the line of thought's interest, or still more if both of these held at once, the hope of knowledge would be vain. Of course it may really be vain. If anyone cares to doubt whether the framework of human logic has any bearing on the nature of things, he may be silenced perhaps, but he cannot be conclusively answered. One may point out to him that the doubt itself is framed in accordance with that logic, but he can reply that thus we are taking advantage of his logic-centric predicament; further, that any argument we can offer accords equally well with his hypothesis and with ours, with the view that we are merely flies caught in a logical net and the view that knowledge reveals reality. And what accords equally well with both hypotheses does not support either to the exclusion of the other. But while such doubt is beyond reach by argument, neither is there anything in its favor. It is a mere suspicion which is, and by its nature must remain, without any positive ground; and as such it can hardly be discussed. Such suspicions aside, we can throw into the scale for our theory the impressive fact of the advance of knowledge. It has been the steadfast assumption of science whenever it came to an unsolved problem that there was a key to it to be found, that if things happened thus rather than

otherwise they did so for a cause or reason, and that if this were not forthcoming it was never because it was lacking, but always because of a passing blindness in ourselves. Reflection has assumed that pursuit of its own immanent end is not only satisfying but revealing, that so far as the immanent end is achieved we are making progress toward the transcendent end as well. Indeed, that these ends coincide is the assumption of every act of thinking whatever. To think is to raise a question; to raise a question is to seek an explanation; to seek an explanation is to assume that one may be had; so to assume is to take for granted that nature in that region is intelligible. Certainly the story of advancing knowledge unwinds as if self-realization in thought meant also a coming nearer to reality.

4. That these processes are really one is the metaphysical base on which our belief in coherence is founded. If one admits that the pursuit of a coherent system has actually carried us to what everyone would agree to call knowledge, why not take this ideal as a guide that will conduct us farther? What better key can one ask to the structure of the real? Our own conviction is that we should take this immanent end of thought in all seriousness as the clue to the nature of things. We admit that it may prove deceptive, that somewhere thought may end its pilgrimage in frustration and futility before some blank wall of the unintelligible. There are even those who evince their superior insight by taking this as a foregone conclusion and regarding the faith that the real is rational as the wishful thinking of the "tender-minded." Their attitude appears to us a compound made up of one part

timidity, in the form of a refusal to hope lest they be disillusioned; one part muddled persuasion that to be skeptical is to be sophisticated; one part honest dullness in failing to estimate rightly the weight of the combined postulate and success of knowledge; one part genuine insight into the possibility of surds in nature. But whatever its motives, it is a view that goes less well with the evidence than the opposite and brighter view. That view is that reality is a system, completely ordered and fully intelligible, with which thought in its advance is more and more identifying itself. We may look at the growth of knowledge, individual or social, either as an attempt by our own minds to return to union with things as they are in their ordered wholeness, or the affirmation through our minds of the ordered whole itself. And if we take this view, our notion of truth is marked out for us. Truth is the approximation of thought to reality. It is thought on its way home. Its measure is the distance thought has travelled, under guidance of its inner compass, toward that intelligible system which unites its ultimate object with its ultimate end. Hence at any given time the degree of truth in our experience as a whole is the degree of system it has achieved. The degree of truth of a particular proposition is to be judged in the first instance by its coherence with experience as a whole, ultimately by its coherence with that further whole, all-comprehensive and fully articulated, in which thought can come to rest.

5. But it is time we defined more explicitly what coherence means. To be sure, no fully satisfactory definition can be given; and as Dr. Ewing says, "it is wrong to tie down the advocates of the coherence theory to a precise definition. What they are doing is to describe an ideal that has never yet been completely clarified but is none the less immanent in all our thinking." Certainly this ideal goes far beyond mere consistency. Fully coherent knowledge would be knowledge in which every judgment entailed, and was entailed by, the rest of the system. Probably we never find in fact a system where there is so much of interdependence. What it means may be clearer if we take a number of familiar systems and arrange them in a series tending to such coherence as a limit. At the bottom would be a junk-heap, where we could know every item but one and still be without any clue as to what that remaining item was. Above this would come a stone-pile, for here you could at least infer that what you would find next would be a stone. A machine would be higher again, since from the remaining parts one could deduce not only the general character of a missing part, but also its special form and function. This is a high degree of coherence, but it is very far short of the highest. You could remove the engine from a motorcar while leaving the other parts intact, and replace it with any one of thousands of other engines, but the thought of such an interchange among human heads or hearts shows at once that the interdependence in a machine is far below that of the body. Do we find then in organic bodies the highest conceivable coherence? Clearly not. Though a human hand, as Aristotle said, would hardly be a hand when detached from the body, still it would be something definite enough; and we can conceive systems in which even this something would be gone. Abstract a number from the num-

ber series and it would be a mere un-recognizable *x;* similarly, the very thought of a straight line involves the thought of the Euclidean space in which it falls. It is perhaps in such systems as Euclidean geometry that we get the most perfect examples of coherence that have been constructed. If any prop-osition were lacking, it could be sup-plied from the rest; if any were altered, the repercussions would be felt through the length and breadth of the system. Yet even such a system as this falls short of ideal system. Its postulates are unproved; they are independent of each other, in the sense that none of them could be derived from any other or even from all the others together; its clear necessity is bought by an abstractness so extreme as to have left out nearly everything that belongs to the character of actual things. A completely satisfac-tory system would have none of these defects. No proposition would be arbi-trary, every proposition would be en-tailed by the others jointly and even singly,[1] no proposition would stand out-side the system. The integration would be so complete that no part could be seen for what it was without seeing its relation to the whole, and the whole

---

[1] Coherence can be defined without this point, which, as Dr. Ewing remarks (*Ideal-ism,* 231), makes the case harder to estab-lish. In no mathematical system, for example, would anyone dream of trying to deduce all the other propositions from any proposition taken singly. But when we are describing an ideal, such a fact is not decisive, and I follow Joachim in holding that in a perfectly co-herent system every proposition would entail all others, if only for the reason that its meaning could never be fully understood without apprehension of the system in its entirety.

itself could be understood only through the contribution of every part.

6. It may be granted at once that in common life we are satisfied with far less than this. We accept the demon-strations of the geometer as complete, and do not think of reproaching him be-cause he begins with postulates and leaves us at the end with a system that is a skeleton at the best. In physics, in biology, above all in the social sciences, we are satisfied with less still. We test judgments by the amount of coherence which in that particular subject-matter it seems reasonable to expect. We apply, perhaps unconsciously, the advice of Aristotle, and refrain from asking demonstration in the physical sciences, while in mathematics we refuse to accept less. And such facts may be thought to show that we make no actual use of the ideal standard just described. But how-ever much this standard may be relaxed within the limits of a particular science, its influence is evident in the grading of the sciences generally. It is precisely in those sciences that approach most nearly to system as here defined that we achieve the greatest certainty, and pre-cisely in those that are most remote from such system that our doubt is greatest whether we have achieved scientific truth at all. Our immediate exactions shift with the subject-matter; our ultimate standard is unvarying.

7. Now if we accept coherence as the test of truth, does that commit us to any conclusions about the *nature* of truth or reality? I think it does, though more clearly about reality than about truth. It is past belief that the fidelity of our thought to reality should be rightly mea-sured by coherence if reality itself were not coherent. To say that the nature of

things may be *in*coherent, but we shall approach the truth about it precisely so far as our thoughts become coherent, sounds very much like nonsense. And providing we retained coherence as the test, it would still be nonsense even if truth were conceived as correspondence. On this supposition we should have truth when, our thought having achieved coherence, the correspondence was complete between that thought and its object. But complete correspondence between a coherent thought and an incoherent object seems meaningless. It is hard to see, then, how anyone could consistently take coherence as the test of truth unless he took it also as a character of reality.

8. Does acceptance of coherence as a test commit us not only to a view about the structure of reality but also to a view about the nature of truth? This is a more difficult question. As we saw at the beginning of the chapter, there have been some highly reputable philosophers who have held that the answer to "What is the test of truth?" is "Coherence," while the answer to "What is the nature or meaning of truth?" is "Correspondence." These questions are plainly distinct. Nor does there seem to be any direct path from the acceptance of coherence as the test of truth to its acceptance as the nature of truth. Nevertheless there is an indirect path. If we accept coherence as our test, we must use it everywhere. We must therefore use it to test the suggestion that truth *is* other than coherence. But if we do, we shall find that we must reject the suggestion as leading to *in*coherence. Coherence is a pertinacious concept and, like the well-known camel, if one lets it get its nose

under the edge of the tent, it will shortly walk off with the whole.

Suppose that, accepting coherence as the test, one rejects it as the nature of truth in favor of some alternative; and let us assume, for example, that this alternative is correspondence. This, we have said, is incoherent; why? Because if one holds that truth is correspondence, one cannot intelligibly hold either that it is tested by coherence or that there is any dependable test at all. Consider the first point. Suppose that we construe experience into the most coherent picture possible, remembering that among the elements included will be such secondary qualities as colors, odors, and sounds. Would the mere fact that such elements as these are coherently arranged prove that anything precisely corresponding to them exists "out there"? I cannot see that it would, even if we knew that the two arrangements had closely corresponding patterns. If on one side you have a series of elements a, b, c, . . . , and on the other a series of elements α, β, γ, . . . , arranged in patterns that correspond, you have no proof as yet that the *natures* of these elements correspond. It is therefore impossible to argue from a high degree of coherence within experience to its correspondence in the same degree with anything outside. And this difficulty is typical. If you place the nature of truth in one sort of character and its test in something quite different, you are pretty certain, sooner or later, to find the two falling apart. In the end, the only test of truth that is not misleading is the special nature or character that is itself constitutive of truth.

Feeling that this is so, the adherents

of correspondence sometimes insist that correspondence shall be its own test. But then the second difficulty arises. If truth does consist in correspondence, no test can be sufficient. For in order to know that experience corresponds to fact, we must be able to get at that fact, unadulterated with idea, and compare the two sides with each other. And we have seen in the last chapter that such fact is not accessible. When we try to lay hold of it, what we find in our hands is a judgment which is obviously not itself the indubitable fact we are seeking, and which must be checked by some fact beyond it. To this process there is no end. And even if we did get at the fact directly, rather than through the veil of our ideas, that would be no less fatal to correspondence. This direct seizure of fact presumably gives us truth, but since that truth no longer consists in correspondence of idea with fact, the main theory has been abandoned. In short, if we can know fact only through the medium of our own ideas, the original forever eludes us; if we can get at the facts directly, we have knowledge whose truth is not correspondence. The theory is forced to choose between skepticism and self-contradiction.

Thus the attempt to combine coherence as the test of truth with correspondence as the nature of truth will not pass muster by its own test. The result is *in*coherence. We believe that an application of the test to other theories of truth would lead to a like result. The argument is: assume coherence as the test, and you will be driven by the incoherence of your alternatives to the conclusion that it is also the nature of truth.

METAPHYSICS

One of the major idealist systems was produced by the American thinker Josiah Royce. The following selection is a statement of a central argument Royce developed for his position. Following Berkeley, he first turns to an analysis of experience and concludes that all experience is ideal or mind related. It is but a vast system of ideas that forces itself upon us.

Such an analytic statement ends, however, in a dilemma, for perhaps there lies beyond this system of ideas an unknowable, inscrutable *x*. Royce therefore turns to the second part of his argument to state his theory of synthetic idealism. Here, through his ingenious "argument from error," he asserts the existence of an inclusive, infinite problem-solver or Self that—even when we are in deepest doubt and uncertainty—possesses in unity our finite ideas and the objects that would make them true. Everything finite is dark and obscure, Royce concludes, but the existence of the Infinite Self is perfectly sure.

4 Reality and Idealism
Josiah Royce (1855-1916)

Idealism has two aspects. It is, for the first, a kind of analysis of the world, an analysis which so far has no absolute character about it, but which undertakes, in a fashion that might be acceptable to any skeptic, to examine what you mean by all the things, whatever they are, that you believe in or experience. This idealistic analysis consists merely in a pointing out, by various devices, that the world of your knowledge, whatever it contains, is through and through such stuff as ideas are made of, that you never in your life believed in anything definable *but* ideas, that, as Berkeley put it, "this whole choir of heaven and furniture of earth" is nothing for any of us but a system of ideas which govern our belief and our conduct. . . .

The other aspect of idealism is the one which gives us our notion of the absolute Self. To it the first is only preparatory. This second aspect is the one which from Kant, until the present time, has formed the deeper problem of thought. Whenever the world has become more conscious of its significance, the work of human philosophy will be, not nearly ended (Heaven forbid an end!), but for the first time fairly begun. For then, in critically estimating our passions, we shall have some truer sense of whose passions they are.

I begin with the first and the less significant aspect of idealism. Our world,

The selection is from Josiah Royce, *The Spirit of Modern Philosophy* (Boston: Houghton Mifflin Company, 1893), pp. 350–380, with omissions.

I say, whatever it may contain, is such stuff as ideas are made of. This preparatory sort of idealism is the one that, as I just suggested, Berkeley made prominent, and, after a fashion familiar. I must state it in my own way, although one in vain seeks to attain novelty in illustrating so frequently described a view.

Here, then, is our so real world of senses, full of light and warmth and sound. If anything could be solid and external, surely, one at first will say, it is this world. Hard facts, not mere ideas, meet us on every hand. Ideas any one can mould as he wishes. Not so facts. In idea socialists can dream out Utopias, disappointed lovers can imagine themselves successful, beggars can ride horses, wanderers can enjoy the fireside at home. In the realm of facts, society organizes itself as it must, rejected lovers stand for the time defeated, beggars are alone with their wishes, oceans roll drearily between home and the wanderer. Yet this world of fact is, after all, not entirely stubborn, not merely hard. The strenuous will can mould facts. We can form our world, in part, according to our ideas. Statesmen influence the social order, lovers woo afresh, wanderers find the way home. . . .

But this bright and beautiful sense-world of ours,—what, amongst these many possible sorts of reality, does that embody? Are the stars and the oceans, the walls and the pictures, real as the maiden's heart is real,—embodying the ideas of somebody, but none the less stubbornly real for that? Or can we make something else of their reality? For, of course, that the stars and the oceans, the walls and the pictures have *some* sort of stubborn reality, just as the minds of our fellows have, our analysis so far does not for an instant think of denying. Our present question is, what sort of reality? Consider, then, in detail, certain aspects of the reality that seems to be exemplified in our sense-world. The sublimity of the sky, the life and majesty of the ocean, the interest of a picture,—to what sort of real facts do these belong? Evidently here we shall have no question. So far as the sense-world is beautiful, is majestic, is sublime, this beauty and dignity exist only for the appreciative observer. If they exist beyond him, they exist only for some other mind, or as the thought and embodied purpose of some universal soul of nature. A man who sees the same world, but who has no eye for the fairness of it, will find all the visible facts, but will catch nothing of their value. At once, then, the sublimity and beauty of the world are thus truths that one who pretends to insight ought to see, and they are truths which have no meaning except for such a beholder's mind, or except as embodying the thought of the mind of the world. So here, at least, is so much of the outer world that is ideal, just as the coin or the jewel or the bank note or the bond has its value not alone in its physical presence, but in the idea that it symbolizes to a beholder's mind, or to the relatively universal thought of the commercial world. But let us look a little deeper. Surely, if the objects yonder are unideal and outer, odors and tastes and temperatures do not exist in these objects in just the way in which

they exist in us. Part of the being of these properties, at least, if not all of it, is ideal and exists for us, or at best is once more the embodiment of the thought or purpose of some world-mind. About tastes you cannot dispute, because they are not only ideal but personal. For the benumbed tongue and palate of diseased bodily conditions, all things are tasteless. As for temperatures, a well-known experiment will show how the same water may seem cold to one hand and warm to the other. But even so, colors and sounds are at least in part ideal. Their causes may have some other sort of reality; but colors themselves are not in the things, since they change with the light that falls on the things, vanish in the dark (whilst the things remained unchanged), and differ for different eyes. And as for sounds, both the pitch and the quality of tones depend for us upon certain interesting peculiarities of our hearing organs, and exist in nature only as voiceless sound-waves trembling through the air. All such sense qualities, then, are ideal. The world yonder may—yes, must—have attributes that give reasons why these qualities are thus felt by us; for so we assume. The world yonder may even be a mind that thus expresses its will to us. But these qualities need not, nay, cannot resemble the ideas that are produced in us, unless, indeed, that is because these qualities have place as ideas in some world-mind. . . .

But now, at this point, the Berkeleyan idealist goes one step further. The real outside world that is still left unexplained and unanalyzed after its beauty, its warmth, its odors, its tastes, its colors, and its tones, have been relegated to the realm of ideal truths, what do you now *mean* by calling it real? No doubt it *is* known as somehow real, but *what* is this reality *known as* being? If you know that this world is still there and outer, as by hypothesis you know, you are bound to say *what* this outer character implies for your thought. And here you have trouble. Is the outer world, as it exists outside of your ideas, or of anybody's ideas, something having shape, filling space, possessing solidity, full of moving things? That would in the first place seem evident. The sound isn't outside of me, but the sound-waves, you say, are. The colors are ideal facts; but the ether-waves don't need a mind to know them. Warmth is ideal, but the physical fact called heat, this playing to and fro of molecules, is real, and is there apart from any mind. But once more, *is* this so evident? What do I *mean* by the shape of anything, or by the size of anything? Don't I mean just the idea of shape or of size that I am obliged to get under certain circumstances? What is the meaning of any property that I give to the real outer world? How can I express that property except in case I think it in terms of my ideas? As for the sound-waves and the ether-waves, what are they but things ideally conceived to explain the facts of nature? The conceptions have doubtless their truth, but it is an ideal truth. What I mean by saying that the things yonder have shape and size and trembling molecules, and that there is air with sound-waves, and ether with light-waves in it,—what I *mean* by all this is that experience forces upon me, directly or indirectly, a vast system of ideas, which may indeed be founded in truth beyond me, which in fact *must* be founded in such truth if my experience has any sense, but which, like my

ideas of color and of warmth, are simply expressions of how the world's order must appear to me, and to anybody constituted like me. . . .

Thus, all the reality that *we* attribute to our world, in so far as *we* know and can tell what we mean thereby, becomes ideal. There is, in fact, a certain system of ideas, forced upon us by experience, which we have to use as the guide of our conduct. This system of ideas we can't change by our wish; it is for us as overwhelming a fact as guilt, or as the bearing of our fellows towards us, but we know it only *as* such a system of ideas. And we call it the world of matter. John Stuart Mill very well expressed the puzzle of the whole thing, as we have now reached the statement of this puzzle, when he called matter a mass of "permanent possibilities of experience" for each of us. Mill's definition has its faults, but is a very fair beginning. You know matter as something that either now gives you this idea or experience, or that would give you some other idea or experience under other circumstances. A fire, while it burns, is for you a permanent possibility of either getting the idea of an agreeable warmth, or of getting the idea of a bad burn, and you treat it accordingly. A precipice amongst mountains is a permanent possibility of your experiencing a fall, or of your getting a feeling of the exciting or of the sublime in mountain scenery. . . . And this acceptance of actual experience, this belief in possible experience, constitutes all that you mean by your faith in the outer world. . . .

What I have desired thus far is merely to give each of you, as it were, the sensation of being an idealist in this first and purely analytical sense of the word idealism. The sum and substance of it all is, you see, this: you know your world in fact as a system of ideas about things, such that from moment to moment you find this system forced upon you by experience. Even matter you know just as a mass of coherent ideas that you cannot help having. Space and time, as you think them, are surely ideas of yours. Now, what more natural than to say that *if* this be so, the real world beyond you must in itself be a system of somebody's ideas? If it is, then you can comprehend what its existence means. If it isn't, then since all you can know of it is ideal, the real world must be utterly unknowable, a bare *x*. Minds I can understand, because I myself am a mind. An existence that has no mental attribute is wholly opaque to me. So far, however, from such a world of ideas, existent beyond me in another mind, seeming to coherent thought essentially *un*real, ideas and minds and their ways, are, on the contrary, the hardest and stubbornest facts that we can name. *If* the external world is in itself mental, then, be this reality a standard and universal thought, or a mass of little atomic minds constituting the various particles of matter, in any case one can comprehend what it is, and will have at the same time to submit to its stubborn authority as the lover accepts the reality of the maiden's moods. If the world *isn't* such an ideal thing, then indeed all our science, which is through and through concerned with our mental interpretations of things, can neither have objective validity, nor make satisfactory progress towards truth. For a science is concerned with ideas, the world beyond all ideas is a bare *x*.

But with this bare *x*, you will say,

this analytical idealism after all leaves me, as with something that, in spite of all my analyses and interpretations, may after all be there beyond me as the real world, which my ideas are vainly striving to reach, but which eternally flees before me. So far, you will say, what idealism teaches is that the real world can only be interpreted by treating it as if it were somebody's thought. So regarded, the idealism of Berkeley and of other such thinkers is very suggestive, yet it doesn't tell us what the true world is, but only that *so much* of the true world as we ever get into our comprehension has to be conceived in ideal terms. . . . Are we not just where we started?

No; there lies now just ahead of us the goal of a synthetic idealistic conception, which will not be content with this mere analysis of the colors and forms of things, and with the mere discovery that all these are for us nothing but ideas. In this second aspect, idealism grows bolder, and fears not the profoundest doubt that may have entered your mind as to whether there is any world at all, or as to whether it is in any fashion knowable. State in full the deepest problem, the hardest question about the world that your thought ever conceived. In this new form idealism offers you a suggestion that indeed will not wholly answer nor do away with every such problem, but that certainly will set the meaning of it in a new light. What this new light is, I must in conclusion seek to illustrate.

Note the point we have reached. *Either,* as you see, your real world yonder is through and through a world of ideas, an outer mind that you are more or less comprehending through your experience, *or else,* in so far as it is real and outer it is unknowable, and inscrutable *x,* an absolute mystery. The dilemma is perfect. . . . Well, try the darker choice that the dilemma gives you. The world yonder shall be an *x,* an unknowable something, outer, problematic, foreign, opaque. And you,—you shall look upon it and believe in it. Yes, you shall for argument's sake first put on an air of resigned confidence, and say, "I do not only fancy it to be an extra-mental and unknowable something there, an impenetrable *x,* but I know it to be such. I can't help it. I didn't make it unknowable. I regret the fact. But there it is. I have to admit its existence. But I know that I shall never solve the problem of its nature." Ah, its nature is a *problem,* then. But what do you mean by this *"problem"?* Problems are, after a fashion, rather familiar things, that is, in the world of ideas. There are problems soluble and problems insoluble in that world of ideas. It is a soluble problem if one asks what whole number is the square root of 64. The answer is 8. It is an insoluble problem if one asks me to find what whole number is the square root of 65. There is, namely, no such whole number. . . . Any fair question could be answered by one who knew enough. No fair question has an unknowable answer. But now, *if* your unknowable world out there is a thing of wholly, of absolutely problematic and inscrutable nature, is it so because you don't *yet* know enough about it, or because in its very nature and essence it is an absurd thing, an *x* that *would* answer a question, which actually it is nonsense to ask? Surely one must choose the former alternative. The real world may

be unknown; it can't be essentially unknowable.

This subtlety is wearisome enough, I know, just here, but I shall not dwell long upon it. Plainly *if* the unknowable world out there is through and through in its nature a really inscrutable problem, this must mean that in nature it resembles such problems as, What is the whole number that is the square root of 65? Or, What two adjacent hills are there that have no valley between them? For in the world of thought such are the *only* insoluble problems. All others either may now be solved, or would be solved if we knew more than we now do. But, once more, *if* this unknowable is only just the real world as now unknown to us, but capable some time of becoming known, then remember that, as we have just seen, only a mind can ever become an object known to a mind. If I know you as external to me, it is only because you are minds. If I can come to know *any* truth, it is only in so far as this truth is essentially mental, is an idea, is a thought, that I can ever come to know it. Hence, if that so-called unknowable, that unknown outer world there, ever could, by any device, come within our ken, then it is already an ideal world. For just that is what our whole idealistic analysis has been proving. Only ideas are knowable. And nothing absolutely unknowable can exist. For the absolutely unknowable, the *x* pure and simple, the Kantian thing in itself, simply cannot be admitted. The notion of it is nonsense. The assertion of it is a contradiction. . . .

Once more, then, to sum up here, *if,* however vast the world of the unknown, only the essentially knowable can exist, and *if* everything knowable is an idea, a mental somewhat, the content of some mind, then once for all we are the world of ideas. Your deepest doubt proves this. Only the nonsense of that inscrutable *x,* of that Abracadabra, of that Snark, the Unknowable of whose essence you make your real world, prevents you from seeing this.

To return, however, to our dilemma. *Either* idealism, we said, *or* the unknowable. What we have now said is that the absolutely unknowable is essentially an absurdity, a non-existent. For any fair and statable problem admits of an answer. *If* the world exists yonder, its essence is then already capable of being known by some mind. If capable of being known by a mind, this essence is then already essentially ideal and mental. . . .

But with this result we come in presence of a final problem. All this, you say, depends upon my assurance that there is after all a real and therefore an essentially knowable and rational world yonder. Such a world would have to be in essence a mind, or a world of minds. But after all, how does one ever escape from the prison of the inner life? Am I not in all this merely wandering amidst the realm of my own ideas? *My* world, of course, isn't and can't be a mere *x,* an essentially unknowable thing, just because it *is* my world, and I have an idea of it. But, then does not this mean that *my* world is, after all, forever just *my* world, so that I never get to any truth beyond myself? Isn't this result very disheartening? My world is thus a world of ideas, but alas! how do I then ever reach those ideas of the minds beyond me?

The answer is a simple, but in one sense a very problematic one. You, in one sense, namely, never *do* or can get beyond your own ideas, nor ought you to wish to do so, because in truth all those other minds that constitute your outer and real world are in essence one with your own self. This whole world of ideas is essentially *one* world, and so it is essentially the world of one self and *That art Thou.*

The truth and meaning of this deepest proposition of all idealism is now not at all remote from us. The considerations, however, upon which it depends are of the dryest possible sort, as commonplace as they are deep.

Whatever objects you may think about, whether they are objects directly known to you, or objects infinitely far removed, objects in the distant stars, or objects remote in time, or objects near and present, such objects, then, as a number with fifty places of digits in it, or the mountains on the other side of the moon, or the day of your death, or the character of Cromwell, or the law of gravitation, or a name that you are just now trying to think of and have forgotten, or the meaning of some mood or feeling or idea now in your mind,— all such objects, I insist, stand in a certain constant and curious relation to your mind whenever you are thinking about them,—a relation that we often miss because it is so familiar. What is this relation? Such an object, while you think about it, needn't be, as popular thought often supposes it to be, the *cause* of your thoughts concerning it. Thus, when you think about Cromwell's character, Cromwell's character isn't just now *causing* any ideas in you, isn't, so to speak, doing anything to you. Cromwell is dead, and after life's fitful fever his character is a very inactive thing. Not as the *cause,* but as the *object* of your thought is Cromwell present to you. Even so, if you choose now to think of the moment of your death, that moment is somewhere off there in the future, and you can make it your object, but it isn't now an active cause of your ideas. The moment of your death has no present physical existence at all, and just now causes nothing. So, too, with the mountains on the other side of the moon. When you make them the object of your thought, they remain indifferent to you. They do not affect you. You never saw them. But all the same you can think about them.

Yet this thinking *about* things is, after all, a very curious relation in which to stand to things. In order to think *about* a thing, it is *not* enough that I should have an idea in me that merely resembles that thing. This last is a very important observation. I repeat, it is *not* enough that I should merely have an idea in me that resembles the thing whereof I think. I have, for instance, in me the idea of a pain. Another man has a pain just like mine. Say we both have toothache; or have both burned our fingertips in the same way. Now my idea of pain is just like the pain in him, but I am not on that account necessarily thinking about *his* pain, merely because what I am thinking about, namely my own pain, resembles his pain. No; to think about an object you must not merely have an idea that resembles the object, but you must *mean* to have your idea resemble that object. Stated in other form, to think of an object you must consciously aim at that object, you

must pick out that object, you must already in some measure possess that object enough, namely, to identify it as what you mean. But how can you *mean,* how can you *aim at,* how can you *possess,* how can you *pick out,* how can you *identify* what is not already present in essence to your own hidden self? Here is surely a deep question. When you aim at yonder object, be it the mountains in the moon or the day of your death, you really say, "I, as my real self, as my larger self, as my complete consciousness, already in deepest truth possess that object, have it, own it, identify it. And that, and that alone, makes it possible for me in my transient, my individual, my momentary personality, to mean yonder object, to inquire about it, to be partly aware of it and partly ignorant of it." You can't mean what is utterly foreign to you. You mean an object, you assert about it, you talk about it, yes, you doubt or wonder about it, you admit your private and individual ignorance about it, only in so far as your larger self, your deeper personality, your total of normal consciousness already *has* that object. Your momentary and private wonder, ignorance, inquiry, or assertion, about the object, implies, asserts, presupposes, that your total self is in full and immediate possession of the object. This, in fact, is the very nature of that curious relation of a thought to an object which we are now considering. The self that is doubting or asserting, or that is even feeling its private ignorance about an object, and that still, even in consequence of all this, is *meaning,* is *aiming at* such object, is in essence identical with the self for which this object exists in its complete and consciously known truth. . . .

In this way I suggest to you the proof which a rigid analysis of the logic of our most commonplace thought would give for the doctrine that in the world there is but *one* Self, and that it is *his* world which we all alike are truly meaning, whether we talk of one another or of Cromwell's character or of the fixed stars or of the far-off eons of the future. The relation of my thought to its object has, I insist, this curious character, that *unless* the thought and its object are parts of one larger thought, I can't even be *meaning* that object yonder, can't even be in error about it, can't even doubt its existence. You, for instance, are part of one larger self with me, or else I can't even be meaning to address you as outer beings. You are part of one larger self along with the most mysterious or most remote fact of nature, along with the moon, and all the hosts of heaven, along with all truth and all beauty. Else could you not even intend to speak of such objects beyond you. For whatever you speak of you will find that your world is meant by you as just your world. Talk of the unknowable, and it forthwith becomes your unknowable, your problem, whose solution, unless the problem be a mere nonsense question, your larger self must own and be aware of. The deepest problem of life is, "What is this deeper self?" And the only answer is, *It is the self that knows in unity all truth.* This, I insist, is no hypothesis. It is actually the presupposition of your deepest doubt. And that is why I say: Everything finite is more or less obscure, dark, doubtful. Only the Infinite Self, the problem-solver, the complete thinker, the one who knows what we mean even when we are most confused and ignorant, the

one who includes us, who has the world present to himself in unity, before whom all past and future truth, all distant and dark truth is clear in one eternal moment, to whom far and forgot is near, who thinks the whole of nature, and in whom are all things, the Logos, the world-possessor,—only his existence, I say, is perfectly sure. . . .

And now, as to the unity of this Self. Can there be many such organic selves, mutually separate unities of moments and of the objects that these moments mean? Nay, were there *many* such, would not their manifoldness be a truth? Their relations, would not these be real? Their distinct places in the world-order, would not these things be objects of possible true or false thoughts? If so, must not there be once more the inclusive real Self for whom these truths were true, these separate selves interrelated, and their variety absorbed in the organism of its rational meaning?

There is, then, at last, but one Self, organically, reflectively, consciously inclusive of all the selves, and so of all truth. I have called this self, Logos, problem-solver, all-knower. Consider, then, last of all, his relation to problems. In the previous lecture we doubted many things; we questioned the whole seeming world of the outer order; we wondered as to space and time, as to nature and evolution, as to the beginning and the end of things. Now he who wonders is like him who doubts. Has his wonder any rationality about it? Does he *mean* anything by his doubt? Then the truth that he means, and about which he wonders, has its real constitution. As wonderer, he in the moment possesses not this solving truth; he appeals to the self who can solve. That self must possess the solution just as surely as the problem has a meaning. The real nature of space and time, the real beginning of things, where matter was at any point of time in the past, what is to become of the world's energy: these are matters of truth, and truth is necessarily present to the Self as in one all-comprehending self-completed moment, beyond which is naught, within which is the world.

The world, then, is such stuff as ideas are made of. Thought possesses all things. But the world isn't unreal. It extends infinitely beyond our private consciousness, because it is the world of an universal mind. What facts it is to contain only experience can inform us. There is no magic that can anticipate the work of science. Absolutely the *only* thing sure from the first about this world, however, is that it is intelligent, rational, orderly, essentially comprehensible, so that all its problems are somewhere solved, all its darkest mysteries are known to the supreme Self. This Self infinitely and reflectively transcends our consciousness, and therefore, since it includes us, it is at the very least a person, and more definitely conscious than we are; for what it possesses is self-reflecting knowledge, and what is knowledge aware of itself, but consciousness? Beyond the seeming wreck and chaos of our finite problems, its eternal insight dwells, therefore, in absolute and supreme majesty. Yet it is not far from every one of us. There is no least or most transient thought that flits through a child's mind, or that troubles with the faintest line of care a maiden's face, and that still does not contain and embody something of this divine Logos.

ETHICS

Idealist ethics has generally centered on an ideal of individual development or personal worth. Values, as T. H. Green wrote, exist "in, of, and for persons"; and the norm of life, as Hegel suggested, is to "be a person and respect others as persons." The theory developed by idealists from premises such as these is usually called—as it is by F. H. Bradley, the author of the following selection—self-realization ethics.

Morality, Bradley holds, is coextensive with the realization of an ideal self. The self to be realized is not, it should be noted carefully, this or that feeling, or a self simply to be pleased. If I wish to achieve my true moral being, I must realize something beyond my present fragmentary being. What should I realize? The first part of Bradley's answer is, "my station and its duties"—that is, my place within the state and society. This is an essential part of the moral life; for man is a social animal, he finds his being only in society, and apart from society he is but an impossible abstraction.

Yet there is a content to this self beyond "my station" in the form of an ideal good that is more than social. Morality for Bradley is ultimately the realization of the self as the *good will*—a will, that is, that realizes an end above particular men, that is superior to them, and that confronts them as a law or obligation. The good will is also a single, "concrete" universal—a universal that is not only above but also in particular details. Finally, the good will remains an ideal, partly perhaps but never fully real.

5 Morality and Self-Realization

F. H. Bradley (1846-1924)

It is a moral duty to realize everywhere the best self, which for us in this sphere is an ideal self; and, asking what morality is, we so far must answer, it is coextensive with self-realization in the sense of the realization of the ideal self in and by us. And thus we are led to the enquiry, what is the *content* of this ideal self.

. . . We can at once gather that the good self is the self which realizes (1) a social, (2) a non-social ideal; the self, first, which does, and, second, which does not directly and immediately involve relation to others. Or from another point of view, what is aimed at is the realization in me (1) of the ideal which is realized in society, of my station and its duties, or (2) of the ideal which is not there fully realized; and this is (a) the perfection of a social and (b) of a non-social self. Or again (it is all the same thing) we may divide into (1) duties to oneself which are not regarded as social duties, (2) duties to oneself which are so regarded, these latter being (a) the duties of my station which I happen to be in, (b) duties beyond that station. Let us further explain.

The content of the good self, we see,

has a threefold origin; and (1) the first and most important contribution comes from what we have called my station and its duties, and of this we have spoken already at some length. We saw that the notion of an individual man existing in his own right independent of society was an idle fancy, that a human being is human because he has drawn his being from human society, because he is the individual embodiment of a larger life; and we saw that this larger life, of the family, society, or the nation, was a moral will, an universal the realization of which in his personal will made a man's morality. We have nothing to add here except in passing to call attention to what we lately advanced, viz. that the good man is good throughout all his life and not merely in parts; and further to request the reader to turn to himself and ask himself in what his better self consists. He will find, if we do not mistake, that the greater part of it consists in his loyalty, and according to the spirit, performing his duties and filling his place as the member of a family, society, and the state. He will find that, when he has satisfied the demands of these spheres upon him, he will in the main have covered the claims of what he calls his good self. The basis and foundation of the ideal self is the self which is true to my station and its duties.

But (2) we saw also that, if we in-

The selection is from Essay VI, "Ideal Morality," in F. H. Bradley, *Ethical Studies* (New York: G. E. Stechert & Co.; London: Henry S. King & Co., 1876), pp. 197–209, with omissions.

vestigate our good self, we find something besides, claims beyond what the world expects of us, a will for good beyond what we see to be realized anywhere. The good in my station and its duties was visibly realized in the world, and it was mostly possible to act up to that real ideal; but this good beyond is only an ideal; for it is not wholly realized in the world we see, and, do what we may, we can not find it realized in ourselves. It is what we strive for and in a manner do gain, but never attain to and never possess. And this ideal self (so far as we are concerned with it here) is a social self. The perfect types of zeal and purity, honor and love, which, figured and presented in our own situation and circumstances, and thereby unconsciously specialized, become the guides of our conduct and law of our being, are social ideals. They directly involve relation to other men, and, if you remove others, you immediately make the practice of these virtues impossible. . . .

But (3) there remains in the good self a further region we have not yet entered on; an ideal, the realization of which is recognized as a moral duty, but which yet in its essence does not involve direct relation to other men. The realization for myself of truth and beauty, the living for the self which in the apprehension, the knowledge, the sight, and the love of them finds its true being, is (all those who know the meaning of the words will bear me out) a moral obligation, which is not felt as such only so far as it is too pleasant.

It is a moral duty for the artist or the enquirer to lead the life of one, and a moral offence when he fails to do so. But on the other hand it is impossible,

without violent straining of the facts, to turn these virtues into social virtues or duties to my neighbor. No doubt such virtues do as a rule lead indirectly to the welfare of others, but this is not enough to make them social; their social bearing is indirect, and does not lie in their very essence. The end they aim at is a single end of their own, the content of which does not necessarily involve the good of other men. This we can see from supposing the opposite. If that were true, then it would not be the duty of the enquirer, as such, simply to enquire, or of the artist, as such, simply to produce the best work of art; but each would have to consider ends falling outside his science or art, and would have no right to treat these latter as ends in themselves. "Nor has he," may be the confident answer. I reply that to me this is a question of fact, and to me it is a fact that the moral consciousness recognizes the perfecting of my intellectual or artistic nature by the production of the proper results, as an end in itself and not merely as a means. The pursuit of these ends, apart from what they lead to, is approved as morally desirable, not perhaps by the theory, but, I think, by the instinctive judgment of all persons worth considering; and if, and while, this fact stands, for me at least it is not affected by doctrines which require that it should be otherwise. To say, without society science and art could not have arisen, is true. To say, apart from society the life of an artist or man of science can not be carried on, is also true; but neither truth goes to show that society is the ultimate end, unless by an argument which takes the basis of a result as its final cause, and which would prove the physical and physiological conditions of society to be the end for which it existed. Man is not man at all unless social, but man is not much above the beasts unless more than social. . . .

The field of morality we find is the whole field of life; its claim is as wide as self-realization, and the question raised before now presents itself, Are morality and self-realization the same and not different? This appears at first sight to be the case. The moral end is to realize the self, and all the forms of the realizing of the self are seen to fall within the sphere of morality; and so it seems natural to say that morality is the process of self-realization, and the most moral man is the man who most fully and energetically realizes human nature. Virtue is excellence, and the most excellent is the most virtuous.

If we say this, however, we come into direct collision with the moral consciousness, which clearly distinguishes moral from other excellence, and asserts that the latter is not in itself moral at all; and we find the deliverance of that consciousness in the emphatic maxim that nothing is morally good save a good will. This maxim we shall forthwith take to be true, and so proceed.

Morality then will be the realization of the self as the good will. It is not self-realization from all points of view, though all self-realization can be looked at from this one point of view; for all of it involves will, and, so far as the will is good, so far is the realization moral. Strictly speaking and in the proper sense, morality is self-realization within the sphere of the personal will. We see this plainly in art and science, for there we have moral excellence, and that excellence does not lie in mere skill or mere success, but in single-mindedness and devotion to what seems best as against what we merely happen to like. . . .

The general end is self-realization, the making real of the ideal self; and for morality, in particular, the ideal self is the good will, the identification of my will with the ideal as an universal will. The end for morals is a will, and my will, and an universal will, and one will. Let us briefly refer on these heads to the moral consciousness.

Nothing, we have seen, is good but a good will. The end for morals is not the mere existence of any sort of ideal indifferently, but it is the realization of an ideal will in my will. The end is the ideal willed by me, the willing of the ideal in and by my will, and hence an ideal will. And my will as realizing the ideal is the good will. A will which obeys no law is not moral, a law which is not willed is nothing for morality. Acts, so far as they spring from the good will, are good, and a temper and habits and character are good so far as they are a present good will, result from it and embody it; and what issues from a good character must thus likewise be morally good.

That the good will for morality is my will is obvious enough, and it is no less plain that it is presented as universal. That does not mean that everybody does or has to do what I do, but it means that, if they were I, they must do as I have to do, or else be immoral; it means that my moral will is *not* the mere will of myself as this or that man, but something above it and beyond it. And further, again, the good will is presented as one will; in collisions, going to our moral consciousness, we are told that, if we knew it, there is a right, that the collision is for us, and is not for the good will. We can not bring before us two diverse good wills, or one good will at cross purposes and not in harmony with itself; and we feel sure that, if our will were but one with the universal, then we too should be one with ourselves, with no conflict of desires, but a harmony and system.

Such is the will presented to itself by the moral consciousness, but for the moral consciousness that is ideal and not real. Within the sphere of morality the universal remains but partially realized: it is something that for ever wants to be, and yet is not.

We saw that the will of the social organism might be called an universal will, and a will which was visibly real, as well as ideal; but we saw too that the sphere of my station and its duties did not cover the whole good self; and further, even within that sphere, and apart from difficulties of progress, for morality in the strict sense ideal and real remain apart. The bad self is not extinguished, and in myself I see an element of will wherein the universal is unrealized, and against which it therefore remains (so far as my morality is concerned) a mere idea, for, even if we assume that society gets no hurt, yet I do not come up to my special type.

For morals then the universal is not realized within my station, and furthermore the moral consciousness does not say that it is realized anywhere at all. The claim of the ideal is to cover the whole field of reality, but our conscience tells us that we will it here, and that there again we do not will it, here it is realized, and there it is not realized, and we can not point to it in ourselves or others and say, Here is the universal incarnate, and fully actual by and as the will of this or that man; and indeed we see that for the ideal self to be in the world as the expressed will of this or that spiritualized animal is quite out of the question.

SOCIAL PHILOSOPHY

Idealistic value theory relies heavily on the Kantian principle previously mentioned in the introduction, namely, respect for personality. This observation holds for idealistic social philosophy as well. True political community does not consist in power alone; it is rather an order for the support of persons' powers and capacities. Idealists therefore argue that there must be rights because personality ought to be respected and developed. This possession of rights depends in turn on a common consciousness of a social good.

In the following selection, Ernest Barker develops the meaning of part of that good, the idea of justice. Influenced especially by the English idealist T. H. Green (1836–1882), Barker defines justice as that right order of relationships among persons which guarantees to all of them the external conditions of their personal development. His position is a form of self-realization theory raised to the social level, and justice is thus an ideal of concrete rationality for society.

6 Justice and Personality

Ernest Barker (1874-1960)

It has already been noted that the root idea of the word *jus*, and therefore also the words *justus* and *justitia*, is the idea of joining or fitting, the idea of a bond or tie. Primarily, the joining or fitting implied in this root idea is that between *man and man* in an organized system of human relations. But we may also conceive of the "just" and "justice" as connected with, and expressed in, a joining or fitting between *value and value* in a general sum and synthesis of values. We recognize a number of different values as necessary to an organized system of human relations. There is the value of liberty: there is the value of equality: there is the value of fraternity, or (as it may also be called, and is perhaps better called) co-operation. All these values are present in any system of law; but they are present in different degrees at different periods of time, and there is a constant process of adjustment and readjustment between their claims. The claims of liberty have to be adjusted to those of equality; and the claims of both have also to be adjusted to those of co-operation. From this point of view the function of justice may be said to be that of adjusting, joining, or fitting the different political values. Justice is the reconciler and the synthesis of political values: it is their union in an adjusted and integrated whole: it is, in Aristotle's words, "What answers to the whole of goodness . . . being the exercise of goodness as a whole . . . towards one's

neighbour."[1] We must presently inquire into each of the values. But before we can do so, it is necessary to inquire into the origin and nature of the general notion of justice—the notion of the "first" or "total" value in which the others are all combined; by which they are all controlled; and in virtue of which their different claims (if and so far as a conflict arises) are reconciled and adjusted.

How do we discover, and from what source do we draw, the total notion of justice—the general and controlling idea of the right and the just—which we feel that the law of the State should express? We acknowledge that justice will justify law to us; we admit that, in virtue of this justification, it finally ties and obliges us to law. But what is the source of its justifying grace and obliging power? . . .

Can we find this principle in ethics? If we answer in the affirmative, the moral standard of the community, precipitated in and enforced by the general moral conscience, will be the source of a notion of justice, containing a system or synthesis of values, which will be in its turn the impersonal source of positive law. We shall accordingly hold that if law is to have value as well as validity—

The selection is from Ernest Barker, *Principles of Social and Political Theory* (Oxford: The Clarendon Press, 1951). Used by permission of The Clarendon Press.

[1] *Ethics*, Book V, c. ii, ¶ 10 (1130^b, 18-19).

value all round, and not some single "broken arc" of value called by the name of "solidarity" or by some other such name—it must satisfy, in the last resort, the demands of the general moral conscience, issuing and expressed in a general all-round notion of what is just and right in the conduct of human relations. In order that law may be valid, it is enough that it should satisfy the canon of declaration, recognition, and enforcement by a constituted authority acting on behalf of the community. In order that it may have value, over and above validity, law must also satisfy— *as much as it can, and so far as its strength avails*—the canon of conformity to the demands of moral conscience as expressed in the general notion of justice. In other words, and in simpler terms, law will have value only if it expresses and realizes—*so far as it can and in such ways as it can*—a rule of right for human relations ultimately derived from ethics.

Here we touch a difficulty, which the provisos already stated are meant to meet in advance. Law is not ethics; and legality, or obedience to law, is not the same as morality. Law is concerned with external acts, and its demands are satisfied by such acts because they are all that its sanctions, themselves external acts of physical compulsion, can possibly secure. Ethics is concerned not only with external acts, but also with internal motive: its essence, as Aristotle said, is "a state of character, concerned with choice," which is freely determined in its choice by its own internal motive; and the demands of ethics are not satisfied unless an internal motive is present as well as an external act. An act is legal, whatever its motive, so long as it is the act demanded by the law. An act is not moral, whatever its outward show may be, if it is not inspired by an internal motive and does not proceed from a "state of a character concerned with choice."

But though we must draw a distinction between the nature of ethics and the nature of law, it does not follow that such a distinction abolishes any relation. Law and ethics are both concerned with what should be, and they both speak in the imperative mood: they both deal, in the main, with identical areas of life— marriage and its sanctities, the keeping of faith and the honouring of pledges, the duty of consideration for others, and man's general duty to his neighbour. How shall we express their relation? We may attempt two alternative methods of expression, and seek to discover which of the two expresses the relation best.

The first method of expression is based on the fact that law is a uniform rule of action binding on all men alike. Men in general run through the whole gamut of the moral scale: some act on this, and some on that standard: one standard is lower, and another higher. What law does, it may be argued, is to establish a moral minimum which every man must attain. It establishes, as it were, a lowest common measure of conduct which all can compass and which can therefore be made a uniform rule of action for all. If law bids me attach and keep burning a rear light on my bicycle when I am riding it in the dark, that is a lowest common measure of consideration for others, and it may, as such, be legally imposed. If law proceeds to fine me for riding without a rear light, it stimulates me into a disposition to obey the moral minimum—a disposition which itself is not moral (even though it results in obedience to the moral rule of consideration for others) because it is based on the negative and non-moral factor of force, and not on the positive and moral factor of an inward motive of spontaneous consideration. Law, when it is so considered, may be regarded as a schoolmaster to bring us to morality, through the enforcement of habits of action by the use of coercive discipline.

But there is an obvious objection to this view of law. A moral minimum, enforced by non-moral means, may have *some* relation to ethics; but it is not a relation which can stand the test of scrutiny, or prove itself to be anything more than a superficial relation. If law is connected with ethics in the sense that it is meant to enforce the rules of ethics on some sort of common standard, ought not the standard initially to be something higher than a mere minimum, and ought we not to be constantly engaged in screwing the strings tighter and tighter, in order to produce a fuller and truer note? And, even more, ought not the standard, whatever its pitch, to be enforced by means, such as reformatory punishment and moral education, which will themselves have a moral quality because they tend to promote a moral disposition? These questions suggest that if once we adopt the idea that law is a moral minimum, we shall soon be led to seek to obliterate any distinction between law and ethics, and to substitute law for ethics, with the result of eliminating ethics.

We may therefore turn to another method of expressing the relation between law and ethics. This second method, like the first, is based on the fact that law deals only with men in the mass, and is in its nature no more than a uniform rule of action binding equally on all alike. But the corollary which we now draw from that fact is that the only thing which law can get from man in the mass is external conduct, because the only thing which it can apply to men in the mass is external force. From this point of view, and bearing in mind the word "external," we arrive at another method of expressing the relation between law and ethics. We conclude that law is related to ethics in the sense that it seeks to secure the set of external conditions necessary for moral action, or the general framework of external order in which the moral conscience can act and determine itself most easily and most freely. Law, from this point of view, is not the lowest common measure of ethics, or the lowest story in the house of ethics: it is rather the best and highest set of conditions, set round the house and forming, as it were, a fence for its protection, which has to be assembled, and firmly established, before moral action can find a free space for its play and in order that moral development may unfold its energies freely. All moral development is inevitably confronted by external obstacles or hindrances: it is the function of law "to remove the obstacles" or "hinder the hindrances". . . .

The course of the argument has led to the conclusion that the idea of justice, which is the impersonal source of law, is an idea which itself has its source in ethics and ethical principles. But the foundation of ethics, and the source of all ethical principles, is the value and the worth of individual personality. The moral world is a world of individual persons, each intrinsically valuable, but all existing in time, and all accordingly subject to the conditions of a time-process. The intrinsic value of each personality is the basis of political thought, just as (and just because) it is the basis of moral thought; and worth of persons —individual persons; *all* individual persons—is the supreme worth in the State. Existing under, and subject to, the conditions of a time-process, these persons —not fixed substances, but so many *growing* nuclei—are engaged in a motion of development, which is the turning of capacity into energy or (as we may also say) of "potency" into "act." The end of any national society is to foster and encourage, in and through partnership, the highest possible development of all the capacities of personality in all of its members; and this end is the justice, or "right ordering," of such a society, and may accordingly be called by the name of social justice.[2] Similarly the end of any legal association or State, which is based and superimposed on a national society, is to assemble and establish the external conditions required by every citizen for the development of his capacities; and this end is the justice, or right ordering, of such a legal association, and may accordingly be called legal justice. . . .

---

[2] The term "social justice," in common usage, tends to be applied only to economics, and to be used only to denote a just distribution of economic duties and rewards. Justice of this economic order is indeed a necessary part of "social justice" in the larger sense of that term; for a just distribution of economic duties and rewards is a necessary means to the fostering and encouraging of general personal development. But social justice, in its broader sense, is a matter of something more than merely economic duties and rewards.

Justice, as we are now in a position to see, is a term of synthesis. It is the final principle which controls the general distribution of rights and the various principles of their distribution. It is, in a word, the general right ordering of human relations in, and by, the association of the State. As such, it gives to each person rights, as his share in the whole system, and it thus "adjusts" person to person. As such, again, it gives to each principle of distribution (liberty, equality, and co-operation) its share and weight in determining the distribution actually made, and it thus "adjusts" principle to principle. This idea of justice as the general "right ordering of human relations," or the final adjustment of persons and principles, may appear to be an abstract conception if we compare it with actual concrete law, which is its visible expression and actual embodiment. But it is not abstract; nor does it reside merely in the speculative mind of the thinker, seeking, by an effort of his own reason, to separate and distil some sort of quintessence from the matter and practice of ordinary life. The idea of justice resides in *all* minds, and it has been created and developed through the ages by a process of historical social thought, which has made it a common inheritance. In that sense, and from that point of view, it is not an abstract conception but a social reality: an actual content of actual minds: a content progressively greater and clearer as those minds think out more fully and consciously the problems of a general right ordering of human relations. This justice is not morality, and its code is not that of ethics; it is not a rule of the inward life, but a rule of the outward life—the life of the relations between the members of an ·organized Society acting as such. On the other hand, this rule of the outward life of relations is vitally and intimately connected with the inward moral life: it is a condition, or set of conditions, needed and designed for the free movement of that life: it is a removal of the obstacles, or a hindrance of the hindrances, which may impede that movement. If justice is not morality it is based upon it. If its code is not that of ethics, it is a code which, as we have seen, is ultimately derived from ethics.

To elucidate the meaning of a term such as justice, built and vested with associations by an historical process of social thought, we shall do well to go back to its origin and the root from which it has grown. That root, which appears in many branches and has been prolific of many growths, would seem to be the notion of "joining" (as in the Latin *jungere* or the Greek *zeugnunai*): of "binding," or "fitting," or "tying together."[3] Justice is thus, in its original notion, the quality of aptitude of joining: it ties together whatever it touches. Primarily, it ties *men* together, by the common bond of a right and "fitting" order of relations, under which each has his position in the order and receives his due place (*suum cuique*); each has rights as his share of the general Right pervading and constituting the order; and each owns *jura* as the exemplification and concrete expression in his own

case of the general *jus*. Accordingly the *Institutes* of Justinian define justice, considered as a subjective feeling and a consequent will for the general right and fitting order, as *constans et perpetua voluntas suum cuique tribuendi*. Similarly the *Institutes* define the three precepts of *jus*, considered as the objective expression of the right order in a recognized and enforced body of rules, as consisting in *honeste vivere* ("living," as we say, "up to one's position"), *alterum non laedere* (not injuring the position of another), and *suum cuique tribuere* (actually and positively respecting another's position and rights). Aristotle, almost a thousand years earlier, had distinguished three different species of justice, as the *Institutes* afterwards distinguished and defined three precepts of *jus*. The first is "distributive" justice, which gives each person his proper position and due share in the political community: this is analogous to Justinian's *suum cuique tribuere*, but it also differs, as it is concerned only with the distribution by the city-state among its members of *public* or official position, and not with the giving of *general* position in the shape of a share in general rights. The second is "corrective" justice, which corrects a loss of position and rights involuntarily sustained in the course of transactions between individual members of the community:[4] this is analogous to Justinian's *alterum non laedere*. The third is "commutative" justice, or

---

[3] The original Indo-European root was *yug*, which may be traced in the English "yoke." The Romans, as has already been noted, still used the word *jus* in the general sense of a bond or tie, as when they spoke of *jus amicitiae* (the bond of friendship), or *jura necessitudinis* (the ties of kinship).

[4] Aristotle cites, as examples of loss thus involuntarily sustained, clandestine injuries such as theft or perjury (leading to the loss of a man's goods or good name), and open and violent injuries such as assault or murder. In Aristotle's own terminology the one term "rectificatory" (or "diorthotic") is

justice in exchange, which determines the proportion of one sort of goods or services to be rendered in return for another sort in voluntary transactions of buying and selling or letting and hiring: this has no analogy with any of Justinian's three precepts—unless it be taken as another form of Justinian's *suum cuique tribuere.*

Such is the primary way in which justice performs its function of "joining" and "fitting together." But there is also a second and further way. Justice is a joining or fitting together not only of persons, but also of principles. It joins and knits together the claims of the principle of liberty with those of the principle of equality, and both with those of the principle of fraternity or co-operation: it adjusts them to one another in a right order of *their* relations. Equality may quarrel with liberty; for if its application be pushed to the length of what is called a "classless" society, with absolute equality of possessions, it is at once brought into conflict with the liberty of each to try himself out in the effort of acquiring for himself some individual "equipment." Similarly the principle of liberty may quarrel with that of co-operation: on the one hand, men may stand on the claims of their liberty (whether the civil liberty of the ordinary individual, or the economic liberty of the worker) to the detriment

of the claims of the community for the co-operation of all its members; on the other hand, a party may press the claims of co-operation to the length of demanding the common provision and common possession of the whole equipment of life, and it may press them thereby to the detriment of the claims of the individual for civil liberty and personal freedom of effort. But not only may there be conflicts between one principle and another; there may also be internal conflicts inside the area of a single principle. In the area of liberty, for example, as the argument has previously suggested, civil liberty may be pleaded in support of claims which run contrary to those of economic liberty; and similarly political liberty may be on occasion the enemy, even if it is generally the friend, of either civil or economic liberty. There must therefore be some final principle transcending that of liberty, as it also transcends the principles of equality and co-operation: a principle which can balance each of these principles against the others, as it can also balance against one another the different and possibly divergent modes of interpretation that may be present within the area even of a single principle: a final principle which, in a word, *suum cuique tribuit.* That final principle is justice, which balances, and thus reconciles (and thus, in the issue, "joins"), the different claims. This balancing and reconciling, in its turn, implies some final and ultimate value in the light of which, and by reference to which, it is possible to strike a balance and achieve a reconciliation; for you can only balance different and possibly conflicting claims if you have something behind them all in terms of which you can measure the weight to be

---

used to cover the two sorts of justice distinguished in the text as "corrective" and "commutative." Using that one term, he then proceeds to distinguish (1) the form of rectificatory justice which deals with losses involuntarily sustained, and (2) the form of rectificatory justice which is concerned with the voluntary transactions of exchange. But the meaning is made clearer if separate names are given to these two separate forms.

assigned to each. That final and ultimate value, on the basis of the argument previously advanced, is the highest possible development of the capacities of personality in the greatest possible number of persons. Justice is therefore an order of persons, and an order of the principles regulating the distribution of rights to persons, which is measured and determined by this final and ultimate value.

ESTHETICS

Idealists have produced a variety of esthetic theories, and many of them are extremely important in the history of thought about art. Among these theories is that developed by the Italian philosopher Benedetto Croce. Central to his view is the definition of art as intuition. Intuition he believes to be not some vague feeling or hunch, but rather a realized and formed object. It is not, that is, merely emotion, but rather a total subjective mood wherein *what* is expressed comes into being in the very process of expression. Thus intuition also involves expression, for art is produced only when the spirit creates from the relatively formless materials of experience expressive images. Three further points should be noted. First, for Croce, it is feeling, not thought, which gives art its symbolism. Yet, secondly, art is a kind of knowledge—namely, knowledge of the individual. And last, the unity of art is found in a lyrical content, as embodied in the representation.

7 Art as Intuition
Benedetto Croce (1866-1952)

The question as to what is art, I will say at once, in the simplest manner, that art is *vision* or *intuition*. The artist produces an image or a phantasm; and he who enjoys art turns his gaze upon the point to which the artist has pointed, looks through the chink which he has opened, and reproduces that image in himself. "Intuition," "vision," "contemplation," "imagination," "fancy," "figurations," "representations," and so on, are words continually recurring, like synonyms, when discoursing upon art, and they all lead the mind to the same conceptual sphere which indicates general agreement.

But this reply, that art is intuition, obtains its force and meaning from all that it implicitly denies and from which it distinguishes art. What negations are implicit in it? I shall indicate the principal, or at least those that are the most important for us at this present moment of our culture.

It denies, above all, that art is a *physical fact:* for example, certain determined colors, or relations of colors; certain definite forms of bodies; certain definite sounds, or relations of sounds;

The selection is from Benedetto Croce, *Breviary of Esthetic,* The Rice Institute Pamphlet, II (1915), pp. 229–237 and 245–250. Quoted by permission of the Rice Institute.

certain phenomena of heat or of electricity—in short, whatsoever be designated as "physical." The inclination toward this error of physicizing art is already present in ordinary thought, and as children who touch the soap-bubble and would wish to touch the rainbow, so the human spirit, admiring beautiful things, hastens spontaneously to trace out the reasons for them in external nature, and proves that it must think, or believes that it should think, certain colors beautiful and certain other colors ugly, certain forms beautiful and certain other forms ugly. But this attempt has been carried out intentionally and with method on several occasions in the history of thought: from the "canons" which the Greek theoreticians and artists fixed for the beauty of bodies, through the speculations as to the geometrical and numerical relations of figures and sounds, down to the researches of the estheticians of the nineteenth century (Fechner, for example), and to the "communications" presented in our day by the inexpert, at philosophical, psychological, and natural science congresses, concerning the relations of physical phenomena with art. And if it be asked why art cannot be a physical fact, we must reply, in the first place, that physical facts *do not possess reality,* and that art, to which so many devote their whole lives and which fills all with a divine joy, is *supremely real;* thus it cannot be a physical fact, which is something unreal. This sounds at first paradoxical, for nothing seems more solid and secure to the ordinary man than the physical world; but we, in the seat of truth, must not abstain from the good reason and substitute for it one less good, solely because the first should

have the appearance of a lie; and besides, in order to surpass what of strange and difficult may be contained in that truth, to become at home with it, we may take into consideration the fact that the demonstration of the unreality of the physical world has not only been proved in an indisputable manner and is admitted by all philosophers (who are not crass materialists and are not involved in the strident contradictions of materialism), but is professed by these same physicists in the spontaneous philosophy which they mingle with their physics, when they conceive physical phenomena as products of principles that are beyond experience, of atoms or of ether, or as the manifestation of an Unknowable: besides, the matter itself of the materialists is a supermaterial principle. Thus physical facts reveal themselves, by their internal logic and by common consent, not as reality, but as a *construction of our intellect for the purposes of science.* Consequently, the question whether art be a physical fact must rationally assume this different signification: that is to say, *whether it be possible to construct art physically.* And this is certainly possible, for we indeed carry it out always, when, turning from the sense of a poem and ceasing to enjoy it, we set ourselves, for example, to count the words of which the poem is composed and to divide them into syllables and letters; or, disregarding the esthetic effect of a statue, we weigh and measure it: a most useful performance for the packers of statues, as is the other for the typographers who have to "compose" pages of poetry; but most useless for the contemplator and student of art, to whom it is neither useful nor licit to allow himself to be "distracted" from his proper object. Thus art is not a physical fact in this second sense, either; which amounts to saying that when we propose to ourselves to penetrate its nature and mode of action, to construct it physically is of no avail.

Another negation is implied in the definition of art as intuition: if it be intuition, and intuition is equivalent to *theory* in the original sense of contemplation, art cannot be a utilitarian act; and since a utilitarian act aims always at obtaining a pleasure and therefore at keeping off a pain, art, considered in its own nature, has nothing to do with the *useful* and with *pleasure* and *pain,* as such. It will be admitted, indeed, without much difficulty, that a pleasure as a pleasure, any sort of pleasure, is not of itself artistic; the pleasure of a drink of water that slakes thirst, or a walk in the open air that stretches our limbs and makes our blood circulate more lightly, or the obtaining of a longed-for post that settles us in practical life, and so on, is not artistic. Finally, the difference between pleasure and art leaps to the eyes in the relations that are developed between ourselves and works of art, because the figure represented may be dear to us and represent the most delightful memories, and at the same time the picture may be ugly; or, on the other hand, the picture may be beautiful and the figure represented hateful to our hearts, or the picture itself, which we approve as beautiful, may also cause us rage and envy, because it is the work of our enemy or rival, for whom it will procure advantage and on whom it will confer new strength: our practical interests, with their relative pleasures and pains, mingle and sometimes become confused with art and disturb, but are

never *identified* with, our esthetic interest. At the most it will be affirmed, with a view to maintaining more effectively the definition of art as the pleasurable, that it is not the pleasurable in general, but a *particular* form of the pleasurable. But such a restriction is no longer a defence, it is indeed an abandonment of that thesis; for given that art is a particular form of pleasure, its distinctive character would be supplied, not by the pleasurable, but by what distinguishes that pleasurable from other pleasurables, and it would be desirable to turn the attention to that distinctive element—more than pleasurable or different from pleasurable. Nevertheless, the doctrine that defines art as the pleasurable has a special denomination (hedonistic esthetic), and a long and complicated development in the history of esthetic doctrines: it showed itself in the Graeco-Roman world, prevailed in the eighteenth century, reflowered in the second half of the nineteenth, and still enjoys much favor, being especially well received by beginners in esthetic, who are above all struck by the fact that art causes pleasure. The life of this doctrine has consisted of proposing in turn one or another class of pleasures, or several classes together (the pleasure of the superior senses, the pleasure of play, of consciousness of our own strength, of criticism, etc., etc.), or of adding to it elements differing from the pleasurable, the useful for example (when understood as distinct from the pleasurable), the satisfaction of cognoscitive and moral wants, and the like. And its progress has been caused just by this restlessness, and by its allowing foreign elements to ferment in its bosom, which it introduces through the necessity of somehow bringing itself into agreement with the reality of art, thus attaining to its dissolution as hedonistic doctrine and to the promotion of a new doctrine, or at least to drawing attention to its necessity. And since every error has its element of truth (and that of the physical doctrine has been seen to be the possibility of the physical "construction" of art as of any other fact), the hedonistic doctrine has its eternal element of truth in the placing in relief the hedonistic accompaniment, or pleasure, common to the esthetic activity as to every form of spiritual activity, which it has not at all been intended to deny in absolutely denying the identification of art with the pleasurable, and in distinguishing it from the pleasurable by defining it as intuition.

A third negation, effected by means of the theory of art as intuition, is that art is a *moral act;* that is to say, that form of practical act which, although necessarily uniting with the useful and with pleasure and pain, is not immediately utilitarian and hedonistic, and moves in a superior spiritual sphere. But the intuition, in so far as it is a theoretic act, is opposed to the practical of any sort. And in truth, art, as has been remarked from the earliest times, does not arise as an act of the will; good will, which constitutes the honest man, does not constitute the artist. And since it is not the result of an act of will, so it escapes all moral discrimination, not because a privilege of exemption is accorded to it, but simply because moral discrimination cannot be applied to art. An artistic image portrays an act morally praiseworthy or blameworthy; but this image, as image, is neither morally praiseworthy nor blameworthy. Not only

is there no penal code that can condemn an image to prison or to death, but no moral judgment, uttered by a rational person, can make of it its object: we might just as well judge the square moral or the triangle immoral as the Francesca of Dante immoral or the Cordelia of Shakespeare moral, for these have a purely artistic function, they are like musical notes in the souls of Dante and of Shakespeare. Further, the moralistic theory of art is also represented in the history of esthetic doctrines, though much discredited in the common opinion of our times, not only on account of its intrinsic demerit, but also, in some measure, owing to the moral demerit of certain tendencies of our times, which render possible, owing to psychological dislike, that refutation of it which should be made—and which we here make— solely for logical reasons. The end attributed to art, of directing the good and inspiring horror of evil, of correcting and ameliorating customs, is a derivation of the moralistic doctrine; and so is the demand addressed to artists to collaborate in the education of the lower classes, in the strengthening of the national or bellicose spirit of a people, in the diffusion of the ideals of a modest and laborious life; and so on. These are all things that art cannot do, any more than geometry, which, however, does not lose anything of its importance on account of its inability to do this; and one does not see why art should do so, either. That it cannot do these things was partially perceived by the moralistic estheticians also; who very readily effected a transaction with it, permitting it to provide pleasures that were not moral, provided they were not openly dishonest, or recommending it to employ to a good end the dominion that, owing to its hedonistic power, it possessed over souls, to gild the pill, to sprinkle sweetness upon the rim of the glass containing the bitter draught—in short, to play the courtezan (since it could not get rid of its old and inborn habits), in the service of holy church or of morality: *meretrix ecclesiae.* On other occasions they have sought to avail themselves of it for purposes of instruction, since not only virtue but also science is a difficult thing, and art could remove this difficulty and render pleasant and attractive the entrance into the ocean of science—indeed, lead them through it as through a garden of Armida, gaily and voluptuously, without their being conscious of the lofty protection they had obtained, or of the crisis of renovation which they were preparing for themselves. We cannot now refrain from a smile when we talk of these theories, but should not forget that they were once a serious matter corresponding to a serious effort to understand the nature of art and to elevate the conception of it; and that among those who believed in it (to limit ourselves to Italian literature) were Dante and Tasso, Parini and Alfieri, Manzoni and Mazzini. And the moralistic doctrine of art was and is and will be perpetually beneficial by its very contradictions; it was and will be an effort, however unhappy, to separate art from the merely pleasing, with which it is sometimes confused, and to assign to it a more worthy post: and it, too, has its true side, because, if art be beyond morality, the artist is neither this side of it nor that, but under its empire, in so far as he is a man who cannot withdraw himself from his duties of man, and must look upon art itself—

art, which is not and never will be moral —as a mission to be exercized as a priestly office.

Again (and this is the last and perhaps the most important of all the general negations that it suits me to recall in relation to this matter), with the definition of art as intuition, we deny that it has the character of *conceptual knowledge.* Conceptual knowledge, in its true form, which is the philosophical, is always realistic, aiming at establishing reality against unreality, or at lowering unreality by including it in reality as a subordinate moment of reality itself. But intuition means, precisely, indistinction of reality and unreality, the image with its value as mere image, the pure ideality of the image; and opposing the intuitive or sensible knowledge to the conceptual or intelligible, the esthetic to the noetic, it aims at claiming the autonomy of this more simple and elementary form of knowledge, which has been compared to the dream (the dream, and not the sleep) of the theoretic life, in respect to which philosophy would be the waking. And indeed, whoever should ask, when examining a work of art, whether what the artist has expressed be metaphysically and historically true or false, asks a question that is without meaning, and commits an error analogous to his who should bring the airy images of the fancy before the tribunal of morality: without meaning, because the discrimination of true and false always concerns an affirmation of reality, or a judgment, but it cannot fall under the head of an image or of a pure subject, which is not the subject of a judgment, since it is without qualification or predicate. It is useless to object that the individuality of the image cannot subsist without reference to the universal, of which that image is the individuation, because we do not here deny that the universal, as the spirit of God, is everywhere and animates all things with itself, but we deny that the universal is rendered logically explicit and is thought in the intuition. Useless also is the appeal to the principle of the unity of the spirit, which is not broken, but, on the contrary, strengthened by the clear distinction of fancy from thought, because from the distinction comes opposition, and from opposition concrete unity. . . . Certainly art is symbol, all symbol—that is, all significant; but symbol of what? What does it mean? The intuition is truly artistic, it is truly intuition, and not a chaotic mass of images, only when it has a vital principle that animates it, making it all one with itself; but what is this principle?

The answer to such a question may be said to result from the examination of the greatest ideal strife that has ever taken place in the field of art (and is not confined to the epoch that took its name from it and in which it was predominant): the strife between *romanticism* and *classicism*. Giving the general definition, here convenient, and setting aside minor and accidental determinations, romanticism asks of art, above all, the spontaneous and violent effusion of the affections, of love and hate, of anguish and jubilation, of desperation and elevation; and is willingly satisfied and pleased with vaporous and indeterminate images, broken and allusive in style, with vague suggestions, with approximate phrases, with powerful and troubled sketches: while classicism loves the peaceful soul, the wise design, figures studied in their characteristics and precise in outline, ponderation, equi-

librium, clarity; and resolutely tends toward *representation,* as the other tends toward *feeling.* And whoever puts himself at one or the other point of view finds crowds of reasons for maintaining it and for confuting the opposite point of view; because (say the romantics), What is the use of an art, rich in beautiful images, which, nevertheless, does not speak to the heart? And if it do speak to the heart, what is the use if the images be not beautiful? And the others will say, What is the use of the shock of the passions, if the spirit do not rest upon a beautiful image? And if the image be beautiful, if our taste be satisfied, what matters the absence of those emotions which can all of them be obtained outside art, and which life does not fail to provide, sometimes in greater quantity than we desire?—But when we begin to feel weary of the fruitless defence of both partial views; above all, when we turn away from the ordinary works of art produced by the romantic and classical schools, from works convulsed with passion or coldly decorous, and fix them on the works, not of the disciples, but of the masters, not of the mediocre, but of the supreme, we see the contest disappear in the distance and find ourselves unable to call the great portions of these works, romantic or classic or representative, because they are both classic and romantic, feelings and representations, a vigorous feeling which has become all most brilliant representation. Such, for example, are the works of Hellenic art, and such those of Italian poetry and art: the transcendentalism of the Middle Ages became fixed in the bronze of the Dantesque *terzina;* melancholy and suave fancy, in the transparency of the songs and sonnets of Petrarch; sage experience of life and badinage with the fables of the past, in the limpid *ottava rima* of Ariosto; heroism and the thought of death, in the perfect blank-verse hendecasyllabics of Foscolo; the infinite variety of everything, in the sober and austere songs of Giacomo Leopardi. Finally (be it said in parenthesis and without intending comparison with the other examples adduced), the voluptuous refinements and animal sensuality of international decadentism have received their most perfect expression in the prose and verse of an Italian, D'Annunzio. All these souls were profoundly passionate (all, even the serene Lodovico Ariosto, who was so amorous, so tender, and so often represses his emotion with a smile); their works of art are the eternal flower that springs from their passions.

These expressions and these critical judgments can be theoretically resumed in the formula, that what gives coherence and unity to the intuition is feeling: the intuition is really such because it represents a feeling, and can only appear from and upon that. Not the idea, but the feeling, is what confers upon art the airy lightness of the symbol: an aspiration enclosed in the circle of a representation—that is art; and in it the aspiration alone stands for the representation, and the representation alone for the aspiration. Epic and lyric, or drama and lyric, are scholastic divisions of the indivisible: art is always lyrical—that is, epic and dramatic in feeling. What we admire in genuine works of art is the perfect fanciful form which a state of the soul assumes; and we call this life, unity, solidity of the work of art. . . . A celebrated sentence uttered by an English critic, and become one of the commonplaces of journalism, states that "all the arts tend to the condition of music"; but it would have been more accurate to say that all the arts are music, if it be thus intended to emphasize the genesis of esthetic images in feeling, excluding from their number those mechanically constructed or realistically ponderous. And another not less celebrated utterance of a Swiss semi-philosopher, which has had the like good or bad fortune of becoming trivial, discovers that "every landscape is a state of the soul": which is indisputable, not because the landscape is landscape, but because the landscape is art.

Artistic intuition, then, is always *lyrical* intuition: this latter being a word that is not present as an adjective or definition of the first, but as a synonym, another of the synonyms that can be united to the several that I have mentioned already, and which, all of them, designate the intuition. And if it be sometimes convenient that instead of appearing as a synonym, it should assume the grammatical form of the adjective, that is only to make clear the difference between the intuition-image, or nexus of images (for what is called image is always a nexus of images, since image-atoms do not exist any more than thought-atoms), which constitutes the organism, and, as organism, has its vital principle, which is the organism itself, —between this, which is true and proper intuition, and that false intuition which is a heap of images put together in play or intentionally or for some other practical purpose, the connection of which, being practical, shows itself to be not organic, but mechanic, when considered from the esthetic point of view. But the word *lyric* would be redundant save in this explicative or polemical sense; and art is perfectly defined when it is simply defined as *intuition*.

PHILOSOPHY OF MAN

Many theories of consciousness in contemporary philosophy tend to deny any conscious acts or distinct reality of mind. One of these, the Identity theory, we studied under materialism, and other such theories will be studied later. Most idealists, with H. D. Lewis, reject such reductionism, and seek to maintain that reality. Lewis grants that the conscious self is elusive, and that a theory of conscious identity is difficult to come by. Yet he maintains, despite these difficulties, that we all know what it is to be a conscious mind in the very act of our being conscious. Indeed, conscious experience at all its levels is directly known, and as well known to be nonmaterial. Given these facts, Lewis is also led to hold a Cartesian-like dualism and a theory of mind-body interactionism.

8 The Elusive Self
H. D. Lewis (1910-   )

Let me now return to the point with which I was already concerned a little earlier, namely that there are two major senses of self-identity. There is, in the first place, the sense of self-identity which I have described as the most radical or basic one. This is the sense in which one knows oneself as one ultimate indivisible being in the course of having any experience whatsoever. I know myself now as one being who just could not be any other. The question of my being or becoming some other person just could not arise, I am myself whatever my experience is like. But there is also a sense in which I am continually subject to change. Every instant I change; a moment ago I was the person who was looking at this tree, I am

now looking at the lawn. My thoughts and sensations change all the time. In terms of what I undergo or experience or do I am never the same person. I may, moreover, from time to time, undergo drastic changes of interests or aptitude or other dispositional traits. These are sometimes so substantial that we are apt to say—'He is quite a different person'. But we also want to say that these changes happen to the same person, and we certainly do this normally in the absence of radical changes. An audience does not suspect that the person who is talking to them at one time is other than the person who started the lecture, and they may not have serious doubts that he is the person who was giving a lecture in the same course last week or last year. How is self-identity in this sense established, and what are the limits of it?

One could go a good deal of the way here by noting that it would be absurd

The selection is from H. D. Lewis, *The Elusive Self* (London: George Allen & Unwin, Ltd.; New York: Humanities Press, Inc., 1969), Chapter XI, with omissions. Used by permission of the publishers.

to suppose that I could have my present understanding and aptitudes without a good deal at least of the experience and history with which I am normally credited. My general understanding and knowledge could not come about without any antecedents, they could not just emerge out of nothing. They are only acquired through a certain continuous experience over a number of years, however much they may also presuppose hereditary traits or a certain natural endowment. My more precise and specific aptitudes and information require that I should have had precise experiences which make up the course of the life I would generally be thought to have lived. But when we pass beyond establishing the sort of continuity which my life must be thought to have involved in this way and ask what sustains the impact of one experience on another and makes possible the continuous course of a person's life, then we have to do more than note the relation of one experience to another, we must account for it. It does not seem to explain itself or be just an ultimate fact about our experience which we recognize. Philosophical analysis has to go further.

It is at this point that I, like Professor Shoemaker,[1] have to have recourse to the facts of memory. But the idea of memory alone will not do the trick, at least not in the sense of noting that I am able to recall or in some other way be assured of some past event in my history. Memory does involve recalling, in a way that has at least the appearance of directness, something that occurred

in the past. Whether this is some sort of direct contact or should be thought of as vivid impressions which we immediately and with justification take to be an assurance of a past event need not be settled. For the point I want to stress is that this could not be memory in the strict sense, (or, alternatively, could not afford assurance of our continued identity) unless the impression of the past event contains within it a recognition of its involving the same distinctive awareness of myself as a unique being which I have in my experience at this moment. It is this, and this alone, in the last resort, that guarantees the presumption I have that the past experience is an experience of the same person as I know myself to be now.

The guarantee in question cannot be obtained from any feature of the event which I do recall, however peculiar. For there is no inherent reason why I should not have vivid and dependable impressions of past events (however this dependability is constituted) without their being past events in which I have participated. There could be clairvoyant knowledge of past events in which I had no part or which happened before I was born. This is why some have toyed with the possibility of more than one person having 'memories', in some after life or re-incarnated state, which are in all respects identical. Suppose, it is said, two persons come to life with the memories of Guy Fawkes. We could not in that case say that either of them was Guy Fawkes. I agree, although I would withhold the word memory, in such cases, and speak instead of dependable impressions or something of that sort. But this possibility cannot really arise if we think of memory proper, for this in-

---

[1 Lewis's discussion here is related to Sydney Shoemaker's book, *Self-Knowledge and Self-Identity* (Ithaca: Cornell University Press, 1963). *Ed.*]

volves the recognition of the past occurrence as one in which I find the consciousness of myself as the person I am now. I re-live, as it were, the past event, or recapture it, in the form which involves the peculiar awareness I now have of myself as one unique being wholly incapable of being any other.

There is, in this way, a linkage with the past event, on its inner side as it were, independently of the sort of event it happens to be in other ways. We do not thus, in the ultimate analysis, look for linkages of content, for those could be fortuitous. Nor do we seek to rectify this by appealing to bodily continuity. For that is conceivably consistent with a change of occupant of a particular body. The essential linkage is not in extraneous matters of this sort. It is, usually at least, firm and more immediately dependable. I recognize myself in the past experience to be the person I am now, not, as I have stressed, because of any particular content of the experience it is, but more expressly in the proper reconstruction of the experience as a whole. I recall, in other words, not just what happened but its happening to me as the person I know myself to be now.

This comes very close, in some ways, to Shoemaker's argument that the way we use the word 'memory' is a guarantee of continuous identity. But I am not in fact appealing to the use of the word, nor would I wish to guarantee our use of it, in the sense that Shoemaker has properly in mind, merely on the ground that our use of it implies that it must sometimes be legitimately used. My appeal is rather to what, in fact, we actually find to be the case, namely that we are able to recall some past events in a reasonably dependable way and recognize the normal consciousness we have of ourselves as a feature of those events. This certainly goes beyond Shoemaker's position, as he presents and states it. But one also suspects in this, as in many similar cases of the appeal to our use of words, that more is involved than may at first be apparent. In that case the difference between what Shoemaker really wants to say and my own view may not be as wide as it seems. If my view is right, there can be no sense in which one person could acquire the memories of another. In a subsidiary sense we can all, of course, remember the same things. We can all remember things we have learnt, in a dispositional or some other way. We can all remember the date of the Norman Conquest, and a number of people may also remember things jointly in the sense of having personal memories of situations in which they were all involved. A group of people may remember jointly the holiday they had last year or some escapade of theirs in school. But no one in the strict sense remembers anything other than an experience or activity of his own. Such experiences will often be of situations in which others were involved and we may have good reason to suppose that they have memories of it as well. But what they can remember, in the strict sense, is what they themselves went through, linked very closely as it was with all that we were undergoing as well. Memory in the strict sense is essentially personal.

It is, moreover, memory in this sense that is involved in the first instance in establishing our continued identity. But once the initial linkage is established it can be supplemented in a host of other ways in which bodily continuity will play a considerable part. I can learn a great deal about my own history in other ways than through my own explicit memories. I can rest assured that I travelled to school and attended certain classes on some date in my boyhood in which nothing happened to me sufficiently eventful for me to remember. I have no recollection of this day, and it might be exceptionally hard to revive any. But I can be sure (from the school register if serious question arose) that I attended school on this day and on many similar days when, as I may have good reason to know, my attendance at school was unbroken. I am sure that I was on those days the being I now know myself to be, but I know it now indirectly as a very strong presumption indeed from independent evidence.

This evidence is substantially the same as the evidence I have about other people. I have good reason to believe that my friends have certain thoughts and feelings when they are with me, and I may be fully justified in supposing that they and other people, some of whom I never encounter, have certain experiences at various times. I know about various people in the past in this way; and I can learn from precisely the same sort of evidence that someone having my bodily appearance underwent certain experiences at some date in the past and responded in certain ways. This would, moreover, dovetail into further things known in the same way and forming the meaningful and continuous history of one person. It would be remarkable indeed if some slice of this history had another experient. For how would he know the things he would need to

know to respond as he does if he had not been the being concerned in all the events that dovetail in this way into one another? One would need to presuppose some completely freakish exercises of clairvoyant power on the part of a number of agents having my bodily form in a succession without any crack at all to indicate it. This is such a remote possibility that no one takes it seriously. It is, however, around the central internal awareness of my own identity that anything I learn in other ways about the course of my own life is built. In the absence of it we could do no more than protest that mere association of ideas would not suffice as the explanation of continuous meaningful experience and presuppose some way, a wholly mysterious one, in which various experiences blend as the significant course of a person's life. The proper explanation comes from one's own inner consciousness of the unique being one finds oneself to be in any experience.

But once a continuous course of experience has been credited to me, together with the various aptitudes or dispositions which this involves, then it is possible to give me an identity in a subsidiary or secondary sense which does admit of, indeed requires, characterization or description. I am thus said to be the person who likes this or that, who is prone to be aroused in this or that way, who has witnessed certain scenes at certain times and so forth. This is the sense or level of identity we have in mind from day to day, and it is with this that philosophers have usually concerned themselves in the first instance when raising the problem of self-identity. But I am contending that we cannot give an adequate explanation of this kind of self-identity apart from the peculiar identification of myself as the unique being I am which I have expressly in any experience.

It would be a great mistake, however, to suppose that the two senses in which I may speak of my own identity presuppose two sorts of selves, as has sometimes been thought in speaking of a phenomenal and a noumenal self. The self which is characterized or described, on the basis of the sort of experience I have had and so forth, is the self which I know, in a way that defies characterization, in all experience. Indeed it is not the self which is, strictly speaking, described. What we can describe is the course of certain events and the aptitudes or traits of character disclosed in these. These are events which have happened to the person I find myself to be, and they are the aptitudes I happen to have. To that extent they are descriptions of me and they are the ways in which I would be identified by other persons. Who am I? I am the person who was born in a certain place, brought up and educated at various places, who likes this or that and makes his living in a certain way and so forth. There is no other way in which other persons can identify me. But I could inwardly know myself to be the person I am *if all these things were different.* They do not give the uniqueness of my being the person I am in any experience whatsoever. My experiences are indeed my own, and I must not be thought to be divorced from them, as if I could just exist in a vacuum—or as if experiences could be without being essentially someone's experience. But who the someone is can only be properly known to himself.

There could thus be a radical change in the characteristics by which I am known to others, and my history could have been different. But if I became, or if I had been in the past, a very different sort of person, or if I had lived at other times and places, there would still be the basic sense in which I would know myself to be myself. If, in the event of my having some other existence, I retain no recollection of the present one, I would still have the same sort of basic sense of being myself as I have now, although, of course, I would not any longer know of my having it now.[2] This is what is often overlooked in some criticisms of the idea of survival which look exclusively for identity in terms of characteristics or a history by which I could be described. I do not think in fact that survival is at all probable in a way that is wholly divorced from my present existence, but this is for further considerations in which the worth and purpose of survival has a prominent place. It would not, however, in my view be absurd to suppose that there could be intermediate stages of a number of existences not related by any consciousness of one another and culminating in some stage of being to which they all contributed. This would be in accordance with some notions of reincarnation. But I do not think in fact that it is likely to be the case.

It must be stressed at the same time, as I have done above, that the self which is not to be identified with its characteristics or the course of its experiences must not be thought capable of

---

[2] Some further telling arguments in support of this position may be found in an article entitled 'Can the self survive the death of its mind?' by John Knox Jr. in *Religious Studies*, October 1969.

existing in a void without experience or a nature or character of any sort. I could not exist as pure being without some sort of experience, and I could certainly not have the sort of experience I have as a human being without some relatively stable nature which sustains the continuity of it and determines my responses. I will not stress this further, as the point has already been made above. But there is one consequential issue which should be noted, although it is not altogether peculiar to a position like my own.

Suppose that, in the course of one's life, one lapses into a state of total unconsciousness or insensitivity. This is what is normally understood by the idea of dreamless sleep. In dreamless sleep my body would still be functioning, but I would have no sort of dream experience at all. It is not to the purpose to ask how far it is likely that there is a state of total unconsciousness of this sort or how we would best settle the question. But it is conceivable that there should be dreamless sleep. In that case the question arises of whether I could be said to exist at that time at all. It could be said, of course, that I have a continued existence in the sense that when I begin to be conscious again my dispositional set-up will remain the same. It could be said to persist in the way dispositions normally persist, but unless we resort to a view of substance as a sustainer of dispositions which I do not hold, this would amount to little more than saying that, for some reason we cannot specify or for purely physical conditions, I would in fact continue to have the same dispositional nature, in essentials at least, on becoming conscious as before my lapse into total unconsciousness.

My own inclination, therefore, is to say that in a state of totally dreamless sleep (in the sense that we have no sort of experience while asleep) we simply cease to exist. I do not find this peculiarly disconcerting, although I believe many people find it so. It would almost be like dying and surviving except that my body would not have undergone clinical death—it would have functioned and nothing else. But this does not seem to me specially disturbing. Why should it, provided the normal continuities persist beyond the 'gap' and I have then the consciousness of myself which I normally have in any experience?

It should be evident now how important it is that there should be no ambiguity about the sense in which it is maintained that there is a certain distinctiveness and an elusiveness of consciousness and of our personal identity. This has not been defended in any esoteric way or as the invocation of some peculiar sort of mystery. It is not contended at all that we might, by some special sort of probing or by some peculiar disciplines or technique of meditation, manage to uncover some otherwise obscure element in our nature, some inner core of our personality of which we are normally quite unaware. I have not been suggesting any way in which we might peel off certain layers of our experience or our natures and reveal thus, to our amazement, some undreamed of treasure whose preservation takes precedence over everything else. The self is not alleged to be a mystery in that sense. Let me put it in this way.

It is held in some 'spiritualist' circles (or among some students of psychic phenomena) that our more manifest and gross material body is the outer wrapping, as it were, of finer bodies (more than one apparently) by which we may materialize, for suitable persons on suitable occasions, and function without the physical limitations to which we are normally subject. There may be more in such suppositions than we generally assume, especially if they were restated by people better suited to reflect on the available evidence than those who usually make such claims. But such ideas are obviously fraught with the utmost difficulties, and these by no means arise solely from the slenderness and imprecision of the evidence. But even if such difficulties could be overcome, they would not in any way help us to understand the sort of inwardness or elusiveness of genuinely mental existence with which I am now concerned. The suggestion of more and more ethereal wrappings of our gross physical body affords no proper analogy to the genuine inwardness of the self or person.

My concern at present is not, therefore, with obscure phenomena of the mental life. This is not because I wish to maintain that everything about us is perfectly transparent or evident, in principle, to ordinary or casual inspection. There may be various levels of mental life. Almost everyone would admit some kind of dispositional 'unconscious', that is the modifying of our dispositional tendencies through events of which we have no recollection—indeed something of this kind must be true of all dispositions. There may also be actual unconscious or subconscious processes, although the way we must understand this presents obvious difficulties—I shall not consider them here. If someone wishes to maintain that what occurs to us in this way could be superior to our nor-

mal conscious experience, that we have some entirely different richer life above or beyond the life we normally seem to lead, I should, indeed, be a good deal more sceptical. The repercussions of such a supposition would be very far-reaching and they would raise very grave problems about freedom and responsibility. I mention them here, however, to make it clear that, when I speak, in this book, of the 'inwardness' and elusiveness of persons and their experience, I am not alluding at all to some quality or level of our existence that is not open to us in the ordinary way and a feature of the experience of any person whatsoever. I claim to uncover nothing that is not there plainly for all to see.

All the same I am maintaining that consciousness and our continued identity are, in a very radical sense, mysterious and elusive. They are so in the sense that there is no special way in which they can be characterized. They are evanescent in the sense that they slip through our hands the moment we try to describe them or say what they are; and the core of the criticisms I levelled against influential contemporary thinkers was that they seem determined to look for some specifiable quality of consciousness, in some way akin to observable qualities (a ghost or shadow of them) by which consciousness could be picked out from other things we encounter in the world. This is just what we cannot do. We know what it is to be conscious *in being conscious*, we know quite well what it is to have an experience, but this is so radically different from the reality we find in the external or material world that we can only recognize the difference without saying anything further.

This holds quite independently of any

view we may have about the external world or physical reality. We may incline, as I do, to a Berkeleyan or phenomenalist view of the world of nature. We would then hold that what we perceive, the choir of heaven and the furniture of earth, do not exist unless they are in some way experienced. But this would not in the least make them mental realities themselves. There would still be a radical dichotomy between extended existences (coloured or characterized in some other manner) which in some way confront us, and which we apprehend, and the apprehending of them or the setting ourselves to manipulate them. My view about the irreducible and distinctive nature of consciousness is in no way supported by inclining towards a phenomenalist view of material reality, although the latter view has

importance in some other ways for our full understanding of what I can best characterize here as 'the human situation'. I require no support from a phenomenalist or Berkeleyan view of the world of nature for my insistence on the non-material *sui generis* nature of experience at all its levels. If I looked for such support I should not only weaken, but in fact quite undermine my position.

This was made very plain by Berkeley himself in his insistence that minds are not known by perception but in the altogether different way of notions. This applies not only to our awareness of conscious processes as such but also to each one's awareness of himself as a distinct irreducible entity which I have been specially concerned to stress in this chapter.

PHILOSOPHY OF SCIENCE

In their function as critics of experience, idealists frequently develop distinctive interpretations of science. Such a statement is given in the following selection by Errol E. Harris, author of many books on philosophy and science.

Influenced greatly by Hegel and his dialectical method, Harris accepts initially the notion that knowledge is a whole, and that it is expressed as a system. Science is an explanatory system, a system to be understood as a series or scale of dialectically related forms. Scientific advance is thus a movement from one system to another, and the logic of this advance, Harris believes, is dialectical. Since knowledge does form a whole, though, such advances are one of many phases in our developing awareness of the world.

9 Dialectic and Scientific Method
Errol E. Harris (1908-   )

One of Kant's major contributions to modern philosophy was the recognition that genuine knowledge is never a mere patchwork of items of information, whether gathered from empirical sources or from intellectual, whether inductively inferred or deductively derived from first principles. "If each and every single representation were completely foreign, isolated and separate from every other," he declared, "nothing would ever arise such as knowledge, which is a whole of related and connected elements."[1] Of this fact, Hegel was unshakably convinced. "The Truth," he maintained, "is the whole"; but it is no undifferentiated, featureless whole, no Schellingian night in which all cows are black. "The true form in which the truth exists can only be the scientific system itself" (*Phänomenologie des Geistes*, p. 27).[2]

Further, he did not conceive the system as a static or invariable pattern, but as a dynamic system; a system of activity and development inherent in the very relationship of part to whole, or of the rudimentary to the fully fashioned. In its explicit form it is self-conscious, and of the self-conscious mind he says that it is absolute restlessness—a constant activity of thinking the essential principle of which is dialectic. Moreover, it is only in the fully explicit self-conscious form that the whole is adequately realized as a self-maintaining system. "The Truth," he says, "is the whole, but only that essential reality which has fulfilled itself through its own self-development is the whole."[3] Moreover, the whole when fully realized transpires as the entire dialectical scale through which it has developed itself, and it is to this and the manner of its progression that we must look for the clue to understanding precisely what Hegel means by system.

The whole of which Hegel speaks is not one that can be broken up into mechanically separable parts, and the system that constitutes it is not a mere spatial or mechanical arrangement of such parts. Neither is it a purely formal set of relations between ideas or formulae. It is a continuous scale of forms and categories which generates itself by the dynamic of its own inherent principle of activity, from the most vague, abstract, and indefinite to the most complete, articulate, and explicit elaboration of absolute reality. Each form, at every level, is, he asserts, the Absolute in some partial, and in some degree inadequate, manifestation of itself. Each logical category, which has a place in the system, is a provisional definition of the Absolute. It is that definition which is characteristic of a particular phase in the process of dialectical development.

The selection is from Errol E. Harris, "Dialectic and Scientific Method," *Idealistic Studies*, 3(1973), pp. 1-17, with omissions. Used by permission of the Editor and author.

[1] *Kritik der Reinen Vernunft*, A.97.

[2] References to the German text are to the Glockner *Jubiläumsausgabe*.

[3] *Phänomenologie*, p. 24.

Hence the progression is not simply from the fragmentary to the complete (though any such progression is one aspect of the process), but is from the vague and confused to the more precise and discriminate. At every stage the whole is in some sense, or manner, or degree, present, for at every stage we have what Kant called a whole of related and connected elements. But the whole is not at every stage explicitly articulated, and the series of forms is constituted by the successive stages of explication engendered from the less to the more adequate self-manifestations of what is ultimately real and true.

The movement is generated by the very inadequacy of the primitive forms. For every entity strives to become self-sufficient; and in those which are finite, incomplete, or in other respects deficient, their very shortcomings give rise to internal conflicts and oppositions which can be resolved only by further self-development and explication. Similarly at the level of development at which consciousness arises and this process becomes explicit as knowledge, finite objects are found wanting just so far as they do not satisfy the mind's demand for, and nisus towards, coherent wholeness; and contradictions arise, oppositions are generated, and resolutions are achieved by synthesis and reconciliation. The progression is consequently one that proceeds by the generation of contradictions and their resolution. It is the continual assertion of the negative aspect involved in finiteness and insufficiency and its supersession by a more adequate form in which the particular deficiency is supplied and the negation is negated.

For this reason Hegel calls the principle of the dialectic one of absolute negativity; and it is because of the generation of internal contradiction through inadequacy of the finite form, the generation of consequent opposition to an other which is constituted by what is lacking from the original, that the triadic appearance of the dialectical stages results. "Thesis, antithesis and synthesis" was not Hegel's own formula for the dialectical movement, but it does summarize what results from it, even though it is not always apparent and by no means always rigidly exemplified in Hegel's exposition.

System, then, is a series or scale of dialectically related forms, each automatically generating the next, by its inherent nisus to overcome its own shortcomings and the contradictions to which they give rise. It is system of this kind that constitutes what Hegel calls "science" or *Wissenschaft*, and it is to this that he is referring when he writes: ". . . knowledge is only real and can only be expounded as a science or system."[4] Each form, because the whole is implicit in it, is itself a whole of some sort. Thus the logic of the dialectic is a logic of development and what develops is always a totality.

The gamut of categories that results from the dialectical process is a scale of forms in which each is a specific exemplification of the totality which is developing, but is an exemplification at a particular level of adequacy (or inadequacy) or degree of explicitness. At the same time the successive forms are mutually related as opposites because of the difference in adequacy between them: the first as relatively false to that which it

---

4 *Phänomenologie*, p. 27.

is its purport to present, and the other as relatively true. As Hegel puts it, the later is "the truth of" the earlier. Every category of the *Logic* is an exemplification of the Idea at a specific level of explicit thought; every category of Nature-philosophy is a specific natural form at a particular level of realization of integral wholeness; and every form of sentience, feeling, and consciousness is a specific form of mind (*Geist*) at a definite level of self-development. Yet each of them, as well as each major division of philosophical reflection, is in some respect, or in some sense, opposed to its neighbor, and in some degree to every other. I believe that this can be demonstrated in detail, but my present purpose is only to bring out the fact that the dialectical system is a scale of forms such as R. G. Collingwood described in his *Essay on Philosophical Method*, in which the forms are mutually related in three ways at once, as degrees of realization of a universal principle, as specifications of that same universal, and as opposites. Such a logical structure Collingwood finds characteristic of all philosophical thinking, and typical of every philosophical system. My object is to show that it is not confined to philosophy but is also the form of scientific theory and scientific advance. . . .

A scientific theory, it was said above, is an explanatory system. The current view of explanation is that it consists simply of deduction, within a deductive system, of the fact or hypothesis to be explained, from a higher level hypothesis couched in theoretical terms. The meaning of these terms is specifiable (according to the doctrine) only by translation into the empirical terms descriptive of the observable facts. This is an odd view of explanation, for we normally mean by that word the setting of the *explicandum* in a context which will make it more intelligible. But if the facts to be explained supply the meaning of the explicatory terms, it is difficult to see how the latter can render the former more intelligible. It is sometimes alleged that explanation is the same as analysis; but analysis is itself a vague term with several applications and meanings, not all of them intuitively obvious. If it is taken literally to mean dissection or separation into elementary parts it is unlikely to provide what explanation demands, especially when the *explicandum* is something the nature of which is determined by its structure, for the pattern of structure would be destroyed by such analysis.

If, however, we take our cue from Kant and see knowledge always as a whole of related and connected elements, we are more likely to hold that explanation involves both analysis and synthesis: analysis to lay bare and expose the elements, synthesis to reveal the relations and connections. And if these again are determined by some general principle of organization, the synoptic view will be more important than the analytic. The psychologist J. J. Gibson is probably nearer the truth when he writes, "The progress of learning is from indefinite to definite, not from sensation to percept" (where "sensation" may be correlated with atomic element and "percept" with structured object). If the progress of learning is the same as, or analogous to, the advancement of knowledge, we should then say that it moves from the vaguer and more confused to the more definite and integrated, and this is, in fact, what we find.

The most satisfactory accounts of perception that we have, whether psychological or epistemological, show it to be an activity of structuring vague and confused sentient elements to form coherent and systematically ordered objects, and these again are recognizable and significant to the extent to which they fit into a wider context of mutually related objects. Our awareness of individual entities in our environment develops *pari passu* with our comprehension of that environment as a world of objects ordered in space and time, as well as in other respects. This presupposition of an ordered world implicit in the perception of ordinary material things is prior to, and is involved in, all scientific observation; so that there is no observation wholly free from theoretical presupposition. Science, moreover, is the fruit of an intellectual effort to render the world of common perception—what we call "the world of common sense"—more intelligible. It arises out of puzzling experiences and develops as the resolution of initial problems gives rise to further questions. Human knowledge, in short, is always a system of some kind, but is never a fixed system established for all time. It is a constantly developing process—a continuing activity of discovery and enlightenment.

From what has been said it will follow that the logical character of this process of discovery will be that characteristic of the development of a whole. Ordinary perception—the common-sense awareness of the world—is already a whole of related and connected elements. Incoherences in this structure give rise to problems which stimulate the scientific enterprise; and this consists in successive efforts to discover the coherent structure underlying the apparent discrepancies, and generates a series of theories of increasing explanatory power. Let us look at examples of this process in more detail.

Common sense accepts the familiar fact of motion as natural and unproblematic, and yet does not reject the conception of a static world as a possibility. We perceive things at rest and also things in motion and transfer the resulting ideas of them at will without undue shock. The Biblical poet speaks of the mountains skipping like lambs and hills like lambkins, and his reader, while he may be incredulous, does not find the image impossible. Further our own sense of effort in moving both our own bodies and others gives rise to a conception of a cause of motion. It seems obvious that something should act on a body at rest in order to move it; for rest seems to be the more natural condition which calls for no explanation, while motion carries with it the idea of activity.

Common experience seems to show that to be moved a body must be pushed or pulled, but falling bodies move without apparent impulsion. Here is a discrepancy in the manifest behavior of things which demands explanation. Such an explanation was devised by the Ancients and set out systematically by Aristotle. We are all aware that, far-reaching as it was, Aristotle's theory led to contradictions when applied to the behavior of projectiles, and the subsequent efforts to resolve these conflicts gave rise to the theories first of impetus and later of inertia and gravitation. . . .

The common-sense view of the world is a more or less systematic totality, but is rather less so than more. The conflicts which become apparent in it on reflection lead to the scientific endeavor to explain what is puzzling. This produces more consistent and more tightly knit systems ordering the observed facts in an intelligible way. But these systems again are partial, being restricted in scope, and (frequently for that very reason), as their implications are developed they evince new contradictions. The efforts to resolve these lead to more comprehensive and more widely interconnected systems, uniting the lesser ones and removing their inner conflicts. Thus Newton's system united the areas of celestial and terrestrial mechanics, Maxwell's system united optics and electro-dynamics, Einstein's combines all these in a single system of physical geometry. The sciences, as they structure and elaborate their own fields, tend to unite and to constitute a single system. In each case we have a whole of related and connected elements, and knowledge advances through a series of such wholes, each at a higher level of integration, articulation and clarity— each successive system being more widely and more penetratingly efficient as a means of explanation.

The next point we must notice is that the establishment of a new hypothesis is not effected by a search for (or discovery of) a large number of similar confirmatory observations, but is achieved by the construction of a body of varying evidence, the diverse factors in which are interdependent and mutually supporting. The term "corroboration" is more applicable to such mutual support of diverse phenomena than to the mere repetition of similar cases. The true empirical method actually practiced by scientists is that of marshaling diverse pieces of evidence which dovetail into

one another to form a system, and it is better described as construction than as induction. It may be carried out by a series of mathematical calculations based on empirical records, as Kepler constructed the orbit of Mars; or by a series of observations prompted by pertinent questions, like those Harvey made to work out the function of the heart and the circulation of the blood; or by a series of experiments directed towards proving a specific relationship of processes, as were conducted by Lavoisier in his discovery of oxidation in combustion and his disproof of the phlogiston theory.

In none of these examples do we find the scientist accumulating like instances of a general rule. Kepler worked with calculated positions of the planet none of which could strictly be observed, for nobody can directly observe the position of a planet in space relative to the sun, and Kepler could work this out only from angular measurements made of appearances in the heavens. When he had done so he had to construct the orbit more or less as one constructs a jigsaw puzzle out of displaced pieces. The various calculations did not give a collection of similar instances of a frequent conjunction of object or events, but a range of differences among which a pattern had to be found. Similarly Harvey did not simply observe a number of like instances of vascular activity. He examined the anatomy of the heart and its valves, the position of the vessels and the valves in the veins, the action of the heart in living creatures, the behavior of the blood in a ligatured limb, and numerous other diverse phenomena. He calculated the rate of flow and the quantities of blood passing through the heart in a given time. And all the varied evidence so gathered he welded into a structure of interlocking parts "so bound together that nothing . . . could be moved from its place without producing confusion in all the other parts." Uranus had been seen twenty times before Sir William Herschel "discovered" the planet, yet this repetition of observation led to no recognition of a new planet. It was only after its position had been charted over a period and its orbit calculated that the "discovery" became an established fact—only, in short, when the phenomena had been fitted into the astronomical system.

The method of science, then, is one of constructing systems. A scientific theory is a systematization of empirical facts according to one, or a few, principles of organization (cf. Newton's laws of motion), and it is established by the marshaling of a system of evidence, diverse in its detail but interlocking and mutually corroborative. The history of scientific advance is a progression from one such system to another, each structured by a conceptual scheme which orders the facts, and which, in large measure, by ordering, constitutes them —makes them what they are. The supersession of one system by its successor is occasioned by the discovery of conflicts within the former, as its implications are developed and its details worked out, and the consequent attempts of thinkers to devise a modified conceptual scheme which will organize the phenomena more coherently.

The process of scientific advance is thus a succession of wholes or systems, like the Hegelian dialectical system, and

the series of conceptual schemes which emerge in it are related to one another as the Hegelian forms and categories are related. In the first place, the development, despite appearances in some cases, is continuous. Secondly, the consecutive systems are specifications of a universal—each is an example of a general type of scientific theory. And thirdly, each system comes to be in opposition to the one it supersedes. They are thus at once degrees in a scale of progressively more satisfactory explanations, species of a special kind or area of explanatory theory, and opposite or rival theories of a certain range of phenomena. The progress of science thus constitutes a scale of forms in a manner comparable to that demonstrated by Collingwood in the case of the history of philosophy. . . .

The history of science thus presents us with a progress which is genuinely continuous, but in which successive main theories relate to each other as opposed and revolutionary, yet at the same time the later sublates (*aufhebt*) the earlier by preserving and transforming significant elements in it. The next succeeding revolution tends to unite these sublated elements so as to resolve the opposition which was most strident in the earlier theories. Consequently, we have an Hegelian triad, but this structure need not be, and should not be regarded as, rigid; for the actual candidates for the places of thesis, antithesis, and synthesis may well be varied. Newton synthesizes Aristotle and Buridan, Einstein synthesizes Ptolemaic Aristotelianism and Newtonianism. It is not the triadic relation that is fundamental but the successive negation of negation involved in the generation of oppositions (through inadequacy) and their resolution in more coherent systems. The triad is the natural result, but it is incidental.[5]

The progress of science, therefore, generates a scale of forms, each being a theory of some field of experience the function of which is to organize the relevant phenomena into a self-consistent system. In the first instance the principle (or principles) of organization are enunciated more or less in the abstract, or in a general form which requires articulation and development. This it receives in the course of application, in the attempt to iron out minor difficulties, during the period that Thomas Kuhn calls "normal science," or the period of "puzzle-solving."[6] Some of these difficulties can be removed with relative ease and without serious modification of the system. But others are more stubborn and if they are overcome it is usually at the cost of considerable revision. Frequently this sort of change reveals a crack in the fabric of the theory which, in the course of time, brings to light intolerable contradictions. It is at this point that scientists cast around for new hypotheses. They

are usually variations of the old ones suggested by the discrepant facts[7] (as Kepler's ovoid orbit was a variation on the circle produced by means of an epicycle turning in the opposite direction and prompted by the discrepancy of eight minutes of arc), and they succeed when they bring to light a new pattern in which the formerly recalcitrant phenomena find harmonious place. This new pattern is the next in the scale of forms, related to its predecessor first as an alternative theory, secondly as a more adequate explanation of the facts and so a higher degree of truth, and thirdly as a correction of errors (hence a theory opposed to the faulty one), yet a correction which does not totally reject what was earlier accepted, but preserves, modified and improved, the elements of truth contained in the prior view.

A scale of this kind is dialectical and the logic which impels it from one stage to the next is a dialectical logic—a logic of construction and of development appropriate to a continuous movement of evolution. It is that principle of absolute restlessness of which Hegel speaks, inherent in rational self-reflection and critical thought. In short, it is the principle of that systematic self-development which is science, "the true form in which the truth exists"[8]—though we must remember that, for Hegel, empirical science is but a part of the total system, an essential part, no doubt, but one which leads on through the same perpetual drive of self-reflection to the phil-

---

[5] Hegel does not himself make this point, but it is no less true of his triads. For instance, the opposition of Being and Essence is reconciled in the Notion, yet that, as concrete, is opposed to either of the other two as abstract, and abstract and concrete are united and reconciled in the Absolute Idea. Again, Organism synthesizes Mechanism and Chemism, but the organic is opposed to the inorganic and finds synthesis with it in the psychophysical.

[6] See Thomas S. Kuhn, *The Structure of Scientific Revolutions* (Chicago: University of Chicago Press, 1962). *Ed.*]

[7] It must, however, be borne in mind that there are no "facts" independent of, or neutral with respect to, theory.

[8] *Phänomenologie*, Preface, p. 27.

osophical sciences of logic, philosophy of nature, and philosophy of mind. The last-named presents natural science as a stage, which it undoubtedly is, of the development of consciousness—a phase of our awareness of the world, in which we view it as an external object to be observed and described in terms of coherent categories of rational understanding.

PHILOSOPHY OF RELIGION

One of the arguments for the existence of God that has become classical is known as the moral argument. It is frequently associated with idealism, and is especially important for axiological idealism. This latter position holds that values, while experienced subjectively, have nevertheless an objective reference to a validity and status beyond themselves. Values, that is, are binding even when they are unacknowledged, compelling even when ignored. But this means that an objective moral order cannot exist in matter (which bears no ideal) nor in finite minds alone (which cannot bear objective, compelling obligations). An objective moral order can exist only for a Supreme Mind who is the Source and Conserver of Value.

Like cosmological arguments for God, the moral argument moves from finite experience to the infinite. Weaker than they because it may seem that an objective moral order can be easily denied, the moral argument is in fact the stronger. Having acknowledged the moral ideal, Sorley believes the argument adds the important point that existence must be posited with it or its very validity and status remain inexplicable.

10 The Moral Argument for God
W. R. Sorley (1855-1935)

The result so far is that the events of the world as a causal system are not inconsistent with the view that this same world is a moral order, that its purpose is a moral purpose. The empirical discrepancies between the two orders, and the obstacles which the world puts in the way of morality, are capable of explanation when we allow that ideals of goodness have not only to be discovered by finite minds, but that for their realisation they need to be freely accepted by individual wills and gradually organised in individual characters. If this principle still leaves many particular difficulties unresolved, it may at least be claimed that it provides the general plan of an explanation of the relation of moral value to experience, and that a larger knowledge of the issues of life than is open to us might be expected to show that the particular difficulties also are not incapable of solution.

This means that it is possible to regard God as the author and ruler of the world, as it appears in space and time, and at the same time to hold that the moral values of which we are conscious and the moral ideal which we come to apprehend with increasing clearness express his nature. But the question remains, Are we to regard morality—its values, laws, and ideal—as belonging to a Supreme Mind, that is, to God? It is as an answer to this question that the specific Moral Argument enters. And here I cannot do better than give the argument in the words of Dr Rashdall:

"An absolute Moral Law or moral ideal cannot exist *in* material things. And it does not exist in the mind of this or that individual. Only if we believe in the existence of a Mind for which the true moral ideal is already in some sense real, a Mind which is the source of whatever is true in our own moral judgments, can we rationally think of the moral ideal as no less real than the world itself. Only so can we believe in an absolute standard of right and wrong, which is as independent of this or that man's actual ideas and actual desires as the facts of material nature. The belief in God, though not (like the belief in a real and an active self) a postulate of there being any such thing as Morality at all, is the logical presupposition of an 'objective' or absolute Morality. A moral ideal can exist nowhere and nohow but in a mind; an absolute moral ideal can exist only in a Mind from which all Reality is derived.[1] Our moral ideal can only claim objective validity in so far as it can rationally be regarded as the revelation of a moral ideal eternally existing in the mind of God."[2]

The argument as thus put may be looked upon as a special and striking

---

The selection is from W. R. Sorley, *Moral Values and the Idea of God,* 2nd ed. (London: Cambridge University Press, 1918, 1921), pp. 346–352. Used by permission of the publisher.

[1] "Or at least a mind by which all Reality is controlled."—Dr Rashdall's footnote.

[2] H. Rashdall, *The Theory of Good and Evil* (1907), vol. 11, p. 212.

extension of the cosmological argument. In its first and most elementary form the cosmological argument seeks a cause for the bare existence of the world and man: to account for them there must be something able to bring them into being: God is the First Cause. Then the order of nature impresses us by its regularity, and we come by degrees to understand the principles of its working and the laws under which the material whole maintains its equilibrium and the ordered procession of its changes: these laws and this order call for explanation, and we conceive God as the Great Lawgiver. But beyond this material world, we understand relations and principles of a still more general kind; and the intellect of man recognises abstract truths so evident that, once understood, they cannot be questioned, while inferences are drawn from these which only the more expert minds can appreciate and yet which they recognise as eternally valid. To what order do these belong and what was their home when man as yet was unconscious of them? Surely if their validity is eternal they must have had existence somewhere, and we can only suppose them to have existed in the one eternal mind: God is therefore the God of Truth. Further, persons are conscious of values and of an ideal of goodness, which they recognise as having undoubted authority for the direction of their activity; the validity of these values or laws and of this ideal, however, does not depend upon their recognition: it is objective and eternal; and how could this eternal validity stand alone, not embodied in matter and neither seen nor realised by finite minds, unless there were an eternal mind whose thought and will were

therein expressed? God must therefore exist and his nature be goodness.

The argument in this its latest phase has a new feature which distinguishes it from the preceding phases. The laws or relations of interacting phenomena which we discover in nature are already embodied in the processes of nature. It may be argued that they have their reality therein: that in cognising them we are simply cognising an aspect of the actual world in space and time, and consequently that, if the mere existence of things does not require God to account for it (on the ground urged by Hume that the world, being a singular event, justifies no inference as to its cause), then, equally, we are not justified in seeking a cause for those laws or relations which are, after all, but one aspect of the existing world. It may be urged that the same holds of mathematical relations: that they are merely an abstract of the actual order, when considered solely in its formal aspect. It is more difficult to treat the still more general logical relations in the same fashion; but they too receive verification in reality and in our thought so far as it does not end in confusion. But it is different with ethical values. Their validity could not be verified in external phenomena; they cannot be established by observation of the course of nature. They hold good for persons only: and their peculiarity consists in the fact that their validity is not in any way dependent upon their being manifested in the character or conduct of persons, or even on their being recognised in the thoughts of persons. We acknowledge the good and its objective claim upon us even when we are conscious that our will has not yielded to the claim; and we admit that its validity existed before we recognised it.

This leading characteristic makes the theistic argument founded upon moral values or the moral law both stronger in one respect and weaker in another respect than the corresponding argument from natural law and intelligible relations. It is weaker because it is easier to deny the premiss from which it starts —that is, the objective validity of moral law—than it is to deny the objective validity of natural or mathematical or logical relations. But I am here assuming the objective validity of morality as already established by our previous enquiries; and it is unnecessary to go back upon the question. And, granted this premiss, the argument adds an important point. Other relations and laws (it may be said, and the statement is true of laws of nature at any rate) are embodied in actually existing objects. But the same cannot be said of the moral law or moral ideal. We acknowledge that there are objective values, although men may not recognise them, that the moral law is not abrogated by being ignored, and that our consciousness is striving towards the apprehension of an ideal which no finite mind has clearly grasped, but which is none the less valid although it is not realised and is not even apprehended by us in its truth and fulness. Where then is this ideal? It cannot be valid at one time and not at another. It must be eternal as well as objective. As Dr Rashdall urges, it is not in material things, and it is not in the mind of this or that individual; but "it can exist nowhere and nohow but in a mind"; it requires therefore the mind of God.

Against this argument, however, it may be contended that it disregards the distinction between validity and existence. Why is it assumed that the moral ideal must exist somehow and somewhere? Validity, it may be said, is a unique concept, as unique as existence, and different from it. And this is true. At the same time it is also true that the validity of the moral ideal, like all validity, is a validity for existents. Without this reference to existence there seems no meaning in asserting validity. At any rate it is clear that it is for existents— namely, for the realm of persons—that the moral ideal is valid. It is also true that the perfect moral ideal does not exist in the volitional, or even in the intellectual, consciousness of these persons: they have not achieved agreement with it in their lives, and even their understanding of it is incomplete. Seeing then that it is not manifested by finite existents, how are we to conceive its validity? Other truths are displayed in the order of the existing world; but it is not so with moral values. And yet the system of moral values has been acknowledged to be an aspect of the real universe to which existing things belong. How are we to conceive its relation to them? A particular instance of goodness can exist only in the character of an individual person or group of persons; an idea of goodness such as we have is found only in minds such as ours. But the ideal of goodness does not exist in finite minds or in their material environment. What then is its status in the system of reality?

The question is answered if we regard the moral order as the order of a Supreme Mind and the ideal of goodness as belonging to this Mind. The difficulty for this view is to show that the Mind which is the home of good-ness may also be regarded as the ground of the existing world. That reality as a whole, both in its actual events and in its moral order, can be consistently re-garded as the expression of a Supreme Mind is the result of the present argu-ment.

CRITIQUE

Idealism, as we have seen, has a variety of forms and expressions, and there are other varieties such as those found in the Orient that we have not explored. Central to all idealistic philosophies, though, is the thesis of the primacy of mind.

This thesis is the focus of the following influential article by G. E. Moore. Moore was an earlier representative of analytic or linguistic philosophy, which we shall study in Section VI. In this article, Moore interprets the idealistic thesis in Berkeleian terms, that *esse* is *percipi*, which he takes as necessary to all idealisms. But this notion, Moore finds, is unacceptable. In his careful, analytic way, he examines in turn the meanings of *percipi*, is, and *esse*. From this examination he concludes that idealists are trying to maintain that subject and object are con-nected in experience. Moore believes that this proposal does not succeed, because it fails to distinguish the *act* of experience from the *content* of experience. From this distinction Moore concludes that while he may not have shown the falsity of idealism, he has demonstrated that the argument for idealism fails.

11 The Refutation of Idealism
G. E. Moore (1873-1958)

Modern Idealism, if it asserts any gen-eral conclusion about the universe at all, asserts that it is *spiritual*. There are two points about this assertion to which I wish to call attention. These points are that, whatever be its exact meaning, it is certainly meant to assert (1) that the universe is very different indeed from what it seems, and (2) that it has quite a large number of properties which it does not seem to have. Chairs and ta-bles and mountains *seem* to be very different from us; but, when the whole universe is declared to be spiritual, it is certainly meant to assert that they are far more like us than we think. The idealist means to assert that they are *in some sense* neither lifeless nor uncon-scious, as they certainly seem to be; and I do not think his language is so grossly deceptive, but that we may assume him to believe that they really are very dif-ferent indeed from what they seem. And secondly when he declares that they are *spiritual*, he means to include in that term quite a large number of

The selection is from G. E. Moore, "The Refutation of Idealism," in *Mind*, n.s., 12 (1903), pp. 433–453, with omissions.

different properties. When the whole universe is declared to be spiritual, it is meant not only that it is in some sense *conscious*, but that it has what we recognise in ourselves as the *higher* forms of consciousness. That it is intelligent; that it is purposeful; that it is not mechanical; all these different things are commonly asserted of it. In general, it may be said, this phrase 'reality is spiritual' excites and expresses the belief that the *whole* universe possesses *all the qualities* the possession of which is held to make us so superior to things which seem to be inanimate: at least, if it does not possess exactly those which we possess, it possesses not one only, but several others, which, by the same ethical standard, would be judged equal to or better than our own. When we say it is *spiritual* we mean to say that it has quite a number of excellent qualities, different from any which we commonly attribute either to stars or planets or to cups and saucers.

Now why I mention these two points is that when engaged in the intricacies of philosophic discussion, we are apt to overlook the vastness of the difference between this idealistic view and the ordinary view of the world, and to overlook the number of *different* propositions which the idealist must prove. It is, I think, owing to the vastness of this difference and owing to the number of different excellences which Idealists attribute to the universe, that it seems such an interesting and important question whether Idealism be true or not. But, when we begin to argue about it, I think we are apt to forget what a vast number of arguments this interesting question must involve: we are apt to assume, that if one or two points be made

on either side, the whole case is won. I say this lest it should be thought that any of the arguments which will be advanced in this paper would be sufficient to disprove, or any refutation of them sufficient to prove, the truly interesting and important proposition that reality is spiritual. For my own part I wish it to be clearly understood that I do not suppose that anything I shall say has the smallest tendency to prove that reality is not spiritual: I do not believe it possible to refute a single one of the many important propositions contained in the assertion that it is so. Reality may be spiritual, for all I know; and I devoutly hope it is. But I take 'Idealism' to be a wide term and to include not only this interesting conclusion but a number of arguments which are supposed to be, if not sufficient, at least *necessary*, to prove it. Indeed I take it that modern Idealists are chiefly distinguished by certain arguments which they have in common. That reality is spiritual has, I believe, been the tenet of many theologians; and yet, for believing that alone, they should hardly be called Idealists. There are besides, I believe, many persons, not improperly called Idealists, who hold certain characteristic propositions, without venturing to think them quite sufficient to prove so grand a conclusion. It is, therefore, only with Idealistic *arguments* that I am concerned; and if any Idealist holds that *no* argument is necessary to prove that reality is spiritual, I shall certainly not have refuted him. I shall, however, attack at least one argument, which, to the best of my belief, is considered necessary to their position by *all* Idealists. And I wish to point out a certain advantage which this procedure gives me—an advantage which justifies the assertion that, if my arguments are sound, they will have refuted Idealism. If I can refute a single proposition which is a necessary and essential step in all Idealistic arguments, then, no matter how good the rest of these arguments may be, I shall have proved that Idealists have *no reason whatever* for their conclusion. . . .

The subject of this paper is, therefore, quite uninteresting. Even if I prove my point, I shall have proved nothing about the Universe in general. Upon the important question whether Reality is or is not spiritual my argument will not have the remotest bearing. I shall only attempt to arrive at the truth about a matter, which is in itself quite trivial and insignificant, and from which, so far as I can see and certainly so far as I shall say, no conclusions can be drawn about any of the subjects about which we most want to know. The only importance I can claim for the subject I shall investigate is that it seems to me to be a matter upon which not Idealists only, but all philosophers and psychologists also, have been in error, and from their erroneous view of which they have inferred (validly or invalidly) their most striking and interesting conclusions. And that it has even this importance I cannot hope to prove. If it has this importance, it will indeed follow that all the most striking results of philosophy —Sensationalism, Agnosticism and Idealism alike—have, for all that has hitherto been urged in their favour, no more foundation than the supposition that a chimera lives in the moon. It will follow that, unless new reasons never urged hitherto can be found, all the most important philosophic doctrines have as little claim to assent as the most

superstitious beliefs of the lowest savages. Upon the question what we have *reason* to believe in the most interesting matters, I do therefore think that my results will have an important bearing; but I cannot too clearly insist that upon the question whether these beliefs are true they will have none whatever.

The trivial proposition which I propose to dispute is this: that *esse* is *percipi*. This is a very ambiguous proposition, but, in some sense or other, it has been very widely held. That it is, in some sense, essential to Idealism, I must for the present merely assume. What I propose to show is that, in all the senses ever given to it, it is false.

But, first of all, it may be useful to point out briefly in what relation I conceive it to stand to Idealistic arguments. That wherever you can truly predicate *esse* you can truly predicate *percipi*, in some sense or other, is, I take it, a necessary step in all arguments, properly to be called Idealistic, and, what is more, in all arguments hitherto offered for the Idealistic conclusion. If *esse* is *percipi*, this is at once equivalent to saying that whatever is, is experienced; and this, again, is equivalent, in a sense, to saying that whatever is, is something mental. But this is not the sense in which the Idealist *conclusion* must maintain that Reality is *mental*. The Idealist *conclusion* is that *esse* is *percipere*; and hence, whether *esse* be *percipi* or not, a further and different discussion is needed to show whether or not it is also *percipere*. And again, even if *esse* be *percipere*, we need a vast quantity of further argument to show that what has *esse* has also those higher mental qualities which are denoted by spiritual. This is why I said that the question I should discuss, namely, whether or not *esse* is *percipi*, must be utterly insufficient either to prove or to disprove that reality is spiritual. But, on the other hand, I believe that every argument ever used to show that reality is spiritual has inferred this (validly or invalidly) from '*esse* is *percipere*' as one of its premisses; and that this again has never been pretended to be proved except by use of the premiss that *esse* is *percipi*. The type of argument used for the latter purpose is familiar enough. It is said that since whatever is, is experienced, and since some things are which are not experienced by the individual, these must at least form part of some experience. Or again that, since an object necessarily implies a subject, and since the whole world must be an object, we must conceive it to belong to some subject or subjects, in the same sense in which whatever is the object of our experience belongs to us. Or again, that, since thought enters into the essence of all reality, we must conceive behind it, in it, or as its essence, a spirit akin to ours, who think: that 'spirit greets spirit' in its object. Into the validity of these inferences I do not propose to enter: they obviously require a great deal of discussion. I only desire to point out that, however correct they may be, yet if *esse* is not *percipi*, they leave us as far from a proof that reality is spiritual, as if they were all false too.

But now: Is *esse percipi*? There are three very ambiguous terms in this proposition, and I must begin by distinguishing the different things that may be meant by some of them.

And first with regard to *percipi*. This term need not trouble us long at present. It was, perhaps, originally used to mean 'sensation' only; but I am not going to be so unfair to modern Idealists—the only Idealists to whom the term should now be applied without qualification—as to hold that, if they say *esse* is *percipi*, they mean by *percipi* sensation only. On the contrary I quite agree with them that, if *esse* be *percipi* at all, *percipi* must be understood to include not sensation only, but that other type of mental fact, which is called 'thought'; and, whether *esse* be *percipi* or not, I consider it to be the main service of the philosophic school, to which modern Idealists belong, that they have insisted on distinguishing 'sensation' and 'thought' and on emphasising the importance of the latter. Against Sensationalism and Empiricism they have maintained the true view. But the distinction between sensation and thought need not detain us here. For, in whatever respects they differ, they have at least this in common, that they are both forms of consciousness or, to use a term that seems to be more in fashion just now, they are both ways of experiencing. Accordingly, whatever *esse* is *percipi* may mean, it does *at least* assert that whatever is, is *experienced*. And since what I wish to maintain is, that even this is untrue, the question whether it be experienced by way of sensation or thought or both is for my purpose quite irrelevant. If it be not experienced at all, it cannot be either an object of thought or an object of sense. It is only if being involves 'experience' that the question, whether it involves sensation or thought or both, becomes important. I beg, therefore, that *percipi* may be understood, in what follows, to refer merely to what is *common* to sensation and thought. . . .

I will leave [this topic] for the present to consider the next ambiguity in the statement: *Esse* is *percipi*. What does the copula mean? What can be meant by saying that Esse *is* percipi? There are just three meanings, one or other of which such a statement *must* have, if it is to be true; and of these there is only one which it can have, if it is to be important. (1) The statement may be meant to assert that the word 'esse' is used to signify nothing either more or less than the word 'percipi': that the two words are precise synonyms: that they are merely different names for one and the same thing: that what is meant by *esse* is absolutely identical with what is meant by *percipi*. I think I need not prove that the principle *esse* is *percipi* is *not* thus intended merely to define a word; nor yet that, if it were, it would be an extremely bad definition. But if it does *not* mean this, only two alternatives remain. The second is (2) that what is meant by *esse*, though not absolutely identical with what is meant by *percipi*, yet *includes* the latter as a *part* of its meaning. If this were the meaning of 'esse is percipi,' then to say that a thing was real would not be the same thing as to say that it was experienced. That it was *real* would mean that it was experienced and *something else besides:* 'being experienced' would be *analytically essential* to reality, but would not be the whole meaning of the term. From the fact that a thing was real we should be able to infer, by the law of contradiction, that it was experienced; since the latter would be *part* of what is meant by the former. But, on the other hand, from the fact a thing was experienced we should *not* be able to infer that it was real; since it would not follow from the fact that it had one of the attributes essential to reality, that it *also* had the other or others. . . .

And this is (3) the third possible meaning of the assertion *esse is percipi*: and, as we now see, the only important one. *Esse* is *percipi* asserts that wherever you have *x* you also have *percipi* that whatever has the property *x* also has the property that it is *experienced*. And this being so, it will be convenient if, for the future, I may be allowed to use the term '*esse*' to denote *x alone*. I do not wish thereby to beg the question whether what we commonly mean by the world 'real' does or does not include *percipi* as well as *x*. I am quite content that my definition of 'esse' to denote *x*, should be regarded merely as an arbitrary verbal definition. Whether it is so or not, the only question of interest is whether from *x percipi* can be inferred, and I should prefer to be able to express this in the form: can *percipi* be inferred from *esse?* Only let it be understood that when I say *esse*, that term will not for the future *include percipi*: it denotes only that *x*, which Idealists, perhaps rightly, include *along with percipi* under *their* term *esse*. That there is such an *x* they must admit on pain of making the proposition an *absolute* tautology; and that from this *x percipi* can be inferred they must admit, on pain of making it a perfectly barren analytic proposition. Whether *x* alone should or should not be called *esse* is not worth a dispute: what is worth dispute is whether *percipi* is necessarily connected with *x*.

We have therefore discovered the ambiguity of the copula in *esse* is *percipi*, so far as to see that this principle asserts two distinct terms to be so related, that whatever has the *one*, which I call *esse*, has *also* the property that it is experienced. It asserts a necessary connexion between *esse* on the one hand and *percipi* on the other; these two words denoting each a distinct term, and *esse* denoting a term in which that denoted by *percipi* is not included. We have, then in *esse* is *percipi*, a *necessary synthetic* proposition which I have undertaken to refute. And I may say at once that, understood as such, it cannot be refuted. If the Idealist chooses to assert that it is merely a self-evident truth, I have only to say that it does not appear to me to be so. But I believe that no Idealist ever has maintained it to be so. Although this—that two distinct terms are necessarily related—is the only sense which 'esse is percipi' can have if it is to be true and important, it *can* have another sense, if it is to be an important falsehood. I believe that Idealists all hold this important falsehood. They do not perceive that *Esse* is *percipi* must, if true, be *merely* a self-evident synthetic truth: they either identify with it or give as a reason for it another proposition which must be false because it is self-contradictory. Unless they did so, they would have to admit that it was a perfectly unfounded assumption; and if they recognised that it was *unfounded*, I do not think they would maintain its truth to be evident. *Esse* is *percipi*, in the sense I have found for it, *may* indeed be true; I cannot refute it: but if this sense were clearly apprehended, no one, I think, would *believe* that it was true.

Idealists, we have seen, must assert that whatever is experienced, is *necessarily* so. And this doctrine they commonly express by saying that 'the object of experience is inconceivable apart from the subject.' I have hitherto been concerned with pointing out what meaning this assertion must have, if it is to be an important truth. I now propose to show that it may have an important

meaning, which must be false, because it is self-contradictory.

It is a well-known fact in the history of philosophy that *necessary* truths in general, but especially those of which it is said that the opposite is inconceivable, have been commonly supposed to be *analytic*, in the sense that the proposition denying them was self-contradictory. It was in this way, commonly supposed, before Kant, that many truths could be proved by the law of contradiction alone. This is, therefore, a mistake which it is plainly easy for the best philosophers to make. Even since Kant many have continued to assert it; but I am aware that among those Idealists, who most properly deserve the name, it has become more fashionable to assert that truths are *both* analytic and synthetic. Now with many of their reasons for asserting this I am not concerned: it is possible that in some connexions the assertion may bear a useful and true sense. But if we understand 'analytic' in the sense just defined, namely, what is proved by the law of contradiction *alone*, it is plain that, if 'synthetic' means what is *not* proved by this alone, no truth can be both analytic and synthetic. Now it seems to me that those who do maintain truths to be both, do nevertheless maintain that they are so in this as well as in other senses. It is, indeed, extremely unlikely that so essential a part of the historical meaning of 'analytic' and 'synthetic' should have been entirely discarded, especially since we find no express recognition that it is discarded. In that case it is fair to suppose that modern Idealists have been influenced by the view that certain truths can be proved by the law of contradiction alone. I admit they also expressly declare that they can *not:* but this is by no means sufficient to prove that they do not also think they are; since it is very easy to hold two mutually contradictory opinions. What I suggest then is that Idealists hold the particular doctrine in question, concerning the relation of subject and object in experience, because they think it is an analytic truth in this restricted sense that it is proved by the law of contradiction alone.

I am suggesting that the Idealist maintains that object and subject are necessarily connected, mainly because he fails to see that they are *distinct*, that they are *two*, at all. When he thinks of 'yellow' and when he thinks of the 'sensation of yellow,' he fails to see that there is anything whatever in the latter which is not in the former. This being so, to deny that yellow can ever *be* apart from the sensation of yellow is merely to deny that yellow can ever be other than it is; since yellow and the sensation of yellow are absolutely identical. To assert that yellow is necessarily an object of experience is to assert that yellow is necessarily yellow—a purely identical proposition, and therefore proved by the law of contradiction alone. Of course, the proposition also implies that experience is, after all, something distinct from yellow—else there would be no reason for insisting that yellow is a sensation: and that the argument thus both affirms and denies that yellow and sensation of yellow are distinct, is what sufficiently refutes it. But this contradiction can easily be overlooked, because though we are convinced, in other connexions, that 'experience' does mean something and something most important, yet we are never distinctly aware *what* it means, and thus in every particu-

lar case we do not notice its presence. The facts present themselves as a kind of antinomy: (1) Experience *is* something unique and different from anything else; (2) Experience of green is entirely indistinguishable from green; two propositions which cannot both be true. Idealists, holding both, can only take refuge in arguing from the one in some connexions and from the other in others.

But I am well aware that there are many Idealists who would repel it as an utterly unfounded charge that they fail to distinguish between a sensation or idea and what I will call its object. And there are, I admit, many who not only imply, as we all do, that green is distinct from the sensation of green, but expressly insist upon the distinction as an important part of their system. They would perhaps only assert that the two form an inseparable unity. But I wish to point out that many, who use this phrase, and who do admit the distinction, are not thereby absolved from the charge that they deny it. For there is a certain doctrine, very prevalent among philosophers nowadays, which by a very simple reduction may be seen to assert that two distinct things both are and are not distinct. A distinction is asserted; but it is *also* asserted that the things distinguished form an 'organic unity.' But, forming such a unity, it is held, each would not be what it is *apart from its relation to the other*. Hence to consider either by itself is to make an *illegitimate abstraction*. The recognition that there are 'organic unities' and 'illegitimate abstractions' in this sense is regarded as one of the chief conquests of modern philosophy. But what is the sense attached to these terms? An abstraction is illegitimate, when and only when we attempt to assert of *a part*—of something abstracted—that which is true only of the *whole* to which it belongs: and it may perhaps be useful to point out that this should not be done. But the application actually made of this principle, and what perhaps would be expressly acknowledged as its meaning, is something much the reverse of useful. The principle is used to assert that certain abstractions are *in all cases* illegitimate; that whenever you try to assert *anything whatever* of that which is *part* of an organic whole, what you assert can only be true of the whole. And this principle, so far from being a useful truth, is necessarily false. For if the whole can, nay *must*, be substituted for the part in all propositions and for all purposes this can only be because the whole is absolutely identical with the part. When, therefore, we are told that green and the sensation of green are certainly distinct but yet are not separable, or that it is an illegitimate abstraction to consider the one apart from the other, what these provisos are used to assert is, that though the two things are distinct yet you not only can but must treat them as if they were not. Many philosophers, therefore, when they admit a distinction, yet (following the lead of Hegel) boldly assert their right, in a slightly more obscure form of words, *also* to deny it. The principle of organic unities, like that of combined analysis and synthesis, is mainly used to defend the practice of holding *both* of two contradictory propositions, wherever this may seem convenient. In this, as in other matters, Hegel's main service to philosophy has consisted in giving a name to and erecting into a principle, a type of fallacy to which experience had shown philosophers, along with the rest of mankind, to be addicted. No wonder that he has followers and admirers.

I have shown then, so far, that when the Idealist asserts the important principle '*Esse* is *percipi*' he must, if it is to be true, mean by this that: Whatever is experienced also *must* be experienced. And I have also shown that he *may* identify with, or give as a reason for, this proposition, one which must be false, because it is self-contradictory. But at this point I propose to make a complete break in my argument. '*Esse* is *percipi*,' we have seen, asserts of two terms, as distinct from one another as 'green' and 'sweet,' that whatever has the one has also the other: it asserts that 'being' and 'being experienced' are necessarily connected: that whatever *is* is *also* experienced. And this, I admit, cannot be directly refuted. But I believe it to be false; and I have asserted that anybody who saw that '*esse* and *percipi*' *were* as distinct as 'green' and 'sweet' would be no more ready to believe that whatever *is* is *also* experienced, than to believe that whatever is green is also sweet. I have asserted that no one would believe that '*esse* is *percipi*' if they saw how different *esse* is from *percipi*: but *this* I shall not try to prove. I have asserted that all who do believe that '*esse* is *percipi*' identify with it or take as a reason for it a self-contradictory proposition: but this I shall not try to prove. I shall only try to show that certain propositions which I assert to be believed, are false. That they are believed, and that without this belief '*esse* is *percipi*' would not be believed either, I must leave without a proof. . . .

[But] at this point I need not conceal

my opinion that no philosopher has ever yet succeeded in avoiding this self-contradictory error: that the most striking results both of Idealism and of Agnosticism are only obtained by identifying blue with the sensation of blue: that *esse* is held to be *percipi*, solely because *what is experienced* is held to be identical with *the experience of it*. That Berkeley and Mill committed this error will, perhaps, be granted: that modern Idealists make it will, I hope, appear more probable later. But that my opinion is plausible, I will now offer two pieces of evidence. The first is that language offers us no means of referring to such objects as "blue" and "green" and "sweet," except by calling them sensations: it is an obvious violation of language to call them "things" or "objects" or "terms." And similarly we have no natural means of referring to such objects as "causality" or "likeness" or "identity," except by calling them "ideas" or "notions" or "conceptions." But it is hardly likely that if philosophers had clearly distinguished in the past between a sensation or idea and what I have called its object, there should have been no separate name for the latter. They have always used the same name for these two different "things" (if I may call them so): and hence there is some probability that they have supposed these "things" *not* to be two and different, but one and the same. And, secondly, there is a very good reason why they should have supposed so, in the fact that when we refer to introspection and try to discover what the sensation of blue is, it is very easy to suppose that we have before us only a single term. The term "blue" is easy enough to distinguish, but the other element which I have called "consciousness"—that which sensation of blue has in common with sensation of green—is extremely difficult to fix. That many people fail to distinguish it at all is sufficiently shown by the fact that there are materialists. And, in general, that which makes the sensation of blue a mental fact seems to escape us: it seems, if I may use a metaphor, to be transparent—we look through it and see nothing but the blue; we may be convinced that there *is something* but *what* it is no philosopher, I think, has yet clearly recognised.

But this was a digression. The point I had established so far was that in every sensation or idea we must distinguish two elements, (1) the "object," or that in which one differs from another; and (2) "consciousness," or that which all have in common—that which makes them sensations or mental facts. This being so, it followed that when a sensation or idea exists, we have to choose between the alternatives that either object alone, or consciousness alone, or both, exist; and I showed that of these alternatives one, namely that the object only exists, is excluded by the fact that what we mean to assert is certainly the existence of a mental fact. There remains the question: Do both exist? Or does the consciousness alone? And to this question one answer has hitherto been given universally: That both exist.

This answer follows from the analysis hitherto accepted of the relation of what I have called "object" to "consciousness" in any sensation or idea. It is held that what I call the object is merely the "content" of a sensation or idea. It is held that in each case we can distinguish two elements and two only, (1) the fact that there is feeling or experience, and (2) *what* is felt or experienced; the sensation or idea, it is said, forms a whole, in which we must distinguish two "inseparable aspects," "content" and "existence." I shall try to show that this analysis is false; and for that purpose I must ask what may seem an extraordinary question: namely what is meant by saying that one thing is "content" of another? It is not usual to ask this question; the term is used as if everybody must understand it. But since I am going to maintain that "blue" is *not* the content of the sensation of blue, and what is more important, that, even if it were this analysis would leave out the most important element in the sensation of blue, it is necessary that I should try to explain precisely what it is that I shall deny.

What then is meant by saying that one thing is the "content" of another? First of all I wish to point out that "blue" is rightly and properly said to be part of the content of a blue flower. If, therefore, we also assert that it is part of the content of the sensation of blue, we assert that it has to the other parts (if any) of this whole the same relation which it has to the other parts of a blue flower—and we assert only this: we cannot mean to assert that it has to the sensation of blue any relation which it does not have to the blue flower. And we have seen that the sensation of blue contains at least one other element beside blue—namely, what I call "consciousness," which makes it a sensation. So far then as we assert that blue is the content of the sensation, we assert that it has to this "consciousness" the same relation which it has to the other parts of a blue flower: we do assert this, and

we assert no more than this. Into the question what exactly the relation is between blue and a blue flower in virtue of which we call the former part of its "content" I do not propose to enter. It is sufficient for my purpose to point out that it is the general relation most commonly meant when we talk of a thing and its qualities; and that this relation is such that to say the thing exists implies that the qualities also exist. The *content* of the thing is *what* we assert to exist, when we assert *that* the thing exists.

When, therefore, blue is said to be part of the content of the "sensation of blue," the latter is treated as if it were a whole constituted in exactly the same way as any other "thing." The "sensation of blue," on this view, differs from a blue bead or a blue beard, in exactly the same way in which the two latter differ from one another: the blue bead differs from the blue beard, in that while the former contains glass, the latter contains hair; and the "sensation of blue" differs from both in that, instead of glass or hair, it contains consciousness. The relation of the blue to the consciousness is conceived to be exactly the same as that of the blue to the glass or hair: it is in all three cases the *quality* of a thing. . . .

The true analysis of a sensation or idea is as follows. The element that is common to them all, and which I have called 'consciousness,' really *is* consciousness. A sensation is, in reality, a case of 'knowing' or 'being aware of' or 'experiencing' something. When we know that the sensation of blue exists, the fact we know is that there exists an awareness of blue. And this awareness is not merely, as we have hitherto seen it must be, itself something distinct and unique, utterly different from blue: it also has a perfectly distinct and unique relation to blue, a relation which is *not* that of thing or substance to content, nor of one part of content to another part of content. This relation is just that which we mean in every case by 'knowing.' To have in your mind 'knowledge' of blue is *not* to have in your mind a 'thing' or 'image' of which blue is the content. To be aware of the sensation of blue is *not* to be aware of a mental image—of a "thing," of which 'blue' and some other element are constituent parts in the same sense in which blue and glass are constituents of a blue bead. It is to be aware of an awareness of blue; awareness being used, in both cases, in exactly the same sense. This element, we have seen, is certainly neglected by the 'content' theory: that theory entirely fails to express the fact that there is, in the sensation of blue, this unique relation between blue and the other constituent. And what I contend is that this omission is *not* mere negligence of expression, but is due to the fact that though philosophers have recognised that *something* distinct is meant by consciousness, they have never yet had a clear conception of *what* that something is. They have not been able to hold *it* and *blue* before their minds and to compare them, in the same way in which they can compare *blue* and *green*. And this for the reason I gave above: namely that the moment we try to fix our attention upon consciousness and to see *what*, distinctly, it is, it seems to vanish: it seems as if we had before us a mere emptiness. When we try to introspect the sensation of blue, all we can see is the blue: the other element is as if it were diaphanous. Yet it *can* be distin-guished if we look attentively enough, and if we know that there is something to look for. My main object in this paragraph has been to try to make the reader *see* it; but I fear I shall have succeeded very ill.

It being the case, then, that the sensation of blue includes in its analysis, beside blue, *both* a unique element 'awareness' *and* a unique relation of this element to blue, I can make plain what I meant by asserting, as two distinct propositions, (1) that blue is probably not part of the content of the sensation at all, and (2) that, even if it were, the sensation would nevertheless not be the sensation *of* blue, if blue had only this relation to it. The first hypothesis may now be expressed by saying that, if it were true, then, when the sensation of blue exists, there exists a *blue awareness*: offence may be taken at the expression, but yet it expresses just what should be and is meant by saying that blue is, in this case, a *content* of consciousness or experience. Whether or not, when I have the sensation of blue, my consciousness or awareness is thus blue, my introspection does not enable me to decide with certainty: I only see no reason for thinking that it is. But whether it is or not, the point is unimportant, for introspection *does* enable me to decide that something else is also true: namely that I am aware *of* blue, and by this I mean, that my awareness has to blue a quite different and distinct relation. It is possible, I admit, that my awareness is blue *as well* as being *of* blue: but what I am quite sure of is that it is *of* blue; that it has to blue the simple and unique relation the existence of which alone justifies us in distinguishing knowledge of a thing from the thing known, indeed in distinguishing mind from matter. And this result I may express by saying that what is called the *content* of a sensation is in very truth what I originally called it—the sensation's *object*.

But, if all this be true, what follows? . . .

Now I think I am not mistaken in asserting that the reason why Idealists suppose that everything which *is* must be an inseparable aspect of some experience, is that they suppose some things, at least, to be inseparable aspects of *their* experience. And there is certainly nothing which they are so firmly convinced to be an inseparable aspect of their experience as what they call the *content* of their ideas and sensations. If, therefore, *this* turns out in every case, whether it be also the content or not, to be at least *not* an inseparable aspect of the experience of it, it will be readily admitted that nothing else which *we* experience ever is such an inseparable aspect. But if we never experience anything but what is *not* an inseparable aspect of *that* experience, how can we infer that anything whatever, let alone *everything*, is an inseparable aspect of *any* experience? How utterly unfounded is the assumption that *"esse* is *percipi"* appears in the clearest light.

SUMMARY

The German writer Georg Lichtenberg (1742–1799) once observed that in youth we may smile at idealism, with increasing maturity we may find it meaningful, and with full maturity we may find that idealism acquires a strength difficult to overcome. This, of course, is a biographical observation, not an argument; but it does suggest the question of what kind of case can be made for idealism.

This is the question which Charles Hartshorne faces in the following selection. Like other writers, he comments on the varieties of idealism, noting that what unites them is the denial of material realities. He also notes that some arguments for idealism have rightly been criticized. But he takes careful notice of Moore's argument, suggesting that it does not hold: indeed, one cannot refute all idealisms by rejecting one proposition. Given its sometimes forceful critics, idealism's best strategy is to resist all philosophical attempts to confine mind to one corner or phase of the universe. One of Hartshorne's own convictions in this regard is that idealism should reject the traditional (Cartesian) dictum that mind—so central a concept for idealism—has an unextended or nonspatial reality.

12 The Case for Idealism
Charles Hartshorne (1897-)

By 'idealism' I shall mean, in Ewing's phrase, the attempt or claim to "interpret reality in terms of mind."[1] Or, it is the doctrine that reality is essentially psychical. The terms 'panpsychism' or 'psychicalism' can also be used. "Psychical" means having such functions as feeling, perception, memory, volition, thought. For idealism, whatever lacks all of these functions is only an appearance of or abstraction from what does possess some or all of them. In still other words, reality, or what there is, consists of cases, forms, aspects, kinds of "experiencing," and of nothing else. This I take as the central affirmation of idealists. Ewing gives many samples of idealistic writing, omitting Leibniz for no apparent reason; also omitting Peirce and Whitehead, among others. As a result, his selections, though most useful, scarcely begin to cover the variety of forms which idealism has taken. Yet his book makes wonderfully clear why idealism has fallen into disrepute, considering the strange aberrations with which it has historically associated itself.

Idealists deny any literally insentient, thoughtless matter taken as more than an abstraction from things which in their concreteness, and taken one by one, are at least sentient. Schopenhauer is a marginal case, admitting only "blind" will as coextensive with reality. Kant is also marginal, since he refuses to characterize things in themselves as either psychical or not psychical. But he does limit the knowable to appearances, i.e., experiences. Moreover the only hints—ethical or religious—he gives concerning the noumena favor idealism.

In the foregoing deliberately broad definitions it is not assumed that such terms as 'feeling', 'experience', 'memory', 'thought', refer only to human instances, or even only to vertebrate animals—or to these plus some supreme, "absolute" or divine form of mind or spirit. All such restrictions upon the scope of psychical terms raise issues more specific than I intend by the option, idealism or not idealism. The same is true of views restricting idealism to one side of such alternatives as monism vs. pluralism, internal vs. external relations, optimism vs. pessimism, determinism (even if by final causes) vs. various gradations of indeterminism. It is indeed remarkable how many metaphysical and epistemological issues (I have counted fifteen without trying to be exhaustive) divide idealists from idealists, granted my definition of the label.

As some use words, an "idealist" is one who believes that all relations are intrinsic to both or all their terms, or that everything depends upon everything else. But many idealists (by my definition) deny this. For some writers, an idealist is a person who thinks that, in knowing, one knows only one's own

The selection is from Charles Hartshorne, "The Case for Idealism," *The Philosophical Forum* (New Series), 1(1968), pp. 7-23, with omissions. Used by permission of the Editor.

[1] See A. C. Ewing's *The Idealistic Tradition* (Glencoe, Illinois, 1957), p. 25.

mental states, or at least knows only these directly. Or, that physical objects are only human, or human and divine, ideas. Yet some idealists reject this view, and by a reasonable definition of terms are epistemological realists. Some psychicalists declare the "unreality of space and time," others do nothing of the sort. Idealists have been theists or atheists, Christians, Hindus, or Buddhists, nominalists or realists, *a priori* rationalists or empiricists, dialectical philosophers or anti-dialecticians. They have held causal theories of perception or acausal theories. They have been essentially literary or artistic in their interests, or essentially scientific, even distinguished contributors to physics or biology. They have thought in terms of 'substance', or (Buddhists, Whitehead) have objected to this concept, taking events or momentary actualities as reality in its basic concrete form. They have been deeply agnostic (Kant) or startlingly gnostic (Hegel).

What follows from this immense array of internal differences in the idealists' camp? One thing follows immediately: one cannot refute (or establish) idealism as such by refuting (or establishing) one or more of the many doctrines upon which idealists have disagreed—unless these doctrines can be shown to follow from (or to entail) idealism itself. G. E. Moore, a noted opponent of idealistic claims, said once that he "devoutly hoped" that idealism (the view that reality is essentially "spiritual") was true. He contended only that it failed to follow from any evidence offered for it.

What can be validly inferred from the idealistic thesis, and from what can it be inferred? These are the crucial ques-

tions, and it is amazing how seldom they were clearly discussed by either the proponents or opponents of historic idealistic systems. One thing does follow from the thesis that reality and mind (i.e., experience or the psychical) are the same. This is that either reality is easy to understand, or mind is not easy to understand. The history of thought refutes the first supposition; so the second only is left. But then is it surprising that idealists have had trouble agreeing as to how the "mind" which they equate with reality is to be conceived? Idealists may have differed because their doctrine forced them to face the genuine, concrete, ultimate reality, not some artificial, abstract simplification. They have rightly located the central mystery, but its mysteriousness remains.

On both sides of the historic controversies one can see the wish to make things simple and obvious. For Berkeley it is enough to point out that nature is thinkable and perceivable only as human (and divine) ideas. His critics are happy to see that 'idea' may mean *either* a case of thinking or perceiving *or* something thought about or perceived, so that the argument rests on an ambiguity. For Green one has only to see that 'reality' means a system of relations and that "relations are the work of thought," to which James replies that relations are perceived or felt and are no inventions of "intelligence." For Bradley the proof of idealism is that relations are contradictory, hence unreal, and that the only model of relationless reality we have is feeling. For Russell the point is that relations are indispensable, and so are terms, which must be independent of the relations. For Blanshard the clue is the insight, "to understand is to see to be necessary." But Nagel finds it plain that this is a false view of understanding. None of these writers has clearly shown the truth or the falsity of idealism as such, or the logical connection between this issue and the others mentioned.

Perhaps at long last it is time to consider dispassionately the logical rather than merely historical relations of the idealistic thesis to other doctrines debated among philosophers.

The idealistic question essentially concerns the mind-matter distinction. To reject idealism is to raise the question: dualism or materialism? (The theory of "neutral stuff" can, by a suitable definition of matter, be included under materialism.) Idealism, in short, is one of the two forms of antidualism, materialism being the other. What connection has the joint rejection of dualism and materialism in favor of idealistic monism (not opposed to a pluralism of individuals) with the other topics discussed above? Clearly it depends, at least in part, upon how the structure of mind or experience is conceived. If, for instance, this structure is deterministic, then idealists should be determinists, if not then not. If and only if the apparent plurality of minds is genuine, should idealists be pluralists. If mind is immutable, then so, for idealism, is reality. But is mind immutable? This seems anything but obvious. If it is the function of mind in knowing to create or alter the known, then of course the things we know are, insofar, creatures of our thinking or perceiving. But, as Santayana pointed out, in now being aware of our previous experiences, we can hardly be creating these past experiences. So, as applied to memory at least, the supposedly idealistic doctrine of knowing is untrue to mind or experiencing itself. Yet how can this show the falsity of idealism as such? Some idealists agree entirely on this point with Santayana.

Many critics of the psychicalist theory have thought to show, if not its falsity, at least its problematic status, by finding fallacies in many of the arguments offered by idealists. And certainly a good many are fallacious. But do they exhaust the possibilities?

How would one show that a certain idea is adequate to explicate "reality"? Would it not be by showing that the idea in question can take all the forms which reality is known, or even can be conceived, to take? Thus if mind can be concrete and also abstract, extended and also inextended, dependent and also independent, singular and also plural, valuable and also trifling, simple and also complex, long-enduring and also momentary, fixed and also changeable, actual and also potential, with quality as well as quantity (and with as great a range of qualities and quantities as you please), contingent as well as necessary, conditioned as well as unconditioned, a part of reality and also reality as a whole—if mind can be on both sides of every genuine contrast, in the sense in which reality can be so (even unrealities are at least mistaken but really occurrent ideas, fancies or what not), then there is no need to assume some additional principle. What is in no sense psychical will be what is in no sense real. How 'psychical' can retain any useful meaning, in spite of this equivalence with 'reality', we shall consider below.

Opposition to idealism must consist in attempts to put mind on one side only of "genuine contrasts" (such that reality is on both sides). Descartes' denial that not mind but only matter can be extended is the paradigm of anti-idealism, calamitously accepted by many idealists. When Aristotle contrasted mind as actuality of an organic body to its matter as potentiality he was taking a somewhat anti-idealistic position. But when, for instance, he said that the soul was "in a manner all things" he was taking an almost idealistic one. Similarly, when Plato defined the soul as the self-moved, and the source of all motion, but implied a contrast with matter as incapable of self-motion, he was stopping short of complete idealism. For idealism, either every reality is self-moved, or mind is not in every case of form self-moved. An idealist does not view mind as what is left over when one abstracts from behavior of matter in motion; rather, he takes matter in motion to be also mind in some form. When (if he did) Plato associated soul with eternal ideas *rather than* with changing bodies, he was insofar anti-idealistic. If mind is reality, then it has all the forms of reality, not just some of them. It is inextended only if nothing is extended, wholly actual only if nothing is potential, pure form only if nothing is anything but form. *If* mind needs something to mold, control, or form, something potential for further determinations, then mind itself must be the form, the forming, and that which is formed. It may not be the same individual mind, or the same kind or aspect of mind, which is on both sides of every contrast, but it must be mind in some case, kind, or aspect.

If the above is sound, there are two opposite strategies for an idealist. He may hold that mind is on one side only

of at least certain seemingly basic contrasts, but urge that the other side is "unreal," i.e., that these contrasts are not what I have been calling "genuine." And this procedure may seem to be helped by the consideration that the unreality in question is a problem only because there is at least an appearance of its presence, appearance being something mental. The objections to this strategy, however, are widely recognized, especially in the West. I cannot see it as a valid procedure, with one exception to be discussed presently.

The other strategy is to resist every attempt to confine mind to one aspect, corner, or species of thinkable reality. I believe that this strategy is capable of great power. . . .

If reality simply is mind, in various forms and aspects, the word 'mind'—or 'experience', 'the psychical'—must, some will object, lose all distinctive meaning. Are not ideas essentially contrasts? If just everything is psychical, then is not "psychical" a synonym for "something, anything you please"? In a sense yes, in a sense no. There are three aspects of the 'no'. First, the doctrine is not that everything is, in the same sense, psychical. For instance, if 'X is psychical' means 'X at least feels', then obviously many things are not psychical. A crowd of persons does not literally feel, only the persons in the crowd feel. Also abstractions—for instance, feeling as such—do not feel. The idea of a triangle does not itself think, but is only an aspect of cases of thinking. Concrete reality *concretely* instances the psychical, abstract reality *abstractly* instances it: individual reality is an *individual* instance, aggregate reality an *aggregate* instance. Or, actual reality is actual feeling or experiencing, potential reality is potential feeling.

The second reason why it is not a meaningless duplication of words to equate reality and experience is this: the equation reminds us that every concept, even so general a one as 'reality', must be related somehow to experience. The most general ideas are still ideas, and experience gives them their sense. If we cannot take 'experience' to have a sense as general as 'reality', what meaning can we attach to this latter word?

We understand that there is more in the world than we ourselves experience partly by taking into account what others experience. If we are to believe that there is more than any human being experiences, can we do this otherwise than by implicitly or explicitly grasping a meaning for 'experience' or 'knowledge' wider than the human? The escape from the egocentric predicament is not by dismissing the very idea of a subject, but by recognizing a variety of subjects, actual and possible. The alternative to egoism is altruism; the remedy for self-centeredness is sociality. We transcend species-centeredness (if we do) by recognizing a society wider than the human. What is wrong with phenomenalism or Berkeleyanism is its arbitrary cutting off of the social conception of objectivity at the limits of humanity, or of terrestrial animal life—whether or not God is added. Indeed, if the idea of mind or "spirit" can span the gulf (in some sense infinite) between man and God, how can it fail to cover the finite though vast difference between man and molecule? And how can even the least creature fail to exhibit some lowly degree of that which in eminent form is deity—assuming we can distinguish

deity from the mere unknown. A dualism of mind and mere matter, as Berkeley saw, is subtly incompatible with theism. But so is the notion that minds can deal directly only with ideas, rather than with other and in some cases vastly different minds.

Epistemic transcendence is most clearly grasped in the social case. *You* are not merely idea or feeling in me, for you have your own ideas and feelings. Who can establish limits to the generalization of transcendence in this social sense? Or prove that there is any other kind? Or that any problem is illuminated by supposing that there is? I admit I see no such problem.

A third reply to the appeal—in itself entirely in order—to the "principle of contrast" is that mind has degrees. Experiences vary in intensity, complexity, spatiotemporal scope, extent of creative freedom, and awareness of alternative possibilities. The lower limit of diminishing degrees, for idealism, coincides with nonentity. No experience at all, human or nonhuman, means no concrete reality at all. But very low degrees will, for many purposes, be equivalent to none at all. Idealism can claim to find a place for all the contrasts we have any need to make.

Anti-idealism implies a criterion for the total absence of experience in some parts of nature. I know of no such criterion that is both nonquestion-begging and conceivably applicable in experience, except through the confusion spoken of above between 'not observably present' and 'observably not present'. For example, it is arbitrary to say that, since our feelings require nervous systems, without such systems there can be no feeling. Of course there could not be our specific kind of feelings, or even the metazoan animal kind, in single cells or molecules. But there are structural and behavioral analogies between metazoan response to stimuli and an amoeba's response or even an atom's. Moreover, the push-pull, purely mechanical account of physical action has been shown to be what Leibniz held it was, a myth due to the grossness of our perceptual discrimination, masking vast numbers of nonmechanical relationships. On all levels environmental changes influence internal changes in individuals; and this is the general formula for perceptual behavior. To say that the formula is more general than the idea of mental experience can be is merely to declare idealism false by definition. For *idealism is the doctrine that mind is as protean and multiform as the reality that mind is trying to know.*

Idealism has sometimes been defined as the equation, "to be is to be perceived." If the phrase means that, supposing *A* perceives *X, X* could not have existed if *A* had failed to perceive it, realists have shown how implausible it is. This is especially clear in the case of human memory, which in its pure form is our way of perceiving our own experiences (introspection being explicable as deliberate, short-term retrospection). The remembered events are presupposed, rather than produced, by the remembering. Moreover, there is little interest in perceiving things unless more than one person can perceive the same things. It is counterintuitive to suppose that perception gives a merely private world. On the other hand, there does seem to be a connection of meaning between reality and perceivability. Furthermore, the point of the possibility

implied here is that there will be some actualizations or other. So perhaps to be is indeed to be perceived—but by whom? By someone or other, or some set of subjects or other, no matter which, so long as they are capable of perceiving the thing. Thus the reality of anything requires that the class of perceivers of that very thing should not be empty, but it does not require just this perceiver or that, or even that the perceivers be human. Things are there, not solely for human beings, but for birds, insects, who can say what else? . . .

It is time to face the Cartesian (really Augustinian) dictum, often put forth as self-evident, that mind is inextended. This has been deliberately rejected by men with every conceivably relevant form of competence concerning both space and mind. Thus—to mention a few—Fechner, James, Troland were psychologists of note; Clifford, Varisco, Peirce and Whitehead were philosophizing mathematicians; Burger is a physicist; Sewall Wright is a great geneticist, a mathematican with a fine knowledge of natural science in general. Many others could be named who see no need to deny the reality of extension in order to explain the world idealistically. I myself reached an idealistic view of the physical world at the age of twenty, and it did not then, and does not now, seem to me that I was in effect declaring spatiality to be unreal. Whatever the status of the Cartesian dogma, self-evident it is not. Only careful argument will do on a question discussed with such immense care as, for instance, Whitehead has discussed it in *Process and Reality*, or Peirce in Vols. I and VI of the *Collected Papers*.

Naturally one can find abstract aspects of mind or experience which cannot be supposed, in any direct clear sense, to occupy space. Thus virtue has no definite, unique, size or shape. Concepts in general are like this. But an actual concrete experience, including elements of thought, perception, memory, desire, is not nowhere, nor yet somewhere in a point. Where then, if not somewhere in a region? Experiences have spatio-temporal relations, for in the modern view space is simply a network of cause-effect relations; and if one rejects (rightly I think) epiphenomenalism and mere materialism one must see even human experiences as entering into such relations, with both temporal and spatial aspects, as truly, though not as obviously or simply, as any events whatever.

If the proper strategy of idealism is the one I have suggested, those critics of historical idealistic systems who have attacked one-sided doctrines of interdependence, or of the exclusive reality of the inextended, eternal, or absolute, have been idealism's friends in disguise. And those idealists who have tried to explain away one side of categorial contrasts in order to leave the field to mind were anti-idealistic in spite of themselves. Immense confusion has resulted from the failure to distinguish clearly between the two essentially opposite ways of defending the idealistic thesis. To explain basic contraries through mind is one thing, to explain them away

as unreal is another. Only the latter has had much attention from the critics.

Idealistic speculation began about three centuries ago in the West with Leibniz. More than a thousand years earlier it had reached fairly sharp formulation in Asia, especially in Mahayana Buddhism. In all that time the question concerning the equivalence of mind and reality was argued only as an issue entangled with others whose necessary connection with *this* issue was never made clear. I have attempted in this sketch to show how confusion resulted from this procedure, and to suggest the direction in which a remedy is to be sought.

Like every philosophical view, idealism needs to be tested by its compatibility with the principle that meaning implies contrast, and hence that the truth is not to be looked for in crassly one-sided positions, such as extreme monism or pluralism, doctrines of universal interdependence or universal independence, absolute optimism or absolute pessimism, eternalism or temporalism, a priorism or empiricism, rationalism or intuitionism.

The subject of Moore's "devout hope" deserves more balanced and adequate reflection than it could receive in the battles of the first quarter of this century by which the hold of an extraordinarily one-sided and counter-intuitive form of idealistic metaphysics was broken.

BIBLIOGRAPHICAL NOTE

Among the best introductory surveys of idealism are two works by Josiah Royce, *Lectures on Modern Idealism* (New Haven, 1923), and, in the relevant chapters, *The Spirit of Modern Philosophy* (New York, 1892). An anthology edited by A. C. Ewing, *The Idealistic Tradition* (Glencoe, Illinois, 1957), presents an interesting collection of papers and includes a bibliography that the student may consult for intensive reading in idealism. Among the major idealistic works and authors not included in the preceding selections are: F. H. Bradley, *Appearance and Reality* (London, 1893); and, especially for idealistic moral and political philosophy, the works of T. H. Green. An interesting variant of idealism is the position known as personal idealism or personalism. For material on personalism, see Borden Parker Bowne, *Metaphysics* (New York, 1882), and *Personalism* (Boston, 1908), and the book by Edgar Sheffield Brightman, *Person and Reality* (New York, 1958). A collection of Brightman's articles is found in Steinkraus and Beck (eds.), *Studies in Personalism* (Cape Cod, 1975). One major philosophical figure, Immanuel Kant, can be classified as idealistic only with great qualification, yet his influence on idealism, as on all of modern philosophy, has been extensive. The student will find his major works, especially the *Critique of Pure Reason*, difficult but rewarding. Another thinker who defies easy classification, Alfred North Whitehead, developed a variant of idealism called the philosophy of organism or, sometimes, panpsychism. Among his important works are *Science and the Modern World* (New York, 1925) and *Adventures of Ideas* (New York, 1933). Discussions of idealism are found in such books as G. W. Cunningham, *The Idealistic Argument in Recent British and American Philosophy* (New York, 1933), and A. C. Ewing, *Idealism: A Critical Survey* (London, 1934). More recent studies of idealism that have concentrated on social philosophy include John E. Smith, *Royce's Social Infinite* (New York, 1950); A. J. M. Milne, *The Social Philosophy of English Idealism* (London, 1962); Melvin Richter, *The Politics of Conscience: T. H. Green and His Age* (Cambridge, Mass., 1964); and Peter Fuss, *The Moral Philosophy of Josiah Royce* (Cambridge, Mass., 1965). The student may find interesting the papers in Clifford Barrett (ed.), *Contemporary Idealism in America* (New York, 1932), and in Buford and Howie (eds.), *Contemporary Studies in Philosophical Idealism* (Cape Cod, 1974). Finally, much material on idealism is available in the recently established journal, *Idealistic Studies.*

Chapter Five

Positivism

Hume · Poincaré · Ayer · Pearson
Stevenson · Lévy-Bruhl · Richards
Schlick · Popper · Ewing · Feigl

The term "positivism" was first associated with the doctrines of the eccentric French thinker Auguste Comte (1798–1857). By it he meant that the highest form of knowledge is simple description of sensory experience. He based this view on an evolutionary "law of three stages," which he believed he had discovered in 1822. The three stages are the *theological,* where spiritual, anthropomorphic beings are appealed to to explain natural phenomena; the *metaphysical,* where these beings are depersonalized and become forces and essences; and the *positive,* where explanation of phenomena proceeds by scientific description.[1] Although this law is Comte's discovery, the basic ideas of positivism are found in numerous thinkers; and actually, contemporary positivists rely very little on Comte's thought in the development of their philosophies.

Like naturalism, positivism holds that science alone provides reliable knowledge of nature; indeed, in some ways it goes farther than naturalism in its emphasis on science. But it differs from naturalism in two fundamental ways: its analysis of science is based more on logic than on the psychological categories of doubt and belief; and it is more explicitly—even at times vehemently—antimetaphysical.

Central to the positivist's analysis of knowledge is the distinction between analytic and synthetic propositions. Analytic propositions are those whose truth value depends on the terms occurring in them, as, "No bachelors are married"; synthetic propositions are those that refer to facts and whose truth depends on a relation to them, as, "There is gold in Siberia." The positivist believes that the

---

[1] The student may find this view developed in Comte's book, *The Positive Philosophy* (tr. Harriet Martineau) (New York: Calvin Blanchard, 1855).

former group, made up of propositions that contain no factual content, really consists only of tautologies. With them, truth and falsehood can be determined by logical and linguistic analysis. The second group, containing all propositions having factual meanings, belongs entirely to the sciences; and there are no factual propositions, the positivist holds, except scientific ones.

This division itself rules out metaphysical statements as cognitive or meaningful. Yet there is another positivistic doctrine, derived from an analysis of the "meaning of factual meaning," that is even more explicitly antimetaphysical. This is the verifiability theory of meaning. Many attempts have been made to formulate the theory accurately; in essence, they all seek to define the meaning of an empirical concept by reference to the sensory observations that will verify or disconfirm it. When a proposition involves such reference, it is meaningful and open to scientific inquiry; when it does not, it is (unless it is a logical truth) only a pseudo statement, noncognitive and nonsense.

A third positivist doctrine follows from the preceding ideas. All statements are divided into three groups: cognitive, such as those of logic and science; directive, which includes the uses of language for purposes of action; and emotive, the use of language to express emotion. It is in these latter two groups that positivists put many of the propositions of traditional philosophy, including ethical, metaphysical, and theological statements.

The student may well ask after reading these three theses, What then is the task of philosophy? The positivist replies that philosophy is not a separate, identifiable body of statements, but rather an activity of analysis. He eschews speculation and the attempt to find ultimate meanings, and concentrates rather on the analysis, first, of key terms in scientific inquiry, and second, of discourse generally. Philosophy, guided by the analytic-synthetic distinction and the verification principle, is thus analysis, and its object of study is primarily language.

The original positivism of Comte and some of his nineteenth-century followers is identifiable by its concern with science. Contemporary positivism is in many ways much more sophisticated, for it utilizes the recent developments in logic in conducting its analyses. It is for this reason frequently called logical positivism. It has also, because of its stress on scientific inquiry, been termed logical empiricism. These different names, however, all refer to the same distinctive position in contemporary philosophy.

INTRODUCTION

The writings of the British philosopher David Hume are a major source of some of the ideas just outlined. In the following selection, Hume makes the distinction between analytic and synthetic propositions, or, as he calls them, relations of ideas and matters of fact. The truth or falsehood of the former, he observes, can be determined "by the mere operation of thought." But what of the second group? Hume sees no self-contradiction in the statement, "The sun will not rise tomorrow," hard as it may be to believe it. How then do we come to accept this belief? Hume answers, through experience.

The next question to ask concerns the basis of reasonings from experience. Hume finds this basis to be the principle of causality, for it is this principle which allows the distinct events of experience to be tied together in some meaningful way. What kind of principle is it? It is not a priori, for every effect is distinct from its cause, and no reasoning can take one from a cause to its precise effect. Is the principle then derived from experience? To ask this question, however, is to become involved in a logical circle: experience is based and depends on the causal principle; hence experience cannot be utilized to warrant it.

Hume therefore concludes in a metaphysically skeptical position. Metaphysical propositions like causality rest on no rational grounds whatsoever. If we use such ideas (and for Hume we do), their only ground can be the psychological principle of custom or habit.

1 Knowledge and Causality
David Hume (1711-1776)

All the objects of human reason or inquiry may naturally be divided into two kinds, to wit, *Relations of Ideas,* and *Matters of Fact.* Of the first kind are the sciences of Geometry, Algebra, and Arithmetic, and, in short, every affirmation which is either intuitively or demonstratively certain. *That the square of the hypotenuse is equal to the square of the two sides,* is a proposition which expresses a relation between these figures. *That three times five is equal to the half of thirty,* expresses a relation between these numbers. Propositions of this kind are discoverable by the mere operation of thought, without dependence on what is anywhere existent in the universe. Though there never were a circle or tri-

The selection is from Hume's *An Inquiry Concerning the Human Understanding,* in *The Philosophical Works of David Hume,* 4 vols. (Boston: Little, Brown and Co., 1854), Vol. IV, pp. 30–54, with omissions.

angle in nature, the truths demonstrated by Euclid would for ever retain their certainty and evidence.

Matters of fact, which are the second objects of human reason, are not ascertained in the same manner; nor is our evidence of their truth, however great, of a like nature with the foregoing. The contrary of every matter of fact is still possible; because it can never imply a contradiction, and is conceived by the mind with the same facility and distinctness, as if ever so conformable to reality. *That the sun will not rise tomorrow* is no less intelligible a proposition, and implies no more contradiction, than the affirmation, *that it will rise.* We should in vain, therefore, attempt to demonstrate its falsehood. Were it demonstratively false, it would imply a contradiction, and could never be distinctly conceived by the mind.

It may therefore be a subject worthy

of curiosity, to inquire what is the nature of that evidence, which assures us of any real existence and matter of fact, beyond the present testimony of our senses, or the records of our memory. This part of philosophy, it is observable, had been little cultivated either by the ancients or moderns; and therefore our doubts and errors, in the prosecution of so important an inquiry, may be the more excusable, while we march through such difficult paths without any guide or direction. They may even prove useful, by exciting curiosity, and destroying that implicit faith and security which is the bane of all reasoning and free inquiry. The discovery of defects in the common philosopher, if any such there be, will not, I presume, be a discouragement, but rather an incitement, as is usual, to attempt something more full and satisfactory than has yet been proposed to the public.

All reasonings concerning matter of fact seem to be founded on the relation of *Cause and Effect*. By means of that relation alone we can go beyond the evidence of our memory and senses. If you were to ask a man why he believes any matter of fact which is absent, for instance, that his friend is in the country, or in France, he would give you a reason, and this reason would be some other fact: as a letter received from him, or the knowledge of his former resolutions and promises. A man, finding a watch or any other machine in a desert island, would conclude that there had once been men in that island. All our reasonings concerning fact are of the same nature. And here it is constantly supposed, that there is a connection between the present fact and that which is inferred from it. Were there nothing to bind them together, the inference would

be entirely precarious. The hearing of an articulate voice and rational discourse in the dark, assures us of the presence of some person: why? because these are the effects of the human make and fabric, and closely connected with it. If we anatomize all the other reasonings of this nature, we shall find that they are founded on the relation of cause and effect, and that this relation is either near or remote, direct or collateral. Heat and light are collateral effects of fire, and the one effect may justly be inferred from the other.

If we would satisfy ourselves, therefore, concerning the nature of that evidence which assures us of matters of fact, we must inquire how we arrive at the knowledge of cause and effect.

I shall venture to affirm, as a general proposition which admits of no exception, that the knowledge of this relation is not, in any instance, attained by reasonings *a priori;* but arises entirely from experience, when we find, that any particular objects are constantly conjoined with each other. Let an object be presented to a man of ever so strong natural reason and abilities; if that object be entirely new to him, he will not be able, by the most accurate examination of its sensible qualities, to discover any of its causes or effects. Adam, though his rational faculties be supposed, at the very first, entirely perfect, could not have inferred from the fluidity and transparency of water that it would suffocate him; or from the light and warmth of fire that it would consume him. No object ever discovers, by the qualities which appear to the senses, either the causes which produced it, or the effects which will arise from it; nor can our reason, unassisted by experience, ever draw any inference concerning real existence and matter of fact.

This proposition, *that causes and effects are discoverable, not by reason, but by experience,* will readily be admitted with regard to such objects as we remember to have once been altogether unknown to us; since we must be conscious of the utter inability which we then lay under of foretelling what would arise from them. Present two smooth pieces of marble to a man who has no tincture of natural philosophy; he will never discover that they will adhere together in such a manner as to require great force to separate them in a direct line, while they make so small a resistance to a lateral pressure. Such events as bear little analogy to the common course of nature, are also readily confessed to be known only by experience; nor does any man imagine that the explosion of gunpowder, or the attraction of a loadstone, could ever be discovered by arguments *a priori.* In like manner, when an effect is supposed to depend upon an intricate machinery or secret structure of parts, we make no difficulty in attributing all our knowledge of it to experience. Who will assert that he can give the ultimate reason, why milk or bread is proper nourishment for a man, not for a lion or tiger?

But the same truth may not appear at first sight to have the same evidence with regard to events, which have become familiar to us from our first appearance in the world, which bear a close analogy to the whole course of nature, and which are supposed to depend on the simple qualities of objects, without any secret structure of parts. We are apt to imagine, that we could discover these effects by the mere operation of our reason without experience. We fancy, that we were brought on a sudden into this world, we could at first have inferred, that one billiard-ball would communicate motion to another upon impulse; and that we needed not to have waited for the event, in order to pronounce with certainty concerning it. Such is the influence of custom, that where it is strongest, it not only covers our natural ignorance, but even conceals itself, and seems not to take place, merely because it is found in the highest degree.

But to convince us, that all the laws of nature, and all the operations of bodies, without exception, are known only by experience, the following reflections may perhaps suffice. Were any object presented to us, and were we required to pronounce concerning the effect which will result from it, without consulting past observation; after what manner, I beseech you, must the mind proceed in this operation? It must invent or imagine some event which it ascribes to the object as its effect; and it is plain that this invention must be entirely arbitrary. The mind can never possibly find the effect in the supposed cause, by the most accurate scrutiny and examination. For the effect is totally different from the cause, and consequently can never be discovered in it. Motion in the second billiard-ball is a quite distinct event from motion in the first; nor is there any thing in the one to suggest the smallest hint of the other. A stone or piece of metal raised into the air, and left without any support, immediately falls: but to consider the matter *a priori,* is there anything we discover in this situation which can beget the idea of a downward, rather than an upward, or any other motion, in the stone or metal?

And as the first imagination or invention of a particular effect, in all natural operations, is arbitrary, where we consult not experience; so must we also esteem the supposed tie or connection between the cause and effect which binds them together, and renders it impossible, that any other effect could result from the operation of that cause. When I see, for instance, a billiard-ball moving in a straight line towards another; even suppose motion in the second ball should by accident be suggested to me as the result of their contact or impulse; may I not conceive that a hundred different events might as well follow from that cause? May not both these balls remain at absolute rest? May not the first ball return in a straight line, or leap off from the second in any line or direction? All these suppositions are consistent and conceivable. Why then should we give the preference to one, which is no more consistent or conceivable than the rest? All our reasonings *a priori* will never be able to show us any foundation for this preference.

In a word, then, every effect is a distinct event from its cause. It could not, therefore, be discovered in the cause; and the first invention or conception of it, *a priori,* must be entirely arbitrary. And even after it is suggested, the conjunction of it with the cause must appear equally arbitrary; since there are always many other effects, which, to reason, must seem fully as consistent and natural. In vain, therefore, should we pretend to determine any single event, or infer any cause or effect, without the assistance of observation and experience. . . .

But we have not yet attained any tolerable satisfaction with regard to the question first proposed. Each solution still gives rise to a new question as difficult as the foregoing, and leads us on to further inquiries. When it is asked, *What is the nature of all our reasonings concerning matter of fact?* the proper answer seems to be, that they are founded on the relation of cause and effect. When again it is asked, *What is the foundation of all our reasonings and conclusions concerning that relation?* it may be replied in one word, *experience.* But if we still carry on our sifting humor, and ask, *What is the foundation of all conclusions from experience?* this implies a new question, which may be of more difficult solution and explication. Philosophers that give themselves airs of superior wisdom and sufficiency, have a hard task when they encounter persons of inquisitive dispositions, who push them from every corner to which they retreat, and who are sure at last to bring them to some dangerous dilemma. The best expedient to prevent this confusion, is to be modest in our pretensions, and even to discover the difficulty ourselves before it is objected to us. By this means we may make a kind of merit of our very ignorance.

I shall content myself in this section with an easy task, and shall pretend only to give a negative answer to the question here proposed. I say then, that even after we have experience of the operations of cause and effect, our conclusions from that experience are *not* founded on reasoning, or any process of the understanding. This answer we must endeavor both to explain and to defend.

It must certainly be allowed, that nature has kept us at a great distance from all her secrets, and has afforded us only the knowledge of a few superficial qualities of objects; while she conceals from us those powers and principles on which the influence of those objects entirely depends. Our senses inform us of the color, weight, and consistence of bread; but neither sense nor reason can ever inform us of those qualities which fit it for the nourishment and support of a human body. Sight or feeling conveys an idea of the actual motion of bodies, but as to that wonderful force or power which would carry on a moving body for ever in a continued change of place, and which bodies never lose but by communicating it to others; of this we cannot form the most distant conception. But notwithstanding this ignorance of natural powers and principles, we always presume when we see like sensible qualities, that they have like secret powers, and expect that effects similar to those which we have experienced will follow from them. If a body of like color and consistence with that bread which we have formerly eaten, be presented to us, we make no scruple of repeating the experiment, and foresee, with certainty, like nourishment and support. Now, this is a process of the mind or thought, of which I would willingly know the foundation. It is allowed on all hands, that there is no known connection between the sensible qualities and the secret powers; and consequently, that the mind is not led to form such a conclusion concerning their constant and regular conjunction, by anything which it knows of their nature. As to past *Experience,* it can be allowed to give *direct* and *certain* information of those precise objects only, and that precise period of time which fell under its cognizance: but why this experience should be extended to future times, and to other objects, which, for

aught we know, may be only in appearance similar, this is the main question on which I would insist. . . .

If we be, therefore, engaged by arguments to put trust in past experience, and make it the standard of our future judgment, these arguments must be probable only, or such as regard matter of fact and real existence, according to the division above mentioned. But that there is no argument of this kind, must appear, if our explication of that species of reasoning be admitted as solid and satisfactory. We have said that all arguments concerning existence are founded on the relation of cause and effect; that our knowledge of that relation is derived entirely from experience; and that all our experimental conclusions proceed upon the supposition, that the future will be conformable to the past. To endeavor, therefore, the proof of this last supposition by probable arguments, or arguments regarding existence, must be evidently going in a circle, and taking that for granted which is the very point in question. . . .

When a man says, *I have found, in all past instances, such sensible qualities, conjoined with such secret powers;* and when he says, *similar sensible qualities will always be conjoined with similar secret powers;* he is not guilty of a tautology, nor are these propositions in any respect the same. You say that the one proposition is an inference from the other: but you must confess that the inference is not intuitive, neither is it demonstrative. Of what nature is it then? To say it is experimental, is begging the question. For all inferences from experience suppose, as their foundation, that the future will resemble the past, and that similar powers will be conjoined with similar sensible qualities. If there be any suspicion that the course of nature may change, and that the past may be no rule for the future, all experience becomes useless, and can give rise to no inference or conclusion. It is impossible, therefore, that any arguments from experience can prove this resemblance of the past to the future: since all these arguments are founded on the supposition of that resemblance. Let the course of things be allowed hitherto ever so regular, that alone, without some new argument or inference, proves not that for the future it will continue so. In vain do you pretend to have learned the nature of bodies from your past experience. Their secret nature, and consequently all their effects and influence, may change, without any change in their sensible qualities. This happens sometimes, and with regard to some objects: why may it not happen always, and with regard to all objects? What logic, what process of argument secures you against this supposition? My practice, you say, refutes my doubts. But you mistake the purport of my question. As an agent, I am quite satisfied in the point; but as a philosopher, who has some share of curiosity, I will not say skepticism, I want to learn the foundation of this inference. No reading, no inquiry has yet been able to remove my difficulty, or give me satisfaction in a matter of such importance. Can I do better than propose the difficulty to the public, even though, perhaps, I have small hopes of obtaining a solution? We shall at least, by this means, be sensible of our ignorance, if we do not augment our knowledge. . . .

Suppose a person, though endowed with the strongest facilities of reason and reflection, to be brought on a sudden into this world; he would, indeed, immediately observe a continual succession of objects, and one event following another; but he would not be able to discover any thing further. He would not at first, by any reasoning, be able to reach the idea of cause and effect; since the particular powers, by which all natural operations are performed, never appear to the senses; nor is it reasonable to conclude, merely because one event in one instance precedes another, that therefore the one is the cause, the other the effect. Their conjunction may be arbitrary and casual. There may be no reason to infer the existence of one, from the appearance of the other: and, in a word, such a person without more experience, could never employ his conjecture or reasoning concerning any matter of fact, or be assured of any thing beyond what was immediately present to his memory and senses.

Suppose again, that he has acquired more experience, and has lived so long in the world as to have observed similar objects or events to be constantly conjoined together; what is the consequence of this experience? He immediately infers the existence of one object from the appearance of the other: yet he has not, by all his experience, acquired any idea or knowledge of the secret power, by which the one object produces the other; nor is it, by any process of reasoning, he is engaged to draw this inference; but still he finds himself determined to draw it; and though he should be convinced that his understanding has no part in the operation, he would nevertheless continue in the same course of thinking. There is some other principle which determines him to form such a conclusion.

This principle is *Custom* or *Habit*. For

wherever the repetition of any particular act or operation produces a propensity to renew the same act or operation, without being impelled by any reasoning or process of the understanding, we always say, that this propensity is the effect of *Custom*. By employing that word, we pretend not to have given the ultimate reason of such a propensity. We only point out a principle of human nature, which is universally acknowledged, and which is well known by its effects. Perhaps we can push our inquiries no further, or pretend to give the cause of this cause; but must rest contented with it as the ultimate principle, which we can assign, of all our conclusions from experience. It is sufficient satisfaction, that we can go so far without repining at the narrowness of our faculties; because they will carry us no further. And, it is certain, we here advance a very intelligible proposition at least, if not a true one, when we assert, that after the constant conjunction of two objects, heat and flame, for instance, weight and solidity, we are determined by custom alone to expect the one from the appearance of the other. This hypothesis seems even the only one which explains the difficulty, why we draw from a thousand instances, an inference which we are not able to draw from one instance, that is in no respect different from them. Reason is incapable of any such variation. The conclusions which it draws from considering one circle, are the same which it would form upon surveying all the circles in the universe. But no man, having seen only one body move after being impelled by another, could infer, that every other body will move after a like impulse. All inferences from experience, therefore, are effects of custom, not of reasoning. . . .

What then is the conclusion of the whole matter? A simple one; though, it must be confessed, pretty remote from the common theories of philosophy. All belief of matter of fact or real existence is derived merely from some present object to the memory or senses, and a customary conjunction between that and some other object; or, in other words, having found, in many instances, that any two kinds of objects, flame and heat, snow and cold, have always been conjoined together: if flame or snow be presented anew to the senses, the mind is carried by custom to expect heat or cold, and to *believe* that such a quality does exist, and will discover itself upon a nearer approach. This belief is the necessary result of placing the mind in such circumstances. It is an operation of the soul, when we are so situated, as unavoidable as to feel the passion of love, when we receive benefits; or hatred, when we meet with injuries. All these operations are a species of natural instincts, which no reasoning or process of the thought and understanding is able either to produce or to prevent.

2 Truth and Experiment
Henri Poincaré (1854-1912)

Closely related to—in fact, intimately bound with—positivism's antimetaphysical stance is the theme that science alone can give us knowledge of our universe. Indeed, since science is given exclusive authority for empirical statements, the belief that metaphysics could give any knowledge is necessarily rejected. The theme itself has been given a number of statements. Henri Poincaré, physicist and philosopher, holds that "experiment is the sole source of truth"; and he goes on to observe that it is experiment alone that can reveal novelty and achieve certainty.

A good experiment, Poincaré writes, is one that enables the scientist to predict future experience and to achieve generalizations about experience. These goals are made more attainable by mathematical techniques that can direct generalization and so increase the productivity of science. Generalization, however, raises the questions of the unity of nature and simplicity of explanation. The former question, Poincaré believes, involves no difficulty; the latter does, for scientific explanation proceeds by resolving the complex into the simple and elementary. But how can the scientist know that he has achieved the truly elementary phenomenon? This problem, Poincaré concludes, can also only be resolved by experiment.

The Role of Experiment and Generalization. Experiment is the sole source of truth. It alone can teach us something new; it alone can give us certainty. These are two points that cannot be questioned. But then, if experiment is everything, what place is left for mathematical physics? What can experimental physics do with such an auxiliary —an auxiliary, moreover, which seems useless, and even may be dangerous?

However, mathematical physics exists. It has rendered undeniable service, and that is a fact which has to be explained. It is not sufficient merely to observe; we

The selection is from Henri Poincaré *Science and Hypothesis* (tr. J. Larmor) (New York: The Walter Scott Publishing Co., Ltd., 1905), pp. 140–159, with omissions.

must use our observations, and for that purpose we must generalize. This is what has always been done, only as the recollection of past errors has made man more and more circumspect, he has observed more and more and generalized less and less. Every age has scoffed at its predecessor, accusing it of having generalized too boldly and too naïvely. Descartes used to commiserate the Ionians. Descartes in his turn makes us smile, and no doubt some day our children will laugh at us. Is there no way of getting at once to the gist of the matter, and thereby escaping the raillery which we foresee? Cannot we be content with experiment alone? No, that is impossible; that would be a complete misunderstanding of the true character of science.

The man of science must work with method. Science is built up of facts, as a house is built of stones; but an accumulation of facts is no more a science than a heap of stones is a house. Most important of all, the man of science must exhibit foresight. Carlyle has written somewhere something after this fashion. "Nothing but facts are of importance. John Lackland passed by here. Here is something that is admirable. Here is a reality for which I would give all the theories in the world." Carlyle was a compatriot of Bacon, and, like him, he wished to proclaim his worship of *the God of Things as they are.*

But Bacon would not have said that. That is the language of the historian. The physicist would most likely have said: "John Lackland passed by here. It is all the same to me, for he will not pass this way again."

We all know that there are good and bad experiments. The latter accumulate in vain. Whether there are a hundred or a thousand, one single piece of work by a real master—by a Pasteur, for example—will be sufficient to sweep them into oblivion. Bacon would have thoroughly understood that, for he invented the phrase *experimentum crucis;* but Carlyle would not have understood it. A fact is a fact. A student has read such and such a number on his thermometer. He has taken no precautions. It does not matter; he has read it, and if it is only the fact which counts, this is a reality that is as much entitled to be called a reality as the peregrinations of King John Lackland. What, then, is a good experiment? It is that which teaches us something more than an isolated fact. It is that which enables us to predict, and to generalize. Without generaliza-

tion, prediction is impossible. The circumstances under which one has operated will never again be reproduced simultaneously. The fact observed will never be repeated. All that can be affirmed is that under analogous circumstances an analogous fact will be produced. To predict it, we must therefore invoke the aid of analogy—that is to say, even at this stage, we must generalize. However timid we may be, there must be interpolation. Experiment only gives us a certain number of isolated points. They must be connected by a continuous line, and this is a true generalization. But more is done. The curve thus traced will pass between and near the points observed; it will not pass through the points themselves. Thus we are not restricted to generalizing our experiment, we correct it; and the physicist who would abstain from these corrections, and really content himself with experiment pure and simple, would be compelled to enunciate very extraordinary laws indeed. Detached facts cannot therefore satisfy us, and that is why our science must be ordered, or, better still, generalized.

It is often said that experiments should be made without preconceived ideas. That is impossible. Not only would it make every experiment fruitless, but even if we wished to do so, it could not be done. Every man has his own conception of the world, and this he cannot so easily lay aside. We must, for example, use language, and our language is necessarily steeped in preconceived ideas. Only they are unconscious preconceived ideas, which are a thousand times the most dangerous of all. Shall we say, that if we cause others to intervene of which we are fully conscious, that we shall only aggravate the evil? I do not think so. I am inclined to think that they will serve as ample counterpoises—I was almost going to say antidotes. They will generally disagree, they will enter into conflict one with another, and *ipso facto,* they will force us to look at things under different aspects. This is enough to free us. He is no longer a slave who can choose his master.

Thus, by generalization, every fact observed enables us to predict a large number of others; only, we ought not to forget that the first alone is certain, and that all the others are merely probable. However solidly founded a prediction may appear to us, we are never *absolutely* sure that experiment will not prove it to be baseless if we set to work to verify it. But the probability of its accuracy is often so great that practically we may be content with it. It is far better to predict without certainty, than never to have predicted at all. We should never, therefore, disdain to verify when the opportuniy presents itself. But every experiment is long and difficult, and the laborers are few, and the number of facts which we require to predict is enormous; and besides this mass, the number of direct verifications that we can make will never be more than a negligible quantity. Of this little that we can directly attain we must choose the best. Every experiment must enable us to make a maximum number of predictions having the highest possible degree of probability. The problem is, so to speak, to increase the output of the scientific machine. I may be permitted to compare science to a library which must go on increasing indefinitely; the librarian has limited funds for his purchases,

and he must, therefore, strain every nerve not to waste them. Experimental physics has to make the purchases, and experimental physics alone can enrich the library. As for mathematical physics, her duty is to draw up the catalogue. If the catalogue is well done the library is none the richer for it; but the reader will be enabled to utilize its riches; and also by showing the librarian the gaps in his collection, it will help him to make a judicious use of his funds, which is all the more important, inasmuch as those funds are entirely inadequate. That is the role of mathematical physics. It must direct generalization, so as to increase what I called just now the output of science. By what means it does this, and how it may do it without danger, is what we have now to examine.

The Unity of Nature. Let us first of all observe that every generalization supposes in a certain measure a belief in the unity and simplicity of Nature. As far as the unity is concerned, there can be no difficulty. If the different parts of the universe were not as the organs of the same body, they would not react one upon the other; they would mutually ignore each other, and we in particular should only know one part. We need not, therefore, ask if Nature is one, but how she is one.

As for the second point, that is not so clear. It is not certain that Nature is simple. Can we without danger act as if she were?

There was a time when the simplicity of Mariotte's law was an argument in favor of its accuracy: when Fresnel himself, after having said in a conversation with Laplace that Nature cares naught for analytical difficulties, was compelled to explain his words so as not to give offence to current opinion. Nowadays, ideas have changed considerably; but those who do not believe that natural laws must be simple, are still often obliged to act as if they did believe it. They cannot entirely dispense with this necessity without making all generalization, and therefore all science, impossible. It is clear that any fact can be generalized in an infinite number of ways, and it is a question of choice. The choice can only be guided by considerations of simplicity. Let us take the most ordinary case, that of interpolation. We draw a continuous line as regularly as possible between the points given by observation. Why do we avoid angular points and inflections that are too sharp? Why do we not make our curve describe the most capricious zigzags? It is because we know beforehand, or think we know, that the law we have to express cannot be so complicated as all that. The mass of Jupiter may be deduced either from the movements of his satellites, or from the perturbations of the major planets, or from those of the minor planets. If we take the mean of the determinations obtained by these three methods, we find three numbers very close together, but not quite identical. This result might be interpreted by supposing that the gravitation constant is not the same in the three cases; the observations would be certainly much better represented. Why do we reject this interpretation? Not because it is absurd, but because it is uselessly complicated. We shall only accept it when we are forced to, and it is not imposed upon us yet. To sum up, in most cases every law is held to be simple until the contrary is proved. . . .

No doubt, if our means of investigation became more and more penetrating, we should discover the simple beneath the complex, and then the complex from the simple, and then again the simple beneath the complex, and so on, without ever being able to predict what the last term will be. We must stop somewhere, and for science to be possible we must stop where we have found simplicity. That is the only ground on which we can erect the edifice of our generalizations. But, this simplicity being only apparent, will the ground be solid enough? That is what we have now to discover.

For this purpose let us see what part is played in our generalizations by the belief in simplicity. We have verified a simple law in a considerable number of particular cases. We refuse to admit that this coincidence, so often repeated, is a result of mere chance, and we conclude that the law must be true in the general case.

Kepler remarks that the positions of a planet observed by Tycho are all on the same ellipse. Not for one moment does he think that, by a singular freak of chance, Tycho had never looked at the heavens except at the very moment when the path of the planet happened to cut that ellipse. What does it matter then if the simplicity be real or if it hide a complex truth? Whether it be due to the influence of great numbers which reduces individual differences to a level, or to the greatness or the smallness of certain quantities which allow of certain terms to be neglected—in no case is it due to chance. This simplicity, real or apparent, has always a cause. We shall therefore always be able to reason in the same fashion, and if a simple law has been observed in several particular cases, we may legitimately suppose that it still will be true in analogous cases. To refuse to admit this would be to attribute an inadmissible role to chance. However, there is a difference. If the simplicity were real and profound it would bear the test of the increasing precision of our methods of measurement. If, then, we believe Nature to be profoundly simple, we must conclude that it is an approximate and not a rigorous simplicity. This is what was formerly done, but it is what we have no longer the right to do. The simplicity of Kepler's laws, for instance, is only apparent; but that does not prevent them from being applied to almost all systems analogous to the solar system, though that prevents them from being rigorously exact.

Role of Hypothesis. Every generalization is a hypothesis. Hypothesis therefore plays a necessary role, which no one has ever contested. Only, it should always be as soon as possible submitted to verification. It goes without saying that, if it cannot stand this test, it must be abandoned without any hesitation. This is, indeed, what is generally done; but sometimes with a certain impatience. Ah well! this impatience is not justified. The physicist who has just given up one of his hypotheses should, on the contrary, rejoice, for he found an unexpected opportunity of discovery. His hypothesis, I imagine, had not been lightly adopted. It took into account all the known factors which seem capable of intervention in the phenomenon. If it is not verified, it is because there is something unexpected and extraordinary about it, because we are on the point of finding something unknown and new. Has the hypothesis thus rejected been sterile? Far from it.

It may be even said that it has rendered more service than a true hypothesis. Not only has it been the occasion of a decisive experiment, but if this experiment had been made by chance, without the hypothesis, no conclusion could have been drawn; nothing extraordinary would have been seen; and only one fact the more would have been catalogued, without deducing from it the remotest consequence.

Now, under what conditions is the use of hypothesis without danger? The proposal to submit all to experiment is not sufficient. Some hypotheses are dangerous—first and foremost those which are tacit and unconscious. And since we make them without knowing them, we cannot get rid of them. Here again, there is a service that mathematical physics may render us. By the precision which is its characteristic, we are compelled to formulate all the hypotheses that we would unhesitatingly make without its aid. Let us also notice that it is important not to multiply hypotheses indefinitely. If we construct a theory based upon multiple hypotheses, and if experiment condemns it, which of the premisses must be changed? It is impossible to tell. Conversely, if the experiment succeeds, must we suppose that it has verified all these hypotheses at once? Can several unknowns be determined from a single equation?

We must also take care to distinguish between the different kinds of hypotheses. First of all, there are those which are quite natural and necessary. It is difficult not to suppose that the influence of very distant bodies is quite negligible, that small movements obey a linear law, and that effect is a continuous function of its cause. I will say as much for the conditions imposed by symmetry. All these hypotheses affirm, so to speak, the common basis of all the theories of mathematical physics. They are the last that should be abandoned. There is a second category of hypotheses which I shall qualify as indifferent. In most questions the analyst assumes, at the beginning of his calculations, either that matter is continuous, or the reverse, that it is formed of atoms. In either case, his results would have been the same. On the atomic supposition he has a little more difficulty in obtaining them—that is all. If, then, experiment confirms his conclusions, will he suppose that he has proved, for example, the real existence of atoms? . . .

These indifferent hypotheses are never dangerous provided their characters are not misunderstood. They may be useful, either as articles for calculation, or to assist our understanding by concrete images, to fix the ideas, as we say. They need not therefore be rejected. The hypotheses of the third category are real generalizations. They must be confirmed or invalidated by experiment. Whether verified or condemned, they will always be fruitful; but, for the reasons I have given, they will only be so if they are not too numerous.

Origin of Mathematical Physics. Let us go further and study more closely the conditions which have assisted the development of mathematical physics. We recognize at the outset that the efforts of men of science have always tended to resolve the complex phenomenon given directly by experiment into a very large number of elementary phenomena, and that in three different ways.

First, with respect to time. Instead of embracing in its entirety the progressive development of a phenomenon, we simply try to connect each moment with the one immediately preceding. We admit that the present state of the world only depends on the immediate past, without being directly influenced, so to speak, by the recollection of a more distant past. Thanks to this postulate, instead of studying directly the whole succession of phenomena, we may confine ourselves to writing down its *differential equation;* for the laws of Kepler we substitute the law of Newton.

Next, we try to decompose the phenomena in space. What experiment gives us is a confused aggregate of facts spread over a scene of considerable extent. We must try to deduce the elementary phenomenon, which will still be localized in a very small region of space. . . .

When we have discovered in which direction to seek for the elementary phenomena, by what means may we reach it? . . . Evidently the best means of reaching the elementary phenomenon would be experiment. It would be necessary by experimental artifices to dissociate the complex system which nature offers for our investigations and carefully to study the elements as dissociated as possible; for example, natural white light would be decomposed into monochromatic lights by the aid of the prism, and into polarized lights by the aid of the polarizer. Unfortunately, that is neither always possible nor always sufficient, and sometimes the mind must run ahead of experiment. I shall only give one example which has always struck me rather forcibly. If I decompose white light, I shall be able to isolate a portion of the spectrum, but however small it may be, it will always be a certain width. In the same way the natural lights which are called *monochromatic* gives us a very fine ray, but a ray which is not, however, infinitely fine. It might be supposed that in the experimental study of the properties of these natural lights, by operating with finer and finer rays, and passing on at last to the limit, so to speak, we should eventually obtain the properties of a rigorously monochromatic light. That would not be accurate. I assume that two rays emanate from the same source, that they are first polarized in planes at right angles, that they are then brought back again to the same plane of polarization, and that we try to obtain interference. If the light were *rigorously* monochromatic, there would be interference; but with our nearly monochromatic lights, there will be no interference, and that, however narrow the ray may be. For it to be otherwise, the ray would have to be several million times finer than the finest known rays.

Here then we should be led astray by proceeding to the limit. The mind has to run ahead of the experiment, and if it has done so with success, it is because it has allowed itself to be guided by the instinct of simplicity. The knowledge of the elementary fact enables us to state the problem in the form of an equation. It only remains to deduce from it by combination the observable and verifiable complex fact. That is what we call *integration,* and it is the province of the mathematician. It might be asked, why in physical science generalization so readily takes the mathematical form.

The reason is now easy to see. It is not only because we have to express numerical laws; it is because the observable phenomenon is due to the superposition of a large number of elementary phenomena which are *all similar to each other;* and in this way differential equations are quite naturally introduced. It is not enough that each elementary phenomenon should obey simple laws: all those that we have to combine must obey the same law; then only is the intervention of mathematics of any use. Mathematics teaches us, in fact, to combine like with like. Its object is to divine the result of a combination without having to reconstruct that combination element by element. If we have to repeat the same operation several times, mathematics enables us to avoid this repetition by telling the result beforehand by a kind of induction. This I have explained before in the chapter on mathematical reasoning. But for that purpose all these operations must be similar; in the contrary case we must evidently make up our minds to working them out in full one after the other, and mathematics will be useless. It is therefore, thanks to the approximate homogeneity of the matter studied by physicists, that mathematical physics came into existence. In the natural sciences the following conditions are no longer to be found:—homogeneity, relative independence of remote parts, simplicity of the elementary fact; and that is why the student of natural science is compelled to have recourse to other modes of generalization.

EPISTEMOLOGY

The verification principle, which provides the criterion for meaningful empirical or factual statements, has been mentioned above in the introduction as one of the theses of positivism. Professor A. J. Ayer gives an account of the principle in the following selection. A statement is factually meaningful, he says, if we know what observations would lead us to accept it as true or false. More technically, an experiential proposition is one such "some experiential propositions can be deduced from it in conjunction with certain other premises without being deducible from those other premises alone." From this principle, it follows that metaphysical statements are nonsensical, and also that meaningful empirical statements are best tested for their truth by science.

The concept of truth is the second subject of the selection. Here the question, "What is truth?" needs careful attention, for it is really a request for an analysis and translation. Analysis shows that the phrase "is true" is logically superfluous: to say " 'Queen Anne is dead' is true" is only to assert that Queen Anne is dead. Thus "true" and "false" connote nothing, only functioning as marks of assertion and denial. And this means, finally, that the traditional problem of truth, involving qualities or relations, is a mistaken one.

3   Verifiability and Truth
A. J. Ayer (1910-   )

The criterion which we use to test the genuineness of apparent statements of fact is the criterion of verifiability. We say that a sentence is factually significant to any given person, if, and only if, he knows how to verify the proposition which it purports to express—that is, if he knows what observations would lead him, under certain conditions, to accept the proposition as being true, or reject it as being false. If, on the other hand,

The selection is from A. J. Ayer, *Language, Truth and Logic* (London: Victor Gollancz, Ltd.; New York: Dover Publications, Inc., 1949), pp. 35–37, 38–40, and 87–89. Reprinted by permission of Victor Gollancz, Ltd., and of Dover Publications, Inc.

the putative proposition is of such a character that the assumption of its truth, or falsehood, is consistent with any assumption whatsoever concerning the nature of his future experience, then, as far as he is concerned, it is, if not a tautology, a mere pseudo-proposition. The sentence expressing it may be emotionally significant to him; but it is not literally significant. And with regard to questions the procedure is the same. We enquire in every case what observations would lead us to answer the question, one way or the other; and, if none can be discovered, we must conclude that the sentence under consideration does not, as far as we are concerned, express a genuine question, however strongly its grammatical appearance may suggest that it does.

As the adoption of this procedure is an essential factor in the argument of this book, it needs to be examined in detail.

In the first place, it is necessary to draw a distinction between practical verifiability, and verifiability in principle. Plainly we all understand, in many cases believe, propositions which we have not in fact taken steps to verify. Many of these are propositions which we could verify if we took enough trouble. But there remain a number of significant propositions, concerning matters of fact, which we could not verify even in we chose; simply because we lack the practical means of placing ourselves in the situation where the relevant observations could be made. A simple and familiar example of such a proposition is the proposition that there are mountains on the farther side of the moon.[1] No rocket has yet been invented which would enable me to go and look at the farther side of the moon, so that I am unable to decide the matter by actual observation. But I do know what observations would decide it for me, if, as is theoretically conceivable, I were once in a position to make them. And therefore I say that the proposition is verifiable in principle, if not in practice, and is accordingly significant. On the other hand, such a metaphysical pseudo-proposition as "the Absolute enters into, but is itself incapable of, evolution and progress,"[2] is not even in principle verifiable. For one cannot conceive of an observation which would enable one to determine whether the Absolute did, or did not, enter into evolution and progress. Of course it is possible that the author of such a remark is using English words in a way in which they are not commonly used by English-speaking people, and that he does, in fact, intend to assert something which could be empirically verified. But until he makes us understand how the proposition that he wishes to express would be verified, he fails to communicate anything to us. And if he admits, as I think the author of the remark in question would have admitted, that his words were not intended to express either a tautology or a proposition which was capable, at least in principle, of being verified, then it follows that he has made an utterance which has no literal significance even for himself. . . .

To make our position clearer, we may formulate it in another way. Let us call a proposition which records an actual or possible observation an experimental proposition. Then we may say that it is the mark of a genuine factual proposition, not that it should be equivalent to an experiential proposition, or any finite number of experiential propositions, but simply that some experiential propositions can be deduced from it in conjunction with certain other premises without being deducible from those other premises alone.[3]

This criterion seems liberal enough.

[1] This example has been used by Professor Schlick to illustrate the same point.

[2] A remark taken at random from *Appearance and Reality*, by F. H. Bradley.

[3] This is an over-simplified statement, which is not literally correct. I give what I believe to be the correct formulation in the Introduction, p. 13. [Ayer's reformulation is that a statement is directly verifiable if it is an observation-statement, or is such that, with other observation-statements, it entails at least one observation-statement not deducible from the others alone. *Ed.*]

In contrast to the principle of conclusive verifiability, it clearly does not deny significance to general propositions or to propositions about the past. Let us see what kinds of assertion it rules out.

A good example of the kind of utterance that is condemned by our criterion as being not even false but nonsensical would be the assertion that the world of sense-experience was altogether unreal. It must, of course, be admitted that our senses do sometimes deceive us. We may, as the result of having certain sensations, expect certain other sensations to be obtainable which are, in fact, not obtainable. But, in all such cases, it is further sense-experience that informs us of the mistakes that arise out of sense-experience. We say that the senses sometimes deceive us, just because the expectations to which our sense-experiences give rise do not always accord with what we subsequently experience. That is, we rely on our senses to substantiate or confute the judgements which are based on our sensations. And therefore the fact that our perceptual judgements are sometimes found to be erroneous has not the slightest tendency to show that the world of sense-experience is unreal. And, indeed, it is plain that no conceivable observation, or series of observations, could have any tendency to show that the world revealed to us by sense-experience was unreal. Consequently, anyone who condemns the sensible world as a world of mere appearance, as opposed to reality, is saying something which, according to our criterion of significance, is literally nonsensical.

An example of a controversy which the application of our criterion obliges us to condemn as fictitious is provided by those who dispute concerning the number of substances that there are in the world. For it is admitted both by monists, who maintain that reality is one substance, and by pluralists, who maintain that reality is many, that it is impossible to imagine any empirical situation which would be relevant to the solution of their dispute. But if we are told that no possible observation could give any probability either to the assertion that reality was one substance or to the assertion that it was many, then we must conclude that neither assertion is significant. We shall see later on that there are genuine logical and empirical questions involved in the dispute between monists and pluralists. But the metaphysical question concerning "substance" is ruled out by our criterion as spurious. . . .

We have already remarked that all questions of the form, "What is the nature of *x*?" are requests for a definition of a symbol in use, and that to ask for a definition of a symbol *x* in use is to ask how the sentences in which *x* occurs are to be translated into equivalent sentences, which do not contain *x* or any of its synonyms. Applying this to the case of "truth" we find that to ask, "What is truth?" is to ask for such a translation of the sentence "(the proposition) *p* is true."

It may be objected here that we are ignoring the fact that it is not merely propositions that can be said to be true or false, but also statements and assertions and judgements and assumptions and opinions and beliefs. But the answer to this is that to say that a belief, or a statement, or a judgement, is true is always an elliptical way of ascribing truth to a proposition, which is believed, or stated, or judged. Thus, if I say that the Marxist's belief that capitalism leads to war is true, what I am saying is that the proposition, believed by Marxists, that capitalism leads to war is true; and the illustration holds good when the word "opinion" or "assumption," or any of the others in the list, is substituted for the word "belief." And, further, it must be made clear that we are not hereby committing ourselves to the metaphysical doctrine that propositions are real entities.[4] Regarding classes as a species of logical constructions, we may define a proposition as a class of sentences which have the same intensional significance for anyone who understands them. Thus, the sentences, "I am ill," "Ich bin krank," "Je suis malade," are all elements of the proposition "I am ill." And what we have previously said about logical constructions should make it clear that we are not asserting that a proposition is a collection of sentences, but rather that to speak about a given proposition is a way of speaking about certain sentences, just as to speak about sentences, in this usage, is a way of speaking about particular signs.

Reverting to the analysis of truth, we find that in all sentences of the form "p is true," the phrase "is true" is logically superfluous. When, for example, one says that the proposition "Queen Anne is dead" is true, all that one is saying is that Queen Anne is dead. And similarly, when one says that the proposition "Oxford is the capital of England" is false, all that one is saying is that Oxford is not the capital of England. Thus, to say that a proposition is true is just to assert it, and to say that it is false is just to assert its contradictory. And this indicates that

the terms "true" and "false" connote nothing, but function in the sentence simply as marks of assertion and denial. And in that case there can be no sense in asking us to analyse the concept of "truth."

This point seems almost too obvious to mention, yet the preoccupation of philosophers with the "problem of truth" shows that they have overlooked it. Their excuse is that references to truth generally occur in sentences whose grammatical forms suggest that the word "true" does stand for a genuine quality or relation. And a superficial consideration of these sentences might lead one to suppose that there was something more in the question "What is truth?" than a demand for the analysis of the sentence "p is true." But when one comes to analyse the sentences in question, one always finds that they contain sub-sentences of the form "p is true" or "p is false," and that when they are translated in such a way as to make these sub-sentences explicit, they contain no other mention of truth. Thus, to take two typical examples, the sentence "A proposition is not made true by being believed" is equivalent to "for no value of p or x, is 'p is true' entailed by 'x believes p' ": and the sentence "Truth is sometimes stranger than fiction" is equivalent to "There are values of p and q such that p is true and q is false and p is more surprising than q." And the same result would be yielded by any other example one cared to take. In every case the analysis of the sentence would confirm our assumption that the question "What is truth?" is reducible to the question "What is the analysis of the sentence 'p is true'?" And it is plain that this question raises no genuine problem, since we

---

[4] For a criticism of this doctrine, see G. Ryle, "Are there propositions?" *Aristotelian Society Proceedings, 1929–30.*

have shown that to say that p is true is simply a way of asserting p.[5]

We conclude, then, that there is no problem of truth as it is ordinarily conceived. The traditional conception of truth as a "real quality" or a "real relation" is due, like most philosophical mistakes, to a failure to analyse sentences correctly. There are sentences, such as the two we have just analysed, in which the word "truth" seems to stand for something real; and this leads the speculative philosopher to enquire what this "something" is. Naturally he fails to obtain a satisfactory answer, since his question is illegitimate. For our analysis has shown that the word "truth" does not stand for anything, in the way which such a question requires.

[5] Cf. F. P. Ramsey on "Facts and Propositions," *The Foundations of Mathematics*, pp. 142–143.

METAPHYSICS

Positivism rests on the claim that science has an unlimited field of inquiry, that all facts are scientific facts, and that a complete interpretation of the universe is the goal of scientific activity. Karl Pearson, English mathematician and scientist, develops this claim in the following selection. The formal validity of a scientific conception, he writes, is determined by its self-consistency and by its deducibility from the perceptions of a normal human being. The material of science is coextensive with the universe in the sense that all things are open to scientific inquiry.

These assertions lead Pearson to hold that no discipline is exempt from scientific controls, even though it may claim a knowledge superior to science. In particular he discusses metaphysics, which he compares to poetry as an imaginative activity. Yet the metaphysician is really more dangerous than the poet because he makes truth claims for his visions. Pearson believes that the metaphysician is a sinister member of the community, and he concludes by stating that science rather than philosophy offers the better training for modern citizenship.

4 The Rejection of Metaphysics

Karl Pearson (1857-1936)

The reader may perhaps feel that I am laying stress upon *method* at the expense of material content. Now this is the peculiarity of scientific method, that when once it has become a habit of

The selection is from Karl Pearson, *The Grammar of Science* (London: Adam and Charles Black, 1900), pp. 12–14, 53–55, and 14–19.

mind, that mind converts *all* facts whatsoever into science. The field of science is unlimited; its material is endless, every group of natural phenomena, every phase of social life, every stage of past or present development is material for science. *The unity of all science consists alone in its method, not in its material.* The man who classifies facts of any kind whatever, who sees their mutual relation and describes their sequences, is applying the scientific method and is a man of science. The facts may belong to the past history of mankind, to the social statistics of our great cities, to the atmosphere of the most distant stars, to the digestive organs of a worm, or to the life of a scarcely visible bacillus. It is not the facts themselves which form science, but the method in which they are dealt with. The material of science is coextensive with the whole physical universe, not only that universe as it now exists, but with its past history and the past history of all life therein. When every fact, every present or past phenomenon of that universe, every phase of present or past life therein, has been examined, classified, and co-ordinated with the rest, then the mission of science will be completed. What is this but saying that the task of science can never end till man ceases to be, till history is no longer made, and development itself ceases?

It might be supposed that science has made such strides in the last two centuries, and notably in the last fifty years, that we might look forward to a day when its work would be practically accomplished. At the beginning of this century it was possible for an Alexander von Humboldt to take a survey to the entire domain of then extant science. Such a survey would be impossible for any scientist now, even if gifted with more than Humboldt's powers. Scarcely any specialist of today is really master of all the work which has been done in his own comparatively small field. Facts and their classification have been accumulating at such a rate, that nobody seems to have leisure to recognize the relations of sub-groups to the whole. It is as if individual workers in both Europe and America were bringing their stones to one great building and piling them on and cementing them together without regard to any general plan or to their individual neighbor's work; only where some one has placed a great cornerstone, is it regarded, and the building then rises on this firmer foundation more rapidly than at other points, till it reaches a height at which it is stopped for want of side support. Yet this great structure, the proportions of which are beyond the ken of any individual man, possesses a symmetry and unity of its own, notwithstanding its haphazard mode of construction. This symmetry and unity lie in scientific method. The smallest group of facts, if properly classified and logically dealt with, will form a stone which has its proper place in the great building of knowledge, wholly independent of the individual workman who has shaped it. Even when two men work unwittingly at the same stone they will but modify and correct each other's angles. In the face of all this enormous progress of modern science, when in all civilized lands men are applying the scientific method to natural, historical, and mental facts, we have yet to admit that the goal of science is and must be infinitely distant.

For we must note that when from a sufficient if partial classification of facts a simple principle has been discovered which describes the relationship and sequences of any group, then this principle or law itself generally leads to the discovery of a still wider range of hitherto unregarded phenomena in the same or associated fields. Every great advance of science opens our eyes to facts which we had failed before to observe, and makes new demands on our powers of interpretation. This extension of the material of science into regions where our great-grandfathers could see nothing at all, or where they would have declared human knowledge impossible, is one of the most remarkable features of modern progress. Where they interpreted the motion of the planets of our own system, we discuss the chemical constitution of stars, many of which did not exist for them, for their telescopes could not reach them. Where they discovered the circulation of the blood, we see the physical conflict of living poisons within the blood, whose battles would have been absurdities for them. Where they found void and probably demonstrated to their own satisfaction that there was void, we conceive great systems in rapid motion capable of carrying energy through brick walls as light passes through glass. Great as the advance of scientific knowledge has been, it has not been greater than the growth of the material to be dealt with. The goal of science is clear—it is nothing short of the complete interpretation of the universe. But the goal is an ideal one—it marks the *direction* in which we move and strive, but never a stage we shall actually reach. The universe grows ever larger as we learn to understand more of our own corner of it. . . .

In order that a conception may have scientific validity, it must be self-consistent, and deducible from the perceptions of the normal human being. For instance, a centaur is not a self-consistent conception; as soon as our knowledge of human and equine anatomy became sufficiently developed, the centaur became an unthinkable thing—a self-negating idea. As the man-horse is seen to be a compound ble of sense-impressions, which are ir-

reconcilable anatomically, so the man-god, whose cruder type is Hercules, is also seen to be a chimera, a self-contradictory conception, as soon as we have clearly defined the physical and mental characteristics of man. But even if an individual mind has reached a conception, which at any rate for that mind is perfectly self-consistent, it does not follow that such a conception must have scientific validity, except as far as science may be concerned with the analysis of that individual mind. When a person conceives that one color—green—suffices to describe the flowers and leaves of a rose-tree in my garden, I know that his conception may, after all, be self-consistent, it may be in perfect harmony with his sense-impressions. I merely assert that his perceptive faculty is *abnormal,* and hold him to be color-blind. I may study the individual abnormality scientifically, but his conception has no scientific validity, for it is not deducible from the perceptions of the normal human being. Here indeed we have to proceed very cautiously if we are to determine what self-consistent conceptions have scientific validity. Above all, we must note that a conception does not cease to be valid because it has not been deduced by the majority of normal human beings from their perceptions. The conception that a new individual will originate from the union of a male and female cell may never have actually been deduced by a majority of normal human beings from their perceptions. But if any normal human being be trained in the proper methods of observation, and be placed in the right circumstances for investigating, he will draw from his perceptions this conception and not its negation. It is in this sense, therefore, that we are to understand the assertion that a conception to have scientific validity must be *deducible* from the perceptions of the normal human being.

The preceding paragraph shows us how important it is that the observations and experiments of science should be repeated as often and by as many observers as possible, in order to ensure that we are dealing with what has validity for all normal human beings, and not with the result of an abnormal perceptive faculty. It is not only, however, in experiments or observations which can be repeated easily, but still more in those which it is very difficult or impossible to repeat, that a great weight of responsibility lies upon the recorder and the public which is called upon to accept his results. An event may have occurred in the presence of a limited number of observers. That the event itself cannot recur, and that it is totally out of accord with our customary experience, are not in themselves sufficient grounds for disregarding it scientifically. Yet what an onus is laid on the individual observers to test whether their perceptive faculties were normal on the occasion, and whether their conceptions of what took place were justified by their perceptions! Still greater onus is laid on men at large to criticize and probe the evidence given by such observers, to question whether they were men trained to observe, and calm and collected at the time of the reported event. Were they not, perhaps, in an exalted state of mind, biassed by preconceptions or hindered by the physical surroundings from clear perception? In short, were or were not their perceptive faculties in a normal condition, and were or were not the circumstances such that normal perception was possible? It can

scarcely be questioned that when the truth or falsehood of an event or observation may have important bearings on conduct, over-doubt is more socially valuable than over-credulity. In an age like our own, which is essentially an age of scientific inquiry, the prevalence of doubt and criticism ought not to be regarded with despair or as a sign of decadence. It is one of the safeguards of progress;—*la critique est la vie de la science* [criticism is the life of science], I must again repeat. One of the most fatal (and not so impossible) features for science would be the institution of a scientific hierarchy which would brand as heretical all doubt as to its conclusions, all criticism of its results. . . .

Now I want to draw the reader's attention to two results which flow from the above considerations, namely: that the material of science is coextensive with the whole life, physical and mental, of the universe, and furthermore that the limits to our perception of the universe are only apparent, not real. It is no exaggeration to say that the universe was not the same for our great-grandfathers as it is for us, and that in all probability it will be utterly different for our great-grandchildren. The universe is a variable quantity, which depends upon the keenness and structure of our organs of sense, and upon the fineness of our powers and instruments of observation. We shall see more clearly the important bearing of this latter remark when we come to discuss more closely in another chapter how the universe is largely the construction of each individual mind. For the present we must briefly consider the former remark, which defines the unlimited scope of science. To say that there are certain fields—for example, *metaphysics*—from which science is excluded, wherein its methods have no application, is merely to say that the rules of methodical observation and the laws of logical thought do not apply to the facts, if any, which lie within such fields. These fields, if indeed such exist, must lie outside any intelligible definition which can be given of the word *knowledge.* If there are facts, and sequences to be observed among those facts, then we have all the requisites of scientific classification and knowledge. If there are no facts, or no sequences to be observed among them, then the possibility of *all* knowledge disappears. The greatest assumption of everyday life—the inference which the metaphysicians tell us is wholly beyond science—namely, that other beings have consciousness as well as ourselves, seems to have just as much or as little *scientific* validity as the statement that an earth-grown apple would fall to the ground if carried to the planet of another star. Both are beyond the range of experimental demonstration, but to assume uniformity in the characteristics of brain "matter" under certain conditions seems as scientific as to assume uniformity in the characteristics of stellar "matter." Both are only working hypotheses and valuable in so far as they simplify our description of the universe. Yet the distinction between science and metaphysics is often insisted upon, and not unadvisedly, by the devotees of both. If we take any group of physical or biological facts—say, for example, electrical phenomena or the development of the ovum—we shall find that, though physicists or biologists may differ to some extent in their measurements or in their hypotheses, yet in the fundamental principles and sequences the professors

of each individual science are in practical agreement among themselves. A similar if not yet so complete agreement is rapidly springing up in both mental and social science, where the facts are more difficult to classify and the bias of individual opinion is much stronger. Our more thorough classification, however, of the facts of human development, our more accurate knowledge of the early history of human societies, of primitive customs, laws, and religions, our application of the principle of natural selection to man and his communities, are converting anthropology, folklore, sociology, and psychology into true sciences. We begin to see indisputable sequences in groups of both mental and social facts. The causes which favor the growth or decay of human societies become more obvious and more the subject of scientific investigation. Mental and social facts are thus not beyond the range of scientific treatment, but their classification has not been so complete, nor for obvious reasons so unprejudiced, as those of physical or biological phenomena.

The case is quite different with metaphysics and those other supposed branches of human knowledge which claim exemption from scientific control. Either they are based on an accurate classification of facts, or they are not. But if their classification of facts were accurate, the application of the scientific method ought to lead their professors to a practically identical system. Now one of the idiosyncrasies of metaphysicians lies in this: that each metaphysician has his own system, which to a large extent excludes that of his predecessors and colleagues. Hence we must conclude that metaphysics are built either on air or on quicksands—either they start from no foundation in facts at all, or the superstructure has been raised before a basis has been found in the accurate classification of facts. I want to lay special stress on this point. There is no short cut to truth, no way to gain a knowledge of the universe except through the gateway of scientific method. The hard and stony path of classifying facts and reasoning upon them is the only way to ascertain truth. It is the reason and not the imagination which must ultimately be appealed to. The poet may give us in sublime language an account of the origin and purport of the universe, but in the end it will not satisfy our esthetic judgment, our idea of harmony and beauty, like the few facts which the scientist may venture to tell us in the same field. The one will agree with all our experiences past and present, the other is sure, sooner or later, to contradict our observation because it propounds a dogma, where we are yet far from knowing the whole truth. Our esthetic judgment demands harmony between the representation and the represented, and in this sense science is often more artistic than modern art.

The poet is a valued member of the community, for he is known to be a poet; his value will increase as he grows to recognize the deeper insight into nature with which modern science provides him. The metaphysician is a poet, often a very great one, but unfortunately he is not known to be a poet, because he strives to clothe his poetry in the language of reason, and hence it follows that he is liable to be a dangerous member of the community. The danger at the present time that metaphysical dogmas may check scientific research is, perhaps,

not very great. The day has gone by when the Hegelian philosophy threatened to strangle infant science in Germany;—that it begins to languish at Oxford is a proof that it is practically dead in the country of its birth. The day has gone by when philosophical or theological dogmas of any kind can throw back for generations the progress of scientific investigation. There is no restriction now on research in any field, or on the publication of the truth when it has been reached. But there is nevertheless a danger which we cannot afford to disregard, a danger which retards the spread of scientific knowledge among the unenlightened, and which flatters obscurantism by discrediting the scientific method. There is a certain school of thought which finds the laborious process by which science reaches truth too irksome; the temperament of this school is such that it demands a short and easy cut to knowledge, where knowledge can only be gained, if at all, by the long and patient toiling of many groups of workers, perhaps through several centuries. There are various fields at the present day wherein mankind is ignorant, and the honest course for us is simply to confess our ignorance. This ignorance may arise from the want of any proper classification of facts, or because supposed facts are themselves inconsistent, unreal creations of untrained minds. But because this ignorance is frankly admitted by science, an attempt is made to fence off these fields as ground which science cannot profitably till, to shut them up as a preserve whereon science has no business to trespass. Wherever science has succeeded in ascertaining the truth, there, according to the school we have referred to, are the "legitimate problems of science." Wherever science is yet ignorant, there, we are told, its method is inapplicable; there some other relation than cause and effect (than the same sequence recurring with the like grouping of phenomena), some new but undefined relationship rules. In these fields, we are told, problems become philosophical and can only be treated by the method of philosophy. The philosophical method is opposed to the scientific method; and here, I think, the danger I have referred to arises. We have defined the scientific method to consist in the orderly classification of facts followed by the recognition of their relationship and recurring sequences. The scientific judgment is the judgment based upon this recognition and free from personal bias. If this were the philosophical method there would be no need of further discussion, but as we are told the subject matter of philosophy is not the "legitimate problem of science," the two methods are presumably not identical. Indeed the philosophical method seems based upon an analysis which does not start with the classification of facts, but reaches its judgments by some obscure process of internal cogitation. It is therefore dangerously liable to the influence of individual bias; it results, as experience shows us, in an endless number of competing and contradictory systems. It is because the so-called philosophical method does not, when different individuals approach the same range of facts, lead, like the scientific, to practical unanimity of judgment, that science, rather than philosophy, offers the better training for modern citizenship.

ETHICS

In the following selection, Professor Charles L. Stevenson turns to the problem of value, particularly ethical value. He describes his task as a philosopher to be analysis and clarification of ethical questions such as, "Is X good?" and he lays down certain conditions to be met by his analysis. It must account for ethical disagreement, show the connection between ethical judgments and action, and be so stated that goodness is not verifiable by science (as he says, "ethics is not psychology").

Two uses of language must be distinguished: a descriptive use that expresses belief, and a dynamical use that is related to interests, attitudes, and emotions. Ethical judgments belong to the second group, for their major use is to suggest, to create an influence on the hearer of the judgment. To speak or ask about the goodness of anything, then, is to ask about its influence relative to human interests. Incidentally, it is because of this emphasis on influence rather than the description found in traditional interest theories that Stevenson rejects them. The language of ethics, therefore, is one of persuasion; and ethical disagreements are disagreements in attitude, not in belief. Stevenson's subtle analysis reflects the positivist position, but it also looks forward to the view of philosophy we shall consider in the next part.

5 Ethics as Emotive

Charles L. Stevenson (1908-   )

Ethical questions first arise in the form "Is so and so good?" or "Is this alternative better than that?" These questions are difficult partly because we don't quite know what we are seeking. We are asking, "Is there a needle in that haystack?" without even knowing just what a needle is. So the first thing to do is to examine the questions themselves. We must try to make them clearer, either by defining the terms in which they are expressed, or by any other method that is available.

The present paper is concerned wholly with this preliminary step of making ethical questions clear. In order to help answer the question "Is X good?" we must *substitute* for it a question which is free from ambiguity and confusion.

It is obvious that in substituting a clearer question we must not introduce some utterly different kind of question. It won't do (to take an extreme instance of a prevalent fallacy) to substitute for "Is X good?" the question "Is X pink with yellow trimmings?" and then point out how easy the question really is. This would beg the original question, not help answer it. On the other hand, we must not expect the substituted question to be strictly "identical" with the original one. The original question may embody hypostatization, anthropomorphism, vague-

ness, and all the other ills to which our ordinary discourse is subject. If our substituted question is to be clearer, it must remove these ills. The questions will be identical only in the sense that a child is identical with the man he later becomes. Hence we must not demand that the substitution strike us, on immediate introspection, as making no change in meaning.

Just how, then, must the substituted question be related to the original? Let us assume (inaccurately) that it must result from replacing "good" by some set of terms which define it. The question then resolves itself to this: How must the defined meaning of "good" be related to its original meaning?

I answer that it must be *relevant*. A defined meaning will be called "relevant" to the original meaning under these circumstances: Those who have understood the definition must be able to say all that they then want to say by using the term in the defined way. They must never have occasion to use the term in the old, unclear sense. (If a person did have to go on using the word in the old sense, then to this extent his meaning would not be clarified, and the philosophical task would not be completed.) It frequently happens that a word is used so confusedly and ambiguously that we must give it *several* defined meanings, rather than one. In this case only the whole set of defined meanings will be called "relevant," and any one of them will be called "partially relevant." This is not a rigorous treatment of *relevance*,

The selection is from C. L. Stevenson, "The Emotive Meaning of Ethical Terms," *Mind,* 46 (1937), pp. 14–16 and 18–30, with omissions. Used by permission of the Editor and the author.

by any means; but it will serve for the present purposes.

Let us now turn to our particular task —that of giving a relevant definition of "good.". . .

There are certain requirements, however, with which this "vital" sense has been expected to comply—requirements which appeal strongly to our common sense. It will be helpful to summarize these. . . .

In the first place, we must be able sensibly to *disagree* about whether something is "good." This condition rules out Hobbes's definition. For consider the following argument: "This is good." "That isn't so; it's not good." As translated by Hobbes, this becomes: "I desire this." "That isn't so, for *I* don't." The speakers are not contradicting one another, and think they are, only because of an elementary confusion in the use of pronouns. The definition, "good" means *desired by my community,* is also excluded, for how could people from different communities disagree?

In the second place, "goodness" must have, so to speak, a magnetism. A person who recognizes X to be "good" must *ipso facto* acquire a stronger tendency to act in its favor than he otherwise would have had. This rules out the Humian type of definition. For according to Hume, to recognize that something is "good" is simply to recognize that the majority approve of it. Clearly, a man may see that the majority approve of X without having, himself, a stronger tendency to favor it. This requirement excludes any attempt to define "good" in terms of the interest of people *other* than the speaker.

In the third place, the "goodness" of anything must not be verifiable solely by use of the scientific method. "Ethics must not be psychology." This restriction rules out all of the traditional interest theories, without exception. . . .

Let us now turn to my own analysis of ethical judgments. First let me present my position dogmatically, showing to what extent I vary from tradition.

I believe that the three requirements, given above, are perfectly sensible; that there is some *one* sense of "good" which satisfies all three requirements; and that no traditional interest theory satisfies them all. But this does not imply that "good" must be explained in terms of a Platonic Idea, or of a Categorical Imperative, or of an unique, unanalyzable property. On the contrary, the three requirements can be met by a *kind* of interest theory. *But we must give up a presupposition which all the traditional interest theories have made.*

Traditional interest theories hold that ethical statements are *descriptive* of the existing state of interest—that they simply *give information* about interests. (More accurately, ethical judgments are said to describe what the state of interests is, was, or will be, or to indicate what the state of interests *would* be under specified circumstances.) It is this emphasis on description, on information, which leads to their incomplete relevance. Doubtless there is always *some* element of description in ethical judgments, but this is by no means all. Their major use is not to indicate facts, but to *create an influence.* Instead of merely describing people's interests, they *change* or *intensify* them. They *recommend* an interest in an object, rather than state that the interest already exists. . . .

Thus ethical terms are *instruments* used in the complicated interplay and readjustment of human interests. This can be seen plainly from more general observations. People from widely separated communities have different moral attitudes. Why? To a great extent because they have been subject to different social influences. Now clearly this influence doesn't operate through sticks and stones alone; words play a great part. People praise one another, to encourage certain inclinations, and blame one another, to discourage others. Those of forceful personalities issue commands which weaker people, for complicated instinctive reasons, find it difficult to disobey, quite apart from fears of consequences. Further influence is brought to bear by writers and orators. Thus social influence is exerted, to an enormous extent, by means that have nothing to do with physical force or material reward. The ethical terms facilitate such influence. Being suited for use in *suggestion,* they are a means by which men's attitudes may be led this way or that. The reason, then, that we find a greater similarity in the moral attitudes of one community than in those of different communities is largely this: ethical judgments propagate themselves. One man says "This is good"; this may influence the approval of another person, who then makes the same ethical judgment, which in turn influences another person, and so on. In the end, by a process of mutual influence, people take up more or less the same attitudes. Between people of widely separated communities, of course, the influence is less strong; hence different communities have different attitudes.

These remarks will serve to give a general idea of my point of view. We must now go into more detail. There are several questions which must be answered: How does an ethical sentence acquire its power of influencing people —why is it suited to suggestion? Again, what has this influence to do with the *meaning* of ethical terms? And finally, do these considerations really lead us to a sense of "good" which meets the requirements mentioned in the preceding section?

Let us deal first with the question about *meaning.* This is far from an easy question, so we must enter into a preliminary inquiry about meaning in general. Although a seeming digression, this will prove indispensable.

Broadly speaking, there are two different *purposes* which lead us to use language. On the one hand we use words (as in science) to record, clarify, and communicate *beliefs.* On the other hand we use words to give vent to our feelings (interjections), or to create moods (poetry), or to incite people to actions or attitudes (oratory).

The first use of words I shall call "descriptive"; the second, "dynamic." Note that the distinction depends solely upon the *purpose* of the *speaker.*

When a person says "Hydrogen is the lightest known gas," his purpose *may* be simply to lead the hearer to believe this, or to believe that the speaker believes it. In that case the words are used descriptively. When a person cuts himself and says "Damn," his purpose is not ordinarily to record, clarify, or communicate any belief. The word is used dynamically. The two ways of using words, however, are by no means mutually exclusive. This is obvious from the fact that our purposes are often complex. Thus when one says "I want you to close the door," part of his purpose, ordinarily, is to lead the hearer to believe that he has this want. To that extent the words are used descriptively. But the major part of one's purpose is to lead the hearer to *satisfy* the want. To that extent the words are used dynamically. . . .

We must now proceed to an important question: What has the dynamic use of words to do with their *meaning?* One thing is clear—we must not define "meaning" in a way that would make meaning vary with dynamic usage. If we did, we should have no use for the term. All that we could say about such "meaning" would be that it is very complicated, and subject to constant change. So we must certainly distinguish between the dynamic use of words and their meaning. . . .

There will be a kind of meaning, however, in the sense above defined, which has an intimate relation to dynamic usage. I refer to "emotive" meaning (in a sense roughly like that employed by Ogden and Richards).[1] The emotive meaning of a word is a tendency of a word, arising through the history of its usage, to produce (result from) *affective* responses in people. It is the immediate aura of feeling which hovers about a word. Such tendencies to produce affective responses cling to words very tenaciously. It would be difficult, for instance, to express merriment by using the interjection "alas." Because of the persistence of such affective tendencies (among other reasons) it becomes feasible to classify them as "meanings."

Just *what* is the relation between emotive meaning and the dynamic use of words? Let us take an example. Suppose

that a man is talking with a group of people which includes Miss Jones, age 59. He refers to her, without thinking, as an "old maid." Now even if his purposes are perfectly innocent—even if he is using the words purely descriptively—Miss Jones won't think so. She will think he is encouraging the others to have contempt for her, and will draw in her skirts, defensively. The man might have done better if instead of saying "old maid" he had said "elderly spinster." The latter words could have been put to the same descriptive use, and would not so readily have caused suspicions about the dynamic use.

"Old maid" and "elderly spinster" differ, to be sure, only in emotive meaning. From the example it will be clear that certain words, because of their emotive meaning, are suited to a certain kind of dynamic use—so well suited, in fact, that the hearer is likely to be misled when we use them in any other way. The more pronounced a word's emotive meaning is, the less likely people are to use it purely descriptively. Some words are suited to encourage people, some to discourage them, some to quiet them, and so on.

Even in these cases, of course, the dynamic purposes are not to be identified with any sort of meaning; for the emotive meaning accompanies a word much more persistently than do the dynamic purposes. But there is an important contingent relation between emotive meaning and dynamic purpose: the former assists the latter. Hence if we define emotively laden terms in a way that neglects their emotive meaning, we are likely to be confusing. *We lead people to think that the terms defined are used dynamically less often than they are.*

---

[1] See *The Meaning of Meaning,* by C. K. Ogden and I. A. Richards.

Let us now apply these remarks in defining "good." This word may be used morally or non-morally. I shall deal with the non-moral usage almost entirely, but only because it is simpler. The main points of the analysis will apply equally well to either usage.

As a preliminary definition, let us take an inaccurate approximation. It may be more misleading than helpful, but will do to begin with. Roughly, then, the sentence "X is good" means *We like X.* ("We" includes the hearer or hearers.)

At first glance this definition sounds absurd. If used, we should expect to find the following sort of conversation: A. "This is good." B. "But I *don't* like it. What led you to believe that I did?" The unnaturalness of B's reply, judged by ordinary word-usage, would seem to cast doubt on the relevance of my definition.

B's unnaturalness, however, lies simply in this: he is assuming that "We like it" (as would occur implicitly in the use of "good") is being used descriptively. This won't do. When "We like it" is to take the place of "This is good," the former sentence must be used not purely descriptively, but dynamically. More specifically, it must be used to promote a very subtle (and for the non-moral sense in question, a very easily resisted) kind of *suggestion.* To the extent that "we" refers to the hearer, it must have the dynamic use, essential to suggestion, of leading the hearer to *make* true what is said, rather than merely to believe it. And to the extent that "we" refers to the speaker, the sentence must have not only the descriptive use of indicating belief about the speaker's interest, but the quasi-interjectory, dynamic function of giving direct expression to the interest. (This immediate expression of feelings assists in the process of suggestion. It is difficult to disapprove in the face of another's enthusiasm.)

For an example of a case where "We like this" is used in the dynamic way that "This is good" is used, consider the case of a mother who says to her several children, "One thing is certain, *we all like to be neat.*" If she really believed this, she wouldn't bother to say so. But she is not using the words descriptively. She is *encouraging* the children to like neatness. By telling them that they like neatness, she will lead them to *make* her statement true, so to speak. If, instead of saying "We all like to be neat" in this way, she had said "It's a good thing to be neat," the effect would have been approximately the same.

But these remarks are still misleading. Even when "We like it" is used for suggestion, it isn't quite like "This is good." The latter is more subtle. With such a sentence as "This is a good book," for example, it would be practically impossible to use instead "We like this book." When the latter is used, it must be accompanied by so exaggerated an intonation, to prevent its becoming confused with a descriptive statement, that the force of suggestion becomes stronger, and ludicrously more overt, than when "good" is used.

The definition is inadequate, further, in that the definiens has been restricted to dynamic usage. Having said that dynamic usage was different from meaning, I should not have to mention it in giving the *meaning* of "good."

It is in connection with this last point that we must return to emotive meaning. The word "good" has a pleasing emotive meaning which fits it especially for the dynamic use of suggesting favorable interest. But the sentence "We like it" has no such emotive meaning. Hence my definition has neglected emotive meaning entirely. Now to neglect emotive meaning is likely to lead to endless confusions, as we shall presently see; so I have sought to make up for the inadequacy of the definition by letting the restriction about dynamic usage take the place of emotive meaning. What I should do, of course, is to find a definiens whose emotive meaning, like that of "good," simply does *lead* to dynamic usage.

Why didn't I do this? I answer that it isn't possible, if the definition is to afford us increased clarity. No two words, in the first place, have quite the same emotive meaning. The most we can hope for is a rough approximation. But if we seek for such an approximation for "good," we shall find nothing more than synonyms, such as "desirable" or "valuable"; and these are profitless because they do not clear up the connection between "good" and favorable interest. If we reject such synonyms, in favor of non-ethical terms, we shall be highly misleading. For instance: "This is good" has something like the meaning of "I *do* like this; do so as well." But this is certainly not accurate. For the imperative makes an appeal to the conscious efforts of the hearer. Of course he can't like something just by trying. He must be led to like it through suggestion. Hence an ethical sentence differs from an imperative in that it enables one to make changes in a much more subtle, less fully conscious way. Note that the ethical sentence centers the hearer's attention not on his interest, but on the object of interests, and thereby facilitates suggestion. Because of its subtlety,

moreover, an ethical sentence readily permits counter-suggestion, and leads to the give and take situation which is so characteristic of arguments about values.

Strictly speaking, then, it is impossible to define "good" in terms of favorable interest if emotive meaning is not to be distorted. Yet it is possible to say that "This is good" is *about* the favorable interest of the speaker and the hearer or hearers, and that it has a pleasing emotive meaning which fits the words for use in suggestion. This is a rough description of meaning, not a definition. But it serves the same clarifying function that a definition ordinarily does; and that, after all, is enough.

A word must be added about the moral use of "good." This differs from the above in that it is about a different kind of interest. Instead of being about what the hearer and speaker *like,* it is about a stronger sort of approval. When a person *likes* something, he is pleased when it prospers, and disappointed when it doesn't. When a person *morally approves* of something, he experiences a rich feeling of security when it prospers, and is indignant, or "shocked" when it doesn't. These are rough and inaccurate examples of the many factors which one would have to mention in distinguishing the two kinds of interest. In the moral usage, as well as in the non-moral, "good" has an emotive meaning which adapts it to suggestion.

And now, are these considerations of any importance? Why do I stress emotive meanings in this fashion? Does the omission of them really lead people into errors? I think, indeed, that the errors resulting from such omissions are enormous. In order to see this, however, we must return to the restrictions, mentioned in [the beginning], with which the "vital" sense of "good" has been expected to comply.

The first restriction, it will be remembered, had to do with disagreement. Now there is clearly some sense in which people disagree on ethical points; but we must not rashly assume that all disagreement is modelled after the sort that occurs in the natural sciences. We must distinguish between "disagreement in belief" (typical of the sciences) and "disagreement in interest." Disagreement in belief occurs when A believes p and B disbelieves it. Disagreement in interest occurs when A has a favorable interest in X, when B has an unfavorable one in it, and when neither is content to let the other's interest remain unchanged.

Let me give an example of disagreement in interest. A. "Let's go to a cinema tonight." B. "I don't want to do that. Let's go to the symphony." A continues to insist on the cinema, B on the symphony. This is disagreement in a perfectly conventional sense. They can't agree on where they want to go, and each is trying to redirect the other's interest. (Note that imperatives are used in the example.)

It is disagreement in *interest* which takes place in ethics. When C says "This is good," and D says "No, it's bad," we have a case of suggestion and counter-suggestion. Each man is trying to redirect the other's interest. There obviously need be no domineering, since each may be willing to give ear to the other's influence; but each is trying to move the other none the less. It is in this sense that they disagree. Those who argue that certain interest theories make no provision for disagreement have been misled, I believe, simply because the traditional

theories, in leaving out emotive meaning, give the impression that ethical judgments are used descriptively only; and of course when judgments are used purely descriptively, the only disagreement that can arise is disagreement *in belief*. Such disagreement may be disagreement in belief *about* interests; but this is not the same as disagreement *in* interest. My definition doesn't provide for disagreement in belief about interests, any more than does Hobbes's; but that is no matter, for there is no reason to believe, at least on common-sense grounds, that this kind of disagreement exists. There is only disagreement *in* interest. (We shall see in a moment that disagreement in interest does not remove ethics from sober argument—that this kind of disagreement may often be resolved through empirical means.)

The second restriction, about "magnetism," or the connection between goodness and actions, requires only a word. This rules out *only* those interest theories which do *not* include the interest of the speaker, in defining "good." My account does include the speaker's interest; hence is immune.

The third restriction, about the empirical method, may be met in a way that springs naturally from the above account of disagreement. Let us put the question in this way: When two people disagree over an ethical matter, can they completely resolve the disagreement through empirical considerations, assuming that each applies the empirical method exhaustively, consistently, and without error?

I answer that sometimes they can, and sometimes they cannot; and that at any rate, even when they can, the relation between empirical knowledge and ethical judgments is quite different from the one which traditional interest theories seem to imply.

This can best be seen from an analogy. Let's return to the example where A and B couldn't agree on a cinema or a symphony. The example differed from an ethical argument in that imperatives were used, rather than ethical judgments; but was analogous to the extent that each person was endeavoring to modify the other's interest. Now how would these people argue the case, assuming that they were too intelligent just to shout at one another?

Clearly, they would give "reasons" to support their imperatives. A might say, "But you know, Garbo is at the Bijou." His hope is that B, who admires Garbo, will acquire a desire to go to the cinema when he knows what play will be there. B may counter, "But Toscanini is guest conductor tonight, in an all-Beethoven programme." And so on. Each supports his imperative (*"Let's* do so and so") by reasons which may be empirically established.

To generalize from this: disagreement in interest may be rooted in disagreement in belief. That is to say, people who disagree in interest would often cease to do so if they knew the precise nature and consequences of the object of their interest. To this extent disagreement in interest may be resolved by securing agreement in belief, which in turn may be secured empirically.

This generalization holds for ethics. If A and B, instead of using imperatives, had said, respectively, "It would be *better* to go to the cinema," and "It would be better to go to the symphony," the reasons which they would advance would be roughly the same. They would each

give a more thorough account of the object of interest, with the purpose of completing the redirection of interest which was begun by the suggestive force of the ethical sentence. On the whole, of course, the suggestive force of the ethical statement merely exerts enough pressure to start such trains of reasons, since the reasons are much more essential in resolving disagreement in interest than the persuasive effect of the ethical judgment itself.

Thus the empirical method is relevant to ethics simply because our knowledge of the world is a determining factor to our interests. But note that empirical facts are not inductive grounds from which the ethical judgment problematically follows. (This is what traditional interest theories imply.) If someone said "Close the door," and added the reason "We'll catch cold," the latter would scarcely be called an inductive ground of the former. Now imperatives are related to the reasons which support them in the same way that ethical judgments are related to reasons.

Is the empirical method *sufficient* for attaining ethical agreement? Clearly not. For empirical knowledge resolves disagreement in interest only to the extent that such disagreement is rooted in disagreement in belief. Not all disagreement in interest is of this sort. For instance: A is of a sympathetic nature, and B isn't. They are arguing about whether a public dole would be good. Suppose that they discovered all the consequences of the dole. Isn't it possible, even so, that A will say that it's good, and B that it's bad? The disagreement in interest may arise not from limited factual knowledge, but simply from A's sympathy and B's coldness. Or again, suppose, in the above argument, that A was poor and unemployed, and that B was rich. Here again the disagreement might not be due to different factual knowledge. It would be due to the different social positions of the men, together with their predominant self-interest.

When ethical disagreement is not rooted in disagreement in belief, is there *any* method by which it may be settled? If one means by "method" a *rational* method, then there is no method. But in any case there is a "way." Let's consider the above example, again, where disagreement was due to A's sympathy and B's coldness. Must they end by saying, "Well, it's just a matter of our having different temperaments"? Not necessarily. A, for instance, may try to *change* the temperament of his opponent. He may pour out his enthusiasms in such a moving way—present the sufferings of the poor with such appeal—that he will lead his opponent to see life through different eyes. He may build up, by the contagion of his feelings, an influence which will modify B's temperament, and create in him a sympathy for the poor which didn't previously exist. This is often the only way to obtain ethical agreement, if there is any way at all. It is persuasive, not empirical or rational; but that is no reason for neglecting it. There is no reason to scorn it, either, for it is only by such means that our personalities are able to grow, through our contact with others.

The point I wish to stress, however, is simply that the empirical method is instrumental to ethical agreement only to the extent that disagreement in interest is rooted in disagreement in belief. There is little reason to believe that all disagreement is of this sort. Hence the empirical method is not sufficient for ethics. In any case, ethics is not psychology, since psychology doesn't endeavor to *direct* our interests; it discovers facts about the ways in which interests are or can be directed, but that's quite another matter.

To summarize this section: my analysis of ethical judgments meets the three requirements for the "vital" sense of "good" that were mentioned in [the beginning]. The traditional interest theories fail to meet these requirements simply because they neglect emotive meaning. This neglect leads them to neglect dynamic usage, and the sort of disagreement that results from such usage, together with the method of resolving the disagreement. I may add that my analysis answers Moore's objection about the open question. Whatever scientifically knowable properties a thing may have, it *is* always open to question whether a thing having these (enumerated) qualities is good. For to ask whether it is good is to ask for *influence*. And whatever I may know about an object, I can still ask, quite pertinently, to be influenced with regard to my interest in it.

SOCIAL PHILOSOPHY

Values, it should be emphasized, are not unimportant in human life for the positivist, despite his emphasis on science. But positivism insists that they be understood scientifically within the context of human life. A contributor to sociological research as well as a writer on philosophical topics, Lucien Lévy-Bruhl is a spokesman for positivism's view of social ideals. In the following selection, his argument may be divided into three parts. First, he rejects natural law theories of ethics and justice with the argument that an elementary knowledge of sociology shows that ideals of justice grow out of social realities. Second, he shows how the rule of justice develops in societies. And third, he admonishes societies to follow the positivist endorsement of science. "To be truly rational," he concludes, "our action on social reality ought not to be guided by an abstract ideal . . . but by the results of science."

6 Justice and Social Reality
Lucien Lévy-Bruhl (1857-1939)

Buckle[1] maintained, supporting his argument by a large number of facts, that the progress of human societies depended chiefly on the discovery of new scientific truths, and in no way on the discovery of ethical truths, since they were transmitted from generation to generation, and even from civilization to civilization, always alike by their formulae, if not in their applications. According to him as far back as history permits us to go, we find societies already in possession of the fundamental principles of ethics although entirely ignorant of the sciences of nature. That conception is not new. The ancient philosophers, especially the stoics, had already made it a commonplace. It is in opposition to what we have tried to establish, for, at bottom it is only a slightly

different expression of the belief in a natural law and in natural ethics. We may then, if we desire, consider it refuted by what precedes it. As, however, it claims to rest on observation, it will not perhaps be useless to criticize it in itself and to examine the value and bearing of the facts which it invokes.

Those facts are, in general, borrowed from civilizations which in comparison with those that are more familiar appear far remote in time and consequently relatively primitive: Egypt, Assyria, Babylon (three or four thousand years before Christ). A certain number of texts exist which testify that there was a conscience at that period, open to the idea of justice and to respect for the rights of others, and also to the duty of assisting others and of protecting the weak. But those civilizations, however remote they seem to us, were already very complex, highly developed, remarkably differentiated from the social point of view, and of an elevated type in organization. We do not know absolutely what space of time separated them from a condition analogous to that in which the inferior

The selection is from Lucien Lévy-Bruhl, *Ethics and Moral Science*, tr. Elizabeth Lee (London: Archibald Constable and Co., Ltd., 1905).

[1] Henry Thomas Buckle (1821-62), English historian and author of *History of Civilization*, a volume developing the view discussed here by Lévy-Bruhl. *Ed.*]

societies of Africa, America and Australia are at the present time; but we shall not be greatly in error if we conclude it to be very considerable. The alleged facts would tend to prove that wherever human societies have reached a high degree of civilization, the ethical relations of men between themselves testify to it. The contrary would indeed be surprising; and the same statement may be made in regard to their economic relations, their art, language and religion. It is an immediate consequence of the solidarity which unites the different fundamental series of social phenomena. The solidarity, doubtless, is not always equally apparent and intercurring causes may favour or retard the development of this or that series; but in a general way, and if we are careful to take into account the perturbations which may arise from the most diverse causes, the law is verified.

Consequently, by reason of the same law, it would be most unlikely that the conscience would be greatly differentiated and be master of itself in a society in which civilization was still low and savage. How is it that one single social series will evolve in isolation to a high degree of complexity and differentiation, while others remain at a much lower stage? How is it to be imagined that with a dull mentality, not yet admitting of abstract thought or generalization, in the absence of an advanced division of labour, of a clearly defined feeling of the opposition possible between the individual and the group, subtle ideas like those of reparative and distributive justice, individual responsibility, respect for law could, I will not say be expressed, but be formed?

To suppose so would be to grant the hypothesis of a special revelation; and it was exactly that hypothesis which we found when we reached the deepest root of the idea of "natural ethics." But we also saw that the hypothesis was not supported by the facts. Doubtless wherever human groups exist, relations also exist between their members which may be described as ethical, that is, acts permitted or forbidden beyond those (small in number) which are indifferent, are to be found as well as feelings of blame, admiration, reprobation, esteem for the perpetrators of the acts. But there is a long distance between those facts and the conscious and considered knowledge of "ethical truths," and especially of truths comparable to those which play so large a part in civilized societies. In the societies called primitive, the presence of an individual conscience possessing those truths itself, would be a sort of miracle. So far as we know that miracle nowhere occurs.

Besides, even in more elevated societies the external resemblance of the formulae should not hide from us the internal difference of the "ethical truths" they express. For instance, it is frequently stated that the essential rules of justice were as well known in the most remote civilized antiquity as in our own time: *Neminem laedere; suum cuique tribuere.* Perhaps: but all that may be legitimately concluded is, that since the days of that remote antiquity language has permitted an abstract expression of the essential ethical relations. The resemblance stops there. It lies only in generality and abstraction of the formula. If there was also resemblance in its signification the meaning of the terms would be almost the same in different civilizations. Now that is not at all the case. How is *neminem* to be understood? To what acts may *laedere* be applied? In half civilized societies, the stranger is not included in *neminem*. The boat cast up by the storm on a foreign shore is pillaged, the men who sailed it murdered, or brought into slavery, without anyone finding an infraction of the rule *neminem laedere*. Such examples abound not only in the past but with us, and in our day. The manner in which the natives of even civilized colonies, like the Annamites, are generally treated by Europeans, shows that "ethical truths" suffer a singular eclipse outside the land of their origin. Similarly for the rule *suum cuique tribuere*. How is *suum* defined? In a society where caste exists, justice consists in treating everyone according to his caste, the Brahmin as a Brahmin, the pariah as a pariah; with a number of half civilized races, it consists in regarding female children as an importunate charge, and women as beasts of burden; in feudal society it consisted in regarding the villain as liable to taxation and statute labour at pleasure. Even in more developed societies, certain applications of the formula of justice call forth protestation from a smaller number of consciences, while others are not disturbed by them. The manufacturer who considers that he is not making sufficient profit may close his mill from one day to the next and consider that he "is wronging no one," since he paid his workmen, now unemployed, for the work done by them up to that day. In the middle of the nineteenth century at the time of the rapid development of manufactures in England, and of the horrible sacrifice of women and children working sixteen or eighteen hours a day in the factories, it does not seem that the masters were conscious of violating the rule of justice; *suum cuique tribuere*. Did they not pay suitable wages?

Those formulae, taken in the abstract, do not possess the power attributed to them of expressing at all times and in all lands the eternal essence of justice. Considered in themselves they are empty. They only receive their signification and their ethical value from their content, which is not provided *a priori* by a sort of ethical intuition nor by an immediate estimation of general utility.[2] It comes to them from the social reality existing at each epoch, and which imposes on every individual the manner in which he ought to behave in a given case. Thus they represent the expressions of ethics of such or such society at a particular time, and not expressions of "ethical truth" in itself. They say equally to the Egyptian, contemporary with the earliest dynasties, to the Assyrian of the time of Sargon, to the Greek of the time of Thucydides, to the baron and prelate of the eleventh century: "You must be just and render to each man his own." But these cases and others that might be put forward, have nothing in common except the formula bidding men conform to definite rules of action under penalty of social punishments, precise or vague, which are echoed in every individual conscience.

The effective progress of social justice cannot then be attributed to a pre-existing conception of justice in men's minds as its decisive or even principal cause. Undoubtedly when progress in morals or in laws is realized, it was demanded, for a long, and sometimes for a very long time, by a certain number of con-

---

[2 The reference is to utilitarianism, and ethical theory which defines the good in terms of the utility of actions toward maximizing pleasure and reducing pain. *Ed.*]

sciences. But why do those consciences feel the need of it? It is not a fresh result drawn from the formula of justice known before, for why should the result be felt at that particular moment, and not have been perceived sooner? The deduction then is merely apparent. The actual fact of which it is the abstract manifestation is, most often, a profound modification produced in another series of social phenomena, and almost always in the economic series. Thus slavery and serfdom, after being regarded as normal phenomena, as excellent institutions necessary to the social order, were gradually eliminated by the economic transformation of European societies, and excluded from what is right by the conscience and condemned in the name of morality. It is thus that the condition of the proletariat under the rule of the modern capitalist, after being long regarded by economists as normal, inevitable and even in a certain sense, providential, is regarded quite differently now that the proletariat, having become conscious of its strength, exacts and obtains more humane conditions of life. The common conscience begins to acknowledge that the claims of the proletariat are just. The economic transformation once begun, the idea of the necessity of realizing a better justice will doubtless help immensely in quickening the movement. But the idea itself would never have been born, and would certainly not have been developed, or have acquired strength enough to obtain millions of adherents, if the whole of the conditions in which society found itself had not caused it to arise. Just as historical materialism is difficult to maintain if it claims to subordinate all evolution of society to its economic life, so is it true

that no series of social phenomena, ethical and juridical phenomena no more than the rest, are developed independently of the other series.

Justice and more generally ethics should be conceived as a "becoming." There is nothing *a priori* to authorize the affirmation that becoming is a progress and an uninterrupted progress. To admit that postulate would be to return to the idea of natural ethics. It would merely take a different form. Instead of supposing that justice was revealed directly in the conscience of every man coming into the world, we should imagine that it was revealed successively in the historical evolution of civilized societies. But the hypothesis, although thus projected into time, would not change its character. It would remain at bottom teleological, religious, and anthropocentric. From the scientific point of view the study of the facts does not prove that the evolution of human societies, not even of higher societies, is such that each series of phenomena, and all together, only vary in the sense of "better." On the contrary, it shows that a multitude of causes, internal and external, may check the development of one or several series, or cause it or them to deviate, and consequently all the others. If we consider the successive conditions of a portion of the ancient world (Spain, Italy, and Gaul) between the first century of the Christian era and the twelfth, it is difficult to assert that the progress towards better conditions has been uninterrupted. No matter from what point of view we regard it (economic, intellectual, moral, political, or any other), it is incontestable that the change, in the whole mass, was rather a retrogression than a progress. For by reason of the law of solidarity of the social series, a change for the worse in social relations from the ethical point of view and a corresponding obscuration of the conscience and the idea, was produced simultaneously. That is exactly what happened. Arabian civilization, that of India, of China, furnishes analogous examples.

Thus the variable content of "ethical truths" does not, even among the most civilized peoples, undergo an uninterrupted process of purification. It evolves parallel to the general evolution of the society. It loses its old elements and demands new ones. Sometimes from one point of view it loses what it would have been better to keep or keeps what would have been better lost. In fact, it acquires what it would have been better for it not to have incorporated. The ever possible eventuality could only be excluded by the care of an omnipotent Providence who guided social evolution: it is perfectly compatible with the principle of the conditions of existence. Consequently, the conscience of a given time, in relation to the whole mass of the social reality of that time, will never provide the general formula of justice with a content that will be worthy of the respect demanded for it in all its parts. By what it prescribes, by what it forbids, and even by what it never dreams of prescribing or forbidding, it necessarily retains more or less important traces of what may be called the social superstition and ignorance of that epoch. Supersition—in the etymological sense of the word—whenever it is a question of the distinction of classes, of old-established obligations, or interdictions, is now under the sway of the prevailing ideas and beliefs, now rejected by the conscience, but it nevertheless persists. Ignorance is insufficiently warned by facts, and our justice remains indifferent to the budding laws that have not as yet the strength to impose themselves.

It is futile to imagine that the waving of a magic wand will rid us of that superstition and ignorance. So far as ignorance is concerned, the impossibility is manifest. How could we learn the modifications of justice that will be exacted by changes still in the distance, and scarcely traced by the whole mass of social conditions, when very often we do not even discern those which are quite near us, and more than half accomplished? And that proves once again how chimerical is the idea of a justice absolute and immutable in itself; for at every new period of social life justice assumes a form that preceding periods could not foresee, and which would never be realized if the evolution of society was different. For instance, we can quite well imagine that the rule of capitalist production had not been set up in Western Europe; in that case a large part of what social justice now demands would never have been conceived. Similarly, whatever the greater number of liberal and socialistic economists may say, we are now in profound ignorance of the social rule which will take the place of ours in a more or less distant future, and consequently of the modifications that the content of "ethical truths" will undergo. We can only slightly remedy our ignorance. We can only (but even that is not to be neglected) make as complete and as objective a study as possible of the present ethical reality. We can determine the meaning, the power, the character, socially useful or harmful, of the different other, of the laws which are in jeopardy, of the laws that are coming into being.

Thus we may render the transitions less difficult to men's minds, less painful in the facts, and help to secure that the evolution of our society—if it is too ambitious to talk of the evolution of humanity—may take as much as possible the form of progress and of pacific progress.

As to "superstitions" (in the sense we gave the word just now), we can only weaken them very gradually, especially the oldest of them, which, being transmitted from generation to generation, ended by acquiring a power comparable to that of instinct. There should, too, be no illusion as regards the word "superstition" or "survival." We do not regard it as the eighteenth century philosophers did, who, in the name of a rational abstract ideal, pitilessly condemned all the traditions that could not be reconciled with that ideal. To imitate them would be to recognize "natural ethics," the existence of which seemed evident to them, and which seems to us incompatible with the reality of facts. It is not for us to undertake a rational crusade against the "superstitions" which still live in our conscience. It is true that all or nearly all is superstition since every-thing is a heritage of the past, and of a past that sometimes goes back beyond history. It matters little that the beliefs that are at the root of a custom are ill-founded, that the reasons which have led to such an interdiction have no longer any meaning in our eyes. If that custom or that interdiction has had a favourable influence on the progress of society, if it is so closely mingled with its life that it cannot be torn away without destroying the whole, in the name of what principle should we undertake to uproot it? To be truly rational, our action on social reality ought to be guided not by an abstract ideal—which claims to have an absolute value and merely expresses the exactions of the conscience to-day—but by the results of science. When science has determined for each of the obligations of the conscience, how it was established, strengthened, imposed, what effect it has produced, and what part it still plays in social life, we shall know in what degree it is expedient—and possible—to modify it. That will be the work of "the rational art" that we conceive to be the methodical application of the results obtained by ethical speculation become scientific.

ESTHETICS

For the positivist, the language of value is emotive, never cognitive. In discussing the language of poetry, I. A. Richards distinguishes the pseudo-statement from statements proper. The latter are always scientific, and hence always subject to verification. Pseudo-statements, however, though frequently having the form of scientific statements, serve only to organize or release human attitudes, not to make true descriptive judgments. Poetry, in dealing in pseudo-statements, is not in the business of making true statements, and it tends toward the ridiculous if it tries. In fact, if the pseudo-statement—in poetry or any other "emotive" activity—is confused with the scientific, we revert to a primitive and magical view of the world.

7 Art and Belief
I. A. Richards (1893-   )

The business of the poet . . . is to give order and coherence, and so freedom, to a body of experience. To do so through words which act as its skeleton, as a structure by which the impulses which make up the experience are adjusted to one another and act together. The means by which words do this are many and varied. To work them out is a problem for linguistic psychology, that embarrassed young heir to philosophy. What little can be done shows already that most critical dogmas of the past are either false or nonsense. A little knowledge is not here a danger, but clears the air in a remarkable way.

Roughly and inadequately, even in the dim light of present knowledge, we can say that words work in the poem in two main fashions. As sensory stimuli and as (in the *widest* sense) symbols. We must refrain from considering the sensory side of the poem, remarking only that it is *not* in the least independent of the other side, and that it has for definite reasons prior importance in most poetry. We must confine ourselves to the other function of words in the poem, or rather, omitting much that is of secondary relevance, to one form of that function, let me call it *pseudo-statement.*

The selection is from I. A. Richards, *Science and Poetry,* rev. ed. (London: Kegan Paul, Trench, Trubner and Co., Ltd., 1935), pp. 61–74 and 92–94. Used by permission of the executors of the estate of Mr. C. K. Ogden, and the author.

It will be admitted—by those who distinguish between scientific statement, where truth is ultimately a matter of verification as this is understood in the laboratory, and emotive utterance, where "truth" is primarily acceptability *by* some attitude, and more remotely is the acceptability *of* this attitude itself —that it is *not* the poet's business to make scientific statements. Yet poetry has constantly the air of making statements, and important ones; which is one reason why some mathematicians cannot read it. They find the alleged statements to be *false.* It will be agreed that their approach to poetry and their expectations from it are mistaken. But what exactly is the other, the right, the poetic, approach and how does it differ from the mathematical?

The poetic approach evidently limits the framework of possible consequences into which the pseudo-statement is taken. For the scientific approach this framework is unlimited. Any and every consequence is relevant. If any of the consequences of a statement conflicts with acknowledged fact then so much the worse for the statement. Not so with the pseudo-statement when poetically approached. The problem is—just how does the limitation work? One tempting account is in terms of a supposed universe of discourse, a world of make-believe, of imagination, of recognized fictions common to the poet and his readers. A pseudo-statement which fits into this system of assumptions would be regarded as "poetically true"; one which does not, as "poetically false." This attempt to treat "poetic truth" on the model of general "coherence theories" is very natural for certain schools of logicians but is inadequate, on the wrong lines from the outset. To mention two objections, out of many; there is no means of discovering what the "universe of discourse" is on any occasion, and the kind of coherence which must hold within it, supposing it to be discoverable, is not an affair of logical relations. Attempt to define the system of propositions into which

O Rose, thou art sick!

must fit, and the logical relations which must hold between them if it is to be "poetically true"; the absurdity of the theory becomes evident.

We must look further. In the poetic approach the relevant consequences are not logical or to be arrived at by a partial relaxation of logic. Except occasionally and by accident logic does not enter at all. They are the consequences which arise through our emotional organization. The acceptance which a pseudo-statement receives is entirely governed by its effects upon our feelings and attitudes. Logic only comes in, if at all, in subordination, as a servant to our emotional response. It is an unruly servant, however, as poets and readers are constantly discovering. A pseudo-statement is "true" if it suits and serves some attitude or links together attitudes which on other grounds are desirable. This kind of "truth" is so opposed to scientific "truth" that it is a pity to use so similar a word, but at present it is difficult to avoid the malpractice.[1]

This brief analysis may be sufficient to indicate the fundamental disparity and opposition between pseudo-statements as they occur in poetry and statements as they occur in science. A pseudo-statement is a form of words which is justified entirely by its effect in releasing or organizing our impulses and attitudes (due regard being had for the better or worse organizations of these *inter se*); a statement, on the other hand, is justified by its truth, that is, its correspondence, in a highly technical sense, with the fact to which it points.

Statements true and false alike do, of course, constantly touch off attitudes and action. Our daily practical existence is largely guided by them. On the whole true statements are of more service to us than false ones. None the less we do not and, at present, cannot order our emotions and attitudes by true statements alone. Nor is there any probability that we ever shall contrive to do so. This is one of the great new dangers to which civilization is exposed. Countless pseudo-statements—about God, about the universe, about human nature, the relations of mind to mind, about the soul, its rank and destiny—pseudo-statements which are pivotal points in the organization of the mind, vital to its well-being, have suddenly become, for sincere, honest and informed minds, impossible to believe as for centuries they have been

---

[1] A pseudo-statement, as I use the term, is not necessarily false in any sense. It is merely a form of words whose scientific truth or falsity is irrelevant to the purpose in hand.

"Logic" in this paragraph is, of course, being used in a limited and conventional, or popular, sense.

believed.[2] The accustomed incidences of the modes of believing are changed irrecoverably; and the knowledge which has displaced them is not of a kind upon which an equally fine organization of the mind can be based.

This is the contemporary situation. The remedy, since there is no prospect of our gaining adequate knowledge, and since indeed it is fairly clear that scientific knowledge cannot meet this need, is to cut our pseudo-statements free from that kind of belief which is appropriate to verified statements. So released they will be changed, of course, but they can still be the main instruments by which we order our attitudes to one another and to the world. This is not a desperate remedy, for, as poetry conclusively shows, even the most important among our attitudes can be aroused and maintained without any believing of a factual or verifiable order entering in at all. We need no such beliefs, and indeed we must have none, if we are to read *King Lear*. Pseudo-statements to which we attach no belief and statements

---

[2] See Appendix. For the mind I am considering here the question "Do I believe *x?*" is no longer the same. Not only the "What" that is to be believed but the "How" of the believing has changed—through the segregation of science and its clarification of the techniques of proof. This is the danger; and the remedy suggested is a further differentiation of the "Hows." To these differences correspond differences in the senses of "is so" and "being" where, as is commonly the case, "is so" and "being" assert believings. As we admit this, the world that "is" divides into worlds incommensurable in respect of so called "degrees of reality." Yet, and this is all-important, these worlds have an order, with regard to one another, which is the order of the mind; and interference between them imperils sanity.

proper, such as science provides, cannot conflict. It is only when we introduce inappropriate kinds of believing into poetry that danger arises. To do so is from this point of view a profanation of poetry.

Yet an important branch of criticism which has attracted the best talents from prehistoric times until today consists of the endeavor to persuade men that the functions of science and poetry are identical, or that the one is a "higher form" of the other, or that they conflict and we must choose between them.

The root of this persistent endeavor has still to be mentioned; it is the same as that from which the Magical View of the world arose. If we give to a pseudo-statement the kind of unqualified acceptance which belongs by right only to certified scientific statements—and those judgments of the routine of perception and action from which science derives—, if we can contrive to do this, the impulses and attitudes with which we respond to it gain a notable stability and vigor. Briefly, if we can contrive to believe poetry, then the world *seems,* while we do so, to be transfigured. It used to be comparatively easy to do this, and the habit has become well established. With the extension of science and the neutralization of nature it has become difficult as well as dangerous. Yet it is still alluring; it has many analogies with drug-taking. Hence the endeavors of the critics referred to. Various subterfuges have been devised along the lines of regarding Poetic Truth as figurative, symbolic; or as more immediate, as a truth of Intuition transcending common knowledge; or as a higher form of the same truth that science yields. Such attempts to use poetry as a denial or as a corrective of science are very common. One point can be made against them all: they are never worked out in detail. There is no equivalent of Mill's *Logic* expounding any of them. The language in which they are framed is usually a blend of obsolete psychology and emotive exclamations.

The long-established and much-encouraged habit of giving to emotive utterances—whether pseudo-statements simple, or looser and larger wholes taken as saying something figuratively —the kind of assent which we give to unescapable facts, has for most people debilitated a wide range of their responses. A few scientists, caught young and brought up in the laboratory, are free from it; but then, as a rule, they pay no *serious* attention to poetry. For most men the recognition of the neutrality of nature brings about—through this habit —a divorce from poetry. They are so used to having their responses propped up by beliefs, however vague, that when these shadowy supports are removed they are no longer able to respond. Their attitudes to so many things have been forced in the past, over-encouraged. And when the world-picture ceases to assist there is a collapse. Over whole tracts of natural emotional response we are today like a bed of dahlias whose sticks have been removed. And this effect of the neutralization of nature is perhaps only in its beginnings. However, human nature has a prodigious resilience. Love poetry seems able to out-play psychoanalysis.

A sense of desolation, of uncertainty, of futility, of the groundlessness of aspirations, of the vanity of endeavor, and a thirst for a life-giving water which seems suddenly to have failed, are the signs in consciousness of this necessary reorganization of our lives.[3] Our attitudes and impulses are being compelled to become self-supporting; they are being driven back upon their biological justification, made once again sufficient to themselves. And the only impulses which seem strong enough to continue unflagging are commonly so crude that, to more finely developed individuals they hardly seem worth having. Such people cannot live by warmth, food, fighting, drink, and sex alone. Those who are least affected by the change are those who are emotionally least removed from the animals. As we shall see at the close

---

[3] My debt to *The Waste Land* here will be evident. The original footnote seems to have puzzled Mr. Eliot and some other readers. Well it might! In saying, though, that he "had effected a complete severance between his poetry and all beliefs" I was referring not to the poet's own history, but to the technical detachment of the poetry. And the way in which he then seemed to me to have "realized what might otherwise have remained a speculative possibility" was by finding a new order through the contemplation and exhibition of disorder.

"Yes! Very funny this terrible thing is. A man that is born falls into a dream like a man who falls into the sea. If he tries to climb out into the air as inexperienced people endeavor to do, he drowns—*nicht wahr?* . . . No! I tell you! The way is to the destructive element submit yourself, and with the exertions of your hands and feet in the water make the deep, deep sea keep you up. So if you ask me how to be? In the destructive element immerse . . . that was the way." *Lord Jim,* p. 216. Mr. Eliot's later verse has sometimes shown still less "dread of the unknown depths." That, at least, seems in part to explain to me why *Ash Wednesday* is better poetry than even the best sections of *The Waste Land.*

of this essay, even a considerable poet may attempt to find relief by a reversion to primitive mentality.

It is important to diagnose the disease correctly and to put the blame in the right quarter. Usually it is some alleged "materialism" of science which is denounced. This mistake is due partly to clumsy thinking, but chiefly to relics of the Magical View. For even if the Universe were "spiritual" all through (whatever that assertion might mean; all such assertions are probably nonsense), that would not make it any more accordant to human attitudes. It is not what the universe is made of but how it works, the law it follows, which makes verifiable knowledge of it incapable of spurring on our emotional responses, and further, the nature of knowledge itself makes it inadequate. The contact with things which we therein establish is too sketchy and indirect to help us. We are beginning to know too much about the bond which unites the mind to its object in knowledge[4] for that old dream of a perfect knowledge which would guarantee perfect life to retain its sanction. What was thought to be pure knowledge, we see now to have been shot through with hope and desire, with fear and wonder; and these intrusive elements indeed gave it all its power to support our lives. In knowledge, in the "How?" of events, we can find hints by which to take advantage of circumstances in our favor and avoid mischances. But we can-

not get from it a *raison d'être* or a justification of more than a relatively lowly kind of life.

The justification, on the reverse, of any attitude lies, not in the object, but in itself, in its serviceableness to the whole personality. Upon its place in the whole system of attitudes, which is the personality, all its worth depends. This is as true for the subtle, finely compounded attitudes of the civilized individual as for the simpler attitudes of the child.

In brief, the imaginative life is its own justification; and this fact must be faced, although sometimes—by a lover, for example—it may be very difficult to accept. When it is faced, it is apparent that all the attitudes to other human beings and to the world in all its aspects, which have been serviceable to humanity, remain as they were, as valuable as ever. Hesitation felt in admitting this is a measure of the strength of the evil habit I have been describing. But many of these attitudes, valuable as ever, are, now that they are being set free, more difficult to maintain, because we still hunger after a basis in belief.

Appendix[5]

Two chief words seem likely occasions of misunderstanding in the above; and they have in fact misled some readers. One is *Nature,* the other is *Belief.*

---

[4] Verifiable scientific knowledge, of course. Shift the sense of "knowledge" to include hope and desire and fear as well as reference, and what I am saying would no longer be true. But then the relevant sense of "true" would have changed too. Its sanction would no longer be verifiability.

[5] This appendix, added in the second edition, was directed by Mr. Richards toward certain misunderstandings which arose among readers of the first edition. He has treated the subjects of this entire selection further in such works as *Speculative Instruments* (Chicago, 1955) and *How to Read a Page* (New York, 1942). *Ed.*]

Nature is evidently as variable a word as can be used. Its senses range from the mere inclusive THAT, in which we live and of which we are a part, to whatever would correspond to the most detailed and interconnected account we could attain of this. Or we omit ourselves (and other minds) and make Nature *either* what influences us (in which case we should not forget our metabolism), *or* an object we apprehend (in which case there are as many Natures as there are types of apprehension we care to distinguish). And what is "natural" to one culture is strange and artificial to another. (See *Mencius on the Mind,* chap. III.) More deceptively, the view here being inseparable from the eye, and this being a matter of habitual speculation, we may talk, as we think, the same language and yet put very different things into Nature; and what we then find will not be unconnected with what we have put in. I have attempted some further discussion of these questions in Chapters VI and VII of *Coleridge on Imagination.*

Belief. Two "beliefs" may differ from one another: (1) In their objects (2) In their statements or expressions (3) In their modes (4) In their grounds (5) In their occasions (6) In their connections with other "beliefs" (7) In their links with possible action (8) And in other ways. Our chief evidence usually for the beliefs of other people (and often for our own) must be some statement or other expression. But very different beliefs may fittingly receive the same expression. Most words used in stating any speculative opinion are as ambiguous as "Belief"; and yet by such words belief-objects must be distinguished.

But in the case of "belief" there is an additional difficulty. Neither it nor its partial synonyms suggest the great variety of the attitudes (3) that are commonly covered (and confused) by the term. They are often treated as though they were mere variations in degree. Of what? Of belief, it would be said. But this no better than the parallel trick of treating all varieties of love as a mere more or less only further differentiated by their objects. Such crude oversimplifications distort the structure of the mind and, although favorite suasive devises with some well-intentioned preachers, are disastrous.

There is an ample field here awaiting a type of dispassionate inquiry which it has seldom received. A world threatened with ever more and more leisure should not be too impatient of important and explorable subtleties.

Meanwhile, as with "Nature," misunderstanding should neither provoke nor surprise. I should not be much less at my reader's mercy if I were to add notes doubling the length of this little book. On so vast a matter, even the largest book could contain no more than a sketch of how things have seemed to be sometimes to the writer.

PHILOSOPHY OF MAN

The mind-body problem, Professor Schlick asserts, cannot exist for the positivist, for the space-time concepts used in science are suitable for describing any reality whatever. In rejecting this dualism, he rejects many others such as inner and outer and psychological and physical as well. Fundamentally, all reality is "physical," a word to be defined by the science of the physical, namely physics. Eschewing metaphysical notions of being, Schlick says that the physical is the scientific conception necessary for describing reality. But what procedures, even if only methodological, can lead to a scientific study of consciousness? The means for accomplishing it is to associate consciousness with brain processes. And this is best done by considering consciousness and brain as one reality, absolutely identical. A parallelism of psychological and physical concepts still remains, of course; but the coherent view of the universe produced by science disallows the conversion of this methodological dualism into a metaphysical one.

8 Psycho-Physical Identity
Moritz Schlick (1882-1936)

The problem which has been at the centre of all metaphysics in more modern philosophy, that is, since about the time of Descartes, is the question of the relationship of the spiritual to the physical, the "soul" to the body. In my opinion it is one of those problems which owe their existence to a false formulation of the question. In fact, from the standpoint which we have reached in the foregoing investigations, a picture of the world unfolds before us without those dark nooks and crannies in which the peculiar difficulties which we fear, and call the psycho-physical problem, could hide. From that standpoint the problem is solved even before it can be stated. We are now going to prove this. But in order to reach complete satisfaction, we must also reveal the source of the error which was able to make the body-soul question into a worrying problem.

The selection is from Moritz Schlick, "Allgemeine Erkenntnislehre" (tr. Gillian Brown), in G. N. A. Vesey (ed.), *Body and Mind* (New York: Humanities Press, Inc.; London: George Allen and Unwin, Ltd., 1964). Used by permission of the publishers.

We have already firmly limited the concept of the mental: it meant what is "absolutely known," which was identical with the "contents of consciousness"; and the meaning of this expression surely needs no more detailed explanation now. Up to now, however, there was no real need to define the physical. We must now make up for this, and we shall see that in actual fact it is only necessary to give a clear presentation of the characteristics which constitute the concept of the physical in order to reach complete clarity on the supposed problem.

The universe appeared to us as an infinite multiplicity of qualities. Those among them which belong in the context of consciousness we called subjective; they are the given and the known. Opposite them stand the objective qualities, as not given and not known. The former are of course what we call *mental,* having already used this name for them. Should we now describe the latter, the objective qualities, as the physical? It would certainly be the term nearest at hand, but we could only use it if the concept thus defined meant exactly what we mean in ordinary speech by the expression "physical." But when we look more closely we see that this is not the case.

It is true that by the term "physical" we usually mean everything (it may, incidentally, be a thing, quality, event, or something else) which cannot be ascribed to the inner world of a conscious being, and which, therefore, belongs neither in the context of one's own "I," nor in that of another consciousness. Consequently the objective qualities (the qualities which are not given and not known) seem to come under this concept of the physical, at least if we disregard the doctrine of those philosophers who think that an "unconscious mind" (which would be objective but not physical) has to be reckoned with. Yet everyone, in ordinary life as well as in the sciences, has counted other characteristics, too, in the concept of the physical, characteristics which in fact are considered to be the essential ones, but which, not sufficiently clarified, are put in quite the wrong place; one must blame them for the fact that the "psycho-physical problem" has arisen at all: they are the characteristics of *spatiality*.

The physical and the extended are not only almost always considered as belonging inseparably together, but often enough as absolutely identical; this is known to be the case in Descartes. Spatial extension always belonged to the definition of the physical body; Kant actually used the sentence: "all bodies have extension in space" as an example of an analytical judgment. This wrong sense completely ignores the difference upon which we should lay the greatest stress: that is, the difference between the spatial as visible reality and "space" as a scheme of order in the objective world. We described the latter, for want of a better expression, as objective or transcendental space, but stressed at the same time that this introduced a figurative meaning of the word "space," which cannot be distinguished carefully enough from the original meaning, where "space" refers exclusively to something visible. But the important result of the investigations undertaken earlier was that it is this visible spatiality of the extra-mental world which does not belong among the objective qualities.

For we know that, in fact, imaginable *extension* is a characteristic of the *subjective* qualities; spatiality in this sense, therefore, possesses not an objective but, on the contrary, a psychic, subjective existence. In the popular concept of the physical, characteristics are supposed to be united which are in reality not compatible; the concept is supposed to be loaded with both the thing-in-itself (that is, no contents of consciousness), and also with the visible, perceptible characteristic of extension. Since the two are incompatible, this concept of the physical (corporeal, material) must give rise to contradictions; these contradictions are just what constitute the psycho-physical problem.

All great philosophical problems rest in fact upon disturbing, tormenting contradictions, and they appear outwardly in certain antithetical concepts; if one can reconcile them one solves the philosophical problem. Such pairs of antithetical concepts are, for example, freedom-necessity, egoism-altruism, and essence-appearance; and our pair of concepts, physical-mental, or body-soul, or matter-mind, or whatever names may be given them, also belongs with them.

Therefore we have recognized that the traditional concept of the physical cannot be completed and is falsely formulated. Should we now, as in fact we ought to do, reject the use of the word entirely, and declare: there are no physical bodies at all? That would naturally not be right, for there must obviously be some sphere where the word can legitimately be used, since otherwise it could not have gained the eminently practical and methodical significance which it has actually developed. The subject of "physical science" must somehow be able to be specified and limited. Up to now we have established, negatively at least, that we should fail in our object if we simply allowed the term "physical" to describe all *non-psychic* qualities. The results of earlier investigations give us the means of solving the problem positively, too.

In order to establish the true sense of the word "physical," there seems to me to be only *one* possible way. The question of the true significance of the word can only be a question of the significance which the word actually has, that is, which it has in that science which deals expressly with the physical as its specific subject—that is, in physical science. A solution of the problem which constructs a special concept of the physical deliberately contrived to avoid any conflict with the mental, cannot be satisfactory. The concept of the physical must be drawn from the individual science which found it in its crude form in prescientific thought and brought it to exactness and clarity.[1]

[1] For this reason R. Reininger's essay (*The Psychophysical Problem,* Vienna, 1916) in which a philosophical concept of the physical is specially created, does not seem to me to solve the actual question.

First and foremost, however, it is important to show proof that a body-soul problem cannot exist for us at all, that we need not fear a contradictory antithesis between body and mind if we persist in the view to which the investigations in the previous chapters have led us.

The world is a varied construction made of connected qualities; part of it is perceptible to my (or anyone else's) consciousness, and this I call subjective or mental; another part is not directly perceptible to our consciousness and this part I call objective or extra-mental— the concept of the physical does not enter into it at this stage. We must emphatically reject the misunderstanding which ascribes to each a different degree of reality, characterizing qualities of one type as mere "manifestations" of qualities of the other. They should rather be considered as, so to speak, equivalent, one type belonging just as much to the general coherent pattern of the universe as the other. We cannot say that on principle a difference exists between the roles they play in the world. In that coherent whole everything is interdependent, every happening is a function of all the other happenings, and it is irrelevant whether objective or subjective qualities are concerned. Whether I see red or experience joy will depend just as much upon my own earlier experiences, therefore on mental qualities, as on the presence of certain extra-mental qualities which can be perceived by me by the methods described earlier. And, conversely, the latter will also depend on the change of the former, they are for example certainly functions of my "will" experiences, for objective events are without doubt influenced by my actions; for example, tendencies that are struggling with each when I have the sensations produced by the firing of a revolver, and hear the report, then something definitely happens in the extra-mental world. Without question a universal interdependence, a "reciprocal action" exists among the qualities of the universe, therefore also between those which belong to my consciousness and those extra-mental qualities which are described by the physical concept "bodies outside my body."

This is all quite natural and fits in without difficulty or force into the picture of the world which we have gained; there is no problem here, and no motive exists which would urge one to make any other assumption, for example to question whether perhaps instead of a universal and general cohesion of reality, a "pre-established harmony" exists between consciousness and the "external world." Only from a completely false position can one ask a question formulated in this way.

It might therefore seem that we ought to take the part, in the body-soul question, of those philosophers who assert that there is psycho-physical reciprocal action. But in fact this is not so. It is obvious to us that we can assume a reciprocal action between the experiences of consciousness, and extra-mental events, that is, between "inner world" and "external world." But whether this reciprocal action can be described as psycho-"physical" can only be decided when we have reached agreement on the concept of the physical. Up to now, at least, we have found no reason for calling the extra-mental world *as such* "physical," and we must remember that even those people who pose the body-soul problem and try to solve it mean by "physical" something *other* than these extra-mental qualities of ours; for they take as a basis the accepted notion of the visible body spatially extended. However, we have just established that this concept of the body is in itself contradictory. We must now see how we can express without contradiction *what* the traditional concept of the physical is really supposed to mean. If we do so we shall, at the same time, at last establish the meaning which we shall in future have to give to the word "physical."

To this end we need only look back at the developments of the previous section, which showed us how natural science builds up its purely quantitative picture of the world. In this picture of the world the concept of physical matter arose by eliminating "the secondary qualities," a concept of matter without quality but with extension, which has dominated speculation in the field of natural philosophy from Democritus to Descartes, and up to and beyond Kant.

The modern development of physical science has radically altered and refined that picture of the world; the concept of extended "substance" now no longer stands at the centre of physical science, but instead the more general concept of the space-time process. In that context, however, the concept of the physical can be deduced with both clarity and certainty: reality is *"physical," insofar as it is described by the spatial-temporal-quantitative system of concepts of the natural sciences.* We perceived earlier that the scientific picture of the world is only a system of signs which we associate with the qualities, and complexes of qualities, which together as a coherent whole form the universe. Besides, the expression "picture of the world" is not without dangers; we should rather say instead "concept of the world," for the word "picture" is better confined to something visible, imaginable, and the representation of the world given in physical science is in no way presentable, but a completely abstract structure, a mere scheme of order. Naturally the component parts of the physical concept of the world are, like all concepts, represented in our thought processes by intuitive images. And it is obvious that to illustrate objective spatial relationships mainly such images are used as belong to a visible space, for example to that of the sense of sight (though the latter is by no means the sole possibility, just as indeed the objective temporal order is not always represented in our minds by intuitive happenings in time, but is illustrated just as well—in graphic representations—by, for example, visual space ideas).

Not only does unclear epistemological thought easily confuse the concept with the real object which it describes, but also with the intuitive images which represent the concept in our consciousness. When we think of the scientific concept of a certain body, we do so through images, for example visual pictures, which bear the intuitive characteristic of extension. The strict *concept* of the body, on the other hand, contains none of this, but only certain numbers which state the "measurements," the "shape" of the body. That does not mean—as shown in detail—an objective presence of spatial-visible qualities in the real object (these belong only to the perceptions and the images, not to something extra-mental), but it means instead that order which cannot be seen or represented, in which the objective qualities of the world follow each other.

We have therefore three kinds of realms to distinguish from each other, and it is by confusing them and mixing them up that the psycho-physical problem has actually been caused: (1) reality itself (the complexes of qualities, the things-in-themselves), (2) the quantitative concepts of natural science allied to reality, forming in their totality the concept of the world given by physical science, and (3) the intuitive images through which the quantities in (2) are represented in our consciousness. Naturally (3), here, is part of (1), that is, a subsidiary part of that part of reality which we call our consciousness.

Now in which of these three realms is the physical to be found? The answer is very easily, and it seems to me quite unequivocally, indicated. No one will argue with us when we say that we always mean something *real* when we talk of the physical, so the word refers without any doubt to objects in the *first* realm. But obviously not directly and unconditionally, for it only refers to those real objects which are associated, or, rather, can be associated, with concepts from the *second* realm. This is all that can be said at the outset, and then the question remains quite open as to whether *collectively* the objects in the first realm can be considered as described by the scientific system of concepts of the second realm, or whether this system is perhaps only possible for a *part* of reality—in other words, whether or not the *whole* world can be interpreted as being something physical. Therefore when we define the physical, the third realm and the psychic in general (which is after all a part of the first realm) do not enter into it at all.

There is above all not the slightest reason for ascribing to this partial reality any distinctive role in regard to its capacity for being described by scientific concepts, for example for assuming that the boundary of the physical, therefore of the real, which can be described by space-time concepts—supposing such a boundary should exist—would coincide with the boundary between experienced and not-experienced reality, that is, between psychic and extra-psychic qualities.

But the simplest hypothesis, which is virtually forced on us by empirical findings to be mentioned immediately, is this: that a boundary of this kind does not exist at all, but rather that the space-time concepts are suited to describing any reality whatever, without exception, and therefore the realities of consciousness too. The fact that we also describe the latter as "psychological" concepts offers no cause for intellectual difficulty, creates no kind of antithesis between physical and mental.

"Physical" consequently means not a special kind of reality, but a special way of describing reality, namely the scientific conception necessary for a knowledge of reality. "Physical" should not be misunderstood as being an attribute which belongs to one part of reality and not to another: it is rather a word for a kind of abstract construction, just as "geographical" or "mathematical" do not describe any peculiar qualities of real things, but rather just describe one way of presenting them by means of concepts. Physical science is the system of exact concepts which allies our knowledge to everything real. To *everything* real, for, according to our hypothesis, in principle *the entire world* can be de-scribed by that system of concepts. Nature is everything, everything real is natural. Mind, the life of consciousness, is not antithetical to nature, but a piece cut out of the totality of the natural.

That we have found the right interpretation here, becomes clear subsequently, when we take a critical look at the other attempts to find a definition for the physical which cannot be disputed.

Modern philosophers who deal with the question try mainly to find the difference between the physical and the spiritual in a difference of points of view. Two philosophers so differently orientated as Mach and Wundt agree that physical science and psychology deal with the *same* objects, which they treat in different ways. If we pay attention, says Mach, to the dependence of an "element" upon those elements which form my body, then it is a mental object, a sensation; if, however, we examine its dependence on other "elements," then we are in physical science, and it is a physical object. "Not the *subject,* but *the direction which the investigation takes* is different in both fields" (*Analysis of Sensations,* p. 14). Now in the last and earlier sections we have convinced ourselves that the essence of physical investigation is not correctly given by this definition. Elements directly known are never themselves included in physical theories, they are under all circumstances eliminated, and only what is substituted for them is called physical. But it is the quantity concepts which take the place of the known qualities. These stay in themselves, and from every point of view, mental. The yellow of this sunflower, the harmony of the sound of that bell are spiritual quantities, "yellow" and "sound" are psychological concepts; physical laws do not deal with them, but instead with frequencies of oscillation, amplitudes and other such quantities, and these are never made up of subjective qualities.

Wundt describes the standpoint of natural science as that of indirect experience in contrast to that of psychology as of direct experience, and stresses "that the expressions external and inner experience indicate not different objects but different points of view which we use in the interpretation and scientific elaboration of experience, which is in itself unified." (*Outline of Psychology,* p. 3.) But the concept of indirect experience is not suitable for defining the physical either. Wundt says it comes into being "by means of the abstraction of the subjective factor contained in every real experience"; therefore natural science considers "the *objects* of experience when seen as independent of the subject" . . . the physical would therefore coincide with the objective, and a definition would be reached which we have already had to reject as unusable, and which after close consideration only makes sense if one presupposes that not only the points of view but also the *objects* are different.

So it seemed more promising when defining the physical to stress that in contrast to the spiritual it is not a reality directly experienced, but that in fact we only reach it by means of the mental, and it seems more promising to construe the expressions direct and indirect experience in this sense. But then one must note the fact that mental qualities can also be the objects of indirect experience, namely those which are part of someone else's consciousness, for we know that we are only able to reach them by drawing conclusions by analogy. The obvious answer was that the physical is that reality which *on principle* is *only* accessible through indirect experience. This is what Münsterberg is getting at in his attempt at definition (*Principles of Psychology,* I, p. 72, 1900) when he says "mental" means "what can be experienced by only one subject, physical what can be experienced in common by several subjects." A. Messer supports him (*Introduction to Epistemology,* 1909, p. 121). This definition could serve as an indisputable definition only if the words "able to be experienced" here meant the same thing both times, if it were one and the same kind of experience through which both realms were made known to us. But this after all is not the case, for a spiritual quality is known absolutely and directly and always to only the one subject who experiences it; in the case of an extramental object, on the other hand, able to be experienced does not mean at the same time able to be lived, its connection with us is indirect, and it can be connected in the same way to many subjects at the same time. Again, however, the same is true of the mental life of other individuals: as many subjects as you like can possess indirect experience of it. Admittedly, this is quite a different kind of experience but this difference is the crux of the matter, and so long as it is not comprehended through the definition, then we have not reached a limit between the physical and spiritual. Consequently Münsterberg's formulation does not take us a step further.

E. Mach, too (*Knowledge and Error,* 3rd ed., p. 6), attempted to define it: "The totality of what is present in space for *everyone* may be described as the physical, and what is only perceptible to *one* person directly may be described as the mental." But nothing exists which corresponds to this definition of the physical, for, as we convinced ourselves earlier, on principle the identical element is never known to two different individuals.

Nothing is achieved, either, by distinguishing two kinds of experience as "inner" and "external"; in fact this tends to lead to errors for the same reasons as those which we earlier considered in connection with "inner perception." Furthermore, if we count sensory perception as "external" experience, as usually happens, then in this way the sensory qualities themselves are drawn into the realm of the physical; and that we have already recognized as inadmissible.

Even if these different attempts at defining the physical are corrected, by putting in place of the two kinds of experience of perception, by which people try to distinguish between physical and psychical, the indisputable antithesis of reality known and not known, we still have not obtained a usable definition of the concept of the physical. For the same reasons stand in our way as those which prevented us from simply describing the real qualities not known as physical: these transcendental qualities lack, as shown, all the characteristics which for both the scientific and the popular concept of the physical are in fact the essential ones.

As we have already remarked several times, quite definite experiences of extension prove that physical concepts can be applied to define reality directly experienced, that is, the mental; and in the previous section we already decided that the only possibility of a *complete* knowl-

edge of the mental is to use the quantitative concepts of the natural sciences to describe mental qualities and the ideas associated with them. And empiricism shows with great clarity the way in which this must be done: it is the complex of concepts of certain "cerebral processes" which must be associated with the world of consciousness. We know that the processes of our consciousness only take place undisturbed if certain parts of the brain are intact. Destruction of the occipital lobe destroys the faculty of sight, destruction of the temporal part of the brain removes the ability to form representations of words, and so on. All that we can learn from these discoveries is that an inner connection exists between the physical object "brain" and the reality experienced, "contents of consciousness." If one wanted to interpret this connection only as reciprocal cal is to be *known* at all, that is, to be described in concepts reducible to each other. We cannot, on any account, consider *all* cerebral processes as signs of consciousness, for in a sleeping or unconscious brain there is no spiritual life as far as we know. But we do not even know *how* these physical processes, to which mental data, that is, subjective qualities cohering in a context, correspond, differ from those physical processes which are symbols of *objective* qualities, that is, those adhering to no consciousness.

Thus purely epistemological reasons lead us to the standpoint of psycho-physical parallelism. We want to be quite clear about the character of this parallelism: it is not metaphysical, does not mean a parallel movement of two kinds of being (as in Geulincx), or two attributes of a single substance (as in Spinoza), or two kinds of manifestation of one and the same "being" (as in Kant), but instead it is an epistemological parallelism between on the one hand a psychological system of concepts and on the other a physical system of concepts. The "physical world" *is* in fact the world described by the system of quantitative concepts of natural science.

PHILOSOPHY OF SCIENCE

The basic thread running through statements of positivism is the primacy of science; and central to the positivistic interpretation of science is the principle of verifiability. As with many philosophical doctrines, this principle has been interpreted in a number of historically important statements, some of which we have covered in the preceding selections. The reason for some variation in these statements is that positivists have tried to be exact in their formulations of the principle.

One of the more important of these statements has been developed by Karl Popper. With other positivists, Popper is concerned with formulating a criterion of meaning which will be consistent with science, eliminate nonsense, and remove metaphysical baggage. He believes he finds this criterion in the notion of falsifiability, by which he means that a statement or theory is meaningful if it is in principle falsifiable, and also that every genuine test of a theory involves the attempt to falsify or refute it.

9 Scientific Theory and Falsifiability
Karl Popper (1902-   )

I

When I received the list of participants in this course and realized that I had been asked to speak to philosophical colleagues I thought, after some hesitation and consultation, that you would probably prefer me to speak about those problems which interest me most, and about those developments with which I

The selection is from Karl Popper, "Philosophy of Science: A Personal Report," in *British in Mid-Century*, ed. C. A. Mace (London: George Allen and Unwin, Ltd., 1957), with omissions. Used by permission of the publisher.

am most intimately acquainted. I therefore decided to do what I have never done before: to give you a report about my own work in the philosophy of science, since the autumn of 1919 when I first began to grapple with the problem, *'When should a theory be ranked as scientific?'* or *'Is there a criterion of the scientific character or status of a theory?'*

The problem which troubled me at the time was neither, 'When is a theory true?' nor, 'When is a theory acceptable?' My problem was different. *I wished to distinguish between science and pseudo-*

science; knowing very well that science often errs, and that pseudo-science may happen to stumble on the truth.

I knew, of course, the most widely accepted answer to my problem: that science is distinguished from pseudo-science—or from 'metaphysics'—by its *empirical method*, which is essentially *inductive*, proceeding from observation and experiment. But this did not satisfy me. On the contrary, I often formulated my problem as one of distinguishing between a genuinely empirical method and a non-empirical or even a pseudo-empirical method—that is to say, a method which, although it appeals to observation and experiment, nevertheless does not come up to scientific standards. The latter method may be exemplified by astrology, with its stupendous mass of empirical evidence based on observation—on horoscopes and on biographies.

But as it was not the example of astrology which led me to my problem I should perhaps briefly describe the atmosphere in which my problem arose and the examples by which it was stimulated. After the collapse of the Austrian Empire there had been a revolution in Austria: the air was full of revolutionary slogans and ideas, and new and often wild theories. Among the theories which interested me Einstein's theory of relativity was no doubt by far the most important. Three others were Marx's theory of history, Freud's psycho-analysis, and Alfred Adler's so-called 'individual psychology'.

There was a lot of popular nonsense talked about these theories, and especially about relativity (as still happens even today) but I was fortunate in those who introduced me to the study of this theory. We all—the small circle of students to which I belonged—were thrilled with the result of Eddington's eclipse observations which in 1919 brought the first important confirmation of Einstein's theory of gravitation. It was a great experience for us, and one which had a lasting influence on my intellectual development.

The three other theories I have mentioned were also widely discussed among students at that time. I myself happened to come into personal contact with Alfred Adler, and even to co-operate with him in his social work among the children and young people in the working-class districts of Vienna where he had established social guidance clinics.

It was during the summer of 1919 that I began to feel more and more dissatisfied with these three theories—the Marxist theory of history, psycho-analysis, and individual psychology; and I began to feel dubious about their claims to scientific status. My problem perhaps first took the simple form, 'What is wrong with Marxism, psycho-analysis, and individual psychology? Why are they so different from physical theories, from Newton's theory, and especially from the theory of relativity?'

To make this contrast clear I should explain that few of us at the time would have said that we believed in the *truth* of Einstein's theory of gravitation. This shows that it was not my doubting the *truth* of those other three theories which bothered me, but something else. Yet neither was it that I merely felt mathematical physics to be more *exact* than the sociological or psychological type of theory. Thus what worried me was neither the problem of truth, at that stage at least, nor the problem of exactness or measurability. It was rather that I felt that these other three theories, though posing as sciences, had in fact more in common with primitive myths than with science; that they resembled astrology rather than astronomy.

I found that those of my friends who were admirers of Marx, Freud, and Adler, were impressed by a number of points common to these theories, and especially by their apparent *explanatory power*. These theories appeared to be able to explain practically everything that happened within the fields to which they referred. The study of any of them seemed to have the effect of an intellectual conversion or revelation, opening your eyes to a new truth hidden from those not yet initiated. Once your eyes were thus opened you saw confirming instances everywhere: the world was full of *verifications* of the theory. Whatever happened always confirmed it. Thus its truth appeared manifest; and unbelievers were clearly people who did not want to see the manifest truth; who refused to see it, either because it was against their class interest, or because of their repressions which were still 'un-analysed' and crying aloud for treatment.

The most characteristic element in this situation seemed to me the incessant stream of confirmations, of observations which 'verified' the theories in question; and this point was constantly emphasized by their adherents. A Marxist could not open a newspaper without finding on every page confirming evidence for his interpretation of history; not only in the news, but also in its presentation—which revealed the class bias of the paper— and especially of course in what the paper did *not* say. The Freudian analysts emphasized that their theories were

constantly verified by their 'clinical observations'. As for Adler, I was much impressed by a personal experience. Once, in 1919, I reported to him a case which to me did not seem particularly Adlerian, but which he found no difficulty in analysing in terms of his theory of inferiority feelings, although he had not even seen the child. Slightly shocked, I asked him how he could be so sure. 'Because of my thousandfold experience,' he replied; whereupon I could not help saying: 'And with this new case, I suppose, your experience has become thousand-and-one-fold.'

What I had in mind was that his previous observations may not have been much sounder than this new one; that each in its turn had been interpreted in the light of 'previous experience', and at the same time counted as additional confirmation. What, I asked myself, did it confirm? No more than that a case could be interpreted in the light of the theory. But this means very little, I reflected, since every conceivable case could be interpreted in the light of Adler's theory, or equally of Freud's. I may illustrate this by two very different examples of human behaviour: that of a man who pushes a child into the water with the intention of drowning it; and that of a man who sacrifices his life in an attempt to save the child. Each of these two cases can be explained with equal ease in Freudian and in Adlerian terms. According to Freud the first man suffered from repression (say, of some component of his Oedipus complex), while the second man had achieved sublimation. According to Adler the first man suffered from feelings of inferiority (producing perhaps the need to prove to himself that he dared to commit some crime), and so did the second man (whose need was to prove to himself that he dared to rescue the child). I could not think of any human behaviour which could not be interpreted in terms of either theory. It was precisely this fact—that they always fitted, that they were always confirmed—which in the eyes of their admirers constituted the strongest argument in favour of these theories. It began to dawn on me that this apparent strength was in fact their weakness.

With Einstein's theory the situation was strikingly different. Take one typical instance—Einstein's prediction, just then confirmed by the findings of Eddington's expedition. Einstein's gravitational theory had led to the result that light must be attracted by heavy bodies (such as the sun), precisely as material bodies were attracted. As a consequence it could be calculated that light from a distant fixed star whose apparent position was close to the sun would reach the earth from such a direction that the star would seem to be slightly shifted away from the sun; or, in other words, that stars close to the sun would look as if they had moved a little away from the sun, and from one another. This is a thing which cannot normally be observed since such stars are rendered invisible in daytime by the sun's overwhelming brightness; but during an eclipse it is possible to take photographs of them. If the same constellation is photographed at night one can measure the distances on the two photographs, and check the predicted effect.

Now the impressive thing about this case is the *risk* involved in a prediction of this kind. If observation shows that the predicted effect is definitely absent, then the theory is simply refuted. The theory is *incompatible with certain possible results of observation*—in fact with results which everybody before Einstein would have expected.[1] This is quite different from the situation I have previously described, when it turned out that the theories in question were compatible with the most divergent human behaviour, so that it was practically impossible to describe any human behaviour that might not be claimed to be a verification of these theories.

These considerations led me in the winter of 1919–20 to conclusions which I may now reformulate as follows.

(1) It is easy to obtain confirmations, or verifications, for nearly every theory—if we look for confirmations.

(2) Confirmations should count only if they are the result of *risky predictions*; that is to say, if, unenlightened by the theory in question, we should have expected an event which was incompatible with the theory—an event which would have refuted the theory.

(3) Every 'good' scientific-theory is a prohibition: it forbids certain things to happen. The more a theory forbids, the better it is.

(4) A theory which is not refutable by any conceivable event is nonscientific. Irrefutability is not a virtue of a theory (as people often think) but a vice.

(5) Every genuine *test* of a theory is an attempt to falsify it, or to refute it. Testability is falsifiability; but there are degrees of testability: some theories are more testable, more exposed to refutation, than others; they take, as it were, greater risks.

---

[1] This is a slight oversimplification, for about half of the Einstein effect may be derived from the classical theory, provided we assume a ballistic theory of light.

(6) Confirming evidence should not count *except when it is the result of a genuine test of the theory*; and this means that it can be presented as a serious but unsuccessful attempt to falsify the theory. (I now speak in such cases of 'corroborating evidence'.)

(7) Some genuinely testable theories, when found to be false, are still upheld by their admirers—for example by introducing *ad hoc* some auxiliary assumption, or by re-interpreting the theory *ad hoc* in such a way that it escapes refutation. Such a procedure is always possible, but it rescues the theory from refutation only at the price of destroying, or at least lowering, its scientific status. (I later described such a rescuing operation as a *'conventionalist twist'* or a *'conventionalist stratagem'*.)

One can sum up all this by saying that *the criterion of the scientific status of a theory is its falsifiability, or refutability, or testability.*

II

I may perhaps exemplify this with the help of the various theories so far mentioned. Einstein's theory of gravitation clearly satisfied the criterion of falsifiability. Even if our measuring instruments at the time did not allow us to pronounce on the results of the tests with complete assurance, there was clearly a possibility of refuting the theory.

Astrology did not pass the test. Astrologers were greatly impressed, and misled, by what they believed to be confirming evidence—so much so that they were quite unimpressed by any unfavourable evidence. Moreover, by making their interpretations and prophecies sufficiently vague they were able to explain away anything that might have been a refutation of the theory had the theory and the prophecies been more precise. In order to escape falsification they destroyed the testability of their theory. It is a typical soothsayer's trick to predict things so vaguely that the predictions can hardly fail: that they become irrefutable.

The Marxist theory of history, in spite of the serious efforts of some of its founders and followers, ultimately adopted this soothsaying practice. In some of its earlier formulations (for example in Marx's analysis of the character of the 'coming social revolution') their predictions were testable, and in fact falsified.[2] Yet instead of accepting the refutations the followers of Marx reinterpreted both the theory and the evidence in order to make them agree. In this way they rescued the theory from refutation; but they did so at the price of adopting a device which made it irrefutable. They thus gave a 'conventional twist' to the theory; and by this stratagem they destroyed its much advertised claim to scientific status.

The two psycho-analytic theories were in a different class. They were simply non-testable, irrefutable. There was no conceivable human behaviour which could contradict them. This does not mean that Freud and Adler were not seeing certain things correctly: I personally do not doubt that much of what they say is of considerable importance, and may well play its part one day in a psychological science which is testable.

[2] See, for example, my *Open Society and Its Enemies*, ch. 15, section iii, and notes 13–14.

But it does mean that those 'clinical observations' which analysts naively believe confirm their theory cannot do this any more than the daily confirmations which astrologers find in their practice.[3] And

as for Freud's epic of the Ego, the Super-ego, and the Id, no substantially stronger claim to scientific status can be made for it than for Homer's collected stories from Olympus. These theories describe some facts, but in the manner of myths. They contain most interesting psychological suggestions, but not in a testable form.

At the same time I realized that such myths may be developed, and become testable; that historically speaking all—or very nearly all—scientific theories originate from myths, and that a myth may contain important anticipations of scientific theories. Examples are Empedocles' theory of evolution by trial and error, or Parmenides' myth of the unchanging block universe in which nothing ever happens and which, if we add another dimension, becomes Einstein's block universe (in which, too, nothing ever happens, since everything is, four-dimensionally speaking, determined and laid down from the beginning). I thus felt that if a theory is found to be non-scientific, or 'metaphysical' (as we might say), it is not thereby found to be unimportant, or insignificant, or 'meaningless', or 'nonsensical'.[4] But it cannot claim to be backed by empirical evidence in the scientific sense—although it may easily be, in some genetic sense, the 'result of observation'.

---

[3] 'Clinical observations', like all other observations, are *interpretations in the light of theories* (see below, sections iv ff.); and for this reason alone they are apt to seem to support those theories in the light of which they were interpreted. But real support can be obtained only from observations undertaken as tests (by 'attempted refutations'); and for this purpose pose *criteria of refutation* have to be laid down beforehand: it must be agreed which observable situations, if actually observed, mean that the theory is refuted. But what kind of clinical responses would refute to the satisfaction of the analyst not merely a particular analytic diagnosis but psychoanalysis itself? And have such criteria ever been discussed or agreed upon by analysts? Is there not, on the contrary, a whole family of analytic concepts, such as 'ambivalence' (I do suggest that there is no such thing as ambivalence), which would make it difficult, if not impossible, to agree upon such criteria? Moreover, how much headway has been made in investigating the question of the extent to which the (conscious or unconscious) expectations and theories held by the analyst influence the 'clinical responses' of the patient? (To say nothing about the conscious attempts to influence the patient by proposing interpretations to him, etc.) Years ago I introduced the term *'Oedipus effect'* to describe the influence of a theory or expectation or prediction *upon the event which it predicts* or describes: it will be remembered that the causal chain leading to Oedipus' parricide was started by the oracle's prediction of this event. This is a characteristic and recurrent theme of such myths, but one seems to have failed to attract the interest of the analysts, perhaps not accidentally. (The problem of confirmatory dreams suggested by the analyst is discussed by Freud, for example in *Gesammelte Schriften*, in, 1925, where he says on p. 314: 'If anybody asserts that most of the dreams which can be utilized in an analysis . . . owe their

origin to [the analyst's] suggestion, then no objection can be made from the point of view of analytic theory. Yet there is nothing in this fact', he surprisingly adds, 'which would detract from the reliability of our results.')

[4] The case of astrology, nowadays a typical pseudo-science, may illustrate this point. It was attacked, by Aristotelians and other rationalists, down to Newton's day, for the wrong reason—for its now accepted assertion

(There were a great many other theories of this pre-scientific or pseudo-scientific character, some of them, unfortunately, as influential as the Marxist interpretation of history; for example, the racialist interpretation of history—another of those impressive and all-explanatory theories which act upon weak minds like revelations.)

---

that the planets had an 'influence' upon terrestrial ('sublunar') events. In fact Newton's theory of gravity, and especially the lunar theory of the tides, was historically speaking an offspring of astrological lore. Newton, it seems, was most reluctant to adopt a theory which came from the same stable as for example the theory that 'influenza' epidemics are due to an astral 'influence'. And Galileo, no doubt for the same reason, actually rejected the lunar theory of the tides; and his misgivings about Kepler may easily be explained by his misgivings about astrology.

Thus the problem which I tried to solve by proposing the criterion of falsifiability was neither a problem of meaningfulness or significance, nor a problem of truth or acceptability. It was the problem of drawing a line (as well as this can be done) between the statements, or systems of statements, of the empirical sciences, and all other statements—whether they are of a religious or of a metaphysical character, or simply pseudo-scientific. Years later—it must have been in 1928 or 1929—I called this first problem of mine the '*problem of demarcation*'. The criterion of falsifiability is a solution to this problem of demarcation, for it says that statements or systems of statements, in order to be ranked as scientific, must be capable of conflicting with possible or conceivable, observations.

PHILOSOPHY OF RELIGION

We have still to see application made of positivistic theses to the problems of religion. This is done with boldness and clarity in the following selection by A. J. Ayer. Having disposed of metaphysics, he proceeds to show that religious knowledge is in a similar manner to be dismissed. Consider the existence of God. This proposition cannot be proved demonstratively because the argument would rest on an empirical premise, and no empirical premise is certain. Nor can God's existence be shown even as a matter of probability; for if one took his existence as an empirical hypothesis, it would mean that other experiential propositions could be deduced from it—which is not the case. Finally, the argument from religious experience or mysticism is invalid because the mystic does not render the object of his experience intelligible; and failing this, the argument for God can be neither meaningful nor verifiable.

In sum, if God is a metaphysical term, then to say that he exists is neither true nor false, but nonsense. The same generalization applies to other religious terms like soul and immortality. Such a position, in making religious assertions meaningless (rather than taking them as false), is neither agnostic nor atheistic, but positivistic.

10 Verification and Religion

A. J. Ayer (1910-   )

This mention of God brings us to the question of the possibility of religious knowledge. We shall see that this possibility has already been ruled out by our treatment of metaphysics. But, as this is a point of considerable interest, we may be permitted to discuss it at some length.

It is now generally admitted, at any rate by philosophers, that the existence of a being having the attributes which define the god of any non-animistic religion cannot be demonstratively proved. To see that this is so, we have only to ask ourselves what are the premises from which the existence of such a god could be deduced. If the conclusion that a god exists is to be demonstratively certain, then these premises must be certain; for, as the conclusion of a deductive argument is already contained in the premises, any uncertainty there may be about the truth of the premises is necessarily shared by it. But we know that no empirical proposition can ever be anything more than probable. It is only *a priori* propositions that are logically certain. But we cannot deduce the existence of a god from an *a priori* proposition. For we know that the reason why *a priori* propositions are certain is that they are tautologies. And from a set of tautologies nothing but a further tautology can be

The selection is from A. J. Ayer, pp. 114-120 of *Language, Truth and Logic* (London: Victor Gollancz, Ltd.; New York: Dover Publications, Inc., 1949). Reprinted by permission of Victor Gollancz, Ltd., and of Dover Publications, Inc., New York, New York.

validly deduced. It follows that there is no possibility of demonstrating the existence of a god.

What is not so generally recognized is that there can be no way of proving that the existence of a god, such as the God of Christianity, is even probable. Yet this also is easily shown. For if the existence of such a god were probable, then the proposition that he existed would be an empirical hypothesis. And in that case it would be possible to deduce from it, and other empirical hypotheses, certain experiential propositions which were not deducible from those other hypotheses alone. But in fact this is not possible. It is sometimes claimed, indeed, that the existence of a certain sort of regularity in nature constitutes sufficient evidence for the existence of a god. But if the sentence "God exists" entails no more than that certain types of phenomena occur in certain sequences, then to assert the existence of a god will be simply equivalent to asserting that there is the requisite regularity in nature; and no religious man would admit that this was all he intended to assert in asserting the existence of a god. He would say that in talking about God, he was talking about a transcendent being who might be known through certain empirical manifestations, but certainly could not be defined in terms of those manifestations. But in that case the term "god" is a metaphysical term. And if "god" is a metaphysical term, then it cannot be even probable that a god exists. For to say that "God exists" is to make a metaphysical utterance which cannot be either true or false. And by the same criterion, no sentence which purports to describe the nature of a transcendent god can possess any literal significance.

It is important not to confuse this view of religious assertions with the view that is adopted by atheists, or agnostics.[1] For it is characteristic of an agnostic to hold that the existence of a god is a possibility in which there is no good reason either to believe or disbelieve; and it is characteristic of an atheist to hold that it is at least probable that no god exists. And our view that all utterances about the nature of God are nonsensical, so far from being identical with, or even lending any support to, either of these familiar contentions, is actually incompatible with them. For if the assertion that there is a god is nonsensical, then the atheist's assertion that there is no god is equally nonsensical, since it is only a significant proposition that can be significantly contradicted. As for the agnostic, although he refrains from saying either that there is or that there is not a god, he does not deny that the question whether a transcendent god exists is a genuine question. He does not deny that the two sentences "There is a transcendent god" and "There is no transcendent god" express propositions one of which is actually true and the other false. All he says is that we have no means of telling which of them is true, and therefore ought not to commit ourselves to either. But we have seen that the sentences in question do not express propositions at all. And this means that agnosticism also is ruled out.

---

[1] This point was suggested to me by Professor H. H. Price.

Thus we offer the theist the same comfort as we gave to the moralist. His assertions cannot possibly be valid, but they cannot be invalid either. As he says nothing at all about the world, he cannot justly be accused of saying anything false, or anything for which he has insufficient grounds. It is only when the theist claims that in asserting the existence of a transcendent god he is expressing a genuine proposition that we are entitled to disagree with him.

It is to be remarked that in cases where deities are identified with natural objects, assertions concerning them may be allowed to be significant. If, for example, a man tells me that the occurrence of thunder is alone both necessary and sufficient to establish the truth of the proposition that Jehovah is angry, I may conclude that, in his usage of words, the sentence "Jehovah is angry" is equivalent to "It is thundering." But in sophisticated religions, though they may be to some extent based on men's awe of natural process which they cannot sufficiently understand, the "person" who is supposed to control the empirical world is not himself located in it; he is held to be superior to the empirical world, and so outside it; and he is endowed with superempirical attributes. But the notion of a person whose essential attributes are nonempirical is not an intelligible notion at all. We may have a word which is used as if it named this "person," but, unless the sentences in which it occurs express propositions which are empirically verifiable, it cannot be said to symbolize anything. And this is the case with regard to the word "god," in the usage in which it is intended to refer to a transcendent object. The mere existence of the noun is enough to foster the illusion that there is a real, or at any rate a possible entity corresponding to it. It is only when we enquire what God's attributes are that we discover that "God," in this usage, is not a genuine name.

It is common to find belief in a transcendent god conjoined with belief in an after-life. But, in the form which it usually takes, the content of this belief is not a genuine hypothesis. To say that men do not ever die, or that the state of death is merely a state of prolonged insensibility, is indeed to express a significant proposition, though all the available evidence goes to show that it is false. But to say that there is something imperceptible inside a man, which is his soul or his real self, and that it goes on living after he is dead, is to make a metaphysical assertion that there is a transcendent god.

It is worth mentioning that, according to the account which we have given of religious assertions, there is no logical ground for antagonism between religion and natural science. As far as the question of truth or falsehood is concerned, there is no opposition between the natural scientist and the theist who believes in a transcendent god. For since the religious utterances of the theist are not genuine propositions at all, they cannot stand in any logical relation to the propositions of science. Such antagonism as there is between religion and science appears to consist in the fact that science takes away one of the motives which make men religious. For it is acknowledged that one of the ultimate sources of religious feeling lies in the inability of men to determine their own destiny; and science tends to destroy the feeling of awe with which men regard an alien world, by making them believe that they can understand and anticipate the course of natural phenomena, and even to some extent control it. The fact that it has recently become fashionable for physicists themselves to be sympathetic towards religion is a point in favor of this hypothesis. For this sympathy towards religion marks the physicists' own lack of confidence in the validity of their hypotheses, which is a reaction on their part from the anti-religious dogmatism of nineteenth-century scientists, and a natural outcome of the crisis through which physics has just passed.

It is not within the scope of this enquiry to enter more deeply into the causes of religious feeling, or to discuss the probability of the continuance of religious belief. We are concerned only to answer those questions which arise out of our discussion of the possibility of religious knowledge. The point which we wish to establish is that there cannot be any transcendent truths of religion. For the sentences which the theist uses to express such "truths" are not literally significant.

An interesting feature of this conclusion is that it accords with what many theists are accustomed to say themselves. For we are often told that the nature of God is a mystery which transcends the human understanding. But to say that something transcends the human understanding is to say that it is unintelligible. And what is unintelligible cannot significantly be described. Again, we are told that God is not an object of reason but an object of faith. This may be nothing more than an admission that the existence of God must be taken on trust, since it cannot be proved. But it may also be an assertion that God is the object of a purely mystical intuition, and cannot therefore be defined in terms which are intelligible to the reason. And I think there are many theists who would assert this. But if one allows that it is impossible to define God in intelligible terms, then one is allowing that it is impossible for a sentence both to be significant and to be about God. If a mystic admits that the object of his vision is something which cannot be described, then he must also admit that he is bound to talk nonsense when he describes it.

For his part, the mystic may protest that his intuition does reveal truths to him, even though he cannot explain to others what these truths are; and that we who do not possess this faculty of intuition can have no ground for denying that it is a cognitive faculty. For we can hardly maintain *a priori* that there are no ways of discovering true propositions except those which we ourselves employ. The answer is that we set no limit to the number of ways in which one may come to formulate a true proposition. We do not in any way deny that a synthetic truth may be discovered by purely intuitive methods as well as by the rational method of induction. But we do say that every synthetic proposition, however it may have been arrived at, must be subject to the test of actual experience. We do not deny *a priori* that the mystic is able to discover truths by his own special methods. We wait to hear what are the propositions which embody his discoveries, in order to see whether they are verified or confuted by our empirical observations. But the mystic, so far from producing propositions which are empirically verified, is unable to produce any intelligible propositions at all. And therefore we say that his intuition has not revealed to him any facts. It is no use his saying that he has apprehended facts but is unable to express them. For we know that if he really had acquired any information, he would be able to express it. He would be able to indicate in some way or other how the genuineness of his discovery might be empirically determined. The fact that he cannot reveal what he "knows," or even himself devise an empirical test to validate his "knowledge," shows that his state of mystical intuition is not a genuinely cognitive state. So that in describing his vision the mystic does not give us any information about the external world; he merely gives us direct information about the condition of his own mind.

These considerations dispose of the argument from religious experience, which many philosophers still regard as a valid argument in favor of the existence of a god. They say that it is logically possible for men to be immediately acquainted with God, as they are immediately acquainted with a sense-content, and that there is no reason why one should be prepared to believe a man when he says that he is seeing a yellow patch, and refuse to believe him when he says that he is seeing God. The answer to this is that if the man who asserts that he is seeing God is merely asserting that he is experiencing a peculiar kind of sense-content, then we do not for a moment deny that his assertion may be true. But, ordinarily, the man who says that he is seeing God is saying not merely that he is experiencing a religious emotion, but also that there exists a transcendent being who is the object of this emotion; just as the man who says that he sees a yellow patch is ordinarily saying not merely that his visual sense-field contains a yellow sense-content, but also that there exists a yellow object to which the sense-content belongs. And it is not irrational to be prepared to believe a man when he asserts the existence of a yellow object, and to refuse to believe him when he asserts the existence of a transcendent god. For whereas the sentence "There exists here a yellow-colored material thing" expresses a genuine synthetic proposition which could be empirically verified, the sentence "There exists a transcendent god" has, as we have seen, no literal significance.

We conclude, therefore, that the argument from religious experience is altogether fallacious. The fact that people have religious experiences is interesting from the psychological point of view, but it does not in any way imply that there is such a thing as religious knowledge, any more than our having moral experiences implies that there is such a thing as moral knowledge. The theist, like the moralist, may believe that his experiences are cognitive experiences, but, unless he can formulate his "knowledge" in propositions that are empirically verifiable, we may be sure that he is deceiving himself. It follows that those philosophers who fill their books with assertions that they intuitively "know" this or that moral or religious "truth" are merely providing material for the psychoanalyst. For no act of intuition can be said to reveal a truth about any matter of fact unless it issues in verifiable propositions. And all such propositions are to be incorporated in the system of empirical propositions which constitutes science.

CRITIQUE

The verification principle, so central to positivism, has not been without its critics, and one of the more important of them is the British philosopher, A. C. Ewing. Ewing finds the principle fraught with difficulties. Fundamentally, he finds that the principle itself is incapable of verification, and thus of truth, in the sense demanded by the principle; for no sense experience or observation can confirm or falsify it. It turns out itself to be nonsense. Perhaps it is useful nonsense, but this, Ewing replies, is unacceptable. Nor do other proposals suggested for the principle—that it is analytically true, that it provides a criterion of meaning—fare any better. And, it may further be noted, if the verification principle is rejected, the positivist's rejection of metaphysics is undercut as well. Finally, Ewing concludes, if the verification principle is to be made the basis of a philosophy, there must be reasons for it, and these reasons have not been forthcoming.

11 Meaninglessness
A. C. Ewing (1899-1974)

In this article I intend to examine the conditions under which a sentence may be said to be meaningless. I have been stimulated to do so by a belief that present-day thinkers are often far too ready to dismiss a philosophical statement as meaningless, and particularly by my opposition to the theory that the meaning of all statements is to be analysed solely in terms of verification by sense-experience. (Note that only sentences can be properly said to have meaning, not propositions. A proposition is what certain sorts of sentences mean and cannot again itself have meaning except in a quite different sense of the word, such as that in which the 'meaning' of something is equivalent to its implications. A meaningful sentence[1] is a sentence which expresses a proposition, a meaningless sentence is a sentence which expresses no proposition. 'Statement', on the other hand, is used both to stand for a proposition and for a sentence expressing a proposition. I shall use it in the latter sense. I am not hereby intending to imply that propositions are separate subsistent entities; this is not a theory which I hold, but I have no time to discuss the question here.) In this article I shall use the term *positivist* for short to mean simply 'upholder of any of the verification theories which I shall consider'. I shall use 'meaning' in the same sense in which it would be used, say, in the *Strand Magazine*.[2]

I shall first take the extremer form of the theory, according to which a statement is said to be verifiable, and therefore to have meaning, if and only if its truth could be conclusively established by sense-experience. 'Sense-experience' is used to include (*a*) sense-perception, (*b*) introspection of images and emotions. Positivists would not usually admit that the occurrence of 'mental acts' could be verified by experience, and would presumably have either to regard these as logical constructions out of sense-data and images, or deny their existence altogether. Still less would the term cover apprehension of 'non-natural' properties or relations. Now I should have thought the first duty of any advocate of a verification theory of meaning would be to inquire how his theory itself was to be verified, and I propose to be a good positivist in this one case at least and put the question myself. How could we verify the statement that all meaningful statements are verifiable?

The first difficulty is that it is a universal proposition and therefore can never be conclusively established merely by experience; but we shall relax the condition, as probably most positivists themselves would, so far as to allow of progressive and incomplete verification, and count the verification theory of meaning as verified for all practical purposes if an adequate number of samples

---

The selection is from A. C. Ewing, "Meaninglessness," *Mind*, n.s. 46 (1937), pp. 347 *ff.*, with omissions. Used by permission of Basil Blackwell, Publisher.

[1] Of this kind

[2] This sentence is taken from *Wisdom*.

of all the different kinds of meaningful statements we can think of are found on examination to be verifiable and we are unable to think of any which are not verifiable. I doubt the consistency of this but I will be as charitable as possible and let it pass. How could the theory then be verified in this sense? It would no doubt be verified if we could take examples of all the different kinds of statements which have ever been made, find by direct inspection what was meant by them, and then discover that they were all verifiable. But I do not think the positivist would or could admit that we can always detect the meanings of statements by direct inspection. If we always can, why all the difficulties about analysis? And it is not by any means sufficient for the purpose that we should *sometimes* be able to do so, for what has to be verified is a proposition about all, not about some, meaningful statements. I doubt in fact whether the positivist would even admit that meaning is the sort of thing that could ever be detected by direct inspection. Further, if we relied on the meaning that statements seem to have when we try to inspect their meaning directly, I do not see how we could ever become positivists. It is surely not by direct inspection of the propositions in question that a positivist learns that propositions about other people's toothache are really propositions about his own sense-data, or that so-called propositions about the past are merely rules for the prediction of those experiences in the future which would verify them. Surely they only come to such conclusions because they first assume the general principle that all meaningful statements are verifiable and then deduce that, since

statements about other people can be verifiable only if they are analysed as statements about one's own sense-data, they must be thus analysed. No doubt they can find examples of meaningful statements which are directly verifiable. Perhaps even all meaningful statements on certain kinds of topics are thus verifiable, *e.g.* all singular propositions about one's present sense-data; but to argue that, because this is true of all of one kind of propositions, it is true of other kinds is as dangerous as to argue that because cats always live on the land, and cats and whales are both mammals, whales must also live on the land. Finally, I do not see how the positivists could establish the truth of their view even in a single case merely by sense-experience. For how can we ever know by sense-experience that there is not a part of the meaning of a statement that we cannot verify? The fact that we do not have any sense-experience of such a part proves nothing, since the point at issue is whether there is something in what we mean beyond sense-experience; and how can we know by sense-experience that there is not?

It therefore seems impossible that the verification theory could be verified in the way suggested, and I cannot conceive what other way there could be of verifying it. For according to the fundamental principles of those who hold the theory it could not be established by any sort of *a priori* argument, and therefore it must presumably be established, if at all, by the empirical examination of particular cases. Now, not merely is it the case that it has not in fact been verified in that way; we have just seen that it is logically impossible that it could be so verified. The statement that all meaningful statements are verifiable is therefore not itself verifiable. It follows that if it is true it is meaningless. But a sentence cannot possibly be both true and meaningless. Therefore the sentence in question cannot be true, but must be either meaningless or false. According to my view it is the latter.

Perhaps it will be said that, although the verification theory is nonsense, it is important and useful nonsense, while the kind of nonsense I talk is unimportant and useless nonsense. But if the statement that it is important and useful nonsense is to be accepted this statement in turn ought to be verified by sense-experience, and how that could possibly be done puzzles me. It might be held that it is useful because it helps to solve philosophical problems; but how can we tell by sense-experience whether a philosophical problem is solved or not? The mere fact that we do not feel an emotion of puzzlement does not prove that we have reached a solution. Otherwise unlettered peasants would have solved all philosophical problems far better than philosophers, and persistent neglect to think would be the golden method for attaining success in philosophy. Also the method prescribed might easily remove the emotion of puzzlement in some men but not in others, and be useful for some philosophical problems but misleading for others.

It might be suggested that the statement of the verification theory should be regarded as a tautology and therefore as meaningless only in the comparatively innocuous sense in which all correct *a priori* statements are meaningless according to the theory. But, if this line were taken, it would be necessary to show that some formal contradiction was committed by denying the theory; and this is not claimed. The only *a priori* propositions that the theory admits are analytic tautologies, if these indeed can be called propositions, but the statement of the theory itself is essentially synthetic. It gives new information, and information not capable of formal proof. The theory therefore cannot, if it is true, be known *a priori*. No *a priori* arguments for it are possible on its own showing since it is synthetic, and it therefore cannot be meaningful even in the modified sense in which a positivist might admit analytic *a priori* statements to be so. It can be meaningful only in the sense in which synthetic statements are supposed to be, i.e. in the sense of being verifiable by sense-experience, and this I claim to have shown it can never be. It is true that it might be deduced analytically from some definition of meaning, but the definition itself must, like all definitions, be synthetic. A proposition giving an analysis must be distinguished from an analytic proposition, or, to put the same thing in different language, a proposition true by definition is not the same as a definition. There can be no self-contradiction in denying a given analysis of the meaning of a term unless some definition is already presupposed, thus begging the question; for there certainly is no analytic logically necessary connection between a word and the analysis of its meaning, and this undoubtedly applies to the word, meaning, itself. That certain marks or noises express propositions and others do not is surely a synthetic proposition if any is. No doubt a positivist can decide to use 'meaning' in any way he chooses, but then he will not be giving an analysis of the ordinary sense of 'meaning', but inventing an arbitrary usage of his own. However this can hardly be what he is doing, for he certainly claims that those who use meaning in a sense in which unverifiable statements are meaningful are committing an error, attributing to certain statements a property they do not possess.

The positivist is thus debarred from giving *a priori* reasons for his theory because it is synthetic, and also from giving empirical reasons because it cannot be based on an empirical inspection of meaning. His only refuge is to make his theory a purely arbitrary convention which therefore requires no justification. But, if this is allowed, a philosopher may assert anything whatever he pleases. The positivist is excused from having to prove his theory, but only at the expense of admitting that there is no more ground for accepting it than there is for accepting any theory whatever. Even such an argument as that it is simpler than other accounts or more useful for establishing deductive systems would be an appeal to a criterion conformity with which certainly cannot be discovered by sense-experience. And it remains true that his theory could mean nothing on its own showing, being neither an *a priori* analytic proposition nor one verifiable by sense-experience.

Now if a theory means nothing I really cannot be expected to refute it. Perhaps it is a very good lyrical expression of the positivist's emotions, but while not wishing to show any lack of sympathy towards his emotions I cannot see that this of itself could make it a useful contribution to philosophy. I add the autobiographical detail that I have never had any emotion myself of which it seemed to me at all a suitable expression. Or perhaps it is a command to treat only those propositions as meaningful which are verifiable; but with all due respect to the positivists I do not see why I should obey their commands unless they can show me that I (or the world) will gain by my doing so. . . .

It is sometimes asserted that the verification theory ought to be accepted because it is the only theory which provides a definition of meaning. But how do the positivists know that meaning is not indefinable? Some terms must be indefinable, and such a fundamental term as meaning is surely one of the most likely terms to be so. Further, can the mere absence of an alternative definition of meaning be any possible justification for giving a definition of meaning which would make meaningless many statements that prior to the definition were held by everybody to have meaning? If a definition does this it is, *prima facie* at any rate, not an account of the way in which the word defined is usually used by people. The definition has not made the *definiens* co-extensive with the *definiendum*, and can only be justified if an *independent argument* is given to show that in the cases where meaning is attributed to statements which cannot be verified the term 'meaning' does not mean anything. If we are content to give definitions that cover only part of the extension of the term defined and then deny that the term as applied to the remainder of its extension has any meaning merely because otherwise it will not fit our definition, as the people who use this argument for the verification theory propose to do, we need never have any difficulty in finding definitions of anything; but surely it is a more philosophic course to suppose that either the term is indefinable or a right definition has not been found yet than to be content with definitions of this kind.

Further this reminds me that I have not stated the verification doctrine in its most common form, simply because this form seemed to me even less plausible than the others and I wished to give my opponents a fair run for their money. As most usually stated, however, the theory asserts not only that no meaningful statements are unverifiable but that the meaning of a statement just is its verification (or its method of verification). And if we use the argument that we must have a definition of meaning and the verification theory is the only definition that has ever been suggested, we must conclude not merely that all meaningful statements are verifiable but that their verification (or method of verification) is identical with their meaning. Otherwise the theory would not be giving a *definition* of meaning. To this extremer form of the theory there seem to me to be two objections that are not applicable to the milder forms which do not actually equate verification with meaning but only use it as a test of meaning. The first objection is that verification presupposes something which is verified, and this cannot itself be the verification but must be a proposition which cannot be reduced without residuum to its own verification. To say that what I mean in asserting a proposition is its verification seems to me parallel to saying 'I lie' when what is said to be a lie is not a previous proposition but the proposition 'I lie' itself. There is nothing to which the 'it' in 'its verification' refers unless there is a proposition to be verified over and above the verification of it.

For what has to be verified is never the sentence but what it means. The sentence is a mere set of noises or black marks which occur and are experienced whether it is true or false, meaningful or meaningless.

Secondly, the belief in the occurrence of an event is very often verified by observing not it but its effects and concluding from them to the event as cause. It will follow that in these cases, if the meaning is identical with its verification, the event will be its own effects. Positivists abominate the entailment view of causation, but, if they were consistent with this definition of meaning, they would have to hold not only that the cause entails but that it analytically entails its effect. I think that an entailment view of causation is true, but even if I am right in this it is quite certain that the entailment, if present, must be synthetic not analytic.

Finally, even if there were reasons for a verification theory, I submit that, if it leads to such consequences as that propositions about other human beings are really only propositions about one's own sense-data, or that all propositions supposed to be about the past are really only about the possible future events which, if they occurred, would verify the propositions, this constitutes an objection to the theory which should outweigh even very strong arguments on its behalf. To me the conclusions in question seem absolutely incredible. Another objection to the theory is that the truth of some statements about metaphysics may be seen logically to entail the truth of others, but how could anything be entailed by a sentence which meant nothing?

I do not believe in saying 'Peace'

when there is no peace, and so I have attacked the verification theory mercilessly, but I am not blind to its merits, which I shall now briefly mention. In order to understand a statement fully, it is, I agree, essential that we should have some idea as to the general kind of way in which it would be justified if it were true, and I am prepared to admit that it is often very useful to ask about a philosophical statement both: How could it be established if it were true? and: What difference, if any, would it make to experience if it were true? Sometimes to ask these questions may even lead us to the conclusion that the statement does not really express a proposition. For, I admit, it does sometimes happen that philosophers are led through verbal confusions into making statements which are meaningless. What I do refuse to admit is that *all* statements which cannot be established or refuted by sense-experience are meaningless. The asking of these questions may help us to get rid of some metaphysics, but not of all metaphysics. The great majority of metaphysical statements that have been made by philosophers in the past are, I think, false or ungrounded, but not meaningless. A few are true or near the truth.

This rejection of metaphysics comes from the unwarranted narrowing down of 'justification' to 'justification by sense-experience.' If we want a criterion to determine when a statement has meaning, it is arguable that 'verifiability' will do if we mean by this that a statement to have a meaning must be such that we can think of some conceivable method by which it might be supported (I think it is too strong to say 'proved') or refuted. But, even so, we are not justified in assuming that the only way of sup-

porting a proposition must be by sense-experience or by inductive argument from sense-experience. Take the proposition that there is a necessary being. That would be proved by the so-called first cause argument if the latter were valid, and the verification of it in my wider sense would consist in going through the argument and seeing whether it was valid. The verification of its contradictory—There is no necessary being—would consist in seeing, as many people think they can see, that there are no existential *a priori* propositions. Suppose, however, we do not find either the argument for or the argument against the existence of a necessary being conclusive. The proposition will still be verifiable potentially if we can see what sort of argument would establish it if it were valid, or what sort of additional premises would be required to make the argument valid. Thus I might see that if we assumed that there was a reason for everything there must be a necessary being, i.e. a being which is its own reason, but I might be uncertain whether we were justified in holding that there was a reason for everything. Again I might see that no *a priori* proposition I knew was existential, and yet be doubtful whether I could see positively that *a priori* existential propositions were impossible. In that case the proposition could still be said to be verifiable in my extended sense of verifiability because I could see what would make it true, just as a proposition about the other side of the moon which we cannot practically verify is still said to be verifiable in the narrower sense of verifiability because we know the experience which, if it could occur, would verify it. I am not sure whether we need or can expect to have a criterion (still less a single criterion) for determining whether statements have a meaning, but if people *must* have a criterion I make them a present of this one. But why beg the whole question of epistemology by identifying verifiability with verifiability by sense-experience at the start?

The positivist has no doubt also done philosophy a good service by carrying out the empiricist principle more consistently than even Hume. For a philosopher should try to investigate the consequences of any possible hypothesis and in particular should try to be an empiricist if he can and as long as he can, because we must not lightly assume the presence of an *a priori* synthetic element in knowledge where an empirical explanation will serve. But I should add that in working out the logical consequences of empiricism the positivist has provided its *reductio ad absurdum*.

Finally I am prepared to grant that we cannot form any idea of anything unless we have either immediately experienced it or it is a logical construction from what we have immediately experienced. Only I use 'experience' in a wide sense according to which seeing that one proposition entails another or that something possesses the non-natural property, good, or being in immediate relation with God, will, if they occur, all be experiences. We can have no right to rule out such experiences in advance as impossible unless we know *a priori* that there cannot be any experiences which are not reducible to sense-experience; and how the positivist could know this, especially on his theory of *a priori* knowledge, is quite beyond my power to conceive. Further, even if I were willing to narrow down experience to suit him, I should still maintain that he had gone too far. For even if we

could not meaningfully talk about anything except qualities or relations given in experience in his narrower sense, and logical constructions from these, it would not follow that it was impossible to make significant statements which could yet not be verified by experience, since it is perfectly possible, for anything we can see, that the same quality actually experienced by us should also qualify existents which no human being, perhaps no being at all, could ever experience. And it is likewise possible that complex characteristics which we never experience may be constructed out of simpler characteristics which we do experience, and that these characteristics may qualify existents which can never be experienced, at any rate by human beings, perhaps not at all. It may be very hard to justify any such assertions, but they are surely significant. If the positivist wishes to dispute this he must disclose some formal contradiction in the supposition. . . .

But it is time to bring this paper to a close. The subject discussed is an extremely important one. The positivists claim to settle once for all by a consistent use of their verification doctrine all the great philosophical issues of the past —the issues between empiricism and rationalism, realism and idealism, pluralism and monism, naturalism and theism, but before they have the least right to do this the verification doctrine must itself be justified. My aim in this paper has been to show both that it cannot be true, because if it were true, it would be meaningless, which is self-contradictory, and that even if *per impossibile* it could be true there is no more ground for believing it than there is for believing the damnatory clauses of the Athanasian creed. If even only the second contention is right, it follows that the verification theory as a universal principle ought to be sternly dismissed from service in philosophical controversy and never used as the major premiss of an argument to show that various sentences uttered by opponents of the positivists are meaningless. For, even if it may be true, a 'may be' without grounds is not enough for a philosopher. We have no right to assume principles which are not self-evident and for which there are no reasons. If a verification theory is to be made the basis of your philosophy there must be reasons for it, and I want to know what the positivist thinks these reasons to be.

SUMMARY

Much of positivism may appear to the student to be only negative and destructive, for it seems to be restrictive in its application of the word "knowledge" and to rule out as nonsense many of the questions that human beings have considered to be of supreme importance. Professor Feigl addresses himself to this sentiment in the following selection, noting that the philosophy for which he speaks is not negativism, but positivism. It is positive because, in eliminating verbal magic and pseudo-problems, it frees thought for the steady advance of science. In his summary restatement of the verification principle, he observes that positivism merely holds that if there are differences, they must make a difference—if there is meaning, it must make for meaningfulness. Such a principle, Feigl believes, can and must be retained despite Ewing's criticisms. To eliminate meaninglessness and metaphysical baggage remains positivism's valued contribution to science and philosophy.

12   The Meaning of Positivism
Herbert Feigl (1902-   )

Positivism, Not Negativism.   Probably the most decisive division among philosophical attitudes is the one between the worldly and the other-worldly types of thought. Profound differences in personality and temperament express them-

selves in the ever changing forms these two kinds of outlook assume. Very likely there is here an irreconcilable divergence. It goes deeper than disagreement in doctrine; at bottom it is a difference in basic aim and interest. Countless frustrated discussions and controversies since antiquity testify that logical argument and empirical evidence are unable to resolve the conflict. In the last analysis this is so because the very issue of the jurisdictive power of the appeal to logic and experi-

The selection is from Herbert Feigl, "Logical Empiricism," in Dagobert D. Runes (ed.), *Twentieth-Century Philosophy* (New York: Philosophical Library, Inc., 1943), pp. 373–377, 381–384, and 386–387. Used by permission of the author and the publisher.

ence (and with it the question of just what empirical evidence can establish) is at stake.

It seems likely that this situation in philosophy will continue as long as human nature in its relations to its cultural environment remains what it has been for the last three or four thousand years. The tough-minded and the tender-minded, as William James described them so brilliantly, are perennial types, perennially antagonistic. There will always be those who find this world of ours, as cruel and deplorable as it may be in some respects, an exciting, fascinating place to live in, to explore, to adjust to, and to improve. And there will always be those who look upon the universe of experience and nature as an unimportant or secondary thing in comparison with something more fundamental and more significant. This tendency of thought may express itself theologically or metaphysically. It may lead to a faith in extra-mundane existence, or it may in various attenuated fashions assert merely the supremacy of some rational or intuitive principles.

Empiricism, Skepticism, Naturalism, Positivism, and Pragmatism are typical thought movements of the worldly, tough-minded variety. Respect for the facts of experience, open-mindedness, an experimental trial-and-error attitude, and the capacity for working within the frame of an incomplete, unfinished world view distinguish them from the more impatient, imaginative, and often aprioristic thinkers in the tender-minded camp. Among the latter are speculative metaphysicians, intuitionists, rationalists, and absolute idealists. An amusing anecdote concerning two celebrated contemporary philosophers has become widely known. One considers the other muddle-headed and the other thinks the one simple-minded. This fairly epitomizes the history of philosophy, that grandiose "tragicomedy of wisdom." Plato and Protagoras, St. Thomas and William of Ockham, Spinoza and Hobbes, Leibniz and Locke, Kant and Hume, Hegel and Comte, Royce and James, Whitehead and Russell are in many regards, though of course not in every feature, outstanding examples of that basic difference.

Inasmuch as this divergence of attitudes establishes a continuum of positions between extremes, there is also among the tough-minded thinkers a gradation of shades from a nominalistic, pan-scientific radicalism to a more liberal, flexible form of empiricism. Typical among the radicals is the use of the phrase "nothing but." We are familiar with this expression from earlier doctrines, such as *materialism:* "Organisms are nothing but machines." "Mind is nothing but matter." "The history of ideas is only an epiphenomenon of the economic processes." We also know it from *phenomenalism:* "Matter is nothing but clusters of sensations." Or from *nominalism:* "Universals are mere words." Or from *ethical skepticism* and *relativism:* "Good and evil are no more than projections of our likes and dislikes."

One of the great merits of logical empiricism lies in the fact that it is conscious of the danger of these reductive fallacies. It may not always have been able to avoid them. A young and aggressive movement in its zeal to purge thought of confusions and superfluous entities, naturally brandishes more destructive weapons than it requires for its genuinely constructive endeavor. But that is a socio-psychological accident which in time will become less important. The future of empiricism will depend on its ability to avoid both the *reductive* fallacies of a narrowminded positivism—stigmatized as *negativism*—as well as the *seductive* fallacies of metaphysics. Full maturity of thought will be attained when neither aggressive destruction nor fantastic construction, both equally infantile, characterize the philosophic intellect. The alternative left between a philosophy of the "Nothing But" and a philosophy of the "Something More" is a philosophy of the "What is What." Thus an attitude of *reconstruction* is emerging: an attitude which recognizes that analysis is vastly different from destruction or reduction to absurdity, an attitude that is favorable to the integration of our knowledge, as long as that integration is carried on in the truly scientific spirit of caution and open-mindedness. The reconstructive attitude demands that we describe the world in a way that does not impoverish it by artificial reductions, and it thus requires that we make important distinctions wherever there is an objective need for them. But, on the other hand, the empiricist will with equal decision reject wishful thinking of all sorts, the reading into experience of features which are incapable of test and the multiplication of entities beyond necessity.

It would be puerile optimism to hope that out of such revision and reform should grow a generally accepted philosophy to end all philosophies. But what may seem questionable as an historical prediction may yet be justifiable as a working attitude in a living enterprise. The spirit of enlightenment, the spirit of Galileo, of Hume, and of the French Encyclopedists is fully alive again in the contemporary encyclopedists of a unified science. These modern logical empiricists hope to have freed themselves from the naïveté and dogmatism of the various nineteenth-century materialists and monists. They are conscious of their philosophy's role as a turning point in the history of critical thought. Nevertheless, they do not claim originality, for they are aware that the empirical and analytic trend in philosophy is no less persistent than the speculative and intuitive approach, though it is admittedly less spectacular and popular. The tradition they now represent has centered its chief inquiries around the two humble questions, "What do you mean?" and "How do you know?" The systematic pursuit of meaning by the Socratic method and the searching scrutiny of the foundations of knowledge are thus again declared the genuine task of philosophy, a task which differs from the quest for truth as carried on by science and yet is most intimately related to it.

Neither the construction of a world view nor a vision of a way of living is the primary aim. If through the progress of knowledge and through social, political, and educational reform one or the other objective is pursued, philosophy in its critical and clarifying capacity may aid or guide such developments. But it cannot, by mere reflective analysis, *prescribe or produce* them. Quackish and dilettantish projects in both directions have always been abundant and cheap in the market of ideas. The main contribution that philosophical reconstruction can make in this regard lies in the direction of an education toward maturer ways of thinking, thinking which possesses the virtues characteristic of science: clarity and consistency, testability and adequacy, precision and objectivity. Immature attitudes are associated with attempts to explain experience in ways which lack the distinguishing marks of science. Certain of these pre-scientific mores of explanation, like the magical, the animistic, and the mythological, are nearly defunct; others, like the theological and the metaphysical, still prevail.

Throughout its history, philosophy has been the particular stronghold of verbal magic. By purely verbal means it has tried to explain things which only science could explain or which cannot be explained at all. In the process it creates its own perplexities, and at its worst it attempts the "solution" of these pseudo-problems—problems arising only out of linguistic confusion—by means of pseudo-techniques—more verbal magic. Analysis teaches us that all this is altogether unnecesssary. Thus, if a little levity be permitted, we may define philosophy as the disease of which it should be the cure. . . .

The Criterion of Factual Meaning and the Critique of Metaphysics. The most important, the most widely debated, and, unfortunately, the most frequently misunderstood regulative principle used by Logical Empiricism is the criterion of factual meaningfulness. The purpose of this criterion is to delimit the type of expression which has possible reference to fact from the other types which do not have this kind of significance: the emotive, the logico-mathematical, the purely formal, and—if there should be such—the completely nonsignificant.

If it is the ostensive steps that connect a purely formal array of signs (e.g., words) with something outside of language, no sign or combination of signs can have factual meaning without this reference to experience. Furthermore, if a sentence is considered true when it corresponds to an existing state of affairs, a sentence is factually meaningful only if we are in principle capable of recognizing such states of affairs as would either validate or invalidate the sentence. If we cannot possibly conceive of what would have to be the case in order to confirm or disconfirm an assertion we would not be able to distinguish between its truth and its falsity. In that case we would simply not know what we are talking about. C. S. Pierce's pragmatic maxim, formulated in his epoch-making essay, *How to make our ideas clear,* has essentially the same import. We may paraphrase it crudely: A difference that is to be a difference (i.e., more than merely a verbal or an emotive one) must *make* a difference. Or, a little more precisely: If and only if assertion and denial of a sentence imply a difference capable of observational (experiential, operational, or experimental) test, does this sentence have factual meaning. Another useful formulation is Ayer's: "It is the mark of a genuine factual proposition . . . that some experiential propositions can be deduced from it in conjunction with certain other premises without being deducible from these other premises alone." This is simply empiricism brought up to date. The psychologistic formulations, an example of which may be found in Hume (ideas must have their basis and origin in impressions), are replaced by logical ones. The most helpful exposition of these concepts for physical scientists was given by P. W. Bridgman. Realizing the close relationship between knowledge and action, or as Dewey would put it, the place of meaning in the context of inquiry, he asks by what procedures we decide the validity of our assertions. Thus Bridgman maintains that concepts and assertion are meaningless if no operations can be specified that define the former and test the latter. . . .

Thus in a general classification of sentences and expressions we distinguish today: (1) Logically true sentences, also called analytic sentences. (2) Logically false sentences, also called contradictions. These sentences are true or false, respectively, by virtue of their form. Even if descriptive empirical terms are contained in them they function only "vacuously," and their factual reference is irrelevant to the validity of the sentence. (3) Factually true and (4) factually false sentences whose validity depends upon their correspondence to observed fact. In the majority of instances this correspondence or non-correspondence is only incompletely and indirectly indicated by whatever is immediately observable. Therefore these sentences are usually not *known* to be true or false but are considered to be confirmed or disconfirmed to an extent which may vary considerably with the accumulation of favorable or unfavorable evidence. (5) Emotive expressions without cognitive meaning and the emotive components of otherwise cognitive expressions. Pictorial, figurative, and metaphorical expressions, exclamations, interjections, words of praise or blame, appeals, suggestions, requests, imperatives, commands, questions, and prayers belong to this category. Even in definitions we recognize a motivational element: the resolution or invitation to use a term in a certain way.

In the light of the preceding distinctions, we may say that an expression is devoid of empirical meaning (i.e., of factual reference) or, briefly, is *factually meaningless,* if it belongs to any one or several of the following five groups: (a) Expressions violating the syntactical formation-rules of a given language; (b) Analytic sentences; (c) Contradictory sentences; (d) Sentences containing extra-logical terms for which no experiential or operational definitions can be provided; (e) Sentences whose confirmability, i.e., even indirect and incomplete testability-in-principle, is logically excluded by the assumptions of the system of which they are a part. . . .

To the empiricist one of the most gratifying trends in the history of science is the gradual liberation of theory from metaphysical bondage. The ideas of absolute space, time, and substance, of numbers as real entities, of the cause-effect relation as an intrinsic necessity, of vital forces and entelechies, and of all manner of obscure faculties and mythical powers have gradually disappeared from respectable science as it was seen that they were either ad hoc explanations or samples of verbal legerdemain or both. One incident in this process of growing epistemological sophistication must suffice for illustration. When after many experiments (Fizeau, Michelson-Morley, de Sitter, Toruton-Noble) physicists realized that it was hopeless to look for effects of the universal ether upon moving bodies, some of them were nevertheless not ready to give up the ether hypothesis. H. A. Lorentz, certainly one of the greatest physicists, pardoned the ether of its undiscoverability by postulating an ingenious set of assumptions, which jointly guaranteed that whatever effects might be produced by the ether, such effects would be exactly cancelled by other counter-effects. Einstein very soon afterwards realized that by this token the stationary-ether hypothesis had become not only scientifically superfluous but strictly meaningless as well. An essentially similar situation prevailed long before in the Newton-Leibniz controversy regarding absolute space and time in which Leibniz used arguments very much like those of the modern pragmatists and positivists.

A word of warning should not be amiss here. The danger of a fallaciously reductive use of the meaning-criterion is great, especially in the hands of young iconoclasts. It is only too tempting to push a very difficult problem aside and by stigmatizing it as meaningless to discourage further investigation. If, for example, some of the extremely tough-minded psychologists relegate questions such as those concerning the instincts, the unconscious, or the relative roles of constitution and environment to the limbo of metaphysics, then they cut with Ockham's razor far into the flesh of knowledge instead of merely shaving away the metaphysical whiskers. No meaningful problem is in principle insoluble, but there is no doubt that the human race will leave a great many problems unsolved.

BIBLIOGRAPHICAL NOTE

For earlier statements of positivism, see the works of Auguste Comte, especially *A General View of Positivism*, English translation (London, 1908), as well as the writings of Lévy-Bruhl, E. Littre, Ernst Mach, and H. Poincaré. A survey of recent positivism is given in V. Kraft, *The Vienna Circle* (New York, 1953). Introductory textbooks of positivistic persuasion include Richard von Misis, *Positivism: A Study in Human Understanding* (Cambridge, 1951); Arthur Pap, *Elements of Analytic Philosophy* (New York, 1949); and Hans Reichenbach, *The Rise of Scientific Philosophy* (Berkeley, 1951). A. J. Ayer's *Language, Truth and Logic*, 2d ed. (London, 1949), is an influential and readable book. More advanced treatments of philosophical problems are found in the writings of such thinkers as Rudolf Carnap, Otto Neurath, and Moritz Schlick. Their important papers, together with others of equal interest, are collected in such anthologies and compilations as H. Feigl and W. Sellars (eds.), *Readings in Philosophical Analysis* (New York, 1949); H. Feigl and M. Brodbeck (eds.), *Readings in the Philosophy of Science* (New York, 1953); *International Encyclopedia of Unified Science*; and *Minnesota Studies in the Philosophy of Science*. Deserving of special mention is A. J. Ayer's *Logical Positivism* (Glencoe, Illinois, 1959), a broad anthology with excellent bibliographical material. R. L. Hawkins, *Positivism in the United States* (Cambridge, 1938), may be of special interest to the student. The works of W. V. O. Quine develop a version of positivism, with much emphasis on language and linguistics. Work of The Society for Exact Philosophy, some of whose papers are published in the journal *Nous*, continues to reflect positivism. Critical studies include J. R. Weinberg, *An Examination of Logical Positivism* (New York, 1936); C. E. M. Joad, *A Critique of Logical Positivism* (London, 1950); G. Bergmann, *The Metaphysics of Logical Positivism* (Madison, Wis., 1954, 1967); and Leszek Kolakowski, *The Alienation of Reason* (tr. N. Guterman) (New York, 1968), which is valuable as a history of positivist thought as well.

Chapter Six

Linguistic Philosophy

Ryle · Wittgenstein · Austin
Wisdom · Hare · Hart · Weitz
Strawson · Findlay · Waismann

Philosophy, we have seen, has been variously defined, and its proper task and subject matter have been variously characterized. In what is called linguistic philosophy or, sometimes, analytic philosophy, we find a rather different position, and one most difficult to describe in brief compass. Not so much a philosophy definable in terms of commonly accepted theses, it is rather a school or position through its temper of mind and its approach to problems.

Linguistic philosophy owes much to positivism, from which it in part developed. It would agree with positivism in the latter's emphasis on analysis as against speculation; that therefore philosophy is not a body of propositions but an activity; and that the object of its analytic concern is language.

Opposed to these agreements, however, are certain crucial differences. First, linguistic philosophers generally reject the verification principle. They find it either a kind of metaphysical proposition—and they reject all metaphysics—or highly reductive in viewing meaning solely in reference to sense-experience. To use a slogan of this philosophy, "the meaning is the use," not verification. Secondly, analysts reject a rigid interpretation of the analytic-synthetic distinction. Within certain types of discourse, to be sure, this distinction can be maintained; but in actual and living languages, it does not hold. Thirdly, linguistic philosophers reject any simple classification of uses of language and insist rather that sentences perform an indefinitely large number of tasks. To use a second slogan, "every statement has its own logic"; that is, the uses and functions of words are richer and more varied than a rigid classification would imply.

But why this exclusive concern with analysis and ordinary language? And what is analysis? The answer to the first question rests on the observation that language can give rise to puzzlement because some expressions, as Professor Gilbert Ryle has written, are "systematically misleading."[1] Consider an illustration: the statement, "Mr. Baldwin is a politician," is not misleading, for it states a fact in a straightforward way. The statement, "Mr. Baldwin is objective," however, though similar in structure, does not exhibit the form of the fact and is misleading without analysis. Traditional philosophy, the linguistic philosopher holds, has been particularly susceptible to error because of such expressions. He therefore is concerned with language because certain expressions are misleading and give rise to puzzles; and what he deals with is not problems or theories but puzzlement.

This type of analysis aims, not at ontology or the traits of experience, but rather at clearing up linguistic confusion, preventing the misuse and misconception of language, and exposing absurd theories. The selections that follow define and articulate, as well as show applications of, this philosophical approach. To conclude with Professor Ryle, "we can often succeed in stating [a] fact in a new form of words which does exhibit what the other failed to exhibit. And I am for the present inclined to believe that this is what philosophical analysis is, and that this is the sole and whole function of philosophy."

---

[1] See his article, "Systematically Misleading Expressions," *Proceedings of the Aristotelian Society,* 1931–1932.

INTRODUCTION

To explain the elucidation and analysis practiced by linguistic philosophers, the following review article by Professor Ryle is included in this introduction. Ryle is discussing the work of Ludwig Wittgenstein, who is a major influence on contemporary philosophy. Wittgenstein's influence is really twofold. In his earlier book, *Tractatus Logico-Philosophicus,* he developed a number of ideas—including the view of logical truths as tautologies and of meaning as certain complexes of words—that contributed to the development of logical positivism. In a second, posthumous book, *Philosophical Investigations,* Wittgenstein breaks with positivism in two important respects: he now defines meaning as the rules for the employment of an expression; and, related to this, language is seen to have an indefinite variety of uses.

In both of these works—though with differences, of course—the task of philosophy is seen as meaning-elucidation. Analysis must disclose the logical architecture or structure that may be concealed in the ordinary uses of language. This elucidation prevents us from falling into philosophical quandaries and puzzlement.

1 Philosophical Elucidation

Gilbert Ryle (1900-   )

What of the philosopher?

He had no formal training in philosophy. His ferments came from his own insides. I do not know just what shape his initial perplexities about mathematics took. Anyhow he consulted Frege[2] and Russell, and studied their logico-mathematical writings; the central problems of his *Tractatus,* though not the same as theirs, were clearly reactions to their doctrines.

Frege and Russell tried to show that all pure mathematics derives from the completely general truths of formal logic, i.e., that these truths stand to arithmetical truths as Euclid's axioms to his theorems. But what was the point of trying to demonstrate this continuity between logic and arithmetic? Surely the truths of mathematics are as well established as anyone could demand, so what is gained, except for tidiness, by underpinning them with an ulterior foundation?

At that time reflective mathematicians were in trouble. Their science seemed all limbs and no body. The very vigor of these branches was generating cross-purposes between them. The notion of number itself seemed to take as many shapes as there were branches of the science of number. Mathematics felt like a caravanserai, not a house.

Its external relations with other sciences also were precarious. John Stuart Mill had likened the truths of mathematics to those of the natural sciences: they are generalizations from experience, susceptible of overthrow by unexpected exceptions. It would be much more surprising to find an exception to $7 + 5 = 12$ than to find a black swan, but only much more. Which is absurd. For another thing, many thinkers, when asked, "Of what entities is mathematics the science?" were giving a psychological answer. The physical world contains countless sorts of things, but it does not contain numbers. There are nine planets, and the earth has one moon. But you cannot see 9 or 1. So, if numbers are not physical things, what else is there for them to be, save ideas in our minds or thoughts or something of the sort? But then arithmetic ought to make allowances for the differences between what goes on in lunatic and in sane minds; in visualizers' and in non-visualizers' minds, and so on. Which is absurd.

Because mathematics needed, internally, coordination between its members and, externally, autonomy from the inductive sciences, especially psychology, its affiliation to logic felt like a rescue operation. Mathematics could be saved from internal discord and from external pressures by becoming part of the unchallengeable science of logic.

But what sort of science is this?

The selection is from Gilbert Ryle's review article on Wittgenstein published in *Scientific American,* 197 (Sept., 1957), pp. 251-259. Used by permission of the publisher of *Scientific American.*

[1 The reference is to F. L. G. Frege (1848-1925), regarded by many as the greatest logician of the nineteenth century. *Ed.*]

What sort of truths are the truths of logic? What sorts of information does logic give us about what sorts of entities? That is, I think, the central problem of Wittgenstein's *Tractatus logico-philosophicus.*

The truths and falsehoods of the natural sciences are truths and falsehoods about what exists and happens in the world. Their truth or falsehood depends upon what is the case with things in the world. But the truths of logic give us no information about the world. "Either it is raining or it is not raining" exemplifies a logical truism, but it tells us nothing about the weather. It is true whatever the weather. "Socrates is mortal" gives us important information or misinformation about Socrates, but "*If* all men are mortal and Socrates is a man, *then* he is mortal" gives us an applied logical truth, which is true whether or not he is mortal.

The truths of the natural sciences are factual truths, while those of logic are purely formal. Their truth is neutral between the world as it is and as it might have been. This formal nature of logical truths shows itself in another way. The truism "Either it is raining or it is not" remains true if for "raining" we substitute "snowing," "freezing" or anything you please. For any proposition whatsoever, either it or its negative is true. The force of "either . . . , or not . . ." is indifferent to the material fillings of the clauses that it links, so long as the clauses are the same. Hence truths of logic can be expressed most cleanly if we algebraize away all material elements like "Socrates," "mortal," and "it is raining." This leaves, for example, "For any *p,* either *p* or not-*p.*"

Thus logic is unconcerned with the actual truth or falsity of the factual statements which can be draped on its skeletons. Nonetheless logic is essentially concerned with the truth-or-falsity of these statements, since it has to work out how the truth or falsity of one *would* follow, if another *were* true or *were* false. That Jack went up the hill would have to be true *if* Jack and Jill went up the hill; and from the falsity of "Jack went up the hill" would follow the falsity of "Jack and Jill went up the hill."

Well then, why should we not answer the original problem by saying that the subject matter of logic consists of truths-or-falsehoods, and that it has to discover in them their formal properties which secure that one would be true if another were true? But then what sorts of entities are truths-or-falsehoods, and what sorts of properties are these formal properties?

When I say "It is raining," my words convey something to you. You understand them even though you do not know that it is raining. They make sense, even if it is not raining. So the actual state of the weather is one thing; the truth-or-falsehood that it is raining is something else. In getting the meaning of my words, you are getting not what the state of the weather is, but what-it-is-being-represented-as-being. But what enables expressions to represent things as they are, or as they are not? What enables a complex of symbols to *mean* something *vis à vis* some actual matter of fact? Consider a simple map representing, truly or falsely, the relative positions and distances of three towns: A, B and C. The dot "A" is one inch higher on the page than the dot "B," and this is two inches higher than the dot "C." This map might tell you that the town A is north of B, which is north of C, and that B is 20 miles from C and 10 from A. How does it do this? By an understood code by which lettered dots stand for towns, the top of the page for north and an inch for 10 miles. It is the way in which the dots are situated on the page that says how the towns are related to one another on the ground. In this case the map, if true, is in certain respects photographically like the corresponding stretch of ground. But with a different code the same dots might represent or misrepresent the heights of three peaks, or the degrees below boiling point of three saucepans. Representation can, but need not, be photographic. The notes played by the musician are not *like* the black marks on his score, yet the arrangement of the latter, by a complex code, may faithfully represent the arrangement of the former.

The "codes" which enable different arrangements of words to represent different states of affairs are enormously complicated, and they vary among different tongues. In English, if you wish to say that Brutus killed Caesar you must put "Brutus" before the verb and "Caesar" after it. Not so in Latin, which achieves the same result by different word terminations. But without applying some syntactical rule or other you cannot say anything, not even anything false. Symbol-structures can represent and misrepresent the structures of actual states of affairs because, though the representing structure is not usually *like* the represented structure, they are still structurally analogous to one another. A sentence has a meaning if its syntax *could* be the structural analogue of an

actual state of affairs, even though, when false, it actually has no such factual counterpart. Caesar did not kill Brutus, but "Caesar killed Brutus" makes sense, since there is, so to speak, room in reality, though unfilled room, for this uncommitted murder.

Not all complexes of words or dots or gestures convey truths or falsehoods. An unorganized jumble of words or dots makes no sense. Even a sequence of words with an orthodox grammar can make nonsense. Lewis Carroll concocted many such sentences; for example, "The Cheshire cat vanished leaving only her grin behind her." Sometimes serious thinkers inadvertently construct senseless sentences. Early geometricians seriously held that Euclidean points are round. A truth-or-falsehood, then, is an organized complex of symbols representing, by analogy of structure, a counterpart actual-or-possible state of affairs. It is, for example, a sentence "in its projective relation to the world." To find out whether it is actually true or actually false we have to match it against its should-be counterpart state of affairs in the world.

Already we can see how Wittgenstein's account of what it is to make sense, that is, to be true-or-false, led to the famous principle of verifiability, by which the logical positivists ostracized as nonsensical the pronouncements of metaphysicians, theologians and moralists. Observation and experiment are our ways of matching the propositions of, say, astronomy against the stellar facts. Where observation and experiment are excluded, our pretended truths-or-falsehoods have no anchorage in facts and so say nothing. They are nothing but disguised gibberish.

What of the truths of logic, the status of which it had been Wittgenstein's main task to fix? Are these also disguised gibberish? Or are they salved by being classed with the most general truths of natural science? Wittgenstein steers between this Scylla and this Charybdis.

An everyday "either-or" statement, like "Either Jack climbed the hill or Jill did," leaves it open which climbed the hill; but it still rules out something that might have been the case, namely, the climbing of the hill by neither of them. But if we ask of an "either-or" truism of logic, like " 'Either Jack climbed the hill or he did not'; what is ruled out by *this* assertion?" we see that the only thing ruled out is Jack's neither climbing nor not climbing the hill. And this is not something which might have been but just happens not to be the case. An ordinary factual assertion gives the "yes" or the "no" answer to a question; it invites us to select the one and to forswear the other. But a truth of logic gives us nothing forswearable to forswear, and so nothing selectable to select. It is factually empty, or "tautological."

It does not, however, follow that the truths of logic are of no use simply because they are uninformative. They serve to show up, by contrast with their own absolute hospitality, the ways in which ordinary statements convey, by their relative shut-doored-ness, positive information or misinformation.

The truths of logic, then, are not nonsensical, though they are empty of information or misinformation. Their business is to *show* us, by evaporation of content, how our ordinary thoughts and assertions are organized.

I pass over Wittgenstein's accounts of the connections and differences between logic and mathematics and between logic and mechanics, important though these are for showing up, by contrast, the positive nature of logic. But I must not pass over his account of the relations between logic and philosophy. For, as his title *Tractatus logico-philosophicus* hints, his book was secondarily concerned to fix the status of philosophy. What sorts of things can philosophers tell us—philosophers as distinct from logicians and from scientists? Are the truths of philosophy factual or formal truths?

Earlier philosophers, if they tried at all to place philosophy, had tended to treat it either as psychology or as non-empirical cosmology. But Russell and others realized that philosophy was neither a natural science nor yet a supernatural science. Russell had emphasized the close connection between logic and philosophy by treating all seriously philosophical questions as problems for "logical analysis," as if logic supplied the lines of latitude and longitude, while philosophy had to fill in the geographical detail.

In partly the same way Wittgenstein, having separated off all philosophical from any scientific questions, describes the positive function of philosophy as "elucidatory." Its function is to disclose that logical architecture of our ordinary and scientific thoughts which our vernaculars conceal but which the designed symbolism of logic would expose. But now there breaks out a seemingly disastrous difference between logic and philosophy. The formulae of logic, though they tell us nothing, still show us, so to speak, at their limit the positive force of the "ors," "ands," "alls" and so forth on which our ordinary truths and falsehoods are built. But philosophical pronouncements are in a worse state, since their elucidatory mission is to *tell* us what sort of sense or nonsense belongs to the propositions of the sciences and of daily life; and this is not the sort of thing that can conceivably be told. The meanings, that is, the truths or falsehoods that we express, cannot then be lifted out of their expressions. We can talk sense, but we cannot talk sense about the sense that we talk.

Consider again my map in which the situations of three dots on the page told you, truly or falsely, the situations of three towns. Now I ask you to draw another map which is to tell me not about things on the ground, but about the information or misinformation conveyed by the first map. It is to tell me whether the first map is accurate or inaccurate, and especially it is to tell me the cartographical code by which the three original dots represent the compass bearings and distances of the towns. You will promptly protest that you cannot make a map of what another map says or of how it says it. What an ordinary map alleges about the earth's surface is not another bit of that surface and so a second map could not map it. The significance-conditions which an ordinary map exemplifies are not *stated* by these or any other maps.

Similarly, we normally know when a sentence expresses a truth-or-falsehood, and when it is nonsensical. We read the composition of an actual-or-possible state of affairs out of the composition of the sentence. But we are debarred from *stating* this correlation. Attempts to state it would be attempts to stand

outside the significance-conditions of statements. They would therefore break these conditions, and so be nonsense.

Philosophical elucidation advances only over the ruins of its attempted articulations. The sort of clarity that we seek we achieve in becoming conscious of what makes us stammer. Critics quickly pointed out that Wittgenstein managed to say many important and understandable things. So perhaps the language of maps has limitations from which the language of words is exempt; and perhaps the notion of sense is wider than the notion of truth-or-falsehood to empirical fact.

Wittgenstein left many manuscripts which are now in process of being published. The first book to be so published was his *Philosophical Investigations.* This has the German text faced by a quite good English translation. . . .

How does the later differ from the earlier Wittgenstein? First, his central problem is different. He is no longer exercised about the status of logic. It is philosophy now that is pestering him for justice. Next he had in the *Tractatus* been scanning the notions of sense and nonsense through the perforated screen of logic. Through its apertures he could see only elementary atoms of truth and falsehood being combined into molecular truths and falsehoods by the operations of "and," "or" and "not." The only discernible differences between sayables were in their degrees and patterns of compositeness. All their other differences had been algebraized away. But now he forsakes this screen. He examines those differences between sayables which will not reduce to degrees of compositeness. Where he had examined the algebraized skeletons of statements in which only the logical constants were left functioning, now he watches the functioning of the live expressions with which we say real things. One thing that he quickly remarks is this. Not all sayables are truths or falsehoods. The logician attends only to assertable premises and conclusions. But not all saying is asserting. There is questioning, advising, entreating, ordering, reassuring, rebuking, joking, warning, commiserating, promising, deploring, praising, parodying. We talk a lot to infants and dogs, but we do not make statements to them.

In the *Tractatus* we were told, in effect, that only those sentences made positive sense which could be the premises or conclusions of a bit of natural science. In the *Philosophical Investigations* the door is opened to anything that anyone might say. We are home, again, in the country of real discourse.

The central notion of sense or meaning has correspondingly thawed. In the *Tractatus* truths-or-falsehoods seemed to be icicles of printer's ink; and their coordination with states of affairs in the real world resembled the congruence between the structures of two crystals. But sentences are normally things said, not written, by one person to another. So now Wittgenstein constantly discusses such questions as "How do children, in real life, actually learn to understand this or that expression?" and "How would we teach a savage to count, or tell the time?" Talking sense and following the sense talked by others are things that we have learned how to do; so the notion of sense comes out of the fog if we constantly ask just what we must have learned, and just how we must have learned it in order to be

able to communicate. Most of Part I of the *Philosophical Investigations* is concerned with questions about sense, understanding, grasping, mastering, interpreting, etc.

One device that Wittgenstein constantly uses is that of exploring imaginary situations in which people have to think up and teach ways of communicating. A builder, for example, wants his inarticulate assistant to pass him bricks and slabs. How would he teach him to distinguish between the orders "Brick" and "Slab"? How would he teach him to bring *two* or *five* bricks, that is, to understand number-words? Wittgenstein calls these imaginary lingo-creations "language-games." This is unfortunate because many readers think he implies that talking is a sort of *playing*. In fact the central idea behind the label "language-game" is the notion of *rules*. Learning to communicate is like learning to play chess or tennis in this respect, that in both we have to master written or unwritten rules—and there are many different, but interlocking, sorts of rules to be learned in both. The chess player has had to learn what moves are allowed, what moves in what situations would be tactical mistakes, and even what moves in what situations would be unsporting. A crude generalization of Wittgenstein's new account of sense or meaning is that the meaning of an expression is the rules for the employment of that expression; that is, the rules licensing or banning its coemployment with other expressions, those governing its effective employment in normal and abnormal communication-situations, and so on. The dynamic notion of rules to be mastered has replaced the notion of an imposed structural congruence.

With his new notion of meaning, Wittgenstein is in a position to say new things about the philosopher's task of meaning-elucidation. But in the main he avoids trying to give any general account of what sort of task this is, or why and when it needs to be done, though there are passages in which he does enigmatically give such an account. Rather, especially in Part II of *Philosophical Investigations,* he tries to demonstrate in examples what philosophical quandaries are like, how to get out of them and what sideslips of thought get us into them. He is trying to teach us methods of operation, rather than give us the answer to a question in an examination.

I do not think that anybody could read the *Philosophical Investigations* without feeling that its author had his finger on the pulse of the activity of philosophizing. We can doubt whether his hinted diagnosis will do; not that he has located, by touch, that peculiar and important intellectual commotion—philosophical puzzlement.

2   Language and Meaning
Ludwig Wittgenstein (1889-1951)

The proper object of philosophy being language, it is necessary to get some understanding of it. To do this, Wittgenstein writes of "language-games," by which expression he wishes to call attention to the fact that speaking a language is part of an activity or of a form of life. In order to know more of language, however, Wittgenstein asks that we look closely at the actual uses of language. These uses are found to be greatly varied, so much so that no reduction of them to a set classification of uses is possible. Only "family resemblances," not a common essence, exist among them.

Not only do the uses of language have no single structure, but, in the same way, meanings have no fixed, single structure or boundary. Rather, they can be known and determined solely by a study of the ordinary meanings of a language. To put it another way, Wittgenstein holds that "an expression has meaning only in the stream of life." The meaning of a word, that is, is its use in the language.

Philosophy, Wittgenstein holds, cannot interfere with the actual use of language. It can rather "only put things before us" in the sense of putting words, sometimes torn by the philosopher from their place in ordinary language, back into their everyday use. Therefore philosophy, Wittgenstein concludes, is not a set of theses but rather more like the treatment of an illness, aiming to remove the disease of puzzlement.

1. *"Cum ipsi (majors homines) appellabant rem aliquam, et cum secundum eam vocem corpus ad aliquid movebant, videbam, et tenebam hoc ab eis vocari rem illam, quod sonabant, cum eam vellent ostendere. Hoc autem eos velle ex motu corporis aperiebatur: tamquam verbis naturalibus omnium*

gentium, quae fiunt voltu et nutu oculorum, ceterorumque membrorum actu, et sonitu vocis indicante affectionem animi in petendis, habendis, rejiciendis, fungiendisve rebus. Ita verba in variis sententiis locis suis posita, et crebro audita, quarum rerum signa essent, paulatim colligebam, measque jam voluntates, edomito in eis signis ore, per haec enuntiabam." (Augustine, Confessions, *I. 8.*)[1]

These words, it seems to me, give us a particular picture of the essence of human language. It is this: the individual words in language name objects—sentences are combinations of such names.—In this picture of language we

---

The selection includes various sections from Part I of *Philosophical Investigations* (tr. G. E. M. Anscombe) (Oxford: Basil Blackwell & Mott, Ltd.; New York: The Macmillan Company, 1953). Used by permission of the publishers.

Wittgenstein expressed the wish that his German text always be available to his readers. His publisher, Basil Blackwell of Oxford, in granting permission to use this material, wishes it to be noted that this text, with an English translation, is available in the full edition.

[1] "When they (my elders) named some object, and accordingly moved towards something, I saw this and I grasped that the thing was called by the sound they uttered when they meant to point it out. Their intention was shewn by their bodily movements, as it were the natural language of all peoples: the expression of the face, the play of the eyes, the movement of other parts of the body, and the tone of voice which expresses our state of mind in seeking, having, rejecting, or avoiding something. Thus, as I heard words repeatedly used in their proper places in various sentences, I gradually learnt to understand what objects they signified; and after I had trained my mouth to form these signs, I used them to express by own desires."

find the roots of the following idea: Every word has a meaning. This meaning is correlated with the word. It is the object for which the word stands.

Augustine does not speak of there being any difference between kinds of word. If you describe the learning of language in this way you are, I believe, thinking primarily of nouns like "table," "chair," "bread," and of people's names, and only secondarily of the names of certain actions and properties; and of the remaining kinds of word as something that will take care of itself.

Now think of the following use of language: I send someone shopping. I give him a slip marked "five red apples." He takes the slip to the shopkeeper, who opens the drawer marked "apples"; then he looks up the word "red" in a table and finds a color sample opposite it; then he says the series of cardinal numbers—I assume that he knows them by heart—up to the word "five" and for each number he takes an apple of the same color as the sample out of the drawer.—It is in this and similar ways that one operates with words.—"But how does he know where and how he is to look up the word 'red' and what he is to do with the word 'five'?"—Well, I assume that he *acts* as I have described. Explanations come to an end somewhere.—But what is the meaning of the word "five"?—No such thing was in question here, only how the word "five" is used.

2. That philosophical concept of meaning has its place in a primitive idea of the way language functions. But one can also say that it is the idea of a language more primitive than ours.

Let us imagine a language for which the description given by Augustine is right. The language is meant to serve for communication between a builder A and an assistant B. A is building with buildingstones: there are blocks, pillars, slabs and beams. B has to pass the stones, and that in the order in which A needs them. For this purpose they use a language consisting of the words "block," "pillar," "slab," "beam." A calls them out;—B brings the stone which he has learned to bring at such-and-such a call.—Conceive this as a complete primitive language.

3. Augustine, we might say, does describe a system of communication; only not everything that we call language is this system. And one has to say this in many cases where the question arises, "Is this an appropriate description or not?" The answer is: "Yes, it is appropriate, but only for this narrowly circumscribed region, not for the whole of what you were claiming to describe."

It is as if someone were to say: "A game consists in moving objects about on a surface according to certain rules . . ."—and we replied: You seem to be thinking of board games, but there are others. You can make your definition correct by expressly restricting it to those games.

8. Let us now look at an expansion of language (2). Besides the four words "block," "pillar," etc., let it contain a series of words used as the shopkeeper in (1) used the numerals (it can be the series of letters of the alphabet); further, let there be two words, which may as well be "there" and "this" (because this roughly indicates their purpose), that are used in connection with a pointing gesture; and finally a number of

color samples. A gives an order like: "d—slab—there." At the same time he shews the assistant a color sample, and when he says "there" he points to a place on the building site. From the stock of slabs B takes one for each letter of the alphabet up to "d," of the same color as the sample, and brings them to the place indicated by A.—On other occasions A gives the order "this —there." At "this" he points to a building stone. And so on.

9. When a child learns this language, it has to learn the series of "numerals" a, b, c, . . . by heart. And it has to learn their use.—Will this training include ostensive teaching of the words?—Well, people will, for example, point to slabs and count: "a, b, c slabs."—Something more like the ostensive teaching of the words "block," "pillar," etc. would be the ostensive teaching of numerals that serve not to count but to refer to groups of objects that can be taken in at a glance. Children do learn the use of the first five or six cardinal numerals in this way.

Are "there" and "this" also taught ostensively?—Imagine how one might perhaps teach their use. One will point to places and things—but in this case the pointing occurs in the *use* of the words too and not merely in learning the use.—

10. Now what do the words of this language *signify?*—What is supposed to shew what they signify, if not the kind of use they have? And we have already described that. So we are asking for the expression "This word signifies *this*" to be made a part of the description. In other words the description ought to take the form: "The word . . . signifies. . . ."

Of course, one can reduce the description of the use of the word "slab" to the statement that this word signifies this object. This will be done when, for example, it is merely a matter of removing the mistaken idea that the word "slab" refers to the shape of building-stone that we in fact call a "block"—but the kind of *"referring"* this is, that is to say the use of these words for the rest, is already known.

Equally one can say that the signs "a," "b," etc. signifiy numbers; when for example this removes the mistaken idea that "a," "b," "c," play the part actually played in language by "block," "slab," "pillar." And one can also say that "c" means this number and not that one; when for example this serves to explain that the letters are to be used in the order a, b, c, d, etc. and not in the order a, b, d, c.

But assimilating the descriptions of the uses of words in this way cannot make the uses themselves any more like one another. For, as we see, they are absolutely unlike.

11. Think of the tools in a tool-box: there is a hammer, pliers, a saw, a screwdriver, a rule, a glue-pot, glue, nails and screws.—The functions of words are as diverse as the functions of these objects. (And in both cases there are similarities.)

Of course, what confuses us is the uniform appearance of words when we hear them spoken or meet them in script and print. For their *application* is not presented to us so clearly. Especially not, when we are doing philosophy!

12. It is like looking into the cabin of a locomotive. We see handles all looking more or less alike. (Naturally, since they are all supposed to be handled.) But one is the handle of a crank which can be moved continuously (it regulates the opening of a valve); another is the handle of a switch, which has only two effective positions, it is either off or on; a third is the handle of a brake-lever, the harder one pulls on it, the harder it brakes; a fourth, the handle of a pump: it has an effect only so long as it is moved to and fro.

19. It is easy to imagine a language consisting only of orders and reports in battle.—Or a language consisting only of questions and expressions for answering yes and no. And innumerable others. —And to imagine a language means to imagine a form of life. . . .

20. But now it looks as if when someone says "Bring me a slab" he could mean this expression as *one* long word corresponding to the single word "Slab!"—Then can one mean it sometimes as one word and sometimes as four? And how does one usually mean it?—I think we shall be inclined to say: we mean the sentence as *four* words when we use it in contrast with other sentences such as *"Hand* me a slab," "Bring *him* a slab," "Bring *two* slabs," etc.; that is, in contrast with sentences containing the separate words of our command in other combinations.—But what does using one sentence in contrast with others consist in? Do the others, perhaps, hover before one's mind? *All* of them? And *while* one is saying the one sentence, or before, or afterwards?—No. Even if such an explanation rather tempts us, we need only think for a moment of what actually happens in order to see that we are going astray here. We say that we use the command

in contrast with other sentences because *our language* contains the possibility of those other sentences. Someone who did not understand our language, a foreigner, who had fairly often heard someone giving the order: "Bring me a slab!" might believe that this whole series of sounds was one word corresponding perhaps to the word for "building-stone" in his language. If he himself had then given this order perhaps he would have pronounced it differently, and we should say: he pronounces it so oddly because he takes it for a *single* word.—But then, is there not also something different going on in him when he pronounces it,—something corresponding to the fact that he conceives the sentence as a *single* word?—Either the same thing may go on in him, or something different. For what goes on in you when you give such an order? Are you conscious of its consisting of four words *while* you are uttering it? Of course you have a *mastery* of this language—which contains those other sentences as well—but is this having a mastery something that *happens* while you are uttering the sentence?—And I have admitted that the foreigner will probably pronounce a sentence differently if he conceives it differently; but what we call his wrong conception *need* not lie in anything that accompanies the utterance of the command.

The sentence is "elliptical," not because it leaves out something that we think when we utter it, but because it is shortened—in comparison with a particular paradigm of our grammar.—Of course one might object here: "You grant that the shortened and the unshortend sentence have the same sense. —What is this sense, then? Isn't there

a verbal expression for this sense?"— But doesn't the fact that sentences have the same sense consist in their having the same *use?*—(In Russian one says "Stone red" instead of "the stone is red"; do they feel the copula to be missing in the sense, or attach it in *thought?*)

23. But how many kinds of sentence are there? Say assertion, question, and command?—There are *countless* kinds: countless different kinds of use of what we call "symbols," "words," "sentences." And this multiplicity is not something fixed, given once for all; but new types of language, new language-games, as we may say, come into existence, and others become obsolete and get forgotten. (We can get a *rough picture* of this from the changes in mathematics.)

Here the term "language-*game*" is meant to bring into prominence the fact that the *speaking* of language is part of an activity, or of a form of life.

Review the multiplicity of language-games in the following examples, and in others:

Giving orders, and obeying them—

Describing the appearance of an object, or giving its measurements—

Constructing an object from a description (a drawing)—

Reporting an event—

Speculating about an event—

Forming and testing a hypothesis—

Presenting the results of an experiment in tables and diagrams—

Making up a story; and reading it—

Play-acting—

Singing catches—

Guessing riddles—

Making a joke; telling it—

Solving a problem in practical arithmetic—

Translating from one language into another—

Asking, thanking, cursing, greeting, praying.

—It is interesting to compare the multiplicity of the tools in language and of the ways they are used, the multiplicity of kinds of word and sentence, with what logicians have said about the structure of language. (Including the author of the *Tractatus Logico-Philosophicus.*)

43. For a *large* class of cases—though not for all—in which we employ the word "meaning" it can be defined thus: the meaning of a word is its use in the language.

And the *meaning* of a name is sometimes explained by pointing to its *bearer*.

65. Here we come up against the great question that lies behind all these considerations.—For someone might object against me: "You take the easy way out! You talk about all sorts of language-games, but have nowhere said what the essence of a language-game, and hence of language, is: what is common to all these activities, and what makes them into language or parts of language. So you let yourself off the very part of the investigation that once gave you yourself most headache, the part about the *general form of propositions* and of language."

And this is true.—Instead of producing something common to all that we call language, I am saying that these phenomena have no one thing in common which makes us use the same word for all,—but that they are *related* to one another in many different ways. And it is because of this relationship, or these relationships, that we call them all "language." I will try to explain this.

66. Consider for example the proceedings that we call "games." I mean board-games, card-games, ball-games, Olympic games, and so on. What is common to them all?—Don't say: "There *must* be something common, or they would not be called 'games' "—but *look and see* whether there is anything common to all.—For if you look at them you will not see something that is common to *all,* but similarities, relationships, and a whole series of them at that. To repeat: don't think, but look! —Look for example at board-games, with their multifarious relationships. Now pass to card-games; here you find many correspondences with the first group, but many common features drop out, and others appear. When we pass next to ball-games, much that is common is retained, but much is lost.—Are they all "amusing"? Compare chess with noughts and crosses. Or is there always winning and losing, or competition between players? Think of patience. In ball games there is winning and losing; but when a child throws his ball at the wall and catches again, this feature has disappeared. Look at the parts played by skill and luck; and at the difference between skill in chess and skill in tennis. Think now of games like ring-a-ring-of-roses; here is the element of amusement, but how many other characteristic features have disappeared! And we can go through the many, many other groups of games in the same way; can see how similarities crop up and disappear.

And the result of this examination is: we see a complicated network of similarities overlapping and criss-crossing: sometimes overall similarities, sometimes similarities of detail.

67. I can think of no better expression to characterize these similarities

than "family resemblances"; for the various resemblances between members of a family: build, features, color of eyes, gait, temperament, etc. etc. overlap and criss-cross in the same way.—And I shall say: "games" form a family.

And for instance the kinds of number form a family in the same way. Why do we call something a "number"? Well, perhaps because it has a—direct—relationship with several things that have hitherto been called number; and this can be said to give it an indirect relationship to other things we call the same name. And we extend our concept of number as in spinning a thread we twist fibre on fibre. And the strength of the thread does not reside in the fact that some one fibre runs through its whole length, but in the overlapping of many fibres.

But if someone wished to say: "There is something common to all these constructions—namely the disjunction of all their common properties"—I should reply: Now you are only playing with words. One might as well say: "Something runs through the whole thread—namely the continuous overlapping of those fibres."

108. We see that what we call "sentence" and "language" have not the formal unity that I imagined, but are families of structures more or less related to one another.—But what becomes of logic now? Its rigor seems to be giving way here.—But in that case doesn't logic altogether disappear?—For how can it lose its rigor? Of course not by our bargaining any of its rigor out of it.—The *preconceived* idea of crystalline purity can only be removed by turning our whole examination round. (One might say: the axis of reference of our examination must be rotated, but about the fixed point of our real need.)

The philosophy of logic speaks of sentences and words in exactly the sense in which we speak of them in ordinary like when we say e.g. "Here is a Chinese sentence," or "No, that only looks like writing; it is actually just an ornament" and so on.

We are talking about the spatial and temporal phenomenon of language, not about some non-spatial, non-temporal phantasm. [Note in margin: Only it is possible to be interested in a phenomenon in a variety of ways.] But we talk about it as we do about the pieces in chess when we are stating the rules of the game, not describing their physical properties.

The question "What is a word really?" is analogous to "What is a piece in chess?"

109. It was true to say that our considerations could not be scientific ones. It was not of any possible interest to us to find out empirically "that, contrary to our preconceived ideas, it is possible to think such-and-such"—whatever that may mean. (The conception of thought as a gaseous medium.) And we may not advance any kind of theory. There must not be anything hypothetical in our considerations. We must do away with all *explanation,* and description alone must take its place. And this description gets its light, that is to say its purpose—from the philosophical problems. These are, of course, not empirical problems; they are solved, rather, by looking into the workings of our language, and that in such a way as to make us recognize those workings: *in despite of* an urge to misunderstand them. The problems are solved, not by giving new information,

but by arranging what we have always known. Philosophy is a battle against the bewitchment of our intelligence by means of language.

116. When philosophers use a word —"knowledge," "being," "object," "I," "proposition," "name"—and try to grasp the *essence* of the thing, one must always ask oneself: is the word ever actually used in this way in the language-game which is its original home?—

What *we* do is to bring words back from their metaphysical to their everyday use.

123. A philosophical problem has the form: "I don't know my way about."

124. Philosophy may in no way interfere with the actual use of language; it can in the end only describe it.

For it cannot give it any foundation either.

It leaves everything as it is.

It also leaves mathematics as it is, and no mathematical discovery can advance it. A "leading problem of mathematical logic" is for us a problem of mathematics like any other.

125. It is the business of philosophy, not to resolve a contradiction by means of a mathematical or logico-mathematical discovery, but to make it possible for us to get a clear view of the state of mathematics that troubles us: the state of affairs *before* the contradiction is resolved. (And this does not mean that one is side-stepping a difficulty.)

The fundamental fact here is that we lay down rules, a technique, for a game, and that then when we follow the rules, things do not turn out as we had assumed. That we are therefore as it were entangled in our own rules.

This entanglement in our rules is what we want to understand (i.e. get a clear view of).

It throws light on our concept of *meaning* something. For in those cases things turn out otherwise than we had meant, foreseen. That is just what we say when, for example, a contradiction appears: "I didn't mean it like that."

The civil status of a contradiction, or its status in civil life: there is the philosophical problem.

126. Philosophy simply puts everything before us, and neither explains nor deduces anything.—Since everything lies open to view there is nothing to explain. For what is hidden, for example, is of no interest to us.

One might also give the name "philosophy" to what is possible *before* all new discoveries and inventions.

127. The work of the philosopher consists in assembling reminders for a particular purpose.

128. If one tried to advance *theses* in philosophy, it would never be possible to question them, because everyone would agree to them.

255. The philosopher's treatment of a question is like the treatment of an illness.

EPISTEMOLOGY

What is truth? as the ancient question puts it. This problem has concerned us in four previous selections under epistemology. As a linguistic philosopher turns to it, his first and primary concern is with the use of "true" in language. Giving the careful attention to language required to unravel some of the puzzles connected with the word, Professor Austin proceeds first to ask what it is that true is used for. Distinguishing sentence and statement, he finds that it is the latter that can be true. But when is a statement true? Roughly, Professor Austin says, when it corresponds to the facts. This answer, however, can be misleading, and much of the selection works at refining it.

Students will also note that Austin rejects the view that "is true" is logically superfluous. Two types of consideration are important in this rejection, one centering around "is false," another showing that many words like true are used as it is but are not seen as superfluous. Austin's conclusion is thus a revised version of the correspondence theory of truth.

3 Truth

J. L. Austin (1911-1960)

1. "What is truth?" said jesting Pilate, and would not stay for an answer. Pilate was in advance of his time. For "truth" itself is an abstract noun, a camel, that is, of a logical construction, which cannot get past the eye even of a grammarian. We approach it cap and categories in hand: we ask ourselves whether Truth is a substance (the Truth, the Body of Knowledge), or a quality (something like the colour red, inhering in truths), or a relation ("correspondence").[1] But philosophers should take something more nearly their own size to strain at. What needs discussing rather is the use, or certain uses, of the word "true." *In vino,* possibly, *"veritas,"* but in a sober symposium *"verum."*

2. What is it that we say is true or is false? Or, how does the phrase "is true" occur in English sentences? The answers appear at first multifarious. We say (or are said to say) that beliefs are true, that descriptions or accounts are true, that propositions or assertions or statements are true, and that words or sentences are true: and this is to mention only a selection of the more obvious candidates. Again, we say (or are said to say) "It is true that the cat is on the mat," or "It is true to say that the cat is on the mat," or " 'The cat is on the mat' is true." We also remark on occa-

The selection is reprinted from J. L. Austin, "Truth," *Proceedings of the Aristotelian Society,* Supplementary Vol. 24 (1950), by courtesy of the Editor of The Aristotelian Society. Copyright 1950 The Aristotelian Society.

[1] It is sufficiently obvious that "truth" is a substantive, "true" an adjective and "of" in "true of" a preposition.

sion, when someone else has said something, "Very true" or "That's true" or "True enough."

Most (though not all) of these expressions, and others besides, certainly do occur naturally enough. But it seems reasonable to ask whether there is not some use of "is true" that is primary, or some generic name for that which at bottom we are always saying "is true." Which, if any, of these expressions is to be taken *au pied de la lettre?* To answer this will not take us long, nor, perhaps, far: but in philosophy the foot of the letter is the foot of the ladder.

I suggest that the following are the primary forms of expression:

> It is true (to say) that the cat
> is on the mat.
> That statement (of his, etc.)
> is true.
> The statement that the cat is
> on the mat is true.

But first for the rival candidates.

(*a*) Some say that "truth is primarily a property of beliefs." But it may be doubted whether the expression "a true belief" is at all common outside philosophy and theology: and it seems clear that a man is said to hold a true belief when and in the sense that he believes (in) *something which* is true, or believes that *something which* is true is true. Moreover if, as some also say, a belief is "of the nature of a picture," then it is of the nature of what cannot be true, though it may be, for example, faithful.[2]

(*b*) True descriptions and true ac-counts are simply varieties of true statements or of collections of true statements, as are true answers and the like. The same applies to propositions too, in so far as they are genuinely said to be true (and not, as more commonly, sound, tenable and so on).[3] A proposition in law or in geometry is something portentous, usually a generalisation, that we are invited to accept and that has to be recommended by argument: it cannot be a direct report on current observation—if you look and inform me that the cat is on the mat, that is not a proposition though it is a statement. In philosophy, indeed, "proposition" is sometimes used in a special way for "the meaning or sense of a sentence or family of sentences": but whether we think a lot or little of this usage, a proposition in this sense cannot, at any rate, be what we say is true or false. For we never say "The meaning (or sense) of this sentence (or of these words) is true": what we do say is what the judge or jury says, namely that *"The words taken in this sense, or if we assign to them such and such a meaning, or so interpreted or understood, are true."*

(*c*) Words and sentences are indeed said to be true, the former often, the latter rarely. But only in certain senses. Words as discussed by philologists, or by lexicographers, grammarians, linguists, phoneticians, printers, critics (stylistic or textual) and so on, are not true or false: they are wrongly formed, or ambiguous or defective or untranslatable or unpronounceable or misspelled or archaistic or corrupt or what not.[4] Sen-

---

[2] A likeness is true *to* life, but not true *of* it. A *word* picture can be true, just because it is *not* a picture.

[3] Predicates applicable also to "arguments," which we likewise do not say are true, but, for example, valid.

[4] Peirce made a beginning by pointing out

tences in similar contexts are elliptic or involved or alliterative or ungrammatical. We may, however, genuinely say "His closing words were very true" or "The third sentence on page 5 of his speech is quite false": but here "words" and "sentence" refer, as is shown by the demonstratives (possessive pronouns, temporal verbs, definite descriptions, etc.), which in this usage consistently accompany them, to the words or sentence *as used by a certain person on a certain occasion.* That is, they refer (as does "Many a true word spoken in jest") to *statements.*

A statement is made and its making is a historic event, the utterance by a certain speaker or writer of certain words (a sentence) to an audience with reference to a historic situation, event or what not.[5]

A sentence is made *up of* words, a statement is made *in* words. A sentence is not English or not good English, a statement is not in English or not in good English. Statements are made, words or sentences are used. We talk of *my* statement, but of *the English* sen-

tence (if a sentence is mine, I coined it, but I don't coin statements). The *same* sentence is used in making *different* statements (I say "It is mine," you say "It is mine"): it may also be used on two occasions or by two persons in making the *same* statement, but for this the utterance must be made with reference to the same situation or event.[6] We speak of "the statement that S," but of "the sentence 'S'," not of "the sentence that S."[7]

When I say that a statement is what is true, I have no wish to become wedded to one word. "Assertion," for example, will in most contexts do just as well, though perhaps it is slightly wider. Both words share the weakness of being rather solemn (much more so than the more general "what you said" or "your words"),—though perhaps we are generally being a little solemn when we

---

that there are two (or three) different senses of the word "word," and adumbrated a technique ("counting" words) for deciding what is a "different sense." But his two senses are not well defined, and there are many more, —the "vocable" sense, the philologist's sense in which "grammar" is the same word as "glamour," the textual critic's sense in which the "the" in 1.254 has been written twice, and so on. With all his 66 divisions of signs, Peirce does not, I believe, distinguish between a sentence and a statement.

[5] "Historic" does not, of course, mean that we cannot speak of future or possible statements. A "certain" speaker need not be any definite speaker. "Utterance" need not be public utterance,—the audience may be the speaker himself.

[6] "The same" does not always mean the same. In fact it has no meaning in the way that an "ordinary" word like "red" or "horse" has a meaning: it is a (the typical) device for establishing and distinguishing the meanings of ordinary words. Like "real," it is part of our apparatus *in* words for fixing and adjusting the semantics *of* words.

[7] Inverted commas show that the words, though uttered (in writing), are not to be taken as a statement by the utterer. This covers two possible cases, (i) where what is to be discussed is the sentence (ii) where what is to be discussed is a statement made elsewhen in the words "quoted." Only in case (i) is it correct to say simply that the token is doing duty for the type (and even here it is quite incorrect to say that "The cat is on the mat" is the *name* of an English sentence,—though possibly *The Cat is on the Mat* might be the title of a novel, or a bull might be known as *Catta est in matta*). Only in case (ii) is there something true or false, *viz.* (not the quotation but) the statement made in the words quoted.

discuss the truth of anything. Both have the merit of clearly referring to the historic use of a sentence by an utterer, and of being therefore precisely not equivalent to "sentence." For it is a fashionable mistake to take as primary "(The sentence) 'S' is true (in the English language)." Here the addition of the words "in the English language" serves to emphasize that "sentence" is not being used as equivalent to "statement," so that it precisely is not what can be true or false (and moreover, "true in the English language" is a solecism, mismodelled presumably, and with deplorable effect, on expressions like "true in geometry").

3. When is a statement true? The temptation is to answer (at least if we confine ourselves to "straightforward" statements): "When it corresponds to the facts." And as a piece of standard English this can hardly be wrong. Indeed, I must confess I do not really think it is wrong at all: the theory of truth is a series of truisms. Still, it can at least be misleading.

If there is to be communication of the sort that we achieve by language at all, there must be a stock of symbols of some kind which a communicator ("the speaker") can produce "at will" and which a communicatee ("the audience") can observe: these may be called the "words," though, of course, they need not be anything very like what we should normally call words—they might be signal flags, etc. There must also be something other than the words, which the words are to be used to communicate about: this may be called the "world." There is no reason why the world should not include the words, in every sense except the sense of the actual statement itself which on any particular occasion is being made about the world. Further, the world must exhibit (we must observe) similarities and dissimilarities (there could not be the one without the other): if everything were either absolutely indistinguishable from anything else or completely unlike anything else, there would be nothing to say. And finally (for present purposes —of course there are other conditions to be satisfied too) there must be two sets of conventions:

Descriptive conventions correlating the words (= sentences) which the *types* of situation, thing, event, etc., to be found in the world.

Demonstrative conventions correlating the words (= statements) with the *historic* situations, etc., to be found in the world.[8]

A statement is said to be true when the historic state of affairs to which it is correlated by the demonstrative conventions (the one to which it "refers") is of a type[9] with which the sentence

---

[8] Both sets of conventions may be included together under "semantics." But they differ greatly.

[9] "Is of a type with which" means "is sufficiently like those standard states of affairs with which." Thus, for a statement to be true one state of affairs must be *like* certain others, which is a natural relation, but also *sufficiently* like to merit the same "description," which is no longer a purely natural relation. To say "This is red" is not the same as to say "This is like those," nor even as to say "This is like those which were called red." That things are *similar,* or even "exactly" similar, I may literally see, but that they are the *same* I cannot literally see—in

used in making it is correlated by the descriptive conventions.[10]

3*a*. Troubles arise from the use of the word "facts" for the historic situations, events, etc., and in general, for the world. For "fact" is regularly used in conjunction with "that" in the sentences "The fact is that S" or "It is a fact that S" and in the expression "the fact that S," all of which imply that it would be true to say that S.[11]

This may lead us to suppose that

(i) "fact" is only an alternative expression for "true statement." We note that when a detective says "Let's look at the facts" he doesn't crawl round the carpet, but proceeds to utter a string of statements: we even talk of "stating the facts";

(ii) for every true statement there exists "one" and its own precisely corresponding fact—for every cap the head it fits.

It is (i) which leads to some of the mistakes in "coherence" or formalist theories; (ii) to some of those in "correspondence" theories. Either we suppose that there is nothing there but the true statement itself, nothing to which it corresponds, or else we populate the world with linguistic *Doppelgänger* (and grossly overpopulate it—every nugget of "positive" fact overlaid by a massive concentration of "negative" facts, every tiny detailed fact larded with generous general facts, and so on).

When a statement is true, there is, *of course,* a state of affairs which makes it true and which is *toto mundo* distinct from the true statement about it: but equally of course, we can only *describe* that state of affairs *in words* (either the

---

calling them the same colour a convention is involved additional to the conventional choice of the name to be given to the colour which they are said to be.

[10] The trouble is that sentences contain words or verbal devices to serve both descriptive and demonstrative purposes (not to mention other purposes), often both at once. In philosophy we mistake the descriptive for the demonstrative (theory of universals) or the demonstrative for the descriptive (theory of monads). A sentence as normally distinguished from a mere word or phrase is characterised by its containing a minimum of verbal demonstrative devices (Aristotle's "reference to time"); but many demonstrative conventions are non-verbal (pointing, etc.), and using these we can make a statement in a single word which is not a "sentence." Thus, "languages" like that of (traffic, etc.) *signs* use quite distinct media for their descriptive and demonstrative elements (the sign on the post, the site of the post). And however many verbal demonstrative devices we use as auxiliaries, there must *always* be a non-verbal *origin* for these coordinates, which is the point of utterance of the statement.

[11] I use the following *abbrevations:*—

S   *for* the cat is on the mat.
ST   *for* it is true that the cat is on the mat.
tst   *for* the statement that.

I take tstS as my example throughout and not, say, tst Julius Caesar was bald or tst all mules are sterile, because these latter are apt in their different ways to make us over-

look the distinction between sentence and statement: we have, apparently, in the one case a sentence capable of being used to refer to only one historic situation, in the other a statement without reference to at least (or to any particular) one.

If space permitted other types of statement (existential, general, hypothetical, etc.) should be dealt with: these raise problems rather of meaning than of truth, though I feel uneasiness about hypotheticals.

same or, with luck, others). I can only describe the situation in which it is true to say that I am feeling sick by saying that it is one in which I am feeling sick (or experiencing sensations of nausea)[12]: yet between stating, however, truly that I am feeling sick and feeling sick there is a great gulf fixed.[13]

"Fact that" is a phrase designed for use in situations where the distinction between a true statement and the state of affairs about which it is a truth is neglected; as it often is with advantage in ordinary life, though seldom in philosophy—above all in discussing truth, where it is precisely our business to prise the words off the world and keep them off it. To ask "Is the fact that S the true statement that S or that which it is true of?" may beget absurd answers. To take an analogy: although we may sensibly ask "Do we *ride* the word 'elephant' or the animal?" and equally sensibly "Do we *write* the word or the animal?" it is nonsense to ask "Do we *define* the word or the animal?" For defining an elephant (supposing we ever do this) is a compendious description of an operation involving both word and animal (do we focus the image or the battleship?); and so speaking about "the fact that" is a compendious way of speaking about a situation involving both words and world.[14]

3b. "Corresponds" also gives trouble, because it is commonly given too restricted or too colourful a meaning, or one which in this context it cannot bear. The only essential point is this: that the correlation between the words (= sentences) and the type of situation, event, etc., which is to be such that when a statement in those words is made with reference to a historic situation of that type the statement is then true, is *absolutely and purely* conventional. We are absolutely free to appoint *any* symbol to describe *any* type of situation, so far as merely being true goes. In a small one-spade language tst nuts might be true in exactly the same circumstances as the statement in English that the National Liberals are the people's choice.[15] There is no need whatsoever for the words used in making a true statement to "mirror" in any way, however indirect, any feature whatsoever of the situation or event; a statement no more needs, in order to be true, to reproduce the "multiplicity," say, or the "structure" or "form" of the reality, than a word needs to be echoic or writing pictographic. To suppose that it does, is to fall once again into the error of reading back into the world the features of language.

The more rudimentary a language, the more, very often, it will tend to have a "single" word for a highly "complex" type of situation: this has such disadvan-

---

[12] If this is what was meant by " 'It is raining' is true if and only if it is raining," so far so good.

[13] It takes two to make a truth. Hence (obviously) there can be no criterion of truth in the sense of some feature detectable in the statement itself which will reveal whether it is true or false. Hence, too, a statement cannot without absurdity refer to itself.

[14] "It is true that S" and "It is a fact that S" are applicable in the same circumstances; the cap fits when there is a head it fits. Other words can fill the same role as "fact"; we say, *e.g.,* "The situation is that S."

[15] We could use "nuts" even now as a code-word: but a code, as a transformation of a language, is distinguished from a language, and a code-word despatched is not (called) "true."

tages as that the language becomes elaborate to learn and is incapable of dealing with situations which are non-standard, unforeseen, for which there may just be no word. When we go abroad equipped only with a phrase-book, we may spend long hours learning by heart:

A^i-moest-fa^{i}nd-^{e}tschâ^{r}woum^{e}n,
Ma^i-hwîl-iz-wau^{r}pt (bènt),

and so on and so on, yet faced with the situation where we have the pen of our aunt, find ourselves quite unable to say so. The characteristics of a more developed language (articulation, morphology, syntax, abstractions, etc.), do not make statements in it any more capable of being true or capable of being any more true, they make it more adaptable, more learnable, more comprehensive, more precise and so on; and *these* aims may no doubt be furthered by making the language (allowance made for the nature of the medium) "mirror" in conventional ways features descried in the world.

Yet even when a language does "mirror" such features very closely (and does it ever?) the truth of statements remains still a matter, as it was with the most rudimentary languages, of the words used being the ones *conventionally appointed* for situations of the type to which that referred to belongs. A picture, a copy, a replica, a photograph— these are *never* true in so far as they are reproductions, produced by natural or mechanical means: a reproduction can be accurate or lifelike (true *to* the original), as a gramophone recording or a transcription may be, but not true (*of*) as a record of proceedings can be. In the

same way a (natural) sign *of* something can be infallible or unreliable but only an (artificial) sign *for* something can be right or wrong.[16]

There are many intermediate cases between a true account and a faithful picture, as here somewhat forcibly contrasted, and it is from the study of these (a lengthy matter) that we can get the clearest insight into the contrast. For example, maps: these may be called pictures, yet they are highly conventionalised pictures. If a map can be clear or accurate or misleading, like a statement, why can it not be true or exaggerated? How do the "symbols" used in map-making differ from those used in statement-making? On the other hand, if an air-mosaic is not a map, why is it not? And when does a map become a diagram? These are the really illuminating questions.

4. Some have said that—

To say that an assertion is true is not to make any further assertion at all.

In all sentences of the form "*p* is true" the phrase "is true" is logically superfluous.

To say that a proposition is true is just to assert it, and to say that it is false is just to assert its contradictory.

But wrongly. TstS (except in paradoxical cases of forced and dubious manufacture) refers to the world or

---

[16] Berkeley confuses these two. There will not be books in the running brooks until the dawn of hydro-semantics.

any part of it exclusive of tstS, *i.e.,* of itself.[17] TstST refers to the world or any part of it *inclusive* of tstS, though once again exclusive of itself, *i.e.,* of tstST. That is, tstST refers to something to which tstS cannot refer. TstST does not, certainly, include any statement referring to the world exclusive of tstS which is not included already in tstS— more, it seems doubtful whether it does include that statement about the world exclusive of tstS which is made when we state that S. (If I state that tstS is true, should we really agree that I have stated that S? Only "by implication."[18]) But all this does not go any way to show that tstST is not a statement different from tstS. If Mr. Q writes on a notice-board "Mr. W is a burglar," then a trial is held to decide whether Mr. Q's published statement that Mr. W is a burglar is a libel: finding "Mr. Q's statement was true (in substance and in fact)." Thereupon a second trial is held, to decide whether Mr. W is a burglar, in which Mr. Q's statement is no longer under consideration: verdict "Mr. W is a burglar." It is an arduous business to hold a second trial: why is it done if the verdict is the same as the previous finding?[19]

What is felt is that the evidence considered in arriving at the one verdict is the same as that considered in arriving at the other. This is not strictly correct. It is more nearly correct that whenever tstS is true then tstST is also true and conversely, and that whenever tstS is false tstST is also false and conversely.[20] And it is argued that the words "is true" are logically superfluous because it is believed that generally if any two statements are always true together and always false together then they must mean the same. Now whether this is in general a sound view may be doubted: but even if it is, why should it not break down in the case of so obviously "peculiar" a phrase as "is true"? Mistakes in philosophy notoriously arise through thinking that what holds of "ordinary" words like "red" or "growls" must also hold of extraordinary words like "real" or "exists." But that "true" is just such another extraordinary word is obvious.[21]

There is something peculiar about the "fact" which is described by tstST, something which may make us hesitate to call it a "fact" at all; namely, that the relation between tstS and the world which tstST asserts to obtain is a *purely conventional* relation (one which "thinking makes so"). For we are aware that this relation is one which we could alter at will, whereas we like to restrict the

---

[17] A statement may refer to "itself" in the sense, *e.g.,* of the sentence used or the utterance uttered in making it ("statement" is not exempt from all ambiguity). But paradox does result if a statement purports to refer to itself in a more full-blooded sense, purports, that is, to state that it itself is true, or to state what it itself refers to ("This statement is about Cato").

[18] And "by implication" tstST asserts something about the making of a statement which tstS certainly does not assert.

[19] This is not quite fair: there are many legal and personal reasons for holding two

trials,—which, however, do not affect the point that the issue being tried is not the same.

[20] Not *quite* correct, because tstST is only in place at all when tstS is envisaged as made and has been verified.

[21] *Unum, verum, bonum*—the old favourites deserve their celebrity. There *is* something odd about each of them. Theoretical theology is a form of onomatolatry.

word "fact" to *hard* facts, facts which are natural and unalterable, or anyhow not alterable at will. Thus, to take an analogous case, we may not like calling it a fact that the word elephant means what it does, though we can be induced to call it a (soft) fact—and though, of course, we have no hesitation in calling it a fact that contemporary English speakers use the word as they do.

An important point about this view is that it confuses falsity with negation: for according to it, it is the same thing to say "He is not at home" as to say "It is false that he is at home." (But what if no one has said that he *is* at home? What if he is lying upstairs dead?) Too many philosophers maintain, when anxious to explain away negation, that a negation is just a second order affirmation (to the effect that a certain first order affirmation is false), yet, when anxious to explain away falsity, maintain that to assert that a statement is false is just to assert its negation (contradictory). It is impossible to deal with so fundamental a matter here.[22] Let me

assert the following merely. Affirmation and negation are exactly on a level, in this sense, that no language can exist which does not contain conventions for both and that both refer to the world equally directly, not to statements about the world: whereas a language can quite well exist without any device to do the work of "true" and "false." Any satisfactory theory of truth must be able to cope equally with falsity[23]: but "is false" can only be maintained to be logically superfluous by making this fundamental confusion.

5. There is another way of coming to see that the phrase "is true" is not logically superfluous, and to appreciate what sort of a statement it is to say that a certain statement is true. There are numerous other adjectives which are in

[22] The following two sets of logical axioms are, as Aristotle (though not his successors) makes them, quite distinct:
  (*a*) No statement can be both true and false.
  No statement can be neither true nor false.
  (*b*) Of two contradictory statements—
  Both cannot be true.
  Both cannot be false.
The second set demands a definition of contradictories, and is usually joined with an unconscious postulate that for every statement there is one and only one other statement such that the pair are contradictories. It is doubtful how far any language does or must contain contradictories, however defined, such as to satisfy both this postulate and the set of axioms (*b*).

Those of the so-called "logical paradoxes" (hardly a genuine class) which concern "true" and "false" are *not* to be reduced to cases of self-contradiction, any more than "S but I do not believe it" is. A statement to the effect that it is itself true is every bit as absurd as one to the effect that it is itself false. There are *other* types of sentence which offend against the fundamental conditions of all communication in ways *distinct from* the way in which "This is red and is not red" offends, —*e.g.*, "This does (I do) not exist," or equally absurd "This exists (I exist)." There are more deadly sins than one; nor does the way to salvation lie through any hierarchy.

[23] To be false is (not, of course, to correspond to a non-fact, but) to mis-correspond with a fact. Some have not seen how, then, since the statement which is false does not describe the fact with which it mis-corresponds (but misdescribes it), we know which fact to compare it with: this was because they thought of all linguistic conventions as descriptive,—but it is the demonstrative conventions which fix which situation it is to which the statement refers. No statement can state what it itself refers to.

the same class as "true" and "false," which are concerned, that is, with the relations between the words (as uttered with reference to a historic situation) and the world, and which nevertheless no one would dismiss as logically superfluous. We say, for example, that a certain statement is exaggerated or vague or bald, a description somewhat rough or misleading or not very good, an account rather general or too concise. In cases like these it is pointless to insist on deciding in simple terms whether the statement is "true or false." Is it true or false that Belfast is north of London? That the galaxy is the shape of a fried egg? That Beethoven was a drunkard? That Wellington won the battle of Waterloo? There are various *degrees and dimensions* of success in making statements: the statements fit the facts always more or less loosely, in different ways on different occasions for different intents and purposes. What may score full marks in a general knowledge test may in other circumstances get a gamma. And even the most adroit of languages may fail to "work" in an abnormal situation or to cope, or cope reasonably simply, with novel discoveries: is it true or false that the dog goes round the cow?[24] What, moreover, of the large class of cases where a statement is not so much false (or true) as out of place, *inept* ("All the signs of bread" said when the bread is before us)?

We become obsessed with "truth" when discussing statements, just as we become obsessed with "freedom" when discussing conduct. So long as we think that what has always and alone to be decided is whether a certain action was done freely or was not, we get nowhere: but so soon as we turn instead to the numerous other adverbs used in the same connexion ("accidentally," "unwillingly," "inadvertently," etc.), things become easier, and we come to see that no concluding inference of the form "Ergo, it was done freely (or not freely)" is required. Like freedom, truth is a bare minimum or an illusory ideal (the truth, the whole truth and nothing but the truth about, say, the battle of Waterloo or the *Primavera*).

6. Not merely is it jejune to suppose that all a statement aims to be is "true," but it may further be questioned whether every "statement" does aim to be true at all. The principle of Logic, that "Every proposition must be true or false," has too long operated as the simplest, most persuasive and most pervasive form of the descriptive fallacy. Philosophers under its influence have forcibly interpreted all "propositions" on the model of the statement that a certain thing is red, as made when the thing concerned is currently under observation.

[24] Here there is much sense in "coherence" (and pragmatist) theories of truth, despite their failure to appreciate the trite but central point that truth is a matter of the relation beween words and world, and despite their wrong-headed *Gleichschaltung* of all varieties of statemental failure under the one head of "partly true" (thereafter wrongly equated with "part of the truth"). "Correspondence" theorists too often talk as one would who held that every map is either accurate or inaccurate; that accuracy is a single and the sole virtue of a map; that every country can have but one accurate map; that a map on a larger scale or showing different features must be a map of a different country; and so on.

Recently, it has come to be realized that many utterances which have been taken to be statements (merely because they are not, on grounds of grammatical form, to be classed as commands, questions, etc.) are not in fact descriptive, nor susceptible of being true or false. When is a statement not a statement? When it is a formula in a calculus: when it is a performatory utterance: when it is a value-judgment: when it is a definition: when it is part of a work of fiction—there are many such suggested answers. It is simply not the business of such utterances to "correspond to the facts" (and even genuine statements have other businesses besides that of so corresponding).

It is a matter for decision how far we should continue to call such masqueraders "statements" at all, and how widely we should be prepared to extend the uses of "true" and "false" in "different senses." My own feeling is that it is better, when once a masquerader has been unmasked, *not* to call it a statement and *not* to say it is true or false. In ordinary life we should not call most of them statements at all, though philosophers and grammarians may have come to do so (or rather, have lumped them all together under the term of art "proposition"). We make a difference between "You said you promised" and "You stated that you promised": the former can mean that you said "I promise," whereas the latter must mean that you said "I promised": the latter, which we say you "stated," is something which is true or false, whereas for the former, which is not true or false, we use the wider verb to "say." Similarly, there is a difference between "You say this is (call this) a good picture" and "You

state that this is a good picture." Moreover, it was only so long as the real nature of arithmetical formulae, say, or of geometrical axioms remained unrecognised, and they were thought to record information about the world, that it was reasonable to call them "true" (and perhaps even "statements,"—though were they ever so called?): but once their nature has been recognized, we no longer feel tempted to call them "true" or to dispute about their truth or falsity.

In the cases so far considered the model "This is red" breaks down because the "statements" assimilated to it are not of a nature to correspond to facts at all,—the words are not descriptive words, and so on. But there is also another type of case where the words *are* descriptive words and the "proposition" does in a way have to correspond to facts, but precisely not in the way that "This is red" and similar statements setting up to be true have to do.

In the human predicament, for use in which our language is designed, we may wish to speak about states of affairs which have not been observed or are not currently under observation (the future, for example). And although we *can* state anything "as a fact" (which statement will then be true or false[25]) we need not do so: we need only say "The cat *may be* on the mat." This utterance is quite different from tstS,—it is not a statement at all (it is not true or false; it is compatible with "The cat may *not* be on the mat"). In the same way, the situation in which we discuss whether and state that tstS is *true* is

_____

[25] Though it is not yet in place to call it either. For the same reason, one cannot lie or tell the truth about the future.

different from the situation in which we discuss whether it is *probable* that S. Tst it is probable that S is out of place, inept, in the situation where we can make tstST, and, I think, conversely. It is not our business here to discuss probability: but is worth observing that the phrases "It is true that" and "It is probable that" are in the same line of business,[26] and in so far incompatibles.

7. In a recent article in *Analysis* Mr. Strawson has propounded a view of truth which it will be clear I do not accept. He rejects the "semantic" account of truth on the perfectly correct ground that the phrase "is true" is not used in talking about *sentences,* supporting this with an ingenious hypothesis as to how meaning may have come to be confused with truth: but this will not suffice to show what he wants,— that "is true" is not used in talking about (or that "truth is not a property of") *anything.* For it *is* used in talking about *statements* (which in his article he does not distinguish clearly from sentences). Further, he supports the "logical superfluity" view to this extent, that he agrees that to say that ST is not to make any further assertion at all, beyond the assertion that S: but he disagrees with it in so far as he thinks that to say that ST *is* to *do* something more than just to assert that S,—it is

namely to *conform* or to *grant* (or something of that kind) the assertion, made or taken as made already, that S. It will be clear that and why I do not accept the first part of this: but what of the second part? I agree that to say that ST "is" very often, and according to the all-important linguistic occasion, to confirm tstS or to grant it or what not; but this cannot show that to say that ST is not also and at the same time to make an assertion about tstS. To say that I believe you "is" on occasion to accept your statement; but it is also to make an assertion, which is not made by the strictly performatory utterance "I accept your statement." It is common for quite ordinary statements to have a performatory "aspect": to say that you are a cuckold may be to insult you, but it is also and at the same time to make a statement which is true or false. Mr. Strawson, moreover, seems to confine himself to the case where I *say* "Your statement is true" or something similar, —but what of the case where you state that S and I *say* nothing but *"look and see"* that your statement is true? I do not see how this critical case, to which nothing analogous occurs with strictly performatory utterances, could be made to respond to Mr. Strawson's treatment.

One final point: if it is admitted (*if*) that the rather boring yet satisfactory relation between words and world which has here been discussed does genuinely occur, why should the phrase "is true" not be our way of describing it? And if it is not, what else is?

---

[26] Compare the odd behaviours of "was" and "will be" when attached to "true" and to "probable."

METAPHYSICS

The writer of the following selection, John Wisdom, has produced several papers of great importance to the linguistic movement. He views philosophy as less like trying to discover elusive facts than getting out of a maze. Puzzlement leads to the asking of philosophical questions, but these are really requests for a ruling on the use of sentences where ordinary language gives no clear answer. Philosophical statements, then, are verbal recommendations made in response to such questions. Yet they are more than this, for they clarify and give us a better understanding of the language we use. "Philosophical theories are illuminating . . . when they suggest or draw attention to a terminology which reveals likenesses and differences which are concealed by ordinary language." They may be likened to a net that catches some similarities but allows others to slip away. Thus "philosophical theories exhibit both linguistic confusion and linguistic penetration."

This view of philosophy is utilized by Wisdom as he turns to the problems of metaphysics and the verification principle. He finds that the verification principle, so often used against metaphysics, is actually a metaphysical principle itself; for it is a recommendation about meaning, designed to be illuminating. (The opposite principle is called by Wisdom the Idiosyncrasy Platitude: namely, every statement has its own sort of meaning.) Like all metaphysics, the principle is concerned with "reduplication questions"; are X facts to be identified with Y facts? It is this question which leads the metaphysician to his metaphysical statements. So identified, however, metaphysics must not be confused with crude falsehoods or nonsense; it is, rather, suggestions of how language might be used to reveal the hidden in the actual use of language.

4 Metaphysics and Verification

John Wisdom (1904-   )

"The meaning of a statement is the method of its verification." Some philosophers bring out this principle with confidence and satisfaction, others are

The selection is from John Wisdom, "Metaphysics and Verification," *Mind,* 46 (1937), pp. 452–498, with omissions. Reprinted in *Philosophy and Psychoanalysis* (Oxford: Basil Blackwell; New York: Philosophical Library, 1953). Used by permission of the author, the Editor of *Mind,* and the publishers.

utterly opposed to it and cannot understand how anyone can be so wrongheaded as to insist upon what so little reflection shows to be so palpably untrue. This conflict is of the greatest importance in philosophy today, and it is easy to see why. The Verification Principle is the generalization of a very large class of metaphysical theories, namely all naturalistic, empirical, positivistic theories. While its opposite, which I venture to call the Idiosyncrasy

Platitude, is the generalization of all common-sense, realist, transcendental theories. The verification principle is the generalization of such theories as: A cherry is nothing but sensations and possibilities of more; A mind is nothing but a pattern of behavior; There are no such things as numbers only numerals, and the laws of logic and mathematics are really rules of grammar; Beauty is nothing but the features in respect of which a thing is beautiful, and the feelings these arouse. According to the idiosyncrasy platitude every sort of statement has its own sort of meaning, and when philosophers ask "What is the analysis of X-propositions?" the answer is that they are ultimate, that "everything is what it is and not another thing" (Butler, quoted by Moore on the title-page of *Principia Ethica*). This principle is the generalization of theories such as: Ethical propositions involve value predicates and are ultimate; Psychological propositions are not reducible to physiological propositions, they are ultimate; Mathematical propositions are necessary synthetic propositions—an ultimate sort of proposition; Statements about nations are not to be reduced to statements about individuals, they are about a certain sort of concrete universal.

There are not other answers to these metaphysical questions. Consequently most or all metaphysical conflict finds expression in "Shall we or shall we not accept the principle that the meaning of a statement is the method of its verification?" and sometimes "Is the verification principle true?" I do not at all wish to suggest that we cannot get on with metaphysical questions without first dealing with this question. On the contrary if I were forced to consider either first the verification principle and then other metaphysical theories or first the other theories and then the principle, I should much prefer the latter plan. In fact an intermediate plan is best—first an examination of easier metaphysical and nearly metaphysical questions, then a mention of the verification principle, then an attack upon the more difficult theories, then a more thorough investigation of the verification principle, then a return to the theories. . . .[1]

But now suppose someone were to ask "Is the verification principle true?" What would you do? I myself should at once ask for the question to be put in the wider, less answer-fixing form "Shall we accept the verification principle?" For I believe the other form misleads us as to the general nature of the question asked. I believe that this is of the utmost importance because I be-

---

[1] On the whole the process of thought has been from the more specific theories to the more general, from the doctrine that analytic propositions are verbal to the doctrine that all necessary propositions are verbal, and from this and such theories as those mentioned above to the verification principle, rather than deductively downwards from it. I admit that in the writings of those supporters of the principle who are positivists (I have in mind such writings as those of Ayer and Schlick) there is to be found ground for Dr. Ewing's accusation that the procedure has been from the principle to the specific theories. Such a procedure, once the verification principle has been recommended by the specific cases, is perfectly satisfactory in a way I shall try to explain. But when the verification principle is regarded as an equation and the "deductions" treated as deductions (calculations) then such a procedure leads to what it has led to—insistence and contrainsistence without end—dead-lock.

lieve that once its general nature is apparent the question "Is it true or not?" vanishes into insignificance while its important metaphysical merits and demerits will have become apparent in the process. . . .

Well, shall we accept the verification principle? What is it to accept it? When people bring out with a dashing air the words "The meaning of a statement is really simply the method of its verification," like one who says "The value of a thing is really simply its power in exchange,"[2] in what sort of way are they using words? What is the general nature of their theory?

The answer is "It is a metaphysical theory." True, it is a peculiar metaphysical theory as appears from the fact that we are inclined to say: It is not so much a metaphysical theory as a recipe for framing metaphysical theories; It is not a metaphysical theory, it is a mnemonic device for getting from metaphysical theories which have been illuminating in easy metaphysical difficulties to theories which shall work in harder cases, a mnemonic device reminding us how to meet objections to positivistic theories; It is a recommendation to so use "mean" that S means the same as S′ provided they are verified in the same way, where this recommendation is not for the purpose of metaphysically illuminating the use of "meaning" but for another metaphysical purpose, namely the illumination of the use of expressions which on the recommended use of "meaning" will be said to mean the same. It is this "altruism"

---

[2] Indeed one might put the verification principle in the form "the meaning of symbols is really simply their power in prediction."

which makes the verification principle a peculiar metaphysical theory. But it is the *likeness* of the verification principle to metaphysical theories which I now want to emphasize and explain. It is like not only to such theories as "A mind is really simply a pattern of behavior," "Goodness is a matter of causing approval," but also to such theories as "We never really know that what we see is real and not a dream," "We never really know what is going on in another person's mind," "Nothing is really the same from moment to moment," "All words are vague." It is to emphasize this likeness that I call the verification principle a metaphysical theory. I should be prepared to argue that there is nothing incorrect in calling it this. But that is neither here nor there. What we are concerned with is its metaphysical nature. And to illuminate this I say that it is a sort of metaphysical theory; and for our purpose it does not matter whether it is a sort of metaphysical theory (*a*) in the way that a hackney is a sort of horse, or (*b*) in 'the way that a motor cycle is, because it is a sort of tireless horse on wheels. If (*a*) my statement is correct; if (*b*) it is not. But this correctness is of no importance. For I make the statement to draw attention to certain likenesses, and whether they suffice or no for the proper application of "metaphysical" does not affect their existence. I say that the verification principle is a metaphysical principle because I want (1) to draw the attention of those who accept it to the deplorably old-fashioned clothes in which it presents itself. Indeed it resembles not only positivistic theories but also the worst transcendental theories by appearing in the disguise either of a scientific discovery removing popular illusion, or of a logical equation (incorrect) from which deductions may be made. No wonder our conservative friends cannot accept it. I want (2) to draw the attention of those who reject it to the fact that because they are taken in by its disguise they fail to recognize the merits which like other metaphysical theories it conceals. Both those who accept it and those who reject it do not realize what they are doing because they do not notice that it is disguised. But metaphysics reveals the hidden, plucks the mask of appearance from the face of reality—and we shall now see what a metaphysical theory really is and thus the general nature of the verification principle.

To say that the verification principle is a sort of metaphysical theory would be already extremely illuminating if we had already an adequate grasp of the ultimate nature of metaphysical theories, but lacking this we must go on. It is possible to go on in either of the two following ways: We may examine the nature of the verification principle and thus throw light on the nature of other metaphysical theories, or we may examine the nature of other metaphysical theories and thus throw light on the nature of the verification principle. Let us adopt the latter plan and work from the specific to the general. Then applying our results in a direct examination of the verification principle we shall obtain a review of the whole of metaphysics because the verification principle is the generalization of one set of answers to metaphysical questions while its opposite is the generalization of the opposing answers. . . .

Let us now take an example from another class of metaphysical questions. These arise, not from the "queerness" of the form of the class of propositions which is felt to be queer, but because of the queerness of the category of what they are about. These are apt to present themselves in the form "What is X?" "What are X's?" where "X" is a name for the puzzling category, or a name for a species of that category. We have for example, "What are characteristics? What are numbers? What are abstract, necessary propositions about?" and we have "What are chairs and tables? What are material things?" "What is a nation? Is it something over and above the individuals of that nation?" "What is Time?"

Suppose we offer an answer to the last on the lines suggested by Moore. We say, "Well, when we speak about time, what are we talking about? Such facts as this—that lunch is over, supper to come, that Smith's anger is past and so on. Let us call such facts 'temporal facts.' Then 'Time is unreal,' can be translated into the concrete (Moore's phrase) by 'There are no temporal facts.' " When we read this, we draw a breath of relief. This is the stuff. With this translation into the concrete, we get "the cash value" (Broad), the predictive power, of the statement "Time is unreal." What a contrast to the answer "Time is an abstract entity, super-sensible, having a sort of existence all its own." For the latter answer only tells us that time is not brown or yellow, not big or little, not to be found in the bathroom, and like Space only different. Such an answer only emphasizes what ordinary language suggests that, besides the facts that lunch is over and his anger past, there is the fact that Time is real. True, Moore did not *find* a definition, but he showed how it was a mere accident of language that we could not provide a definition and thus remove an uneasy feeling about Time, just as we did when we had the uneasy feeling that though the class of all men is not to be identified with its members, yet there were not in addition to the facts about men, *e.g.,* that men exist, that all are mortal, facts about the class of men, *e.g.,* that it exists, has members, has members which are mortal.

We may say here that Moore meets a philosophical request, even, if you like, a metaphysical request, not indeed by finding but by creating an analytic definition.

I do not wish to deny this any more than I wish to deny that Russell did the same with his definition of number.[3] They both translated sentences which trouble us into others which do not.

But of course there will be people dissatisfied with this answer. They fall into two very different classes: In the first place, some will say "What is meant by 'Time is real' is different from what is meant by 'Either lunch is over, or my supper yet to come, or his anger is past, or something of that sort (i.e., and so on).' What I have in mind when I say 'Time is unreal,' is very different from what I have in mind if I say 'Either lunch is over or etc.'" And yet these same people, some of them, will not be satisfied by any definition which does not put "Time is unreal" in terms of individual events. So they reject every

[3 Russell's definition is: "The number of a class is the class of all those classes that are similar to it." It is discussed in Chapter II of his *Introduction to Mathematical Philosophy* (London, 1919). *Ed.*]

definition either on the ground that it is incorrect or on the ground that it is not sufficiently profound. The nature of this difficulty in metaphysics and the light it throws upon its nature will appear later.

In the second place, there are people who will say that even the definition in terms of individual events or temporal facts is not sufficiently profound; they ask that the definition should be taken further. And if we say "By temporal facts we mean such facts as 'Smith's anger is past' and so on" they complain (*a*) against the "specimen" fact as again involving time, or (*b*) against the phrase "and so on." It is soon clear that there is nothing to be done for them with regard to (*a*). We may try saying "His anger is past" means "He was angry and is not." But it is a hopeless game. The reply will be that "He was angry" involves Time again. And of course it involves it if any sentence using a verb with a tense involves Time. And it is now apparent that this is how the metaphysician uses "involves Time." He cannot translate sentences which work like the ones with tenses into sentences involving only a timeless "is" such as "Red is a color." But this is what he wants. Nothing short of it will do, nothing else will be a reduction of temporal facts to non-temporal. No new language will help. Suppose we invent a new language with no time-indicating words such as "was," "will be" and no time-indicating endings such as "ed." Now the new sentences, if they are to provide translations, must do the work the old did; so there must be differences between those which correspond to the old "was"-sentences and those which correspond to the old "will be"-sentences. We might put them in different colored inks (compare Ramsey's writing negatives as positives upside down). But then the new sentences would surely again express temporal propositions.

I am well aware that there is nothing novel in the conclusion that temporal propositions are unanalyzable, and that this unanalyzability is not a matter of our being unable to do or find the analysis but of the nature of the facts. Prof. Broad supports far more fully and carefully than I have done this very conclusion about temporal facts. . . .

In general: The metaphysically-minded person feels that the actual world is made up solely of positive, specific, determinate, concrete, contingent, individual, sensory facts, and that the appearance of a penumbra of fictional, negative, general, indeterminate, abstract, necessary, super-individual, physical facts is somehow only an appearance due to a lack of penetration upon our part. And he feels that there are not, in addition to the ways of knowing the nonpenumbral facts, additional ways of knowing employed for ascertaining the penumbral facts. At the same time the penumbral do not seem to be identical with the nonpenumbral and thus *do* seem to call for extra ways of knowing.

Now this feeling of taking the same reality twice over (McTaggart), this feeling of superfluous entities (Russell), this feeling of metaphysical double vision has been removed in certain cases by definition. . . . We can imagine someone wondering how we know that when (1) there are two white goats and four black in a field then (2) there are six goats in the field or there exists a class *goats-in-that-field* which has six members. Definition removes these

troubles. Take the last case. When we saw that the two sentences meant the same or that the meaning of the one included the meaning of the other, then the appearance of plurality was explained by the plurality of sentences, while the assurance of identity was justified in the single meaning made true by a single fact. And with the disappearance of the ontological puzzle the epistemological puzzle vanished also. No wonder the definition model fascinated.

But unfortunately, as we have seen, there are cases where definitions cannot be found, where no ingenuity reveals non-penumbral sentences which we can feel sure mean the same as the penumbrals. And yet we cannot feel that the facts which make the penumbral true are anything but the positive, concrete etc. non-penumbral facts which make up the actual world. Indeed there are cases where we know that there are no non-penumbral sentences which mean the same in the ordinary use of "mean the same" as the penumbral, while yet some of us feel that there is no difference between the facts which make those penumbral sentences true and those which make the non-penumbral sentences true. Some people come down on one side of the fence, some on the other. Thus Broad argues from the fact that the question "Fido behaves in all respects intelligently, but is he intelligent?" is not silly like "Smith is rich, but is he wealthy?" to the conclusion that the question is synthetic like "I have given Smith 2 ounces of arsenic, but will it kill him?" That is, he concludes that the sentences "Fido behaves in all respects intelligently" and "Fido is intelligent" do not mean the same, do not stand for the same proposition, do not stand for the same fact. To do this is to represent the question "Smith still breathes, and he nods, smiles, and talks as usual, but does he really think and feel?" as like the question "Smoke still comes from the chimneys, the lights go on in the evenings, but have the inhabitants fled?" Has Smith's soul left his body but arranged with the nervous system that appearances shall be kept up in its absence? Has his *rha* flown? And yet we feel that the question is *not* like this—yet surely it must be, for Broad's premises are true and there is no logical slip. . . .

To sum up: The metaphysician is concerned with certain fundamental ontological and epistemological reduplication questions: Are X facts to be identified with Y facts? How do we get from knowledge of the latter to knowledge of the former?

Usually, even as questions of logic, there is no right or wrong answer to these questions. I should be inclined to say this in every case where the question is in the form in which reduplication is most intolerable, namely, "Are X facts nothing but Y facts or are they something over and above Y facts?" Sometimes in the form in which reduplication is less intolerable, namely, "Do X sentences mean the same as Y sentences" (taken as a question of logic) there is a correct answer "No."

But in either case the metaphysical dispute is resolved by explaining what induces each disputant to say what he does. This is done as follows: 1. Explain the nature of the question or request; (*a*) Negatively—remove the wrong idea that it is a question of fact whether natural *or logical;* (*b*) Positively—give the right idea by showing

how, as in other disputes of this unanswerable sort, the questions are really requests for a description of (1) those features of the use of the expressions involved in the questions which incline one to answer "Yes," and of (2) those features of their use which incline one to answer "No." In the case of ontological questions such as "Are X facts to be identified with Y facts?" "Do X sentences mean the same as Y sentences?" "Does the sentence S stand for the same fact as the sentence S′?" the expressions involved are, of course, (*a*) the expressions "X facts," "Y facts," "X sentences," "Y sentences," "The sentence S" and so on, and (*b*) the *connectives* "stand for the same fact," "mean the same" and so on. In the case of epistemological questions, expressions such as "know," "rational," take the place of the connectives.

2. Second there is the work of providing the descriptions that are really wanted.

Fortunately when the nature of the questions has been explained, then the nature of the "answers," "theories" and "reasons" which they have been "offering" and "advancing" becomes clear to the disputants. And then it becomes clear how much of the work of providing the descriptions has been already done, though under the disguise of a logical dispute. Thus the metaphysical paradoxes appear no longer as crude falsehoods about how language is actually used, but as penetrating suggestions as to how it might be used so as to reveal what, by the actual use of language, is hidden. And metaphysical platitudes appear as timely reminders of what is revealed by the actual use of language and would be hidden by the new. To take an example which we have ourselves come upon: Some have said "Analytic propositions are verbal," others have said "They are not," and, in supporting these "views," they have between them done all that is primarily asked for by one who asks "Are analytic propositions verbal or are they not?"

Thus it appears how it is that, to give metaphysicians what they want, we have to do little more than remove the spectacles through which they look at their own work. Then they see how those hidden identities and diversities which lead to the "insoluble" reduction questions about forms, categories and predicates, have already been revealed, though in a hidden way.

ETHICS

Linguistic philosophers who work in ethics have generally understood their goal to be, not to add to the stock of man's moral knowledge or to make moral pronouncements (sometimes called normative ethics), but rather to attend to the analysis of our ethical utterances and of key words like "good" (metaethics). It is just such an analysis which is given below by R. M. Hare. Following the earlier work of G. E. Moore, Hare denies that "good" can be identified with any natural property like yellow or pleasant. Moore called this the naturalistic fallacy because it is always possible to ask whether *that* property is good. Rather, Hare says, good and similar words are the names of "supervenient" properties. By this, Hare means that good applies to many classes of objects, not just a single class. Further, in the uses of value words like good, the paramount meaning is evaluative, and describing is only a secondary function. In such a distinction is shown the logical peculiarity of good, whose primary function is to commend something to us.

5 The Logic of "Good"

R. M. Hare *(1919-   )*

"Naturalism"

5.2. Let me illustrate one of the most characteristic features of value-words in terms of a particular example. It is a feature sometimes described by saying that "good" and other such words are the names of "supervenient" or "consequential" properties. Suppose that a picture is hanging upon the wall and we are discussing whether it is a good picture; that is to say, we are debating whether to assent to, or dissent from, the judgment "P is a good picture." It must be understood that the context makes it clear that we mean by "good picture" not "good likeness" but "good work of art"—though both these uses would be value-expressions.

First let us notice a very important peculiarity of the word "good" as used in this sentence. Suppose that there is another picture next to P in the gallery (I will call it Q). Suppose that either P is a replica of Q or Q of P, and we do not know which, but do know that both were painted by the same artist at about the same time. Now there is one thing that we cannot say; we cannot say "P is exactly like Q in all respects save this

one, that P is a good picture and Q not." If we were to say this, we should invite the comment, "But how can one be good and the other not, if they are exactly alike? There must be some *further* difference between them to make one good and the other not." Unless we at least admit the relevance of the question "What makes one good and the other not?" we are bound to puzzle our hearers; they will think that something has gone wrong with our use of the word "good." Sometimes we cannot specify just what it is that makes one good and the other not; but there always must be something. Suppose that in the attempt to explain our meaning we said: "I didn't say that there *was* any other difference between them; there is just this one difference, that one is good and the other not. Surely you would understand me if I said that one was *signed* and the other not, but that there was otherwise no difference? So why shouldn't I say that one was *good* and the other not, but that there was otherwise no difference?" The answer to this protest is that the word "good" is not like the word "signed"; there is a difference in their logic. . . .

5.4. Let us then ask whether 'good' behaves in the way that we have noticed for the same reason that 'rectangular' does; in other words, whether there are certain characteristics of pictures which are defining characteristics of a good picture, in the same way as "having all its angles 90 degrees and being a rec-

---

The selection is taken from Part II of *The Language of Morals* (Oxford: The Clarendon Press, 1952). Used by permission of Clarendon Press and the author.

[In giving his permission, Professor Hare wishes to call the reader's attention to the fact that full understanding of his position requires, of course, a reading of his entire argument. *Ed.*]

tilinear plane figure" are defining characteristics of a rectangle. Moore thought that he could prove that there were no such defining characteristics for the word "good" as used in morals. His argument has been assailed since he propounded it; and it is certainly true that the formulation of it was at fault. But it seems to me that Moore's argument was not merely plausible; it rests, albeit insecurely, upon a secure foundation; there is indeed something about the way in which, and the purposes for which, we use the word "good" which makes it impossible to hold the sort of position which Moore was attacking, although Moore did not see clearly what this something was. Let us, therefore, try to restate Moore's argument in a way which makes it clear why "naturalism" is untenable, not only for the moral use of "good" as he thought, but also for many other uses.

Let us suppose for the sake of argument that there are some "defining characteristics" of a good picture. It does not matter of what sort they are; they can be a single characteristic, or a conjunction of characteristics, or a disjunction of alternative characteristics. Let us call the group of these characteristics C. "P is a good picture" will then mean the same as "P is a picture and P is C." For example, let C mean "Having a tendency to arouse in people who are at that time members of the Royal Academy (or any other definitely specified group of people), a definitely recognizable feeling called 'admiration'." The words "definitely specified" and "definitely recognizable" have to be inserted, for otherwise we might find that words in the *definiens* were being used evaluatively, and this would make the defini-

tion no longer "naturalistic." Now suppose that we wish to say that the members of the Royal Academy have good taste in pictures. To have good taste in pictures means to have this definitely recognizable feeling of admiration for those pictures, and only those pictures, which are good pictures. If therefore we wish to say that the members of the Royal Academy have good taste in pictures, we have, according to the definition, to say something which means the same as saying that they have this feeling of admiration for pictures which have a tendency to arouse in them this feeling.

Now this is not what we wanted to say. We wanted to say that they admired good pictures; we have succeeded only in saying that they admired pictures which they admired. Thus if we accept the definition we debar ourselves from saying something that we do sometimes want to say. What this something is will become apparent later; for the moment let us say that what we wanted to do was to *commend* the pictures which the members of the Royal Academy admired. Something about our definition prevented our doing this. We could no longer commend the pictures which they admired, we could only say that they admired those pictures which they admired. Thus our definition has prevented us, in one crucial case, from commending something which we want to commend. That is what is wrong with it.

Let us generalize. If "P is a good picture" is held to mean the same as "P is a picture and P is C," then it will become impossible to commend pictures for being C; it will be possible only to say that they are C. It is important to realize that this difficulty has nothing to do with the particular example that I have chosen. It is not because we have chosen the wrong defining characteristics; it is because, whatever defining characteristics we choose, this objection arises, that we can no longer commend an object for possessing those characteristics.

Let us illustrate this by another example. I am deliberately excluding for the moment moral examples because I want it to be clear that the logical difficulties which we are encountering have nothing to do with morals in particular, but are due to the general characteristics of value-words. Let us consider the sentence "S is a good strawberry." We might naturally suppose that this means nothing more than "S is a strawberry and S is sweet, juicy, firm, red, and large." But it then becomes impossible for us to say certain things which in our ordinary talk we do say. We sometimes want to say that a strawberry is a good strawberry because it is sweet, etc. This —as we can at once see if we think of ourselves saying it—does not mean the same as saying that a strawberry is a sweet, etc., strawberry because it is sweet, etc. But according to the proposed definition this is what it would mean. Thus here again the proposed definition would prevent our saying something that we do succeed in saying meaningfully in our ordinary talk. . . .

Meaning and Criteria

6.2. It is a characteristic of "good" that it can be applied to any number of different classes of objects. We have good cricket-bats, good chronometers, good fire-extinguishers, good pictures, good sunsets, good men. The same is true of the word "red"; all the objects I have just listed might be red. We have to ask first whether, in explaining the meaning of the word "good" it would be possible to explain its meaning in all of these expressions at once, or whether it would be necessary to explain "good cricket-bat" first, and then go on to explain "good chronometer" in the second lesson, "good fire-extinguisher" in the third, and so on; and if the latter, whether in each lesson we should be teaching something entirely new—like teaching the meaning of "fast dye" after we had in a previous lesson taught the meaning of "fast motor-car"—or whether it would be just the same lesson over again, with a different example— like teaching "red dye" after we had taught "red motor-car." Or there might be some third possibility.

The view that "good chronometer" would be a completely new lesson, even though the day before we had taught "good cricket-bat," runs at once into difficulties. For it would mean that at any one time our learner could only use the word "good" in speaking of classes of objects which he had learnt so far. He would never be able to go straight up to a new class of objects and use the word "good" of one of them. When he had learnt "good cricket-bat" and "good chronometer," he would not be able to manage "good fire-extinguisher"; and when he had learnt the latter, he would still be unable to manage "good motor-car." But in fact one of the most noticeable things about the way we use "good" is that we are able to use it for entirely new classes of objects that we have never called "good" before. Suppose that someone starts collecting cacti for the first time and puts one on his mantel-piece—the only cactus in the country. Suppose then that a friend sees it, and says "I must have one of those"; so he sends for one from wherever they grow, and puts it on his mantel-piece, and when his friend comes in, he says, "I've got a better cactus than yours." But how does he know how to apply the word in this way? He has never learnt to apply "good" to cacti; he does not even know any *criteria* for telling a good cactus from a bad one (for as yet there are none); but he has learnt to use the word "good," and having learnt that, he can apply it to any class of objects that he requires to place in order of merit. He and his friend may dispute about the criteria of good cacti; they may attempt to set up rival criteria; but they could not even do this unless they were from the start under no difficulty in using the word "good." Since, therefore, it is possible to use the word "good" for a new class of objects without further instruction, learning the use of the word for one class of objects cannot be a different lesson from learning it for another class of objects—though learning the criteria of goodness in a new class of objects may be a new lesson each time. . . .

To teach *what makes* a member of any class a good member of the class is indeed a new lesson for each class of objects; but nevertheless the word "good" has a constant meaning which, once learnt, can be understood no matter what class of objects is being discussed. We have, as I have already said, to make a distinction between the meaning of the word "good" and the criteria for its application. . . .

Description and Evaluation

7.1. . . . There are two sorts of things that we can say, for example, about strawberries; the first sort is usually called *descriptive*, the second sort *evaluative*. Examples of the first sort of remark are, "This strawberry is sweet" and "This strawberry is large, red, and juicy." Examples of the second sort of remark are "This is a good strawberry" and "This strawberry is just as strawberries ought to be." The first sort of remark is often given as a reason for making the second sort of remark; but the first sort does not by itself entail the second sort, nor vice versa. Yet there seems to be some close logical connexion between them. Our problem is: "What is this connexion?" for no light is shed by saying that there is a connexion, unless we can say what it is.

The problem may also be put in this way: if we knew all the descriptive properties which a particular strawberry had (knew, of every descriptive sentence relating to the strawberry, whether it was true or false), and if we knew also the meaning of the word "good," then what else should we require to know, in order to be able to tell whether a strawberry was a good one? Once the question is put in this way, the answer should be apparent. We should require to know, what are the criteria in virtue of which a strawberry is to be called a good one, or what are the characteristics that make a strawberry a good one, or what is the standard of goodness in strawberries. We should require to be given the major premises. We have already seen that we can know the meaning of "good strawberry" without knowing any of these latter things—though there is also a sense of the sentence "What does it mean to call a strawberry a good one?" in which we should not know the answer to it, unless we also knew the answer to these other questions. It is now time to elucidate and distinguish these two ways in which we can be said to know what it means to call an object a good member of its class. This will help us to see more clearly both the differences and the similarities between "good" and words like "red" and "sweet."

Since we have been dwelling for some time on the differences, it will do no harm now to mention some of the similarities. For this purpose, let us consider the two sentences: "M is a red motor-car" and "M is a good motor-car." . . .

The first similarity between "M is a red motor-car" and "M is a good motor-car" is that both can be, and often are, used for conveying information of a purely factual or descriptive character. If I say to someone "M is a good motor-car," and he himself has not seen, and knows nothing of M, but does on the other hand know what sorts of motor-car we are accustomed to call "good" (knows what is the accepted standard of goodness in motor-cars), he undoubtedly receives information from my remark about what sort of motor-car it is. He will complain that I have misled him, if he subsequently discovers that M will not go over 30 m.p.h., or uses as much oil as petrol, or is covered with rust, or has large holes in the roof. His reason for complaining will be the same as it would have been if I had said that the car was red and he subsequently discovered that it was black. I should have led him to expect the motor-car to be of a certain description when in fact it was of a quite different description.

The second similarity between the two sentences is this. Sometimes we use

them, not for actually conveying information, but for putting our hearer into a position subsequently to use the word "good" or "red" for giving or getting information. Suppose, for example, that he is utterly unfamiliar with motor-cars in the same sort of way as most of us are unfamiliar with horses nowadays, and knows no more about motor-cars than is necessary in order to distinguish a motor-car from a hansom cab. In that case, my saying to him "M is a good motor-car" will not give him any information about M, beyond the information that it is a motor-car. But if he is able then or subsequently to examine M, he will have learnt something. He will have learnt that some of the characteristics which M has, are characteristics which make people—or at any rate me—call it a good motor-car. This may not be to learn very much. But suppose that I make judgments of this sort about a great many motor-cars, calling some good and some not good, and he is able to examine all or most of the motor-cars about which I am speaking; he will in the end learn quite a lot, always presuming that I observe a consistent standard in calling them good or not good. He will eventually, if he pays careful attention, get into the position in which he knows, after I have said that a motor-car is a good one, what sort of a motor-car he may expect it to be—for example fast, stable on the road, and so on.

Now if we were dealing, not with "good," but with "red," we should call this process "explaining the meaning of the word"—and we might indeed, in a sense, say that what I have been doing is explaining what one means by "a good motor-car." This is a sense of "mean" about which, as we have seen, we must be on our guard. The processes, however, are very similar. I might explain the meaning of "red" by continually saying of various motor-cars "M is a red motor-car," "N is not a red motor-car," and so on. If he were attentive enough, he would soon get into a position in which he was able to use the word "red" for giving or getting information, at any rate about motor-cars. And so, both with "good" and with "red," there is this process, which in the case of "red" we may call "explaining the meaning," but in the case of "good" may only call it so loosely and in a secondary sense; to be clear we must call it something like "explaining or conveying or setting forth the standard of goodness in motor-cars."

The standard of goodness, like the meaning of "red," is normally something which is public and commonly accepted. When I explain to someone the meaning of "red motor-car," he expects, unless I am known to be very eccentric, that he will find other people using it in the same way. And similarly, at any rate with objects like motor-cars where there is a commonly accepted standard, he will expect, having learnt from me what is the standard of goodness in motor-cars, to be able, by using the expression "good motor-car," to give information to other people, and get it from them, without confusion.

A third respect in which "good motor-car" resembles "red motor-car" is the following: both "good" and "red" can vary as regards the exactitude or vagueness of the information which they do or can convey. We normally use the expression "red motor-car" very loosely. Any motor-car that lies somewhere between the unmistakably purple and the unmistakably orange could without abuse of language be called a red motor-car. And similarly, the standard for calling motor-cars good is commonly very loose. There are certain characteristics, such as inability to exceed 30 m.p.h., which to anyone but an eccentric would be sufficient conditions for refusing to call it a good motor-car; but there is no precise set of accepted criteria such that we can say "If a motor-car satisfies these conditions, it is a good one; if not, not." And in both cases we could be precise if we wanted to. We could, for certain purposes, agree not to say that a motor-car was "really red" unless the redness of its paint reached a certain measurable degree of purity and saturation; and similarly, we might adopt a very exact standard of goodness in motor-cars. We might refuse the name "good motor-car" to any car that would not go round a certain race-track without mishap in a certain limited time, that did not conform to certain other rigid specifications as regards accommodation, etc. This sort of thing has not been done for the expression "good motor-car"; but, as Mr. Urmson has pointed out, it has been done by the Ministry of Agriculture for the expression "super apple."[1]

It is important to notice that the exactness or looseness of their criteria does absolutely nothing to distinguish words like "good" from words like "red." Words in both classes may be descriptively loose or exact, according to how rigidly the criteria have been laid down by custom or convention. It certainly is not true that value-words are

---

[1] *Mind*, lix (1950), 152 (also in *Logic and Language*, ii, ed. Flew, 166).

distinguished from descriptive words in that the former are looser, descriptively, than the latter. There are loose and rigid examples of both sorts of word. Words like "red" can be extremely loose, without becoming to the least degree evaluative; and expressions like "good sewage effluent" can be the subject of very rigid criteria, without in the least ceasing to be evaluative. . . .

7.4. It is time now to justify my calling the descriptive meaning of "good" secondary to the evaluative meaning. My reasons for doing so are two. First, the evaluative meaning is constant for every class of object for which the word is used. When we call a motor-car or a chronometer or a cricket-bat or a picture good, we are commending all of them. But because we are commending all of them for different reasons, the descriptive meaning is different in all cases. We have knowledge of the evaluative meaning of "good" from our earliest years; but we are constantly learning to use it in new descriptive meanings, as the classes of objects whose virtues we learn to distinguish grow more numerous. Sometimes we learn to use "good" in a new descriptive meaning through being taught it by an expert in a particular field—for example, a horseman might teach me how to recognize a good hunter. Sometimes, on the other hand, we make up a new descriptive meaning for ourselves. This happens when we start having a standard for a class of objects, certain members of which we have started needing to place in order of merit, but for which there has hitherto been no standard, as in the "cactus" example (6.2). . . .

The second reason for calling the evaluative meaning primary is, that we can use the evaluative force of the word in order to *change* the descriptive meaning for any class of objects. This is what the moral reformer often does in morals; but the same process occurs outside morals. It may happen that motor-cars will in the near future change considerably in design (e.g., by our seeking economy at the expense of size). It may be that then we shall cease giving the name "a good motor-car" to a car that now would rightly and with the concurrence of all be allowed that name. How, linguistically speaking, would this have happened? At present, we are roughly agreed (though only roughly) on the necessary and sufficient criteria for calling a motor-car a good one. If what I have described takes place, we may begin to say "No cars of the nineteen-fifties were really good; there weren't any good ones till 1960." Now here we cannot be using "good" with the same descriptive meaning as it is now generally used with; for some of the cars of 1950 do indubitably have those characteristics which entitle them to the name "good motor-car" in the 1950 descriptive sense of that word. What is happening is that the evaluative meaning of the word is being used in order to shift the descriptive meaning; we are doing what would be called, if "good" were a purely descriptive word, redefining it. But we cannot call it that, for the evaluative meaning remains constant; we are rather altering the standard. This is similar to the process called by Professor Stevenson "persuasive definition";[2] the process is not necessarily, however, highly coloured with emotion.

---

[2] *Ethics and Language*, ch. ix.

Commending and Choosing

8.1. It is now time to inquire into the reasons for the logical features of "good" that we have been describing, and to ask why it is that it has this peculiar combination of evaluative and descriptive meaning. The reason will be found in the purposes for which it, like other value-words, is used in our discourse. . . .

I have said that the primary function of the word "good" is to commend. We have, therefore, to inquire what commending is. When we commend or condemn anything, it is always in order, at least indirectly, to guide choices, our own or other people's, now or in the future. Suppose that I say "The South Bank Exhibition is very good." In what context should I appropriately say this, and what would be my purpose in so doing? It would be natural for me to say it to someone who was wondering whether to go to London to see the Exhibition, or, if he was in London, whether to pay it a visit. It would, however, be too much to say that the reference to choices is always as direct as this. An American returning from London to New York, and speaking to some people who had no intention of going to London in the near future, might still make the same remark. In order, therefore, to show that critical value-judgments are all ultimately related to choices, and would not be made if they were not so related, we require to ask, for what purpose we have standards.

It has been pointed out by Mr. Urmson that we do not speak generally of "good" wireworms. This is because we never have any occasion for choosing between wireworms, and therefore require no guidance in so doing. We therefore need to have no standards for wire-worms. But it is easy to imagine circumstances in which this situation might alter. Suppose that wireworms came into use as a special kind of bait for fishermen. Then we might speak of having dug up a very good wireworm (one, for example, that was exceptionally fat and attractive to fish), just as now, no doubt, sea-fishermen might talk of having dug up a very good lug-worm. We only have standards for a class of objects, we only talk of the virtues of one specimen as against another, we only use value-words about them, when occasions are known to exist, or are conceivable, in which we, or someone else, would have to choose between specimens. We should not call pictures good or bad if no one ever had the choice of seeing them or not seeing them (or of studying them or not studying them in the way that art students study pictures, or of buying them or not buying them). Lest, by the way, I should seem to have introduced a certain vagueness by specifying so many alternative kinds of choices, it must be pointed out that the matter can, if desired, be made as precise as we require; for we can specify, when we have called a picture a good one, within what class we have called it good; for example, we can say "I meant a good picture to study, but not to buy."

Some further examples may be given. We should not speak of good sunsets, unless sometimes the decision had to be made, whether to go to the window to look at the sunset; we should not speak of good billiard-cues, unless sometimes we had to choose one billiard-cue in preference to another; we should not speak of good men unless we had the choice, what sort of men to try to become. Leibniz, when he spoke of "the best of all possible worlds," had in mind a creator choosing between the possibilities. The choice that is envisaged need not ever occur, nor even be expected ever to occur; it is enough for it to be envisaged as occurring, in order that we should be able to make a value-judgment with reference to it. It must be admitted, however, that the most useful value-judgments are those which have reference to choices that we might very likely have to make.

8.2. It should be pointed out that even judgments about past choices do not refer merely to the past. As we shall see, all value-judgments are covertly universal in character, which is the same as to say that they refer to, and express acceptance of, a standard which has an application to other similar instances. If I censure someone for having done something, I envisage the possibility of him, or someone else, or myself, having to make a similar choice again; otherwise there would be no point in censuring him. Thus, if I say to a man whom I am teaching to drive "You did that manœuvre badly" this is a very typical piece of driving-instruction; and driving-instruction consists in teaching a man to drive not in the past but in the future; to this end we censure or commend past pieces of driving, in order to impart to him the standard which is to guide him in his subsequent conduct.

When we commend an object, our judgment is not solely about that particular object, but is inescapably about objects like it. Thus, if I say that a certain motor-car is a good one, I am not merely saying something about that particular motor-car. To say something about that particular car, merely, would

not be to commend. To commend, as we have seen, is to guide choices. Now for guiding a particular choice we have a linguistic instrument which is not that of commendation, namely, the singular imperative. If I wish merely to tell someone to choose a particular car, with no thought of the kind of car to which it belongs, I can say "Take that one." If instead of this I say "That is a good one," I am saying something more. I am implying that if any motor-car were just like that one, it would be a good one too; whereas by saying "Take that one," I do not imply that, if my hearer sees another car just like that one, he is to take it too. But further, the implication of the judgment "That is a good motor-car" does not extend merely to motor-cars *exactly* like that one. If this were so, the implication would be for practical purposes useless; for nothing is exactly like anything else. It extends to every motor-car that is like that one in the *relevant* particulars; and the relevant particulars are its virtues— those of its characteristics for which I was commending it, or which I was calling good about it. Whenever we commend, we have in mind something about the object commended which is the reason for our commendation. It therefore always makes sense, after someone has said "That is a good motor-car," to ask "What is good about it?" or "Why do you call it good?" or "What features of it are you commending?" It may not always be easy to answer this question precisely, but it is always a legitimate question. If we did not understand why it was always a legitimate question, we should not understand the way in which the word "good" functions. . . .

We thus have to distinguish two questions that can always be asked in eluci-dation of a judgment containing the word "good." Suppose that someone says "That is a good one." We can then always ask (1) "Good what—sports car or family car or taxi or example to quote in a logic-book?" Or we can ask (2) "What makes you call it good?" To ask the first question is to ask for the class within which evaluative compari-sons are being made. Let us call it the class of comparison. To ask the second question is to ask for the virtues or "good-making characteristics." . . .

8.3. Now since it is the purpose of the word "good" and other value-words to be used for teaching standards, their logic is in accord with this purpose. We are therefore in a position at last to ex-plain the feature of the word "good" which I pointed out at the beginning of this investigation. The reason why I cannot apply the word "good" to one picture, if I refuse to apply it to another picture which I agree to be in all other respects exactly similar, is that by doing this I should be defeating the purpose for which the word is designed. I should be commending one object, and so pur-porting to teach my hearers one stand-ard, while in the same breath refusing to commend a similar object, and so un-doing the lesson just imparted. By seek-ing to impart two inconsistent stand-ards, I should be imparting no standard at all. The effect of such an utterance is similar to that of a contra-diction; for in a contradiction, I say two inconsistent things, and so the effect is that the hearer does not know what I am trying to say. . . .

SOCIAL PHILOSOPHY

If we properly define the concept of justice, Hart argues in the following selection, we find that it is a concept of appraisal, and thus that it belongs to the class of moral words. As a specific form of excellence attributed to laws, its closest con-ceptual relative is the concept of fairness. The specific character of justice is expressed in the traditional principle of treating like cases alike, different cases differently. But this principle needs to be supplemented by determining what differences among human beings are relevant to applying the concept of justice.

Hart therefore distinguishes two parts of the idea of justice. The first is the invariant formal principle expressed by treating like cases alike, the second is the varying criterion of relevant differences. The latter principle takes one somewhat outside the law, for differences in political and moral outlooks are reflected in the application of the criterion. These observations, resulting from Hart's use of analytic techniques, are directed toward bringing greater clarity to the concept of justice as well as to certain puzzles which arise as men apply the concept in concrete appraisals of laws and decisions.

6 The Principles of Justice

H. L. A. Hart (1907-   )

The terms most frequently used by lawyers in the praise or condemnation of law or its administration are the words "just" and "unjust" and very often they write as if the ideas of justice and morality were coextensive. There are indeed very good reasons why justice should have a most prominent place in the criticism of legal arrangements; yet it is important to see that it is a distinct segment of morality, and that laws and the administration of laws may have or lack excellences of different kinds. Very little reflection on some common types of moral judgment is enough to show this special character of justice. A man guilty of gross cruelty to his child would often be judged to have done something morally *wrong, bad*, or even *wicked* or to have disregarded his moral *obligation* or duty to his child. But it would be strange to criticize his conduct as *unjust*. This is not because the word "unjust" is too weak in condemnatory force, but because the point of moral criticism in terms of justice or injustice is usually different from, and more specific than, the other types of general moral criticism which are appropriate in this particular case and are expressed by words like "wrong," "bad," or "wicked." "Unjust" would become appropriate if the man had arbitrarily

selected one of his children for severer punishment than those given to others guilty of the same fault, or if he had punished the child for some offence without taking steps to see that he really was the wrongdoer. Similarly, when we turn from the criticism of individual conduct to the criticism of law, we might express our approval of a law requiring parents to send their children to school, by saying that it was a good law and our disapproval of a law forbidding the criticism of the Government, as by calling it a bad law. Such criticisms would not normally be couched in terms of "justice" and "injustice." "Just," on the other hand, would be the appropriate expression of approval of a law distributing the burden of taxation according to wealth; so "unjust" would be appropriate for the expression of disapproval of a law which forbade coloured people to use the public means of transport or the parks. That just and unjust are more specific forms of moral criticism than good and bad or right and wrong, is plain from the fact that we might intelligibly claim that a law was good because it was just, or that it was bad because it was unjust, but not that it was just because good, or unjust because bad.

The distinctive features of justice and their special connexion with law begin to emerge if it is observed that most of the criticisms made in terms of just and unjust could almost equally well be conveyed by the words "fair" and "unfair."

The selection is from H. L. A. Hart, *The Concept of Law* (Oxford: The Clarendon Press, 1961). Used by permission of The Clarendon Press.

Fairness is plainly not coextensive with morality in general; references to it are mainly relevant in two situations in social life. One is when we are concerned not with a single individual's conduct but with the way in which *classes* of individuals are treated, when some burden or benefit falls to be distributed among them. Hence what is typically fair or unfair is a "share." The second situation is when some injury has been done and compensation or redress is claimed. These are not the only contexts where appraisals in terms of justice or fairness are made. We speak not only of distributions or compensations as just or fair but also of a judge as just or unjust; a trial as fair or unfair; and a person as justly or unjustly convicted. These are derivative applications of the notion of justice which are explicable once the primary application of justice to matters of distribution and compensation is understood.

The general principle latent in these diverse applications of the idea of justice is that individuals are entitled in respect of each other to a certain relative position of equality or inequality. This is something to be respected in the vicissitudes of social life when burdens or benefits fall to be distributed; it is also something to be restored when it is disturbed. Hence justice is traditionally thought of as maintaining or restoring a *balance* or *proportion*, and its leading precept is often formulated as "Treat like cases alike"; though we need to add to the latter "and treat different cases differently." So when, in the name of justice, we protest against a law forbidding coloured people the use of the public parks, the point of such criticism is that such a law is bad, because in distribut-

ing the benefits of public amenities among the population it discriminates between persons who are, in all relevant respects, alike. Conversely, if a law is praised as just because it withdraws from some special section some privilege or immunity, e.g. in taxation, the guiding thought is that there is no such relevant difference between the privileged class and the rest of the community as to entitle them to the special treatment. These simple examples are, however, enough to show that, though "Treat like cases alike and different cases differently" is a central element in the idea of justice, it is by itself incomplete and, until supplemented, cannot afford any determinate guide to conduct. This is so because any set of human beings will resemble each other in some respects and differ from each other in others and, until it is established what resemblance and differences are relevant, "Treat like cases alike" must remain an empty form. To fill it we must know when, for the purposes in hand, cases are to be regarded as alike and what differences are relevant. Without this further supplement we cannot proceed to criticize laws or other social arrangements as unjust. It is not unjust for the law when it forbids homicide to treat the red-haired murderers in the same way as others; indeed it would be as unjust if it treated them differently, as it would be if it refused to treat differently the sane and the insane.

There is therefore a certain complexity in the structure of the idea of justice. We may say that it consists of two parts: a uniform or constant feature, summarized in the precept "Treat like cases alike"; and a shifting or varying criterion used in determining when, for any given purpose, cases are alike or different. In this respect justice is like the notion of what is genuine, or tall, or warm, which contain an implicit reference to a standard which varies with the classification of the thing to which they are applied. A tall child may be the same height as a short man, a warm winter the same temperature as a cold summer, and a fake diamond may be a genuine antique. But justice is far more complicated than these notions because the shifting standard of relevant resemblance between different cases incorporated in it not only varies with the type of subject to which it is applied, but may often be open to challenge even in relation to a single type of subject.

In certain cases, indeed, the resemblances and differences between human beings which are relevant for the criticism of legal arrangements as just or unjust are quite obvious. This is preeminently the case when we are concerned not with the justice or injustice of the *law* but of its *application* in particular cases. For here the relevant resemblances and differences between individuals, to which the person who administers the law must attend, are determined by the law itself. To say that the law against murder is justly applied is to say that it is impartially applied to all those and only those who are alike in having done what the law forbids; no prejudice or interest has deflected the administrator from treating them "equally." Consistently with this the procedural standards such as *"audi alteram partem"* "let no one be a judge in his own cause" are thought of as requirements of justice, and in England and America are often referred to as principles of Natural Justice. This is so because they are guarantees of impartiality or objectivity, designed to secure that the law is applied to all those and only to those who are alike in the relevant respect marked out by the law itself.

The connexion between this aspect of justice and the very notion of proceeding by rule is obviously very close. Indeed, it might be said that to apply a law justly to different cases is simply to take seriously the assertion that what is to be applied in different cases is the same general rule, without prejudice, interest, or caprice. This close connexion between justice in the administration of the law and the very notion of a rule has tempted some famous thinkers to identify justice with conformity to law. Yet plainly this is an error unless "law" is given some specially wide meaning; for such an account of justice leaves unexplained the fact that criticism in the name of justice is not confined to the administration of the law in particular cases, but the laws themselves are often criticized as just or unjust. Indeed there is no absurdity in conceding that an unjust law forbidding the access of coloured persons to the parks has been justly administered, in that only persons genuinely guilty of breaking the law were punished under it and then only after a fair trial.

When we turn from the justice or injustice of the administration of the law to the criticism of the law itself in these terms, it is plain that the law itself cannot now determine what resemblances and differences among individuals the law must recognize if its rules are to treat like cases alike and so be just. Here accordingly there is much room for doubt and dispute. Fundamental differences, in general moral and political outlook, may lead to irreconcilable differences and disagreement as to what characteristics of human beings are to be taken as relevant for the criticism of law as unjust. Thus, when in the previous example we stigmatized as unjust a law forbidding coloured people access to the parks, this was on the footing that, at least in the distribution of such amenities, differences of colour are irrelevant. Certainly in the modern world, the fact that human beings, of whatever colour, are capable of thought, feeling, and self-control, would be generally though not universally accepted as constituting crucial resemblances between them to which the law should attend. Hence, in most civilized countries there is a great measure of agreement that both the criminal law (conceived not only as restricting liberty but as providing protection from various sorts of harm) and the civil law (conceived as offering redress for harm), would be unjust if in the distribution of these burdens and benefits they discriminated between persons, by reference to such characteristics as colour or religious belief. And if, instead of these well-known *foci* of human prejudice, the law discriminated by reference to such obvious irrelevancies as height, weight, or beauty it would be both unjust and ludicrous. If murderers belonging to the established church were exempt from capital punishment, if only members of the peerage could sue for libel, if assaults on coloured persons were punished less severely than those on whites, the laws would in most modern communities be condemned as unjust on the footing that *prima facie* human beings should be treated alike and these privileges and immunities rested on no relevant ground.

Indeed so deeply embedded in modern man is the principle that *prima facie*

human beings are entitled to be treated alike that almost universally where the laws do discriminate by deference to such matters as colour and race, lip service at least is still widely paid to this principle. If such discriminations are attacked they are often defended by the assertion that the class discriminated against lack, or have not yet developed, certain essential human attributes; or it may be said that, regrettable though it is, the demands of justice requiring their equal treatment must be overridden in order to preserve something held to be of greater value, which would be jeopardized if such discriminations were not made. Yet though lip service is now general, it is certainly possible to conceive of a morality which did not resort to these often disingenuous devices to justify discrimination and inequalities, but openly rejected the principle that *prima facie* human beings were to be treated alike. Instead, human beings might be thought of as falling naturally and unalterably into certain classes, so that some were naturally fitted to be free and others to be their slaves or, as Aristotle expressed it, the living instruments of others. Here the sense of *prima facie* equality among men would be absent. Something of this view is to be found in Aristotle and Plato, though even there, there is more than a hint that any full defence of slavery would involve showing that those enslaved lacked the capacity for independent existence or differed from the free in their capacity to realize some ideal of the good life.

It is therefore clear that the criteria of relevant resemblances and differences may often vary with the fundamental moral outlook of a given person or society. Where this is so, assessments of the justice or injustice of the law may be met with counter-assertions inspired by a different morality. But sometimes a consideration of the object which the law in question is admittedly designed to realize may make clear the resemblances and differences which a just law should recognize and they may then be scarcely open to dispute. If a law provides for the relief of poverty then the requirement of the principle that "Like cases be treated alike" would surely involve attention to the *need* of different claimants for relief. A similar criterion of need is implicitly recognized when the burden of taxation is adjusted by a graded income tax to the wealth of the individuals taxed. Sometimes what is relevant are the *capacities* of persons for a specific function with which the exercise of the law in question may be concerned. Laws which exclude from the franchise, or withhold the power to make wills or contracts from children, or the insane, are regarded as just because such persons lack the capacity, which sane adults are presumed to have, to make a rational use of these facilities. Such discriminations are made on grounds which are obviously relevant, whereas discriminations in these matters between the sexes or between persons of different colour are not; though of course it has been argued in defence of the subjection of women, or coloured people, that women or coloured people lack the white male's capacity for rational thought and decision. To argue thus is of course to admit that equal capacity for a particular function is the criterion of justice in the case of such law, though in the absence of any evidence that such capacity is lacking in women or coloured persons, again only lip service is paid to this principle.

So far we have considered the justice or injustice of laws which may be viewed as *distributing* among individuals burdens and benefits. Some of the benefits are tangible, like poor relief, or food rations; others are intangible, like the protection from bodily harm given by the criminal law, or the facilities afforded by laws relating to testamentary or contractual capacity, or the right to vote. From distribution in this wide sense, we must distinguish *compensation* for injury done by one person to another. Here the connexion between what is just and the central precept of justice "Treat like cases alike and different cases differently" is certainly less direct. Yet it is not too indirect to be traced and may be seen in the following way. The laws which provide for the compensation by one person of another for torts or civil injuries might be considered unjust for two different reasons. They might, on the one hand, establish unfair privileges or immunities. This would be so if only peers could sue for libel, or if no white person were liable to a coloured person for trespass or assault. Such laws would violate, in a straightforward way, principles of fair distribution of the rights and duties of compensation. But such laws might also be unjust in a quite different way: for while making no unfair discriminations they might fail altogether to provide a remedy for certain types of injury inflicted by one person on another, even though morally compensation would be thought due. In this matter the law might be unjust while treating all alike.

The vice of such laws would then not be the maldistribution, but the refusal to all alike, of compensation for injuries which it was morally wrong to inflict on others. The crudest case of such unjust refusal of redress would be a system in which no one could obtain damages for physical harm wantonly inflicted. It is worth observing that *this* injustice would still remain even if the criminal law prohibited such assaults under penalty. Few instances of anything so crude can be found, but the failure of English law to provide compensation for invasions of privacy, often found profitable by advertisers, has often been criticized in this way. Failure to provide compensation where morally it is held due is, however, also the gravamen of the charge of injustice against technicalities of the law of tort or contract which permit "unjust enrichment" of the expense of another by some action considered morally wrong.

The connexion between the justice and injustice of the compensation for injury, and the principle "Treat like cases alike and different cases differently," lies in the fact that outside the law there is a moral conviction that those with whom the law is concerned have a right to mutual forbearance from certain kinds of harmful conduct. Such a structure of reciprocal rights and obligations proscribing at least the grosser sorts of harm, constitutes the basis, though not the whole, of the morality of every social group. Its effect is to create among individuals a moral and, in a sense, an artificial equality to offset the inequalities of nature. For when the moral code forbids one man to rob or use violence on another even when superior strength or cunning would enable him to do so with impunity, the strong and cunning are put on a level with the weak and simple. Their cases are made morally alike. Hence the strong man who disregards morality and takes advantage of his strength to injure another is conceived as upsetting this equilibrium, or order of equality, established by morals; justice then requires that this moral *status quo* should as far as possible be restored by the wrongdoer. In simple cases of theft this would simply involve giving back the thing taken; and compensation for other injuries is an extension of this primitive notion. One who has physically injured another either intentionally or through negligence is thought of as having taken something from his victim; and though he has not literally done this, the figure is not too far fetched: for he has profited at his victim's expense, even if it is only by indulging his wish to injure him or not sacrificing his ease to the duty of taking adequate precautions. Thus when laws provide compensation where justice demands it, they recognize indirectly the principle "Treat like cases alike" by providing for the restoration, after disturbance, of the moral *status quo* in which victim and wrongdoer are on a footing of equality and so alike. Again, it is conceivable that there might be a moral outlook which did not put individuals on a footing of reciprocal equality in these matters. The moral code might forbid Barbarians to assault Greeks but allow Greeks to assault Barbarians. In such cases a Barbarian may be thought morally bound to compensate a Greek for injuries done though entitled to no such compensation himself. The moral order here would be one of inequality in which victim and wrongdoer were treated differently. For such an outlook, repellant though it may be to us, the law would be just only if it reflected this difference and treated different cases differently.

In this brief outline of justice we have considered only some of its simpler applications in order to show the specific form of excellence attributed to laws which are appraised as just. Not only is this distinct from other values which laws may have or lack, but sometimes the demands of justice may conflict with other values. This may occur, when a court, in sentencing a particular offender for a crime which has become prevalent, passes a severer sentence than that passed in other similar cases, and avowedly does this "as a warning." There is here a sacrifice of the principle "Treat like cases alike" to the general security or welfare of society. In civil cases, a similar conflict between justice and the general good is resolved in favour of the latter, when the law provides no remedy for some moral wrong because to enforce compensation in such cases might involve great difficulties of proof, or overburden the courts, or unduly hamper enterprise. There is a limit to the amount of law enforcement which any society can afford, even when moral wrong has been done. Conversely the law, in the name of the general welfare of society, may enforce compensation from one who has injured another, even where morally, as a matter of justice, it might not be thought due. This is often said to be the case when liability in tort is strict, i.e. independent of the intention to injure or failure to take care. This form of liability is sometimes defended on the ground that it is in the interest of "society" that those accidentally injured should be compensated; and it is claimed that the easiest way of doing this is to place the burden on those whose activities, however carefully controlled, result in such accidents. They commonly have deep pockets and opportunities to insure. When this defence is made, there is in it

an implicit appeal to the general welfare of society which, though it may be morally acceptable and sometimes even called "*social* justice," differs from the primary forms of justice which are concerned simply to redress, as far as possible, the *status quo* as between two individuals.

An important juncture point between ideas of justice and social good or welfare should be noticed. Very few social changes or laws are agreeable to or advance the welfare of all individuals alike. Only laws which provide for the most elementary needs, such as police protection or roads, come near to this. In most cases the law provides benefits for one class of the population only at the cost of depriving others of what they prefer. Provision for the poor can be made only out of the goods of others; compulsory school education for all may mean not only loss of liberty for those who wish to educate their children privately, but may be financed only at the cost of reducing or sacrificing capital investment in industry or old-age pensions or free medical services. When a choice has been made between such competing alternatives it may be defended as proper on the ground that it was for the "public good" or the "common good." It is not clear what these phrases mean, since there seems to be no scale by which contributions of the various alternatives to the common good can be measured and the greater identified. It is, however, clear that a choice, made without prior consideration of the interests of all sections of the community would be open to criticism as merely partisan and unjust. It would, however, be rescued from *this* imputation if the claims of all had been impartially considered before legislation, even though in the result the claims of one section were subordinated to those of others.

Some might indeed argue that all that in fact could be meant by the claim that a choice between the competing claims of different classes or interests was made "for the common good," was that the claims of all had been thus impartially surveyed before decision. Whether this is true or not, it seems clear that justice in this sense is at least a necessary condition to be satisfied by any legislative choice which purports to be for the common good. We have here a further aspect of distributive justice, differing from those simple forms which we have discussed. For here what is justly "distributed" is not some specific benefit among a class of claimants to it, but impartial attention to and consideration of competing claims to different benefits.

ESTHETICS

Is esthetic theory, in the sense of stating a true definition of art, possible? Writing under the direct influence of Wittgenstein, Professor Weitz answers, No. Theory is never possible in esthetics, and it is wrong in principle. To understand this denial, it must be remembered from Wittgenstein that how we view our concepts is exceedingly important. More specifically, we must begin, not with the question, "What is art?" but rather with, "What sort of concept is 'art'?" The latter question generates an inquiry elucidating the concept; and like all elucidation, it gives the relation between the use of the concept and the conditions under which it can be correctly employed.

Professor Weitz likens his treatment of "art" to Wittgenstein's analysis of games. If we look at what we call art, we find only resemblances rather than common properties. This means that "art" has an "open texture" in that it has no fixed boundary of application and the conditions for its application are never final. When we use and apply "art," we do so on the basis of a decision.

Esthetic theory must, therefore, elucidate the concept of art by describing the conditions for its employment. In doing this, it may learn from traditional esthetic theories. It must not fail to recognize, however, that they are only recommendations to us to attend to certain features of art.

7   Theory and Art
Morris Weitz (1916-   )

Theory has been central in esthetics and is still the preoccupation of the phi-

The selection is from Morris Weitz, "The Role of Theory in Aesthetics," *Journal of Aesthetics and Art Criticism*, 15 (1956), pp. 27–28 and 30–35. Used by permission of the Editor.

losophy of art. Its main avowed concern remains the determination of the nature of art which can be formulated into a definition of it. It construes definition as the statement of the necessary and sufficient properties of what is being defined, where the statement purports to be a true or false claim about the essence of art, what characterizes and distinguishes it from everything else. Each of the great theories of art—Formalism, Voluntarism, Emotionalism, Intellectualism, Intuitionism, Organicism—converges on the attempt to state the defining properties of art. Each claims that it is the true theory because it has formulated correctly into a real definition the nature of art; and that the others are false because they have left out some necessary or sufficient property. Many theorists contend that their enterprise is no mere intellectual exercise but an absolute necessity for any understanding of art and our proper evaluation of it. Unless we know what art is, they say, what are its necessary and sufficient properties, we cannot begin to respond to it adequately or to say why one work is good or better than another. Esthetic theory, thus, is important not only in itself but for the foundations of both appreciation and criticism. Philosophers, critics, and even artists who have written on art, agree that what is primary in esthetics is a theory about the nature of art.

Is esthetic theory, in the sense of a true definition or set of necessary and sufficient properties of art, possible? If nothing else does, the history of esthetics itself should give one enormous pause here. For, in spite of the many theories, we seem no nearer our goal today than we were in Plato's time. Each age, each art-movement, each philosophy of art, tries over and over again to establish the stated ideal only to be succeeded by a new or revised theory, rooted, at least in part, in the repudiation of preceding ones. Even today, almost everyone interested in esthetic matters is still deeply

wedded to the hope that the correct theory of art is forthcoming. We need only examine the numerous new books on art in which new definitions are proffered; or, in our own country especially, the basic textbooks and anthologies to recognize how strong the priority of a theory of art is.

In this essay I want to plead for the rejection of this problem. I want to show that theory—in the requisite classical sense—is *never* forthcoming in esthetics, and that we would do much better as philosophers to supplant the question, "What is the nature of art?" by other questions, the answers to which will provide us with all the understanding of the arts there can be. I want to show that the inadequacies of the theories are not primarily occasioned by any legitimate difficulty such e.g., as the vast complexity of art, which might be corrected by further probing and research. Their basic inadequacies reside instead in a fundamental misconception of art. Esthetic theory—all of it—is wrong in principle in thinking that a correct theory is possible because it radically misconstrues the logic of the concept of art. Its main contention that "art" is amenable to real or any kind of true definition is false. Its attempt to discover the necessary and sufficient properties of art is logically misbegotten for the very simple reason that such a set and, consequently, such a formula about it, is never forthcoming. Art, as the logic of the concept shows, has no set of necessary and sufficient properties, hence a theory of it is logically impossible and not merely factually difficult. Esthetic theory tries to define what cannot be defined in its requisite sense. But in recommending the repudiation of esthetic theory I shall not argue from this, as too many others have done, that its logical confusions render it meaningless or worthless. On the contrary, I wish to reassess its role and its contribution primarily in order to show that it is of the greatest importance to our understanding of the arts. . . .

The problem with which we must begin is not "What is art?," but "What sort of concept is 'art'?" Indeed, the root problem of philosophy itself is to explain the relation between the employment of certain kinds of concepts and the conditions under which they can be correctly applied. If I may paraphrase Wittgenstein, we must not ask, What is the nature of any philosophical x? or even, according to the semanticist, What does "x" mean?—a transformation that leads to the disastrous interpretation of "art" as a name for some specifiable class of objects; but rather, What is the use or employment of "x"? What does "x" do in the language? This, I take it, is the initial question, the begin-all if not the end-all of any philosophical problem and solution. Thus, in esthetics, our first problem is the elucidation of the actual employment of the concept of art, to give a logical description of the actual functioning of the concept, including a description of the conditions under which we correctly use it or its correlates.

My model in this type of logical description or philosophy derives from Wittgenstein. It is also he who, in his refutation of philosophical theorizing in the sense of constructing definitions of philosophical entities, has furnished contemporary esthetics with a starting point for any future progress. In his new work, *Philosophical Investigations,* Wittgenstein raises as an illustrative question, What is a game? The traditional philosophical, theoretical answer would be in terms of some exhaustive set of properties common to all games. To this Wittgenstein says, let us consider what we call "games": "I mean board-games, card-games, ball-games, Olympic games, and so on. What is common to them all —Don't say: 'there *must* be something common, or they would not be called "games" ' but *look and see* whether there is anything common to all.—For if you look at them you will not see something that is common to *all,* but similarities, relationships, and a whole series of them at that . . ."

Card games are like board games in some respects but not in others. Not all games are amusing, nor is there always winning or losing or competition. Some games resemble others in some respects —that is all. What we find are no necessary and sufficient properties, only "a complicated network of similarities overlapping and crisscrossing," such that we can say of games that they form a family with family resemblances and no common trait. If one asks what a game is, we pick out sample games, describe these, and add, "This and *similar things* are called 'games.' " This is all we need to say and indeed all any of us knows about games. Knowing what a game is is not knowing some real definition or theory but being able to recognize and explain games and to decide which among imaginary and new examples would or would not be called "games."

The problem of the nature of art is like that of the nature of games, at least in these respects: If we actually look and see what it is that we call "art," we will also find no common properties—

only strands of similarities. Knowing what art is is not apprehending some manifest or latent essence but being able to recognize, describe, and explain those things we call "art" in virtue of these similarities.

But the basic resemblance between these concepts is their open texture. In elucidating them, certain (paradigm) cases can be given, about which there can be no question as to their being correctly described as "art" or "game," but no exhaustive set of cases can be given. I can list some cases and some conditions under which I can apply correctly the concept of art but I cannot list all of them, for the all-important reason that unforeseeable or novel conditions are always forthcoming or envisageable.

A concept is open if its conditions of application are emendable and corrigible; i.e., if a situation or case can be imagined or secured which would call for some sort of *decision* on our part to extend the use of the concept to cover this, or to close the concept and invent a new one to deal with the new case and its new property. If necessary and sufficient conditions for the application of a concept can be stated, the concept is a closed one. But this can happen only in logic or mathematics where concepts are constructed and completely defined. It cannot occur with empirically-descriptive and normative concepts unless we arbitrarily close them by stipulating the ranges of their uses.

I can illustrate this open character of "art" best by examples drawn from its sub-concepts. Consider questions like "Is Dos Passos' *U.S.A.* a novel?" "Is V. Woolf's *To the Lighthouse* a novel?" "Is Joyce's *Finnegan's Wake* a novel?"

On the traditional view, these are construed as factual problems to be answered yes or no in accordance with the presence or absence of defining properties. But certainly this is not how any of these questions is answered. Once it arises, as it has many times in the development of the novel from Richardson to Joyce (e.g., "Is Gide's *The School for Wives* a novel or a diary?"), what is at stake is no factual analysis concerning necessary and sufficient properties but a decision as to whether the work under examination is similar in certain respects to other works, already called "novels," and consequently warrants the extension of the concept to cover the new case. The new work is narrative, fictional, contains character delineation and dialogue but (say) it has no regular time-sequence in the plot or is interspersed with actual newspaper reports. It is like recognized novels, A, B, C . . . , in some respects but not like them in others. But then neither were B and C like A in some respects when it was decided to extend the concept applied to A to B and C. Because work $N + 1$ (the brand new work) is like A, B, C . . . N in certain respects—has strands of similarity to them—the concept is extended and a new phase of the novel engendered. "Is N 1 a novel?" then, is no factual, but rather a decision problem, where the verdict turns on whether or not we enlarge our set of conditions for applying the concept.

What is true of the novel is, I think, true of every sub-concept of art: "tragedy," "comedy," "painting," "opera," etc., of "art" itself. No "Is X a novel, painting, opera, work of art, etc.?" question allows of a definitive answer in the sense of a factual yes or no report. "Is this *collage* a painting or not?" does not rest on any set of necessary and sufficient properties of painting but on whether we decide—as we did! —to extend "painting" to cover this case.

"Art," itself, is an open concept. New conditions (cases) have constantly arisen and will undoubtedly constantly arise; new art forms, new movements will emerge, which will demand decisions on the part of those interested, usually professional critics, as to whether the concept should be extended or not. Estheticians may lay down similarity conditions but never necessary and sufficient ones for the correct application of the concept. With "art" its conditions of application can never be exhaustively enumerated since new cases can always be envisaged or created by artists, or even nature, which would call for a decision on someone's part to extend or to close the old or to invent a new concept. (E.g., "It's not a sculpture, it's a mobile.")

What I am arguing, then, is that the very expansive, adventurous character of art, its ever-present changes and novel creations, makes it logically impossible to ensure any set of defining properties. We can, of course, choose to close the concept. But to do this with "art" or "tragedy" or "portraiture," etc., is ludicrous since it forecloses on the very conditions of creativity in the arts.

Of course there are legitimate and serviceable closed concepts in art. But these are always those whose boundaries of conditions have been drawn for a *special* purpose. Consider the difference, for example, between "tragedy" and "(extant) Greek tragedy." The first is open and must remain so to allow for the possibility of new conditions, e.g., a play in which the hero is not noble or fallen or in which there is no hero but other elements that are like those of plays we already call "tragedy." The second is closed. The plays it can be applied to, the conditions under which it can be correctly used are all in, once the boundary, "Greek," is drawn. Here the critic can work out a theory or real definition in which he lists the common properties at least of the extant Greek tragedies. Aristotle's definition, false as it is as a theory of all the plays of Aeschylus, Sophocles, and Euripides, since it does not cover some of them, properly called "tragedies," can be interpreted as a real (albeit incorrect) definition of this closed concept; although it can also be, as it unfortunately has been, conceived as a purported real definition of "tragedy," in which case it suffers from the logical mistake of trying to define what cannot be defined—of trying to squeeze what is an open concept into an honorific formula for a closed concept.

What is supremely important, if the critic is not to become muddled, is to get absolutely clear about the way in which he conceives his concepts; otherwise he goes from the problem of trying to define "tragedy," etc., to an arbitrary closing of the concept in terms of certain preferred conditions or characteristics which he sums up in some linguistic recommendation that he mistakenly thinks is a real definition of the open concept. Thus, many critics and estheticians ask, "What is tragedy?," choose a class of samples for which they may give a true account of its common properties, and then go on to construe this account of the chosen closed class as a true definition or theory of the whole open class of tragedy. This, I think, is the logical mechanism of most of the so-called theories of the sub-concepts of art: "tragedy," "comedy," "novel," etc. In effect, this whole procedure, subtly deceptive as it is, amounts to a transformation of correct criteria for *recognizing* members of certain legitimately closed classes of works of art into recommended criteria for *evaluating* any putative member of the class.

The primary task of esthetics is not to seek a theory but to elucidate the concept of art. Specifically, it is to describe the conditions under which we employ the concept correctly. Definition, reconstruction, patterns of analysis are out of place here since they distort and add nothing to our understanding of art. What, then, is the logic of "X is a work of art?"

As we actually use the concept, "Art" is both descriptive (like "chair") and evaluative (like "good"); i.e., we sometimes say, "This is a work of art," to describe something and we sometimes say it to evaluate something. Neither use surprises anyone.

What, first, is the logic of "X is a work of art," when it is a descriptive utterance? What are the conditions under which we would be making such an utterance correctly? There are no necessary and sufficient conditions but there are the strands of similarity conditions, i.e., bundles of properties, none of which need be present but most of which are, when we describe things as works of art. I shall call these the "criteria of recognition" of works of art. All of these have served as the defining criteria of the individual traditional theories of art; so we are already familiar

with them. Thus, mostly, when we describe something as a work of art, we do so under the conditions of there being present some sort of artifact, made by human skill, ingenuity, and imagination, which embodies in its sensuous, public medium—stone, wood, sounds, words, etc.—certain distinguishable elements and relations. Special theorists would add conditions like satisfaction of wishes, objectification or expression of emotion, some act of empathy, and so on; but these latter conditions seem to be quite adventitious, present to some but not to other spectators when things are described as works of art. "X is a work of art and contains *no* emotion, expression, act of empathy, satisfaction, etc.," is perfectly good sense and may frequently be true. "X is a work of art and . . . was made by no one," or . . . "exists only in the mind and not in any publicly observable thing," or . . . "was made by accident when he spilled the paint on the canvas," in each case of which a normal condition is denied, are also sensible and capable of being true in certain circumstances. None of the criteria of recognition is a defining one, either necessary or sufficient, because we can sometimes assert of something that it is a work of art and go on to deny any one of these conditions, even the one which has traditionally been taken to be basic, namely, that of being an artifact: Consider, "This piece of driftwood is a lovely piece of sculpture." Thus, to say of anything that it is a work of art is to commit oneself to the presence of *some* of these conditions. One would scarcely describe X as a work of art if X were not an artifact, or a collection of elements sensuously presented in a medium, or a product of human skill, and so on. If none of the conditions were present, if there were no criteria present for recognizing something as a work of art, we would not describe it as one. But, even so, no one of these or any collection of them is either necessary or sufficient.

The elucidation of the descriptive use of "Art" creates little difficulty. But the elucidation of the evaluative use does. For many, especially theorists, "This is a work of art" does more than describe; it also praises. Its conditions of utterance, therefore, include certain preferred properties or characteristics of art. I shall call these "criteria of evaluation." Consider a typical example of this evaluative use, the view according to which to say of something that it is a work of art is to imply that it is a *successful* harmonization of elements. Many of the honorific definitions of art and its subconcepts are of this form. What is at stake here is that "Art" is construed as an evaluative term which is either identified with its criterion or justified in terms of it. "Art" is defined in terms of its evaluative property, e.g., successful harmonization. On such a view, to say "X is a work of art" is (1) to say something which is taken *to mean* "X is a successful harmonization" (e.g., "Art *is* significant form") or (2) to say something praiseworthy *on the basis* of its successful harmonization. Theorists are never clear whether it is (1) or (2) which is being put forward. Most of them, concerned as they are with this evaluative use, formulate (2), i.e., that feature of art that *makes* it art in the praise-sense, and then go on to state (1), i.e., the definition of "Art" in terms of its art-making feature. And this is clearly to confuse the conditions under which we say something evaluatively with the meaning of what we say. "This is a work of art," said evaluatively, cannot mean "This is a successful harmonization of elements"—except by stipulation—but at most is said in virtue of the art-making property, which is taken as a (the) criterion of "Art," when "Art" is employed to assess. "This is a work of art," used evaluatively, serves to praise and not to affirm the reason why it is said.

The evaluative use of "Art," although distinct from the conditions of its use, relates in a very intimate way to these conditions. For, in every instance of "This is a work of art" (used to praise), what happens is that the criterion of evaluation (e.g., successful harmonization) for the employment of the concept of art is converted into a criterion of recognition. This is why, on its evaluative use, "This is a work of art" implies "This has P," where "P" is some chosen art-making property. Thus, if one chooses to employ "Art" evaluatively, as many do, so that "This is a work of art and not (esthetically) good" makes no sense, he uses "Art" in such a way that he refuses to *call* anything a work of art unless it embodies his criterion of excellence.

There is nothing wrong with the evaluative use; in fact, there is good reason for using "Art" to praise. But what cannot be maintained is that theories of the evaluative use of "Art" are true and real definitions of the necessary and sufficient properties of art. Instead they are honorific definitions, pure and simple, in which "Art" has been redefined in terms of chosen criteria.

But what makes them—these honorific definitions—so supremely valuable is not their disguised linguistic recommendations; rather it is the *debates* over the reasons for changing the criteria of the concept of art which are built into the definitions. In each of the great theories of art, whether correctly understood as honorific definitions or incorrectly accepted as real definitions, what is of the utmost importance are the reasons proffered in the argument for the respective theory, that is, the reasons given for the chosen or preferred criterion of excellence and evaluation. It is this perennial debate over these criteria of evaluation which makes the history of esthetic theory the important study it is. The value of each of the theories resides in its attempt to state and to justify certain criteria which are either neglected or distorted by previous theories. Look at the Bell-Fry theory again. Of course, "Art is significant form" cannot be accepted as a true, real definition of art; and most certainly it actually functions in their esthetics as a redefinition of art in terms of the chosen condition of significant form. But what gives it its esthetic importance is what lies behind the formula: In an age in which literary and representational elements have become paramount in painting, *return* to the plastic ones since these are indigenous to painting. Thus, the role of the theory is not to define anything but to use the definitional form, almost epigrammatically, to pin-point a crucial recommendation to turn our attention once again to the plastic elements in painting.

Once we, as philosophers, understand this distinction between the formula and what lies behind it, it behooves us to deal generously with the traditional theories of art; because incorporated in every one of them is a debate over and argument for emphasizing or centering upon some particular feature of art which has been neglected or perverted. If we take the esthetic theories literally, as we have seen, they all fail; but if we reconstrue them, in terms of their function and point, as serious and argued-for recommendations to concentrate on certain criteria of excellence in art, we shall see that esthetic theory is far from worthless. Indeed, it becomes as central as anything in esthetics, in our understanding of art, for it teaches us what to look for and how to look at it in art. What is central and must be articulated in all the theories are their debates over the reasons for excellence in art— debates over emotional depth, profound truths, natural beauty, exactitude, freshness of treatment, and so on, as criteria of evaluation—the whole of which converges on the perennial problem of what makes a work of art good. To understand the role of esthetic theory is not to conceive it as definition, logically doomed to failure, but to read it as summaries of seriously made recommendations to attend in certain ways to certain features of art.

PHILOSOPHY OF MAN

How do we come to have a concept of ourselves? And how shall we understand this concept? P. F. Strawson begins the following selection by noting some of the puzzles that are connected with it. Fundamental to them is the fact that we ascribe to ourselves both conscious activities like thinking and feeling, and material characteristics. We do this because, while conscious beings, we are also uniquely related to our own bodies. Two theories suggest themselves about this double ascription, Cartesian dualism and the "no-subject" view. The former posits two substances to account for the two kinds of ascription, the second holds only to the physical and denies any conscious subject, believing that a mental subject theory results from linguistic confusion.

But both these theories, Strawson argues, are unsatisfactory and incoherent. Puzzles in talk about oneself can be overcome only by taking the concept of person as primitive or underived from any other concepts. So to take person is to mean by it a being of whom we can and do ascribe states of consciousness as well as corporeal characteristics. Both predications are proper to the use of the concept.

8 Persons

P. F. Strawson (1919-   )

I. In the *Tractus* (5.631–5.641), Wittgenstein writes of the I which occurs in philosophy, of the philosophical idea of the subject of experiences. He says first: "The thinking, presenting subject—there is no such thing." Then, a little later: "*In an important sense there is no subject.*" This is followed by: "The subject does not belong to the world, but is a limit of the world." And a little later comes the following paragraph: "There is (therefore) really a sense in which in philosophy we can talk non-psychologically of the I. The I occurs in philosophy through the fact that the 'world is my world.' The philosophical I is not the man, not the human body, or the human soul of which psychology treats, but the metaphysical subject, the limit—not a part of the world." These remarks are impressive, but also puzzling and obscure. Reading them, one might think: Well, let's settle for the human body and the human soul of which psychology treats, and which is a part of the world, and let the metaphysical subject go. But again we might think: No, when I talk of myself, I do after all talk of that which has all of my experiences, I do talk of the subject of my experiences—and yet also of something that is part of the world in that it, but not the world, comes to an end when I die. The limit of *my* world is not—and is not so thought of by me— the limit of *the* world. It may be difficult to explain the idea of something which is both a subject of experiences and a part of the world. But it is an idea we have: it should be an idea we can explain.

Let us think of some of the ways in which we ordinarily talk of ourselves, of some of the things which we ordinarily ascribe to ourselves. They are of many kinds. We ascribe to ourselves *actions* and *intentions* (I am doing, did, shall do this); *sensations* (I am warm, in pain); *thoughts* and *feelings* (I think, wonder, want this, am angry, disappointed, contented); perceptions and memories (I see this, hear the other, remember that). We ascribe to ourselves, in two senses, position: *location* (I am on the sofa), and *attitude* (I am lying down). And of course we ascribe to ourselves not only temporary conditions, states, and situations, like most of these, but also enduring characteristics, including such physical characteristics as height, colouring, shape, and weight. That is to say, among the things we ascribe to ourselves are things of a kind that we also ascribe to material bodies to which we would not dream of ascribing others of the things that we ascribe to ourselves. Now there seems nothing needing explanation in the fact that the particular height, colouring, and physical position which we ascribe

The selection is from P. F. Strawson, "Persons," *Minnesota Studies in the Philosophy of Science*, Vol. II. Edited by Herbert Feigl, Michael Scriven, and Grover Maxwell, University of Minnesota Press, Minneapolis. Copyright © 1958 by the University of Minnesota. Used by permission of the publisher.

to ourselves, should be ascribed to *something or other;* for that which one calls one's body is, at least, a body, a material thing. It can be picked out from others, identified by ordinary physical criteria and described in ordinary physical terms. But it can seem, and has seemed, to need explanation that one's states of consciousness, one's thoughts and sensations, are ascribed *to the very same thing* as that to which these physical characteristics, this physical situation, is ascribed. Why are one's states of consciousness ascribed to the very same thing as certain corporeal characteristics, a certain physical situation, etc.? And once this question is raised, another question follows it, viz.: Why are one's states of consciousness ascribed to (said to be of, or to belong to) anything at all? It is not to be supposed that the answers to these questions will be independent of one another.

It might indeed be thought that an answer to both of them could be found in the unique role which each person's body plays in his experience, particularly his perceptual experience. All philosophers who have concerned themselves with these questions have referred to the uniqueness of this role. (Descartes was well enough aware of its uniqueness: "I am *not* lodged in my body like a pilot in a vessel.") In what does this uniqueness consist? Well, of course, in a great many facts. We may summarize some of these facts by saying that for each person there is one body which occupies a certain *causal* position in relation to that person's perceptual experience, a causal position which is in various ways unique in relation to each of the various kinds of perceptual ex-

perience he has; and—as a further consequence—that this body is also unique for him as an *object* of the various kinds of perceptual experience which he has. This complex uniqueness of the single body appears, moreover, to be a contingent matter, or rather a cluster of contingent matters; we can, or it seems that we can, imagine many peculiar combinations of dependence and independence of aspects of our perceptual experience on the physical states or situation of more than one body.

Now I must say, straightaway, that this cluster of apparently contingent facts about the unique role which each person's body plays in his experience does not seem to me to provide, *by itself,* an answer to our questions. Of course these facts explain *something.* They provide a very good reason why a subject of experience should have a *very special regard* for just one body, why he should think of it as unique and perhaps more important than any other. They explain —if I may be permitted to put it so— why I feel *peculiarly attached* to what in fact I call my own body; they even might be said to explain why, granted that I am going to speak of one body as *mine,* I should speak of this body (the body that I do speak of as mine) as mine. But they do not·explain why I should have the concept of *myself* at all, why I should ascribe my thoughts and experiences to *anything.* Moreover, even if we were satisfied with some other explanation of why one's states of consciousness (thoughts and feelings and perceptions) were ascribed to *something,* and satisfied that the facts in question sufficed to explain why the "possession" of a particular body should be ascribed to the *same* thing (i.e., to explain why a particular body should be spoken of as standing in some special relation, called "being possessed by" to that thing), yet the facts in question still do not explain why we should, as we do, ascribe certain corporeal characteristics not simply to the body standing in this special relation to the thing to which we ascribe thoughts, feelings, etc., but to the thing itself to which we ascribe those thoughts and feelings. (For we say "I am bald," as well as "I am cold," "I am lying on the hearthrug" as well as "I see a spider on the ceiling.") Briefly, the facts in question explain why a subject of experience should pick out one body from others, give it, perhaps, an honoured name and ascribe to it whatever characteristics it has; but they do not explain why the experiences should be ascribed to any subject at all; and they do not explain why, if the experiences are to be ascribed to something, they *and* the corporeal characteristics which might be truly ascribed to the favoured body, should be ascribed to the same thing. So the facts in question do not explain the use that we make of the word "I," or how any word has the use that word has. They do not explain the concept we have of a person.

II. A possible reaction at this point is to say that the concept we have is wrong or confused, or, if we make it a rule not to say that the concepts we have are confused, that the usage we have, whereby we ascribe, or seem to ascribe, such different kinds of predicate to one and the same thing, is confusing, that it conceals the true nature of the concepts involved, or something of this sort. This reaction can be found in two very important types of view about these mat-

ters. The first type of view is Cartesian, the view of Descartes and of others who think like him. Over the attribution of the second type of view I am more hesitant; but there is some evidence that it was held, at one period, by Wittgenstein and possibly also by Schlick. On both of these views, one of the questions we are considering, namely: "Why do we ascribe our states of consciousness to the very same thing as certain corporeal characteristics, etc.?" is a question which does not arise; for on both views it is only a linguistic illusion that both kinds of predicate are properly ascribed to one and the same thing, that there is a common owner, or subject of both types of predicate. And on the second of these views, the other question we are considering, namely "Why do we ascribe our states of consciousness to anything at all?" is also a question which does not arise; for on this view, it is only a linguistic illusion that one ascribes one's states of consciousness at all, that there is any proper subject of these apparent ascriptions, that states of consciousness belong to, or are states of anything.

That Descartes held the first of these views is well enough known. When we speak of a person, we are really referring to one or both of two distinct substances (two substances of different types), each of which has its own appropriate type of states and properties; and none of the properties or states of either can be a property or state of the other. States of consciousness belong to one of these substances, and not to the other. I shall say no more about the Cartesian view at the moment—what I have to say about it will emerge later on—except to note again that while it escapes one of our questions, it does not escape, but indeed invites, the other: "Why are one's states of consciousness *ascribed* at all, to *any* subject?"

The second of these views I shall call the "no-ownership" or "no-subject" doctrine of the self. Whether or not anyone has explicitly held this view, it is worth reconstructing, or constructing, in outline.[1] For the errors into which

it falls are instructive. The "no-ownership" theorist may be presumed to start his explanations with facts of the sort which illustrate the unique causal position of a certain material body in a person's experience. The theorist maintains that the uniqueness of this body is sufficient to give rise to the idea that one's experiences can be ascribed to some particular individual thing, can be said to be possessed by, or owned by, that thing. This idea, he thinks, though infelicitously and misleadingly expressed in terms of ownership, would have some validity, would make some sort of sense, so long as we thought of this individual thing, the possessor of the experiences, as the body itself. So long as we thought in this way, then to ascribe a particular state of consciousness to this body, this individual thing, would at least be to say something contingent, something that might be, or might have been, false. It might have been a misascription; for the experience in question might be, or might have been, causally dependent on the state of some other body; in the present admissible, though infelicitous, sense of "belong," it might have belonged to some other individual thing. But now, the theorist suggests, one becomes confused: one slides from this admissible, though infelicitous, sense in which one's experiences may be said to

---

[1] The evidence that Wittgenstein at one time held such a view is to be found in the third of Moore's articles in *Mind* on "Wittgenstein's Lectures in 1930–3" (*Mind*, 1955, especially pp. 13–14). He is reported to have held that the use of "I" was utterly different in the case of "I have a tooth-ache" or "I see a red patch" from its use in the case of "I've got a bad tooth" or "I've got a matchbox." He thought that there were two uses of "I" and that in one of them "I" was replaceable by "this body." So far the view might be Cartesian, but he also said that in the other use (the use exemplified by "I have a tooth-ache" as opposed to "I have a bad tooth"), "I" *does not denote a possessor,* and that no ego is involved in thinking or in having a tooth-ache; and referred with apparent approval to Lichtenberg's dictum that, instead of saying "I think," we (or Descartes!) ought to say "There is a thought" (i.e., "Es denkt").

The attribution of such a view to Schlick would have to rest on his article "Meaning and Verification," Pt. V (*Readings in Philosophical Analysis,* H. Feigl and W. Sellars, eds.). Like Wittgenstein, Schlick quotes Lichtenberg, and then goes on to say: "Thus we see that unless we choose to call our body the owner or bearer of the data (the data of immediate experience)—which seems to be a rather misleading expression—we have to say that the data have no owner or bearer." The full import of Schlick's article is, however, obscure to me, and it is quite likely that a false impression is given by the quotation of a single sentence. I shall say merely that I have drawn on Schlick's article in constructing the case of my hypothetical "no-subject" theorist; but shall not claim to be representing his views.

Lichtenberg's anti-Cartesian dictum is, as the subsequent argument will show, one that I endorse, if properly used. But it seems to have been repeated, without being understood, by many of Descartes' critics.

The evidence that Wittgenstein and Schlick ever held a "no-subject" view seems indecisive, since it is possible that the relevant remarks are intended as criticisms of a Cartesian view rather than as expositions of the true view.

belong to, or be possessed by, some particular thing, to a wholly inadmissible and empty sense of these expressions, and in this new and inadmissible sense, the particular thing which is supposed to possess the experiences is not thought of as a body, but as something else, say an ego.

Suppose we call the first type of possession, which is really a certain kind of causal dependence, "having₁"; and the second type of possession, "having₂"; and call the individual of the first type "B" and the supposed individual of the second type "E." Then the difference is that while it is genuinely a contingent matter that *all my experiences are had₁ by B,* it appears as a necessary truth that *all my experiences are had₂ by E.* But the belief in E and in having₂ by E is an illusion. Only those things whose ownership is logically transferable can be owned at all. So experiences are not owned by anything except in the dubious sense of being causally dependent on the state of a particular body. This is at least a genuine relationship to a thing, in that they might have stood in it to another thing. Since the whole function of E was to own experiences in a logically non-transferable sense of "own," and since experiences are not owned by anything in this sense, for there is no such sense of "own," E must be eliminated from the picture altogether. It only came in because of a confusion.

I think it must be clear that this account of the matter, though it contains *some* of the facts, is not coherent. It is not coherent, in that one who holds it is forced to make use of that sense of possession of which he denies the existence, in presenting his case for the denial.

When he tries to state the contingent fact, which he thinks gives rise to the illusion of the "ego," he has to state it in some such form as "All *my* experiences are had₁ by (uniquely dependent on the state of) body B." For any attempt to eliminate the "my," or some other expression with a similar possessive force, would yield something that was not a contingent fact at all. The proposition that *all* experiences are causally dependent on the state of a single body B, for example, is just false. The theorist means to speak of all the experiences *had by a certain person* being contingently so dependent. And the theorist cannot consistently argue that "all the experiences of person P" *means the same thing* as "all experiences contingently dependent on a certain body B"; for then his proposition would not be contingent, as his theory requires, but analytic. He must mean to be speaking of some class of experiences of the members of which it is in fact contingently true that they are all dependent on body B. And the defining characteristic of this class is in fact that they are "*my* experiences" or "the experiences *of* some person," where the sense of "possession" is the one he calls into question.

This internal incoherence is a serious matter when it is a question of denying what prima facie is the case; that is, that one does genuinely ascribe one's states of consciousness to something, viz., oneself, and that this kind of ascription is precisely such as the theorist finds unsatisfactory, i.e., is such that it does not seem to make sense to suggest, for example, that the identical pain which was in fact one's own might have been another's. We do not have to seek far in order to understand the place of this logically non-transferable kind of ownership in our general scheme of thought. For if we think of the requirements of identifying reference, in speech, to *particular* states of consciousness, or private experiences, we see that such particulars cannot be thus identifyingly referred to except as the states or experiences *of* some identified *person*. States, or experiences, one might say, *owe* their identity as particulars to the identity of the person whose states or experiences they are. And from this it follows immediately that if they can be identified as particular states or experiences at all, they must be possessed or ascribable in just that way which the no-ownership theorist ridicules, i.e., in such a way that it is logically impossible that a particular state or experience in fact possessed by someone should have been possessed by anyone else. The requirements of identity rule out logical transferability of ownership. So the theorist could maintain his position only by denying that we could ever refer to particular states or experiences at all. And *this* position is ridiculous.

We may notice, even now, a possible connection between the no-ownership doctrine and the Cartesian position. The latter is, straightforwardly enough, a dualism of two subjects (two types of subject). The former could, a little paradoxically, be called a dualism too; a dualism of one subject (the body) and one non-subject. We might surmise that the second dualism, paradoxically so called, arises out of the first dualism, non-paradoxically so called; in other words, that if we try to think of that to which one's states of consciousness are ascribed as something utterly different from that to which certain corporeal

characteristics are ascribed, then indeed it becomes difficult to see why states of consciousness should be ascribed, thought of as belonging to, anything at all. And when we think of this possibility, we may also think of another: viz., that both the Cartesian and the no-ownership theorist are profoundly wrong in holding, as each must, that there are two uses of "I" in one of which it denotes something which it does not denote in the other.

III. The no-ownership theorist fails to take account of all the facts. He takes account of some of them. He implies, correctly, that the unique position or role of a single body in one's experience is not a sufficient explanation of the fact that one's experiences, or states of consciousness, are ascribed to something which *has* them, with that peculiar non-transferable kind of possession which is here in question. It may be a necessary part of the explanation, but it is not, by itself, a sufficient explanation. The theorist, as we have seen, goes on to suggest that it is perhaps a sufficient explanation of something else: viz., of our confusedly and mistakenly *thinking* that states of consciousness are to be ascribed to something in this special way. And this suggestion, as we have seen, is incoherent: for it involves the denial that someone's states of consciousness are anyone's. We avoid the incoherence of this denial, while agreeing that the special role of a single body in someone's experience does not suffice to explain why that experience should be ascribed to anybody. The fact that there is this special role does not, by itself, give a sufficient reason why what we think of as a subject of experience should have any use for the conception of himself as such a subject.

When I say that the no-ownership theorist's account fails through not reckoning with all the facts, I have in mind a very simple but, in this question, a very central, thought: viz., that it is a necessary condition of one's ascribing states of consciousness, experiences, to oneself, in the way one does, that one should also ascribe them (or be prepared to ascribe them) to others who are not oneself.[2] This means not less than it

says. It means, for example, that the ascribing phrases should be used in just the same sense when the subject is another, as when the subject is oneself. Of course the thought that this is so gives no trouble to the non-philosopher: the thought, for example, that "in pain" means the same whether one says "I am in pain" or "He is in pain." The dictionaries do not give two sets of meanings for every expression which describes a state of consciousness: a first-person meaning and a second- and third-person meaning. But to the philosopher this thought has given trouble; indeed it has. How could the sense be the same when the method of verification was so different in the two cases— or, rather, when there was a method of verification in the one case (the case of others) and not, properly speaking, in the other case (the case of oneself)? Or, again, how can it be right to talk of *ascribing* in the case of oneself? For surely there can be a question of ascribing only if there is or could be a question of identifying that to which the ascription is made? And though there may be a question of identifying the one who is in pain when that one is another, how can there be such a question when that one is oneself? But this last query answers itself as soon as we remember that we speak primarily to others, for the information of others. In one sense, indeed, there is no question of my having to *tell who it is* who is in pain, when I am. In another sense I may have to *tell who it is,* i.e., to let others know who it is.

What I have just said explains, per-

---

[2] I can imagine an objection to the unqualified form of this statement, an objection which might be put as follows. Surely the idea of a uniquely applicable predicate (a predicate which *in fact* belongs to only one individual) is not absurd. And, if it is not, then surely the most that can be claimed is that a necessary condition of one's ascribing predicates of a certain class to one individual (oneself) is that one should be prepared, or ready, on appropriate occasions, to ascribe them to other individuals, and hence that one should have a conception of what those appropriate occasions for ascribing them would be; but not, necessarily, that one should actually do so on any occasion.

The shortest way with the objection is to admit it, or at least to refrain from disputing it; for the lesser claim is all that the argument strictly requires, though it is slightly simpler to conduct it on the basis of the larger claim. But it is well to point out further that we are not speaking of a single predicate, or merely of some group or other of predicates, but of the whole of an enormous class of predicates such that the applicability of those predicates or their negations determines a major logical type or category of individuals. To insist, at this level, on the distinction between the lesser and the larger claims is to carry the distinction over from a level at which it is clearly correct to a level at which it may well appear idle or, possibly, senseless.

The main point here is a purely logical one: the idea of a predicate is correlative with that of a range of distinguishable indi-

---

viduals of which the predicate can be significantly, though not necessarily truly affirmed.

haps, how one may properly be said to ascribe states of consciousness to oneself, given that one ascribes them to others. But how is it that one can ascribe them to others? Well, one thing is certain: that *if* the things one ascribes states of consciousness to, in ascribing them to others, are thought of as a set of Cartesian egoes to which *only* private experiences can, in correct logical grammar, be ascribed, *then* this question is unanswerable and this problem insoluble. If, in identifying the things to which states of consciousness are to be ascribed, private experiences are to be all one has to go on, then, just for the very same reason as that for which there is, from one's own point of view, no question of telling that a private experience is one's own, there is also no question of telling that a private experience is another's. All private experiences, all states of consciousness, will be mine, i.e., no one's. To put it briefly: one can ascribe states of consciousness to oneself only if one can ascribe them to others; one can ascribe them to others only if one can identify other subjects of experience; and one cannot identify others if one can identify them *only* as subjects of experience, possessors of states of consciousness.

It might be objected that this way with Cartesianism is too short. After all, there is no difficulty about distinguishing bodies from one another, no difficulty about identifying bodies. And does not this give us an indirect way of identifying subjects of experience, while preserving the Cartesian mode? Can we not identify such a subject as, for example, "the subject that stands to that body in the same special relation as I stand to this one"; or, in other words,

"the subject of those experiences which stand in the same unique causal relation to body N as *my* experiences stand to body M"? But this suggestion is useless. It requires me to have noted that *my* experiences stand in a special relation to body M, when it is just the right to speak of *my* experiences at all that is in question. (It requires me to have noted that *my* experiences stand in a special relation to body M; but it requires me to have noted this as a condition of being able to identify other subjects of experience, i.e., as a condition of having the idea of myself as a subject of experience, i.e., as a condition of thinking of any experience as *mine*.) So long as we persist in talking, in the mode of this explanation, of experiences on the one hand, and bodies on the other, the most I may be allowed to have noted is that experiences, *all* experiences, stand in a special relation to body M, that body M is unique in just this way, that this is what makes body M unique among bodies. (This "most" is, perhaps, too much—because of the presence of the word "experiences.") The proffered explanation runs: "Another subject of experience is distinguished and identified as the subject of those experiences which stand in the same unique causal relationship to body N as my experiences stand to body M." And the objection is: "But what is the word 'my' doing in this explanation? (It could not get on without it.)"

What we have to acknowledge, in order to begin to free ourselves from these difficulties, is the *primitiveness* of the concept of a person. What I mean by the concept of a person is the concept of a type of entity such that *both* predicates ascribing states of consciousness *and* predicates ascribing corporeal characteristics, a physical situation, etc. are equally applicable to a single individual of that single type. And what I mean by saying that this concept is primitive can be put in a number of ways. One way is to return to those two questions I asked earlier: viz., (1) why are states of consciousness ascribed to anything at all? and (2) why are they ascribed to the very same thing as certain corporeal characteristics, a certain physical situation, etc.? I remarked at the beginning that it was not to be supposed that the answers to these questions were independent of each other. And now I shall say that they are connected in this way: that a necessary condition of states of consciousness being ascribed at all is that they should be ascribed to the *very same things* as certain corporeal characteristics, a certain physical situation, etc. That is to say, states of consciousness could not be ascribed at all, *unless* they were ascribed to persons, in the sense I have claimed for this word. We are tempted to think of a person as a sort of compound of two kinds of subject—a subject of experiences (a pure consciousness, an ego), on the one hand, and a subject of corporeal attributes on the other.

Many questions arise when we think in this way. But, in particular, when we ask ourselves how we come to frame, to get a use for, the concept of this compound of two subjects, the picture—if we are honest and careful—is apt to change from the picture of two subjects to the picture of one subject and one non-subject. For it becomes impossible to see how we could come by the idea of different, distinguishable, identifiable subjects of experiences—differ-

ent consciousnesses—*if this idea is thought of as logically primitive,* as a logical ingredient in the compound idea of a person, the latter being composed of two subjects. For there could never be any question of assigning an experience, as such, to any subject other than oneself; and therefore never any question of assigning it to oneself either, never any question of ascribing it to a subject at all. So the concept of the pure individual consciousness—the pure ego—is a concept that cannot exist; or, at least, cannot exist as a primary concept in terms of which the concept of a person can be explained or analysed. It can only exist, if at all, as a secondary, non-primitive concept, which itself is to be explained, analysed, in terms of the concept of a person. It was the entity corresponding to this illusory primary concept of the pure consciousness, the ego-substance, for which Hume was seeking, or ironically pretending to seek, when he looked into himself, and complained that he could never discover himself without a perception and could never discover anything but the perception. More seriously—and this time there was no irony, but a confusion, a Nemesis of confusion for Hume—it was this entity of which Hume vainly sought for the principle of unity, confessing himself perplexed and defeated; sought vainly because there is no principle of unity where there is no principle of differentiation. It was this, too, to which Kant, more prespicacious here than Hume, accorded a purely formal ("analytic") unity: the unity of the "I think" that accompanies all my perceptions and therefore might just as well accompany none. And finally it is this, perhaps, of which Wittgenstein spoke when he said of the subject, first, that there is no such thing, and second, that it is not a part of the world, but its limit.

So, then, the word "I" never refers to this, the pure subject. But this does not mean, as the no-ownership theorist must think and as Wittgenstein, at least at one period, seemed to think, that "I" in some cases does not refer at all. It refers, because I am a person among others. And the predicates which would, *per impossible,* belong to the pure subject if it could be referred to, belong properly to the person to which "I" does refer.

The concept of a person is logically prior to that of an individual consciousness. The concept of a person is not to be analysed as that of an animated body or of an embodied anima. This is not to say that the concept of a pure individual consciousness might not have a logically secondary existence, if one thinks, or finds, it desirable. We speak of a dead person—a body—and in the same secondary way we might at least think of a disembodied person, retaining the logical benefit of individuality from having been a person.[3]

---

[3] A little further thought will show how limited this concession is. But I shall not discuss the question now.

PHILOSOPHY OF SCIENCE

A frequent puzzle to the young student of science is how the scientific world about which he is learning is related to the everyday world of his experience. Often this puzzle leads him to make a distinction between the two worlds, one real, the other appearance. The removal of the puzzle is Professor Ryle's concern in the following selection. He warns us first about the words "science" and "world," in a sense deflating them and cautioning us in our use of them. He then proceeds to elucidate and clarify the logical pattern that gives rise to the problem of "two worlds," doing so through an extended analogy between science and an auditor's balance sheet. The auditor, Ryle says, gives information by exhibiting relations among things, not by giving a rival description of them. So too, the scientist does not give a rival description of things such as would make his world real and the everyday world appearance. Rather, the scientist, the poet, and the theologian produce compatible pictures of the same "world"—even though they have different businesses to perform—and they do not give conflicting answers to the same questions. This point, Ryle concludes, is likely to be forgotten if we fail to note the "smothering" effect of words like depict, describe, and explain.

9   Science and Ordinary Language

Gilbert Ryle (1900-   )

We often worry ourselves about the relations between what we call "the world of science" and "the world of real life" or "the world of common sense." Sometimes we are even encouraged to worry about the relations between "the desk of physics" and the desk on which we write.

When we are in a certain intellectual mood, we seem to find clashes between the things that scientists tell us about our furniture, clothes and limbs and the things that we tell about them. We are apt to express these felt rivalries by saying that the world whose parts and members are described by scientists is different from the world whose parts and members we describe ourselves, and yet, since there can be only one world, one of these seeming worlds must be a dummy-world. Moreover, as no one nowadays is hardy enough to say "Bo" to science, it must be the world that we ourselves describe which is the dummy-world. . . .

As a preface to the serious part of the argument I want to deflate two over-inflated ideas, from which derives not the cogency but some of the persuasiveness of the argument for the irreconcilability of the world of science with the everyday world. One is the idea of *science,* the other that of *world.*

(*a*) There is no such animal as "Science." There are scores of sciences. Most of these sciences are such that acquaintanceship with them or, what is even more captivating, hearsay knowledge about them has not the slightest tendency to make us contrast their world with the everyday world. Philology is a science, but not even popularizations of its discoveries would make anyone feel that the world of philology cannot be accommodated by the world of familiar people, things and happenings. Let philologists discover everything discoverable about the structures and origins of the expressions that we use; yet their discoveries have no tendency to make us write off as mere dummies the expressions that we use and that philologists also use. The sole dividedness of mind that is induced in us by learning any of the lessons of philology is akin to that which we sometimes experience when told, say, that our old, familiar paper-weight was once an axe-head used by a prehistoric warrior. Something utterly ordinary becomes also, just for the moment, charged with history. A mere paper-weight becomes also, just for the moment, a death-dealing weapon. But that is all.

Nor do most of the other sciences give us the feeling that we live our daily lives in a bubble-world. Botanists, entomologists, meteorologists, and geologists do not seem to threaten the walls, floors and ceilings of our common dwelling-place. On the contrary, they seem to increase the quantity and improve the arrangement of its furniture.

The selection is from Gilbert Ryle, *Dilemmas,* Chapter V, "The World of Science and the Everyday World" (Cambridge: University Press, 1954), pp. 68–81, with omissions. Used by permission of the publisher.

Nor even, as might be supposed, do all branches of physical science engender in us the idea that our everyday world is a dummy-world. The discoveries and theories of astronomers and astro-physicists may make us feel that the earth is very small, but only by making us feel that the heavens are very big. The gnawing suspicion that both the terrestrial and the super-terrestrial alike are merely painted stage-canvas is not begotten by even hearsay knowledge of the physics of the immense. It is not begotten, either, by hearsay knowledge of the physics of the middle-sized. The theory of the pendulum, the cannon-ball, the water-pump, the fulcrum, the balloon and the steam-engine does not by itself drive us to vote between the everyday world and the so-called world of science. Even the comparatively minute can be accommodated by us without theoretical heart-searchings in our everyday world. Pollen-grains, frost-crystals and bacteria, though revealed only through the microscope, do not by themselves make us doubt whether middle-sized and immense things may not belong where rainbows and mirages or even dreams belong. We always knew that there were things too small to be seen with the naked eye; the magnifying-glass and the microscope have surprised us not by establishing their existence but by disclosing their variety and, in some cases, their importance.

No, there are, I think, two branches of science which, especially when in collusion with one another, produce what I may describe as the "poison-pen effect," the effect of half-persuading us that our best friends are really our worst enemies. One is the physical theory of the ultimate elements of mat-ter; the other is that one wing of human physiology which investigates the mechanism and functioning of our organs of perception. I do not think it makes much difference to the issue whether these ultimate elements of matter are described as the Greek atomists described them or as the twentieth-century nuclear physicist describes them. Nor do I think that it makes much difference whether we consider old-fashioned guesses or recent conclusive discoveries about the mechanism of perception. The upsetting moral drawn by Epicurus, Galileo, Sydenham and Locke is precisely that drawn by Eddington, Sherrington and Russell. The fact that this upsetting moral was once drawn from a piece of speculation and is now drawn from well-established scientific theory makes no difference. The moral drawn is not a piece of good science now, and it was not a piece of bad science then.

So the so-called world of science which, we gather, has the title to replace our everyday world is, I suggest, the world not of science in general but of atomic and subatomic physics in particular, enhanced by some slightly incongruous appendages borrowed from one branch of neuro-physiology.

(*b*) The other idea which needs prefatory deflation is that of *world*. When we hear that there is a grave disparity between our everyday world and the world of science or, a little more specifically, the world of one wing of physical science, it is difficult for us to shake off the impression that there are some physicists who by dint of their experiments, calculations and theorizing have qualified themselves to tell us everything that is really important about the cosmos, whatever that may be.

Where theologians used to be the people to tell us about the creation and management of the cosmos, now these physicists are the experts—for all that in the articles and books that they write for their colleagues and pupils the word "world" seldom occurs, and the grand word "cosmos," I hope, never occurs. There is some risk of a purely verbal muddle here. We know that a lot of people are interested in poultry and would not be surprised to find in existence a periodical called "The Poultry World." Here the word "world" is not used as theologians use it. It is a collective noun used to label together all matters pertaining to poultry-keeping. It could be paraphrased by "field" or "sphere of interest" or "province." In this use there could be no question of a vendetta between the poultry world and the Christian world, since, while "world" could be paraphrased by "cosmos" in the phrase "Christian world," it could not be so paraphrased in the other.

It is obviously quite innocuous to speak of the physicist's world, if we do so in the way in which we speak of the poultry-keeper's world or the entertainment world. We could correspondingly speak of the bacteriologist's world and the marine zoologist's world. In this use there is no connotation of cosmic authority, for the word "world" in this use does not mean "*the* world" or "the cosmos." On the contrary, it means the *department* of interests which physicists' interests constitute.

But this is not the whole story. For while there are hosts of interests, scientific, political, artistic, etc., from which the interests peculiar to physicists are distinguished, while, that is, there are hosts of provinces of interest, which are different from without being rivals of the physicist's province, there remains an important respect in which the subject matters of fundamental physical theory do comprehend or cover the subject matters of all the other natural sciences. The specimens collected by the marine biologist, though of no special interest to the physical theorist, are still, in an indirect way, specimens of what he is specially interested in. So too are the objects studied by the geologist, the mycologist and the philatelist. There is nothing that any natural scientist studies of which the truths of physics are not true; and from this it is tempting to infer that the physicist is therefore talking about everything, and so that he is, after all, talking about the cosmos. So, after all, the cosmos must be described only in his terms, and can only be misdescribed in the terms of any of these other more special sciences or, more glaringly, in theological terms, or most glaringly of all, in the terms of everyday conversation. . . .

I am now going to try to bring out the underlying logical pattern of the view that the truths of physical theory leave no room for the truths of daily life, and this I do by means of a long-drawn out analogy with which I hope you will bear for some little time. An undergraduate member of a college is one day permitted to inspect the college accounts and to discuss them with the auditor. He hears that these accounts show how the college has fared during the year. "You will find," he is told, "that all the activities of the college are represented in these columns. Undergraduates are taught, and here are the tuition-fees that they pay. Their instructors teach, and here are the stipends that they receive. Games are played, and here are the figures; so much for rent of the ground, so much for the wages of the groundsman, and so on. Even your entertainments are recorded; here is what was paid out to the butchers, grocers and fruiterers, here are the kitchen-charges, and here is what you paid in your college battels." At first the undergraduate is merely mildly interested. He allows that these columns give him a different sort of view of the life of the college from the patchwork-quilt of views that he had previously acquired from his own experiences of working in the library, playing football, dining with his friends, and the rest. But then under the influence of the auditor's grave and sober voice he suddenly begins to wonder. Here everything in the life of the college is systematically marshalled and couched in terms which, though colorless, are precise, impersonal and susceptible of conclusive checking. To every plus there corresponds an equal and opposite minus; the entries are classified; the origins and destinations of all payments are indicated. Moreover, a general conclusion is reached; the financial position of the college is exhibited and compared with its position in previous years. So is not this expert's way, perhaps, the right way in which to think of the life of the college, and the other muddled and emotionally charged ways to which he had been used the wrong ways?

At first in discomfort he wriggles and suggests "May not these accounts give us just one part of the life of the college? The chimney-sweep and the inspector of electricity-meters see their little corners of the activities of the college; but no one supposes that what

they have to tell is more than a petty fragment of the whole story. Perhaps you, the auditor, are like them and see only a small part of what is going on." But the auditor rejects this suggestion. "No," he says, "here are the payments to the chimney-sweep at so much per chimney swept, and here are the payments to the Electricity Board at so much a unit. Everybody's part in the college life, including my own, is down here in figures. There is nothing departmental in the college accounts. Everything is covered. What is more, the whole system of accountancy is uniform for all colleges and is, at least in general pattern, uniform for all businesses, government departments and town councils. No speculations or hypotheses are admitted; our results are lifted above the horizons of opinion and prejudice by the sublime Principle of Double Entry. These accounts tell the objective truth about the entire life of the whole college; the stories that you tell about it to your brothers and sisters are only picturesque travesties of the audited facts. They are only dreams. Here are the realities." What is the undergraduate to reply? He cannot question the accuracy, comprehensiveness or exhaustiveness of the accounts. He cannot complain that they cover five or six sides of college life, but do not cover the other sixteen sides. All the sides that he can think of are indeed duly covered.

Perhaps he is acute enough to suspect that there has been some subtle trick played by this word "covered." The tuition he had received last term from the lecturer in Anglo-Saxon was indeed covered, yet the accounts were silent about what had been taught and the auditor betrayed no inquisitiveness about what progress the student had made. He, too, the undergraduate himself, had been covered in scores of sections of the accounts, as a recipient of an Exhibition, as a pupil of the lecturer in Anglo-Saxon and so on. He had been covered, but not characterized or mischaracterized. Nothing was said about him that would not have fitted a much taller Exhibitioner or a much less enthusiastic student of Anglo-Saxon. Nothing had been said about him personally at all. He has not been described, though he has been financially accounted for.

Take a special case. In one way the auditor is very much interested in the books that the librarian buys for the college library. They must be scrupulously accounted for, the price paid for each must be entered, the fact of the actual receipt of the book must be recorded. But in another way the auditor need not be at all interested in these books, since he need not have any idea what the books contain or whether anybody reads them. For him the book is merely what is indicated by the price mark on its jacket. For him the differences between one book and another are differences in shillings. The figures in the section devoted to library accounts do indeed cover every one of the actual books bought; yet nothing in these figures would have been different had these books been different in subject matter, language, style and binding, so long as their prices were the same. The accounts tell neither lies nor the truth about the contents of any of the books. In the reviewer's sense of "describe," they do not describe any of the books, though they scrupulously cover all of the books.

Which, now, is the real and which the bubble-book, the book read by the undergraduate or the book whose price is entered in the library-accounts? Clearly there is no answer. There are not two books, nor yet one real book, side by side with another bubble-book— the latter, queerly, being the one that is useful for examinations. There is just a book available for students, and an entry in the accounts specifying what the college paid for it. There could have been no such entry had there not been the book. There could not be a library stocked with mere book-prices; though also there could not be a well-conducted college which had a library full of books but required no library accounts to be kept.

The library used by the student is the same library as that accounted for by the accountant. What the student finds in the library is what the accountant tells the pounds, shillings and pence of. I am suggesting, you see, that it is in partially the same way that the world of the philologist, the marine-biologist, the astronomer and the housewife is the same world as that of the physicist; and what the pedestrian and the bacteriologist find in the world is what the physicist tells him about in his double-entry notation.

I do not want to press the analogy beyond a certain point. I am not arguing that a scientific theory is in all or many respects like a balance-sheet, but only that it is like a balance-sheet in one important respect, namely that the formulae of the one and the financial entries of the other are constitutionally speechless about certain sorts of matters, just because they are *ex officio* explicit about other, but connected matters.

Everything that the student says about the books in the library may be true, and everything that the accountant says about them may be true. The student's information about the books is greatly unlike the accountant's, and neither is it deducible from the accountant's information, nor vice versa. Yet the student's information is covered, in an important way, by the accounts, although these are constitutionally speechless about the literary and scholarly qualities of books which are just what interest the student. The appearance of a vendetta between the different ways of describing the library is as delusive an appearance as was the appearance of a vendetta between my way of talking about my brother and the economist's way of talking about anybody's brother.[1] For though the accountant is, in some very general sense, telling the college about the books in the library, he is not, in the reviewer's sense of the word, describing or, of course, misdescribing these books at all. He is exhibiting the arithmetical relations holding during the financial year between the total bills paid to the booksellers for books and, somewhat indirectly, the total bills paid to the college for the use of those books. That there are such bills to record and, consequently, such arithmetical relations between their totals, itself logically presupposes that there are books in the library, actually bought from booksellers and actually available for reading by students. It logically presupposes that there are things of which the student's descriptions are either true or false, though these descriptions cannot be read out of the library accounts. Not only

can the full history of the life of the college during the year accommodate both of these kinds of information about the books, but it could not include a page for either kind without having a page for the other. It is not a question of two rival libraries, or of two rival descriptions of one library, but of two different but complementary ways of giving information of very different sorts about the one library. . . .

I hope that this protracted analogy has satisfied you at least that there is a genuine logical door open for us; that at least there is no general logical objection to saying that physical theory, while it covers the things that the more special sciences explore and the ordinary observer describes, still does not put up a rival description of them; and even that for it to be true in its way, there must be descriptions of these other kinds which are true in their quite different way or ways. It need not be a matter of rival worlds of which one has to be a bubble-world, nor yet a matter of different sectors or provinces of one world, such that what is true of one sector is false of the other.

In the way in which a landscape-painter paints a good or bad picture of a range of hills, the geologist does not paint a rival picture, good or bad, of those hills, though what he tells us the geology of are the same hills that the painter depicts or misdepicts. The painter is not doing bad geology and the geologist is not doing good or bad landscape painting. In the way in which the joiner tells us what a piece of furniture is like and gets his description right or wrong (no matter whether he is talking about its color, the wood it is made of, its style, carpentry or period), the nuclear physicist does not proffer a competing description, right or wrong, though what he tells us the nuclear physics of covers what the joiner describes. They are not giving conflicting answers to the same questions or to the same sort of question, though the physicist's questions are, in a rather artificial sense of "about," what the joiner gives his information about. The physicist does not mention the furniture; what he does mention are, so to speak, bills for such goods as, *inter alia,* bits of furniture.

Part of this point is sometimes expressed in this way. As the painter in oils on one side of the mountain and the painter in water-colors on the other side of the mountain produce very different pictures, which may still be excellent pictures of the same mountain, so the nuclear physicist, the theologian, the historian, the lyric poet and the man in the street produce very different, yet compatible and even complementary pictures of one and the same "world." But this analogy is perilous. It is risky enough to say that the accountant and the reviewer both give descriptions of the same book, since in the natural sense of "describe" in which the reviewer does describe or misdescribe the book, the accountant does neither. But it is far riskier to characterize the physicist, the theologian, the historian, the poet and the man in the street as all alike producing "pictures," whether of the

same object or of different objects. The highly concrete word "picture" smothers the enormous differences between the businesses of the scientist, historian, poet and theologian even worse than the relatively abstract word "description" smothers the big differences between the businesses of the accountant and the reviewer. It is just these smothered differences which need to be brought out into the open. If the seeming feuds between science and theology or between fundamental physics and common knowledge are to be dissolved at all, their dissolution can come not from making the polite compromise that both parties are really artists of a sort working from different points of view and with different sketching materials, but only from drawing uncompromising contrasts between their businesses. To satisfy the tobacconist and the tennis-coach that there need be no professional antagonisms between them, it is not necessary or expedient to pretend that they are really fellow-workers in some joint but unobvious missionary enterprise. It is better policy to remind them how different and independent their trades actually are. Indeed, this smothering effect of using notions like *depicting, describing, explaining,* and others to cover highly disparate things reinforces other tendencies to assimilate the dissimilar and unsuspiciously to impute just those parities of reasoning, the unreality of which engenders dilemmas.

PHILOSOPHY OF RELIGION

Concern for the logic of statements in all their variety naturally leads the analyst to religious statements. In the following selection the central problem is the logic of belief in divinity. Professor Wisdom begins by observing that the existence of God is not an experimental or experiential issue in the way it was in the past, for we now find explanations of nature in science. But the issue is more complicated than this. The reasonableness of religious belief is, to be sure, a question of whether there are supporting facts in nature; yet the question is partly scientific and partly metaphysical (in Wisdom's sense of a recommendation based on attitude). Consider the problem through an analogous question, "Do flowers feel?" We would interpret the question, are flowers mindlike enough for us to apply to them the concept "feel"? Similarly, is nature "divinelike" enough for us to apply to it or use the concept "divinity"? These questions can be answered only by a decision about the application of the concepts.

Yet the religious decision is a difficult one to describe. Wisdom offers still another analogy, comparing it to a decision in law, where there may be agreement about the facts but disagreement about their significance. Disagreements about decisions have their own sort of logic: they are neither deductions nor inductions, nor are they arbitrary and irrational. The religious decision, reflecting as it does an attitude toward nature and life, expresses a connection, based on feelings, between nature and higher beings in the universe.

10 Talk about God

John Wisdom (1904-   )

1. *The existence of God is not an experimental issue in the way it was.* An atheist or agnostic might say to a theist "You still think there are spirits in the trees, nymphs in the streams, a God of the world." He might say this because he noticed the theist in time of drought pray for rain and make a sacrifice and in the morning look for rain. But disagreement about whether there are gods is now less of this experimental or betting sort than it used to be. This is due in part, if not wholly, to our better knowledge of why things happen as they do.

It is true that even in these days it is seldom that one who believes in God has no hopes or fears which an atheist has not. Few believers now expect prayer to still the waves, but some think it makes a difference to people and not merely in ways the atheist would admit. Of course with people, as opposed to waves and machines, one never knows

The selection is from John Wisdom's article, "Gods," in Anthony Flew (ed.), *Essays on Logic and Language* (Oxford: Basil Blackwell and Mott, Ltd., 1951), pp. 187–206, with omissions. Used by permission of the publisher.

what they won't do next, so that expecting prayer to make a difference to them is not so definite a thing as believing in its mechanical efficacy. Still, just as primitive people pray in a business-like way for rain so some people still pray for others with a real feeling of doing something to help. However, in spite of this persistence of an experimental element in some theistic belief, it remains true that Elijah's method on Mount Carmel of settling the matter of what god or gods exist would be far less appropriate today than it was then.

2. *Belief in gods is not merely a matter of expectation of a world to come.* Someone may say "The fact that a theist no more than an atheist expects prayer to bring down fire from heaven or cure the sick does not mean that there is no difference between them as to the facts, it does not mean that the theist has no expectations different from the atheist's. For very often those who believe in God believe in another world and believe that God is there and that we shall go to that world when we die."

This is true, but I do not want to consider here expectations as to what one will see and feel after death nor what sort of reasons these logically unique expectations could have. So I want to consider those theists who do not believe in a future life, or rather, I want to consider the differences between atheists and theists in so far as these differences are not a matter of belief in a future life.

3. *What are these differences? And is it that theists are superstitious or that atheists are blind?* A child may wish to sit awhile with his father and he may, when he has done what his father dis-

likes, fear punishment and feel distress at causing vexation, and while his father is alive he may feel sure of help when danger threatens and feel that there is sympathy for him when disaster has come. When his father is dead he will no longer expect punishment or help. Maybe for a moment an old fear will come or a cry for help escape him, but he will at once remember that this is no good now. He may feel that his father is no more until perhaps someone says to him that his father is still alive though he lives now in another world and one so far away that there is no hope of seeing him or hearing his voice again. The child may be told that nevertheless his father can see him and hear all he says. When he has been told this the child will still fear no punishment nor expect any sign of his father, but now, even more than he did when his father was alive, he will feel that his father sees him all the time and will dread distressing him and when he has done something wrong he will feel separated from his father until he has felt sorry for what he has done. Maybe when he himself comes to die he will be like a man who expects to find a friend in the strange country where he is going. But even when this is so, it is by no means all of what makes the difference between a child who believes that his father lives still in another world and one who does not.

Likewise one who believes in God may face death differently from one who does not, but there is another difference between them besides this. This other difference may still be described as belief in another world, only this belief is not a matter of expecting one thing rather than another here or hereafter, it is not a matter of a world to come but of a world that now is, though beyond our senses. . . .

4. *The question "Is belief in gods reasonable?" has more than one source.* It is clear now that in order to grasp fully the logic of belief in divine minds we need to examine the logic of belief in animal and human minds. But we cannot do that here and so for the purposes of this discussion about divine minds let us acknowledge the reasonableness of our belief in human minds without troubling ourselves about its logic. The question of the reasonableness of belief in divine minds then becomes a matter of whether there are facts in nature which support claims about divine minds in the way facts in nature support our claims about human minds.

In this way we resolve the force behind the problem of the existence of gods into two components, one metaphysical and the same which prompts the question "Is there *ever any* behavior which gives reason to believe in *any* sort of mind?" and one which finds expression in "Are there other mind-patterns in nature beside the human and animal patterns which we can all easily detect, and are these other mind-patterns superhuman?"

Such over-determination of a question syndrome is common. Thus, the puzzling questions "Do dogs think?" "Do animals feel?" are partly metaphysical puzzles and partly scientific questions. They are not purely metaphysical; for the reports of scientists about the poor performances of cats in cages and old ladies' stories about the remarkable performances of their pets are not irrelevant. But nor are these questions purely scientific; for the stories

never settle them and therefore they have other sources. One other source is the metaphysical source we have already noticed, namely, the difficulty about getting behind an animal's behavior to its mind, whether it is a nonhuman animal or a human one.

But there's a third component in the force behind these questions, these disputes have a third source, and it is one which is important in the dispute which finds expression in the words "I believe in God," "I do not." This source comes out well if we consider the question "Do flowers feel?" Like the questions about dogs and animals this question about flowers comes partly from the difficulty we sometimes feel over inference from *any* behavior to thought or feeling and partly from ignorance as to what behavior is to be found. But these questions, as opposed to a like question about human beings, come also from hesitation as to whether the behavior in question is *enough* mind-like, that is, is it enough similar to or superior to human behavior to be called "mind-proving"? Likewise, even when we are satisfied that human behavior shows mind and even when we have learned whatever mind-suggesting things there are in nature which are not explained by human and animal minds, we may still ask "But are these things sufficiently striking to be called a mind-pattern? Can we fairly call them manifestations of a divine being?"

"The question," someone may say, "has then become merely a matter of the application of a name. And 'What's in a name?'"

5. *But the line between a question of fact and a question or decision as to the application of a name is not so simple*

as this way of putting things suggests. The question "What's in a name?" is engaging because we are inclined to answer both "Nothing" and "Very much." And this "Very much" has more than one source. We might have tried to comfort Heloise by saying "It isn't that Abelard no longer loves you, for this man isn't Abelard"; we might have said to poor Mr. Tebrick in Mr. Garnet's *Lady into Fox* "But this is no longer Silvia." But if Mr. Tebrick replied "Ah, but it is!" this might come not at all from observing facts about the fox which we have not observed, but from noticing facts about the fox which we had missed, although we had in a sense observed all that Mr. Tebrick had observed. It is possible to have before one's eyes all the items of a pattern and still to miss the pattern. . . .

The line between using a name because of how we feel and because of what we have noticed isn't sharp. "A difference as to the facts," "a discovery," "a revelation," these phrases cover many things. Discoveries have been made not only by Christopher Columbus and Pasteur, but also by Tolstoy and Dostoievsky and Freud. Things are revealed to us not only by the scientists with microscopes, but also by the poets, the prophets, and the painters. What is so isn't merely a matter of "the facts." For sometimes when there is agreement as to the facts there is still argument as to whether defendant did or did not "exercise reasonable care," was or was not "negligent."

And though we shall need to emphasize how much "There is a God" evinces an attitude to the familiar[1] we shall find

---

[1] "Persuasive Definitions," *Mind,* July, 1938, by Charles Leslie Stevenson, should be read here.

in the end that it also evinces some recognition of patterns in time easily missed and that, therefore, difference as to there being any gods is in part a difference as to what is so and therefore as to the facts, though not in the simple ways which first occurred to us.

6. *Let us now approach these same points by a different road.*

6.1. *How it is that an explanatory hypothesis, such as the existence of God, may start by being experimental and gradually become something quite different can be seen from the following story:*

Two people return to their long neglected garden and find among the weeds a few of the old plants surprisingly vigorous. One says to the other "It must be that a gardener has been coming and doing something about these plants." Upon inquiry they find that no neighbor has ever seen anyone at work in their garden. The first man says to the other "He must have worked while people slept." The other says "No, someone would have heard him and besides, anybody who cared about the plants would have kept down these weeds." The first man says "Look at the way these are arranged. There is purpose and a feeling for beauty here. I believe that someone comes, someone invisible to mortal eyes. I believe that the more carefully we look the more we shall find confirmation of this." They examine the garden ever so carefully and sometimes they come on new things suggesting that a gardener comes and sometimes they come on new things suggesting the contrary and even that a malicious person has been at work. Besides examining the garden carefully they also study what happens to gardens left without attention. Each learns all the other learns about this and about the garden. Consequently, when after all this, one says "I still believe a gardener comes" while the other says "I don't" their different words now reflect no difference as to what they have found in the garden, no difference as to what they would find in the garden if they looked further and no difference about how fast untended gardens fall into disorder. At this stage, in this context, the gardener hypothesis has ceased to be experimental, the difference between one who accepts and one who rejects it is now not a matter of the one expecting something the other does not expect. What is the difference between them? The one says "A gardener comes unseen and unheard. He is manifested only in his works with which we are all familiar," the other says "There is no gardener" and with this difference in what they say about the gardener goes a difference in how they feel towards the garden, in spite of the fact that neither expects anything of it which the other does not expect.

But is this the whole difference between them—that the one calls the garden by one name and feels one way towards it, while the other calls it by another name and feels in another way towards it? And if this is what the difference has become then is it any longer appropriate to ask "Which is right?" or "Which is reasonable?"

And yet surely such questions *are* appropriate when one person says to another "You still think the world's a garden and not a wilderness, and that the gardener has not forsaken it" or "You still think there are nymphs of the streams, a presence in the hills, a spirit of the world." Perhaps when a man

sings "God's in His heaven" we need not take this as more than an expression of how he feels. But when Bishop Gore or Dr. Joad writes about belief in God and young men read them in order to settle their religious doubts the impression is not simply that of persons choosing exclamations with which to face nature and the "changes and chances of this mortal life." The disputants speak as if they are concerned with a matter of scientific fact, or of trans-sensual, trans-scientific and metaphysical fact, but still of fact and still a matter about which reasons for and against may be offered, although no scientific reasons in the sense of field surveys for fossils or experiments on delinquents are to the point.

6.2. *Now can an interjection have a logic?* Can the manifestation of an attitude in the utterance of a word, in the application of a name, have a logic? When all the facts are known how can there still be a question of fact? How can there still be a question? Surely as Hume says ". . . after every circumstance, every relation is known, the understanding has no further room to operate"?[2]

6.3. When the madness of these questions leaves us for a moment *we can all easily recollect disputes which though they cannot be settled by experiment are yet disputes in which one party may be right and the other wrong* and in which both parties may offer reasons and the one better reasons than the other. *This may happen in pure and applied mathematics and logic.* Two accountants or two engineers provided with the same

---

[2] Hume, *An Enquiry concerning the Principles of Morals.* Appendix I.

data may reach different results and this difference is resolved not by collecting further data but by going over the calculations again. Such differences indeed share with differences as to what will win a race, the honor of being among the most "settlable" disputes in the language.

6.4. *But it won't do to describe the theistic issue as one settlable by such calculation,* or as one about what can be deduced in this *vertical* fashion from the facts we know. No doubt dispute about God has sometimes, perhaps especially in medieval times, been carried on in this fashion. But nowadays it is not and we must look for some other analogy, some other case in which a dispute is settled but not by experiment.

6.5. *In courts of law* it sometimes happens that opposing counsel are agreed as to the facts and are not trying to settle a question of further fact, are not trying to settle whether the man who admittedly had quarrelled with the deceased did or did not murder him, but are concerned with whether Mr. A who admittedly handed his long-trusted clerk signed blank cheques did or did not exercise reasonable care, whether a ledger is or is not a document, whether a certain body was or was not a public authority.

In such cases we notice that the process of argument is not a *chain* of demonstrative reasoning. It is a presenting and representing of those features of the case which *severally co-operate* in favor of the conclusion, in favor of saying what the reasoner wishes said, in favor of calling the situation by the name by which he wishes to call it. The reasons are like the legs of a chair, not the links of a chain. Consequently al-

though the discussion is *a priori* and the steps are not a matter of experience, the procedure resembles scientific argument in that the reasoning is not *vertically* extensive but *horizontally* extensive—it is a matter of the cumulative effect of several independent premises, not of the repeated transformation of one or two. And because the premises are severally inconclusive the process of deciding the issue becomes a matter of weighing the cumulative effect of one group of severally inconclusive items against the cumulative effect of another group of severally inconclusive items, and thus lends itself to description in terms of conflicting "probabilities." This encourages the feeling that the issue is one of fact—that it is a matter of guessing from the premises at a further fact, at what is to come. But this is a muddle. *The dispute does not cease to be* a priori *because it is a matter of the cumulative effect of severally inconclusive premises.* The logic of the dispute is not that of a chain of deductive reasoning as in a mathematic calculation. But nor is it a matter of collecting from several inconclusive items of information an expectation as to something further, as when a doctor from a patient's symptoms guesses at what is wrong, or a detective from many clues guesses the criminal. It has its own sort of logic and its own sort of end—the solution of the question at issue is a decision, a ruling by the judge. But it is not an arbitrary decision though the rational connections are neither quite like those in vertical deductions nor like those in inductions in which from many signs we guess at what is to come; and though the decision manifests itself in the application of a name it is no more merely the application of a name than is the pinning on of a medal merely the pinning on of a bit of metal. Whether a lion with stripes is a tiger or a lion is, if you like, merely a matter of the application of a name. Whether Mr. So-and-So of whose conduct we have so complete a record did or did not exercise reasonable care is not merely a matter of the application of a name or, if we choose to say it is, then we must remember that with this name a game is lost and won and a game with very heavy stakes. With the judges' choice of a name for the facts goes an attitude, and the declaration, the ruling, is an exclamation evincing that attitude. But *it is an exclamation which not only has a purpose but also has a logic,* a logic surprisingly like that of "futile," "deplorable," "graceful," "grand," "divine.". . .

6.7. *And if we say as we did at the beginning that when a difference as to the existence of a God is not one as to future happenings then it is not experimental and therefore not as to the facts, we must not forthwith assume that there is no right and wrong about it,* no rationality or irrationality, no appropriateness or inappropriateness, no procedure which tends to settle it, *nor even that this procedure is in no sense a discovery of new facts.* After all even in science this is not so. Our two gardeners even when they had reached the stage when neither expected any experimental result which the other did not, might yet have continued the dispute, each presenting and representing the features of the garden favoring his hypothesis, that is, fitting his model for describing the accepted fact; each emphasizing the pattern he wishes to emphasize. True, in science, there is seldom or never a pure instance of this sort of dispute, for nearly always with difference of hypothesis goes some difference of expectation as to the facts. But scientists argue about rival hypotheses with a vigor which is not exactly proportioned to difference in expectations of experimental results.

The difference as to whether a God exists involves our feelings more than most scientific disputes and in this respect is more like a difference as to whether there is beauty in a thing.

7. *The connecting technique.* Let us consider again the technique used in revealing or proving beauty, in removing a blindness, in inducing an attitude which is lacking, in reducing a reaction that is inappropriate. Besides running over in a special way the features of the picture, tracing the rhythms, making sure that this and that are not only seen but noticed, and their relation to each other—besides all this—there are other things we can do to justify our attitude and alter that of the man who cannot see. For features of the picture may be brought out by setting beside it other pictures; just as the merits of an argument may be brought out, proved, by setting beside it other arguments, in which striking but irrelevant features of the original are changed and relevant features emphasized; just as the merits and demerits of a line of action may be brought out by setting beside it other actions. . . .

Imagine that a man picks us some flowers that lie half withered on a table and gently puts them in water. Another man says to him "You believe flowers feel." He says this although he knows that the man who helps the flowers doesn't expect anything of them which he himself doesn't expect; for he himself expects the flowers to be "refreshed" and to be easily hurt, injured, I mean, by rough handling, while the man who puts them in water does not expect them to whisper "Thank you." The Skeptic says "You believe flowers feel" because something about the way the other man lifts the flowers and puts them in water suggests an attitude to the flowers which he feels inappropriate although perhaps he would not feel it inappropriate to butterflies. He feels that this attitude to flowers is somewhat crazy *just as it is sometimes felt that a lover's attitude is somewhat crazy even when this is not a matter of his having false hopes about how the person he is in love with will act.* It is often said in such cases that reasoning is useless. But the very person who says this feels that the lover's attitude is crazy, is inappropriate like some dreads and hatreds, such as some horrors of enclosed places. And often one who says "It is useless to reason" proceeds at once to reason with the lover, nor is this reasoning always quite without effect. We may draw the lover's attention to certain things done by her he is in love with and trace for him a path to these from things done by others at other times which have disgusted and infuriated him. And by this means we may weaken his admiration and confidence, make him feel it unjustified and arouse his suspicion and contempt and make him feel our suspicion and contempt reasonable. It is possible, of course, that he has already noticed the analogies, the connections, we point out and that he has accepted them—that is, he has not denied them nor passed them off. He has recognized them and they have altered his attitude, altered

his love, but he still loves. We then feel that perhaps it is we who are blind and cannot see what he can see.

8. *Connecting and disconnecting.* But before we confess ourselves thus inadequate there are other fires his admiration must pass through. For when a man has an attitude which it seems to us he should not have or lacks one which it seems to us he should have then, not only do we suspect that he is not influenced by connections which we feel should influence him and draw his attention to these, but also we suspect he is influenced by connections which should not influence him and draw his attention to these. It may, for a moment, seem strange that we should draw his attention to connections which we feel should not influence him, and which, since they do influence him, he has in a sense already noticed. But we do—such is our confidence in "the light of reason."

Sometimes the power of these connections comes mainly from a man's mismanagement of the language he is using. This is what happens in the Monte Carlo fallacy, where by mismanaging the laws of chance a man passes from noticing that a certain color or number has not turned up for a long while to an improper confidence that now it soon will turn up. In such cases our showing up of the false connections is a process we call "explaining a fallacy in reasoning." To remove fallacies in reasoning we urge a man to call a spade a spade, ask him what he means by "the State" and having pointed out ambiguities and vaguenesses ask him to reconsider the steps in his argument.

9. *Unspoken connections. Usually, however, wrongheadedness or wrongheartedness in a situation, blindness to*

what is there or seeing what is not, does not arise merely from mismanagement of language but is more due to connections which are not mishandled in language, for the reason that they are not put into language at all. And often these misconnections too, weaken in the light of reason, if only we can guess where they lie and turn it on them. In so far as these connections are not presented in language the process of removing their power is not a process of correcting the mismanagement of language. But it is still akin to such a process; for though it is not a process of setting out fairly what has been set out unfairly, it is a process of setting out fairly what has not been set out at all. And we must remember that the line between connections ill-presented or half-presented in language and connections operative but not presented in language, or only hinted at, is not a sharp one.

Whether or not we call the process of showing up these connections "reasoning to remove bad unconscious reasoning" or not, it is certain that in order to settle in ourselves what weight we shall attach to someone's confidence or attitude we not only ask him for his reasons but also look for unconscious reasons both good and bad; that is, for reasons which he can't put into words, isn't explicitly aware of, is hardly aware of, isn't aware of at all—perhaps it's long experience which he *doesn't* recall which lets him know a squall is coming, perhaps it's old experience which he *can't* recall which makes the cake in the tea mean so much and makes Odette so fascinating.[3]

---

[3] Proust, *Swann's Way,* vol. I, p. 58, vol. II. Phoenix Edition.

I am well aware of the distinction between the question "What reasons are there for the belief that S is P?" and the question "What are the sources of beliefs that S is P?" There are cases where investigation of the rationality of a claim which certain persons make is done with very little inquiry into why they say what they do, into the causes of their beliefs. This is so when we have very definite ideas about what is really logically relevant to their claim and what is not. Offered a mathematical theorem we ask for the proof; offered the generalization that parental discord causes crime we ask for the correlation co-efficients. But even in this last case, if we fancy that only the figures are reasons we underestimate the complexity of the logic of our conclusion; and yet it is difficult to describe the other features of the evidence which have weight and there is apt to be disagreement about the weight they should have. In criticizing other conclusions and especially conclusions which are largely the expression of an attitude, we have not only to ascertain what reasons there are for them but also to decide what things are reasons and how much. This latter process of sifting reasons from causes is part of the critical process for every belief, but in some spheres it has been done pretty fully already. In these spheres we don't need to examine the actual processes to belief and distil from them a logic. But in other spheres this remains to be done. Even in science or on the stock exchange or in ordinary life we sometimes hesitate to condemn a belief or a hunch merely because those who believe it cannot offer the sort of reasons we had hoped for. . . .

10. *Now what happens, what should*

happen, when we inquire in this way into the reasonableness, the propriety of belief in gods? The answer is: A double and opposite-phased change. Wordsworth writes:

. . . And I have felt
A presence that disturbs me with the joy
Of elevated thoughts; a sense sublime
Of something far more deeply interfused,
Whose dwelling is the light of setting
   suns,
And the round ocean and the living air,
And the blue sky, and in the mind of
   man:
A motion and a spirit, that impels
All thinking things, all objects of all
   thought,
And rolls through all things . . .⁴

We most of us know this feeling. But is it well placed like the feeling that here is first-rate work, which we sometimes rightly have even before we have fully grasped the picture we are looking at or the book we are reading? Or is it misplaced like the feeling in a house that has long been empty that someone secretly lives there still? Wordsworth's feeling *is* the feeling that the world is haunted, that something watches in the hills and manages the stars. The child feels that the stone tripped him when he stumbled, that the bough struck him when it flew back in his face. He has to learn that the wind isn't buffeting him, that there is not a devil in it, that he was wrong, that his attitude was inappropriate. And as he learns that the wind wasn't hindering him so he also learns it wasn't helping him. But we know how, though he learns, his attitude lingers. It is plain

---

⁴ *Tintern Abbey.*

that Wordsworth's feeling is of this family.

Belief in gods, it is true, is often very different from belief that stones are spiteful, the sun kindly. For the gods appear in human form and from the waves and control these things and by so doing reward and punish us. But varied as are the stories of the good they have a family likeness and we have only to recall them to feel sure of the other main sources which co-operate with animism to produce them.

What are the stories of the gods? What are our feelings when we believe in God? They are feelings of awe before power, dread of the thunderbolts of Zeus, confidence in the everlasting arms, unease beneath the all-seeing eye. They are feelings of guilt and inescapable vengeance, of smothered hate and of a security we can hardly do without. We have only to remind ourselves of these feelings and the stories of the gods and goddesses and heroes in which these feelings find expression, to be reminded of how we felt as children to our parents and the big people of our childhood. . . .

But here a new aspect of the matter may strike us.⁵ For the very facts which make us feel that now we can recognize systems of super-human, sub-human, elusive, beings for what they are—the persistent projections of infantile phantasies—include facts which make these systems less fantastic. What are these facts? They are patterns in human reactions which are well described by saying that we are as if there were hidden

---

⁵ This different aspect of the matter and the connection between God, the heavenly Father, and "the good father" of the psychoanalysts, was put into my head by some remarks of Dr. Susan Isaacs.

within us powers, persons, not ourselves and stronger than ourselves. That this is so may perhaps be said to have been common knowledge yielded by ordinary observation of people,[6] but we did not know the degree in which this is so until recent study of extraordinary cases in extraordinary conditions had revealed it. I refer, of course, to the study of multiple personalities and the wider studies of psycho-analysts. Even when the results of this work are reported to us that is not the same as tracing the patterns in the details of the cases on which the results are based; and even that is not the same as taking part in the studies oneself. One thing not sufficiently realized is that some of the

things shut within us are not bad but good. . . .

Many have tried to find ways of salvation. The reports they bring back are always incomplete and apt to mislead even when they are not in words but in music or paint. But they are by no means useless; and not the worst of them are those which speak of oneness with God. But in so far as we become one with Him He becomes one with us. St. John says he is in us as we love one another.

This love, I suppose, is not benevolence but something that comes of the oneness with one another of which Christ spoke.[7] Sometimes it momentarily gains strength.[8] Hate and the Devil do too. And what is oneness without otherness?

---

[6] Consider Tolstoy and Dostoievsky—I do not mean, of course, that their observation was ordinary.

[7] *St. John,* xvi: 21.
[8] "The Harvesters" in *The Golden Age,* Kenneth Graham.

CRITIQUE

The following selection is part of a symposium on the problem of meaning. The first participant was Gilbert Ryle, who argued for a theory of meaning along the lines we have been studying in linguistic philosophy; the second was J. N. Findlay, whose contribution is given here. While agreeing with Ryle on some points, Findlay crosses swords with him on the fundamental doctrine that meaning is use. The notion of *use,* he finds, places extraordinary restrictions on one's account of language and the circumstances in which a word is correctly used; and the effort to give an account of language and meaning in terms of merely public operations and behavior is deeply obfuscating. Even the notion of linguistic rule in this philosophy, Findlay believes, is deeply obscure, and the doubts cast on first-person, conscious experience by linguistic philosophers are for him a kind of ultimate, if subtle, refutation of the position. Findlay concludes by suggesting that Wittgenstein was a profound philosopher, but that in his theory of meaning he was profoundly wrong.

11 Use, Usage, and Meaning

J. N. Findlay (1903-   )

I am in great agreement with what I regard as the substantial points in Professor Ryle's paper. His definition of language I think rather arbitrarily narrow: for him it is a 'stock, fund or deposit of words, constructions, *cliché* phrases and so on'. I should have thought it would be wrong not to include in a language the various syntactical and other *rules* which restrict our employment of the capital of expressions mentioned by Professor Ryle, though perhaps I am wrong in thinking he meant to exclude them. That adjectives must agree with the gender of their substantives in certain cases would certainly be held to be part of the French language, as it is not part of the English. There is also, I think, a further arbitrariness in excluding sentences from *language*, and in making them the units of *speech* which are produced when we say things. I think we can and should distinguish between the sentence *Je ne sais quoi* as a mere possibility permitted by the French language; and the same sentence as used or produced by someone to say something. I can in fact see no good reason why one should not have a narrower and a wider conception of a language. On the narrower conception, a language includes a vocabulary and rules, whereas on the wider conception it includes also *all* the possible sentences that could be framed out of the vocabulary in accordance with the rules. In this sense French or English would include all the permissible sentences that could be framed in it, whether anyone ever uttered or wrote or thought them or not. If this conception of a language makes it absurdly wide, the conception of it as a vocabulary plus rules makes it unduly narrow. Certainly, however, I think we want to distinguish between a sentence as a grammatically permissible word-combination, and the utterance or writing down or silent thinking of that sentence by someone on some occasion to make an allegation, raise a query, express a doubt, etc., etc., and in the latter case I find a language of *use* or *employment* more natural than Professor Ryle's language of *production*. I think therefore that Professor Ryle is legislating rather vexatiously in forbidding us to speak of sentences as parts of language, or to say that such sentences can be *used* by speakers. I do not, however, think that this vexatious piece of legislation is in the forefront of Professor Ryle's intentions.

What Professor Ryle is mainly concerned to do seems to me to be to distinguish between grammatical faults in the use of words in constructing sentences, and faults in what may be called 'logical syntax' or 'logical grammar', which involve the use of words to construct perfectly grammatical sentences,

The selection is from J. N. Findlay, "Use, Usage and Meaning," *Proceedings of The Aristotelian Society*, Supplementary Volume 35 (1961), pp. 231–242. Copyright © 1961 The *Aristotelian Society*. Reprinted by permission of the Editor of The Aristotelian Society.

but which none the less violate a deeper set of rules, the rules of sense, the rules of logic, the rules regulating the mutual relations of categories, etc., etc. With all this I am deeply in agreement, because it involves precisely the recognition that different sorts of words, as it were, make different sorts of abstract *cuts* in their subject-matter, or help to execute different sorts of abstract *cuts*—some, as Aristotle might say, tell us *what* things are, others *how* they are, others *how many* they are, others *conjoin*, others *emphasize*, others *bracket*, etc., etc.—and that in making such quite different types of cross-section they become subject to the relations necessarily obtaining among such cross-sections, so that some verbal combinations which are smooth and pretty grammatically none the less make hideous nonsense. Professor Ryle, it seems to me, is here suggesting that it is the relations of different sorts of *meanings* to one another which determine the depth-grammar of words, and that these meanings and their relations are matters that must be *independently* considered if we are to study logical as well as grammatical syntax. If this suggestion is not implicit in his words, perhaps he will explain what sort of abuse of words it is that is logical or depth-grammatical as opposed to merely surface-grammatical abuse. Incidentally, I feel in the context invoked by Ryle that it is doubly tempting to talk of the *use* and *abuse* of grammatical sentences. The sentence is there, a fully-fashioned grammatical entity, and it is its use to express a categorially possible combination of meanings which is at times possible and legitimate, whereas at other times there is really only an abuse.

Having expressed my agreement and disagreement with Ryle, I may perhaps allow myself to dwell a little on the famous dictum which he quotes and which has dominated philosophical discussion for the past twenty years: 'Don't ask for the meaning: ask for the use.' I wish to make against it the not often raised objection that the use for which it bids us ask, is of all things the most obscure, the most veiled in philosophical mists, the most remote from detailed determination or application, in the wide range of philosophical concepts. There is, I think, a use of 'use' which is humdrum and ordinary, but in which a study of the use of expressions is of only limited philosophical importance and interest. There is also a use of 'use' characteristic of the later writings of Wittgenstein which is utterly remote from the humdrum and ordinary, and which has won its way into the acceptance of philosophers largely because it has *seemed* to have the clearness and the straightforwardness of the ordinary use. We are all proof against the glozing deceits of words like 'substance', 'being', 'nothingness', 'consciousness', etc., etc.: we at once see that some occasions of their employment are really only abuses —but we are not yet proof against the fascinations exerted by the singular abuses of so ordinary a term as 'use'. When these abuses are exposed, the whole attitude represented by the slogan quoted by Ryle reveals itself as completely without significant basis, which unfortunately puts an end to all but a limited emphasis on 'use' and 'usage' by philosophers. Since the suggestion that use and usage—in some acceptable sense—*are* philosophically very important, certainly underlies Ryle's paper, I need not apologize for irrelevance in proceeding to demolish this suggestion.

The reason why it is absurd to tell us *not* to attend to the meaning of expressions but to concentrate on their use, is perfectly simple: it is that the notion of use, as it ordinarily exists and is used, presupposes the notion of meaning (in its central and paradigmatic sense), and that it cannot therefore be used to elucidate the latter, and much less to replace or to do duty for it. The notion of use is a *wider* notion than the paradigmatic notion of meaning: it covers many *other* things beside the meaning of an expression, but the meaning-function in its paradigmatic sense is certainly *one* of the things it covers, and it is not possible to give a clear account of use without presupposing this function. What I am saying is simply that we cannot fully say, in a great many cases, how an expression is used, without saying what sort of things it is intended to refer to, or to bring to mind, and just how, or in what angle or light, it purports to refer to them, or to bring them to mind. And in cases where it would be wrong and absurd to say that an expression *independently* brought something to mind, or presented it in a certain light, it would none the less be uncontestably right to say that it *helped* to do such things in some definite manner, so that what was brought to mind would be *different*, or *differently presented*, if the expression were not part of our total utterance. Thus if I make use of the word 'dragon' in a large number of contexts, I use it to refer to a human being or beings, generally mature and female, and I use it also to represent such a human being or beings as being restrictive, uncompromising and somewhat terrifying. And if I *apply* the term in a certain con-

text I see that to which I apply it in the light connoted by my words. And if I use the words 'such a' before uttering the word 'dragon', these words certainly help to suggest that what I am describing is *very* restrictive, *very* uncompromising and *very* terrifying, i.e., they contribute to the force of my description without playing an independent part of it. In saying what the use of my expressions is, I therefore have to say what, in the ordinary diction of logicians, they denote and connote, what their precise reference is or what their general scope, or how they contribute to connotation or denotation, and it is not thought possible to say how many expressions are *used*, without bringing in such connotative and denotative particulars.

The notion of use of course goes far *beyond* that of connotation and denotation, and it is one of the extremely important discoveries of modern semantics that there are *some* expressions whose use, in certain contexts, is *not* to connote or denote anything, nor even to help to do either, but to do such things as give voice to feelings and wishes, evoke certain attitudes in others, or *perform* certain formal social acts, e.g., promises, which have certain definite social consequences, etc., etc. That *not* all expressions, on all occasions of their *use*, perform the functions of reference or characterization, or assist in such performance, is certainly a discovery not to be underestimated, which has cleared the deck of much tangled tackle and many stumbling-blocks. But this kind of *non*-referential, *non*-connotative use is parasitic upon a connotative, referential one, and could hardly exist without it. It is one of Wittgenstein's more irresponsible fancies that there could be a language composed *only* of commands, or *only* of curses, or *only* of greetings. The concept of use also certainly covers all the hidden *implications* and *suggestions* which attach to the writing or utterance of a word or a sentence, but which are not strictly part of what it means or says: thus when I say 'He did not commit this murder' I may use this sentence to imply that he committed certain other murders, that I absolutely believe him to be no murderer, that we live under laws forbidding the taking of life, etc., etc. But all such implications and suggestions are likewise dependent upon the function of directly connoting or denoting something, and are in fact an extension of the same. Use also obviously covers the mere requirements of accidence and syntax, though these, as Ryle has shown, are mere instrumentalities in the task of significant diction.

What is implicit, however, in the slogan 'Don't ask for the meaning: ask for the use' is not that use covers much *more* than the connotative and denotative functions of language, but that it somehow resumes and completely explains the latter, that we can completely see around and see through talk about the reference and connotation of expressions by taking note of the way people operate with such expressions, how they combine them with other expressions to form sentences, and the varying *circumstances* in which producing such sentences is reckoned appropriate or fully justifiable. This study of verbal manoeuvres, and of appropriate and justifying circumstances, must not, however, be confined to the single instant of utterance: it must point *backwards* to the all-important situations in which use was *learnt* or *taught*, and it must point *forwards* to the innumerable situations in

which the utterance in question will again be found *appropriate*, or will be found to be more and more abundantly *justified*. The study of use therefore includes a genealogy and a prognosis of the most indefinite and complex kind, much more extensive than any that occurs in a merely grammatical or philological study. In another respect, however, the slogan gives 'use' an extraordinarily restricted interpretation. The operations involved in use are not to be operations conducted privately in anyone's head, or at least such operations can only be brought into consideration in so far as they can be narrowly tied up with other non-private operations, and the *circumstances* in which such operations are conducted must all be circumstances belonging to what may be called the common public environment, circumstances in which bricks are being assembled into buildings, apples taken from drawers and handed over to customers, railway-signals altered, or hunting expeditions conducted. The sort of change which is a mere change in perspective or in conscious 'light' is *not* among the circumstances mentionable in describing use.

And there is yet another most extraordinary restriction placed upon our account of the *circumstances* in which a word is correctly used: we must not employ the word or its equivalent to explain those circumstances. We must not, e.g., say, that when a man is confronted by three apples in a drawer, or by an apple and another apple and yet another apple, he is then justified in employing the word 'three' in connexion with such apples. The word 'three' may be employed in describing the circumstances justifying countless *other* sorts of utterance, but not the circumstances justifying its *own* employment. In the same way we must never say that it is when a man is confronted by a red object, or has learnt to discriminate its colour, that he is justified in calling it 'red'. Such accounts are held to be wholly trivial and unilluminating, and are moreover held to suggest various deep philosophical fallacies: the belief that meanings exist 'out there' in the things we deal with *before* we find the appropriate words to 'pick them out', or that they exist 'in the mind' or the understanding before we find words to express them. Whatever we suggest by our accounts of use, we must never suggest that there are *pre-existent meanings*. Words enjoy meaning and reference in and by our use of them, and our use cannot be explained in terms of any meaning that antedates the use of words. And since understanding and thinking are defined in terms of the operation with signs, we must never speak as if we could understand or think anything before we dispose of appropriate verbal expressions and have been taught to employ them. The programme of this extreme 'utilitarianism'—as one may perhaps call the use-doctrine—is impressive: it resembles nothing so much as the brave empiricist programme of Locke and Hume, in which no idea was to be admitted into the charmed circle of thought and knowledge without producing a genealogy purer than any required by the Nuremberg laws, exhibiting a proper origin in sensation and reflection, and a derivation from these by approved processes. But, like that brave programme, it faces the crucial objection that it cannot be carried out completely, and that no comprehensive account of use and usage can be given which does not contain some members

of impure origin. That the brave programme was hopeless Wittgenstein himself perhaps obscurely realized, when he wrongly said of the *Brown Book*, the most profound and wonderful of his writings, that it was *nichts wert*. But if success, rather than stimulus and provocation, is the criterion of philosophical value, his judgement was entirely justified.

I need not range far nor cite many instances to make plain the totally unilluminating, indeed deeply obfuscating character of attempts to give a complete account of the use of expressions in terms of merely public operations and circumstances. The very conception of a *rule*, central to the 'utilitarianism' in question, abounds in difficulty. For we are expressly told that to follow a rule is not necessarily to be guided by a spoken or written formula, since each such formula admits of interpretation in terms of another formula, and this in terms of another, and so on indefinitely. Nor is the following of a rule to be identified with any sort of inner personal understanding of that rule which can guide one's subsequent performance, since to hold this would be to accept pre-existent meanings resident in the queer medium of the mind. Nor can the following of a rule be identified with one's actual performance up to a point, since this is always compatible with an infinity of rules. In the end it would seem that following a rule must be an ineffable sort of affair: it must be something that can be accomplished in one's *doing* (in this case, speaking), but not effectively spoken *about*. It is something that one can know how *to do* without being able to know how what one does is done. The conception of a linguistic rule has, in fact, all the irretrievable obscurity of the structural resemblance constitutive of meaning in the *Tractatus*, which cannot be expressed but only *shown*. If it is at least *possible* that a rule should at times be understood or grasped in thought, we can understand what it is like to follow it without thought, but if grasping is a function of following, the whole activity of following dissolves in mystery. I do not myself know how it differs from the most arbitrary irregularity except that it mysteriously *feels* right at every stage, and that others, standing at my side, mysteriously agree in such feelings. And if it is hard to throw light on the following of rules in terms of outward circumstances and performances, how much harder it is to say in what lies conformity to an *open* rule, one which is to be applied over and over *indefinitely*. While the *thought* expressed by the phrase 'and so on indefinitely' is most absolutely simple and easy to entertain, it is a thought *logically* impossible to evince adequately in one's performance. Much has been written, from the standpoint of the use-doctrine, about the difference between closed and open games, but the discussion ends up with very much what it started from, that it is a difference in the *spirit* with which the respective games are played. A man, e.g., using an open arithmetic simply has a system or general rule for constructing numerals *indefinitely*. That a spirit is operative in this case I should not care to deny, but that it consorts well with the use-doctrine, or establishes its superiority, I cannot conceive.

Similar difficulties confront us if we consider the use-account of the use of descriptive adjectives like those of colour. We are forbidden to talk of prior colour-differences in objects, or prior colour-discriminations in persons, as this would involve the grave error of positing pre-existent meanings. We are introduced to imaginary tribal activities which involve the picturesque carrying about of charts of colour samples and their comparison with, or imposition on objects, but these it would seem explain little or nothing, since the charts are dispensable and admit moreover of a wrong use. From the use of charts the tribe progresses to the use of colour samples carried somehow in the mind's eye, and ultimately to the mere unhesitant pronouncement, after sufficient training, of certain colour-words in the presence of certain objects. With this pronouncement others as unhesitatingly agree. From the Scylla of holding that 'blue' stands for a discriminable blueness in objects, or expresses an awareness of blueness in one's mind, one proceeds to the Charybdis of saying that those things are blue which we and others agree, and have been trained, to call so. It is plain, of course, that one must have ultimates somewhere, and it is plain also that there are different possibilities of colour-discrimination corresponding to different possibilities of usage: what is *not* plain is why one should prefer such a strange, secondary ultimate as a *use* to the more obvious, understandable ultimates of discriminating thoughts in the mind, or discriminable features in things.

The most superb example of the problem-increasing character of the use-semantics is, however, to be found in its treatment of cases where men use expressions without obvious reference to any palpable feature of the public environment, when they give voice, e.g., to recollections or anticipations, or describe their personal feelings or impressions, or report their fantasies or their dreams. Here the course is followed of attempting to account for such uses by supposing men to be such as *spontaneously* to want to use expressions taught in certain contexts in contexts where their normal justification is absent, and that these non-normal needs, so strangely universal among us, constitute the basis for a new *secondary* set of linguistic usages, where the sole fact that we agree in feeling certain linguistic urges is the sole criterion of their correctness. Thus children perhaps spontaneously run over the names of objects recently presented to them, or can be encouraged to do so without difficulty: meaning can then be given to the *past tense*, and they can learn to say that they *had* a ball, a stick, a rattle, etc. To 'refer to the past' is merely to learn to employ the past tense in such circumstances, an account as amusingly free in presupposing pastness and temporal passage in the *circumstances* of the learning, as it is firm in denying any non-verbal *understanding* of them. Men then spontaneously begin to use the past tense where there is no such recent provocation: we then give a use to talk about 'remembering', particularly if others agree in such spontaneous inclinations. The reference to the past in memory is therefore not the ultimate, mysterious thing that Husserl, Broad and others have supposed it to be: it merely reflects the strange tendency of men to talk preteritively beyond the limits of recency, and the further linkage of this fact with the readings of instruments, the reports of others, and many other observed matters. It may now happen that men waking from sleep spontaneously talk in the past tense *as if* recalling happenings which no one remembers, and which do not fit in with the observable contemporary state, or with the memory-inclinations of others. The concept of 'dreaming' now makes its *debut* to take care of these extraordinary performances. Malcolm, the admirable exponent of a preposterous analysis, admits[1] that on it dream-language is very odd: it is *as if* one is faithfully recalling something, but one cannot explain this fact by saying that one *did* experience what one is disposed to report, since this would involve an unintelligible hypothesis, one excluded by the guiding assumptions of the doctrine of use. What these queernesses surely show is the profound mistakenness somewhere of these guiding assumptions. To make use of a gnostic principle used by Moore in other contexts: we *know* certain facts about meaning much more absolutely than we can be sure of the premises, or the inferential rules, of semantic arguments designed either to establish them, or to explain them away. Obviously we cannot make straight sense of many linguistic usages without postulating just those preexistent understandings (not confined to matters in the public forefront) and the possibility of communicating such understandings to others, which it is the whole aim of the use-doctrine to exclude.

The use-doctrine may further be objected to for its profoundly circular, question-begging character. This is a point ably made by Mr. Gellner in a book[2] where some of the most profound criticisms of the use-doctrine and its consequences lie hidden under a somewhat popular exterior. To have

[1 The reference is to N. Malcolm, *Dreaming* (London, 1959). *Ed.*]

[2 E. Gellner, *Words and Things* (London, 1959). *Ed.*]

seen an unacceptable, unargued naturalism behind Wittgenstein's brilliant façade of exposition, is no mean insight. By describing the functioning of linguistic expression exclusively in public and social terms, we at once *go too far* in assuming such approaches to be wholly justified and clear, and we also *do not go far enough* in refusing to recognize aspects of language not fitting an approach of this sort, or in 'proving' them to be misguided or senseless. These two lines of objection really coincide, since it is by turning away from aspects of language it cannot readily accommodate that the use-doctrine is unable to see its own difficulties and obscurities. The use-theorists have dwelt much on the profound subtlety of ordinary language, but they have been far from recognizing *how* subtle it actually is. For it not only uses expressions to point to, or to throw light on, ordinary objects, but it also uses them *reflexly*, in the manner studied in Husserl's *Logische Untersuchungen*, to point to or throw light on its own *meanings*, thereby setting up an order of objects as clear-edged and partial as its normal objects are fuzzy and full, and as delicate in their abstraction as they are indispensable for the higher flights of thought. That a phrase like 'the third door on the right' can be used both straightforwardly to refer to a door, and reflexly to refer to its own meaning, is a truth plain to babes, but occasioning headaches to the semantically over-wise and prudent. Ordinary speech further, provides us with an instrument for communicating with others about matters public and common, which is also an instrument for purely personal use, in which different observations, different views, different judgments provide much

the same complementary parallax, and the same corrective or confirmatory testing as in the interpersonal case. But not only is it thus double in its use, it also manages to incorporate the personal in the public use, and the public in the personal, in a regress pursuable as far as even we choose. Thus we all understand other people's first-person talk by analogy with our own, and its imperfect public intelligibility is also perfectly and publicly intelligible, since everyone makes just such first-person statements in his own case. The manner in which we smoothly swing over from another man's perfectly understood use of the first-person pronoun 'I', and replace it with 'he' in reporting the content of his statement, and expect the other man to do the same in regard to us, as well as the children's games in which these proprieties are amusingly violated: all these show an understanding of the antithesis of contrasted privacies, and of their overcoming in a wider publicity, of which the use-semantics betrays no inkling. In the same manner, ordinary speech has in it the germs of what may be called the Cartesian or the Lockean inversion, the reversal of the ordinary approach from outward things to the mind, into an approach to outer things from the facts of our subjective life. Though the language in which we talk of and to ourselves—the best subject-matter and audience—may have had its *source* in contexts of public ostensibility, it can, by a profitable ingratitude, use the personal language thus painfully acquired to cast doubt upon, or to throw light on, its own origin. We may illuminate our understanding and knowledge of public matters in terms of just those personal experiences and pre-existent understandings which talk about public matters first renders possible. And this personal Cartesian or Lockean story can then achieve the widest publicity, since to have back rooms continuous with those opening on the public square is the most universal, most inescapable of predicaments. It is no doubt by a creative transformation that the rumour of the square penetrates backwards, and is re-echoed in the small back rooms, and it is likewise by a creative transformation that these transformed echoes rejoin the rumour of the square. All this, however, unquestionably happens, and it is the task of a philosophical semantics to make sense of it, and not to declare it unintelligible.

Nothing that has been said in the foregoing is meant to reflect on the painstaking, detailed study of linguistic usage, or the actual manner of its teaching, if used to show how we actually come to mean what we undoubtedly do mean, or to throw light on the complexity and subtlety of our meanings, or to show how we come to be misled into supposing we mean what really conflicts with the 'depth-grammar' of our meanings. Our criticisms are only of a radical use-theory carried to extremes, which constructs fables as to how we might have been taught the meanings of words in order to buttress *a priori* doctrines as to what we *must* or *cannot* mean. If anyone thinks such doctrines archaic and superseded, and so not requiring rebuttal, he is wide of the truth. Wittgenstein's accounts of language-games are so arresting, so novel, so subtle in their detailed development, so daring in their frank embrace of the unplausible, so imbued with intellectual seriousness and earnestness, and so great, finally, in their aesthetic appeal, that it is hard to

see through them or around them. They fascinate the philosopher in the same way that Wittgenstein claimed that philosophers were fascinated by the forms of ordinary language, and against such fascination determined steps are necessary. The steps I have taken in this paper may not have been sufficiently subtle, and may have involved certain misunderstandings of detail: I shall hope, at least, to have incited others to do better.

All this should not, of course, be taken as reflecting on the philosophical greatness of Wittgenstein. Wittgenstein is the author of three wholly differing accounts of meaning, all of which merit entire rejection: meaning is *not* reduplication of structure, it is *not* verification or verifiability, it is plainly *not* what he meant by 'use'. It is not these things, though it is of course intimately connected with them all, but it will be best illuminated by construing further the old humdrum notions of connotation and denotation, and by seeking painfully to throw light on the 'thought behind our words', for which, on account of the peculiar categories it involves, it would seem that no adequate surrogate has been, or can be, offered. It is, I surmise, in the 'intentional nature of thought' that the true solution of the problems of meaning is to be found. But by formulating these three inadequate accounts, Wittgenstein has given the semantic problem the central place it deserves in philosophy, and has contributed vastly to its solution. Through his inability to account satisfactorily for certain linguistic performances, he has indicated the precise nodes where language makes its various creative leaps and has thereby given philosophical semantics its opportunity and its task. Moreover, each of Wittgenstein's frequent rhetorical questions is such that, if answered in the sense *not* intended by the question, it will lead to an illuminating result: they are practically all arrows which, if read in the reverse direction, point unerringly to some truth. A philosophy of meaning so valuably wrong does not differ profoundly from one that is systematically right.

SUMMARY

We have seen, even in Findlay's criticisms, that in order to gain understanding of the work of linguistic philosophy, we must keep its conception of philosophy clearly in mind. The following summary by Professor Waismann provides an opportunity to review that conception. Philosophy, he writes, begins in puzzlement, in wonder. Before attempting to answer our questions, however, we must find sense for them. The error of traditional philosophy is that it failed to do this. Finding sense for them means calling to mind the uses and rules of language. But this in turn leads, not to the solution of problems, but to their dissolution. Is this only a negative view of philosophy? No, Professor Waismann concludes, philosophizing leads men to new horizons of thought, to new similarities, and to new questions. Whether such proposed novelty is reply enough to Findlay's censures remains critical to one's evaluation of linguistic philosophy as a whole.

12   Language and Philosophy

Friedrich Waismann (1896-   )

From Plato to Schopenhauer philosophers are agreed that the source of their philosophizing is wonder. What gives rise to it is nothing recondite and rare but precisely those things which stare us in the face: memory, motion, general ideas. (Plato: What does "horse" mean? A single particular horse? No, for it may refer to *any* horse; *all* the horses, the total class? No, for we speak of this or that horse. But if it means neither a single horse nor all horses, what *does* it mean?) The idealist is shaken in just the same way when he comes to reflect that he has, in Schopenhauer's words, "no knowledge of the sun but only of an eye that sees a sun, and no knowledge of the earth but only of a hand that feels an earth." Can it be, then, that nothing whatever is known to us except our own consciousness?

In looking at such questions, it seems as if the mind's eye were growing dim and as if everything, even that which

---

The selection is from F. Waismann, "How I See Philosophy," in H. D. Lewis (ed.), *Contemporary British Philosophy*, Third Series (London: George Allen & Unwin, Ltd.; New York: The Macmillan Company, 1956), pp. 449–451, 453–458, and 461–467, with omissions. Used by permission of the publishers.

ought to be absolutely clear, was becoming oddly puzzling and unlike its usual self. To bring out what seems to be peculiar to these questions one might say that they are not so much questions as tokens of a profound uneasiness of mind. Try for a moment to put yourself into the frame of mind of which Augustine was possessed when he asked: How is it possible to measure time? Time consists of past, present and future. The past can't be measured, it is gone; the future can't be measured, it is not yet here; and the present can't be measured, it has no extension. Augustine knew of course how time is measured and this was not his concern. What puzzled him was how it is *possible* to measure time, seeing that the past hour cannot be lifted out and placed alongside the present hour for comparison. Or look at it this way: what is measured is in the past, the measuring in the present: how can that be?

The philosopher as he ponders over some such problem has the appearance of a man who is deeply disquieted. He seems to be straining to grasp something which is beyond his powers. The words in which such a question presents itself do not quite bring out into the open the real point—which may, perhaps more aptly, be described as the recoil from the incomprehensible. If, on a straight railway journey, you suddenly come in sight of the very station you have just left behind, there will be terror, accompanied perhaps by slight giddiness. That is exactly how the philosopher feels when he says to himself, "Of course time can be measured; but how *can* it?" It is as though, up to now, he had been passing heedlessly over the difficulties, and now, all of a sudden, he notices them and asks himself in alarm, "But how can that be?"

That is a sort of question which we only ask when it is the very facts themselves which confound us, when something about them strikes us as preposterous. . . .

We all have our moments when something quite ordinary suddenly strikes us as queer—for instance, when time appears to us as a curious thing. Not that we are often in this frame of mind; but on some occasions, when we look at things in a certain way, unexpectedly they seem to change as though by magic: they stare at us with a puzzling expression, and we begin to wonder whether they can possibly be the things we have known all our lives.

"Time flows" we say—a natural and innocent expression, and yet one pregnant with danger. It flows "equably," in Newton's phrase, at an even rate. What can this mean? When something moves, it moves with a definite speed (and speed means: rate of change in time). To ask with what speed time moves, i.e., to ask how quickly time changes in time, is to ask the unaskable. It also flows, again in Newton's phrase, "without relation to anything external." How are we to figure that? Does time flow on irrespective of what happens in the world? Would it flow on even if everything in heaven and on earth came to a sudden standstill as Schopenhauer believed? For if this were not so, he said, time would have to stop with the stopping of the clock and move with the clock's movement. How odd: time flows at the same rate and yet without speed; and perhaps even without anything to occur in it? . . .

But isn't the answer to this that what mystifies us lies in the *noun* form "the time"? Having a notion embodied in the form of a noun almost irresistibly makes us turn round to look for what it is "the name of." We are trying to catch the shadows cast by the opacities of speech. A wrong analogy absorbed into the forms of our language produces mental discomfort (and the feeling of discomfort, when it refers to language, is a profound one). "All sounds, all colors . . . evoke indefinite and yet precise emotions, or, as I prefer to think, call down among us certain disembodied powers whose footsteps over our hearts we call emotions" (W. B. Yeats).

Yet the answer is a prosaic one: don't ask what time is but how the *word* "time" is being used. Easier said than done; for if the philosopher rectifies the use of language, ordinary language has "the advantage of being in possession of declensions," to speak with Lichtenberg, and thus renews its spell over him, luring him on into the shadow chase. It is perhaps only when we turn to languages of a widely different grammatical structure that the way towards such possibilities of interpretation is entirely barred. "It is highly probable that philosophers within the domain of the Ural-Altaic languages (where the subject-concept is least developed) will look differently 'into the world' and be found on paths of thought different from those of the Indo-Europeans or Mussulman's" (Nietzsche).

It may be well at this point to remind ourselves that the words "question" and "answer," "problem" and "solution" are not always used in their most trite sense. It is quite obvious that we often have to do something very different to find the way out of a difficulty. A problem of politics is solved by adopting a certain line of action, the problems of novelists perhaps by the invention of devices for presenting the inmost thoughts and feelings of their characters; there is the painter's problem of how to suggest depth or movement on the canvas, the stylistic problem of expressing things not yet current, not yet turned into cliché; there are a thousand questions of technology which are answered, not by the discovery of some truth, but by a practical achievement; and there is of course the "social question." In philosophy, the real problem is not to find the answer to a given question but to find a sense for it. . . .

Many are the types of bewilderment: there is the obsessional doubt—can I ever know that other people have experiences, that they see, hear and feel as I do? Can I be sure that memory does not always deceive me? Are there really material objects and not only sense-impressions "of" them? There is the doubt-like uneasiness—what sort of being is possessed by numbers? There is the anxiety-doubt—are we really free? This doubt has taken many different forms one of which I shall single out for discussion—the question, namely, whether the law of excluded middle,[1] when it refers to statements in the future tense, forces us into a sort of logical Predestination. A typical argument is this. If it is true now that I shall do a certain thing tomorrow, say, jump into the Thames, then no matter how fiercely I resist, strike out with hands and feet like a madman, when the day comes I cannot help jumping into the water; whereas, if this prediction is false now, then whatever efforts I may make, however many times I may nerve and brace myself, look down at the water and say to myself, "One, two, three—," it is impossible

---

[1 A law of logic that A is either B or not-B, e.g., the chair is either red or not-red. *Ed.*]

for me to spring. Yet that the prediction is either true or false is itself a necessary truth, asserted by the law of excluded middle. From this the startling consequence seems to follow that it is already now decided what I shall do tomorrow, that indeed the entire future is somehow fixed, logically preordained. Whatever I do and whichever way I decide, I am merely moving along lines clearly marked in advance which lead me towards my appointed lot. We are all, in fact, marionettes. If we are not prepared to swallow *that,* then—and there is a glimmer of hope in the "then"—there is an alternative open to us. We need only renounce the law of excluded middle for statements of this kind, and with it the validity of ordinary logic, and all will be well. Descriptions of what will happen are, at present, neither true nor false. (This sort of argument was actually propounded by Lukasiewicz in favor of a three-valued logic with "possible" as a third truth-value alongside "true" and "false.")

The way out is clear enough. The asker of the question has fallen into the error of so many philosophers: of giving an answer before stopping to consider the question. For is he clear what he is asking? He seems to suppose that a statement referring to an event in the future is at present undecided, neither true nor false, but that when the event happens the proposition enters into a sort of new state, that of being true. But how are we to figure the change from "undecided" to "true"? Is it sudden or gradual? At what moment does the statement "it will rain tomorrow" begin to be true? When the first drop falls to the ground? And supposing that it will not rain, when will the statement begin

to be false? Just at the end of the day, at 12 P.M. sharp? Supposing that the event *has* happened, that the statement *is* true, will it remain so for ever? If so, in what way? Does it remain uninterruptedly true, at every moment of day and night? Even if there were no one about to give it any thought? Or is it true only at the moment when it is being thought of? In that case, how long does it remain true? For the duration of the thought? We wouldn't know how to answer these questions; this is due not to any particular ignorance or stupidity on our part but to the fact that something has gone wrong with the way the words "true" and "false" are applied here. . . .

Now it begins to look a bit less paradoxical to say that when a philosopher wants to dispose of a question the one thing he must not do is: to give an answer. A philosophic question is not solved: it *dis*solves. And in what does the "dissolving" consist? In making the meaning of the words used in putting the question so clear to ourselves that we are released from the spell it casts on us. Confusion was removed by calling to mind the use of language or, so far as the use *can* be distilled into rules, the rules: it therefore *was* a confusion about the use of language, or a confusion about rules. It is here that philosophy and grammar meet. . . .

What, only criticism and no meat? The philosopher a fog dispeller? If that were all he was capable of I would be sorry for him and leave him to his devices. Fortunately, this is not so. For one thing, a philosophic question, if pursued far enough, may lead to something positive—for instance, to a more profound understanding of language. Take the skeptical doubts as to material objects, other minds, etc. The first reaction is perhaps to say: these doubts are idle. Ordinarily, when I doubt whether I shall finish this article, after a time my doubt comes to an end. I cannot go on doubting for ever. It's the destiny of doubt to die. But the doubts raised by the skeptic never die. Are they doubts? Are they pseudo-questions? They appear so only when judged by the twin standards of common sense and common speech. The real trouble lies deeper: it arises from the skeptic casting doubt on the very facts which underlie the use of language, those permanent features of experience which make concept formation possible, which in fact are precipitated in the use of our most common words. Suppose that you see an object in front of you quite clearly, say, a pipe, and when you are going to pick it up it melts into thin air, then you may feel, "Lord, I'm going mad" or something of the sort (unless the whole situation is such that you have reason to suspect that it was some clever trick). But what, the skeptic may press now, if such experiences were quite frequent? Would you be prepared to *dis*-solve the connection between different sense experiences which form the hard core of our idea of a solid object, to *un*-do what language has done—to part with the category of thing-hood? And would you then be living in a phenomenalist's paradise with color patches and the other paraphernalia of the sense-datum theory, in a disobjected, desubstantialized world? To say in such circumstances, "Look, it's just tabling now" would be a joke (for even in the weakened verb forms "tabling," "chairing" an element of the thing-category lingers on). That is why the skeptic struggles to express himself in a language which is not fit for this purpose. He expresses himself misleadingly when he says that he doubts such-and-such *facts:* his doubts cut so deep that they affect the fabric of language itself. For what he doubts is already embodied in the very forms of speech, e.g. in what is condensed in the use of thing-words. The moment he tries to penetrate those deep-sunken layers, he undermines the language in which he ventilates his qualms—with the result that he seems to be talking nonsense. He is not. But in order to make his doubts fully expressible, language would first have to go into the melting-pot. (We can get a glimmering of what is needed from modern science where all the long-established categories—thing-hood, causality, position—had to be revolutionized. This required nothing less than the construction of some new language, not the expression of new facts with the old one.)

If we look at the matter in this way the attitude of the skeptic is seen in a new light. He considers possibilities which lie far outside the domain of our current experience. If his doubts are taken seriously, they turn into observations which cast a new and searching light on the subsoil of language, showing what possibilities are open to our thought (though not to ordinary language), and what paths might have been pursued if the texture of our experience were different from what it is. These problems are not spurious: they make us aware of the vast background in which any current experiences are embedded, and to which language has adapted itself; thus they bring out the unmeasured sum of experience stored up in the use of our words and syntactical forms. . . .

A whole chapter might be written on the fate of questions, their curious adventures and transformations—how they change into others and in the process remain, and yet do not remain, the same. The original question may split and multiply almost like a character in a dream play. To mention just a few examples: can logic be characterized completely in a formal way, i.e. without bringing in any extraneous ideas such as the use of language and all that goes with it? Can arithmetic be characterized in any such way, entirely "from within"? Or will any interpretation include some *Erdenrest* of the empiric? These questions have given rise to extensive research on mathematical interpretation of formal systems. The query how far logical intuition is correct has got ramified into a bunch of questions pertaining to the theory of logical types, the axiom of choice, etc., indeed to a far more fundamental issue, namely, whether ordinary logic itself is "right" as contrasted with the system of inferences evolved by the intuitionists. Or again, are there undecidable questions in mathematics, not in the restricted sense of Gödel, but undecidable in an absolute sense? Are there natural limits to generalization? It is interesting to watch how from a question of this sort, not too precise, somewhat blurred, new and better defined questions detach themselves, the parent question—in Frege's case philosophic *par excellence*[2]—giving rise to a scientist's progeny. . . .

The question is the first groping step of the mind in its journeyings that lead towards new horizons. The genius of the

philosopher shows itself nowhere more strikingly than in the new kind of question he brings into the world. What distinguishes him and gives him his place is the passion of questioning. That his questions are at times not so clear is perhaps of not so much moment as one makes of it. There is nothing like clear thinking to protect one from making discoveries. It is all very well to talk of clarity, but when it becomes an obsession it is liable to nip the living thought in the bud. This, I am afraid, is one of the deplorable results of Logical Positivism, not foreseen by its founders, but only too striking in some of its followers. Look at these people, gripped by a clarity neurosis, haunted by fear, tonguetied, asking themselves continually, "Oh dear, now does this make perfectly good sense?" Imagine the pioneers of science, Kepler, Newton, the discoverers of non-Euclidean geometry, of field physics, the unconscious, matter waves or heaven knows what, imagine them asking themselves this question at every step—this would have been the surest means of sapping any creative power. No great discoverer has acted in accordance with the motto, "Everything that can be said can be said clearly." And some of the greatest discoveries have even emerged from a sort of primordial fog. (Something to be said for the fog. For my part, I've always suspected that clarity is the last refuge of those who have nothing to say.) . . .

But here a new problem presents itself: How do we know what will satisfy a given question? More generally: How does the answer fit the question? Questions of the current sort ("What is the right time?") show already by their form what sort of answer to expect. They are,

[2 The reference is to the logician Frege's work that—as Waismann points out elsewhere—resulted from philosophic wonder about the nature of arithmetical truths and led to the development of modern logic. *Ed.*]

so to speak, cheques with a blank to be filled; yet not always so: Augustine's question, "How is it possible to measure time?" or Kant's question, "How is geometry possible?" do not trace out the form of the answer. There is no *obvious* link between question and answer, any more than there is in the case of asking "What is a point?" When Hilbert's idea —that the axioms of geometry jointly provide the "implicit definition" of the basic terms—was first propounded it came totally unexpected; no one had ever thought of that before; on the contrary, many people had an uneasy feeling as if this were a way of evading the issue rather than an answer, amongst them no less a man than Frege. He thought the problem still unsolved. . . .

Frege behaves not so very unlike a man mystified by the question, "What is time?" We may suggest converting the latter into the question how the word "time" is being used (which would bring him down to earth). But aren't we cheating him? We seem to be holding out the answer to *one* question, but not to that one which he was asking. He may suspect that we are trying to fob him off with the second best we have in store, his original question still remaining an enigma. Similarly Frege: he considered it a scandal that the questions "What is a point?" "What is a number?" were still unanswered.

In either of these cases, the aim of a discussion, in the absence of a proof, can only be to change the asker's attitude. We may, for instance, scrutinize similar, or partially similar, cases, point out that the form of the answer is not always that of the question; by going patiently over such cases, the vast background of analogies against which the question is seen will slowly change. The turning up of a wide field of language loosens the position of certain standards which are so ingrained that we do not see them for what they are; and if we do this in an effective manner, a mind like Frege's will be released from the obsession of seeking strainingly for an answer to fit the mould. Arguments are used in such a discussion, not as proofs though but rather as means to make him see things he had not noticed before: e.g. to dispel wrong analogies, to stress similarities with other cases and in this way to bring about something like a shift of perspective. However, there is no way of proving him wrong or bullying him into mental acceptance of the proposal: when all is said and done the decision is his.

BIBLIOGRAPHICAL NOTE

Introductory historical surveys of linguistic philosophy, including frequently its relations to positivism, are given in the following volumes: A. J. Ayer *et al.*, *The Revolution in Philosophy* (London, 1956); D. F. Pears (ed.), *The Nature of Metaphysics* (London, 1957); J. Passmore, *A Hundred Years of Philosophy* (London, 1957); J. O. Urmson, *Philosophical Analysis* (Oxford, 1956); and G. J. Warnock, *English Philosophy Since 1900* (London, 1958). Among the books that are considered classics for this position are G. E. Moore's *Philosophical Studies* (London, 1922); L. Wittgenstein, *Tractatus Logico-Philosophicus* (London, 1922), which greatly influenced positivism, his *Philo-*

sophical Investigations (New York, 1953) and *The Blue and Brown Books* (New York, 1958), which are clearly expressive of principles of linguistic philosophy; Gilbert Ryle, *The Concept of Mind* (London, 1949); and John Wisdom, *Other Minds* (Oxford, 1952), *Philosophy and Psycho-Analysis* (Oxford, 1953), and *Paradox and Discovery* (1967). Anthologies of important discussions from a linguistic point of view are: A. G. N. Flew (ed.), *Logic and Language*, First Series (Oxford, 1951), Second Series (Oxford, 1953); M. Macdonald (ed.), *Philosophy and Analysis* (Oxford, 1954); C. A. Mace (ed.), *British Philosophy in the Mid-Century* (London, 1957); Morris Weitz (ed.), *20th-Century Philosophy: The Analytic Tradition* (New York, 1967); and Richard Rorty (ed.), *The Linguistic Turn* (Chicago, 1967). A somewhat advanced survey is F. Waismann, *The Principles of Linguistic Philosophy* (ed. R. Harre) (London, 1965). A bibliography of many articles is given by J. O. Urmson, "Bibliography of Analytic Philosophy," *Revue Internationale de Philosophie*, 7 (1953), and later. E. Gellner's *Words and Things* (London, 1959) and H. D. Lewis (ed.), *Clarity is Not Enough* (London, 1963) contain interesting comments on linguistic approaches to philosophy. Many journals express the linguistic point of view: see especially *Mind* and *Philosophical Analysis*.

Chapter Seven

Existentialism

Pascal · Kierkegaard · Heidegger · Sartre
Nietzsche · Camus · Merleau-Ponty
Jaspers · Tillich · Manser · Heinemann

The term "existentialism" is commonly used to refer to a contemporary type of thinking that emphasizes human existence and the qualities of being that are peculiar to it rather than to nature or the physical world. So characterized, existentialism is sometimes seen as simply a new name for an ancient philosophical tradition. Taken only as a revival of ancient thought, however, it loses what in fact are its distinctive features.

"Emphasis on human existence" is the beginning of a definition of existentialism, but actually it is too vague for use in reference to the modern movement; for existentialism's concern about man grows out of specifically modern conditions and concludes in a quite unique position. Among these conditions are the loss of the individual in mass culture and technology, the consequent alienation of the human person from himself as well as from his productions, and the loss of meaning in life through divisions within the human spirit. The result of these conditions is frequently called the "existential experience." Recorded by many artists and writers as well as philosophers, it is, in sum, an experience of the decomposition of our phenomenal world—first, of all rational concepts, next of objects, then of time and history, until finally all coherence is gone—to the point where one faces only Nothing and experiences only despair. Sometimes also called an experience of crisis, it has arisen in times of social and personal catastrophe in our century.

Whatever the conditions that produce it, however, existentialism is not simply a philosophy of despair. A second expression, "the existentialist attitude," indicates that the existential experience results in an important philosophical alternative. This attitude is directed toward human existence. Other philosophies also study man;

but they view him in terms of some concept or essence derived from reason. The existentialist opposes such traditional conceptualism and its abstract, general concept of existence, for he believes that *what* man is can only be determined from *how* he is; that is, man's essence is to be found only in his concrete existence. The desire to know the meaning of the individual man in a more radical way than other philosophers have sought leads the existentialist to hold that the starting point of philosophy is the concrete situation of man in the world.

Much of existentialist writing aims at describing the whole of human life—not just reason but emotional and conative states as well. Reason and rational structure are not equivalent to human life; feeling, passion, and decision are equally if not more important clues to man's being. Yet existentialism is not simply phenomenology, great as is its reliance on descriptive techniques. It also desires to know the reality of human existence and, for some existentialists, to produce a general theory of being. The phenomenological interest is directed toward an ontological goal, though the latter can be achieved only through the former.

This ontological interest links existentialism with certain aspects of traditional philosophy, though it would agree to some extent with positivism and analysis in their distrust of philosophic rationalism. But it has in turn its doubts about them. In particular, existentialism takes issue with efforts to make philosophy another technology, for this would destroy philosophy; it doubts that science or reason can interpret the whole universe; and it is suspicious of the "disinterestedness" of modern "objective" thought. Its closer tie is with traditional philosophy, which was occupied with the problems of human existence, although, as this introductory sketch has indicated, existentialism's approach to them is unique.

Readers will also find that existentialists do not form a "school" in the usual meaning of the term. Highly individualistic in their writings, they have refused to become a movement in philosophy. Something of a debate on the proper application of the term has therefore developed; and some of the following writers, in fact, would not accept the name existentialist, given its diverse meanings. While taking note of this debate, however, we shall turn directly to the materials; for it is in them that the philosophical significance of the thought of these men will be found.

INTRODUCTION

Although the number of thinkers in the history of ideas who reflected the existentialist position is small, one—the French mathematician and philosopher Blaise Pascal—surely belongs within the stream of existentialism. Caught in the religious strifes of his day, at the same time being a contributor to the rising mathematical science of his century, he was extremely sensitive to the human condition with its frailty, uncertainty, and despair. His *Pensées* provides a good introduction to existentialism.

Two aspects of his thought are reflected in the following selection. There is first the phenomenological or descriptive approach to individual existence. Many of the recurring themes of existentialist thought are found here: the problem of knowing oneself concretely, the distrust of science and reason for existential concerns, the uncertainties of existence, the nothingness of man's being, the elusiveness of finality, the reality of temporality and change, and man's corruption—his untruth—as revealed in disguise, falsehood, and hypocrisy. The second aspect is ontological. Pascal offers a view of man as spirit, yet a spirit in nature. Hence man is a riddle, a paradox: as spirit, his reality is found in his passion for the Eternal; as natural, his being is an insignificant speck between two infinites.

1 The Discovery of Finitude

Blaise Pascal (1623-1662)

One must know oneself. If this does not serve to discover truth, it at least serves as a rule of life, and there is nothing better.

Physical science will not console me for the ignorance of morality in the time of affliction. But the science of ethics will always console me for the ignorance of the physical sciences.

Man's Disproportion. This is where our intuitive knowledge leads us. If it be not true, there is no truth in man; and if it be, he finds therein a great reason for humiliation, because he must abase himself in one way or another. And since he cannot exist without such knowledge, I wish that before entering on deeper researches into nature he would consider her seriously and at leisure, that he would examine himself also, and knowing what proportion

Selected and arranged from C. Kegan Paul (tr.), *The Thoughts of Blaise Pascal* (London: Kegan Paul, Trench and Co., 1888), pp. 19–87.

there is. Let man then contemplate the whole realm of nature in her full and exalted majesty, and turn his eyes from the low objects which hem him round; let him observe that brilliant light set like an eternal lamp to illumine the universe, let the earth appear to him a point in comparison with the vast circle described by that sun, and let him see with amazement that even this vast circle is itself but a fine point in regard to that described by the stars revolving in the firmament. If our view be arrested there, let imagination pass beyond, and it will sooner exhaust the power of thinking than nature that of giving scope for thought. The whole visible world is but an imperceptible speck in the ample bosom of nature. No idea approaches it. We may swell our conceptions beyond all imaginable space, yet bring forth only atoms in comparison with the reality of things. It is an infinite sphere, the center of which is every where, the circumference no where. It is, in short, the greatest sensible mark of the almighty power of God, that imagination loses itself in that thought.

Then, returning to himself, let man consider his own being compared with all that is; let him regard himself as wandering in this remote province of nature; and from the little dungeon in which he finds himself lodged, I mean the universe, let him learn to set a true value on the earth, on its kingdoms, its cities, and on himself.

What is a man in the infinite? But to show him another prodigy no less astonishing, let him examine the most delicate things he knows. Let him take a mite which in its minute body presents him with parts incomparably more minute; limbs with their joints, veins in the limbs, blood in the veins, humors in the blood, drops in the humors, vapors in the drops; let him, again dividing these last, exhaust his power of thought; let the last point at which he arrives be that of which we speak, and he will perhaps think that here is the extremest diminutive in nature. Then I will open before him therein a new abyss. I will paint for him not only the visible universe, but all that he can conceive of nature's immensity in the enclosure of this diminished atom. Let him therein see an infinity of universes of which each has its firmament, its planets, its earth, in the same proportion as in the visible world; in each earth animals, and at the last the mites, in which he will come upon all that was in the first, and still find in these others the same without end and without cessation; let him lose himself in wonders as astonishing in their minuteness as the others in their immensity; for who will not be amazed at seeing that our body, which

before was imperceptible in the universe, itself imperceptible in the bosom of the whole, is now a colossus, a world, a whole, in regard to the nothingness to which we cannot attain.

Who so takes this survey of himself will be terrified at the thought that he is upheld in the material being, given him by nature, between these two abysses of the infinite and nothing, he will tremble at the sight of these marvels; and I think that as his curiosity changes into wonder, he will be more disposed to contemplate them in silence than to search into them with presumption.

For after all what is man in nature? A nothing in regard to the infinite, a whole in regard to nothing, a mean between nothing and the whole; infinitely removed from understanding either extreme. The end of things and their beginnings are invincibly hidden from him in impenetrable secrecy, he is equally incapable of seeing the nothing whence he was taken, and the infinite in which he is engulfed.

What shall he do then, but discern somewhat of the middle of things in an eternal despair of knowing either their beginning or their end? All things arise from nothing, and tend towards the infinite. Who can follow their marvellous course? The author of these wonders can understand them, and none but he.

Of these two infinites in nature, the infinitely great and the infinitely little, man can more easily conceive the great.

Because they have not considered these infinities, men have rashly plunged into the research of nature, as though they bore some proportion to her.

It is strange that they have wished to understand the origin of all that is, and thence to attain to the knowledge of the whole, with a presumption as infinite as their object. For there is no doubt that such a design cannot be formed without presumption or without a capacity as infinite as nature.

If we are well informed, we understand that nature having graven her own image and that of her author on all things, they are almost all partakers of her double infinity. Thus we see that all the sciences are infinite in the extent of their researches, for none can doubt that geometry, for instance, has an infinite infinity of problems to propose. They are also infinite in the number and in the nicety of their premises, for it is evident that those which are finally proposed are not self-supporting, but are based on others, which again having others as their support have no finality.

But we make some apparently final to the reason, just as in regard to material things we call that an indivisible point beyond which our senses can no longer perceive anything, though by its nature this also is infinitely divisible.

Of these two scientific infinities, that of greatness is the most obvious to the senses, and therefore a few persons have made pretensions to universal knowledge. "I will discourse of the all," said Democritus.

But beyond the fact that it is a small thing to speak of it simply, without proving and knowing, it is nevertheless impossible to do so, the infinite multitude of things being so hidden, that all we can express by word or thought is but an invisible trace of them. Hence it is plain how foolish, vain, and ignorant is that title of some books: *De omni scibili*.

But the infinitely little is far less evident. Philosophers have much more frequently asserted they have attained it, yet in that very point they have all stumbled. This has given occasion to such common titles as *The Origin of Creation, The Principles of Philosophy,* and the like, as presumptuous in fact though not in appearance as that dazzling one, *De omni scibili*.

We naturally think that we can more easily reach the center of things than embrace their circumference. The visible bulk of the world visibly exceeds us, but as we exceed little things, we think ourselves more capable of possessing them. Yet we need no less capacity to attain the nothing than the whole. Infinite capacity is needed for both, and it seems to me that whoever shall have understood the ultimate principles of existence might also attain to the knowledge of the infinite. The one depends on the other, and one leads to the other. Extremes meet and reunite by virtue of their distance, to find each other in God, and in God alone.

Let us then know our limits; we are something, but we are not all. What existence we have conceals from us the knowledge of first principles which spring from the nothing, while the pettiness of that existence hides from us the sight of the infinite.

In the order of intelligible things our intelligence holds the same position as our body holds in the vast extent of nature.

Restricted in every way, this middle state between two extremes is common to all our weaknesses.

Our senses can perceive no extreme. Too much noise deafens us, excess of light blinds us, too great distance or nearness equally interfere with our vision, prolixity or brevity equally obscure a discourse, too much truth overwhelms us. I know even those who cannot understand that if four be taken from nothing nothing remains. First principles are too plain for us, superfluous pleasure troubles us. Too many concords are unpleasing in music, and too many benefits annoy, we wish to have wherewithal to overpay our debt. *Beneficia eo usque læta sunt dum videntur exsolvi posse; ubi multum antevenere, pro gratia odium redditur* ["Benefits are pleasing so long as they appear able to be repaid; but when they are excessive in number, then enmity is returned instead of favor"].

We feel neither extreme heat nor extreme cold. Qualities in excess are inimical to us and not apparent to the senses, we do not feel but are passive under them. The weakness of youth and age equally hinder the mind, as also too much and too little teaching . . .

In a word, all extremes are for us as though they were not; and we are not, in regard to them: they escape us, or we them.

This is our true state; this is what renders us incapable both of certain knowledge and of absolute ignorance. We sail on a vast expanse, ever uncertain, ever drifting, hurried from one to the other goal. If we think to attach ourselves firmly to any point, it totters and fails us; if we follow, it eludes our grasp, and flies us, vanishing for ever. Nothing stays for us. This is our natural condition, yet always the most contrary to our inclination; we burn with desire to find a steadfast place and an ultimate fixed basis whereon we may build a tower to reach the infinite. But our whole foundation breaks up, and earth opens to the abysses.

We may not then look for certainty or stability. Our reason is always deceived by changing shows, nothing can fix the finite between the two infinites, which at once enclose and fly from it.

If this be once well understood I think that we shall rest, each in the state wherein nature has placed him. This element which falls to us as our lot being always distant from either extreme, it matters not that a man should have a trifle more knowledge of the universe. If he has it, he but begins a little higher. He is always infinitely distant from the end, and the duration of our life is infinitely removed from eternity, even if it last ten years longer.

In regard to these infinites all finites are equal, and I see not why we should fix our imagination on one more than on another. The only comparison which we can make of ourselves to the finite troubles us.

Were man to begin with the study of himself, he would see how incapable he is of proceeding further. How can a part know the whole? But he may perhaps aspire to know at least the parts with which he has proportionate relation. But the parts of the world are so linked and related, that I think it impossible to know one without another, or without the whole.

Man, for instance, is related to all that he knows. He needs place wherein to abide, time through which to exist, motion in order to live; he needs constituent elements, warmth and food to nourish him, air to breathe. He sees light, he feels bodies, he contracts an alliance with all that is.

To know man then it is necessary to understand how it comes that he needs air to breathe, and to know the air we must understand how it has relation to the life of man, etc.

Flame cannot exist without air, therefore to know one, we must know the other.

All that exists then is both cause and effect, dependent and supporting, mediate and immediate, and all is held together by a natural though imperceptible bond, which unites things most distant and most different. I hold it impossible to know the parts without knowing the whole, or to know the whole without knowing the parts in detail.

I hold it impossible to know one alone without all the others, that is to say impossible purely and absolutely.

The eternity of things in themselves or in God must also confound our brief duration. The fixed and constant immobility of Nature in comparison with the continual changes which take place in us must have the same effect.

And what completes our inability to know things is that they are in their essence simple, whereas we are composed of two opposite natures differing in kind, soul and body. For it is impossible that our reasoning part should be other than spiritual; and should any allege that we are simply material, this would far more exclude us from the knowledge of things, since it is an inconceivable paradox to affirm that matter can know itself, and it is not possible for us to know how it should know itself.

So, were we simply material, we could know nothing whatever, and if we are composed of spirit and matter we cannot perfectly know what is simple, whether it be spiritual or material. For how should we know matter distinctly, since our being, which acts on this knowledge, is partly spiritual, and how should we know spiritual substances clearly since we have a body which weights us, and drags us down to earth.

Moreover what completes our inability is the simplicity of things compared with our double and complex nature. To dispute this point were an invincible absurdity, for it is as absurd as impious to deny that man is composed of two parts, differing in their nature, soul and body. This renders us unable to know all things; for if this complexity be denied, and it be asserted that we are entirely material, it is plain that matter is incapable of knowing matter. Nothing is more impossible than this.

Let us conceive then that this mixture of spirit and clay throws us out of proportion . . .

Hence it comes that almost all philosophers have confounded different ideas, and speak of material things in spiritual phrase, and of spiritual things in material phrase. For they say boldly that bodies have a tendency to fall, that they seek after their center, that they fly from destruction, that they fear a void, that they have inclinations, sympathies, antipathies; and all of these are spiritual qualities. Again, in speaking of spirits, they conceive of them as in a given spot, or as moving from place to place; qualities which belong to matter alone.

Instead of receiving the ideas of these things simply, we color them with our own qualities, and stamp with our complex being all the simple things which we contemplate.

Who would not think, when we declare that all that is consists of mind and matter, that we really understood this combination? Yet it is the one thing we least understand. Man is to himself the most marvellous object in Nature, for he cannot conceive what matter is, still less what is mind, and less than all how a material body should be united to a mind. This is the crown of all his difficulties, yet it is his very being: *Modus quo corporibus adhæret spiritus comprehendi ab homine non potest et hoc tamen home est* ["The manner by which the mind clings to bodies cannot be comprehended by man and yet this is man"].

The nature of man is his whole nature, *omne animal.*

There is nothing we cannot make natural, nothing natural we cannot lose.

Of Self-Love. The nature of self-love and of this human "I" is to love self only, and consider self only. But what can it do? It cannot prevent the object it loves from being full of faults and miseries; man would fain be great and sees that he is little, would fain be happy, and sees that he is miserable, would fain be perfect, and sees that he is full of imperfections, would fain be the object of the love and esteem of men, and sees that his faults merit only their aversion and contempt. The embarrassment wherein he finds himself produces in him the most unjust and criminal passion imaginable, for he conceives a mortal hatred against that truth which blames him and convinces him of his faults. Desiring to annihilate it, yet unable to destroy it in its essence, he destroys it as much as he can in his own knowledge, and in that of others; that is to say, he devotes all his care to the concealment of his faults, both from others and from himself, and he can

neither bear that others should show them to him, nor that they should see them.

It is no doubt an evil to be full of faults, but it is a greater evil to be full of them, yet unwilling to recognize them, because that is to add the further fault of a voluntary illusion. We do not like others to deceive us, we do not think it just in them to require more esteem from us than they deserve; it is therefore unjust that we should deceive them, desiring more esteem from them than we deserve.

Thus if they discover no more imperfections and vices in us than we really have, it is plain they do us no wrong, since it is not they who cause them; but rather they do us a service, since they help us to deliver ourselves from an evil, the ignorance of these imperfections. We ought not to be troubled that they know our faults and despise us, since it is but just they should know us as we are, and despise us if we are despicable.

Such are the sentiments which would arise in a heart full of equity and justice. What should we say then of our own heart, finding in it a wholly contrary disposition? For is it not true that we hate truth, and those who tell it us, and that we would wish them to have an erroneously favorable opinion of us, and to esteem us other than indeed we are?

One proof of this fills me with dismay. The Catholic religion does not oblige us to tell out our sins indiscriminately to all, it allows us to remain hidden from men in general, but she excepts one alone, to whom she commands us to open the very depths of our heart, and to show ourselves to him as we are. There is but this one man in the world whom she orders us to undeceive; she binds him to an inviolable secrecy, so that this knowledge is to him as though it were not. We can imagine nothing more charitable and more tender. Yet such is the corruption of man, that he finds even this law harsh, and it is one of the main reasons which has set a large portion of Europe in revolt against the Church.

How unjust and unreasonable is the human heart which finds it hard to be obliged to do in regard to one man what in some degree it were just to do to all men. For it is just that we should deceive them?

There are different degrees in this dislike to the truth, but it may be said that all have it in some degree, for it is inseparable from self-love. This false delicacy causes those who must needs reprove others to choose so many windings and modifications in order to avoid shocking them. They must needs lessen our faults, seem to excuse them, mix praises with their blame, give evidences of affection and esteem. Yet this medicine is always bitter to self-love, which takes as little as it can, always with disgust, often with a secret anger against those who administer it.

Hence it happens, that if any desire our love, they avoid doing us a service which they know to be disagreeable; they treat us as we would wish to be treated: we hate the truth, and they hide it from us; we wish to be flattered, they flatter us; we love to be deceived, they deceive us.

Thus each degree of good fortune which raises us in the world removes us further from truth, because we fear most to wound those whose affection is most useful, and whose dislike is most dangerous. A prince may be the byword of all Europe, yet he alone knows nothing of it. I am not surprised; to speak the truth is useful to whom it is spoken, but disadvantageous to those who speak it, since it makes them hated. Now those who live with princes love their own interests more than that of the prince they serve, and thus they take care not to benefit him so as to do themselves a disservice.

This misfortune is, no doubt, greater and more common in the higher classes, but lesser men are not exempt from it, since there is always an interest in making men love us. Thus human life is but a perpetual illusion, an interchange of deceit and flattery. No one speaks of us in our presence as in our absence. The society of men is founded on this universal deceit: few friendships would last if every man knew what his friend said of him behind his back, though he then spoke in sincerity and without passion.

Man is then only disguise, falsehood, and hypocrisy, both in himself and with regard to others. He will not be told the truth, he avoids telling it to others, and all these tendencies, so far removed from justice and reason, have their natural roots in his heart.

Contraries. Man is naturally credulous and incredulous, timid and rash.

Description of man: dependency, desire of independence, bodily needs.

The condition of man; inconstancy, weariness, unrest.

Our nature consists in motion; perfect rest is death.

Weariness. Nothing is so insufferable to man as to be completely at rest, without passions, without business, without diversion, without study. He then feels his nothingness, his forlornness, his insufficiency, his dependence, his weakness, his emptiness. There will immediately arise from the depth of his heart weariness, gloom, sadness, fretfulness, vexation, despair.

Contradiction. To despise existence, to die for nothing, to hate our existence.

We run carelessly to the precipice, after we have put something before us to prevent us seeing it.

When I consider the short duration of my life, swallowed up in the eternity before and after, the little space which I fill, and even can see, engulfed in the infinite immensity of spaces whereof I know nothing and which know nothing of me, I am terrified, and wonder that I am here rather than there, for there is no reason why here rather than there, or now rather than then. Who has set me here? By whose order and design have this place and time been destined for me? *Memoria hospitis unius diei praetereuntis* ["Memory of a guest passing by for a day"].

2   Existence and Despair

Soren Kierkegaard (1813-1855)

Important as Pascal is, it is nevertheless necessary to place the real origin of existentialism in the writings of another thinker, Soren Kierkegaard. Kierkegaard's central idea is how one may become a Christian, and much of his writing defends Christianity against false values. His day and age, he believes, has forgotten what it means to be a Christian, or even what it means to *be*. Hence he is led to introduce into Western thought—many believe for the first time—the categories of "individual" and "existence."

By existence Kierkegaard means the striving of a person to fulfill himself. That men must strive points to a tension within their very being. In describing and analyzing the experience of despair, Kierkegaard finds this tension to be a result of the fact that man is a spiritual being, that he is a synthesis of the temporal and eternal, the finite and infinite.

Man is a synthesis, but simply as synthesis he is not a self. Despair arises because man is a synthesis, and ultimately it is despair over this synthesis—that is, over the self itself. Despair reveals that, simply as given, the self with all finite things is meaningless. The recognition of the self's meaninglessness, however, reveals an ultimate meaning by positing the infinite and the eternal. Hence despair also reveals that men are spiritual beings and that they exist before God. Since true selfhood can be attained only when the self is related to the Power that constitutes the synthesis (even though men may try to find substitutes for God in pleasure or duty), despair posits the necessity of genuine endeavor through decision. Only decision or faith can bring meaning into human personality, and the achievement of meaning is the achievement of "subjective truth."

Man is spirit. But what is spirit? Spirit is the self. But what is the self? The self is a relation which relates itself to its own self, or it is that in the relation [which accounts for it] that the relation relates itself to its own self; the self is not the relation but [consists in the fact] that the relation relates itself to its own self. Man is a synthesis of the infinite and the finite, of the temporal and the eternal, of freedom and necessity, in short it is a synthesis. A synthesis is a relation between two factors. So regarded, man is not yet a self.

In the relation between two, the relation is the third term as a negative unity, and the two relate themselves to the relation, and in the relation to the relation; such a relation is that between soul and body, when man is regarded as soul. If on the contrary the relation relates itself to its own self, the relation is then the positive third term, and this is the self.

Such a relation which relates itself to its own self (that is to say, a self) must either have constituted itself or have been constituted by another.

If this relation which relates itself to its own self is constituted by another, the relation doubtless is the third term, but this relation (the third term) is in turn a relation relating itself to that which constituted the whole relation.

Such a derived, constituted, relation is the human self, a relation which relates itself to its own self, and in relat-

The selection is from Soren Kierkegaard, *Fear and Trembling: The Sickness unto Death* (tr. Walter Lowrie), copyright 1941, 1954 by Princeton University Press; Princeton Paperback, 1968, pp. 146–61, with omissions. Reprinted by permission of Princeton University Press.

ing itself to its own self relates itself to another. Hence it is that there can be two forms of despair properly so called. If the human self had constituted itself, there could be a question only of one form, that of not willing to be one's own self, of willing to get rid of oneself, but there would be no question of despairingly willing to be oneself. This formula [i.e. that the self is constituted by another] is the expression for the total dependence of the relation (the self namely), the expression for the fact that the self cannot of itself attain and remain in equilibrium and rest by itself, but only by relating itself to that Power which constituted the whole relation. Indeed, so far is it from being true that this second form of despair (despair at willing to be one's own self) denotes only a particular kind of despair, that on the contrary all despair can in the last analysis be reduced to this. . . .

This then is the formula which describes the condition of the self when despair is completely eradicated: by relating itself to its own self and by willing to be itself the self is grounded transparently in the Power which posited it.

Is despair an advantage or a drawback? Regarded in a purely dialectical way it is both. If one were to stick to the abstract notion of despair, without thinking of any concrete despairer, one might say that it is an immense advantage. The possibility of this sickness is man's advantage over the beast, and this advantage distinguishes him far more essentially than the erect posture, for it implies the infinite erectness or loftiness of being spirit. The possibility of this sickness is man's advantage over the beast; to be sharply observant of the sickness constitutes the Christian's advantage over the natural man; to be healed of this sickness is the Christian's bliss.

So then it is an infinite advantage to be able to despair; and yet it is not only the greatest misfortune and misery to be in despair; no, it is perdition. Ordinarily there is no such relation between possibility and actuality; if it is an advantage to be able to be this or that, it is a still greater advantage to be such a thing. That is to say, being is related to the ability to be as an ascent. In the case of despair, on the contrary, being is related to the ability to be as a fall. Infinite as is the advantage of the possibility, just so great is the measure of the fall. So in the case of despair the ascent consists in not being in despair. Yet this statement is open to misunderstanding. The thing of not being in despair is not like not being lame, blind, etc. In case the not being in despair means neither more nor less than not being this, then it is precisely to be it. The thing of not being in despair must mean the annihilation of the possibility of being this; if it is to be true that a man is not in despair, one must annihilate the possibility every instant. Such is not ordinarily the relation between possibility and actuality. Although thinkers say that actuality is the annihilated possibility, yet this is not entirely true; it is the fulfilled, the effective possibility. Here, on the contrary, the actuality (not being in despair), which in its very form is a negation, is the impotent, annihilated possibility; ordinarily, actuality in comparison with possibility is a confirmation, here it is a negation.

Despair is the disrelationship in a relation which relates itself to itself. But the synthesis is not the disrelationship, it is merely the possibility, or, in the synthesis is latent the possibility of the disrelationship. If the synthesis were the disrelationship, there would be no such thing as despair, for despair would then be something inherent in human nature as such, that is, it would not be despair, it would be something that befell a man, something he suffered passively, like an illness into which a man falls, or like death which is the lot of all. No, this thing of despairing is inherent in man himself; but if he were not a synthesis, he could not despair, neither could he despair if the synthesis were not originally from God's hand in the right relationship.

Whence then comes despair? From the relation wherein the synthesis relates itself to itself, in that God who made man a relationship lets this go as it were out of His hand, that is, in the fact that the relation relates itself to itself. And herein, in the fact that the relation is spirit, is the self, consists the responsibility under which all despair lies, and so lies every instant it exists, however much and however ingeniously the despairer, deceiving himself and others, may talk of his despair as a misfortune which has befallen him, with a confusion of things different, as in the case of vertigo aforementioned, with which, though it is qualitatively different, despair has much in common, since vertigo is under the rubric soul what despair is under the rubric spirit, and is pregnant with analogies to despair. . . .

The concept of the sickness unto death must be understood, however, in a peculiar sense. Literally it means a sickness the end and outcome of which is death. Thus one speaks of a mortal sickness as synonymous with a sickness unto death. In this sense despair cannot be called the sickness unto death. But in the Christian understanding of it death itself is a transition unto life. In view of this, there is from the Christian standpoint no earthly, bodily sickness unto death. For death is doubtless the last phase of the sickness, but death is not the last thing. If in the strictest sense we are to speak of a sickness unto death, it must be one in which the last thing is death, and death the last thing. And this precisely is despair.

Yet in another and still more definite sense despair is the sickness unto death. It is indeed very far from being true that, literally understood, one dies of this sickness, or that this sickness ends with bodily death. On the contrary, the torment of despair is precisely this, not to be able to die. So it has much in common with the situation of the moribund when he lies and struggles with death, and cannot die. So to be sick *unto* death is, not to be able to die—yet not as though there were hope of life; no, the hopelessness in this case is that even the last hope, death, is not available. When death is the greatest danger, one hopes for life; but when one becomes acquainted with an even more dreadful danger, one hopes for death. So when the danger is so great that death has become one's hope, despair is the disconsolateness of not being able to die. . . .

A despairing man is in despair over *something*. So it seems for an instant, but only for an instant; that same instant the true despair manifests itself, or despair manifests itself in its true character. For in the fact that he despaired of *something*, he really despaired of himself, and now would be rid of himself. Thus when the ambitious man whose watchword was "Either Caesar or nothing" does not become Caesar, he is in despair thereat. But this signifies something else, namely, that precisely because he did not become Caesar he now cannot endure to be himself. So properly he is not in despair over the fact that he did not become Caesar, but he is in despair over himself for the fact that he did not become Caesar. This self which, had he become Caesar, would have been to him a sheer delight (though in another sense equally in despair), this self is now absolutely intolerable to him. In a profounder sense it is not the fact that he did not become Caesar which is intolerable to him, but the self which did not become Caesar is the thing that is intolerable; or, more correctly, what is intolerable to him is that he cannot get rid of himself. If he had become Caesar he would have been rid of himself in desperation, but now that he did not become Caesar he cannot in desperation get rid of himself. Essentially he is equally in despair in either case, for he does not possess himself, he is not himself. By becoming Caesar he would not after all have become himself but have got rid of himself, and by not becoming Caesar he falls into despair over the fact that he cannot get rid of himself. Hence it is a superficial view (which presumably has never seen a person in despair, not even one's own self) when it is said of a man in despair, "He is consuming himself." For precisely this it is he despairs of, and to his torment it is precisely this he cannot do, since by despair fire has entered into something that cannot burn, or cannot burn up, that is, into the self.

So to despair over something is not yet properly despair. It is the beginning, or it is as when the physician says of a sickness that it has not yet declared itself. The next step is the declared despair, despair over oneself. A young girl is in despair over love, and so she despairs over her lover, because he died, or because he was unfaithful to her. This is not a declared despair; no, she is in despair over herself. This self of hers, which, if it had become "his" beloved, she would have been rid of in the most blissful way, or would have lost, this self is now a torment to her when it has to be a self without "him"; this self which would have been to her her riches (though in another sense equally in despair) has now become to her a loathsome void, since "he" is dead, or it has become to her an abhorrence, since it reminds her of the fact that she was betrayed. Try it now, say to such a girl, "Thou art consuming thyself," and thou shalt hear her reply, "Oh, no, the torment is precisely this, that I cannot do it."

To despair over oneself, in despair to will to be rid of oneself, is the formula for all despair, and hence the second form of despair (in despair at willing to be oneself) can be followed back to the first (in despair at not willing to be oneself), just as in the foregoing we resolved the first into the second. . . . A despairing man wants despairingly

to be himself. But if he despairingly wants to be himself, he will not want to get rid of himself. Yes, so it seems; but if one inspects more closely, one perceives that after all the contradiction is the same. That self which he despairingly wills to be is a self which he is not (for to will to be that self which one truly is, is indeed the opposite of despair); what he really wills is to tear his self away from the Power which constituted it. But notwithstanding all his despair, this he is unable to do, not withstanding all the efforts of despair, that Power is the stronger, and it compels him to be the self he does not will to be. But for all that he wills to be rid of himself, to be rid of the self which he is, in order to be the self he himself has chanced to choose. To be *self* as he wills to be would be his delight (though in another sense it would be equally in despair), but to be compelled to be *self* as he does not will to be is his torment, namely, that he cannot get rid of himself.

Socrates proved the immortality of the soul from the fact that the sickness of the soul (sin) does not consume it as sickness of the body consumes the body. So also we can demonstrate the eternal in man from the fact that despair cannot consume his self, that this precisely is the torment of contradiction in despair. If there were nothing eternal in a man, he could not despair; but if despair could consume his self, there would still be no despair.

Thus it is that despair, this sickness in the self, is the sickness unto death. The despairing man is mortally ill. In an entirely different sense than can appropriately be said of any disease, we may say that the sickness has attacked the noblest part; and yet the man cannot die. Death is not the last phase of the sickness, but death is continually the last. To be delivered from this sickness by death is an impossibility, for the sickness and its torment . . . and death consist in not being able to die.

This is the situation in despair. And however thoroughly it eludes the attention of the despairer, and however thoroughly the despairer may succeed (as in the case of that kind of despair which is characterized by unawareness of being in despair) in losing himself entirely, and losing himself in such a way that it is not noticed in the least—eternity nevertheless will make it manifest that his situation was despair, and it will so nail him to himself that the torment nevertheless remains that he cannot get rid of himself, and it becomes manifest that he was deluded in thinking that he succeeded. And thus it is eternity must act, because to have a self, to be a self, is the greatest concession made to man, but at the same time it is eternity's demand upon him.

Just as the physician might say that there lives perhaps not one single man who is in perfect health, so one might say perhaps that there lives not one single man who after all is not to some extent in despair, in whose inmost parts there does not dwell a disquietude, a perturbation, a discord, an anxious dread of an unknown something, or of a something he does not even dare to make acquaintance with, dread of a possibility of life, or dread of himself, so that, after all, as physicians speak of a man going about with a disease in him,

this man is going about and carrying a sickness of the spirit, which only rarely and in glimpses, by and with a dread which to him is inexplicable, gives evidence of its presence within. At any rate there has lived no one and there lives no one outside of Christendom who is not in despair, and no one in Christendom, unless he be a true Christian, and if he is not quite that, he is somewhat in despair after all.

This view will doubtless seem to many a paradox, an exaggeration, and a gloomy and depressing view at that. Yet it is nothing of the sort. It is not gloomy; on the contrary, it seeks to throw light upon a subject which ordinarily is left in obscurity. It is not depressing; on the contrary it is uplifting, since it views every man in the aspect of the highest demand made upon him, that he be spirit. Nor is it a paradox; on the contrary, it is a fundamental apprehension consistently carried through, and hence it is no exaggeration. . . .

Not only is despair far more dialectical than an illness, but all its symptoms are dialectical, and for this reason the superficial view is so readily deceived in determining whether despair is present or not. For not to be in despair may mean to be in despair, and it may also mean to be delivered from being in despair. A sense of security and tranquility may mean that one is in despair, precisely this security, this tranquility, may be despair; and it may mean that one has overcome despair and gained peace. In this respect despair is unlike bodily sickness; for not to be sick cannot possibly mean to be sick; but not to be despairing may mean precisely to be despairing. It is not true of despair, as it is of bodily sickness, that the feeling of indisposition is the sickness. By no means. The feeling of indisposition is again dialectical. Never to have been sensible of this indisposition is precisely to be in despair.

This points to the fact, and has its ground therein, that man, regarded as spirit, is always in a critical condition—and if one is to talk of despair, one must conceive of man as spirit. In relation to sickness we talk of a crisis, but not in relation to health. And why not? Because bodily health is an "immediate" qualification, and only becomes dialectical in sickness, when one can speak of the crisis. But spiritually, or when man is regarded as spirit, both health and sickness are critical. There is no such thing as "immediate" health of the spirit. . . .

Therefore it is as far as possible from being true that the vulgar view is right in assuming that despair is a rarity; on the contrary, it is quite universal. It is as far as possible from being true that the vulgar view is right in assuming that everyone who does not think or feel that he is in despair is not so at all, and that only he is in despair who says that he is. On the contrary, one who without affectation says that he is in despair is after all a little bit nearer, a dialectical step nearer to being cured than all those who are not regarded and do not regard themselves as being in despair. But precisely this is the common situation (as the physician of souls will doubtless concede), that the majority of men live without being thoroughly conscious that they are spiritual beings—and to this is referable all the security, contentment with life, etc., etc., which precisely is despair. Those, on the other hand, who say that they are in despair are generally such as have a nature so much more profound that they must become conscious of themselves as spirit, or such as by the hard vicissitudes of life and its dreadful decisions have been helped to become conscious of themselves as spirit—either one or the other, for rare is the man who truly is free from despair.

Ah, so much is said about human want and misery—I seek to understand it, I have also had some acquaintance with it at close range; so much is said about wasted lives—but only that man's life is wasted who lived on, so deceived by the joys of life or by its sorrows that he never became eternally and decisively conscious of himself as spirit, as self, or (what is the same thing) never became aware and in the deepest sense received an impression of the fact that there is a God, and that he, he himself, his self, exists before this God, which gain of infinity is never attained except through despair. And, oh, this misery, that so many live on and are defrauded of this most blessed of all thoughts; this misery, that people employ themselves about everything else, or, as for the masses of men, that people employ them about everything else, utilize them to generate the power for the theater of life, but never remind them of their blessedness; that they heap them in a mass and defraud them, instead of splitting them apart so that they might gain the highest thing, the only thing worth living for, and enough to live in for an eternity—it seems to me that I could weep for an eternity over the fact that such misery exists! And, oh, to my thinking this is one expression the more of the dreadfulness of this most dreadful sickness and misery, namely, its hiddenness—not only that he who suffers from it may wish to hide it and may be able to do so, to the effect that it can so dwell in a man that no one, no one whatever discovers it; no, rather that it can be so hidden in a man that he himself does not know it! And, oh, when the hour-glass has run out, the hour-glass of time, when the noise of worldliness is silenced, and the restless or the ineffectual busyness comes to an end, when everything is still about thee as it is in eternity—whether thou wast man or woman, rich or poor, dependent or independent, fortunate or unfortunate, whether thou didst bear the splendor of the crown in a lofty station, or didst bear only the labor and heat of the day in an inconspicuous lot; whether thy name shall be remembered as long as the world stands (and so was remembered as long as the world stood), or

without a name thou didst cohere as nameless with the countless multitude; whether the glory which surrounded thee surpassed all human description, or the judgment passed upon thee was the most severe and dishonoring human judgment can pass—eternity asks of thee and of every individual among these million millions only one question, whether thou hast lived in despair or not, whether thou wast in despair in such a way that thou didst not know thou wast in despair, or in such a way that thou didst hiddenly carry this sickness in thine inward parts as thy gnawing secret, carry it under thy heart as the fruit of a sinful love, or in such a way that thou, a horror to others, didst rave in despair. And if so, if thou hast lived in despair (whether for the rest thou didst win or lose), then for thee all is lost, eternity knows thee not, it never knew thee, or (even more dreadful) it knows thee as thou art known, it puts thee under arrest by thyself in despair.

EPISTEMOLOGY

The writer of the next selection, Martin Heidegger, has disclaimed the title "existentialist" because the question that concerns him is not human existence but Being in its totality and as such. Yet he continues to be classified with the existentialists because of his approach to the question of Being. He believes this question can be answered only by beginning with the being we can examine—namely, "the being which we ourselves are." Thus we see that, as in the other schools we have examined, existentialism includes a diversity of interests and problems.

In the following essay Heidegger discusses the problem of truth. Traditional definitions of truth center on the idea of correspondence or representation of ideas and objects. But such definitions are primarily of propositional truth, and they also involve difficulties over "representation." Heidegger asks, what can representation mean except: letting something *be* an object to us? If this is done, statements about the object will "right" themselves—and truth is rightness.

For a thing to be revealed and rightness to be possible, there must be freedom. "The essence of truth is freedom," and truth is not, then, originally in the proposition. Freedom is an ex-posing of the nature of what is; truth is a revealing of what is.

But human beings, Heidegger believes, live essentially in error, for the what-is—even and especially of themselves—is not revealed, is not open. Hence their existence is unauthentic and compulsive. To achieve authentic existence, men must live in freedom and truth.

3   The Essence of Truth

Martin Heidegger (1889-   )

What do we ordinarily understand by "truth"? This exalted but at the same time overworked and almost exhausted word "truth" means: that which makes something true into a truth. What is "something true"? We say, for example: "It is a true pleasure to collaborate in the accomplishment of this task." We mean, it is a pure, real joy. The True is the Real. In the same way we speak of "true coin" as distinct from false. False coin is not really what it seems. It is only a "seeming" and therefore unreal. The unreal stands for the opposite of the real. But counterfeit coin too is something real. Hence we say more precisely: "Real coin is genuine coin." Yet both are "real," the counterfeit coin in circulation no less than the genuine. Therefore the truth of the genuine coin cannot be verified by its reality. The question returns: What do "genuine" and "true" mean here? Genuine coin is that real thing whose reality

agrees with (*in der Uebereinstimmung steht mit*) what we always and in advance "really" mean by "coin." Conversely, where we suspect false coin we say: "There is something not quite right here" (*Hier stimmt etwas nicht*). On the other hand we say of something that is "as it should be": "It's right" (*es stimmt*). The *thing* (*Sache*) is right.

We call "true" not only a real pleasure, genuine coin and all actualities of that sort, we also and principally call "true" or "false" our statements concerning such actualities as are themselves true or false in their kind, which may be thus or thus in their reality. A statement is true when what it means and says agrees with the thing of which it speaks. Here too we say: "It's right." Though now it is not the *thing* that is right but the *proposition* (*Satz*).

The True, then, be it a true thing or a true proposition, is that which is right, which corresponds (*das Stimmende*). Being true and truth here mean correspondence, and that in a double sense: firstly the correspondence of a thing with the idea of it as conceived in advance (*dem über sie Vorgemeinten*), and secondly the correspondence of that which

The selection is from Martin Heidegger, "On the Essence of Truth," in Werner Brock (tr.), *Existence and Being* (Chicago: Henry Regnery Co.; London: Vision Press, Ltd., 1949), pp. 321-350, with omissions. Used by permission of the publishers.

is intended by the statement with the thing itself.

The dual aspect of this correspondence is brought out very clearly by the traditional definition of truth: *veritas est adaequatio rei et intellectus.* Which can be taken to mean: truth is the approximation of thing (object) to perception. But it can also mean: truth is the approximation of perception to thing (object). Admittedly the above definition is usually employed only in the formula: *veritas est adaequatio intellectus ad rem.* Yet truth so understood, i.e. *propositional* truth, is only possible on the basis of *objective* truth, the *adaequatio rei ad intellectum.* Both conceptions of the nature of *veritas* always imply "putting oneself right by" (*sich richten nach*) something and thus conceive truth as *rightness* (*Richtigkeit*). . . .

We speak of "agreement" in different senses. We say, for example, seeing two half-crowns lying on the table, that they agree with one another, are like one another. Both agree in identity of appearance. They have this in common and are therefore in this respect alike. Further, we speak of agreement when we say of one of these half-crowns: this coin is round. Here the statement "agrees" with the subject or thing. The relationship now obtains not between thing and thing, but between statement and thing. But in what do statement and thing agree, seeing that the referents are obviously different in appearance? The coin is of metal. The statement is in no sense material. The coin is round. The statement has absolutely nothing spatial about it. With the coin you can buy something. The statement about it can never be legal tender. But despite

the disparity between the two, the above statement agrees with and is true of the coin. And, according to the accepted idea of truth, this agreement is supposed to be an approximation (*Angleichung*). How can something completely unlike —the statement—approximate to the coin? It would have to *become* the coin and present itself entirely in that form. No statement can do that. The moment it succeeded in doing so the statement, as statement, could no longer agree with the thing. In any approximation the statement has to remain, indeed it has first to become, what it is. In what does its nature, so entirely different from any other thing, consist? How can the statement, precisely by insisting on its own nature, approximate to something else, to the thing?

"Approximation" in this instance cannot mean a material likeness between two things unlike in kind. The nature of the approximation is rather determined by the kind of relationship obtaining between statement and thing. So long as this "relationship" remains indeterminate and its nature unfathomed, all argument as to the possibility or impossibility, the kind and degree of approximation, leads nowhere.

The statement about the coin relates "itself" to this thing by representing it and saying of the thing represented "how it is," "what it is like," in whatever respect is important at that moment. The representative statement has its say about the thing represented, stating it to be *such as* it is. This "such-as" (*sowie*) applies to the representation and what it represents. "Representation" means here, if we disregard all "psychological" and "theory of consciousness" preconceptions, *letting something take up a position opposite to us, as an object.* The thing so opposed must, such being its position, come across the open towards us and at the same time stand fast in itself as the thing and manifest itself as a constant. This manifestation of the thing in making a move towards us is accomplished in the open, within the realm of the Overt (*das Offene*), the overt character (*Offenheit*) of which is not initially created by the representation but is only entered into and taken over each time as an area of relationships (*Bezugsbereich*). The relation between representative statement and thing serves to implement that condition (*Verhältnis*) which originally started to vibrate, and now continues to vibrate, as *behavior* (*Verhalten*). But all behavior is characterized by the fact that, obtaining as it does in the open, it must always relate to something manifest *as such* (*ein Offenbares als einsolches*). What is thus, and solely in this narrow sense, made manifest was experienced in the early stages of Western thought as "that which is present" and has long been termed "that which is" (*das Seiende*).

All behavior is "overt" (lit. "stands open": *offen-ständig*) to what-is, and all "overt" relationship is behavior. Man's "overtness" varies with the nature of what-is and the mode of behavior. All working and carrying out of tasks, all transaction and calculation, sustains itself in the open, an overt region within which what-is can expressly take up its stand *as* and *how* it is *what* it is, and thus become capable of expression. This can only occur when what-is represents itself (*selbst vorstellig wird*) with the representative statement, so that the statement submits to a directive enjoin-ing it to express what-is "such-as" or just as it is. By following this directive the statement "rights itself" (*sich richtet nach*) by what-is. Directing itself in this way the statement is right (true). And what is thus stated is rightness (truth).

The statement derives its rightness from the overtness of behavior, for it is only through this that anything manifest can become the criterion for the approximation implicit in the representative statement. Overt behavior must apply this criterion to itself. Which means: it must be for a start something of a criterion for all representation. This is implicit in the overtness of behavior. But if rightness (truth) of statement is only made possible by the overt character of behavior, then it follows that the thing that makes rightness possible in the first place must have a more original claim to be regarded as the essence of truth.

Thus the traditional practice of attributing truth exclusively to the statement as its sole and essential place of origin, falls to the ground. Truth does not possess its original seat in the proposition. At the same time the question arises: on what basis does it become inwardly possible for overt behavior to postulate a criterion—a possibility which alone invests propositional rightness with sufficient status to achieve, in any measure, the essence of truth?

Whence does the representative statement receive its command to "right itself" by the object and thus to be in accord with rightness? Why does this accord (*Stimmen*) at the same time determine (*bestimmen*) the nature of truth? How, in fact, can there be such a thing at all as approximation to pre-established criterion, or a directive enjoining such an accord? Only because this postulate (*Vorgeben*) has already freed itself (*sich freigegeben hat*) and become open to a manifestation operating in this openness—a manifestation which is binding on all representation whatsoever. This "freeing" for the sake of submitting to a binding criterion is only possible as freedom to reveal something already overt (*zum Offenbaren eines Offenen*). Being free in this way points to the hitherto uncomprehended nature of freedom. The overt character of behavior in the sense that it makes rightness a possibility, is grounded in freedom. *The essence of truth is freedom. . . .*

But to turn truth into freedom—is that not to abandon truth to the caprice of man? Can truth be more basically undetermined than by being delivered up to the whim of this wavering reed? The thing that has forced itself time and again on our sound judgment during the course of this exposition so far, now becomes all the more evident: truth is brought down to the subjective level of the human subject. Even if this subject can attain to some kind of objectivity, it still remains human in its subjectivity and subject to human control.

Admittedly, guile and dissimulation, lies and deception, fraud and pretense, in short, all manner of untruth, are ascribed to man. But untruth is the opposite of truth, for which reason it is, as the very negation of truth, its "disessence" rightly kept at a remove from the field of enquiry into the pure essence of truth. This human origin of untruth merely confirms by contrast the essential nature of truth "as such" which holds

sway "over" man and which metaphysics regard as something imperishable and eternal, something that can never be founded on the transitoriness and fragility of humankind. How then can the essence of truth possibly have a stable basis in human freedom?

Resistance to the proposition that the essence of truth is freedom is rooted in prejudices, the most obstinate of which contends that freedom is a property of man and that the nature of freedom neither needs nor allows of further questioning. As for man, we all know what *he* is.

The indication, however, of the essential connection between truth *as rightness,* and freedom, shatters these preconceived notions, provided of course that we are prepared to change our way of thinking. Consideration of the natural affinity between truth and freedom induces us to pursue the question as to the nature of man in one of its aspects —an aspect vouched for by our experience of a hidden ground in man's nature and being, so that we are transported in advance into the original living realm of truth. But at this point it also becomes evident that freedom is the basis of the inner possibility of rightness only because it receives its own essence from that thing of earlier origin: the uniquely essential truth.

Freedom was initially defined as freedom for the revelation of something already overt. How are we to think of the essence of freedom so conceived? The Manifest (*das Offenbare*), to which a representative statement approximates in its rightness, is that which obviously "is" all the time and has some manifest form of behavior. The freedom to reveal something overt lets whatever "is" at the moment *be* what it is. Freedom reveals itself as the "letting-be" of what-is.

We usually talk of "letting be" when, for instance, we stand off from some undertaking we have planned. "We let it be" means: not touching it again, not having anything more to do with it. "Letting be" here has the negative sense of disregarding something, renouncing something, of indifference and even neglect.

The phrase we are now using, namely the "letting-be" of what-is, does not, however, refer to indifference and neglect, but to the very opposite of them. To let something be (*Seinlassen*) is in fact to have something to do with it (*sich einlassen auf*). This is not to be taken merely in the sense of pursuing, conserving, cultivating and planning some actuality casually met with or sought out. To let what-is *be* what it is means participating in something overt and its overtness, in which everything that "is" takes up its position and which entails such overtness. Western thought at its outset conceived this overtness as τὰ ἀληθέα, the Unconcealed. If we "translate ἀλήθεια by "unconcealment" or "revealment" instead of truth, the translation is not only more "literal" but it also requires us to revise our ordinary idea of truth in the sense of propositional correctitude and trace it back to that still uncomprehended quality: the revealedness (*Entborgenheit*) and revelation (*Entbergung*) of what-is. Participation in the revealed nature of what-is does not stop there, it develops into a retirement before it so that what-is may reveal itself as *what* and *how* it is,

and the approximation which represents it in the statement may take it for a criterion. In this manner "letting-be" exposes itself (*setzt sich aus*) to what-is-as-such and brings all behavior into the open (*versetzt ins Offene*). "Letting-be", i.e. freedom, is in its own self "exposing" (*aus-setzend*) and "ex-sistent" (*ek-sistent*).

The nature of freedom, seen from the point of view of the nature of truth, now shows itself as an "exposition" into the revealed nature of what-is.

Freedom is not what common sense is content to let pass under that name: the random ability to do as we please, to go this way or that in our choice. Freedom is not license in what we do or do not do. Nor, on the other hand, is freedom a mere readiness to do something requisite and necessary—and thus in a sense "actual" (*Seiendes*). Over and above all this ("negative" and "positive" freedom) freedom is a participation in the revealment of what-is-as-such (*das Seiende als ein solches*). The revelation of this is itself guaranteed in that ex-sistent participation whereby the overtness of the overt (*die Offenheit des Offenen*), i.e. the "There" (*Da*) of it, *is* what it is.

In this Da-sein there is preserved for mankind that long unfathomed and essential basis on which man is able to ex-sist. "Existence" in this case does not signify *existentia* in the sense of the "occurrence" (*Vorkommen*) and "being" (*Dasein*), i.e. "presence" (*Vorhandensein*) of an "existent" (*eines Seienden*). Nor does "existence" mean, "existentially" speaking, man's moral preoccupation with himself—a preoccupation arising out of his psycho-physical constitution. Ex-sistence, grounded in truth as freedom, is nothing less than exposition into the revealed nature of what-is-as-such. Still unfathomed and not even conscious of the need for any deeper fathoming of its essence, the ex-sistence of historical man begins at that moment when the first thinker to ask himself about the revealed nature of what-is, poses the question: What is what-is? With this question uncon-cealment and revealment are experi-enced for the first time. . . .

But if ex-sistent *Da-sein*, understood as the letting-be of what-is, sets man free for his "freedom" which confronts him, then and only then, with a choice between actual possibilities and which imposes actual necessities upon him, then freedom is not governed by human inclination. Man does not "possess" freedom as a property, it is the contrary that is true: freedom, or ex-sistent, revelatory *Da-sein* possesses man and moreover in so original a manner that it alone confers upon him that relationship with what-is-in-totality which is the basis and distinctive characteristic of his history. Only ex-sistent man is historical. "Nature" has no history.

Freedom, so understood as the let-ting-be of what-is, fulfils and perfects the nature of truth in the sense that truth is the unconcealment and reveal-ment of what-is. "Truth" is not the mark of some correct proposition made by a human "subject" in respect of an "object" and which then—in precisely what sphere we do not know—counts as "true"; truth is rather the revelation of what-is, a revelation through which something "overt" comes into force. All human behavior is an exposition into that overtness. Hence man *is* in virtue of his ex-sistence.

Because all modes of human behavior (*Verhalten*) are, each in its own way, overt and always relate to that which they must (*wozu es sich verhält*), it fol-lows that the restraint (*Verhaltenheit*) of "letting things be," i.e. freedom, must necessarily have given man an inner directive to approximate his ideas (rep-resentations: *Vorstellen*) to what-is at any moment. Man ex-sists, and this now means: historical man has his history and all its possibilities guaranteed him in the revelation of what-is-in-totality. The manner in which the original nature of truth operates (*west*) gives rise to the rare and simple decisions of history.

But because truth is in essence free-dom, historical man, though he lets things be, cannot really let what-is be just *what* it is and *as* it is. What-is is then covered up and distorted. Illusion comes into its own. The essential nega-tion of truth, its "dis-essence" (*Un-wesen*), makes its appearance. But because ex-sistent freedom, being the essence of truth, is not a property of man (it being rather the case that man only ex-sists as the property of this freedom and so becomes capable of history), it follows that the dis-essence of truth can-not, in its turn, simply arise *a posteriori* from the mere incapacity and negligence of man. On the contrary, untruth must derive from the essence of truth. Only because truth and untruth are not *in essence* indifferent to one another, can a true proposition contrast so sharply with its correspondingly untrue proposi-tion. Our quest for the nature of truth only extends into the original realm of interrogation when, having gained a pre-liminary insight into the complete essence of truth, we now include a con-sideration of untruth in the revelation of "essence." The enquiry into the dis-essence of truth is not a subsequent filling of the gap; it is the decisive step towards any adequate posing of the question as to the nature of truth. Yet, how are we to conceive truth's dis-essence as part of its essence? If the essence of truth is not fully displayed into the rightness of a statement, then neither can untruth be equated with the wrongness of an opinion. . . .

Man errs. He does not merely fall into error, he lives in error always because, by ex-sisting, he in-sists and is thus already in error. The error in which he lives is not just something that runs along besides him like a ditch, something he occasionally falls into. No, error is part of the inner structure of *Da-sein*, in which historical man is involved. Error is the theatre for that variable mode of being (*Wende*) where in-sistent ex-sistence, turning and turning about, perpetually forgets and mistakes itself. The dissimulation of what-is concealed in totality comes into force through the revelation of what-is at any moment, and this revelation, because it is a forgetting of the dissimulation, leads to error.

Error is the essential counter-essence (*das wesentliche Gegenwesen*) of the original essence of truth. It opens out as the manifest theatre for all counter-play to essential truth. Error is the open ground, the basis of Wrong (*Irrtum*). Wrong is not just the isolated mistake, it is the empire, the whole history of all the complicated and intricate ways of erring.

All modes of behavior have, according to their overtness and correlation to what-is-in-totality, each their way of erring. Wrong ranges from the com-monest mistake, oversight, miscalculation to going astray and getting utterly lost when it comes to adopting important attitudes and making essential decisions. What we ordinarily understand by "wrong" and moreover, according to the teachings of philosophy—namely the wrongness (*Unrichtigheit*) of a judgment and the falseness of perception, is only one, and that the most superficial, way of erring. The error in which historical man must always walk, which makes his road erratic (*irrig*) is essentially one with the manifest character of what-is. Error dominates man through and through by leading him astray. But, by this self-same aberration (*Beirrung*), error collaborates in the possibility which man has (and can always extract from his ex-sistence) of *not allowing* himself to be led astray, of himself experiencing error and thus not overlooking the mystery of *Da-sein*.

Because man's in-sistent ex-sistence leads to error, and because error always oppresses in one way or another and out of this oppression becomes capable of commanding the mystery, albeit forgotten, it follows that man in his *Da-sein* is *especially* subject to the rule of mystery and his own affliction. Between them, *he lives in an extremity of compulsion.* The total essence of truth, which contains in its own self its "dis-essence," keeps *Da-sein* ever turning this way and that but always into misery. *Da-sein* is, in fact, a turning to misery, a turning into need. From man's *Da-sein* and from this alone comes the revelation of necessity and, as a result, the possibility of turning this necessity into something *needed*, something unavoidable. . . .

The present essay leads the question

concerning the nature of truth beyond the accustomed confines of our fundamental ideas and helps us to consider whether this question of the essence of truth is not at the same time necessarily the question of the truth of essence. Philosophy, however, conceives "essence" as Being. By tracing the inner possibility of a statement's "rightness" back to the ex-sistent freedom of "letting-be" as the very basis of that statement, and by suggesting that the essential core of this basis is to be found in dissimulation and error, we may have indicated that the nature of truth is not just the empty, "general" character of some "abstract" commonplace, but something that is unique in history (itself unique): the self-dissimulation of the unveiling of the "meaning" of what we call "Being," which we have long been accustomed to think of only as "what-is-in-totality."

METAPHYSICS

Existentialists show a unity of philosophical concern in their belief that man's nature or essence can be found only in his concrete, lived experience. In the lecture from which the following selection is taken, the French philosopher Jean-Paul Sartre develops this belief in terms of the statement, "existence precedes essence." There has been much discussion of this view, and there is disagreement over it even among existentialists. The lecture itself shows signs of being a public lecture rather than a careful essay (Jaspers, for example, is mistakenly referred to as a Catholic). Yet Sartre's statement remains a brilliant and incisive summary of his fundamental position.

To say that existence precedes essence means that man first appears and only later defines himself in his experience. There being no antecedent essence to which he must conform, man is both free and responsible for the definition he produces. In his freedom, man exists outside and beyond himself or his essence, and this in fact is existence. Sartre's version of existentialism is an effort to draw all the consequences of an atheistic position; though men experience anguish, forlornness, and despair in their existing, Sartre says that even if God existed, nothing would change.

4 Essence and Existence

Jean-Paul Sartre (1905-   )

Most people who use the word [existentialism] would be rather embarrassed if they had to explain it, since, now that the word is all the rage, even the work of a musician or painter is being called existentialist. A gossip columnist in

The selection is from Jean-Paul Sartre, "Existentialism," in *Existentialism and Human Emotions* (tr. Bernard Frechtman) (New York: Philosophical Library, 1957), pp. 12-51, with omissions. Used by permission of the publisher.

Clartés signs himself *The Existentialist,* so that by this time the word has been so stretched and has taken on so broad a meaning, that it no longer means anything at all. It seems that for want of an advance-guard doctrine analogous to surrealism, the kind of people who are eager for scandal and flurry turn to this philosophy which in other respects does not at all serve their purposes in this sphere.

Actually, it is the least scandalous, the most austere of doctrines. It is intended strictly for specialists and philosophers. Yet it can be defined easily. What complicates matters is that there are two kinds of existentialist; first, those who are Christian, among whom I would include Jaspers and Gabriel Marcel, both Catholic; and on the other hand the atheistic existentialists, among whom I class Heidegger, and then the French existentialists and myself. What they have in common is that they think that existence precedes essence, or, if you prefer, that subjectivity must be the starting point.

Just what does that mean? Let us consider some object that is manufactured, for example, a book or a paper-cutter: here is an object which has been made by an artisan whose inspiration came from a concept. He referred to the concept of what a paper-cutter is and likewise to a known method of production, which is part of the concept, something which is, by and large, a routine. Thus, the paper-cutter is at once an object produced in a certain way and, on the other hand, one having a specific use; and one can not postulate a man who produces a paper-cutter but does not know what it is used for. Therefore, let us say that, for the paper-

cutter, essence—that is, the ensemble of both the production routines and the properties which enable it to be both produced and defined—precedes existence. Thus, the presence of the paper-cutter or book in front of me is determined. Therefore, we have here a technical view of the world whereby it can be said that production precedes existence.

When we conceive God as the Creator, He is generally thought of as a superior sort of artisan. Whatever doctrine we may be considering, whether one like that of Descartes or that of Leibnitz, we always grant that will more or less follows understanding or, at the very least, accompanies it, and that when God creates He knows exactly what He is creating. Thus, the concept of man in the mind of God is comparable to the concept of paper-cutter in the mind of the manufacturer, and, following certain techniques and a conception, God produces man, just as the artisan, following a definition and a technique, makes a paper-cutter. Thus, the individual man is the realization of a certain concept in the divine intelligence.

In the eighteenth century, the atheism of the *philosophes* discarded the idea of God, but not so much for the notion that essence precedes existence. To a certain extent, this idea is found everywhere; we find it in Diderot, in Voltaire, and even in Kant. Man has a human nature; this human nature, which is the concept of the human, is found in all men, which means that each man is a particular example of a universal concept, man. In Kant, the result of this universality is that the wild-man, the natural man, as well as the bourgeois, are circumscribed by the same definition and have the same basic qualities. Thus, here too the essence of man precedes the historical existence that we find in nature.

Atheistic existentialism, which I represent, is more coherent. It states that if God does not exist, there is at least one being in whom existence precedes essence, a being who exists before he can be defined by any concept, and that this being is man, or, as Heidegger says, human reality. What is meant here by saying that existence precedes essence? It means that, first of all, man exists, turns up, appears on the scene, and, only afterwards, defines himself. If man, as the existentialist conceives him, is indefinable, it is because at first he is nothing. Only afterward will he be something, and he himself will have made what he will be. Thus, there is no human nature, since there is no God to conceive it. Not only is man what he conceives himself to be, but he is also only what he wills himself to be after this thrust toward existence.

Man is nothing else but what he makes of himself. Such is the first principle of existentialism. It is also what is called subjectivity, the name we are labeled with when charges are brought against us. But what do we mean by this, if not that man has a greater dignity than a stone or table? For we mean that man first exists, that is, that man first of all is the being who hurls himself toward a future and who is conscious of imagining himself as being in the future. Man is at the start a plan which is aware of itself, rather than a patch of moss, a piece of garbage, or a cauliflower; nothing exists prior to this plan; there is nothing in heaven; man will be what he will have planned to be.

Not what he will want to be. Because by the word "will" we generally mean a conscious decision, which is subsequent to what we have already made of ourselves. I may want to belong to a political party, write a book, get married; but all that is only a manifestation of an earlier, more spontaneous choice that is called "will." But if existence really does precede essence, man is responsible for what he is. Thus, existentialism's first move is to make every man aware of what he is and to make the full responsibility of his existence rest on him. And when we say that a man is responsible for himself, we do not only mean that he is responsible for his own individuality, but that he is responsible for all men.

The word subjectivism has two meanings, and our opponents play on the two. Subjectivism means, on the one hand, that an individual chooses and makes himself; and, on the other, that it is impossible for man to transcend human subjectivity. The second of these is the essential meaning of existentialism. When we say that man chooses his own self, we mean that every one of us does likewise; but we also mean by that that in making this choice he also chooses all men. In fact, in creating the man that we want to be, there is not a single one of our acts which does not at the same time create an image of man as we think he ought to be. To choose to be this or that is to affirm at the same time the value of what we choose, because we can never choose evil. We always choose the good, and nothing can be good for us without being good for all.

If, on the other hand, existence precedes essence, and if we grant that we exist and fashion our image at one and the same time, the image is valid for everybody and for our whole age. Thus, our responsibility is much greater than we might have supposed, because it involves all mankind. If I am a working-man and choose to join a Christian trade-union rather than be a communist, and if by being a member I want to show that the best thing for man is resignation, that the kingdom of man is not of this world, I am not only involving my own case—I want to be resigned for everyone. As a result, my action has involved all humanity. To take a more individual matter, if I want to marry, to have children; even if this marriage depends solely on my own circumstances or passion or wish, I am involving all humanity in monogamy and not merely myself. Therefore, I am responsible for myself and for everyone else. I am creating a certain image of man of my own choosing. In choosing myself, I choose man.

This helps us understand what the actual content is of such rather grandiloquent words as anguish, forlornness, despair. As you will see, it's all quite simple.

First, what is meant by anguish? The existentialists say at once that man is anguish. What that means is this: the man who involves himself and who realizes that he is not only the person he chooses to be, but also a lawmaker who is, at the same time, choosing all mankind as well as himself, can not help escape the feeling of his total and deep responsibility. Of course, there are many people who are not anxious; but we claim that they are hiding their anxiety, that they are fleeing from it. Certainly, many people believe that when

they do something, they themselves are the only ones involved, and when someone says to them, "What if everyone acted that way?" they shrug their shoulders and answer, "Everyone doesn't act that way." But really, one should always ask himself, "What would happen if everybody looked at things that way?" There is no escaping this disturbing thought except by a kind of double-dealing. A man who lies and makes excuses for himself by saying "not everybody does that," is someone with an uneasy conscience, because the act of lying implies that a universal value is conferred upon the lie.

Anguish is evident even when it conceals itself. This is the anguish that Kierkegaard called the anguish of Abraham. You know the story: an angel has ordered Abraham to sacrifice his son; if it really were an angel who has come and said, "You are Abraham, you shall sacrifice your son," everything would be all right. But everyone might first wonder, "Is it really an angel, and am I really Abraham? What proof do I have?"

There was a madwoman who had hallucinations; someone used to speak to her on the telephone and give her orders. Her doctor asked her, "Who is it who talks to you?" She answered, "He says it's God." What proof did she really have that it was God? If an angel comes to me, what proof is there that it's an angel? And if I hear voices, what proof is there that they come from heaven and not from hell, or from the subconscious, or a pathological condition? What proves that they are addressed to me? What proof is there that I have been appointed to impose my choice and my conception of man on humanity? I'll never find any proof or sign to convince me of that. If a voice addresses me, it is always for me to decide that this is the angel's voice; if I consider that such an act is a good one, it is I who will choose to say that it is good rather than bad.

Now, I'm not being singled out as an Abraham, and yet at every moment I'm obliged to perform exemplary acts. For every man, everything happens as if all mankind had its eyes fixed on him and were guiding itself by what he does. And every man ought to say to himself, "Am I really the kind of man who has the right to act in such a way that humanity might guide itself by my actions?" And if he does not say that to himself, he is masking his anguish. . . .

When we speak of forlornness, a term Heidegger was fond of, we mean only that God does not exist and that we have to face all the consequences of this. The existentialist is strongly opposed to a certain kind of secular ethics which would like to abolish God with the least possible expense. About 1880, some French teachers tried to set up a secular ethics which went something like this: God is a useless and costly hypothesis; we are discarding it; but, meanwhile, in order for there to be an ethics, a society, a civilization, it is essential that certain values be taken seriously and that they be considered as having an *a priori* existence. It must be obligatory, *a priori,* to be honest, not to lie, not to beat your wife, to have children, etc., etc. So we're going to try a little device which will make it possible to show that values exist all the same, inscribed in a heaven of ideas, though otherwise God does not exist. In other words—and this, I believe, is the tendency of everything called reformism in France—nothing will be changed if God does not exist. We shall find ourselves with the same norms of honesty, progress, and humanism, and we shall have made of God an outdated hypothesis which will peacefully die off by itself.

The existentialist, on the contrary, thinks it very distressing that God does not exist, because all possibility of finding values in a heaven of ideas disappears along with Him; there can no longer be an *a priori* Good, since there is no infinite and perfect consciousness to think it. Nowhere is it written that the Good exists, that we must be honest, that we must not lie; because the fact is we are on a plane where there are only men. Dostoievsky said, "If God didn't exist, everything would be possible." That is the very starting point of existentialism. Indeed, everything is permissible if God does not exist, and as a result man is forlorn, because neither within him nor without does he find anything to cling to. He can't start making excuses for himself.

If existence really does precede essence, there is no explaining things away by reference to a fixed and given human nature. In other words, there is no determinism, man is free, man is freedom. On the other hand, if God does not exist, we find no values or commands to turn to which legitimize our conduct. So, in the bright realm of values, we have no excuse behind us, nor justification before us. We are alone, with no excuses.

That is the idea I shall try to convey when I say that man is condemned to be free. Condemned, because he did not create himself, in other respects is free; because, once thrown into the world, he is responsible for everything he does. The existentialist does not believe in the power of passion. He will never agree that a sweeping passion is a ravaging torrent which fatally leads a man to certain acts and is therefore an excuse. He thinks that man is responsible for his passion.

The existentialist does not think that man is going to help himself by finding in the world some omen by which to orient himself. Because he thinks that man will interpret the omen to suit himself. Therefore, he thinks that man, with no support and no aid, is condemned every moment to invent man. Ponge, in a very fine article, has said, "Man is the future of man." That's exactly it. But if it is taken to mean that this future is recorded in heaven, that God sees it, then it is false, because it would really no longer be a future. If it is taken to mean that, whatever a man may be, there is a future to be forged, a virgin future before him, then this remark is sound. But then we are forlorn. . . .

As for despair, the term has a very simple meaning. It means that we shall confine ourselves to reckoning only with what depends upon our will, or on the ensemble of probabilities which make our action possible. When we want something, we always have to reckon with probabilities. I may be counting on the arrival of a friend. The friend is coming by rail or street-car; this supposes that the train will arrive on schedule, or that the street-car will not jump the track. I am left in the realm of possibility; but possibilities are to be reckoned with only to the point where my action comports with the ensemble of these possibilities, and no further. The moment the possibilities I am consider-

ing are not rigorously involved by my action, I ought to disengage myself from them, because no God, no scheme, can adapt the world and its possibilities to my will. When Descartes said, "Conquer yourself rather than the world," he meant essentially the same thing. . . .

At heart, what existentialism shows is the connection between the absolute character of free involvement, by virtue of which every man realizes himself in realizing a type of mankind, an involvement always comprehensible in any age whatsoever and by any person whosoever, and the relativeness of the cultural ensemble which may result from such a choice; it must be stressed that the relativity of Cartesianism and the absolute character of Cartesian involvement go together. In this sense, you may, if you like, say that each of us performs an absolute act in breathing, eating, sleeping, or behaving in any way whatever. There is no difference between being free, like a configuration, like an existence which chooses its essence, and being absolute. There is no difference between being an absolute temporarily localized, that is, localized in history, and being universally comprehensible. . . .

Man is constantly outside of himself; in projecting himself, in losing himself outside of himself, he makes for man's existing; and, on the other hand, it is by pursuing transcendent goals that he is able to exist; man, being this state of passing-beyond, and seizing upon things only as they bear upon this passing-beyond, is at the heart, at the center of this passing-beyond. There is no universe other than a human universe, the universe of human subjectivity. This connection between transcendency, as a constituent element of man—not in the sense that God is transcendent, but in the sense of passing beyond—and subjectivity, in the sense that man is not closed in on himself but is always present in a human universe, is what we call existentialist humanism. Humanism, because we remind man that there is no law-maker other than himself, and that in his forlornness he will decide by himself; because we point out that man will fulfill himself as man, not in turning toward himself, but in seeking outside of himself a goal which is just this liberation, just this particular fulfillment.

From these few reflections it is evident that nothing is more unjust than the objections that have been raised against us. Existentialism is nothing else than an attempt to draw all the consequences of a coherent atheistic position. It isn't trying to plunge man into despair at all. But if one calls every attitude of unbelief despair, like the Christians, then the word is not being used in its original sense. Existentialism isn't so atheistic that it wears itself out showing that God doesn't exist. Rather, it declares that even if God did exist, that would change nothing. There you've got our point of view. Not that we believe that God exists, but we think that the problem of His existence is not the issue. In this sense existentialism is optimistic, a doctrine of action, and it is plain dishonesty for Christians to make no distinction between their own despair and ours and then to call us despairing.

ETHICS

The "existential experience" with its loss of meaning and its general nihilism is present in the ethical as well as in all other dimensions of experience. One of the greatest diagnosticians of this nihilism is Friedrich Nietzsche, a thinker whose influence on present existentialism was tremendous. Nietzsche saw Western culture with its science, technology, mass society, and nationalism as tending to create a complete fear of individuality and an absence of meaning and value. He expresses this observation poignantly in his statement, "God is dead, and we have killed him." No belief in an objective moral order, that is, is possible in modern society because of the very activities and institutions that it has produced. But how, then, are meaning and ethical value to be achieved? Nietzsche's answer is, only by the deliberate, creative willing of value by strong personalities. These creators he called *Uebermenschen*.

The following selections expand these themes of existentialist as well as ethical interest. Nietzsche's style is aphoristic but very moving. The individual, the value of honesty or subjective truth, master or creative morality, men who by rejecting the conventional, the dishonest, the mass, and all that subdues individual existence prepare for the *Uebermenschen*: such ideas are clearly developments of the existential experience, and they place Nietzsche within the existentialist position.

5 A New Ethics

Friedrich Nietzsche (1844-1900)

[*The Will to Truth*.] The Will to Truth, which is to tempt us to many a hazardous enterprise, the famous Truthfulness of which all philosophers have hitherto spoken with respect, what questions has this Will to Truth not laid before us! What strange, perplexing, questionable questions! It is already a long story; yet it seems as if it were hardly commenced. Is it any wonder if we at last grow distrustful, lose patience, and turn impatiently away? That this Sphinx teaches us at last to ask questions ourselves? *Who* is it really that puts questions to us here? *What* really is this "Will to Truth" in us? In fact we made a long halt at the question as to the origin of this Will—until at last we came to an absolute standstill before a yet more fundamental question. We inquired about the *value* of this Will. Granted that we want the truth: *why not rather* untruth? And uncertainty? Even ignorance? The problem of the value of truth presented itself before us—or was it we

who presented ourselves before the problem? Which of us is the Œdipus here? Which the Sphinx? It would seem to be a rendezvous of questions and notes of interrogation. And could it be believed that it at last seems to us as if the problem had never been propounded before, as if we were the first to discern it, get a sight of it, and *risk raising* it? For there is risk in raising it; perhaps there is no greater risk. . . .

[*Master and Slave Morality*.] In a tour through the many finer and coarser moralities which have hitherto prevailed or still prevail on the earth, I found certain traits recurring regularly together, and connected with one another, until finally two primary types revealed themselves to me, and a radical distinction was brought to light. There is *master-morality* and *slave-morality;*—I would at once add, however, that in all higher and mixed civilizations, there are also attempts at the reconciliation of the two moralities; but one finds still oftener the confusion and mutual misunderstanding of them, indeed, sometimes their close juxtaposition—even in the same man, within one soul. The distinctions of moral values have either originated in a ruling caste, pleasantly conscious of being different from the ruled—or among the ruled class, the slaves and dependents of all sorts. In the first case, when it is the rulers who determine the conception "good," it is the exalted, proud disposition which is regarded as the distinguishing feature, and that

The selection, except the last three sections, is from Friedrich Nietzsche, *Beyond Good and Evil* (tr. Helen Zimmern) (London: George Allen & Unwin, Ltd.; New York: The Macmillan Company, 1907), pp. 5-6, 227-232, and 8-9. Used by permission of George Allen & Unwin, Ltd. The next to last paragraph before the numbered sections is from *The Dawn of Day* (tr. Johanna Volz) (New York: The Macmillan Company, 1903), p. 170. The last paragraph has been translated from *Die fröhliche Wissenschaft* (Leipzig: C. G. Naumann, 1900), pp. 214-215. The numbered sections have been translated from "Von alten und neuen Tafeln," *Also Sprach Zarathustra* (Leipzig: C. G. Naumann, 1904), pp. 287-291.

which determines the order of rank. The noble type of man separates from himself the beings in whom the opposite of this exalted, proud disposition displays itself: he despises them. Let it at once be noted that in this first kind of morality the antithesis "good" and "bad" means practically the same as "noble" and "despicable";—the antithesis "good" and *"evil"* is of a different origin. The cowardly, the timid, the insignificant, and those thinking merely of narrow utility are despised; moreover, also, the distrustful, with their constrained glances, the self-abasing, the dog-like kind of men who let themselves be abused, the mendicant flatterers, and above all the liars:—it is a fundamental belief of all aristocrats that the common people are untruthful. "We truthful ones"—the nobility in ancient Greece called themselves. It is obvious that everywhere the designations of moral value were at first applied to *men,* and were only derivatively and at a later period applied to *actions*; it is a gross mistake, therefore, when historians of morals start with questions like, "Why have sympathetic actions been praised?" The noble type of man regards *himself* as a determiner of values; he does not require to be approved of; he passes the judgment: "What is injurious to me is injurious in itself"; he knows that it is he himself only who confers honor on things; he is a *creator of values.* He honors whatever he recognizes in himself: such morality is self-glorification. In the foreground there is the feeling of plenitude, of power, which seeks to overflow, the happiness of high tension, the consciousness of a wealth which would fain give and bestow:—the noble man also helps the unfortunate, but not —or scarcely—out of pity, but rather from an impulse generated by the superabundance of power. The noble man honors in himself the powerful one, him also who has power over himself, who knows how to speak and how to keep silence, who takes pleasure in subjecting himself to severity and hardness, and has reverence for all that is severe and hard. "Wotan placed a hard heart in my breast," says an old Scandinavian Saga: it is thus rightly expressed from the soul of a proud Viking. Such a type of man is even proud of *not* being made for sympathy; the hero of the Saga therefore adds warningly: "He who has not a hard heart when young, will never have one." The noble and brave who think thus are the furthest removed from the morality which sees precisely in sympathy, or in acting for the good of others, or in *désintéressement,* the characteristic of the moral; faith in oneself, pride in oneself, a radical enmity and irony towards "selflessness," belong as definitely to noble morality, as do a careless scorn and precaution in presence of sympathy and the "warm heart." —It is the powerful who *know* how to honor, it is their art, their domain for invention. The profound reverence for age and for tradition—all law rests on this double reverence,—the belief and prejudice in favor of ancestors and unfavorable to newcomers, is typical in the morality of the powerful; and if, reversely, men of "modern ideas" believe almost instinctively in "progress" and the "future," and are more and more lacking in respect for old age, the ignoble origin of these "ideas" has complacently betrayed itself thereby. A morality of the ruling class, however, is more especially foreign and irritating to present-day taste in the sternness of its principle that one has duties only to one's equals; that one may act towards beings of a lower rank, towards all that is foreign, just as seems good to one, or "as the heart desires," and in any case "beyond good and evil": it is here that sympathy and similar sentiments can have a place. The ability and obligation to exercise prolonged gratitude and prolonged revenge—both only within the circle of equals,—artfulness in retaliation, *raffinement* of the idea in friendship a certain necessity to have enemies (as outlets for the emotions of envy, quarrelsomeness, arrogance—in fact, in order to be a good *friend*): all these are typical characteristics of the noble morality, which, as has been pointed out, is not the morality of "modern ideas," and is therefore at present difficult to realize, and also to unearth and disclose.—It is otherwise with the second type of morality, *slave-morality*. Supposing that the abused, the oppressed, the suffering, the unemancipated, the weary, and those uncertain of themselves, should moralize, what will be the common element in their moral estimates? Probably a pessimistic suspicion with regard to the entire situation of man will find expression, perhaps a condemnation of man, together with his situation. The slave has an unfavorable eye for the virtues of the powerful; he has a skepticism and distrust, a *refinement* of distrust of everything "good" that is there honored —he would fain persuade himself that the very happiness there is not genuine. On the other hand, *those* qualities which serve to alleviate the existence of sufferers are brought into prominence and flooded with light; it is here that sympathy, the kind, helping hand, the warm heart, patience, diligence, humility, and friendliness attain to honor; for here these are the most useful qualities, and almost the only means of supporting the burden of existence. Slave-morality is essentially the morality of utility. Here is the seat of the origin of the famous antithesis "good" and *"evil"*: —power and dangerousness are assumed to reside in the evil, a certain dreadfulness, subtlety, and strength, which do not admit of being despised. According to slave-morality, therefore, the "evil" man arouses fear; according to master-morality, it is precisely the "good" man who arouses fear and seeks to arouse it, while the bad man is regarded as the despicable being. The contrast attains its maximum when, in accordance with the logical consequences of slave-morality, a shade of depreciation—it may be slight and well-intentioned—at last attaches itself to the "good" man of this morality; because, according to the servile mode of thought, the good man must in any case be the *safe* man: he is good-natured, easily deceived, perhaps a little stupid, *un bonhomme*. Everywhere that slave-morality gains the ascendancy, language shows a tendency to approximate the significations of the words "good" and "stupid."—At last fundamental difference: the desire for *freedom,* the instinct for happiness and the refinements of the feeling of liberty belong as necessarily to slave-morals and morality, as artifice and enthusiasm in reverence and devotion are the regular symptoms of an aristocratic mode of thinking and estimating.—Hence we can understand without further detail why love *as a passion*—it is our European specialty

—must absolutely be of noble origin; as is well known, its invention is due to the Provençal poet-cavaliers, those brilliant ingenious men of the *"gai saber"* to whom Europe owes so much, and almost owes itself.

[*Beyond Good and Evil*] The falseness of an opinion is not for us any objection to it: it is here, perhaps, that our new language sounds most strangely. The question is, how far an opinion is life-furthering, life-preserving, species-preserving, perhaps species-rearing; and we are fundamentally inclined to maintain that the falsest opinions (to which the synthetic judgments *a priori* belong), are the most indispensable to us; that without a recognition of logical fictions, without a comparison of reality with the purely *imagined* world of the absolute and immutable, without a constant counterfeiting of the world by means of numbers, man could not live—that the renunciation of false opinions would be a renunciation of life, a negation of life. *To recognize untruth as a* condition of life: that is certainly to impugn the traditional ideas of value in a dangerous manner, and a philosophy which ventures to do so, has thereby alone placed itself beyond good and evil.

The Panegyrists of Work In the glorification of work, in the incessant chatter about the "blessings of work," I discover the same secret thought as in the praise of the benevolent, impersonal actions, namely, the dread of the individual. At the sight of work—which always implies that severe toil from morning till night—we really feel that such work is the best police, that it keeps everybody in bounds, and effectually

checks the development of reason, of covetousness, of a desire after independence. For it consumes an enormous amount of nervous force, withdrawing it from reflection, brooding, dreaming, care, love, hatred; it always dangles a small object before the eye, affording easy and regular gratifications. Thus a society in which hard work is constantly being performed will enjoy greater security, and security is now worshipped as the supreme deity. And now! Oh horror! the very "workman" has grown dangerous! the world is swarming with "dangerous individuals"! And in their train follows the danger of all dangers—the individual.

Pioneering Men I welcome all signs that a more manly, warlike age is about to begin which, above all, will again bring honor to valor! For it shall prepare the way for a higher age and gather the strength which this higher age will someday need—that age, which shall bear heroism into knowledge and *wage wars* for the sake of ideas and their consequences. For this there is now needed many pioneering valorous men, who cannot spring up out of nothing—any more than out of sand and filth of our present civilization and its metropolitanism: men who understand how to be silent, solitary, resolute, content and steadfast in imperceptible activity: men who then with inner inclination seek after that which is to be *overcome* in them: men in whom cheerfulness, patience, unpretentiousness, and contempt for all great vanities are just as much part of them as magnanimity in victory and forbearance toward the small vanities of the vanquished: men with a keen and free judgment on all victors and on the share of chance in every victory and fame: men with their own festivals, workdays, times of mourning, accustomed and sure in command and likewise ready, where necessary, to obey, in one as in the other equally proud, equally serving their own cause: men in greater danger, more fruitful men, happier men! For, believe me!—the secret of the greatest fruitfulness and the greatest enjoyment of being is: *to live dangerously!* Build your cities on the slopes of Vesuvius! Send your ships into unmapped seas! Live at war with your peers and with yourselves. Be robbers and conquerors, as long as you cannot be rulers and owners, you lovers of knowledge! The time is soon past when it will be enough for you to live hidden like timid deer in the woods. Finally the pursuit of knowledge will stretch out for its due:—it will want to *rule* and *possess,* and you along with it.

1.

[*Old and new values.*] Here I sit and wait, old broken tables around me and also new half written tables. When does my hour come?

—the hour of my descent, of my down-going: for once more I will go unto men.

For that hour I now wait: for first must the signs come to me that it is *my* hour,—namely the laughing lion with the flock of doves.

Meanwhile I talk to myself as one who has time. No one tells me anything new: so I tell my own story to myself.—
—

2.

When I came unto men, I found them relying on an old infatuation: All of them thought they had long known what was good and bad for men.

All discourse about virtue seemed to them an old wearisome business; and whoever wished to sleep well spoke of "good" and "bad" before retiring to rest.

I disturbed this somnolence when I taught: *no one yet knows* what is good and bad:—that is for the creating one!

—But it is he who creates man's goal and gives the earth its meaning and its future: he first posits that something is good or bad.

And I called on them to overturn their old academic chairs, and wherever else that old infatuation had prevailed; I called on them to laugh at their great moralists and saints and poets and world-saviors.

I called on them to laugh at their gloomy sages, and at whomever had sat admonishing on the tree of life like a black scarecrow.

I sat down on their great grave-street beside the carrion and vultures—and I laughed at all their lore and its mellow decaying glory. Truly, like preachers and fools I cried scorn and shame on all their greatness and smallness—that their best is so very small! That their best is so very small!—thus I laughed.

Thus did my wise longing, born in the mountains, cry and laugh in me, truly a wild wisdom—my great pinion-rustling longing.

And often it carried me off and up and away and into the midst of laughter: then I flew quivering like an arrow with sun-intoxicated rapture:

—out into distant futures, which no dream has yet seen, into warmer souths than ever a sculptor dreamed: where gods danced ashamed of all clothes:—
—

that I speak in parables, and halt and stammer like poets: and truly I am ashamed that I must still be a poet!—

Where all becoming seemed to me dancing of gods and wantoning of gods, and the world unloosed and unbridled and fleeing back to itself:—

—as an eternal self-fleeing and re-seeking among the gods, as the blessed self-contradicting, self-communing, and self-fraternizing among the gods:—

Where all time seemed to me a blessed mockery of moments, where necessity was freedom itself, which played happily with the goad of freedom:—

Where I also found again my old devil and arch enemy, the spirit of seriousness, and all it created: constraint, law, necessity and consequence and purpose and will and good and bad:—

For must there not be that which is danced *over*, danced beyond? Must there not, for the sake of the nimble, the nimblest—be moles and clumsy dwarfs?
—

3.

There also it was where I picked up from the path the word "Superman," and that man is something that must be overcome.

—that man is a bridge and not a goal: rejoicing over his noontides and evenings as ways to new rosy dawns:

—the Zarathustra-word of the great noontide, and whatever else I have hung up over men like purple evening afterglows.

Truly, also I made them see new stars along with new nights; and over cloud and day and night I spread out laughter like a gay-colored canopy.

I taught them all *my* poetry and aspiration: to compose and collect into unity what is fragmented in man and riddle and fearful chance,—

—as composer, riddle-reader, and redeemer of chance I taught them to create the future, and all that *was*—, to redeem by creating.

The past of man to redeem and every "It was" to transform, until the Will says: "But so did I will it! So shall I will it—"

—This I called redemption; this alone I taught them to call redemption.— —

Now I await *my* redemption—, that I may go unto them for the last time.

For once more I will go unto men: *among* them I will go down; in dying I will give them my choicest gift!

From the sun I learned this, when it goes down, the exuberant one: it then pours gold into the sea out of inexhaustible riches,—

—so that even the poorest fisherman steers with a *golden* rudder! This I once saw and did not tire of weeping in beholding it.— —

Like the sun Zarathustra will also go down: now he sits here and waits, old broken tables around him, and also new tables,—half written.

4.

Behold, here is a new table; but where are my brethren who will carry it with me to the valley and into hearts of flesh?—

Thus my great love demands of the remotest ones: *be not considerate of your neighbor*! Man is something that must be overcome.

There are many diverse ways and

modes of overcoming: see *you* thereto! But only a buffoon thinks: "man can also be *overleaped*."

Overcome yourself even in your neighbor: and a right which you can seize upon, you shall not allow to be given to you!

What you do no one can do to you again. Lo, there is no requital.

He who cannot command himself shall obey. And many *can* command, but still sorely lack self-obedience!

SOCIAL PHILOSOPHY

Existentialist writing, as we have seen, is suspicious of abstractions and generalities, preferring rather to concentrate on and develop concrete issues in their relation to values. The problem of justice is no exception. Albert Camus finds that formal definitions of justice (for example, treating equals as equal and unequals as unequal) define the concept by the rules of a "crude arithmetic." This crudeness is especially apparent when "justice" issues the sentence of capital punishment, for the resultant dehumanizing of both victim and society is beyond measurement. The months of waiting for execution, the reduction of victim and society to primitive terms, the treatment of the condemned as an object: these and more make capital punishment only premeditated murder.

The death penalty, Camus believes, can never express the meaning of justice. It rather destroys the value of life, and results in a corroding nihilism. But individuals need to be defended against the State's oppressions as symbolized by the death penalty. That is why its abolition must be the first item in the social codes of the future.

6   Justice and Death

Albert Camus (1914-1960)

A punishment that penalizes without forestalling is indeed called revenge. It

The selection is from Albert Camus, *Resistance, Rebellion, and Death* (tr. Justin O'Brien) (New York: Alfred A. Knopf, 1961; London: Hamish Hamilton), pp. 197-230, with omissions. Used by permission of the publishers.

is a quasi-arithmetical reply made by society to whoever breaks its primordial law. That reply is as old as man; it is called the law of retaliation. Whoever has done me harm must suffer harm; whoever has put out my eye must lose an eye; and whoever has killed must die. This is an emotion, and a particularly violent one, not a principle. Retaliation is related to nature and instinct, not to law. Law, by definition, cannot obey the same rules as nature. If murder is in the nature of man, the law is not intended to imitate or reproduce that nature. It is intended to correct it. Now, retaliation does no more than ratify and confer the status of a law on a pure impulse of nature. We have all known that impulse, often to our shame, and we know its power, for it comes down to us from the primitive forests. In this regard, we French, who are properly indignant upon seeing the oil king in Saudi Arabia preach international democracy and call in a butcher to cut off a thief's hand with a cleaver, live also in a sort of Middle Ages without even the consolations of faith. We still define justice according to the rules of a crude arithmetic.[1] Can it be said at least that that arithmetic is exact and that justice, even when elementary, even when limited to legal revenge, is safeguarded by the death penalty? The answer must be no.

[1] A few years ago I asked for the reprieve of six Tunisians who had been condemned to death for the murder, in a riot, of three French policemen. The circumstances in which the murder had taken place made difficult any division of responsibilities. A note from the executive office of the President of the Republic informed me that my appeal was being considered by the appropriate organization. Unfortunately, when that note was addressed to me I had already read two weeks earlier that the sentence had been carried out. Three of the condemned men had been put to death and the three others reprieved. The reasons for reprieving some rather than the others were not convincing. But probably it was essential to carry out three executions where there had been three victims.

Let us leave aside the fact that the law of retaliation is inapplicable and that it would seem just as excessive to punish the incendiary by setting fire to his house as it would be insufficient to punish the thief by deducting from his bank account a sum equal to his theft. Let us admit that it is just and necessary to compensate for the murder of the victim by the death of the murderer. But beheading is not simply death. It is just as different, in essence, from the privation of life as a concentration camp is from prison. It is a murder, to be sure, and one that arithmetically pays for the murder committed. But it adds to death a rule, a public premeditation known to the future victim, an organization, in short, which is in itself a source of moral sufferings more terrible than death. Hence there is no equivalence. Many laws consider a premeditated crime more serious than a crime of pure violence. But what then is capital punishment but the most premeditated of murders, to which no criminal's deed, however calculated it may be, can be compared? For there to be equivalence, the death penalty would have to punish a criminal who had warned his victim of the date at which he would inflict a horrible death on him and who, from that moment onward, had confined him at his mercy for months. Such a monster is not encountered in private life.

There, too, when our official jurists talk of putting to death without causing suffering, they don't know what they are talking about and, above all, they lack imagination. The devastating, degrading fear that is imposed on the condemned for months or years[2] is a

[2] Roemen, condemned to death at the

punishment more terrible than death, and one that was not imposed on the victim. Even in the fright caused by the mortal violence being done to him, most of the time the victim is hastened to his death without knowing what is happening to him. The period of horror is counted out with his life, and hope of escaping the madness that has swept down upon that life probably never leaves him. On the other hand, the horror is parceled out to the man who is condemned to death. Torture through hope alternates with the pangs of animal despair. The lawyer and chaplain, out of mere humanity, and the jailers, so that the condemned man will keep quiet, are unanimous in assuring him that he will be reprieved. He believes this with all his being and then he ceases to believe it. He hopes by day and despairs of it by night.[3] As the weeks pass, hope and despair increase and become equally unbearable. According to all accounts, the color of the skin changes, fear acting like an acid. "Knowing that you are going to die is nothing," said a

condemned man in Fresnes. "But not knowing whether or not you are going to live, that's terror and anguish." Cartouche said of the supreme punishment: "Why, it's just a few minutes that have to be lived through." But it is a matter of months, not of minutes. Long in advance the condemned man knows that he is going to be killed and that the only thing that can save him is a reprieve, rather similar, for him, to the decrees of heaven. In any case, he cannot intervene, make a plea himself, or convince. Everything goes on outside of him. He is no longer a man but a thing waiting to be handled by the executioners. He is kept as if he were inert matter, but he still has a consciousness which is his chief enemy.

When the officials whose job it is to kill that man call him a parcel, they know what they are saying. To be unable to do anything against the hand that moves you from one place to another, holds you or rejects you, is this not indeed being a parcel, or a thing, or, better, a hobbled animal? Even then an animal can refuse to eat. The condemned man cannot. He is given the benefit of a special diet (at Fresnes, Diet No. 4 with extra milk, wine, sugar, jam, butter); they see to it that he nourishes himself. If need be, he is forced to do so. The animal that is going to be killed must be in the best condition. The thing or the animal has a right only to those debased freedoms that are called whims. "They are very touchy," a top-sergeant at Fresnes says without the least irony of those condemned to death. Of course, but how else can they have contact with freedom and the dignity of the will that man cannot do without?

Liberation of France, remained seven hundred days in chains before being executed, and this is scandalous. Those condemned under common law, as a general rule, wait from three to six months for the morning of their death. And it is difficult, if one wants to maintain their chances of survival, to shorten that period. I can bear witness, moreover, to the fact that the examination of appeals for mercy is conducted in France with a seriousness that does not exclude the visible inclination to pardon, insofar as the law and customs permit.

[3] Sunday not being a day of execution, Saturday night is always better in the cell blocks reserved for those condemned to death.

Touchy or not, the moment the sentence has been pronounced the condemned man enters an imperturbable machine. For a certain number of weeks he travels along in the intricate machinery that determines his every gesture and eventually hands him over to those who will lay him down on the killing machine. The parcel is no longer subject to the laws of chance that hang over the living creature but to mechanical laws that allow him to foresee accurately the day of his beheading.

That day his being an object comes to an end. During the three quarters of an hour separating him from the end, the certainty of a powerless death stifles everything else; the animal, tied down and amenable, knows a hell that makes the hell he is threatened with seem ridiculous. The Greeks, after all, were more humane with their hemlock. They left their condemned a relative freedom, the possibility of putting off or hastening the hour of his death. They gave him a choice between suicide and execution. On the other hand, in order to be doubly sure, we deal with the culprit ourselves. But there could not really be any justice unless the condemned, after making known his decision months in advance, had approached his victim, bound him firmly, informed him that he would be put to death in an hour, and had finally used that hour to set up the apparatus of death. What criminal ever reduced his victim to such a desperate and powerless condition?

This doubtless explains the odd submissiveness that is customary in the condemned at the moment of their execution. These men who have nothing more to lose could play their last card, choose to die of a chance bullet or be guillotined in the kind of frantic struggle that dulls all the faculties. In a way, this would amount to dying freely. And yet, with but few exceptions, the rule is for the condemned to walk toward death passively in a sort of dreary despondency. That is probably what our journalists mean when they say that the condemned died courageously. We must read between the lines that the condemned made no noise, accepted his status as a parcel, and that everyone is grateful to him for this. In such a degrading business, the interested party shows a praiseworthy sense of propriety by keeping the degradation from lasting too long. But the compliments and the certificates of courage belong to the general mystification surrounding the death penalty. For the condemned will often be seemly in proportion to the fear he feels. He will deserve the praise of the press only if his fear or his feeling of isolation is great enough to sterilize him completely. Let there be no misunderstanding. Some among the condemned, whether political or not, die heroically, and they must be granted the proper admiration and respect. But the majority of them know only the silence of fear, only the impassivity of fright, and it seems to me that such terrified silence deserves even greater respect. When the priest Bela Just offers to write to the family of a young condemned man a few moments before he is hanged and hears the reply: "I have no courage, even for that," how can a priest, hearing that confession of weakness, fail to honor the most wretched and most sacred thing in man? Those who say nothing but leave a little pool on the spot from which they are taken—who would dare say they died as cowards? And how can we describe the men who reduced them to such cowardice? After all, every murderer when he kills runs the risk of the most dreadful of deaths, whereas those who kill him risk nothing except advancement.

No, what man experiences at such times is beyond all morality. Not virtue, nor courage, nor intelligence, nor even innocence has anything to do with it. Society is suddenly reduced to a state of primitive terrors where nothing can be judged. All equity and all dignity have disappeared. "The conviction of innocence does not immunize against brutal treatment. . . . I have seen authentic bandits die courageously whereas innocent men went to their deaths trembling in every muscle."[4] When the same man adds that, according to his experience, intellectuals show more weakness, he is not implying that such men have less courage than others but merely that they have much imagination. Having to face an inevitable death, any man, whatever his convictions, is torn asunder from head to toe.[5] The feeling of powerlessness and solitude of the condemned man, bound and up against the public coalition that demands his death, is in itself an unimaginable punishment. From this point of view, too, it would be better for the execution to be public. The actor in every man could then come to the aid of the terrified animal and help him cut a figure, even in his own eyes. But darkness and secrecy offer no recourse. In such a disaster, courage, strength of soul, even faith may be disadvantages. As a general rule, a man is undone by waiting for capital punishment well before he dies. Two deaths are inflicted on him, the first being worse than the second, whereas he killed but once. Compared to such torture, the penalty of retaliation seems like a civilized law. It never claimed that the man who gouged out one of his brother's eyes should be totally blinded. . . .

Such, it will be said, is human justice, and, despite its imperfections, it is better than arbitrariness. But that sad evaluation is bearable only in connection with ordinary penalties. It is scandalous in the face of verdicts of death. A classic treatise on French law, in order to excuse the death penalty for not involving degrees, states this: "Human justice has not the slightest desire to assure such a proportion. Why? Because it knows it is frail." Must we therefore conclude that such frailty authorizes us to pronounce an absolute judgment and that, uncertain of ever achieving pure justice, society must rush headlong, through the greatest risks, toward supreme injustice? If justice admits that it is frail, would it not be better for justice to be modest and to allow its judgments sufficient latitude so that a mistake can be corrected?[6] Could not justice concede to the crimi-

---

[4] Bela Just, *La Potence et la Croix* (Fasquelle).

[5] A great surgeon, a Catholic himself, told me that as a result of his experience he did not even inform believers when they had an incurable cancer. According to him, the shock might destroy even their faith.

[6] We congratulated ourselves on having reprieved Sillon, who recently killed his four-year-old daughter in order not to give her to her mother, who wanted a divorce. It was discovered, in fact, during his imprisonment that Sillon was suffering from a brain tumor that might explain the madness of his deed.

nal the same weakness in which society finds a sort of permanent extenuating circumstance for itself? Can the jury decently say: "If I kill you by mistake, you will forgive me when you consider the weaknesses of our common nature. But I am condemning you to death without considering those weaknesses or that nature"? There is a solidarity of all men in error and aberration. Must that solidarity operate for the tribunal and be denied the accused? No, and if justice has any meaning in this world, it means nothing but the recognition of that solidarity; it cannot, by its very essence, divorce itself from compassion. Compassion, of course, can in this instance be but awareness of a common suffering and not a frivolous indulgence paying no attention to the sufferings and· rights of the victim. Compassion does not exclude punishment, but it suspends the final condemnation. Compassion loathes the definitive, irreparable measure that does an injustice to mankind as a whole because of failing to take into account the wretchedness of the common condition.

To tell the truth, certain juries are well aware of this, for they often admit extenuating circumstances in a crime that nothing can extenuate. This is because the death penalty seems excessive to them in such cases and they prefer not punishing enough to punishing too much. The extreme severity of the penalty then favors crime instead of penalizing it. There is not a court session during which we do not read in the press that a verdict is incoherent and that, in view of the facts, it seems either insufficient or excessive. But the jurors are not ignorant of this. However, faced with the enormity of capital punishment, they prefer, as we too should

prefer, to look like fools rather than to compromise their nights to come. Knowing themselves to be fallible, they at least draw the appropriate consequences. And true justice is on their side precisely insofar as logic is not. . . .

In relation to crime, how can our civilization be defined? The reply is easy: for thirty years now, State crimes have been far more numerous than individual crimes. I am not even speaking of wars, general or localized, although bloodshed too is an alcohol that eventually intoxicates like the headiest of wines. But the number of individuals killed directly by the State has assumed astronomical proportions and infinitely outnumbers private murders. There are fewer and fewer condemned by common law and more and more condemned for political reasons. The proof is that each of us, however honorable he may be, can foresee the possibility of being someday condemned to death, whereas that eventuality would have seemed ridiculous at the beginning of the century. Alphonse Karr's witty remark: "Let the noble assassins begin" has no meaning now. Those who cause the most blood to flow are the same ones who believe they have right, logic, and history on their side.

Hence our society must now defend herself not so much against the individual as against the State. It may be that the proportions will be reversed in another thirty years. But, for the moment, our self-defense must be aimed at the State first and foremost. Justice and expediency command the law to protect the individual against a State given over to the follies of sectarianism or of pride. "Let the State begin and abolish the death penalty" ought to be our rallying cry today.

Bloodthirsty laws, it has been said, make bloodthirsty customs. But any society eventually reaches a state of ignominy in which, despite every disorder, the customs never manage to be as bloodthirsty as the laws. Half of Europe knows that condition. We French knew it in the past and may again know it. Those executed during the Occupation led to those executed at the time of the Liberation, whose friends now dream of revenge. Elsewhere States laden with too many crimes are getting ready to drown their guilt in even greater massacres. One kills for a nation or a class that has been granted divine status. One kills for a future society that has likewise been given divine status. Whoever thinks he has omniscience imagines he has omnipotence. Temporal idols demanding an absolute faith tirelessly decree absolute punishments. And religions devoid of transcendence kill great numbers of condemned men devoid of hope.

How can European society of the mid-century survive unless it · decides to defend individuals by every means against the State's oppression? Forbidding a man's execution would amount to proclaiming publicly that society and the State are not absolute values, that nothing authorizes them to legislate definitively or to bring about the irreparable. Without the death penalty, Gabriel Péri and Brasillach would perhaps be among us. We could then judge them according to our opinion and proudly proclaim our judgment, whereas now they judge us and we keep silent. Without the death penalty Rajk's corpse would not poison Hungary; Germany, with less guilt on her conscience, would be more favorably looked upon by Eu-

rope; the Russian Revolution would not be agonizing in shame; and Algerian blood would weigh less heavily on our consciences. Without the death penalty, Europe would not be infected by the corpses accumulated for the last twenty years in its tired soil. On our continent, all values are upset for fear and hatred between individuals and between nations. In the conflict of ideas the weapons are the cord and the guillotine. A natural and human society exercising her right of repression has given way to a dominant ideology that requires human sacrifices. "The example of the gallows," it has been written,[7] "is that a man's life ceases to be sacred when it is thought useful to kill him." Apparently it is becoming ever more useful; the example is being copied; the contagion is spreading everywhere. And together with it, the disorder of nihilism. Hence we must call a spectacular halt and proclaim, in our principles and institutions, that the individual is above the State. And any measure that decreases the pressure of social forces upon the individual will help to relieve the congestion of a Europe suffering from a rush of blood, allowing us to think more clearly and to start on the way toward health. Europe's malady consists in believing nothing and claiming to know everything. But Europe is far from knowing everything, and, judging from the revolt and hope we feel, she believes in something: she believes that the extreme of man's wretchedness, on some mysterious limit, borders on the extreme of his greatness. For the majority of Europeans, faith is lost. And with it, the justifications faith pro-

---

[7] By Francart.

vided in the domain of punishment. But the majority of Europeans also reject the State idolatry that aimed to take the place of faith. Henceforth in mid-course, both certain and uncertain, having made up our minds never to submit and never to oppress, we should admit at one and the same time our hope and our ignorance, we should refuse absolute law and the irreparable judgment. We know enough to say that this or that major criminal deserves hard labor for life. But we don't know enough to decree that he be shorn of his future—in other words, of the chance we all have of making amends. Because of what I have just said, in the unified Europe of the future the solemn abolition of the death penalty ought to be the first article of the European Code we all hope for.

ESTHETICS

Esthetic values, like moral values, are never simply *given* for the existentialist. Rather, they come into being only by a creative decision and act of some creator. In the following selection, Sartre writes that the *esthetic* object, as distinct from the physical thing we call a book or a painting, is present only to a realizing consciousness that has become imaginative. But imaginative consciousness negates the world and grasps or contemplates an *unreality*. Hence the esthetic object, as a product of imagination, is itself an unreality. In turn, beauty is a value only in reference to the imaginary: the real is never beautiful. Beauty, therefore, is a negation of the world.

7 Art as Unreality

Jean-Paul Sartre (1905-   )

The following comments will be concerned essentially with the existential type of the work of art. And we can at once formulate the law that the work of art is an unreality.

This appeared to us clearly from the moment we took for our example, in an entirely different connection, the portrait of Charles VIII. We understood at the very outset that this Charles VIII was an object. But this, obviously, is not the same object as is the painting, the canvas, which are the real objects of the painting. As long as we observe the canvas and the frame for themselves the esthetic object "Charles VIII" will not appear. It is not that it is hidden by the picture, but because it cannot present itself to a realizing consciousness. It will appear at the moment when consciousness, undergoing a radical change in which the world is negated,

The selection is from Jean-Paul Sartre, *The Psychology of Imagination* (tr. Bernard Frechtman) (New York: Philosophical Library, Inc.; London: John F. Rider, 1948), pp. 273–282. Used by permission of the Philosophical Library and The Hutchinson Group.

will itself become imaginative. The situation here is like that of the cubes which can be seen at will to be five or six in number. It will not do to say that when they are seen as five it is because at that time the aspect of the drawing in which they are six is *concealed*. The intentional act that apprehends them as five is sufficient unto itself, it is complete and *exclusive* of the act which grasps them as six. And so it is with the apprehension of Charles VIII as an image which is depicted on the picture. This Charles VIII on the canvas is necessarily the correlative of the intentional act of an imaginative consciousness. And since this Charles VIII, who is an unreality so long he is grasped on the canvas, is precisely the object of our esthetic appreciations (it is he who "moves" us, who is "painted with intelligence, power, and grace," etc.), we are led to recognize that, in a picture, the esthetic object is something *unreal*. This is of great enough importance once we remind ourselves of the way in which we ordinarily confuse the real and the imaginary in a work of art. We often hear it said, in fact, that the artist first has an idea in the form of an image which he then *realizes* on canvas. This mistaken notion arises from the fact that the painter can, in fact, begin with a mental image which is, as such, incommunicable, and from the fact that at the end of his labors he presents the public with an object which anyone can observe. This leads us to believe that there occurred a transition from the imaginary to the real. But this is in no way true. That which is real, we must not fail to note, are the results of the brush strokes, the stickiness of the canvas, its grain, the polish spread over the colors. But all

this does not constitute the object of esthetic appreciation. What is "beautiful" is something which cannot be experienced as a perception and which, by its very nature, is out of the world. We have just shown that it cannot be *brightened*, for instance, by projecting a light beam on the canvas: it is the canvas that is brightened and not the painting. The fact of the matter is that the painter did not *realize* his mental image at all: he has simply constructed a material analogue of such a kind that everyone can grasp the image provided he looks at the analogue. But the image thus provided with an external analogue remains an image. There is no realization of the imaginary, nor can we speak of its *objectification*. Each stroke of the brush was not made *for itself* nor even for the constructing of a coherent real whole (in the sense in which it can be said that a certain lever in a machine was conceived in the interest of the whole and not for itself). It was given together with an unreal synthetic whole and the aim of the artist was to construct a whole of *real* colors which enable this unreal to manifest itself. The painting should then be conceived as a material thing *visited* from time to time (every time that the spectator assumes the imaginative attitude) by an unreal which is precisely the *painted object*. What deceives us here is the real and sensuous pleasure which certain real colors on the canvas give us. Some reds of Matisse, for instance, produce a sensuous enjoyment in those who see them. But we must understand that this sensuous enjoyment, if thought of in isolation—for instance, if aroused by a color in nature—has nothing of the esthetic. It is purely and simply a pleasure of sense. But when the red of the painting is grasped, it is grasped, in spite of everything, as a part of an unreal whole and it is in this whole that it is beautiful. For instance it is the red of a rug by a table. There is, in fact, no such thing as pure color. Even if the artist is concerned solely with the sensory relationships between forms and colors, he chooses for that very reason a rug in order to increase the sensory value of the red: tactile elements, for instance, must be intended through the red, it is a *fleecy* red, because the rug is of a fleecy material. Without this "fleeciness" of the color something would be lost. And surely the rug is painted there *for the red* it justifies and not the red for the rug. If Matisse chose a rug rather than a sheet of dry and glossy paper it is because of the voluptuous mixture of the color, the density and the tactile quality of the wool. Consequently the red can be truly enjoyed only in grasping it as the *red of the rug*, and therefore unreal. And he would have lost his strongest contrast with the green of the wall if the green were not rigid and cold, because it is the green of a wall tapestry. It is therefore in the unreal that the relationship of colors and forms takes on its real meaning. And even when drawn objects have their usual meaning reduced to a minimum, as in the painting of the cubists, the painting is at least not flat. The forms we see are certainly not the forms of a rug, a table, nor anything else we see in the world. They nevertheless do have a density, a material, a depth, they bear a relationship of perspective towards each other. They are *things*. And it is precisely in the measure in which they are things that they are unreal. Cubism has introduced

the fashion of claiming that a painting should not *represent* or *imitate* reality but should constitute an object in itself. As an esthetic doctrine such a program is perfectly defensible and we owe many masterpieces to it. But it needs to be understood. To maintain that the painting, although altogether devoid of meaning, nevertheless is a *real* object, would be a grave mistake. It is certainly not an object of nature. The real object no longer functions as an analogue of a bouquet of flowers or a glade. But when I "contemplate" it, I nevertheless am not in a realistic attitude. The painting is still an *analogue*. Only what manifests itself through it is an unreal collection of *new things*, of objects I have never seen or ever will see, but which are not less unreal because of it, objects which do not exist *in the painting*, nor anywhere in the world, but which manifest themselves by means of the canvas, and which have gotten hold of it by some sort of possession. And it is the configuration of these unreal objects that I designate as *beautiful*. The esthetic enjoyment is real but it is not grasped for itself, as if produced by a real color: it is but a manner of apprehending the unreal object and, far from being directed on the real painting, it serves to constitute the imaginary object through the real canvas. This is the source of the celebrated disinterestedness of esthetic experience. This is why Kant was able to say that it does not matter whether the object of beauty, when experienced as beautiful, is or is not objectively real; why Schopenhauer was able to speak of a sort of suspension of the Will. This does not come from some mysterious way of apprehending the real, which we are able to use occasionally. What happens is that the esthetic object is constituted and apprehended by an imaginative consciousness which posits it as unreal.

What we have just shown regarding painting is readily applied to the art of fiction, poetry and drama, as well. It is self-evident that the novelist, the poet and the dramatist construct an unreal object by means of verbal analogues; it is also self-evident that the actor who plays Hamlet makes use of himself, of his whole body, as an analogue of the imaginary person. Even the famous dispute about the paradox of the comedian is enlightened by the view here presented. It is well known that certain amateurs proclaim that the actor *does not believe* in the character he portrays. Others, leaning on many witnesses, claim that the actor becomes identified in some way with the character he is enacting. To us these two views are not exclusive of each other; if by "belief" is meant actually real it is obvious that the actor does not actually consider himself to be Hamlet. But this does not mean that he does not "mobilize" all his powers to make Hamlet real. He uses all his feelings, all his strength, all his gestures as analogues of the feelings and conduct of Hamlet. But by this very fact he takes the reality away from them. *He lives completely in an unreal way.* And it matters little that he is *actually* weeping in enacting the role. These tears . . . he himself experiences—and so does the audience—as the tears of Hamlet, that is as the analogue of unreal tears. The transformation that occurs here is like that we discussed in the dream: the actor is completely caught up, inspired, by the unreal. It is not the character who becomes real in the actor, it is the actor who *becomes unreal* in his character.[1]

But are there not some arts whose objects seem to escape unreality by their very nature? A melody, for instance, refers to nothing but itself. Is a cathedral anything more than a mass of *real* stone which dominates the surrounding house tops? But let us look at this matter more closely. I listen to a symphony orchestra, for instance, playing the Beethoven Seventh Symphony. Let us disregard exceptional cases—which are besides on the margin of esthetic contemplation—as when I go mainly "to hear Toscanini" interpret Beethoven in his own way. As a general rule what draws me to the concert is the desire "to hear the Seventh Symphony." Of course I have some objection to hearing an amateur orchestra, and prefer this or that well-known musical organization. But this is due to my desire to hear the symphony "played perfectly," because the symphony will then be *perfectly itself.* The shortcomings of a poor orchestra which plays "too fast" or "too slow," "in the wrong tempo," etc., seem to me to rob, to "betray" the work it is playing. At most the orchestra effaces itself before the work it performs, and, provided I have reasons to trust the performers and their conductor, I am confronted by the symphony itself. This everyone will grant me. But now, what is the Seventh Symphony itself? Obviously it is a *thing*, that is something

---

[1] It is in this sense that a beginner in the theatre can say that stage-fright served her to represent the timidity of Ophelia. If it did so, it is because she suddenly turned it into an unreality, that is, that she ceased to apprehend it for itself and that she grasped it as *analogue* for the timidity of Ophelia.

which is before me, which endures, which lasts. Naturally there is no need to show that that thing is a synthetic whole, which does not consist of tones but of a thematic configuration. But is that "thing" real or unreal? Let us first bear in mind that I am listening to the Seventh Symphony. For me that "Seventh Symphony" does not exist in time, I do not grasp it as a dated event, as an artistic manifestation which is unrolling itself in the Châtelet auditorium on the 17th of November, 1938. If I hear Furtwaengler tomorrow or eight days later conduct another orchestra performing the same symphony, I am in the presence of the same symphony once more. Only it is being played either better or worse. Let us now see *how* I hear the symphony: some persons shut their eyes. In this case they detach themselves from the *visual* and dated event of this particular interpretation: they give themselves up to the pure sounds. Others watch the orchestra or the back of the conductor. But they do not see what they are looking at. This is what Revault d'Allonnes calls reflection with auxiliary fascination. The auditorium, the conductor and even the orchestra have disappeared. I am therefore confronted by the Seventh Symphony, but on the express condition of understanding *nothing about it*, that I do not think of the event as an actuality and dated, and on condition that I listen to the succession of themes as an absolute succession and not as a real succession which is unfolding itself, for instance, on the occasion when Peter paid a visit to this or that friend. In the degree to which I hear the symphony it is *not here*, between these walls, at the tip of the violin bows. Nor is it "in the past" as if I thought: this is the work that matured in the mind of Beethoven on such a date. It is completely beyond the real. It has its own time, that is, it possesses an inner time, which runs from the first tone of the allegro to the last tone of the finale, but this time is not a succession of a preceding time which it continues and which happened "before" the beginning of the allegro; nor is it followed by a time which will come "after" the finale. The Seventh Symphony is in no way *in time*. It is therefore in no way real. It occurs *by itself*, but as absent, as being out of reach. I cannot act upon it, change a single note of it, or slow down its movement. But it depends on the real for its appearance: that the conductor does not faint away, that a fire in the hall does not put an end to the performance. From this we cannot conclude that *the* Seventh Symphony has come to an end. No, we only think that the *performance* of the symphony has ceased. Does this not show clearly that the performance of the symphony is its *analogue*? It can manifest itself only through analogues which are dated and which unroll in our time. But to experience it on these analogues the imaginative reduction must be functioning, that is, the real sounds must be apprehended as analogues. It therefore occurs as a perpetual elsewhere, a perpetual absence. We must not picture it (as does Spandrell in *Point Counterpoint* by Huxley—as so many platonisms) as existing in another world, in an intelligible heaven. It is not only outside of time and space—as are essences, for instance—it is outside of the real, outside of existence. I do not hear it actually, I listen to it in the imaginary. Here we find the explanation for the considerable difficulty we always experience in passing from the world of the theatre or of music into that of our daily affairs. There is in fact no passing from one world into the other, but only a passing from the imaginative attitude to that of reality. Esthetic contemplation is an induced dream and the passing into the real is an actual waking up. We often speak of the "deception" experienced on returning to reality. But this does not explain that this discomfort also exists, for instance, after having witnessed a realistic and cruel play, in which case reality should be experienced as comforting. This discomfort is simply that of the dreamer on awakening; an entranced consciousness, engulfed in the imaginary, is suddenly freed by the sudden ending of the play, of the symphony, and comes suddenly in contact with existence. Nothing more is needed to arouse the nauseating disgust that characterizes the consciousness of reality.

From these few observations we can already conclude that the real is never beautiful. Beauty is a value applicable only to the imaginary and which means the negation of the world in its essential structure. This is why it is stupid to confuse the moral with the esthetic. The values of the Good presume being-in-the-world, they concern action in the real and are subject from the outset to the basic absurdity of existence. To say that we "assume" an esthetic attitude to life is to constantly confuse the real and the imaginary. It does happen, however, that we do assume the attitude of esthetic contemplation towards real events or objects. But in such cases everyone of us can feel in himself a sort of recoil in relation to the object contemplated which slips into nothingness so that, from this moment on, it is no longer *perceived*; it functions as an *analogue* of itself, that is, that an unreal image of what it is appears to us through its actual presence. This image can be purely and simply the object "itself" neutralized, annihilated, as when I contemplate a beautiful woman or death at a bull fight; it can also be the imperfect and confused appearance of *what it could be* through what it is, as when the painter grasps the harmony of two colors as being greater, more vivid, *through* the real blots he finds on a wall. The object at once appears to be *in back of* itself, becomes *untouchable*, it is beyond our reach; and hence arises a sort of sad disinterest in it. It is in this sense that we may say that great beauty in a woman kills the desire for her. In fact we cannot at the same time place ourselves on the plane of the esthetic when this unreal "herself" which we admire appears and on the realistic plane of physical possession. To desire her we must forget she is beautiful, because desire is a plunge into the heart of existence, into what is most contingent and most absurd. Esthetic contemplation of *real* objects is of the same structure as paramnesia, in which the real object functions as analogue of itself in the past. But in one of the cases there is a negating and in the other a placing a thing in the past. Paramnesia differs from the esthetic attitude as memory differs from imagination.

PHILOSOPHY OF MAN

The Cartesian dualism of mental and physical substances not only divides man's being, but it also lies at the root of many of the destructive divisions in the modern world. Idealism versus realism and individualism versus collectivism are but two of many possible examples. These divisions can be overcome, Merleau-Ponty believes, only by use of the methods of phenomenology, which alone can be adequate to the complexities of our being-in-the-world. (Embodiment cannot be grasped by scientific thought because it remains impersonal and "objectivist.") After suggesting some failures of classical psychology, Merleau-Ponty finds that a proper understanding of habit is helpful in articulating the phenomenon of embodiment. Habit, he says, is neither in thought, nor in the body alone, but rather in the body as mediator of a world. The body, so viewed, is the domain of our expressive space, and serves as our anchorage in the world.

Merleau-Ponty is known more as a phenomenologist than as an existentialist. Yet his contacts with existentialist writers were close—with Sartre he founded the review *Les Temps modernes*—and many of the themes in his works are influenced by, and an influence on, existentialism. He is generally viewed as an important contributor to contemporary philosophy.

8 The Phenomenon of Embodiment

Maurice Merleau-Ponty (1908-1961)

In its descriptions of the body from the point of view of the self, classical psychology was already wont to attribute to it "characteristics" incompatible with the status of an object. In the first place it was stated that my body is distinguishable from the table or the lamp in that I can turn away from the latter whereas my body is constantly perceived. It is therefore an object which

The selection is from M. Merleau-Ponty, *Phenomenology of Perception* (tr. Colin Smith) (New York: Humanities Press, Inc.; London: Routledge and Kegan Paul, Ltd., 1962), pp. 90-96 and 142-147. Used by permission of the publishers.

does not leave me. But in that case is it still an object? If the object is an invariable structure, it is not one *in spite of* the changes of perspective, but *in* that change or *through* it. It is not the case that ever-renewed perspectives simply provide it with opportunities of displaying its permanence, and with contingent ways of presenting itself to us. It is an object, which means that it is standing in front of us, only because it is observable: situated, that is to say, directly under our hand or gaze, indivisibly overthrown and re-integrated with every movement they make. Otherwise it would be true like an idea and not present like a thing. It is particularly true that an object is an object only in so far as it can be moved away from me, and ultimately disappear from my field of vision. Its presence is such that it entails a possible absence. Now the permanence of my own body is entirely different in kind: it is not at the extremity of some indefinite exploration; it defies exploration and is always presented to me from the same angle. Its permanence is not a permanence in the world, but a permanence from my point of view. To say that it is always near me, always there for me, is to say that it is never really in front of me, that I cannot array it before my eyes, that it remains marginal to all my perceptions, that it is *with* me. It is true that external objects too never turn one of their sides to me without hiding the rest, but I can at least freely choose the side which they are to present to me. They could not appear otherwise than in perspective, but the particular perspective which I acquire at each moment is the outcome of no more than physical necessity, that is to say, of a necessity which I can use and which is not a prison for me: from my window only the tower of the church is visible, but this limitation simultaneously holds out the promise that from elsewhere the whole church could be seen. It is true, moreover, that if I am a prisoner the church will be restricted, for me, to a truncated steeple. If I did not take off my clothes I could never see the inside of them, and it will in fact be seen that my clothes may become appendages of my body. But this fact does not prove that the presence of my body is to be compared to the *de facto* permanence of

certain objects, or the organ compared to a tool which is always available. It shows that conversely those actions in which I habitually engage incorporate their instruments into themselves and make them play a part in the original structure of my own body. As for the latter, it is my basic habit, the one which conditions all the others, and by means of which they are mutually comprehensible. Its permanence near to me, its unvarying perspective are not a *de facto* necessity, since such necessity presupposes them: in order that my window may impose upon me a point of view of the church, it is necessary in the first place that my body should impose upon me one of the world; and the first necessity can be merely physical only in virtue of the fact that the second is metaphysical; in short, I am accessible to factual situations only if my nature is such that there are factual situations for me. In other words, I observe external objects with my body, I handle them, examine them, walk round them, but my body itself is a thing which I do not observe: in order to be able to do so, I should need the use of a second body which itself would be unobservable. When I say that my body is always perceived by me, these words are not to be taken in a purely statistical sense, for there must be, in the way my own body presents itself, something which makes its absence or its variation inconceivable. What can it be? My head is presented to my sight only to the extent of my nose end and the boundaries of my eye-sockets. I can see my eyes in three mirrors, but they are the eyes of someone observing, and I have the utmost difficulty in catching my living glance when a mirror in the street unexpectedly deflects my image back at me. My body in the mirror never stops following my intentions like their shadow, and if observation consists in varying the point of view while keeping the object fixed, then it escapes observation and is given to me as a simulacrum of my tactile body since it imitates the body's actions instead of responding to them by a free unfolding of perspectives. My visual body is certainly an object as far as its parts far removed from my head are concerned, but as we come nearer to the eyes, it becomes divorced from objects, and reserves among them a quasi-space to which they have no access, and when I try to fill this void by recourse to the image in the mirror, it refers me back to an original of the body which is not out there among things, but in my own province, on this side of all things seen. It is no different, in spite of what may appear to be the case, with my tactile body, for if I can, with my left hand, feel my right hand as it touches an object, the right hand as an object is not the right hand as it touches: the first is a system of bones, muscles and flesh brought down at a point of space, the second shoots through space like a rocket to reveal the external object in its place. In so far as it sees or touches the world, my body can therefore be neither seen nor touched. What prevents its ever being an object, ever being "completely constituted"[1] is that it is that by which there are objects. It is neither tangible nor visible in so far as it is that which sees and touches. The body therefore is not the nondescript one among external objects and simply

having the peculiarity of always being there. If it is permanent, the permanence is absolute and is the ground for the relative permanence of disappearing objects, real objects. The presence and absence of external objects are only variations within a field of primordial presence, a perceptual domain over which my body exercises power. Not only is the permanence of my body not a particular case of the permanence of external objects in the world, but the second cannot be understood except through the first: not only is the perspective of my body not a particular case of that of objects, but furthermore the presentation of objects in perspective cannot be understood except through the resistance of my body to all variation of perspective. If objects may never show me more than one of their facets, this is because I am myself in a certain place from which I see them and which I cannot see. If nevertheless I believe in the existence of their hidden sides and equally in a world which embraces them all and co-exists with them, I do so in so far as my body, always present for me, and yet involved with them in so many objective relationships, sustains their co-existence with it and communicates to them all the pulse of its duration. Thus the permanence of one's own body, if only classical psychology had analysed it, might have led it to the body no longer conceived as an object of the world, but as our means of communication with it, to the world no longer conceived as a collection of determinate objects, but as the horizon latent in all our experience and itself ever-present and anterior to every determining thought.

The other "characteristics" whereby

---

[1] Husserl, *Ideen.* T. II (unpublished).

one's own body were defined were no less interesting, and for the same reasons. My body, it was said, is recognized by its power to give me "double sensations": when I touch my right hand with my left, my right hand, as an object, has the strange property of being able to feel too. We have just seen that the two hands are never simultaneously in the relationship of touched and touching to each other. When I press my two hands together, it is not a matter of two sensations felt together as one perceives two objects placed side by side, but of an ambiguous set-up in which both hands can alternate the rôles of "touching" and being "touched." What was meant by talking about "double sensations" is that, in passing from one rôle to the other, I can identify the hand touched as the same one which will in a moment be touching. In other words, in this bundle of bones and muscles which my right hand presents to my left, I can anticipate for an instant the integument or incarnation of that other right hand, alive and mobile, which I thrust towards things in order to explore them. The body catches itself from the outside engaged in a cognitive process; it tries to touch itself while being touched, and initiates "a kind of reflection"[2] which is sufficient to distinguish it from objects, of which I can indeed say that they "touch" my body, but only when it is inert, and therefore without ever catching it unawares in its exploratory function.

It was also said that the body is an affective object, whereas external things are from my point of view merely represented. This amounted to stating a

third time the problem of the status of my own body. For if I say that my foot hurts, I do not simply mean that it is a cause of pain in the same way as the nail which is cutting into it, differing only in being nearer to me; I do not mean that it is the last of the objects in the external world, after which a more intimate kind of pain should begin, an unlocalized awareness of pain itself, related to the foot only by some causal connection and within the closed system of experience. I mean that the pain reveals itself as localized, that it is constitutive of a "pain-infested space." "My foot hurts" means not: "I think that my foot is the cause of this pain," but: "the pain comes from my foot" or again "my foot has a pain." This is shown clearly by the "primitive voluminousness of pain" formerly spoken of by psychologists. It was therefore recognized that my body does not present itself as the objects of external impressions do, and that perhaps even these latter objects do no more than stand out against the affective background which in the first place throws consciousness outside itself.

Finally when the psychologists tried to confine "kinaesthetic sensations" to one's own body, arguing that these sensations present the body's movements to us globally, whereas they attributed the movements of external objects to a mediating perception and to a comparison between successive positions, it could have been objected that movement, expressing a relationship, cannot be felt, but demands a mental operation. This objection, however, would merely have been an indictment of their language. What they were expressing, badly it is true, by "kinaesthetic sensa-

---

[2] Husserl, *Méditations cartésiennes*, p. 81.

tion," was the originality of the movements which I perform with my body: they directly anticipate the final situation, for my intention initiates a movement through space merely to attain the objective initially given at the starting point; there is as it were a germ of movement which only secondarily develops into an objective movement. I move external objects with the aid of my body, which takes hold of them in one place and shifts them to another. But my body itself I move directly, I do not find it at one point of objective space and transfer it to another, I have no need to look for it, it is already with me—I do not need to lead it towards the movement's completion, it is in contact with it from the start and propels itself towards that end. The relationships between my decision and my body are, in movement, magic ones.

If the description of my own body given by classical psychology already offered all that is necessary to distinguish it from objects, how does it come about that psychologists have not made this distinction or that they have in any case seen no philosophical consequence flowing from it? The reason is that, taking a step natural to them, they chose the position of impersonal thought to which science has been committed as long as it believed in the possibility of separating, in observation, on the one hand what belongs to the situation of the observer and on the other the properties of the absolute object. For the living subject his own body might well be different from all external objects; the fact remains that for the unsituated thought of the psychologist the experience of the living subject became itself an object and, far from requiring a fresh definition of being, took its place in universal being. It was the life of the "psyche" which stood in opposition to the real, but which was treated as a second reality, as an object of scientific investigation to be brought under a set of laws. It was postulated that our experience, already besieged by physics and biology, was destined to be completely absorbed into objective knowledge, with the consummation of the system of the sciences. Thenceforth the experience of the body degenerated into a "representation" of the body; it was not a phenomenon but a fact of the psyche. In the matter of living appearance, my visual body includes a large gap at the level of the head, but biology was there ready to fill that gap, to explain it through the structure of the eyes, to instruct me in what the body really is, showing that I have a retina and a brain like other men and like the corpses which I dissect, and that, in short, the surgeon's instrument could infallibly bring to light in this indeterminate zone of my head the exact replica of plates illustrating the human anatomy. I apprehend my body as a subject-object, as capable of "seeing" and "suffering," but these confused representations were so many psychological oddities, samples of a magical variety of thought the laws of which are studied by psychology and sociology and which has its place assigned to it by them, in the system of the real world, as an object of scientific investigation. This imperfect picture of my body, its marginal presentation, and its equivocal status as touching and touched, could not therefore be *structural* characteristics of the body itself; they did not affect the idea of it; they became "distinctive characteristics" of those *contents* of consciousness which make up our representation of the body: these contents are consistent, affective and strangely duplicated in "double sensations," but apart from this the representation of the body is a representation like any other and correspondingly the body is an object like any other. Psychologists did not realize that in treating the experience of the body in this way they were simply, in accordance with the scientific approach, shelving a problem which ultimately could not be burked. The inadequacy of my perception was taken as a *de facto* inadequacy resulting from the organization of my sensory apparatus; the presence of my body was taken as a *de facto presence* springing from its constant action on my receptive nervous system; finally the union of soul and body, which was presupposed by these two explanations, was understood, in Cartesian fashion, as a *de facto union* whose *de jure* possibility need not be established, because the fact, as the starting point of knowledge, was eliminated from the final result. Now the psychologist could imitate the scientist and, for a moment at least, see his body as others saw it, and conversely see the bodies of others as mechanical things with no inner life. The contribution made from the experiences of others had the effect of dimming the structure of his own, and conversely, having lost contact with himself he became blind to the behaviour of others. He thus saw everything from the point of view of universal thought which abolished equally his experience of others and his experience of himself. But as a psychologist he was engaged in a task which by nature pulled him back into

himself, and he could not allow himself to remain unaware to this extent. For whereas neither the physicist nor the chemist are the objects of their own investigation, the psychologist *was himself,* in the nature of the case, the fact which exercised him. This representation of the body, this magical experience, which he approached in a detached frame of mind, was himself; he lived it as he thought it. It is true that, as has been shown,[3] it was not enough for him to be a psyche in order to know this, for this knowledge, like other knowledge, is acquired only through our relations with other people. It does not emerge from any recourse to an ideal of introspective psychology, and between himself and others no less than between himself and himself, the psychologist was able and obliged to rediscover a preobjective relationship. But as a psyche speaking of the psyche, he *was* all that he was *talking* about. This history of the psyche which he was elaborating in adopting the objective attitude was one whose outcome he already possessed within himself, or rather he was, in his existence, its contracted outcome and latent memory. The union of soul and body had not been brought about once and for all in a remote realm; it came into being afresh at every moment beneath the psychologist's thinking, not as a repetitive event which each time takes the psyche by surprise, but as a necessity that the psychologist knew to be in the depths of his being as he became aware of it as a piece of knowledge. The birth of perception from the "sense-data" to the "world" was sup-

---

[3] Guillaume, *L' Objectivité en Psychologie.*

posed to be renewed with each act of perception, otherwise the sense-data would have lost the meaning they owed to this development. Hence the "psyche" was not an object like others: it had done everything that one was about to say of it before it could be said; the psychologist's being knew more about itself than he did; nothing that had happened or was happening according to science was completely alien to it. Applied to the psyche, the notion of fact, therefore, underwent a transformation. The *de facto* psyche, with its "peculiarities," was no longer an event in objective time and in the external world, but an event with which we were in internal contact, of which we were ourselves the ceaseless accomplishment or upsurge, and which continually gathered within itself its past, its body and its world. Before being an objective fact, the union of soul and body had to be, then, a possibility of consciousness itself and the question arose as to what the perceiving subject is and whether he must be able to experience a body as his own. There was no longer a fact passively submitted to, but one assumed. To be a consciousness or rather *to be an experience* is to hold inner communication with the world, the body and other people, to be with them instead of being beside them. To concern oneself with psychology is necessarily to encounter, beneath objective thought which moves among ready-made things, a first opening upon things without which there would be no objective knowledge. . . .

The cultivation of habit as a rearrangement and renewal of the body image presents great difficulties to traditional philosophies, which are always inclined to conceive synthesis as intellectual synthesis. It is quite true that what brings together, in habit, component actions, reactions and "stimuli" is not some external process of association.[4] Any mechanistic theory runs up against the fact that the learning process is systematic: the subject does not weld together individual movements and individual stimuli but acquires the power to respond with a certain type of solution to situations of a certain general form. The situations may differ widely from case to case, and the response movements may be entrusted sometimes to one operative organ, sometimes to another, both situations and responses in the various cases having in common not so much a partial identity of elements as a shared significance. Must we then see the origin of habit in an act of understanding which organizes the elements only to withdraw subsequently?[5] For example, is it not the case that forming the habit of dancing is discovering, by analysis, the formula of the movement in question, and then reconstructing it on the basis of the ideal outline by the use of previously acquired movements, those of walking and running? But before the formula of the new dance can incorporate certain elements of general motility, it must first have had, as it were, the stamp of movement set upon it. As has often been said, it is the body which "catches" (*kapiert*) and "comprehends" movement. The cultivation of habit is indeed the grasping of a significance, but it is the motor

---

[4] See, on this point, *La Structure du Comportement*, pp. 125 and ff.
[5] As Bergson, for example, thinks when he defines habit as "the fossilized residue of a spiritual activity."

grasping of a motor significance. Now what precisely does this mean? A woman may, without any calculation, keep a safe distance between the feather in her hat and things which might break it off. She feels where the feather is just as we feel where our hand is.[6] If I am in the habit of driving a car, I enter a narrow opening and see that I can "get through" without comparing the width of the opening with that of the wings, just as I go through a doorway without checking the width of the doorway against that of my body.[7] The hat and the car have ceased to be objects with a size and volume which is established by comparison with other objects. They have become potentialities of volume, the demand for a certain amount of free space. In the same way the iron gate to the Underground platform, and the road, have become restrictive potentialities and immediately appear passable or impassable for my body with its adjuncts. The blind man's stick has ceased to be an object for him, and is no longer perceived for itself; its point has become an area of sensitivity, extending the scope and active radius of touch, and providing a parallel to sight. In the exploration of things, the length of the stick does not enter expressly as a middle term: the blind man is rather aware of it through the position of objects than of the position of objects through it. The position of things is immediately given through the extent of the reach which carries him to it, which comprises besides the arm's own reach the stick's range of action. If I want to get used to a stick, I try it by touching a few things

with it, and eventually I have it "well in hand," I can see what things are "within reach" or out of reach of my stick. There is no question here of any quick estimate or any comparison between the objective length of the stick and the objective distance away of the goal to be reached. The points in space do not stand out as objective positions in relation to the objective position occupied by our body; they mark, in our vicinity, the varying range of our aims and our gestures. To get used to a hat, a car or a stick is to be transplanted into them, or conversely, to incorporate them into the bulk of our own body. Habit expresses our power of dilating our being in the world, or changing our existence by appropriating fresh instruments.[8] It is possible to know how to type without being able to say where the letters which make the words are to be found on the banks of keys. To know how to type is not, then, to know the place of each letter among the keys, nor even to have acquired a conditioned reflex for each one, which is set in motion by the letter as it comes before our eye. If habit is neither a form of knowledge nor an involuntary action, what then is it? It is knowledge in the hands, which is forthcoming only when bodily effort is made, and cannot be formulated in detachment from that effort. The subject knows where the letters are on the typewriter as we know where one of our limbs is, through a knowledge bred of familiarity

---

[6] Head, *Sensory disturbances from cerebral lesion,* p. 188.

[7] Grünbaum, *Aphasie und Motorik,* p. 395.

[8] It thus elucidates the nature of the body image. When we say that it presents us immediately with our bodily position, we do not mean, after the manner of empiricists, that it consists of a mosaic of "extensive sensations". It is a system which is open on to the world, and correlative with it.

which does not give us a position in objective space. The movement of her fingers is not presented to the typist as a path through space which can be described, but merely as a certain adjustment of motility, physiognomically distinguishable from any other. The question is often framed as if the perception of a letter written on paper aroused the representation of the same letter which in turn aroused the representation of the movement needed to strike it on the machine. But this is mythological language. When I run my eyes over the text set before me, there do not occur perceptions which stir up representations, but patterns are formed as I look, and these are endowed with a typical or familiar physiognomy. When I sit at my typewriter, a motor space opens up beneath my hands, in which I am about to "play" what I have read. The reading of the word is a modulation of visible space, the performance of the movement is. a modulation of manual space, and the whole question is how a certain physiognomy of "visual" patterns can evoke a certain type of motor response, how each "visual" structure eventually provides itself with its mobile essence without there being any need to spell the word or specify the movement in detail in order to translate one into the other. But this power of habit is no different from the general one which we exercise over our body: if I am ordered to touch my ear or my knee, I move my hand to my ear or my knee by the shortest route, without having to think of the initial position of my hand, or that of my ear, or the path between them. We said earlier that it is the body which "understands" in the cultivation of habit. This way of putting it will appear absurd,

if understanding is subsuming a sense-datum under an idea, and if the body is an object. But the phenomenon of habit is just what prompts us to revise our notion of "understand" and our notion of the body. To understand is to experience the harmony between what we aim at and what is given, between the intention and the performance—and the body is our anchorage in a world. When I put my hand to my knee, I experience at every stage of the movement the fulfilment of an intention which was not directed at my knee as an idea or even as an object, but as a present and real part of my living body, that is, finally, as a stage in my perpetual movement towards a world. When the typist performs the necessary movements on the typewriter, these movements are governed by an intention, but the intention does not posit the keys as objective locations. It is literally true that the subject who learns to type incorporates the key-bank space into his bodily space.

The example of instrumentalists shows even better how habit has its abode neither in thought nor in the objective body, but in the body as mediator of a world. It is known[9] that an experienced organist is capable of playing an organ which he does not know, which has more or fewer manuals, and stops differently arranged, compared with those on the instrument he is used to playing. He needs only an hour's practice to be ready to perform his programme. Such a short preparation rules out the supposition that new conditioned reflexes have here been substituted for the existing sets, except where both

---

[9] Cf. Chevalier, *L'Habitude*, pp. 202 and ff.

form a system and the change is all-embracing, which takes us away from the mechanistic theory, since in that case the reactions are mediated by a comprehensive grasp of the instrument. Are we to maintain that the organist analyses the organ, that he conjures up and retains a representation of the stops, pedals and manuals and their relation to each other in space? But during the short rehearsal preceding the concert, he does not act like a person about to draw up a plan. He sits on the seat, works the pedals, pulls out the stops, gets the measure of the instrument with his body, incorporates within himself the relevant directions and dimensions, settles into the organ as one settles into a house. He does not learn objective spatial positions for each stop and pedal, nor does he commit them to "memory." During the rehearsal, as during the performance, the stops, pedals and manuals are given to him as nothing more than possibilities of achieving certain emotional or musical values, and their positions are simply the places through which this value appears in the world. Between the musical essence of the piece as it is shown in the score and the notes which actually sound round the organ, so direct a relation is established that the organist's body and his instrument are merely the medium of this relationship. Henceforth the music exists by itself and through it all the rest exists.[10] There is here no

place for any "memory" of the position of the stops, and it is not in objective space that the organist in fact is playing. In reality his movements during rehearsal are consecratory gestures: they draw affective vectors, discover emotional sources, and create a space of expressiveness as the movements of the augur delimit the *templum*.

The whole problem of habit here is one of knowing how the musical significance of an action can be concentrated in a certain place to the extent that, in giving himself entirely to the music, the organist reaches for precisely those stops and pedals which are to bring it into being. Now the body is essentially an expressive space. If I want to take hold of an object, already, at a point of space about which I have been quite unmindful, this power of grasping constituted by my hand moves upwards towards the thing. I move my legs not as things in space two and a half feet from my head, but as a power of locomotion which extends my motor intention downwards. The main areas of my body are devoted to actions, and participate in their value, and asking why common sense makes the head the seat of thought raises the same problem as asking how the organist distributes, through "organ space," musical significances. But our body is not merely one expressive space among the rest, for that is simply the constituted body. It is the origin of the rest, expressive movement itself, that which causes them to begin to exist as things, under our hands and eyes. Although our body does not impose definite instincts upon us from birth, as it does upon animals, it does at least give to our life the form of generality, and develops our personal acts into stable

---

[10] "As though the musicians were not nearly so much playing the little phrase as performing the rites on which it insisted before it would consent to appear." (Proust, *Swann's Ways, II*, trans. C. K. Scott Moncrieff, Chatto & Windus, p. 180.)

"Its cries were so sudden that the violinist must snatch up his bow and race to catch them as they came." (Ibid., p. 186.)

dispositional tendencies. In this sense our nature is not long-established custom, since custom presupposes the form of passivity derived from nature. The body is our general medium for having a world. Sometimes it is restricted to the actions necessary for the conservation of life, and accordingly it posits around us a biological world; at other times, elaborating upon these primary actions and moving from their literal to a figurative meaning, it manifests through them a core of new significance: this is true of motor habits such as dancing. Sometimes, finally, the meaning aimed at cannot be achieved by the body's natural means; it must then build itself an instrument, and it projects thereby around itself a cultural world. At all levels it performs the same function which is to endow the instantaneous expressions of spontaneity with "a little renewable action and independent existence."[11] Habit is merely a form of this fundamental power. We say that the body has understood, and habit has been cultivated when it has absorbed a new meaning, and assimilated a fresh core of significance.

[11] Valéry, *Introduction à la Méthode de Léonard de Vinci, Variété*, p. 177.

To sum up, what we have discovered through the study of motility, is a new meaning of the word "meaning." The great strength of intellectualist psychology and idealist philosophy comes from their having no difficulty in showing that perception and thought have an intrinsic significance and cannot be explained in terms of the external association of fortuitously agglomerated contents. The *Cogito* was the coming to self-awareness of this inner core. But all meaning was *ipso facto* conceived as an act of thought, as the work of a pure *I,* and although rationalism easily refuted empiricism, it was itself unable to account for the variety of experience, for the element of senselessness in it, for the contingency of contents. Bodily experience forces us to acknowledge an imposition of meaning which is not the work of a universal constituting consciousness, a meaning which clings to certain contents. My body is that meaningful core which behaves like a general function, and which nevertheless exists, and is susceptible to disease. In it we learn to know that union of essence and existence which we shall find again in perception generally, and which we shall then have to describe more fully.

PHILOSOPHY OF SCIENCE

Existentialists rather generally hold that reason, concepts, and science do not grasp the whole of life, and that they may even be instruments that destroy existence and individuality. This theme is explored by Karl Jaspers in the following selection. In former ages, Jaspers observes, philosophy was itself considered a science. Today this view is no longer possible. The name "science" can belong properly only to the sciences. But they need to be purified: all that is pseudo-science and partial science needs to be removed from them. In turn, purified science demands a new and purified philosophy: new, for it must be developed within the new conditions produced by modern science; and purified, for it must grant a full recognition to scientific activity and conclusions. Such recognition, however, indicates that science does not encompass all truth, and that philosophy points beyond scientific objects to the individual in his inward action and freedom. Thus philosophy is the act of becoming conscious of our genuine being.

9   Purity in Science and Philosophy
Karl Jaspers (1883-1969)

Philosophy has from its very beginnings looked upon itself as science, indeed as science par excellence. To achieve the highest and most certain knowledge is the goal that has always animated its devotees.

How its scientific character came to be questioned can be understood only in the light of the development of the specifically modern sciences. These sciences made their greatest strides in the nineteenth century, largely outside philosophy, often in opposition to philosophy, and finally in an atmosphere of indifference to it. If philosophy was still expected to be a science, it was in a different sense than before; it was now expected to be a science in the same sense as those modern sciences that convince by virtue of their accomplishments. If it were unable to do so, it was argued, it had become pointless and might just as well die out.

Some decades ago the opinion was widespread that philosophy had had its

The selection is from Karl Jaspers, "Philosophy and Science," (tr. Ralph Manheim), in *Partisan Review*, 16 (1949), pp. 871 and 878-882. Copyright 1949 by *Partisan Review*. Used by permission of the Editors and the author.

place up to the moment when all the sciences had become independent of it, the original universal science. Now that all possible fields of research have been marked off, the days of philosophy are over. Now that we know how science obtains its universal validity, it has become evident that philosophy cannot stand up against judgment by these criteria. It deals in empty ideas because it sets up undemonstrable hypotheses, it disregards experience, it seduces by illusions, it takes possession of energies needed for genuine investigation and squanders them in empty talk about the whole. . . .

At a time when confusion prevails regarding the meaning of science, three tasks are imperative. . . .

First, the idea that total philosophical knowledge is scientific knowledge must be exposed as false. The sciences themselves critically explode this false total knowledge. It is here that the opposition to philosophy has its root, and in this respect contempt of it is justifiable.

Second, the sciences must be made pure. This can be accomplished through constant struggle and awareness in the course of our scientific activity itself. By and large, the need for basic clarity concerning science and its limits is readily admitted even by those who sin against such clarity in practice. But the essential is to achieve this purity within the specific sciences. This must be done largely through the critical work of the scientists themselves. But the philosopher who wishes to test the truth-meaning of scientific knowledge, to auscultate it, so to speak, must participate in the actual work of these scientists.

Third, a pure philosophy must be worked out in the new conditions that have been created by the modern sciences. This is indispensable for the sake of the sciences themselves. For philosophy is always alive in the sciences and so inseparable from them that the purity of both can be achieved only jointly. The rejection of philosophy usually leads to the unwitting development of a bad philosophy. The concrete work of the scientist is guided by his conscious or unconscious philosophy, and this philosophy cannot be the object of scientific method.

For example: It is impossible to prove scientifically that there should be such a thing as science. Or: The choice of an object of science that is made from among an infinite number of existing objects on the basis of this object itself is a choice that cannot be justified scientifically. Or: The ideas that guide us are tested in the systematic process of investigation, but they themselves do not become an object of direct investigation.

Science left to itself as mere science becomes homeless. The intellect is a whore, said Nicholas of Cusa, for it can prostitute itself to anything. Science is a whore, said Lenin, for it sells itself to any class interest. For Nicholas of Cusa it is Reason, and ultimately the knowledge of God, that gives meaning, certainty, and truth to intellectual knowledge; for Lenin, it is the classless society that promotes pure science. Be that as it may, awareness of all this is the business of philosophical reflection. Philosophy is inherent in the actual sciences themselves; it is their inner meaning that provides the scientist with sustenance and guides his methodical work. He who consolidates this guidance through reflection and becomes conscious of it has reached the stage of explicit philosophizing. If this guidance fails, science falls into gratuitous convention, meaningless correctness, aimless busy-ness, and spineless servitude.

A pure science requires a pure philosophy.

But how can philosophy be pure? Has it not always striven to be science? Our answer is: It is "science" but science of such a sort that in the sense of modern scientific inquiry it is both less and more than science.

Philosophy can be called science in so far as it presupposes the sciences. There is no tenable philosophy outside the sciences. Although conscious of its distinct character, philosophy is inseparable from science. It refuses to transgress against universally binding insight. Anyone who philosophizes must be familiar with scientific method.

Any philosopher who is not trained in a scientific discipline and who fails to keep his scientific interests constantly alive will inevitably bungle and stumble and mistake uncritical rough drafts for definitive knowledge. Unless an idea is submitted to the coldly dispassionate test of scientific inquiry, it is rapidly consumed in the fire of emotions and passions, or else it withers into a dry and narrow fanaticism.

Moreover, anyone who philosophizes strives for scientific knowledge, for it is the only way to genuine nonknowledge, it is as though the most magnificent insights could be achieved only through man's quest for the limit at which cognition runs aground, not seemingly and temporarily but genuinely and definitively, not with a sense of loss and despair but with a sense of genuine internal evidence. Only definitive knowledge can make definitive nonknowledge possible; it alone can achieve the authentic failure which opens up a vista, not merely upon the discoverable existent but upon being itself.

In accomplishing the great task of dispelling all magical conceptions, modern science enters upon the path that leads to the intuition of the true depth, the authentic mystery, which becomes present only through the most resolute knowledge in the consummation of nonknowledge.

Consequently philosophy turns against those who despise the sciences, against the sham prophets who deprecate scientific inquiry, who mistake the errors of science for science itself, and who would even hold science, "modern science," responsible for the evils and the inhumanity of our era.

Rejecting superstitious belief in science as well as contempt of science, philosophy grants its unconditional recognition to modern science. In its eyes science is a marvellous thing which can be relied upon more than anything else, the most significant achievement of man in his history, an achievement that is the source of great dangers but of even greater opportunities and that from now on must be regarded as a prerequisite of all human dignity. Without science, the philosopher knows, his own pursuits eventuate in nothing.

These pursuits can continue to be called scientific because philosophy proceeds methodically and because it is conscious of its methods. But these methods differ from those of science in that they have no object of inquiry. Any specific object is the object of a particular science. Were I to say that the object of philosophy is the whole, the world, being, philosophical critique would answer that such terms do not denote genuine objects. The methods of philosophy are methods of transcending the object. To philosophize is to transcend. But since our thinking is inseparable from objects, the history of philosophy is an account of how the progress of human thought has succeeded in transcending the objects of philosophy. These objects, the great creations of philosophy, function as road signs, indicating the direction of philosophical transcending. Thus there is no substitute for the profound discourse of the metaphysician, which speaks to us from the centuries; to assimilate it from its source in the history of philosophy is not only to know something that once was but to make it come to life.

The mass of sham philosophical knowledge taught in the schools originates in the hypostatization of entities that have served for a time as the signpost of philosophy but are always being transcended by it. Such hypostatized entities are nothing but the *capita mortua,* the ossuaries of the great metaphysical systems. To imagine that they confer knowledge is a philosophical per-version. In philosophizing we must not fall under the spell of the object that we use as a means of transcendence. We must remain masters of our thoughts and not be subjugated by them.

Yet in this intellectual transcendence, which is proper to philosophy and which is analogous to scientific forms, philosophy is less than science. For it does not gain any tangible results or any intellectually binding insight. There is no overlooking the simple fact that while scientific cognition is identical throughout the world, philosophy, despite its claim to universality, is not actually universal in any shape or form. This fact is the outward characteristic of the peculiar nature of philosophical truth. Although scientific truth is universally valid, it remains relative to method and assumptions; philosophical truth is absolute for him who conquers it in historical actuality, but its statements are not universally valid. Scientific truth is one and the same for all—philosophical truth wears multiple historical cloaks; each of these is the manifestation of a unique reality, each has its justification, but they are not identically transmissible.

The one philosophy is the *philosophia perennis* around which all philosophies revolve, which no one possesses, in which every genuine philosopher shares, and which nevertheless can never achieve the form of an intellectual edifice valid for all and exclusively true.

Thus philosophy is not only less but also more than science, namely, as the source of a truth that is inaccessible to scientifically binding knowledge. It is this philosophy that is meant in such definitions as: To philosophize is to learn how to die or to rise to godhead —or to know being *qua* being. The meaning of such definitions is: Philosophical thought is inward action; it appeals to freedom; it is a summons to transcendence. Or the same thing can be formulated differently: Philosophy is the act of becoming conscious of genuine being—or is the thinking of a faith in man that must be infinitely elucidated—or is the way of man's self-assertion through thinking.

But none of these propositions is properly speaking a definition. There is no definition of philosophy, because philosophy cannot be determined by something outside it. There is no genus above philosophy, under which it can be subsumed as a species. Philosophy defines itself, relates itself directly to godhead, and does not justify itself by any kind of utility. It grows out of the primal source in which man is given to himself.

To sum up: The sciences do not encompass all of the truth but only the exact knowledge that is binding to the intellect and universally valid. Truth has a greater scope, and part of it can reveal itself only to philosophical reason. Throughout the centuries since the early Middle Ages, philosophical works have been written under the title "On the Truth"; today the same task still remains urgent, i.e., to gain insight into the essence of truth in its full scope under the present conditions of scientific knowledge and historical experience.

The foregoing considerations also apply to the relation between science and philosophy. Only if the two are strictly distinguished can the inseparable connection between them remain pure and truthful.

PHILOSOPHY OF RELIGION

As a general position, existentialism includes both atheists and theists, and the latter in some variety. The religious value has always been central in man's experience; and a philosophy of concrete experience will explore it avidly.

There is some doubt about applying the technical term "existentialist" to the writer of the following selection, Paul Tillich, for he rejects many of the formulations of other existentialists. Yet if the term is used broadly, he may be included here, for he approaches the problems of religion through concrete experience and its ontology rather than through arguments from nature, or arguments at all. Tillich is here defining and characterizing the concept of faith. Faith, he writes, is the state of being ultimately concerned. It is an act of the total personality and lies at the very center of the self. Man is driven toward faith by the sense of the infinite, which he both possesses and yearns for. Faith is about the unconditioned and ultimate. Idolatrous faith such as worship of the self or the state is about something neither unconditional nor ultimate. It inevitably ends in "existential disappointment." Only the faith of theism can bring existential fulfillment.

10 The Nature of Faith

Paul Tillich (1886-1965)

1. Faith as Ultimate Concern. Faith is the state of being ultimately concerned: the dynamics of faith are the dynamics of man's ultimate concern. Man, like every living being, is concerned about many things, above all about those which condition his very existence, such as food and shelter. But man, in contrast to other living beings, has spiritual concerns —cognitive, esthetic, social, political. Some of them are urgent, often extremely urgent, and each of them as well

The selection is from Paul Tillich, *Dynamics of Faith* (New York: Harper & Brothers; London: George Allen & Unwin, Ltd.), pp. 1-12. Copyright © 1957 by Paul Tillich. Reprinted by permission of Harper & Row, Publishers, Incorporated and George Allen & Unwin, Ltd.

as the vital concerns can claim ultimacy for a human life or the life of a social group. If it claims ultimacy it demands the total surrender of him who accepts this claim, and it promises total fulfillment even if all other claims have to be subjected to it or rejected in its name. If a national group makes life and growth of the nation its ultimate concern, it demands that all other concerns, economic well-being, health and life, family, esthetic and cognitive truth, justice and humanity, be sacrificed. The extreme nationalisms of our century are laboratories for the study of what ultimate concern means in all aspects of human existence, including the smallest concern of one's daily life. Everything is centered in the only god, the nation—a god who certainly proves to be a demon, but who shows clearly the unconditional character of an ultimate concern.

But it is not only the unconditional demand made by that which it one's ultimate concern, it is also the promise of ultimate fulfillment which is accepted in the act of faith. The content of this promise is not necessarily defined. It can be expressed in indefinite symbols or in concrete symbols which cannot be taken literally, like the "greatness" of one's nation in which one participates even if one has died for it, or the conquest of mankind by the "saving race," etc. In each of these cases it is "ultimate fulfillment" that is promised, and it is exclusion from such fulfillment which is threatened if the unconditional demand is not obeyed.

An example—and more than an example—is the faith manifest in the religion of the Old Testament. It also has the character of ultimate concern in demand, threat and promise. The content of this concern is not the nation—although Jewish nationalism has sometimes tried to distort it into that—but the content is the God of justice, who, because he represents justice for everybody and every nation, is called the universal God, the God of the universe. He is the ultimate concern of every pious Jew, and therefore in his name the great commandment is given: "You shall love the Lord your God with all your heart, and with all your soul, and with all your might" (Deut. 6:5). This is what ultimate concern means and from these words the term "ultimate concern" is derived. They state unambiguously the character of genuine faith, the demand of total surrender to the subject of ultimate concern. The Old Testament is full of commands which make the nature of this surrender concrete, and it is full of promises and threats in relation to it. Here also are the promises of symbolic indefiniteness, although they center around fulfillment of the national and individual life, and the threat is the exclusion from such fulfillment through national extinction and individual catastrophe. Faith, for the men of the Old Testament, is the state of being ultimately and unconditionally concerned about Jahweh and about what he represents in demand, threat and promise.

Another example—almost a counterexample, yet nevertheless equally revealing—is the ultimate concern with "success" and with social standing and economic power. It is the god of many people in the highly competitive Western culture and it does what every ultimate concern must do: it demands unconditional surrender to its laws even if the price is the sacrifice of genuine human relations, personal conviction, and creative *eros*. Its threat is social and economic defeat, and its promise—indefinite as all such promises—the fulfillment of one's being. It is the breakdown of this kind of faith which characterizes and makes religiously important most contemporary literature. Not false calculations but a misplaced faith is revealed in novels like *Point of No Return*. When fulfilled, the promise of this faith proves to be empty.

Faith is the state of being ultimately concerned. The content matters infinitely for the life of the believer, but it does not matter for the formal definition of faith. And this is the first step we have to make in order to understand the dynamics of faith.

2. Faith as a Centered Act.

Faith as ultimate concern is an act of the total personality. It happens in the center of the personal life and includes all its elements. Faith is the most centered act of the human mind. It is not a movement of a special section or a special function of man's total being. They all are united in the act of faith. But faith is not the sum total of their impacts. It transcends every special impact as well as the totality of them and it has itself a decisive impact on each of them.

Since faith is an act of the personality as a whole, it participates in the dynamics of personal life. These dynamics have been described in many ways, especially in the recent developments of analytic psychology. Thinking in polarities, their tensions and their possible conflicts, is a common characteristic of most of them. This makes the psychology of personality highly dynamic and requires a dynamic theory of faith as the most personal of all personal acts. The first and decisive polarity in analytic psychology is that between the so-called unconscious and the conscious. Faith as an act of the total personality is not imaginable without the participation of the unconscious elements in the personality structure. They are always present and decide largely about the content of faith. But, on the other hand, faith is a conscious act and the unconscious elements participate in the creation of faith only if they are taken into the personal center which transcends each of them. If this does not happen, if unconscious forces determine the mental status without a centered act, faith does not occur, and compulsions take its place. For faith is a matter of freedom. Freedom is nothing more than the possibility of centered personal acts.

The frequent discussion in which faith and freedom are contrasted could be helped by the insight that faith is a free, namely, centered act of the personality. In this respect freedom and faith are identical.

Also important for the understanding of faith is the polarity between what Freud and his school call ego and superego. The concept of the superego is quite ambiguous. On the one hand, it is the basis of all cultural life because it restricts the uninhibited actualization of the always-driving libido; on the other hand, it cuts off man's vital forces, and produces disgust about the whole system of cultural restrictions, and brings about a neurotic state of mind. From this point of view, the symbols of faith are considered to be expressions of the superego or, more concretely, to be an expression of the father image which gives content to the superego. Responsible for this inadequate theory of the superego is Freud's naturalistic negation of norms and principles. If the superego is not established through valid principles, it becomes a suppressive tyrant. But real faith, even if it uses the father image for its expression, transforms this image into a principle of truth and justice to be defended even against the "father." Faith and culture can be affirmed only if the superego represents the norms and principles of reality.

This leads to the question of how faith as a personal, centered act is related to the rational structure of man's personality which is manifest in his meaningful language, in his ability to know the true and to do the good, in his sense of beauty and justice. All this, and not only his possibility to analyze, to calculate and to argue, makes him a rational being. But in spite of this larger concept of reason we must deny that man's essential nature is identical with the rational character of his mind. Man is able to decide for or against reason, he is able to create beyond reason or to destroy below reason. This power is the power of his self, the center of self-relatedness in which all elements of his being are united. Faith is not an act of any of his rational functions, as it is not an act of the unconscious, but it is an act in which both the rational and the nonrational elements of his being are transcended.

Faith as the embracing and centered act of the personality is "ecstatic." It transcends both the drives of the non-rational unconscious and the structures of the rational conscious. It transcends them, but it does not destroy them. The ecstatic character of faith does not exclude its rational character although it is not identical with it, and it includes nonrational strivings without being identical with them. In the ecstasy of faith there is an awareness of truth and of ethical value; there are also past loves and hates, conflicts and reunions, individual and collective influences. "Ecstasy" means "standing outside of oneself"—without ceasing to be oneself—with all the elements which are united in the personal center.

A further polarity in these elements, relevant for the understanding of faith, is the tension between the cognitive function of man's personal life, on the one hand, and emotion and will, on the other hand. In a later discussion I will try to show that many distortions of the meaning of faith are rooted in the attempt to subsume faith to the one or the other of these functions. At this point it must be stated as sharply and insistently as possible that in every act of faith there is cognitive affirmation, not as the result of an independent process of inquiry but as an inseparable element in a total act of acceptance and surrender. This also excludes the idea that faith is the result of an independent act of "will to believe." There is certainly affirmation by the will of what concerns one ultimately, but faith is not a creation of the will. In the ecstasy of faith the will to accept and to surrender is an element, but not the cause. And this is true also of feeling. Faith is not an emotional outburst: this is not the meaning of ecstasy. Certainly, emotion is in it, as in every act of man's spiritual life. But emotion does not produce faith. Faith has a cognitive content and is an act of the will. It is the unity of every element in the centered self. Of course, the unity of all elements in the act of faith does not prevent one or the other element from dominating in a special form of faith. It dominates the character of faith but it does not create the act of faith.

This also answers the question of a possible psychology of faith. Everything that happens in man's personal being can become an object of psychology. And it is rather important for both the philosopher of religion and the practical minister to know how the act of faith is embedded in the totality of psychological processes. But in contrast to this justified and desirable form of a psychology of faith there is another one which tries to derive faith from something that is not faith but is most frequently fear. The presupposition of this method is that fear or something else from which faith is derived is more original and basic than faith. But this presupposition cannot be proved. On the contrary, one can prove that in the scientific method which leads to such consequences faith is already effective. Faith precedes all attempts to derive it from something else, because these attempts are themselves based on faith.

3.   The Source of Faith.

We have described the act of faith and its relation to the dynamics of personality. Faith is a total and centered act of the personal self, the act of unconditional, infinite and ultimate concern. The question now arises: what is the source of this all-embracing and all-transcending concern? The word "concern" points to two sides of a relationship, the relation between the one who is concerned and his concern. In both respects we have to imagine man's situation in itself and in his world. The reality of man's ultimate concern reveals something about his being, namely, that he is able to transcend the flux of relative and transitory experiences of his ordinary life. Man's experiences, feelings, thoughts are conditioned and finite. They not only come and go, but their content is of finite and conditional concern—unless they are elevated to unconditional validity. But this presupposes the general possibility of doing so; it presupposes the element of infinity in man. Man is able to understand in an immediate personal and central act the meaning of the ultimate, the unconditional, the absolute, the infinite. This alone makes faith a human potentiality.

Human potentialities are powers that drive toward actualization. Man is driven toward faith by his awareness of the infinite to which he belongs, but which he does not own like a possession. This is in abstract terms what concretely appears as the "restlessness of the heart" within the flux of life.

The unconditional concern which is faith is the concern about the unconditional. The infinite passion, as faith has been described, is the passion for the infinite. Or, to use our first term, the ultimate concern is concern about what is experienced as ultimate. In this way we have turned from the subjective meaning of faith as a centered act of the personality to its objective meaning, to what is meant in the act of faith. It would not help at this point of our analysis to call that which is meant in the act of faith "God" or "a god." For at this step we ask: What in the idea of God constitutes divinity? The answer is: It is the element of the unconditional and of ultimacy. This carries the quality of divinity. If this is seen, one can understand why almost every thing "in heaven and on earth" has received ultimacy in the history of human religion. But we also can understand that a critical principle was and is at work in man's religious consciousness, namely, that which is really ultimate over against what claims to be ultimate but is only preliminary, transitory, finite.

The term "ultimate concern" unites the subjective and the objective side of the act of faith—the *fides qua creditur* (the Faith through which one believes) and the *fides quae creditur* (the faith which is believed). The first is the classical term for the centered act of the personality, the ultimate concern. The second is the classical term for that toward which this act is directed, the ultimate itself, expressed in symbols of the divine. This distinction is very important, but not ultimately so, for the one side cannot be without the other. There is no faith without a content toward which it is directed. There is always something meant in the act of faith. And there is no way of having the content of faith except in the act of faith. All speaking about divine matters which is not done in the state of ultimate concern is meaningless. Because that which is meant in the act of faith cannot be approached in any other way than through an act of faith.

In terms like ultimate, unconditional, infinite, absolute, the difference between subjectivity and objectivity is overcome. The ultimate of the act of faith and the ultimate that is meant in the act of faith are one and the same. This is symbolically expressed by the mystics when they say that their knowledge of God is the knowledge God has of himself; and it is expressed by Paul when he says (I Cor. 13) that he will know as he is known, namely, by God. God never can be object without being at the same time subject. Even a successful prayer is, according to Paul (Rom. 8), not possible without God as Spirit praying within us. The same experience expressed in abstract language is the disappearance of the ordinary subject-object scheme in the experience of the ultimate, the unconditional. In the act of faith that which is the source of this act is present beyond the cleavage of subject and object. It is present as both and beyond both.

This character of faith gives an additional criterion for distinguishing true and false ultimacy. The finite which claims infinity without having it (as, e.g., a nation or success) is not able to transcend the subject-object scheme. It remains an object which the believer looks at as a subject. He can approach it with ordinary knowledge and subject it to ordinary handling. There are, of course, many degrees in the endless realm of false ultimacies. The nation is nearer to true ultimacy than is success. Nationalistic ecstasy can produce a state in which the subject is almost swallowed by the object. But after a period the subject emerges again, disappointed radically and totally, and by looking at the nation in a skeptical and calculating way does injustice even to its justified claims. The more idolatrous a faith the less it is able to overcome the cleavage between subject and object. For that is the difference between true and idolatrous faith. In true faith the ultimate concern is a concern about the truly ultimate; while in idolatrous faith preliminary, finite realities are elevated to the rank of ultimacy. The inescapable consequence of idolatrous faith is "existential disappointment," a disappointment which penetrates into the very existence of man! This is the dynamics of idolatrous faith: that it is faith, and as such, the centered act of a personality; that the centering point is something which is more or less on to the periphery; and that, therefore, the act of faith leads to a loss of the center and to a disruption of the personality. The ecstatic character of even an idolatrous faith can hide this consequence only for a certain time. But finally it breaks into the open.

CRITIQUE

Diverse as existential thought is, it has been shown in the preceding selections to be primarily concerned with problems of our developing humanity and the value experiences open to it. In a very broad sense of the word, ethics and ethical problems have been uppermost in the writings of existentialists, however much there have also been ontological and religious analyses. In the following selection, Professor Manser reviews some of the basic theses of existentialism, and then goes on to consider critically such central ethical ideas as moral decision-making, authenticity, and preoccupation with extreme situations. In some ways, he says, the first of these is most serious, for the existentialist analysis leaves us with no concrete advice on what to do. Perhaps indeed this is man's moral situation, though Manser's somewhat paradoxical conclusion is that existentialists are therefore weakest when dealing with ethical matters.

11 Existence and Ethics

A. R. Manser (1924-   )

It is no easy matter to discuss Existentialism before an audience of British philosophers. The very name itself is enough to conjure up visions of woolly metaphysics, of the "systematic misuse of the verb 'to be' ", of which we on this side of the Channel have been laboriously ridding ourselves. It is even surprising that such a topic should be accepted for a joint session; perhaps it is a gesture towards an intellectual "Common Market". Certainly there is room for greater philosophical contact across the Channel, but I am not sure that this is the best subject to form a bridge between two different traditions of thought. For, like many labelled philosophical movements, those who have been so described tend to reject the term "existentialist". Even Sartre, so often regarded as an archetypical example, originally refused the title; Merleau-Ponty reports that when he found that he was continually called one, he decided that he hadn't the right to reject the description, since that was how others saw him. Certainly no major philosophical figure of the present time has set out to *be* an existentialist, just as I suspect no British philosopher has set out to be a linguistic analyst. In both cases, the groupings have been imposed from the outside and usually by those who were hostile to, or ignorant of, the nature of the philosophical enterprise. Hence in this paper I shall in no way be setting out a well-defined doctrine. No doubt many of the things I have to say have been contradicted or denied by one or other of the Existential philosophers. Nevertheless I hope that there will be some resemblance between their views and the sub-

The selection is from A. R. Manser, "Existence and Ethics," *Proceedings of The Aristotelian Society*, Supplementary Volume 37 (1963), pp. 11–26. Copyright © 1963 The Aristotelian Society. Reprinted by permission of the Editor of The Aristotelian Society.

stance of my paper. In any case, I think there are some philosophical points worth discussing which arise from what has been said by Kierkegaard, Heidegger, Marcel, Sartre and Jaspers, to list the five to whom the description is generally applied.

If Existentialism has met with hostility from professional philosophers in this country, it seems to me also to have been unfortunate in its defenders; indeed, these may well be partially responsible for the hostility. The defence consists of accusations of failure to provide spiritual consolation on the part of British philosophy together with brief and often misleading statements of the headier fare provided on the Continent. The titles of books of this character generally refer to crises and predicaments of modern man; the core of the books is a study of the five philosophers I have mentioned, garnished with some literary figures such as Dostoevsky and Kafka. Sometimes there is an attempt to show that many earlier philosophers were 'really' existentialists, just as some enthusiasts of a different persuasion have maintained that many of the great philosophers of the past were 'really' doing analysis. The most popular starting point of such surveys is naturally Augustine. Some Christian apologists, worried by the success of the new philosophy, have even gone so far as to claim that Aquinas was the greatest existentialist of them all; after all, he did stress 'existence' more and 'essence' less than Aristotle. If anyone who talks about existence is to be called an existentialist, then the label has been made meaningless, as in the case of talking of anyone who mentions the importance of language as a linguistic philosopher.

Just as genuine linguistic philosophers don't talk about language in the abstract, but deal with problems that arise from the use of particular bits of language, so genuine existentialists don't talk about existence as such, but about problems that arise for human beings in the course of their existence.

Already there seems to be something peculiar being said, for whereas we undoubtedly do use language, existing is not something that we do. Austin's note in *Sense and Sensibilia* should prevent us from falling into the trap: " 'Exist', of course, is itself extremely tricky. The word is a verb, but it does not describe something that things do all the time, like breathing, only quieter—ticking over, as it were, in a metaphysical sort of way. It is only too easy to start wondering what, then, existing *is*" (p. 68n). "Existence" and "being" are useful words, but their usefulness lies in their general and neutral character. Questions about the existence of anything can only be answered by paying attention to the sort of thing it is; any other sort of enquiry can only lead to the most questionable sort of metaphysics. It is true that Heidegger, in his later work, seems to fall into this trap; he puts "What is Being?" as the central question of philosophy. But in spite of this, existentialists in general seem only concerned with one sort of existence, that of human beings. Questions such as "Why should there be anything rather than nothing?" are not raised by them, and even their use of "nothing" can be seen, by careful examination, to be far from the fallacy committed by the White King with "nobody". The existence of material objects is only of interest to them in so far as it shows up the existence of people. Even

Roquentin's discovery, in *La Nausée*, that the chestnut root exists in its own right is, and is intended by the author to be, an anti-idealist argument of sorts, not very different from Moore's "Proof" of the external world. There is nothing 'metaphysical', in the bad sense of the word, about it. That there is an external world, however, does have some bearing on our existence.

The existentialists, then, are concerned with human existence, and are attempting to make some general statements about it. The first obvious objection is that if this is the case, then they are not talking about *existence*, but about human beings; their subject might be called 'philosophical anthropology', and this might be considered a form of old-fashioned metaphysics. It seems to me that the reply to this accusation would refer to an awareness of existence which they would regard both as the starting point for their enquiry and the justification, if needed, for their name. This awareness is something very different from what Descartes claimed to have achieved with the *Cogito*. I will discuss this point in more detail later, but the main difference lies in the fact that the existentialists stress an emotional awareness, whereas Descartes was concerned with what might be called a logical point. Merely to say "I exist" is to make an empty statement, because there is no possibility of *saying* "I don't exist". Existentialists demand an emotional awareness of existence which is not obtained as a result of a logical process. This awareness is considered to be comparatively rare, because for the greater part of the time we are so immersed in the activities of the world that we direct our attention away

from ourselves and on to the various objects we are occupied with. It is significant that Roquentin's discovery of his existence occurs when he is cut off from most normal human contacts and activities. Again, in situations involving choice, particularly where the choice is an important and difficult one, we may be forced to realise that it is we who are choosing. But, because this awareness is normally unpleasant, we tend to ignore or neglect it; it is much easier to pretend that one is acting because one has to act in that way, or because "they" expect it of one. There are numerous devices of "bad faith" to protect us from this uncomfortable awareness. (I don't think any existentialists would wish to maintain that we ought always to be aware of our existence in this way, that all our decisions should be made in fear and trembling; it is rather that such an awareness is an essential starting point for philosophy.)

The existentialists' search for this sentiment of existence is not undertaken in the interest of abstract metaphysical theory; there is always an ethical purpose behind the enquiry. Indeed, it seems at times as if the claim were that a genuine realisation of my own existence is at the same time a discovery of the right way of life. This sounds like the ethics of "Know thyself"; there are similarities between such a morality and existential morality, some of which I will mention below, but the existentialists would stress that it is the unique individual which is important, that the discovery of existence is not one of a universal "essence" of man which will lead to a recipe for the right way of life or happiness. The catch-phrase "Existence is prior to essence" has, as part of its function, the ruling out of such "metaphysical" moralities. (The phrase is due to Sartre, but he intended it to characterise all 'existential' philosophies.) The stress on the unique individual has led to the claim that there is no single set of ethical precepts which apply to men as such. Some English commentators have interpreted this to mean that an existential moral rule is one which is not universalisable; "I ought to do this" does not imply that anyone else in the same position as me ought to do it. Apart from the question of the propriety of using "ought" in such a way, such a view would seem to be based on a misunderstanding of what the existentialists are looking for; a set of rules would, for them, imply the possibility of bad faith. It has been suggested, with some justification, that their search is one for salvation, in a religious or quasi-religious sense. In fact, the major problem with such writers seems to be that they undoubtedly regard moral questions as immensely important, as the central problem of "existence" and thus of philosophy, but that they by no means succeed in making it clear what solution they are offering to the problems; in some cases, even, it is hard to see what problems are worrying them.

It is, of course, possible to offer a sketch of their views, using their own terminology; such a sketch can be made extremely convincing at a high level of generality. It is in filling in the concrete details of the picture that the difficulties are encountered. The sketch might run as follows: human life is one of action, but authentic action can only spring from a person who is a genuine individual, who fully understands his own

existence, and this understanding is an emotional as much as an intellectual achievement. In the rest of this paper I want to examine this connexion between "existence" and "authenticity" which is the core of existentialism, and to try and set it out in as sympathetic a light as I can. One difficulty in doing so lies in the fact that there is not a simple connexion —there is no deductive pathway from existence to morality once a crude creation theory is rejected—but rather an emotional one. For this reason the writings of existentialists frequently resemble novels rather than traditional works of philosophy. I say that they *resemble* novels because their function, in spite of the resemblance, is philosophical. The position is complicated by the fact that some, such as Sartre and Marcel, produce both works of philosophy and literary works, and in the case of Kierkegaard it is not clear in which category most of his writings are to be placed. In the first two instances, however, it seems possible to distinguish sharply between the two sides; in so far as they succeed as literary artists, their work is not philosophy and *vice versa*. *La Nausée* fails as literature precisely because it is so full of philosophy; it appeals mainly to those who know their philosophical texts and can recognise the numerous allusions to them. Any interest we may have in the characters as human beings is secondary. The primary function of such apparently literary passages is the same as that of the striking examples so often used in contemporary British philosophy; neither is meant merely as a particular fact. We are not expected to be interested in them for their own sake, but for what they indicate. For the existentialists they have the further point that they emphasise the concrete nature of their philosophy, in contrast to what they consider the abstractness of traditional metaphysics, as in Kierkegaard's jibe that the philosopher constructs a palace and lives in a hut beside it.

The existentialist claim might be clearer if expressed, as it often is, in opposition to Descartes, who also claimed to use knowledge of his own existence as the starting point of his philosophy. The *Cogito* served as the foundation on which to construct the system. But the Existentialists consider that the Cartesian *Cogito* is not genuinely "existential". It is true that Descartes needed it in the context of his argument to establish one *particular* existence, and that it was this that differentiated it from the innumerable other "eternal truths" that could be known (*cf. Principles of Philosophy* I, No. 49). But, like them, the *Cogito* was a necessary truth. Hence, though it purports to establish a particular existence, it fails because there is nothing to distinguish the existence it establishes from any other. It may well be that "I am, I exist, is necessarily true each time I pronounce it or that I mentally conceive it", but this is a public truth, the equivalent of a mathematical existence theorem, not a discovery of Descartes' self by Descartes. No doubt it serves to solve the particular problem in philosophy that worried Descartes, but this again makes it more like a theorem than like a piece of genuine self-knowledge. In going through the various moves which led to the *Cogito*, Descartes had not fulfilled the command "Know thyself". The way in which "I" appears in the proof succeeds in abstracting all that is personal from it. For

it is in doing logic and mathematics that we are least personal. Even if I "prove" the theorem for the first time, it is because of the universal element in it that it is called a proof, not because of what "I" have done. Similarly, in constructing the proof I feel that I am discovering something that is there already, not creating something. Hence, the existentialists claim, the *Cogito* is useless for self-knowledge in any real sense of the term.

In fact there is some analogy between existentialism and the Greek moralities of "Know thyself" as well as with the doctrines of psycho-analysis, both of which connect understanding of oneself with a "right way of life". All three might be called "moralities of being" in contrast to "moralities of doing" which are those normally considered under the heading "ethics" in this country. Moralities of being are primarily concerned with the way of life that will lead to happiness for the practitioner, rather than to social harmony. (Though of course they also assume that what leads to the individual's happiness will not be contrary to social harmony.) The analogy between psycho-analysis and existentialism is in fact the closer one; there is even a school of "existential analysts" which claims some success for its techniques, based primarily on the writings of Heidegger. The point of the analogy here is that it is no good for the patient to know that he has a certain complex, in the sense of intellectually accepting the diagnosis given by the analyst of his case. Similarly, the analyst must not merely discover the existence of a certain complex in the way in which an ordinary doctor recognises a disease. He must be able to exhibit the complex to the patient, in order that the latter may understand it fully, for only through such genuine understanding can a cure result. The cure does not result from self-knowledge in general terms, but from detailed knowledge of all the particular features of his own history which were responsible for the complex.

But there is more to the psychoanalytical cure than simple recognition of the past by the patient; this knowledge must be integrated into a new way of life which commits him to a different course of action in the future. Indeed, it might be said that this commitment is a measure of the self-knowledge obtained. Even in the course of the treatment such an emotional understanding must occur as the patient transfers various attitudes to the person of the analyst. Similarly in the case of an ethics of self-knowledge the claim to know oneself will only be allowed if it involves a change of behaviour on the agent's part; mere intellectual assent to a series of propositions is not enough. Freud, in one passage, explicitly connects his own doctrine with such an ethic of self-knowledge: "We hold that whoever has passed successfully through an education for truthfulness towards himself will therefore be protected permanently against the danger of immorality, even if his standard of morality should differ somehow from social convention."

The difference between existentialism and the two views that I have been using as comparisons lies in its denial that there is a common "self" to know, a denial again summed up by the catchphrase "Existence is prior to essence". Man is something to be created in the course of life, not a piece of mechanism which merely has to be repaired in accordance with its original plan in order to function correctly. From the essentialist point of view, self-knowledge, however involved with emotion and action, is knowledge of what men have in common; the Freudian ideal of normality is based on a theory of human nature, as are moralities of "Know thyself". The existentialist objection to this view, and it is an objection put forward by both the Christian and the atheistic branches of the movement, is that if such were the case then there would be a formula, a set of rules, which could be followed mechanically and which would lead to happiness or the right way of life. For them, this is to reduce living to the level of a mere technique far removed from an authentic existence. Kierkegaard, for instance, in his criticism of the "so-called Christians" among his contemporaries, stressed the way in which they made out that Christianity was something easy, demanding very little effort and no radical change in the life of the believer. For him, faith involved an element of risk and hence of commitment. The risk, however, is not the every-day one of failing to achieve the objective, not the sort of risk that is involved in any journey of not getting to the destination. Every time I set off for a trip there is a possibility that I will not reach my goal; a breakdown, accident or some other hindrance may intervene. But such things are purely external and beyond my control, don't affect the nature of my intention to go to a particular place. Kierkegaard was thinking of quite other risks, those involving myself and the possibility that God did not exist; in other words risks which were part of the nature of the project of faith itself. The existence of a set of rules which could be obeyed and would lead to a satisfactory solution would alter the very nature of the project. Other examples which existentialists would give would be getting married or joining a revolutionary political party.

It is decisions like these, involving all the agent's life, that the existentialists want to consider the subject matter of ethics. It is noteworthy that they have little to say about ordinary problems of duty, day to day honesty, promise-keeping and so on. There is some evidence that they would regard these as typically "bourgeois" virtues, shop-keepers' morality, and hence as part of a resolutely inauthentic life. On the other hand, there is no evidence that they wish to advocate deliberately failing to conform to such traditional moral rules for the sake of authenticity. I think they tend to look on such rules rather as manners would be normally considered, conventions which are all very well in promoting social intercourse but which must always be sacrificed if a real ethical point is in conflict with them. It might be said that a kind of reclassification was being carried on; only really radical decisions can be given the honorific title of "ethical" (or "existential"), and which decisions are of this kind can partly be seen from the fact that rules are irrelevant to them. An existentialist slogan might run. "Where there are rules, there is no morality; where there is morality, no rules." Authenticity and rules cannot be found together.

In one sense, of course, it is obvious that any difficult moral decision will be one where there isn't a simple answer provided by existing morality; if there were, it wouldn't be a difficult decision. Nevertheless, I think the existentialists

are attempting to say more than this. Even in the difficult case it is usually possible to see what considerations are relevant to the decision within the normal moral code. They seem to want to cut out any recourse to anything which might be generalised into a system and hence to refuse even to offer advice. Sartre relates that he told the young man worried whether to stay in Occupied France and look after his mother or leave for England and the Free French forces that he just had to choose between these alternatives; the choice would indicate or constitute his commitment and his moral attitude. This attitude is something like the one expressed by the Categorical Imperative, "Act only on that maxim which you can at the same time also will to be universal law", but Kant was convinced that human nature provided definite limitations on the range of possibilities for maxims; some, for him, just couldn't imaginably be so generalised. The existentialists do not provide any such limitations beyond those of authenticity and commitment. "Authenticity" is a term much used in their writings, though never very clearly defined; it seems to involve honesty towards oneself, a recognition of what one *really* is, this constituting an essential foundation for any true commitment. In other words, it is a realisation that one *is* what one makes oneself by one's acts. The opposite is "bad faith", the deliberate or semi-deliberate suppression of self-knowledge by claiming that one has a certain character as the result of heredity or upbringing, and that this cannot be changed by any voluntary means. Partly, no doubt, because of its associations, the term "authentic" seems to have some meaning in the contexts in which it is used, and the devastating analyses Sartre gives of bad faith reinforce this idea. But when an attempt is made to employ the notion to solve a moral dilemma, such as the one just quoted, it gives no assistance whatsoever. It is clear that existentialists are convinced that the attempt to be authentic rules out certain possibilities of action, but it is not clear what possibilities are eliminated nor the precise grounds for their elimination. Sartre, for example, is confident that there couldn't be an authentic anti-semite. Unless some other principles are introduced, there seems no reason why I should not commit myself to such a policy. It is clear that Sartre wouldn't do so, but not that he has philosophic grounds for not doing so.

This is a consequence of the existentialist reduction of human beings to bare existence, their insistence that man has to create himself. It is for this reason that I compared the doctrine to Kant's, paradoxical as it may sound. In choosing what I am to become, I am at the same time, as it were, choosing what I would like everyone else to be as well, and thus creating not only an individual but also the species Man. As this is a matter of producing something new, there can be no formula or general advice. This does not prevent the existentialists from rating some attempts higher than others, as in their condemnation of the bourgeoisie, the settled and comfortable. But this assessment seems more like aesthetic than moral commendation; the existentialist hero, like the great work of art, is working within his own set of rules. And again as in a work of art, imitation of the original will inevitably fail to produce equal

greatness. This aesthetic attitude to ethics seems to run through a great deal of existentialism, paradoxical as it may sound after what I have said about the seriousness of their attitude. But the two things are not unconnected; seriousness of this kind, cut off from any social ties, must result in something like this. And the existentialist emphasis on existence of the individual is bound to lead to a neglect of other people, of the social side of ethics. An extreme version of this aesthetic attitude is represented by Sartre's suggestion, towards the end of *L'Être et le Néant*, that ethics might profitably be considered as a form of play, the establishment of rules for their own sake. Sartre never followed this suggestion up, but then neither has he produced the work on ethics which he promised at the end of that volume. It is not, perhaps, fanciful to suggest also that the existentialist tendency to express themselves in literary form is connected with this same aesthetic attitude.

To say that man has to create himself is not to deny that every person exists from the beginning in a particular "situation", with particular inherited qualities, both physical and mental, is born into a particular social environment which restricts the possibilities of action. But in so far as he is only the product of these forces, the existentialists claim, his existence is in no way different from that of any other object in the physical world, governed by the interaction of numerous causal chains. To become a human being in the full sense of the word involves transcending what is given, either by changing oneself or by actively accepting what one is. The majority of the creatures that can biologically be classified as human beings do not exist fully, are not really aware of their existence, not completely self-conscious. Authenticity, like salvation, is a state which only few attain. And in so far as men are not self-aware, they are incapable of action; it might be said that they react rather then act. Action only counts as such when it involves commitment. It is possible to understand what is meant by this in the case of those acts which involve long-term engagement in projects whose future course is not very determinate, like marrying or joining a church or party. In such a case, the committed person is presumably one who realises something of "what he is letting himself in for" without being able to foresee the exact form it will take, and who nevertheless is willing to stake much of his future on continuing to think in the same way as he does at the moment. It is not so clear what this could mean in commoner types of action, deciding to go to the pictures or help a blind person across the road. I suspect that the shift in the meaning of "ethics" which I have referred to above is such that these actions are considered beneath philosophical consideration.

Awareness of existence only occurs at critical moments. It might be said that I am only conscious of myself when I am about to make a decision that will change myself; at all other times existence is something which remains in the background. It is in this connexion that the notion of "angst", dread or anxiety, is introduced. This is not a worry directed at the external consequences of the decision, the way in which other people are likely to be affected by it. For instance, a commander in war-time has many agonising choices to make,

generally on insufficient evidence. If he is normally conscientious, he will be very worried about these, but he will not necessarily suffer from *angst*. For even if his choice turns out to have been wrong, there will be something which can be said to justify it. *Angst* arises from the totally unjustifiable nature of my existence and of any of the choices of ways of life I may make. In so far as a man is engaged in acting in the world, even though the decisions are agonising ones, there will be no feeling of *angst*, because in these cases his existence is hidden from him. It arises when existence itself is brought into question.

I am aware that this necessarily brief sketch of existentialism has distorted it in many ways, but I hope that it has served to bring out what seems to me the important points, the shifts in the meanings of the words "existence" and "ethics". From the neutral term of ordinary usage, "existence" has become a highly charged emotive one, at least in its application to human beings; existentialists have little interest in, and little to say about, the existence of tables and chairs, electrons and protons. In so far as this is what their procedure involves, I don't think there is any great danger in it, nor need anyone be misled. Indeed, it may be that they are performing a valuable service in stressing the emotional aspects of self-consciousness, as well as in drawing attention to features of moral action that have been neglected in this country. It seems to me that it is not the use made of the term "existence" which is wrong in existentialism, it is what is said *about* it; there is a substantive, rather than a logical, flaw in the system. I have already hinted at the core of my criticism in talking of the apparently "aesthetic" attitude which existentialists seem to adopt, and the two major points that I wish to raise in the remainder of this paper are really developments and specifications of that charge.

First, existentialists err in concentrating most of their attention on the extreme situation, the decision that involves a whole way of life. There is nothing wrong in discussing these in ethics; indeed, there is some justice in the charge that British moralists have recently appeared to forget that there was anything more important in the moral life than wondering whether to return a borrowed book. But by making such situations their central theme the existentialists tend to paint the moral life, if not all life, as nothing but a series of such decisions which have to be made without any possibility of compromise of any sort. In a characteristic passage, Sartre writes: "Such is the real paradox of morality; if I occupy myself with treating as ends in themselves certain human beings, my wife, my son, my friends, the needy beggar I meet in the street, if I really try to carry out all my duties toward them, I shall spend my whole life in doing so, I shall be compelled to *pass over* in silence the injustices of the epoch, the class-struggle, colonialism, anti-semitism, etc., and, in the last resort, to profit from oppression in order to do good." Similarly, he goes on, if I throw myself into the struggle against injustice and oppression, I will be compelled to neglect completely my family and my friends. In times of genuine political revolution, these may be the only alternatives. But for most of the time it would appear that it were possible to arrive at some sort of compromise between the conflicting obligations of public and private duty. No such compromise will be perfectly satisfactory; some tensions are bound to persist. But it seems likely that more will be achieved in this way than by the romantic abandoning of one alternative in favour of the other, a solution which has the advantage of simplicity only. Kierkegaard's treatment of his fiancée seems a good example of this theory put into practice. Perhaps this is the fundamental reason why existentialists find it possible to write novels and plays; extreme situations are the stuff of which such works are made.

The result of this preoccupation with the extreme may well be shown by Heidegger's acceptance of National Socialism and Sartre's of a form of Bolshevism. I don't wish to imply that these are in any way corollaries of existentialism, merely that by thinking of total commitment as the central stuff of ethics, existentialists are liable to confuse themselves into accepting any system which commits them totally, which claims to give an answer to all questions, to lay down a complete way of life. But there seems no reason why commitment should have to be to one thing to the exclusion of others; most people would regard themselves as committed to a number of things, family, political party, perhaps their job, to mention a few. Though there are occasions when two important elements in a life clash, these are fortunately rare. This demand for a single solution on the part of the existentialists has led some critics to say that all forms of existentialism are basically religious. Certainly there seems to be something of the desire for salvation in the demand for authentic existence. Nevertheless I think that if the word "religious" is to be of any use in referring to them, it must serve to distinguish between those who, like Kierkegaard, refer to a transcendent being and those who, like Sartre, feel no need of a deity of any sort.

The second major point of criticism is that, in spite of its pre-occupation with ethics, existentialism completely fails to give any concrete advice on what to do. The command "Be authentic" gives no help on what course of action to commit oneself to; it seems to demand a choice without giving any useful criteria for making that choice. There are situations where this is all that can be done, but to draw attention only to them is not to provide a foundation for ethics. It is perhaps noteworthy in this connexion that existentialists seem happier when they are condemning inauthenticity than they are when trying to give more positive advice. In fact, I am tempted to say that the main value of existentialism lies in its moral pathology, in its analyses of "bad faith" and other moral failings. Authenticity seems a criterion whose main use is in its negative application, like the Kantian Categorical Imperative; and, again like it, to be in some sense parasitic on an already existing moral system. Indeed, it is fairly clear that the existentialists themselves are highly moral men. Sartre, in the passage quoted above, refers to his duties to his family and friends. Presumably these would be the duties that are generally accepted by others of his time, and it is clear that he feels he should at least try to fulfil them. But there seems no connexion between them and the philosoph-

ical doctrine he advances. Indeed, given the stress on the negative correlation between obedience to rules and authentic existence, it might even seem that he should not fulfil them, or not recognise them as "duties".

Indeed, the separation of authentic decision from any kind of rules or criteria reduces it to something which hardly merits the name of "decision". Without an accepted framework within which the decision is made, there seems nothing to distinguish it from an arbitrary act. Ultimately, the existentialists seem to be offering us only a "Do it yourself" kit for ethics, which, apart from representing a failure on a philosophic level, also, I suspect, has dangers on the purely moral plane. This failure does not arise from misuse of language or a lack of attention to its details so much as from an unwillingness or inability to make the connexions between the rather inflated technical terminology employed and concrete cases. The attraction of existentialism, particularly for those with little philosophical sophistication, lies in the way very detailed examples appear to give rise to notions of the highest generality. It is only when an attempt is made to bridge the gap between the two that its weaknesses become apparent. My own paradoxical conclusion is that existentialists are at their weakest when dealing with ethics. Philosophers will find things of value in Kierkegaard's discussions of faith, Heidegger's of time, and in Sartre's analyses of psychological concepts. In ethics they serve mainly to point to the dangers of an inflated terminology, the worst fault of "metaphysics".

SUMMARY

Existentialists, writes F. H. Heinemann in this concluding selection, show the diversity of form and expression found within other philosophic schools. Yet they are "children of the same age," all involved in the same predicament, which to them is one of crisis. Thus in spite of their diversity, they are united in attitude and situation, protesting in their individual ways against tendencies in the present age. Sympathetic yet critical, Heinemann sees this protest as a challenge to all philosophy. Its function is to release us from the predominance of analysis and rationalism, and to stir us to a revaluation of the traditional problems of men. So seen, he concludes, existentialism remains an important, though perhaps not final, expression of our day.

12   The Challenge of Existentialism

F. H. Heinemann (1889-   )

So far we have considered some existentialist philosophers. We had to discuss them just as they are in their diversity and particularity, and some readers may well have wondered whether they are not so different as human beings, so particular in their language and thought and sometimes so antagonistic to each other that one is unable to see what they have in common. "Even if we agree to call them existentialists," one may object, "we fail to see what that existentialism is on which they agree." We have therefore to return to our starting-point and to repeat the question: What is existentialism? Can this question be answered at

all? If it is meant to imply the demand for a real definition, it cannot, for there is no single entity or essence to which this word corresponds. There is not *one* philosophy called existentialism, but several philosophies with profound differences. It is not even possible to make a clear-cut distinction between German philosophers of existence and French existialists, for Marcel is nearer to Jaspers than to Sartre and therefore rightly calls one of his books *Philosophy of Existence;* Sartre is nearer to Heidegger than to Marcel, and Heidegger would like to form a class of his own as eksistentialist. There is no set of principles common to them all, nor do they share a well-defined method comparable to the dialectic of the Hegelians. Nevertheless they belong together. Children of one and the same age, they are faced with the same challenge to which they have to respond, and are involved in the same

The selection is from F. H. Heinemann, *Existentialism and the Modern Predicament* (London: A. & C. Black, Ltd., 1953; New York: Harper & Brothers, 1958), pp. 165-174, 179-180. Copyright © 1953, 1958 by F. H. Heinemann. Used by permission of A. & C. Black, Ltd.

predicament. Though their answers are not identical, they move in parallel directions and are, even if opposed to each other, internally related. In other words, the term "existentialism" points to a certain state of mind, to a specific approach or attitude, to a spiritual movement which is of significance in present circumstances and to a specific mode of thought, in any case to something which is alive.

It is a fundamental mistake to assume that what cannot be defined does not exist. On the contrary, anything which is alive cannot be exhausted by definition. I do not deny for a moment that the emphasis on form, *Gestalt,* definition and measurement was of the greatest importance for the development of European science. But we should never forget that life is inexhaustible and that often the formless, which cannot be defined or measured, is the most valuable part of living beings. It is possible to define existentialism in three ways. The first is by ostensive definition, *i.e.* by pointing to existentialists and their books and by saying that what they are doing is existentialism. That we have done. The second is to describe the situation to which they respond and to interpret these philosophies as an expression of the *Zeitgeist.* The third is to change the form of the question and to search for their *function* rather than for their *essence.*

It can hardly be doubted that these philosophies are specific expressions of the *Zeitgeist,* albeit of the first half of the twentieth century. They express something of that which many feel without being able to formulate it. True, it is the feeling of a minority, but of a minority that counts, because it belongs to the intellectual élite. Whilst the majority accepted, voluntarily or forced, the pseudo-philosophies of Marxism, Bolshevism and Fascism, the existentialists defended the rights of the person. It would, however, be incorrect to interpret existentialism as the antithesis to Marxism and Fascism, for on the one hand its battlefront is broader, and on the other, individual existentialists may well be Marxists or Fascists.

The Marxists are therefore not right if they try to explain existentialism away as a last desperate attempt of a declining bourgeoisie, which just before its ultimate submergence clings to an overemphasized individualism as to a life-belt. Existentialism is not the philosophy of a class, and the problems which it discusses transcend the boundaries of a specific group; they are simply human and they reappear within dictatorial states, even in a more pressing, though perhaps insoluble form. Anyone in Russia or her satellite states who wants to be himself in order to live his own life, express his own thought, and practise his own religion, has to experience the agony of existentialist problems. The Bolshevists hate the existentialists as the potential revolutionaries of the future. In fact, the existentialists are philosophers of resistance. They attempt to resist the collectivizing trend, bound up with machine production, which seems to lead in any society, whether democratic, fascist or socialist, to a depersonalization of man. This resistance takes various forms. Kierkegaard criticizes the modern tendency towards equality and the levelling brought about by public opinion and the rise of the masses. Jaspers protests against the absorption of man by the machinery of the modern welfare state, Marcel against the increased socialization of life, against the extension of the powers of the State, and against the substitution of the registration card for the person. Most of the French existentialists were members of the Resistance, in deadly opposition to the Nazi oppressors.

The philosophies of existence are philosophies of liberation rather than philosophies of freedom. They attempt to liberate man from the domination of external forces, of society, of the state, and of dictatorial power. They want to set man's authentic self free from the shackles of the unauthentic self. We saw that they experience freedom (Sartre) and that they may formulate a philosophy of freedom (Berdyaev).

Existentialism is in all its forms a philosophy of crisis. It expresses the crisis of man openly and directly, whereas other schools, like that of the Logical Positivists, express it indirectly and unconsciously. For this reason, the fact of estrangement in its enormous complexity and many-sidedness became central with them. Today it pervades the relations of persons as well as of groups, of classes and races rather than of nations and religious sects. Science and the arts are out of harmony. Science claims to contain the whole of true knowledge. Art, religion and speculative philosophy cannot accept this claim, and contend that wisdom, nurtured by the experience of generations, may be of greater significance than abstract science. Some schools, like those of Gurdieff and Ouspensky, go still further. They reject science as a guide to human action, and build their "Teaching" on esoteric wisdom allegedly coming down to them from primeval times. Hegel's idealistic and Marx's materialistic alienation have led to institutional

alienation. Human institutions—the state, the government, the civil service, the party, the factory—have become impersonal and anonymous powers of enormous strength which the individual tries in vain to master. Thence arises the growing sense of frustration, anxiety and despair, which pervades the Western hemisphere. At the back of it all is man's estrangement from Nature, deeply felt by Rousseau and the Romantics; but chiefly that estrangement from God, which is in a certain sense the source of all these troubles and therefore remains a recurrent theme from Kierkegaard to Marcel, and is present, even when not discussed, as in the case of Sartre.

Alienation ends in absurdity, because under its domination the acts of individuals and groups become unco-ordinated. Shall we ridicule or praise Sartre and Camus because of their revelation of *homo absurdus* and of the absurd universe? It is not the universe that is absurd, but man, who projects his absurdity into the world. Nothing is absurd except feelings, thoughts, interpretations, actions or productions of man. Many products of contemporary art and literature are undoubtedly absurd, and in that they are a true mirror of our time. It would, however, be unfair to our age to single it out in this manner. Absurdity is at all times a possibility for human beings though not for animals. It is the price man has to pay for the inexhaustibility and indefiniteness of his nature. If, however, it *actually* dominates him, it points to a *cul-de-sac,* it indicates that a point has been reached where the direction has to be changed. The absurd man needs no refutation, he is his own *reductio ad absurdum.* However, genius and madness, exceptional gifts and absurdity, may co-exist. It would therefore be a mistake to reject existentialist doctrines as absurdities; for they merely reveal the fact that life on this planet is on the point of becoming absurd. Wherever one looks, whether at the lives of individuals, communities or nations, one cannot help noticing them. The only trouble is, that we fail to see how absurd we ourselves and some of our actions are becoming. Sometimes I cannot help wondering whether Shakespeare's Puck is still making an ass of many a man who remains quite unaware of his transformation. Are examples really necessary? Everyone knows them: the policy of unconditional surrender followed after a short time by a rearmament of Japan and Germany; the demolition of factories in these countries, which had to be reconstructed after a few months; the United Nations broken up into two hostile camps waging a cold war against each other; and the piling up of arms in both camps for the preservation of peace, but which in very fact enhances the danger of war. "Absurdity of absurdities, all is absurd," seems to be the motto of the contemporary world.

But even if it be granted that existentialism has a representative value by expressing the crisis of our time in its phase of absurdity, the question remains: What then is existentialism? This is the point where we have to change the form of our question. Instead of asking, "What is the essence of existentialism?" we now ask, "What is its function in present circumstances?"

Its first function is to bring about a revaluation of problems and to liberate us from certain traditional problems whether they are material or purely formal and technical. The existentialists maintain that the philosophers of the past overlooked the most pressing problems of man and of human existence. What is the good, they would say, of talking about a transcendent realm of values, if these are not realized here and now in human persons? What alone matters are problems that are lived, directly experienced, suffered and intimately connected with our being; problems in which we are engaged, which form part of ourselves, which we cannot escape. It is a change in the quality of problems, brought about by the climate of the age. The existentialists reject the starting-point of modern philosophers from Descartes to the present time, *e.g.* the thesis that nothing but the data of my consciousness are given to me. However these data are interpreted, either with Descartes as "ideas" in their three forms, with Locke as simple ideas, with Hume as impressions, or with Kant as a "chaos of sensations," they are in each case abstractions. Whitehead is right, these philosophers are the victims of the fallacy of misplaced concreteness, they falsely assume that their data are concrete, whereas in fact they are abstract. If these philosophers try to prove or disprove, on the basis of their hypotheses, the existence or non-existence of material objects, of other minds, or of God, they are discussing pseudo-problems. On this point, that is in rejecting certain problems as pseudo-problems, the existentialists are in agreement with the logical positivists. They go, however, much further. They would say that the attempt of the latter to reduce all problems to linguistic problems may again lead to the replacement of real problems by pseudo-problems.

The existentialists have here the function of liberating us from the predominance of analysis. Nobody denies the importance of analysis, but analysis as such is not enough. Analysis is the breaking up of a material or ideal whole into its parts. It can only break down, but not build up. It has been too easily assumed that the model of arithmetical analysis may be applied in psychology and epistemology, *i.e.* that just as all numbers may be broken down into prime numbers, so all our ideals may be analyzed into simple ideas. That is what I call the fallacy of simplicity. An analysis into simpler elements is possible, but the so-called simple ideas prove to be very complex, if they are not mere abstractions. Each field of inquiry demands a different form of analysis adequate to its problems. Since in psychology and epistemology the whole is more than its parts, the whole, the totality, the overriding meaning disappears in this sort of analysis. The analysts are inclined to disregard synthesis altogether, in spite of the fact that analysis and synthesis are strictly correlative; or if they acknowledge it, they interpret it in a superficial manner as a "collection of ideas." There is a second sense which may be given to analysis. *Analyser, c'est traduire,* said Hippolyte Taine. In fact, if I am of the opinion that nothing but sense-data are given to me, I have to translate statements about external objects into statements about my sensations. I do not wish to discuss this standpoint here. I can only stress one point. The analysis of ethical statements in the first half of the twentieth century has resulted in greater disagreement than ever before, and we are told that "in some cases disagreement about issues so fundamental arose that certain schools of thought find it unrewarding, if not impossible to communicate

with each other." That this should be the case is easily understandable if one notices the arbitrariness of these translations. Stevenson, *e.g.,* would analyze the proposition "this action is right" into: "I approve of it. Do so likewise!" This analysis seems to be completely arbitrary, because the criterion on which the approval is based remains undefined. The danger in all these translations is that they are not equivalent, *i.e.* that they substitute something else foreign to the original meaning. In fact, in both kinds of analysis the negative tendency prevails. In this situation the existentialist would seem to fulfil a useful function by raising the following questions: Is the analysis of ethical statements really the only function of a moral philosopher? Is it not more important to clarify the condition of man, to reveal the danger in which the persons find themselves, to appeal to them to make their own decision and to take the responsibility for their actions, and to discuss the criteria on which the rightness of an action is based? And, generally speaking, is analysis enough? Should we not go on to meta-analysis, *i.e.* to an analysis of analysis on a higher level? Should we not analyze the analyzers? Is it not time to see that analysis without the corresponding synthesis is condemned to remain barren and fruitless? Should we not restrict the sphere of influence of analysis within the realm of philosophy and science? The existentialists remind us that there may be some concrete problems of primary importance which are not discussed by analytic science and by analytic philosophy. They concern the existence of human persons.

All the existentialists stressed the fact of alienation. Did they succeed in overcoming self-estrangement? The problem of estrangement is, as we saw, multi-dimensional. We have therefore to ask whether there is one solution to it, or whether its different aspects call for diverse remedies. Before attempting an answer, the preliminary somewhat unusual question has to be pondered: Is it at all possible to get rid of this affliction? Will not an element of it always remain because of its having, so to say, metaphysical roots? Is it perhaps our permanent fate to remain foreigners on this earth, in spite of our being at home on it? Is this not even more true of man within the Universe? Though a creature of this world, he nevertheless remains foreign in it. Responding consciously and unconsciously to rays from sun and stars, he does not understand the message they may convey. Cosmic alienation is even greater than earth alienation. Pantheists and Yogis may believe that they are nearer to the Unity of all beings than to their neighbors and to the earth, but that is a matter of subjective experience and not of verifiable fact. The highest degree of estrangement, *i.e.* a complete break and an unbridgeable gulf, and the lowest degree, where no feeling of difference is left, are seldom realized, but they mark the limits between which the pendulum of our feeling oscillates. There is a limit to our understanding of other persons. In their inner life they all remain, to a certain degree, foreign to us. Is it to be wondered at that this feeling increases if we meet animals, plants, stones or stars?

From this it follows that alienation cannot be completely eliminated, it can only be reduced to reasonable terms. All we can do is to remove it from the foreground to the background and deprive

it of its central position and of its emotional power, but we have to acquiesce in the fact that alienation somehow belongs to our heritage. It brings, moreover, certain advantages with it. It allows us to keep aloof from others in cases where we do not wish to identify ourselves with their doings. In due degree it is to be welcomed so long as it remains less intense than the opposed feeling of togetherness and participation. Normal alienation is healthy, abnormal alienation is morbid, because if dominant it becomes an impediment to creative work, destroying normal relations and transforming trust into mistrust. Therefore all those solutions which assume the possibility of a complete elimination of estrangement seem to be over-simplifications. Neither Hegel's return of the Mind to itself, nor Marx's proletarian revolution, nor Kierkegaard's repetition understood as a restitution of the *status pristinus,* nor Marcel's absolute hope which does not leave room for any sort of despair, offer a definitive solution of the problem, for in spite of them alienation remains. . . .

Existentialism points here to an urgent problem, or rather to a series of problems, but offers no solution, partly because the problems are so complex and many-sided that no simple solution is possible, and partly because they are, to a certain extent, in principle insoluble. . . .

But whatever the attitude of the individual philosopher to these problems may be, even if he should think that they are not his concern, he should still accept the challenge of existentialism. It should help him to overcome the non-existential philosophy of our time. "Non-existential philosophy" is concerned with words or with symbols and their manipulation, with the clarification of scientific propositions or with talk. The linguistic philosophers started with the rejection of metaphysical problems as pseudo-problems, but, alas! they did not foresee that one day they themselves might be enmeshed in linguistic pseudo-problems which they discuss at great length. Linguistic analysis and the distinction of different kinds of symbols are important, but not enough. Words and symbols are only means to an end, and not the end itself. They cannot serve as a final substitute for thinking, not even as the substitute signs of algebra and symbolic logic. A philosopher cannot help asking what they mean. He knows quite well that the word *reality* has different meanings. But even a hard-boiled Logical Positivist can hardly deny that one of these meanings is predominant in the problem of reality when, *e.g.,* a bomb has fallen near him and smashed his leg. He should see that philosophy has something to do with man. It should be an expression of the whole man and not merely of his intellect. It demands a decision of his will as well. His philosophy should be a response to the challenge of his time. He should not try to evade it, and he should not imagine that he could render it non-existent by doing so. Does he perhaps not see what the challenge of our time is? Can he really overlook it? Or does he not wish to see it for the simple reason that he himself is infected with the mortal disease of our age? Whatever formula one may choose, dehumanization of man, annihilation of man, or the question whether man will survive in the face of nihilistic destruction of all human and moral values, the facts are indisputable. Once more the human world resembles the valley full of bones which Ezekiel saw in his vision. And again is the question put to us: "Son of man, can these bones live?" The integration of the diffused and disintegrated parts into a whole, the rehumanization of man, that is the task with which we are confronted. One cannot expect a philosopher to put new breath into dead bones, but one can expect him to remind human beings of what it means to be man. In short, what we need is not Philosophies of Existence, but Existential Philosophers.

BIBLIOGRAPHICAL NOTE

A number of fine surveys of existentialist thought have been written; among them are F. H. Heinemann, *Existentialism and the Modern Predicament* (New York, 1958), which includes bibliographical materials; H. J. Blackham, *Six Existentialist Thinkers* (New York, 1959); Marjorie Greene, *Dreadful Freedom* (Chicago, 1948; reissued as *Introduction to Existentialism*); Robert Grimsley, *Existentialist Thought* (Cardiff, Wales, 1955); and Emmanuel Mounier, *Existentialist Philosophies* (New York, 1949). The student will want, however, to consult the writings of existentialists themselves, and these surveys will direct him to the major sources. Two recent anthologies include N. Lawrence and D. O'Connor (eds.), *Readings in Existential Phenomenology* (New York, 1967), and G. A. Schrader, Jr. (ed.), *Existential Philosophers* (New York, 1967). A brief sample of primary sources, additional to the writings from which the selections in this text are taken, may be hopeful here. R. Bretall, *A Kierkegaard Anthology* (Princent, 1946), is useful for a first orientation, although it should be supplemented by further reading in Kierkegaard. Among Jaspers' work available in English are *Way to Wisdom* (London, 1951), *The Perennial Scope of Philosophy* (New York, 1949), and *Reason and Existenz* (New York, 1955). Werner Brock's *Existence and Being* (Chicago, 1949) contains four of Heidegger's essays together with a long introductory study of Heidegger's thought. Also available in English translation are Heidegger's *An Introduction to Metaphysics* (New Haven, 1959) and *Being and Time* (New York, 1962). Sartre's major philosophical work, *Being and Nothingness* (New York, 1956), is available in English, along with many of his literary pieces and shorter essays. Many editions of Pascal and Nietzsche are in print. Finally, mention should be made of three other writers of major importance. Gabriel Marcel has attempted to produce a Roman Catholic form of existentialism; for one of his major works, see *The Mystery of Being*, 2 vols. (Chicago, 1950, 1951). The Russian Nicholas Berdyaev, whose works are available in English through Geoffrey Bles, Ltd., has produced a personalistic existentialism. His *Dream and Reality* (London, 1950) contains both a good introduction to his own thought and a bibliography of his other writings. And Albert Camus, French novelist, essayist, and Nobel prize winner, has written many stirring books, in addition to the essay selected above, including *The Myth of Sisyphus* (New York, 1955) and *The Rebel* (New York, 1956). Current work on existentialist themes can be found in many journals, including *Man and World*, *Philosophy and Phenomenological Research*, and *Humanitas*.

GLOSSARY

Many of the key terms met in the readings are defined in the following selected glossary. Its aim is not so much completeness—which would be impossible here—as helpfulness. For further elaboration of these and related words, students should consult a standard philosophical lexicon or dictionary.

Absolute idealism: monistic variant of idealism. The real is one inclusive mind or self, the "Absolute."

Agnosticism: position holding that ultimate propositions are, for mankind, undecidable.

Analysis: a philosophical procedure, variously characterized, for solving problems by translation or resolution to simpler parts.

Analytic: a statement whose denial involves a contradiction; or, a statement whose truth follows, with the help of definitions, from logical principles alone.

A posteriori: lit., "after experience." Used with reference to knowledge derived from experience.

A priori: lit., "before experience." Used with reference to knowledge or concepts supposedly gained independently of experience.

Art: generally, any manipulation of objects to serve human purposes. Fine art is manipulation to produce an esthetic experience.

Atheism: the doctrine which denies the existence of God.

Authoritarianism: view that authority of some type (e.g., Bible, church) is the most reliable source of knowledge.

Axiology: a branch of philosophy that investigates problems of value.

Behaviorism: psychological theory that all knowledge of man must be based on observation of behavior. Also, sometimes, the theory that mind is behavior, thus denying the existence of mind or mental acts.

Category: a principle of explanation, usually considered ultimate in the area of experience to which it applies.

Cause: an event, process, or object productive of change in another. Additionally, in Aristotle, a principle.

Coherence: theory that the criterion of truth is systematic entailment of propositions; also, that the nature of truth is such a coherent system.

Common good: the good for society, as distinguished from the individual good.

Concept: a term defining what is common to the objects to which it applies.

Connotation: that part of the meaning of a word which refers to properties or characteristics rather than to the entities intended. Cf. denotation.

Contingent: that which is possible, hence not necessary, as contingent existence.

Cosmology: a division of metaphysics; lit., study of the cosmos.

Deduction: type of inference where the evidence for the conclusion is exhaustively given in the premises.

Definition: a statement articulating the meaning of a term. May be of many kinds.

Denotation: that part of the meaning of a word which refers to the entities intended.

Determinism: thesis that every event is totally conditioned by its cause or causes.

Dialectic: relating to the interrelationships of concepts. Cf. Hegel.

Efficient cause: in Aristotle, the cause productive of a thing or its changes.

Emotive meaning: a noncognitive form of meaning having an emotional basis and designed to arouse or express emotion.

Empiricism: the theory that knowledge is derived from and tested in experience.

Epiphenomenalism: doctrine that mind is solely by-product or effect of brain.

Epistemology: lit., theory of knowledge.

Essence: the principle in a being that makes it to be *what* it is. In phenomenology, the nature, structure or meaning of a phenomenon.

Esthetics: normative investigation of art and the beautiful.

Ethics: normative science of human conduct.

Existence: the act whereby some essence *is*. Also, the field of human struggle and decision.

Existential proposition: a proposition asserting or denying the existence of some subject.

Existentialism: a philosophical position directed toward articulating human existence.

Final cause: in Aristotle, the end toward which a being or change is directed.

Form, formal cause: the structure or pattern of anything.

Generalization: a proposition covering all instances of the items being referred to.

Hedonism: in ethics, theory that pleasure is the only intrinsic good; in psychology, that man's actions are motivated by desire for pleasure.

Historicism: theory making all knowledge and experience relative to historical circumstance.

Hylomorphic: composed of form and matter. Cf. Aristotle.

Hypostatization: the treatment of an abstraction as a concrete thing or substance.

Hypothesis: proposition suggesting a resolution of a problem.

Ideal: a definition of a value.

Idealism: most generally, the theory which emphasizes the centrality of mind in metaphysics, epistemology, and axiology.

Indeterminism: theory that man has free choice and is not fully determined in his actions. Also, freedomism.

Induction: an inference whose conclusion is derived from a set of particulars.

Inference: a conclusion drawn from premises.

Instrumentalism: alternative name for pragmatism; the theory that mind and ideas are instruments in adjustment.

Intention, intentional act: the reference of consciousness to some specified object.

Intuition, intuitive knowledge: knowledge grasped without mediation.

Logic: the study of arguments.

Logical empiricism: alternative name for logical positivism.

Logical form: the pattern or structure of arguments, as isolated and studied by logicians.

Logical positivism: school holding that all empirical statements are scientific and that the task of philosophy is analysis.

Material cause: in Aristotle, that out of which a being comes.

Materialism: metaphysical theory that matter is the ultimately real.

Metaphysics: philosophical inquiry into being or reality.

Mysticism: epistemological and religious theory that truth is obtained by direct, intuitive experience, usually of the Ultimate.

Natural law: in ethics, a principle of right believed to be derived from the nature of man.

Natural theology: theology based on nature or reason rather than on revelation. Sometimes also called rational theology.

Naturalism: philosophical position holding that nature is all there is,—there is no supernatural being, realm, or entity.

Necessary condition: that without which an event cannot occur.

Nihilism: a philosophy denying the value of human life, sometimes all value experience.

Norm, normative: having reference to what ought to be as against what is; also, what is taken as a true ideal.

Ontology: division of metaphysics concerned with the meaning of being.

Panpsychism: a pluralistic form of idealism; reality is held to be a society of minds or mindlike entities.

Pantheism: a religious position that identifies God and nature.

Particular: opposed to universal; that which is taken as a unit or individual.

Personalism: a variant of idealism that holds that the real is personal or a person.

Phenomenalism: theory that limits human knowledge to phenomena or appearances.

Phenomenology: philosophical discipline directed toward describing the structures of experience.

Philosophy: lit., "love of wisdom." Generally concerned with comprehensive problems, be they of the nature of analysis, description, evaluation, or reality as a whole.

Philosophy of religion: a normative investigation of the truth of religious beliefs and the value of religious practices.

Physicalism: a methodological thesis that explanations be made in terms of physics.

Positivism: generally, the theory that limits valid knowledge to scientific knowledge.

Pragmatism: position in philosophy that defines meaning and knowledge in terms of their function in experience, with reference to adjustment and the resolution of problematic situations.

Primary quality: quality or attribute of an object that is definable in mathematical terms.

Proposition: the meaning of a declarative sentence; an assertion that may be true or false.

Rational psychology: branch of metaphysics that investigates the being of mind; distinguished from empirical psychology.

Rational theology: division of metaphysics that investigates the being and attributes of God on the basis of reason and experience alone. Sometimes called natural theology.

Rationalism: epistemological view that holds that reason is the source and criterion of truth.

Realism: metaphysical view that the real consists of independently existing substances; in epistemology, the theory that the object of knowledge is independent of the act of knowing.

Reductive: as used of explanation, the view that "higher" levels of experience are to be explained through "lower" ones.

Religion: concern about the status of values, devotion to what is believed to be the source of value, and suitable expression of this concern and devotion.

Science: in classical thought, an organized body of knowledge. Currently used chiefly only of the experimental sciences.

Secondary quality: quality or attribute of an object that is dependent on the perceiving mind for its existence.

Semantics: part of the study of language, concerned with the relation of words to things.

Sense-datum: term used for that which is experienced in an act of perceiving. Usually distinguished from a physical object.

Skepticism: a position that doubts or denies the power of intellect to know reality or ultimate truths.

Social philosophy: a normative inquiry into the principles underlying social process.

Solipsism: extreme form of subjectivism holding that one's self or mind and its perceptions are all that exist.

Soul: in Aristotle, the form of a living body that makes it live.

Substance: the real thing referred to by the demonstrative "this."

Sufficient condition: a condition in the presence of which an effect occurs.

Summum bonum: the highest good; the ultimate goal of conduct.

Syllogism: an argument wherein two premises necessitate a conclusion. The basis of classical logic.

Synthetic: a statement referring to actual states of affairs; one whose truth can be determined only by recourse to experience. Opposed to analytic.

Synthetic a priori: esp. in Kant, a universal, necessary proposition which is also empirical and functions in making experience possible.

Tautology: a proposition with no empirical content, whose truth value is determined by linguistic conventions or logic alone.

Teleology: study or doctrine of ends and purposes; also the belief in natural purposes.

Theism: religious position that believes God to be a living, personal being.

Theology: a systematic inquiry into the being and attributes of God.

Transcendent: having reference to what is beyond experience.

Universal: a concept or proposition holding for the entire class to which it refers.

Utilitarianism: ethical theory defining the good by reference to produced pleasures.

Valid, validity: in logic, a conclusion drawn necessarily from a set of premises.

Value: whatever is enjoyed, desired, esteemed, or prized.

Verifiability theory of meaning: theory that the meaning of a synthetic proposition lies in its reference to possible empirical confirmation.

Virtue: a habit of right action; in classical thought, it may be either moral or intellectual.

Wisdom: traditionally, knowledge of first principles and their application to experience.

INDEX

Absolute, the, 207, 210–211, 220, 254
Absolute idealism, 131, 198, 206, **562**
Abstraction, 76, 88–89, 90, 127, 201, 206, 271–272
Accident, 52–54
Actual, actuality, 42–44
Actualism, 99
Agnosticism, **562**
Alienation, 559–560
Analysis, 3, 286, 367, 559, **562**
Analytic, 285–286, 401, **562**
Analytic philosophy (*see* Linguistic philosophy)
A posteriori, **562**
A priori, 137, 289, 348, **562**
Art, 67, 77, 157–163, 239–245, 419–426, **563**
See also Esthetics
Atheism, **562**
Atomism, 56, 114–123, 181
Authority, 130, 134–136, **562**
Axiology, 4, 261, **562**

Beauty, 33–34, 37, 522
Behaviorism, **562**
Being, 5, 39–44, 51–58, 81–82, 92–94, 107–111, 202, 537
Belief, 133–138, 319–320, 329, 332, 383, 453
Body, 9–13, 523–533

Category, **562**
Cause, causation, 40, 57–58, 81–82, 287, 288–290, **563**
Cause, final, **563**
Change, 40–41, 52–55
See also Motion
Classicism, 244
Coherence, 213–219, 386, **563**
Common good, 67, **563**
Concept, **563**
Connotation, **563**
Consciousness, 150, 163–168, 246–253, 340, 429, 435, 528–529
See also Mind
Contemplation, 59
Cosmology, 4

Creation, artistic, 76–82
Custom, 287, 292–293

Deduction, **563**
Definition, 40, **563**
Denotation, **563**
Description, theory of, 26–29
Despair, 483–489, 502
Dialectic, 149, 207, 253–256, **563**
Doubt, 7–11, 130, 133–134
See also Skepticism
Duty, 14–15, 22, 229–230

Efficient cause, 40, 98, **563**
Emotive meaning, 286, 311, **563**
Empiricism, 364, **563**
Epistemology, 4, *44–51, 131–139, 213–219, 301–305, 382–393, 489–497*
See also Knowledge
Error, 9–11, 49–50, 490, 496
Essence, 40, 47, 55–58, 111, 497, 499–500, 556, **563**
Esthetics, 4, *75–82, 157–163, 239–245, 326–332, 419–426, 517–522,* **563**
Ethics, 4, *58–67, 144–148, 186, 228–232,* 234, *311–320,* 324–325, *401–411, 503–510,* 544, 554, **563**
Evil, 97, 99
Evolution, 139–144
Existence, 24–29, 34–35, 55–58, 80–82, 93–94, 111, 201, 482, 494–495, 497, 499–500, 545–546, 552, 557, **563**
Existential proposition, **563**
Existentialism, *463–562,* **563**
Experience, 157–163, 167–168, 187–188, 287, 289–291, 359

Faith, 96–97, 482, 538–543
Final cause, 40, **563**
Form, 40, 44, 47, 54–55, 76–77, 84–85, 99–106, 255, 426
Formal cause, 40, **563**
Forms, theory of, *31–38*
Freedom, 236, 238, 493–497, 506

Generalization, 294–296, **563**
God, 12, 68–69, 72, 80–81, 92–99, 108, 143, 188, 200, 261–265, 347–352, 445–447, 476, 482, 501, 539, 542–543
Good, 13–22, 58, 60, 72–73, 97, 99, 146–148, 312–313, 316–317, 401–411
See also Morality; Value

Happiness, 58, 61–62
Historicism, **563**
History, 347
Hylomorphism, 106, **563**
Hypothesis, 170, 298–299, **563**

Idea, 200–201, 206
Ideal, 229–230, 232, **563**
Idealism, 182–183, *198–284,* **563**
Identity, 246–252
Image, 164–168
Imagination, 47–48, 179–180, 331
Imperative, 15–22
Induction, 124, 130, **563**
Inference, 131–132, **563**
Inquiry, 133–138, 169
Instrumentalism, **563**
See also Pragmatism
Intellect, 46–47, 84–86, 99
See also Mind
Intention, **564**
Intuition, 88, 111, 174, 239, 241, 245, 351, **564**

Judgment, 48–49
Justice, 30, 67–68, 70–75, 149, 232–239, 321–326, 411–419, 514–515

Knowledge, 4, 7–11, 30, 34–36, 44–51, 67, 83, 110–111, 123, 190, 200–201, 209, 243–244, 254, 285, 331
See also Epistemology

Language, 5, 22–29, 125, 128, 286, 367, 374–381, 387–388, 456

Italic page numbers refer to selections, **boldface** numbers to definitions in the Glossary.